THE ROUTLEDGE HANDBOOK OF INTEGRATED REPORTING

This timely handbook provides a current and comprehensive examination of integrated reporting, both practical and research-based. It offers insights and different perspectives from more than 60 authors, including representatives of the International Integrated Reporting Council, Integrated Reporting Committee of South Africa, professional bodies and audit firms, as well as leading academics in the fields of integrated reporting, sustainability reporting and corporate social responsibility.

This collected work provides an in-depth review of the development of integrated reporting, with a focus on the interpretation and guidance provided by the International Integrated Reporting Council. It encourages the development of new thinking and research topics in the area of integrated reporting (such as links between integrated reporting and reports focused on financial and corporate social responsibility matters), as well as showcasing how integrated reporting issues are seen and practiced in different parts of the world. The chapters include reviews of the most recent research, practitioner viewpoints, conceptual pieces, case studies and disclosure analyses.

Accessible and engaging, this handbook will be an invaluable overview for those new to the field or those who are interested in ensuring they are up to date with its developments, as well as those who are concerned with how to construct an integrated report.

Charl de Villiers is an expert on Integrated Reporting; Professor of Accounting, the University of Auckland, New Zealand; a professor at the University of Pretoria, South Africa; an adjunct professor at several other universities; and a research fellow at the Centre for Sustainability Management, Leuphana University Lüneburg, Germany.

Pei-Chi Kelly Hsiao is a lecturer at the School of Accounting, Finance, and Economics, the University of Waikato, New Zealand. Her research interests include corporate disclosure, sustainability accounting, integrated reporting and investment decision-making.

Warren Maroun is a professor at the School of Accountancy, University of the Witwatersrand, South Africa. He has served on integrated reporting working groups for the Independent Regulatory Board for Auditors and Integrated Reporting Committee of South Africa.

"Integrated reporting and the prospect of integrated thinking has attracted huge interest amongst practitioners, researchers and policy setters. It is a potential game changer. This book is a must for all those captivated by the prospect of a reporting framework that influences what organisations focus on – from profit to creating value that encompasses overall well-being and to seeing the organisation as part of society. The book provides critical reflection on the framework, discusses the practicalities of implementation, considers future directions for integrated reporting and assurance and areas for further research. Its authors are leaders that have implemented integrated reporting in their organisations, leading technical experts and leading academic researchers and thinkers."

— *Carol Adams, Integrated Reporting Expert*, Non-executive Director, Professor of Accounting, Durham University, UK, and Swinburne Business School, Australia

THE ROUTLEDGE HANDBOOK OF INTEGRATED REPORTING

Edited by Charl DE VILLIERS, Pei-Chi Kelly HSIAO
and Warren MAROUN

LONDON AND NEW YORK

First published 2020
by Routledge
2 Park Square, Milton Park, Abingdon, Oxon OX14 4RN

and by Routledge
52 Vanderbilt Avenue, New York, NY 10017

Routledge is an imprint of the Taylor & Francis Group, an informa business

British Library Cataloguing-in-Publication Data
A catalogue record for this book is available from the British Library

Library of Congress Cataloging-in-Publication Data
Names: De Villiers, Charl, editor. | Hsiao, Pei-Chi Kelly, editor. | Maroun, Warren, editor.
Title: The Routledge handbook of integrated reporting / edited by Charl de Villiers, Pei-Chi Kelly Hsiao and Warren Maroun.
Description: 1 Edition. | New York : Routledge, 2020. | Includes bibliographical references and index.
Subjects: LCSH: Corporation reports. | Social responsibility of business. | Sustainable development reporting.
Classification: LCC HG4028.B2 R68 2020 (print) | LCC HG4028.B2 (ebook) | DDC 658.15/12–dc23
LC record available at https://lccn.loc.gov/2020003512
LC ebook record available at https://lccn.loc.gov/2020003513

ISBN: 978-0-367-23385-3 (hbk)
ISBN: 978-0-429-27962-1 (ebk)

Typeset in Bembo
by Swales & Willis, Exeter, Devon, UK

CONTENTS

FIGURES

TABLES

CONTRIBUTORS

Editors

Charl de Villiers is Professor of Accounting, Department of Accounting and Finance, the University of Auckland, New Zealand, where his research interests include sustainability accounting and integrated reporting. He is also a professor at the University of Pretoria, South Africa, an adjunct professor at several other universities, and a research fellow at the Centre for Sustainability Management, Leuphana University Lüneburg, Germany. Charl co-edited the Routledge published book *Sustainability Accounting and Integrated Reporting*. He has co-edited several special issues on integrated reporting in academic journals and has published widely on the topic. He has more than 300 research based publications and presentations, including over 80 articles in refereed journals, including in *Accounting, Organisations and Society*; *Journal of Management*; *Accounting, Auditing & Accountability Journal*; *British Accounting Review*; *European Accounting Review*; *Journal of Accounting and Public Policy*; and *Accounting and Business Research*. Charl is the editor-in-chief of *Meditari Accountancy Research* and serves on the editorial board of several other research journals.

Pei-Chi Kelly Hsiao is a lecturer at the School of Accounting, Finance, and Economics, the University of Waikato, New Zealand. Her research interests include corporate disclosure, sustainability accounting, integrated reporting and investment decision-making. Pei-Chi has completed her master's and doctorate degrees on the topic of integrated reporting, and she has published in *Accounting, Auditing & Accountability Journal*; *Accounting & Finance, Meditari Accountancy Research*; and *Sustainability Accounting, Management and Policy Journal*.

Warren Maroun is a professor at the School of Accountancy, University of the Witwatersrand, South Africa. His research interests include: corporate reporting, integrated reporting, external audit and corporate governance with a specific focus on the functioning of mechanisms of accountability. Warren has published over 100 journal articles and other research-based publications including papers in *Accounting, Auditing & Accountability Journal*; *British Accounting Review*; *Accounting Forum*; *Journal of Accounting and Public Policy*; and *Meditari Accountancy Research*. He has contributed to several technical and practitioner-focused reports dealing with different aspects of integrated reporting and has served on integrated reporting working groups for the Independent Regulatory Board for Auditors and Integrated

Reporting Committee of South Africa. He consults widely with practitioners and investors on different aspects of corporate reporting. Warren is a member of the Chartered Institute of Management Accountants and the South African Institute of Chartered Accountants. He holds a PhD from King's College London.

Contributors

Giulia Achilli, PhD, is a lecturer in accounting at Royal Holloway University of London. Her research interests focus on the visual design of accounting and reporting practices, as well as on integrated thinking and reporting.

Elisabeth Albertini is a professor at the IAE Paris – Sorbonne Business School. Before her academic career, she worked for several years in a company that has implemented integrated reporting as a mean of disclosing non-financial information.

Jill Atkins is Chair in Financial Management at the University of Sheffield and a visiting professor at the University of the Witwatersrand. She is a professor of corporate governance with over 100 publications on different forms of environmental, integrated and sustainability reporting.

Carlo Bagnoli is a Full Professor of Strategy Innovation at Ca' Foscari University of Venice. His research interests include the impact of strategy and innovation on integrated reporting and financial disclosure.

Richard Barker is Professor of Accounting, Said Business School, University of Oxford, is a member of the UK's Corporate Reporting Council and a former Research Fellow at the IASB.

Mary E. Barth is Joan E. Horngren Professor of Accounting, Emerita, Stanford Graduate School of Business, researcher on integrated reporting.

Michael Bray is KPMG Fellow in Integrated Reporting at Deakin University. He advises KPMG clients on integrated reporting and assures their integrated reports under the <IR> Framework, and teaches and researches integrated reporting at Deakin University.

Caroline M. Bridges is Senior Tutor, University of Auckland Business School and has worked in public practice and the corporate sector; the research in her PhD examined integrated reporting.

Judy Brown is a professor at the Victoria University of Wellington and an associate editor of *Critical Perspectives on Accounting* and has research expertise in the fields of critical accounting, accounting and democracy, sustainability, integrated reporting and participatory governance.

Michael Büchling is a lecturer in the School of Accountancy, University of the Witwatersrand. He is an assurance and corporate governance researcher focusing specifically on emerging forms of environmental reporting.

Cristiano Busco, PhD, is Professor of Accounting and Integrated Reporting at LUISS Guido Carli University of Rome and at the University of Roehampton. Previously, Cristiano has held positions at the National University of Ireland, Babson College, Manchester Business School, the University of Southern California and the University of Siena.

Steven F. Cahan is Professor of Accounting, University of Auckland. He is a researcher on integrated reporting and a member of the IIRC Academic Oversight Body.

Dannielle Cerbone is a senior lecturer in the School of Accountancy, University of the Witwatersrand. She is a corporate governance and assurance researcher focusing on the development of integrated reporting in emerging economies.

Li Chen is Senior Lecturer in Accounting, University of Auckland, and a researcher on integrated reporting.

Charles H. Cho is Professor of Accounting and the Erivan K. Haub Chair in Business & Sustainability at the Schulich School of Business, York University in Toronto, Canada. His research expertise focuses on different types of non-financial reporting and his work in this particular area has been widely published in high-impact academic journals.

Craig Deegan is Professor of Accounting at RMIT University Australia, is and has been a leader in the area of organisational accountability for social and environmental performance for a number of years, and he is one of the most highly cited accounting researchers internationally.

Derick de Jongh is Associate Professor in the Department of Business Management and Director of the Albert Luthuli Centre for Responsible Leadership at the University of Pretoria. Prior to this position, he founded the Centre for Corporate Citizenship at UNISA in 2002. His quest in life is to prepare the next generation of responsible leaders in service of a sustainable planet.

René de Klerk is Programme Coordinator for the BCom Economics and Law degree at Akademia, a private institute for Higher Learning in South Africa. She is passionate about social and environmental justice and is curious to find out whether integrated reporting and investment decision making can contribute to sustainability.

Jesse Dillard is Adjunct Professor at the Victoria University of Wellington and University of Central Florida and an associate editor of *Critical Perspectives on Accounting* and has research expertise in the fields of interdisciplinary and critical accounting, social and environmental accounting and accountability, sustainability, integrated reporting and management information systems.

Ana Rita Domingues is a PhD student in management, University of Bologna. She has a research interest in sustainability performance assessment and reporting, sustainability indicators and stakeholder engagement.

John Dumay is Associate Professor of Accounting and Finance at Macquarie University Business School, Sydney, and the University of Bologna. He has published widely on integrated reporting and other forms of non-financial reporting and these works are highly cited.

Neil Eccles is a professor in the Institute for Corporate Citizenship at the University of South Africa with an interest in sustainability, business and contradictions, three themes that are all very germane to the integrated reporting discourse.

Martin Farrar is Associate Technical Director (Strategic Sustainability and Management Accounting), AICPA–CIMA. He is one of the management accounting research technical specialists working in the different Management Accounting Practice Areas which includes reporting issues.

Marco Fasan is an associate professor at the Ca' Foscari University of Venice. His research interests include integrated reporting.

Eduardo Flores is Assistant Professor at the University of Sao Paulo in the Accounting & Actuarial Science Department. He is alternate board member of the International Integrated Reporting Council and Coordinator of the Financial and Economic Dimension of the Corporate Sustainability Index (ISE) in Brazil.

John Flower was formerly Professor of Accounting, University of Bristol, and has penned several highly cited critiques of the IIRC.

Sendirella George is a lecturer at the School of Accounting and Commercial Law, Victoria University of Wellington, and has research expertise in the fields of critical accounting, accounting for sustainability and integrated reporting.

Jannik Gerwanski, MSc, is a PhD candidate affiliated to the chair of Accounting, Auditing & Corporate Governance at Leuphana University Lueneburg, and has his primary research interest in integrated reporting, its determinants and its effects.

Fabrizio Granà, PhD, is Assistant Professor in Management Control at ESCP Business School, London. His research interests focus on the role of accounting and reporting practices for sustainable development. In particular, he focuses on integrated thinking and integrated management.

James Guthrie, Member of the Order of Australia, is Distinguished Professor of Accounting, Macquarie Business School. He has been researching and publishing on integrated reporting for nearly a decade.

Julie Harrison is an associate professor at the University of Auckland Business School. She has worked in public practice and the corporate sector; since joining academia in 2000 she has specialised in performance measurement and reporting, most recently in the area of sustainability.

James Hazelton is an associate professor at Macquarie Business School. He has extensive experience in both teaching and researching alternative accounting methods, including IR.

Maria Federica Izzo, PhD, is a lecturer in accounting at LUISS University. Her research interests include corporate reporting, performance measurement and integrated reporting as well as integrated thinking.

Amanpreet Kaur is a lecturer in accounting at the University of South Australia.She has contributed to the sustainability reporting research agenda with a particular focus on stakeholder engagement and integrated planning and reporting practices in the public sector.

Alessandro Lai is Professor of Accounting at Verona University. He has published several articles on integrated reporting, is engaged in research projects on integrated reporting practices and is president of the Italian Body for Business Reporting (OIBR Foundation).

Yvette Lange is Associate Director at PricewaterhouseCoopers (South Africa). She specialises in the assurance of non-financial information and application of integrated reporting frameworks and guidelines.

Matteo La Torre is Postdoc Research Fellow of Accounting, University "G. d'Annunzio" of Chieti-Pescara. He researches on integrated reporting, non-financial reporting and digital advances and has been published in *Meditari Accountancy Research*, *Journal of Intellectual Capital* and *The British Accounting Review*.

Sumit Lodhia is Professor of Accounting, University of South Australia Business School. He has contributed to the integrated reporting literature through publications focusing on the transition to integrated reporting by a customer-owned bank, the role of information and communication technologies to facilitate Integrated Reporting, sustainability and integrated reporting in the public sector, and the readability of integrated reports.

Mercedes Luque-Vilchez, PhD is a researcher and teaching assistant of accounting at the University of Córdoba. Her research interests focus on social and environmental accounting and sustainability reporting practices with a focus on regulation and assurance.

Francesca Manes-Rossi is an associate professor at the University of Naples, Federico II, and has a research interest in sustainability and integrated reporting in public entities, international public sector accounting and auditing standards and performance measurement.

Eleonora Masiero is a PhD working as postdoctoral researcher and lecturer at the Department of Management, at Ca' Foscari University of Venice. Her interest in IR emerged during her PhD studies and was deepened during the following years through researches, meetings and workshops.

Maurizio Massaro is an Associate Professor of Digital Management, Planning and Control at the Ca' Foscari University of Venice. His research interests include management control systems and non-financial information and disclosure.

Rebecca McCaffry is Associate Technical Director (Public Sector Management Accounting), AICPA-CIMA. She is one of the management accounting research technical specialists working in the different Management Accounting Practice Areas which includes reporting issues.

Parvez Mia has completed his PhD from Macquarie Business School where he has investigated cities' environmental disclosure practices which is an important aspect of integrated reporting.

Chiara Mio is Full Professor at the Ca' Foscari University of Venice. She is chair of the ESG Reporting Task Force (Accountancy Europe) and she has published a number of research papers on integrated reporting.

Liz Prescott is on secondment to the IIRC and holds the role of Technical Director, having previously worked in the IIRC's Networks and Relationships, and Stakeholder Engagement teams.

John Purcell, FCPA, is Policy Adviser ESG at CPA Australia, and in this capacity provides technical and policy analysis on emerging forms of corporate disclosure, of which integrated reporting is a key component, including associated regulatory and governance developments.

Nick Ridehalgh is KPMG Australia – National Leader Better Business Reporting. IIRC Ambassador. He is a member of the Working Group that developed the <IR> Framework (2010–2013) and principal of Integrated Reporting Education Australia (an IIRC accredited training collaboration of KPMG, UNSW and Deakin) delivering <IR> training through Chartered Accountants Australia and New Zealand and UNSW.

Leonardo Rinaldi is a senior lecturer in accounting at the School of Business and Management at Royal Holloway University of London. His research explores the causes and consequence of integrated reporting and how it contributes to changing entrenched cultural and political institutions. Leonardo has been co-guest editor of two Special Issues on integrated reporting published in *Accounting, Auditing & Accountability Journal*.

Leigh Roberts is Chief Executive Officer of the Integrated Reporting Committee of South Africa and Chair of the Integrated Reporting Committee Working Group.

Adriana Rossi, PhD, is a research fellow at the University of Siena and Teaching Assistant of Planning & Control at LUISS Guido Carli University of Rome. Her research interests focus on the role of accounting and reporting practices for sustainable development with a focus on sustainability reporting and assurance instruments and integrated thinking.

Rebecca L. Orelli is Associate Professor of Accounting, University of Bologna. She focuses her research on IR in the public sector. She also has a research interest on sustainability and UN SDGs, stakeholder engagement and public value.

Ian Selby is Vice President Global Management Accounting Research and Innovation, leads the global research and innovation operation for CIMA working with businesses, universities and CIMA members in every continent to foster and promote the science of management accounting and he leads the multi-centred and talented R&D and Innovation team, some of whom have contributed to the chapter in this book.

Roger Simnett is a Professor of Accounting at UNSW Sydney, and the current Chair and CEO of the Australian Auditing and Assurance Standards Board, and has previously served on the IIRC working panel.

Peter Simons is Associate Technical Director (Future of Finance), AICPA–CIMA. He is one of the management accounting research technical specialists working in the different Management Accounting Practice Areas which includes reporting issues.

Peter Spence is Associate Technical Director (Performance Management and Cost Accounting), AICPA-CIMA. He is one of the management accounting research technical specialists working in the different Management Accounting Practice Areas which includes reporting issues.

Riccardo Stacchezzini is Associate Professor of Accounting at Verona University. He is engaged in several research projects on integrated reporting, has published articles on integrated reporting practices, and is a member of the European Accounting Association (EAA) Stakeholder Reporting Committee (SRC) and of the scientific committee of the Italian Body for Business Reporting (OIBR Foundation).

Alan Teixeira is Global Director of IFRS Research, Deloitte LLP and Department of Accounting and Finance, University of Auckland. He is a former Senior Technical Director at the IASB who led the development of the Management Commentary Practice Statement and was on the IIRC Task Force that developed the IIRC Framework.

Nick Topazio is Associate Technical Director (Corporate Reporting), AICPA-CIMA He is the Association's Corporate Reporting Research Specialist with extensive knowledge and experience in this research field but more broadly across the different Management Accounting Practice Areas.

Wayne van Zijl is a senior lecturer in the School of Accountancy, University of the Witwatersrand. He is a financial reporting researcher dealing with the evolution of corporate reporting.

Patrick Velte is Professor of Accounting, Auditing & Corporate Governance at Leuphana University Lueneburg. He has published several empirical studies on nonfinancial reporting, especially on integrated reporting during the last years.

Elmar R. Venter is Associate Professor of Accounting, University of Pretoria, and a researcher on integrated reporting.

Belinda Williams is a senior lecturer in accounting, College of Business and Economics, University of Tasmania. She has contributed to the wider voluntary reporting agenda in the public sector with specific focus on research in integrated reporting in local government in recent years.

Mark Yeoman is a senior executive with experience in finance and general management in the retail, financial services, technology and telecommunications sectors. He was involved in the international pilot of integrated reporting and has driven the adoption of integrated reporting in two large organizations.

Shan Zhou is a senior lecturer, University of Sydney. She has been doing research on integrated reporting since her PhD thesis and has published several papers on integrated reporting in leading academic journals.

1

INTRODUCTION TO *THE ROUTLEDGE HANDBOOK OF INTEGRATED REPORTING*

An overview of integrated reporting and this book, which entails different perspectives on a maturing field and a framework for future research

Charl de Villiers

The University of Auckland, and University of Pretoria

Pei-Chi Kelly Hsiao

The University of Waikato

Warren Maroun

University of the Witwatersrand

Abstract

This chapter provides a brief overview of integrated reporting (IR). An integrated report should be a concise account of an organization's future value creation story, including information on financial and non-financial capitals, and referencing the organization's strategy and business model. Integrated reporting started in practice and was later formalized, first in the influential King Report on Corporate Governance, then by the Integrated Reporting Committee of South Africa (IRCSA), and the International Integrated Reporting Council (IIRC). Integrated reporting is now promoted by these institutions, the accounting profession, regulators and other bodies around the world who espouse the theoretical advantages of IR. There is empirical evidence for some of these claims, but IR's critics lament its neoliberal foundations and its potentially negative consequences. These differing viewpoints are reflected in this book. We summarise the range of opinions in this lead chapter, while providing some frameworks for the different perspectives and causal links involved.

Introduction

Integrated reporting (IR) sought to address deficiencies with existing reporting frameworks, which were either dedicated to dealing with financial issues or failed to make the interconnections between economic, environmental and social capitals sufficiently clear. As explained by Mervyn King, in his foreword to the discussion paper by the Integrated Reporting Committee of South Africa (IRCSA):

> [A] string of corporate collapses over the past decade has led many stakeholders to question the relevance and reliability of annual financial reports as a basis for making decisions about an organisation. Reports based largely on financial information do not provide sufficient insight to enable stakeholders to form a comprehensive picture of the organisation's performance and of its ability to create and sustain value, especially in the context of growing environmental, social and economic challenges. Sustainability reports have similarly suffered weaknesses, usually appearing disconnected from the organisation's financial reports, generally providing a backward-looking review of performance, and almost always failing to make the link between sustainability issues and the organisation's core strategy. For the most part, these reports have failed to address the lingering distrust among civil society of the intentions and practices of business. Stakeholders today want forward-looking information that will enable them to more effectively assess the total economic value of an organisation.
>
> *(IRCSA, 2011, p. 1)*

An integrated report is meant to follow a process of integrated thinking within the organization, suggesting that leadership and governance should be aware of the interrelated nature of the financial and non-financial capitals the organization uses to create value (De Villiers and Hsiao, 2018).

Some of the world's leading organizations have been implementing IR practices and disclosure in anticipation of IR becoming a global norm. For example, KPMG (2017) finds that IR has been gaining momentum following the release of the International Integrated Reporting Council's (IIRC) Framework, the International Integrated Reporting Framework (IIRC Framework), in several jurisdictions, including South Africa, Japan, Spain, the Netherlands, Brazil, the United Kingdom, Sweden and Poland. More broadly, the release of at least some form of corporate social responsibility report to complement conventional financial reporting has become generally accepted internationally for both large and mid-cap companies (KPMG, 2012, 2013, 2015, 2017). Emerging economies, in particular, have been devoting considerable attention to expanding their reporting models to address issues such as climate change, human rights and sustainable development (KPMG, 2017). Corporate responsibility reporting and, more recently, IR, is seen as offering an opportunity to attract foreign investment, signal the quality of underlying corporate governance systems, and demonstrate the credibility of these jurisdictions to the international capital market (KPMG, 2017; De Villiers and Maroun, 2018). At the same time, it is hoped that IR will promote a more responsible approach to doing business, which considers stakeholder interests and the importance of protecting the environment (King, 2018). Used in conjunction with existing reporting guidelines, governance systems and management practices, IR has the potential to drive positive organizational change and help with the realization of the United Nations' Sustainable Development Goals (Guthrie et al., 2017; Al-Htaybat and von Alberti-alhtaybat, 2018; McNally and Maroun, 2018).

There are, however, a number of limitations and detractors. As discussed in more detail in Parts II to V of this book, the IIRC may be over-emphasizing financial capital providers to the detriment of stakeholder-centrism and long-term sustainability (see also Flower, 2015; Thomson, 2015). Despite efforts to develop a multi-capital reporting model, conceptualizations of value and value-creation continue to be constrained by economic imperatives (Brown and Dillard, 2014). The possibility of IR forming part of an impression management strategy, which simply obscures unsustainable business practices, cannot be precluded (Haji and Anifowose, 2016; du Toit et al., 2017) while the practical challenges of internalizing and applying the IIRC Framework should not be overlooked (Dumay et al., 2017; McNally et al., 2017).

Consequently, IR is best described as being in a developmental stage (De Villiers et al., 2014; Rinaldi et al., 2018). There is significant variability in how the IIRC Framework is being interpreted and applied, leading to differences in the content, format and structure of even the most recent examples from industry leaders (PwC, 2015; EY, 2018). Rather than 'crystallizing' into a standard reporting typology, IR remains an ambiguous concept, which requires cross-disciplinary advances to support full implementation and realise its potential for promoting long-term value-creation and sustainability.

Given these differences in perspective on, and practice of, IR, *The Routledge Handbook of Integrated Reporting* provides the most current and comprehensive examination of IR at a time when the disparate views on IR could be a sign of a maturing field. The book includes insights from more than 60 authors, provided in 30 chapters. It includes authors who represent the IIRC, IRCSA, professional bodies and audit firms, as well as leading academics in the fields of IR, environmental, corporate social responsibility and sustainability reporting. The councils and professionals mostly promote IR, while the academics fall into different camps, some providing (seemingly) balanced empirical insights, while others provide insights on specialized areas, and yet others critique various aspects of the promotion and implementation of IR. Giving voice to these differing perspectives is a unique feature of this book, because of its openness to the inclusion of these differing perspectives.

The collected work provides an in-depth review of the development of IR, with a focus on the interpretation and guidance provided by the IIRC. The chapters include a detailed discussion on the potential of IR to promote financial stability and holistic value creation. They offer multiple perspectives on this emerging form of reporting and provide insights on current implementation and assurance strategies, the impacts of IR on management and disclosure practices and the relationship between IR and sustainable development. The chapters include reviews of the most recent research, practitioner viewpoints, conceptual pieces, case studies and disclosure analyses. The chapters in the book are written in accessible language; therefore, this handbook is suitable for all readers, regardless of their perspective or level of background knowledge on IR.

Overview of the handbook

The handbook is composed of seven parts, each of which deals with a different aspect of the development, application and future of IR and related practices. Figure 1.1 provides an overview.

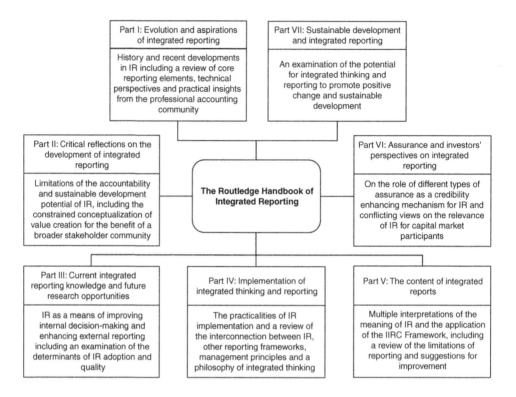

Figure 1.1 Outline of *The Routledge Handbook of Integrated Reporting*

Evolution and aspirations of integrated reporting

Part I, 'Evolution and aspirations of integrated reporting', provides a detailed overview of the development of IR, what it is meant to be, and what it is intended to achieve. The chapters in this section are from practitioners' perspectives and they discuss the events that led up to the formation and development of the IRC, the IIRC and the IIRC Framework. The future of these initiatives is also examined.

Chapter 2 focuses on the IIRC and the IIRC Framework. Bray and Prescott provide a historical overview of the IIRC's developments, its current progress, and its short-, medium- and long-term agendas to achieve global adoption by 2025. Chapter 3 presents an introduction to another key player in the IR movement, the IRC of South Africa. Roberts and colleagues introduce the ten key considerations for a balanced report and provide examples of best practice for each consideration. The guidance offered in this chapter is of interest to both current and prospective integrated report preparers.

Chapters 4 to 6 focus on professional accountancy bodies' advocacy for IR and their contribution to the development of reporting discourse and practice. From the KPMG perspective, in Chapter 4 Bray and Ridehalgh trace the evolution of IR through the four waves of business and accounting, illustrating how the focuses of business and corporate disclosure simultaneously changed across time. The authors share first-hand insights on KPMG's involvement in IR and their plans to support clients through IR implementation and assurance.

Topazio and colleagues present the views of members of the Chartered Institute of Management Accountants (CIMA) on IR and the IIRC Framework in Chapter 5. Emphasis is placed on the potential benefits of adopting the IIRC Framework, which include better understanding of the sources of value creation and enhanced organizational trust and reputation. The chapter highlights the CIMA's involvement with and advocacy for IR and details the latest IR developments. Similarly, from CPA Australia's perspective, in Chapter 6 Purcell advocates for the adoption of the IIRC Framework and integrated thinking for all forms of business organizations. The author describes CPA Australia's IR journey and its research, which supports the preparation of integrated reports.

Critical reflections on the development of integrated reporting

Part II, 'Critical reflections on the development of integrated reporting', challenges some of the perspectives presented by the professional accounting community. Academic contributors reflect on the focus and content of the IIRC Framework and discuss concerns relating to the IIRC having apparently abandoned accountability and sustainability.

The section opens with Deegan's discussion of the accountability notion and the application of a four-step model of accountability to evaluate the IIRC Framework (Chapter 7). Despite the potential to improve reporting practices, the author argues that IIRC falls short of promoting accountability to broad stakeholder groups. Aspects such as the restricted focus on financial capital providers, a defined reporting boundary and the adoption of a weak sustainability perspective undermines the framework's suitability for promoting meaningful reporting. Flower echoes these concerns in Chapter 8 which reflects on the development of the IIRC and its Framework and argues that the organization has abandoned the concept of sustainability. The author suggests that regulatory capture and the need for acceptance have resulted in the IIRC Framework deviating from the original intention of a framework supporting accounting for sustainability. The IIRC is criticised for advocating weak sustainability practices and promoting a business-as-usual attitude.

Brown and colleagues argue that, due to the dominating business case perspective that privileges financial capital providers, the current framing of IR fails to take into account broad stakeholder interests. Chapter 9 re-envisions IR through a critical dialogic accounting and accountability lens to propose a broader reporting initiative, which addresses the need for accountability and sustainability.

Chapters 10 and 11 discuss the similarities of the IIRC Framework with the International Financial Reporting Standards (IFRS) and intellectual capital reporting. Both point to a bleak future for the IIRC Framework. In Chapter 10, Barker and Teixeira discuss whether the IIRC and the International Accounting Standards Board (IASB) have produced competing reporting frameworks. Comparisons of the purpose and guidance provided by these two frameworks lead the authors to conclude that these frameworks do not differ in substance and do compete with each other. Both frameworks anchor on financial capital and the information needs of investors, emphasize the importance of non-financial information, and face the same limitations with reporting on diverse capitals. The authors suggest that the IIRC Framework may become redundant if the International Accounting Standards Board improves its guidance for the preparation of management commentaries. Dumay reaches a similar conclusion in Chapter 11, arguing that IR, as envisioned by the IIRC, suffers the same problems that eventually led to the demise of intellectual capital reporting. Integrated reporting is described as a myth that reinforces the public façade of good corporate citizenship while hiding dishonest behaviours.

Current integrated reporting knowledge and future research opportunities

Departing from normative and critical perspectives of IR, Part III, 'Current integrated reporting knowledge and future research opportunities', reviews the existing IR literature. As there are a number of literature reviews on IR available, the chapters in this section focus on specific research techniques and aspects of IR to provide focused discussions and suggestions for future research.

In Chapter 12, Barth and colleagues survey the existing literature that provides evidence on the dual objectives of IR: improving external information and informing better internal decision-making. They present an overview of agency and non-agency theories, and indicates that, while there is initial evidence of capital market benefits, archival evidence for internal benefits is sparse.

In relation to the external information objective, Chapter 13 by Rossi and colleagues draws on the academic literature and policy and regulatory documents to analyse the current status of IR assurance research and practices. The chapter identifies a number of technical challenges that frustrate efforts to have integrated reports external assured. This leads to suggestions for configuring IR assurance practices and clarifying the roles assurance practitioners in the IR process.

Chapter 14 deals with IR more broadly. Velte and Gerwanski focus on the determinants of IR adoption and disclosure quality, specifically reviewing studies related to internal and external corporate governance mechanisms. The authors identify a number of corporate governance characteristics that potentially affect IR adoption and quality but are yet to be examined in detail. Examples include management demographic and choice of external auditors. Velte and Gerwanski suggest that future research needs to clarify what IR quality is, how it should be measured and how to gauge the factors that contribute to better quality reporting. De Villiers et al. (2017b) address IR measurement and appropriate control measures at length in an article that should be seen as a starting point for any further exploration of these matters.

Chapter 15 complements the private sector research by providing a glimpse of IR in the public sector. Lodhia and colleagues discuss sustainability reporting and its connection with IR and draw on the IR literature to identify potential advantages and challenges of IR in the public sector. A number of research opportunities are noted, including investigating public sector IR in developing countries, comparing public sector IR with private sector IR, and exploring how public sector organizations implement integrated thinking.

Implementation of integrated thinking and reporting

Part IV, 'Implementation of integrated thinking and reporting', explores the process of IR implementation and the impacts IR has on accounting systems. The chapters deal with different conceptualizations of IR and how integrated thinking can be used to strengthen stakeholder engagement.

Chapter 16 evaluates whether organizations should start with integrated thinking or prepare an integrated report first, when implementing the IIRC Framework. Bridges and colleagues present two case studies, representing two organizations that have embarked on their IR journey in opposite ways. The authors conclude that there is no best way of adopting the IIRC Framework. Rather, it is necessary for organizations to have experience with sustainability management and reporting, a reporting champion, and strategies and management focus aligned with value creation of diverse capitals to sustain an integrated approach to business management and reporting.

Similar conclusions are reached by Busco and colleagues. Chapter 17 draws on the experience of a European university to illustrate how the IIRC Framework influenced the design of its social impact assessment tool. The chapter demonstrates the potential of integrating the IIRC Framework with widely accepted impact assessment tools to improve understanding and assessment of organizations' impacts on the capitals used to create stakeholder value.

Chapter 18 discusses the actors and processes involved in preparing an integrated report. A report taxonomy is proposed by Stacchezzini and Lai which sees the report preparation process as dependent on preparers' modes of cognition and stakeholder salience. The authors suggest that embracing the concept of integrated thinking (and considering both investor and stakeholder interests) could encourage a move away from siloed reporting.

Chapter 19 also focuses on cognitive processes, using relevant concepts to conceptualize the relationship between integrated thinking and stakeholder engagement. Rinaldi proposes a processing model to illustrate how integrated thinking can contribute to effective stakeholder engagement, and suggests that the processes of cognitive ease, associative activation and repeated experience can be applied as forms of integrated thinking to enhance stakeholder engagement.

The content of integrated reports

Part V, 'The content of integrated reports', includes studies that have assessed the content of integrated reports. Chapters 20 to 23 investigate the reporting changes following adoption of the IIRC Framework or provide suggestions on how to improve integrated disclosure practices.

A case study by Guthrie and La Torre in Chapter 20 demonstrates that the concept of IR is open to different interpretations and adoptions. There are multiple ways to produce high quality disclosure and the IIRC Framework may not be necessary for this purpose. The case company is acknowledged as an example of 'best practice' for reporting. It has an established history of sustainability reporting, and participated in the IIRC pilot program. However, the company's integrated report omits participation in the program and is stakeholder-orientated rather than investor-centric. While there are external pressures for adoption of the IIRC Framework, the company continued with its own ideas and internally developed reporting practices.

In Chapter 21, Albertini and Cho assess whether integrated reports provide comprehensive information on sustainable value creation. Based on the six capitals outlined in the IIRC Framework, the authors investigate the types of information European companies disclose in their integrated reports. The authors identify a number of concerns from available integrated reports, including bias towards disclosure of positive information, a lack of disclosure on all capitals and problems with comparability.

provides practical insights on producing an integrated report in Chapter 22. The chapter assesses the disclosures of listed South African companies using PwC's IR model and the IIRC Framework. The author recognises the effort reporters have invested in improving their disclosure over time, and identifies opportunities for improvement in terms of reporting on governance aspects, business model outcomes and key performance indicators related to strategic processes.

In Chapter 23, Masiero and colleagues deal specifically with the principle of connectivity. The chapter summarizes a case study to illustrate how organizations can strengthen communication with stakeholders by enhancing textual, intertextual and relational 'connectiveness'. The findings suggest that the use of cross-references and navigation devices, infographics and hyperlinks, social media platforms and seeking stakeholder feedback can stimulate constant dialogue with stakeholders.

Assurance and investors' perspectives on integrated reporting

Part VI, 'Assurance and investors' perspectives on integrated reporting', deals with IR assurance practices and investors' perspectives on IR. Chapter 24 provides an in-depth discussion of the IIRC's assurance discussion papers and responses, and current regulatory guidance and approaches for IR assurance. Zhou and colleagues discuss different pathways to add credibility and trust to an integrated report. The authors focus on four credibility and trust enhancing techniques: the ISA 720 approach; the ISAE 3000 approach; the combined assurance approach and the integrated report assurance approach.

Chapters 25 and 26 focus on investors' perspectives. Fasan and colleagues (2020) assess whether capital market reactions detected in prior IR studies can be attributed to a virtuous circle or a benchmarking effect. The former suggests that analysts are interested in having detailed and updated IR information. The latter posits that analysts following non-IR companies demand IR information because of its value relevance. The study assesses the number of references made to IR themes in conference calls. The findings provide evidence supporting the virtuous circle view, suggesting IR companies cover IR themes more extensively than non-IR companies.

While in Chapter 25, Fasan and colleagues suggest that capital market participants are interested in IR information, in Chapter 26 de Klerk and colleagues argue that they may not be interested in integrated reports. In a South African context, de Klerk and colleagues investigate investment decision-making processes, investors' use of integrated reports and their perceptions of financial stability and sustainability. The findings show that many participants are unaware of IR and few are using integrated reports as an information source for decision-making. There is a level of distrust of corporate reporting. Maximizing financial returns and minimizing risk remain the priority of investors.

Sustainable development and integrated reporting

'Sustainable development and integrated reporting' is the final part of this book. It reflects on the role of IR in progressing towards sustainable development. Contrary to the views expressed in Part II, the chapters in Part VII argue that there is potential for integrated thinking and reporting to promote sustainable business practices and act as a framework for communicating sustainability performance. Chapters 27 to 30 reflect on the United Nations Sustainable Development Goals (SDGs) and measurement of environmental sustainability.

Part VII opens with Busco and colleagues' overview of the SDGs and organizations' role in meeting these goals in Chapter 27. The chapter presents three case studies, which demonstrate how organizations have been re-adapting their strategies and business models to integrate the SDGs into their reporting processes. This process requires changes in operational models and constant innovation in performance measurement and reporting practices. The authors suggest that integrated thinking and reporting is potentially a powerful tool in this regard. Similarly, in Chapter 28, Guthrie and colleagues suggest the IIRC Framework could potentially be used to assess and communicate sustainability practices. The chapter examines an Italian university's journey towards integrating the SDGs into its operations and disclosure. The university followed the GRI guidelines and adopted integrated thinking and reporting, as encouraged by the British Universities Finance

Directors Group. The authors conclude that the IIRC Framework may provide appropriate guidance for introducing integrated thinking and embedding the SDGs into organizational strategies.

The remaining two chapters focus on environmental accounting. In Chapter 29, Büchling and Atkins review different reporting standards for biodiversity that could guide disclosure of natural capital within integrated reports. The authors present a framework for what they refer to as 'extinction accounting' and address the criticism that integrated reports do not provide sufficient detail on the importance of biodiversity to the organization and society as a whole.

Finally, in Chapter 30 Mia and colleagues focus on accounting for greenhouse gases. The chapter provides a detailed overview of accounting for greenhouse gas inventory and discusses measurement and recognition challenges. The authors encourage standardised accounting and reporting guidance, and recommend the adoption of a consumption-based approach and inclusion of all scope 3 emissions to improve the quality of emissions accounting systems.

Discussion and areas for future research

Two recent special issues on IR, one in *Meditari Accountancy Research* (De Villiers et al., 2017a), and the other in the *Accounting, Auditing & Accountability Journal* (Rinaldi, Unerman and De Villiers, 2018) provide interesting new perspectives on IR. Based on the articles published in these special issues and in the broader literature, a model can be constructed to depict the determinants, framing schematics and consequences of IR (see Figure 1.2).

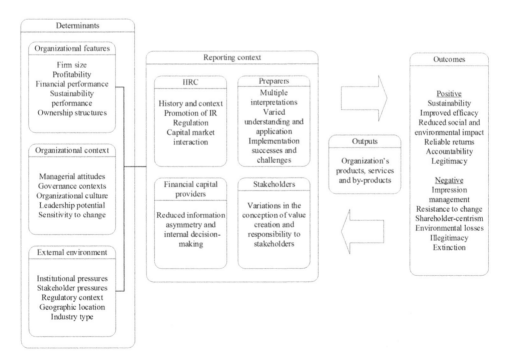

Figure 1.2 Integrated reporting model

Three broad determinants of IR adoption and quality are identified: organizational features, entity-specific contexts and the external environment. The first includes factors such as firm size, profitability and performance. These give an indication of the complexity of the business model, which must be explained to shareholding and non-shareholding stakeholders, and the resources that must be available to prepare an integrated report (De Villiers et al., 2017a; De Villiers and Maroun, 2018). The second assesses the relevance of managerial attitudes to alternate forms of reporting; cultural considerations; organizational leadership, governance structures; and, ultimately, an organization's propensity to change (Stubbs and Higgins, 2014; Guthrie et al., 2017; Al-Htaybat and von Alberti-alhtaybat, 2018; McNally and Maroun, 2018). These factors work hand-in-hand with institutional systems, societal expectations and regulatory requirements. Each can be a source of powerful coercive, normative or mimetic pressures, which influence the decision to prepare an integrated report and the level of commitment to high quality reporting (De Villiers and Maroun, 2018).

Determinants should be understood according to the prevailing reporting context (De Villiers and Lubbe, 2001). In our view, the formation of the IIRC, the technical provisions of the IIRC Framework and its application by professional accounting bodies – dealt with mainly in Part I of this book – provide the discourse for describing and developing specific reporting practices.

As an emerging type of reporting, different conceptualizations of IR are possible. In this context, Part III of this book examines how IR can develop as a mechanism for reducing information asymmetry and informing changes in internal business processes. It can be complemented by existing governance systems and assurance practices to bolster the quality of information being made available to financial capital providers and other stakeholders in both the private and public sectors. The extent to which these benefits are realised will be influenced by how IR is understood and operationalized by preparers (Parts IV and V); users' perceptions of the relevance of IR (Part VI); and the constraining effects of economic paradigms and shareholder-centric conceptions of value (Part II).

From a critical perspective, several chapters in this book consider that IR is part of a compliance exercise designed to placate expectations of at least some environmental and social disclosures to complement financial statements. There are no direct effects on an organization's outputs. Integrated reporting becomes part of the impression management machinery which, paradoxically, contributes to the legitimacy of unsustainable business practices and a failure to achieve sustainable development goals (Flower, 2015; Thomson, 2015). More optimistic accounts are also provided. While integrated reports suffer from several limitations, they can provide a basis for proactively managing environmental and social concerns, changing the way in which organizations do business, and promoting a more holistic understanding of performance and value creation (Part VII).

Finally, the 30 chapters making up this book offer numerous opportunities for additional research. While it is difficult to predict the direction of future research, we use Figure 1.3 to provide a schematic for scholars interested in contributing to IR research and the IR literature.

Starting on the left, there are opportunities to use different research paradigms and different theoretical perspectives to explain the emergence, development and future of IR. For example, studies embedded in the positivist, interpretivist and critical research paradigms can all contribute and provide different perspectives on IR, while stakeholder and agency theory could offer interesting insights into how firm-specific reporting practices are developed, and the role of different types of stakeholders in moderating the manner and

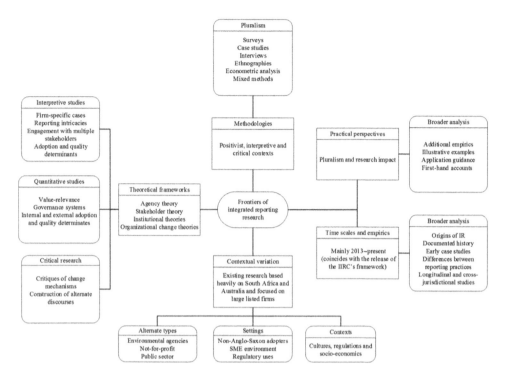

Figure 1.3 Opportunities for future research

extent of reporting on the six capitals outlined by the IIRC. Whether or not stakeholder groups are changing because of IR; how firms define materiality in multi-capital reporting model; and the 'elements' of an integrated report that are most valued by stakeholders could also be fruitful avenues for future research, using different approaches, such as interview-based approaches (De Villiers, 1999) or quantitative methods (De Villiers et al., 2017b).

There have been some studies on the effects of IR on organizational behaviour (Stubbs and Higgins, 2014; Guthrie et al., 2017; McNally and Maroun, 2018). These can be complemented by more detailed reviews of the interconnections among IR, integrated thinking and organizational change. For example:

- How do business models, strategy development, risk assessment and reporting practices interconnect and change over time?
- Why do some firms change rapidly when they adopt IR while others appear to be more 'inert'?
- What strategies are being used to ensure that IR does not become a compliance-approach to reporting?
- How do we know when integrated thinking has taken hold?

An analysis of the various determinants of the adoption and quality of IR would be useful. Possible examples include proxies for firm culture; the operation of corporate governance systems; variations in stakeholder pressure; and the attitudes of institutional investors to emerging forms of corporate reporting. Preparer characteristics are an additional consideration. While the prior research usually draws a distinction between internal and external reporting determinants (Alrazi et al., 2015; De Villiers et al., 2017a), we know relatively little about the impact which power-dynamics, socialization of preparers and the relationships between individual firm members have on the application of IR and the emergence of integrated thinking (Humphrey et al., 2017). The views of IR preparers can potentially be solicited (Adhariani and De Villiers, 2019)

More broadly, it is still unclear why IR becomes generally accepted in some organizations, and in some jurisdictions, while being fiercely resisted by others. The methods used to gain support for emerging forms of corporate reporting at the macro and firm level need to be examined in more detail. The same is true for strategies used to temper change.

To date, research has focused mainly on what Rinaldi et al. (2018) refer to as 'generation', 'elaboration', 'championing' and 'production' of IR. Compared with other types of corporate social responsibility reporting, there is little on the impact of IR. More refined value-relevance models, which control for differences in firm culture, governance systems and relationships with stakeholders, can provide additional insights. These can be complemented by interpretive studies engaging with investors, employee representatives, environmental agencies and other key stakeholders to determine exactly how integrated reports moderate the relationship between firms and their stakeholders and inform decision-making processes.

Several chapters in this book adopt a critical perspective. These chapters highlight the theoretical and practical limitations of IR that may undermine its potential to effect change. These studies provide a useful reference for case studies on exactly how IR fails to achieve its objectives. Both macro- and micro-level factors should be taken into consideration and used to generate clear recommendations for practitioners and standard setters.

When it comes to contextual focus, the majority of the research to date focuses on large listed companies in jurisdictions where IR is relatively established. However, emerging research deals with state-owned enterprises (Montecalvo et al., 2018; Farneti et al., 2019). Further opportunities for research in different settings include, but are not limited to, the following:

- How is the IIRC Framework being interpreted and applied by government agencies, local governments, non-governmental organizations and regulatory bodies?
- What factors influence small and medium-sized firms to adopt IR or to refrain from doing so?
- Are there differences in the attitudes towards IR and conceptualization of value, risk and materiality between different types of organizations which explain successes and failures in the adoption and application of the IIRC Framework?
- Do differences in countries' cultures, socio-political contexts, environmental conditions and economic development have any relevance for the extent to which IR is being practiced in different jurisdictions?

With the release of the IIRC Framework in 2013, and several companies adopting the framework, there are now opportunities for longitudinal studies. These can focus on a single jurisdiction and, as IR becomes more commonplace, include cross-jurisdictional analyses of the drivers, costs and benefits of IR. In addition, the influence of IR on other aspects of reporting can be studied (De Villiers and Sharma, 2019; Sukhari and De Villiers, 2019; Terblanche and De Villiers, 2019).

Finally, while theoretical application is important, this should not come at the expense of empirical development and practical relevance. Documenting changes in reporting practices, exploring alternate bases for measuring report quality and tracking the history of the IIRC will provide important insights on the development of IR, particularly for the practitioner community. To ensure that multiple perspectives are considered, we call for a methodological and theoretical pluralism (consider Dillard and Roslender, 2011; Atkins et al., 2015; De Villiers et al., 2019). Researchers should draw on a range of qualitative and quantitative methods, different theoretical frameworks and alternate sources of data to explore the development, application and consequences of IR. The choice of theory and methods is important but this must not undermine the need for academic research that is practically relevant and a driver of change in its own right.

Overall, with the rapid development of the ideas, frameworks and practice of IR, there are many research opportunities to assess the success, limitations, determinants and consequences of all kinds of IR, the IIRC Framework and the practitioners who promote IR.

References

Adhariani, D., and De Villiers, C. (2019). Integrated reporting: perspectives of corporate report preparers and other stakeholders. *Sustainability Accounting, Management and Policy Journal, 10*(1), 126–156.

Al-Htaybat, K., and von Alberti-alhtaybat, L. (2018). Integrated thinking leading to integrated reporting: case study insights from a global player. *Accounting, Auditing & Accountability Journal, 31*(5), 1435–1460.

Alrazi, B., De Villiers, C., and van Staden, C. J. (2015). A comprehensive literature review on, and the construction of a framework for, environmental legitimacy, accountability and proactivity. *Journal of Cleaner Production, 102*, 44–57.

Atkins, J., Atkins, B., Thomson, I., and Maroun, W. (2015). 'Good' news from nowhere: imagining utopian sustainable accounting. *Accounting, Auditing & Accountability Journal, 28*(5), 651–670.

Brown, J., and Dillard, J. (2014). Integrated reporting: on the need for broadening out and opening up. *Accounting, Auditing & Accountability Journal, 27*(7), 1120–1156.

De Villiers, C. (1999). The decision by management to disclose environmental information: a research note based on interviews. *Meditari Accountancy Research, 7*, 33–48.

De Villiers, C., Dumay, J., and Maroun, W. (2019). Qualitative accounting research: dispelling myths and developing a new research agenda. *Accounting & Finance, 59*(3), 1449–1458.

De Villiers, C., and Hsiao, P.-C. K. (2018). Integrated reporting. In C. De Villiers, and W. Maroun (Eds.), *Sustainability Accounting and Integrated Reporting* (pp. 13–24). London: Routledge.

De Villiers, C., Hsiao, P.-C. K., and Maroun, W. (2017a). Developing a conceptual model of influences around integrated reporting, new insights and directions for future research. *Meditari Accountancy Research, 25*(4), 450–460.

De Villiers, C., and Maroun, W. (2018). *Sustainability Accounting and Integrated Reporting*. London: Routledge.

De Villiers, C., Rinaldi, L., and Unerman, J. (2014). Integrated reporting: insights, gaps and an agenda for future research. *Accounting, Auditing & Accountability Journal, 27*(7), 1042–1067.

De Villiers, C., and Sharma, U. (2019). A critical reflection on the future of financial, intellectual capital, sustainability and integrated reporting. *Critical Perspectives on Accounting*. doi:10.1016/j. cpa.2017.05.003.

De Villiers, C., Venter, E., and Hsiao, P.-C.K. (2017b). Integrated reporting: background, measurement issues, approaches and an agenda for future research. *Accounting & Finance, 57*(4), 937–959.

De Villiers, C. J., and Lubbe, D. S. (2001). Industry differences in corporate environmental reporting in South Africa. *Meditari Accountancy Research, 9*(1), 81–91.

Dillard, J., and Roslender, R. (2011). Taking pluralism seriously: embedded moralities in management accounting and control systems. *Critical Perspectives on Accounting, 22*(2), 135–147.

du Toit, E., van Zyl, R., and Schütte, G. (2017). Integrated reporting by South African companies: a case study. *Meditari Accountancy Research, 25*(4), 654–674.

Dumay, J., Bernardi, C., Guthrie, J., and La Torre, M. (2017). Barriers to implementing the International Integrated Reporting Framework: a contemporary academic perspective. *Meditari Accountancy Research, 25*(4), 461–480.

EY. (2018). *EY's Excellence in Integrated Reporting Awards 2018*. Available at: www.ey.com/Publication/vwLUAssets/ey-excellence-integrated-reporting-awards-2016/$FILE/ey-excellence-integrated-reporting-awards-2016.pdf (accessed: 8 December 2019).

Farneti, F., Casonato, F., Montecalvo, M., and De Villiers, C. (2019). The influence of integrated reporting and stakeholder information needs on the disclosure of social information in a state-owned enterprise. *Meditari Accountancy Research*, 27(4), 556–579.

Fasan, M., Mio, C., and Flores, E. (2020). Assurance and investors' perspectives on integrated reporting – integrated reporting and earnings calls – virtuous circle or benchmarking effect? Preliminary insights. In C. De Villiers, P.-C. K. Hsiao, and W. Maroun (Eds.), *The Routledge Handbook of Integrated Reporting*. London: Routledge.

Flower, J. (2015). The international integrated reporting council: a story of failure. *Critical Perspectives on Accounting*, 27, 1–17.

Guthrie, J., Manes-Rossi, F., and Orelli, R. L. (2017). Integrated reporting and integrated thinking in Italian public sector organisations. *Meditari Accountancy Research*, 25(4), 553–573.

Haji, A. A., and Anifowose, M. (2016). The trend of integrated reporting practice in South Africa: ceremonial or substantive? *Sustainability Accounting, Management and Policy Journal*, 7(2), 190–224.

Humphrey, C., O'Dwyer, B., and Unerman, J. (2017). Re-theorizing the configuration of organizational fields: the IIRC and the pursuit of 'Enlightened' corporate reporting. *Accounting and Business Research*, 47(1), 30–63.

IRCSA. (2011). *Framework for Integrated Reporting and the Integrated Report*. Available at: www.sustainabilitysa.org (accessed: 5 June 2012).

King, M. (2018). Comments on integrated reporting and corporate governance in South Africa. IRCSA Annual Conference, South Africa, 24 July.

KPMG. (2012). *Carrots and Sticks – Promoting Transparency and Sustainability: An Update on Trends in Voluntary and Mandatory Approaches to Sustainability Reporting*. Available at: www.globalreporting.org/resourcelibrary/Carrots-And-Sticks-Promoting-Transparency-And-Sustainbability.pdf (accessed: 30 June 2013).

KPMG. (2013). *The KPMG Survey of Corporate Responsibility Reporting 2013*. Available at: https://assets.kpmg.com/content/dam/kpmg/pdf/2015/08/kpmg-survey-of-corporate-responsibility-reporting-2013.pdf (accessed: 11 December 2016).

KPMG. (2015). *Currents of Change: The KPMG Survey of Corporate Responsibility Reporting 2015*. Available at: https://assets.kpmg.com/content/dam/kpmg/pdf/2016/02/kpmg-international-survey-of-corporate-responsibility-reporting-2015.pdf (accessed: 11 December 2016).

KPMG. (2017). *The Road Ahead: The KPMG Survey of Corporate Responsibility Reporting 2017*. Available at: https://assets.kpmg.com/content/dam/kpmg/xx/pdf/2017/10/kpmg-survey-of-corporate-responsibility-reporting-2017.pdf (accessed: 20 November 2017).

McNally, M.-A., Cerbone, D., and Maroun, W. (2017). Exploring the challenges of preparing an integrated report. *Meditari Accountancy Research*, 25(4), 481–504.

McNally, M.-A., and Maroun, W. (2018). It is not always bad news: illustrating the potential of integrated reporting using a case study in the eco-tourism industry. *Accounting, Auditing & Accountability Journal*, 31(5), 1319–1348.

Montecalvo, M., Farneti, F., and De Villiers, C. (2018). The potential of integrated reporting to enhance sustainability reporting in the public sector. *Public Money & Management*, 38(5), 365–374.

PwC. (2015). *Integrated Reporting Where to Next?* Available at: www.pwc.co.za/en/assets/pdf/integrated-reporting-survey-2015.pdf (accessed: 16 February 2016).

Rinaldi, L., Unerman, J., and De Villiers, C. (2018). Evaluating the integrated reporting journey: insights, gaps and agendas for future research. *Accounting, Auditing & Accountability Journal*, 31(5), 1294–1318.

Stubbs, W., and Higgins, C. (2014). Integrated reporting and internal mechanisms of change. *Accounting, Auditing & Accountability Journal*, 27(7), 1068–1089.

Sukhari, A., and De Villiers, C. (2019). The influence of integrated reporting on business model and strategy disclosures. *Australian Accounting Review*, 29(4), 708–725.

Terblanche, W., and De Villiers, C. (2019). The influence of integrated reporting and internationalisation on intellectual capital disclosures. *Journal of Intellectual Capital*, 20(1), 40–59.

Thomson, I. (2015). 'But does sustainability need capitalism or an integrated report' a commentary on 'The International Integrated Reporting Council: a story of failure' by Flower, J. *Critical Perspectives on Accounting*, 27, 18–22.

PART I

Evolution and aspirations of integrated reporting

2

THE INTERNATIONAL INTEGRATED REPORTING COUNCIL'S AGENDA OF MOVING INTEGRATED REPORTING TOWARDS GLOBAL ADOPTION BY 2025

Michael Bray

KPMG, Deakin University and IIRC

Liz Prescott

IIRC and KPMG

Abstract

The authors examine the evolution of the International Integrated Reporting Council (IIRC) and integrated reporting (IR), starting with the IIRC's formation in 2010 and looking forward towards expected global adoption by 2025. The chapter considers the development and use of the International Integrated Reporting <IR> Framework, the IIRC's progress up to 2018, and goals of the IIRC's Momentum Phase (2018–2020). It then looks at the IIRC's medium-term agenda, through the Global Adoption Phase (2021–2025), and the longer term, post-2025, with the anticipated acceptance of IR as the corporate reporting norm. The distinctive contribution of IR and potential areas for future research are also explored.

The IIRC's aims and current agenda

In this chapter, we examine the evolution and current status of the International Integrated Reporting Council (IIRC) and integrated reporting (IR), providing the foundation for the ongoing aims and agenda of the IIRC. These matters are clearly articulated in the IIRC's 2018 Integrated Report, a must-read for those who wish to understand the IIRC's strategic agenda and goals for IR in the short, medium and long term.

We define time frames with reference to the IIRC's strategic phases of IR adoption. The short term is defined as the remainder of the Momentum Phase (2018 to 2020). The medium term is the expected duration of the Global Adoption Phase (2021 to 2025). The long term is when the IIRC expects IR to be the corporate reporting norm (2025 and beyond).

The chapter assesses the International <IR> Framework (<IR> Framework), the IIRC's key piece of intellectual property. Finally, we summarize the distinctive contribution of IR – *why* IR exists, including its difference from other reporting frameworks and standards – compared to the many other reporting frameworks in existence today. Further, we briefly identify potential areas for future research.

Notwithstanding the authors' roles with the IIRC, they are writing this chapter in their personal capacities and the contents do not necessarily represent the views of the IIRC.

Evolution of IR and the IIRC

The <IR> Framework defines IR as 'a process founded on integrated thinking that results in a periodic integrated report by an organization about value creation over time and related communications regarding aspects of value creation' (IIRC, 2013, p. 33). The integrated report is an outcome of integrated thinking.

In substance, 'integrated thinking' means effective business practice:

- strategy aligned with the organization's purpose, clear strategic objectives, clear understanding of resulting risks and opportunities, sound understanding of stakeholders' needs and interests (the *what* of the business);
- business model and governance aligned with strategy, including strategic management, governance and other key business processes, identification of critical success factors within them and connected resource allocation, to ensure their effective and efficient operation (the *how* of the business); and
- allocation of the resources and relationships available to the organization to activities within the business model and governance (the *with* of the business).

The resulting integrated report will report on the business, and key performance indicators measuring the performance of the business in terms of its what, with, and how in an understandable way for investors and other stakeholders.

If the IIRC successfully achieves its long-term vision, we will live in a world where integrated thinking is embedded within mainstream business practice, facilitated by IR as the corporate reporting norm. An integrated thinking approach will flow to integrated decision-making and actions that lead to better business practice and value creation over time by taking into account the connectivity and interdependencies between a range of factors.

In reality, the journey towards IR began well before the IIRC was formed in 2010. An interpretation of this journey – from a KPMG perspective – is set out in Chapter 4 of this book. That chapter traces the journey towards IR since 1992 in some detail, with reference to Robert Elliott's article 'The third wave breaks on the shores of accounting'.

As the former CEO of the IIRC, Paul Druckman, stated, one of the most profound questions facing capital markets is how to account for climate change and sustainable development. Such accounts are not focused on improving transparency in a narrow sense, but rather emphasize integration of sustainability into corporate strategy, and understanding how a business is creating value and how capital allocation decisions are made.

This question has been contemplated for a number of years, and aptly captures the sentiment behind the growing recognition of the need for IR, and an appropriate body to bring harmony to a patchwork of interconnected voices and interests. The IIRC believes it is that body; a market-led, evidence-based, globally recognized expert on IR, well placed to act as a global centre of excellence for corporate reporting reform.

The IIRC is a global coalition of regulators, investors, companies, standard setters, the accounting profession, academics and NGOs. Together, this coalition shares the view that communication about value creation should be the next step in the evolution of corporate reporting. The IIRC proposes that the cycle of integrated thinking and reporting, resulting in efficient and productive capital allocation, will act as a force for financial stability and sustainability. Its long-term vision is a world in which integrated thinking is embedded within mainstream business practice in both the public and private sectors, facilitated by IR as the corporate reporting norm.

The need for IR

Globalization and interconnectivity mean the world's finances, people and knowledge are inextricably connected, as evidenced by the global financial crisis. In the wake of the crisis, the imperative to promote financial stability and sustainable development by better linking investment decisions, corporate behaviour and corporate reporting became increasingly recognized as a pressing global need.

Evolution in the corporate reporting system to overcome significant information gaps is needed more urgently than ever before. Organizations such as the World Bank and IMF are joining the IIRC in calling for change to overcome the limitations of current requirements and encourage corporate reporting that gives a more comprehensive picture of an organization's strategy, business model, governance, performance and prospects.

Integrated reporting, founded on integrated thinking, provides an opportunity to enhance and integrate aspects of current reporting, which are often spread across a variety of corporate reports and disclosure mechanisms. The more that integrated thinking is embedded into an organization's activities, the more naturally will the connectivity of information flow into management reporting, analysis and decision-making. It also leads to better integration of the information systems that support internal and external reporting and communication, including preparation of the integrated report, for use by investors and other stakeholders.

Integrated reporting is further designed to enhance accountability, stewardship and trust, as well as to harness the information flow and transparency of business that technology has enabled in the modern world. Evidence shows that better long-term investment returns will be facilitated by providing investors with the information they need to make more effective capital allocation decisions.

Formation and early years of the IIRC

The IIRC has a clear vision to make a lasting contribution to financial stability and sustainable development. An essential advantage is the strength of the IIRC coalition, and the reach of individuals and organizations involved in business, investment, finance, accounting, civil society and academia. Being able to draw on the resources of coalition members is a major asset of the IIRC and adds greatly to its authority and credibility.

The lead up to and formation of the IIRC, and its early life to 2013, is summarized in Table 2.1.

Table 2.1 Timeline of the feasibility and creation phrases

	Feasibility Phase			Creation Phase	
2009	2010	2011	2012	2013	
• His Royal Highness, Prince Charles, Prince of Wales convened a meeting of key stakeholders in September to discuss IR and the need to establish an IR body. • The International Integrated Reporting Committee (IIRC) discussed at HRH Prince of Wales' Accounting for Sustainability Forum in December.	Formation of the International Integrated Reporting Committee. Steering committee chaired by Sir Michael Peat, with Professor Mervyn King as Deputy Chairman. Working Group led by Paul Druckman and Ian Ball.	• <IR> Discussion Paper considered rationale for IR, initial proposals for development of <IR> Framework, and next steps towards creation and adoption. • Overwhelming support for IR, endorsing development of global framework. Also concluded that primary audience of integrated reports is investors.	• IIRC Pilot Programme, feeding back to IIRC with progression towards IR. • IIRC re-named International Integrated Reporting Council, with its current governance structure consisting of a representative Council and an operating company overseen by a Board of Directors.	Prototype of <IR> Framework released to demonstrate progress towards defining key concepts and principles that underpin IR.	• Consultation Draft of International <IR> Framework released in April. Launch followed by a 90-day consultation period. • International <IR> Framework released in December.

The 'Feasibility' Phase of 2009–2010 centred on proof of concept. The 'Creation' Phase, from 2011 to 2013, incorporated significant public consultation alongside detailed technical development and market testing. This resulted in global awareness of IR as well as creation of the <IR> Framework itself.

Launch of the International <IR> Framework (2013)

The <IR> Framework is the IIRC's main piece of intellectual property. Its development was led by the IIRC Technical Taskforce, working in conjunction with a Pilot Programme comprising almost 100 businesses and 35 investors around the world. The development approach was market-led and inclusive, and responsive to the fourth wave of business (refer to Chapter 4).

Integrated reporting is an evolution of corporate reporting, with a focus on the value creation, strategic relevance and future orientation of an organization, presented in a concise manner. It improves the quality of information presented by focusing on material matters and makes the reporting process more effective in terms of its strategic alignment, and more efficient in eliminating reporting and other process redundancy. Integrated reporting requires and brings about integrated thinking, enabling a better understanding of the factors that materially affect an organization's ability to create value over time. It can lead to behavioural changes and has been proven to deliver performance improvement throughout an organization.

An integrated report is an outcome – a concise communication about how an organization's strategy, governance, performance and prospects, in the context of its external environment, lead to the creation of value in the short, medium and long term. The <IR> Framework enables a business to bring these elements together through the concept of 'connectivity of information', to best tell an organization's value creation story.

Integrated reporting has been created for any organization that wants to embrace integrated thinking and improve its corporate reporting. Businesses adopting IR have reported breakthroughs in understanding their own value creation, greater collaboration within teams, more informed decision-making and positive impacts on stakeholder relations.

The <IR> Framework is intended to underpin and accelerate the evolution of corporate reporting, reflecting developments in financial and operational governance, management commentary and sustainability reporting. Investors are the primary audience of an integrated report. However, the <IR> Framework stresses that information in the report should be of interest to all stakeholders.

The <IR> Framework comprises:

- Three Fundamental Concepts – Value creation for the organization and for others (for example, customers, employees, regulators and communities) in the short, medium and long term, the capitals, and the value creation process – which underpin the Guiding Principles and Content Elements.
- Seven Guiding Principles. A number of principles, such as materiality, and consistency and comparability, are common to other reporting frameworks. Some are unique to IR – for example, strategic focus and future orientation; connectivity of information; and conciseness.
- Eight Content Elements including governance; business model; risks and opportunities; strategy and resource allocation; and outlook, and

- 19 requirements if a report is to be characterized as an integrated report prepared in accordance with the <IR> Framework.

Since the release of the <IR> Framework in December 2013, the IIRC has focused on achieving a meaningful shift towards adoption of IR. In 2017, a formal consultation focused on implementation of the <IR> Framework was conducted in advance of the IIRC moving to its Momentum Phase. The consultation attracted more than 400 submissions from 19 countries around the world, and covered the different sectors that make up the global coalition for IR.

The Framework Implementation Feedback exercise provided the most up-to-date assessment of global implementation of IR, and its successes and challenges, from those directly involved in its implementation. The feedback indicated that the <IR> Framework stood up well to the challenges of implementation. It also pointed to several opportunities to provide guidance, examples and training and take other actions to help report preparers and other stakeholders more easily implement IR. Those opportunities and actions are being addressed through a two-year Technical Programme running to the end of 2019.

The Breakthrough Phase (2014–2018)

Figure 2.1 visualizes the journey from feasibility to creation of the <IR> Framework, followed by the Breakthrough Phase, which marked the transition towards early adoption of the <IR> Framework. The subsequent Momentum Phase (2018–2020) and Global Adoption Phase (2021–2025) are expected to see IR accepted as the global norm.

In 2014, the IIRC moved into the 'Breakthrough' phase, the objective of which was to achieve a meaningful shift from creation and market testing to development and early adoption of the <IR> Framework by reporting organizations around the world. Some of the developments that characterized the IIRC's Breakthrough Phase were:

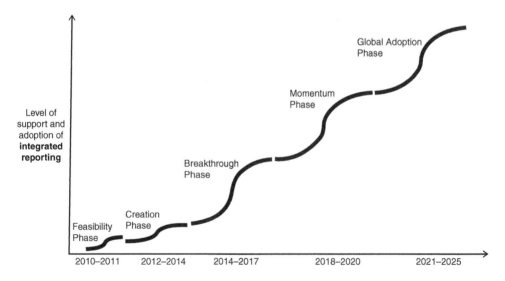

Figure 2.1 The journey from feasibility to creation of the <IR> Framework
Source: IIRC (2019c)

- The formation of the Corporate Reporting Dialogue in June 2014. Integrated reporting acts as an 'umbrella' for corporate reporting, behaviour and decision-making, offering a basis for dialogue and alignment. The Corporate Reporting Dialogue was established to facilitate discussion between the respective participants on their frameworks and standards as the basis for further advancing corporate reporting.
- The creation of various global networks to promote the quality adoption of IR around the world:

  - Business Network, which evolved from the 2011–2013 Pilot Programme;
  - Investor Network, which led to the Investor Statement supporting IR as a route to better understanding performance (IIRC, 2019b);
  - <IR> Technology Initiative, which brings organizations together to look at how technology can underpin new trends in corporate reporting, and in particular, can be applied to assist in the global adoption of IR;
  - <IR> Academic Network (see the section titled Research Opportunities for further information); and
  - <IR> Training Partner Network to deliver the <IR> Training Programme aimed at developing individuals' skills and build capacity for organizations to implement IR.

As 2017 drew to a close, the IIRC based its readiness to enter a new strategic phase on several achievements:

- Adoption of IR in 62 markets, including every G20 economy.
- Embedding of IR in international accountancy qualifications, guaranteeing a pipeline of new finance professionals ready to implement IR.
- Explicit reference to IR in corporate governance codes, and IOSCO Principle 16 was beginning to be used to advocate <IR> adoption.
- Increasing support from pension funds alongside growing interest in the integration of ESG factors within mainstream investment.
- The <IR> Framework increasingly accepted as a permanent feature of corporate reporting, being described as an 'umbrella' and the future of corporate reporting by internationally respected bodies.
- A positive response from the IIRC's 2017 Framework Implementation Feedback, indicating that the principles underlying the Framework stood the test of time.

The IIRC achieved a number of successes in 2018 in relation to the continued momentum towards the global adoption of IR, and marked a significant change in the IIRC's strategic intent as it moved from the Breakthrough to the Momentum Phase.

A snapshot of the IIRC's KPIs disclosed in its 2018 Integrated Report is provided in Table 2.2 (IIRC, 2019a). The table is important as it sets out the IIRC's self-assessment of its progress against the strategic themes previously set and reported to stakeholders. In effect, it self-assesses the IIRC's progress against its strategy and importantly, the table has been subject to Crowe UK LLP's limited assurance engagement on the IIRC's 2018 integrated report. Overall, there is forward progress, even if some metrics are coming off a low base.

The IIRC was able to move from its Breakthrough Phase to its Momentum Phase in 2018 as a number of key countries had joined South Africa in achieving momentum in their IR adoption journeys – for example, Japan and the UK (through its substantively

Table 2.2 The IIRC's KPIs

Strategic Theme	Lead KPI	Measured By	2018	2017	Directional Change
One – Continuous progress in the adoption of integrated thinking and reporting	Number of integrated reports published annually	GNDI Global Director Survey Report – respondents that use the <IR> Framework (of 2,159 respondents)	15%	n/a	n/a
		World Business Council for Sustainable Development member companies sampled annually that produce self-declared integrated reports (158 sampled in 2018)	18%	22%	↙
		WBCSD member companies sampled annually whose report is titled 'Integrated' (158 sampled in 2018)	11%	11%	Unchanged
		JAPAN – KPMG Survey of Integrated Reports in Japan	341	279	↗
		UK – Deloitte survey of UK premium-listed FTSE companies – those clearly considering the IR notion of 'capitals' in their business models	35%	32%	↗
		AUSTRALIA – KPMG's survey of ASX 200 corporate reporting – companies using at least some IR principles	48%	25%	↗
		IIRC estimate – Number of organizations on the path to IR	1,635	n/a	n/a
Two – Mobilize the investor 'pull' for IR	EY's annual global investor survey question –	How useful do you find the following sources of non-financial information when making an investment decision? (Answers for 'integrated reports')			↗
		'Score' out of 4 (4 assigned to 'Essential', 3 to 'Very useful' etc.)	3.0	2.7	
		Essential or very useful	95%	57%	↗
Three – Promote objectives of <IR> in, and facilitate alignment of, corporate reporting system	Stakeholder survey question average 'score' (out of 5)	How connected do you think the current elements of corporate reporting are today?	2.9	2.4	↗
		To what extent do you agree that IR promotes a more connected and efficient approach to corporate reporting?	4.2	4.2	Unchanged
		To what extent do you agree that IR is an 'umbrella' for corporate reporting, providing the context and linkage for other forms of reporting?	4.0	3.8	↗

(Continued)

Table 2.2 (Cont.)

Strategic Theme	Lead KPI	Measured By	2018	2017	Directional Change
Four – Make it easier to adopt IR	Stakeholder survey questions 'score' (out of 5)	To what extent do available guidance and tools address barriers to practical IR adoption?	3.6	n/a	n/a
		What is your view of the quality of research and reports produced by the IIRC and partners as shown on the IIRC website?	3.8	3.9	↙
Five – Foster policy and regulatory environment supporting moves to <IR>	National regulation	Number of countries where there is regulatory signposting to, or alignment to principles of, IR; e.g. through corporate governance or stewardship codes	17	16	↗
	Supranational platforms	Number of key supranational platforms where IR is on the agenda	8	7	↗
Six – Maintain a viable and effective organization	IIRC stakeholder survey question	Average 'score' from IIRC Council, Board & ambassadors (out of 5)			↗
		As a partner or advocate, to what extent is the IIRC effective at building good relationships with you?	4.2	3.8	↗
		What degree of progress do you believe the IIRC is making towards global adoption of IR?	4.0	3.7	↗

equivalent strategic reporting regimes). The combination of the KPIs achieved and other significant breakthroughs described in Table 2.3 signalled that the market was ready for the IIRC to begin its **Momentum Phase**, aimed at delivering accelerated action towards its goal for integrated thinking and reporting.

The 2019 IIRC Integrated Report will cover developments in these and other areas. For instance, the Corporate Reporting Dialogue issued its Phase 1 report on the Better Alignment Project in November 2019, and the IIRC has been involved in the 2019 Japanese B20 and is preparing for the 2020 Saudi Arabian B20 processes.

The what, with and how of the IIRC

Integrated reporting is founded on integrated thinking – better business practice – and built on three Fundamental Concepts. As these relate to the IIRC:

- **Value creation for the organization and for others**, or the '*what*' of the business – the IIRC's strategic objectives, risks and opportunities;
- **The Capitals**, or the '*with*' of the IIRC – the resources and relationships the IIRC uses in its value creation process to implement strategy and realize its overarching Purpose; and
- **Value Creation Process**, the '*how*' of the IIRC – its business model and governance.

We bring these concepts to life using the IIRC as a case study.

Table 2.3 The IIRC's breakthroughs

Strategic Theme	Breakthrough Achieved
One – Continuous progress in the adoption of integrated thinking and reporting	• A number of key countries had joined South Africa in achieving momentum in their IR journeys, including Japan and the UK (through its substantively equivalent strategic reporting regimes). Third-party research also showed continued significant growth of adoption in Australia. • The IIRC's Integrated Thinking & Strategy Special Interest Group formalized its work plan and met a number of times to progress its programme. • Launch of <IR> Academic Database with over 200 pieces of research and analysis. • Deakin University was announced as the inaugural Chair of the IIRC Global Academic Network Oversight Body.
Two – Mobilize the investor 'pull' for IR	• EY (2018) Global Climate Change and Sustainability Services study of institutional investors indicated that investors now considered integrated reports the most useful source of non-financial information, overtaking the annual report, with 94% of respondents finding integrated reports 'essential' or 'very useful'.
Three – Promote objectives of <IR> in, and facilitate alignment of, corporate reporting system	• The Corporate Reporting Dialogue launched its Better Alignment Project, a major two-year initiative aimed at bringing greater consistency, coherence and clarity to the corporate reporting landscape, a major objective of the IIRC's Momentum Phase strategy.
Four – Make it easier to adopt IR	• The IIRC began working on a number of guidance documents to support practical implementation of IR, due for publication in 2019.
Five – Foster policy & regulatory environment supporting moves to <IR>	• The <IR> Technology Initiative produced a guide for Chief Technology Officers to help them to have more meaningful conversations with finance teams to ensure businesses have access to the information they need. • In Japan, the UK and Australia, IR gained increased explicit support from policymakers, setting a more conducive environment for adoption of IR. • The impact of the Securities and Exchange Board of India's 2017 circular asking the top 500 listed companies in India to adopt IR – more than 30 companies adopted IR in 2018. • The IIRC again participated in the B20 group of business leaders advising G20 governments under Argentina's presidency, an involvement that began with the Australian G20 Presidency in 2014.
Six – Maintain a viable and effective organization	• Dominic Barton, Senior Partner and former Global Managing Partner, McKinsey & Company (2009 to 2018), was announced as new Chair of the Council, in October 2018, following the near decade-long, outstanding leadership of the inaugural chair, Judge Professor Mervyn King (2010–2018).

The what: the IIRC's strategy for creating value for itself and for others

The IIRC is encouraging worldwide adoption of IR to improve communication about value creation, advance the evolution of corporate reporting, and make a lasting contribution to financial stability and sustainable development on a global scale.

The IIRC's **mission** is to establish IR, the foundation of which is integrated thinking, within mainstream business practice as the norm in the public and private sectors. Its **vision** is to align capital allocation and corporate behaviour to wider goals of financial stability and sustainable development through the cycle of IR. To facilitate this vision, the **<IR> Framework** was created.

The **objective** of the IIRC is to change the corporate reporting system so that IR becomes the global norm. This objective underlies the IIRC's strategic direction, as embodied in its phased approach to driving implementation of IR through breakthrough, momentum and global adoption. As an organization with noble ambitions but limited resources, the IIRC's delivery model is critical to its success. An approach based only on applying existing staff resources to the strategic themes would, at best, achieve incremental progress – the IIRC seeks a step change in levels of adoption, demand from mainstream investors, regulatory endorsement and improved capital market and corporate reporting systems.

It is therefore vital that the IIRC's strategic partners help amplify its message, advocate for change, both globally and in individual markets, produce persuasive research and lead market-based networks that bring together businesses, investors and regulators. This inclusive, market-based partnership approach will remain the linchpin of the IIRC's strategy delivery and enable delivery on its commitment to be market-led, while multiplying the available resources for its cause.

The with: IIRC's capitals

The IIRC relies primarily on **four capitals**:

- The majority of its **funding** comes from contributions and grants from Council members, Business Network participants and other organizations and mainly goes towards its staff and travel costs. Key supporters are listed on the IIRC website.
- The IIRC's guidance, research and expertise form its **intellectual capital,** the centre-piece being the <IR> Framework, the product of extensive consultation and multi-stakeholder perspectives developed over three years.
- The IIRC's **people** consist of the Board, Council and Ambassadors and a relatively small staff team that coordinate IIRC activities under the oversight and direction of the IIRC Board.
- The IIRC's **relationships**, formed through networks, strategic partnerships and collaborations, are crucial in amplifying the IIRC's efforts, particularly given its small staff team. The 2018 IIRC Integrated Report summarizes the IIRC's stakeholder relationships – by group, their interest(s) and the IIRC's response, including business and other reporter entities; investors; framework developers and standard setters; the accountancy profession; policymakers, regulators and securities exchanges; civil society; academia; and the IIRC team.

The how: the IIRC's governance and business model

Governance

The IIRC's governance structure and processes strike an important balance between the legal authority and responsibilities of the Board and the significant weight and influence of the Council (see Figure 2.2). All activities of the IIRC are coordinated and conducted through the Operating Company of the same name, a non-profit company limited by guarantee, incorporated and based in the UK, subject to oversight by the Board of Directors.

- Members of the IIRC (the Council) are recommended by the Board of Directors, acting in consultation with the Governance and Nominations Committee. The Council is a critical source of advice, expertise, experience, resources and support required for achievement of the IIRC's purpose.
- The members of the Governance and Nominations Committee are appointed by the Council. They serve – effectively as the Council's proxy and subject to the Council's direction if necessary – as members of the Operating Company. In that capacity, they enjoy such powers as are determined by law and the Operating Company's Articles of Association, including the power to appoint and remove the directors. They also advise the IIRC's Board of Directors on governance issues.
- The Board of Directors appoints the Chief Executive Officer (CEO), who is responsible for the IIRC team. A global search for a new CEO was underway at the time of writing.
- The <IR> Framework Panel, appointed by the Board and convened by the IIRC team, meets regularly to provide their input and guidance on outputs from the IIRC's ongoing technical work.
- IIRC Ambassadors support the mission and work of the IIRC by promoting the aims of the IIRC, by engaging locally and leveraging their voice in key markets. There are currently about 50 Ambassadors around the world and this is an area presenting opportunities for further engagement.

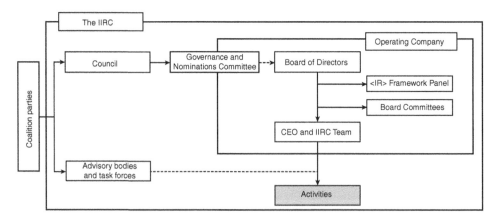

Figure 2.2 The IIRC's governance structure
Source: IIRC (2019d)

- The Integrated Reporting Foundation (a company limited by guarantee) is a registered UK charity. The IIRC is the sole member of the Foundation and appoints the independent Board of Trustees, and also provides administrative support. Financial results of the Foundation are consolidated with the IIRC.

Business model

The business model diagram in its 2018 Integrated Report shows how the IIRC transforms inputs through business activities into outputs and outcomes that aim to fulfil its strategic purpose (see Figure 2.3).

The why: the distinctive contribution of IR

The IIRC's 2018 integrated report communicates the <IR> Framework's points of difference compared to other reporting frameworks and standards. It distinguishes the <IR>

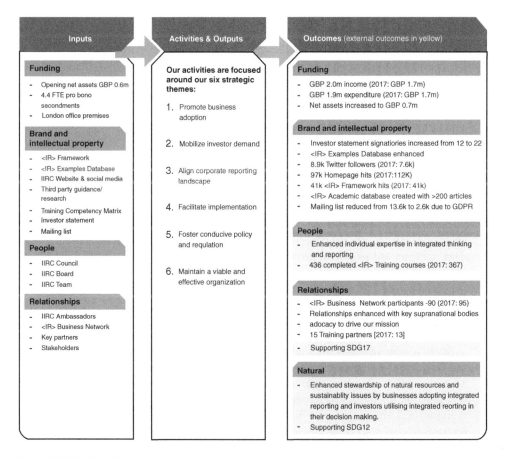

Figure 2.3 The IIRC's business model
Source: IIRC (2019a)

Framework from existing financial, regulatory and sustainability reporting initiatives as follows:

- Grounding in integrated thinking and better business practice, with the integrated report being an outcome of this process. Only IR has this business focus – on the *what* (strategy, risks and opportunities, and stakeholder management), *with* (resources and relationships) and *how* (business model and governance) of the business, and the integration thereof, as well as the *why* – the competitive edge of the business – its integrated thinking.
- Focus on intellectual capital and particular aspects of social and relationship and human capital. Innovation, intellectual property and technology are critically important to today's business models. Integrated reporting ensures organizations are considering the impact of these factors, in addition to financial, manufactured, human and natural capitals. The <IR> Framework also focuses on two other critical aspects of today's business models – customer satisfaction, people engagement/strategic alignment and executive remuneration – not given specific focus by other reporting frameworks, but which provide valuable insights into particular aspects of social and relationship and human capitals.
- Integration of reporting across all six capitals. Only IR has a focus on reporting in integrated fashion across the whole range of capitals that an organization uses to create value, which promotes connected rather than siloed reporting.

The IIRC's 2018 Integrated Report also explains how IR benefits:

- Organizations. Integrated reporting helps organizations to understand and communicate their impact and how they create value in a holistic way. This improves relationships with all stakeholders, reduces the cost of capital and facilitates improved long-term performance and sustainable development.
- Investors and other key stakeholders (e.g. customers, employees and regulators). Integrated reporting provides a comprehensive understanding of businesses and their prospects in the short, medium and long term, particularly enabling better informed investment decisions by providers of all forms of capital, not just financial investors.
- **Society**. Enhanced business and investor performance increases economic prosperity, while appropriate consideration is given to management of all the capitals over the short, medium and long term promotes sustainable development and financial stability.

The benefits to investors have been attested to in research by acclaimed academics in highly respected accounting journals, with teams led by:

- **Professor Mary Barth of Stanford University**. Professor Barth's team found that good IR is positively associated with stock liquidity and firm value. Critically, the team also found that it is likely that this represents a real effect than a capital market effect. That is, good IR stimulates more integrated thinking – better business practice – which is reflected in the integrated report, which is used by investors in their decision-making processes (real effect). It is not just better information being produced that is used by investors (capital market effect). It is enhanced business performance and processes that are generating the better information, which is reflected in integrated reports, and used by investors (Barth, Cahan, Chen and Venter, 2017).

- Professor Roger Simnett of UNSW. Professor Simnett's team found evidence that analysts' forecast errors reduce as a company's level of alignment with the <IR> Framework increases. Further, the improved alignment is associated with a subsequent reduction in the cost of equity capital for certain reporting companies (Zhou, Simnett and Green, 2017).

This brief analysis of research findings is not intended to denigrate other forms of reporting (financial and sustainability reporting are and will remain critically important), nor to say that an IR journey cannot start from a sustainability report. Indeed, many experienced sustainability reporters highlight the benefits of having well established internal controls and reporting processes for capturing non-financial information prior to beginning their IR journey. Equally, it can start from an existing form of Management Commentary, for instance: a Management Discussion and Analysis in North America; a Strategic Report in the UK; or an Operating and Financial Review in Australia).

Regardless of the starting point, IR is not interchangeable with other reporting forms, for instance, an integrated report is not a sustainability report, but it can include sustainability information that is material to the organization's ability to create value in the short, medium and long term.

Widespread adoption of the <IR> Framework can add two benefits to the global economy:

- International consistency in reporting to investors. Investors operate across national boundaries. National or even regional reporting mechanisms not aligned to a global flagship reporting framework impede investment analysis. The IIRC believes that the flagship global framework is IR. The fragmentation of today's national investor reporting mechanisms and the proliferation of reporting frameworks, a problem that has afflicted financial and sustainability reporting over many decades, can be overcome by embracing IR. Integrated reporting is a suitable anchor point for national investor reporting mechanisms, and through the <IR> Framework, a guide to implementation at the organizational level. One flagship reporting framework for reporting to investors (which also benefits other stakeholders) will also enable a consistent global approach to assurance, one that will be facilitated by the IAASB. (2019) Extended External Reporting Assurance Guidance. This will bring uniformity when attesting to the credibility of integrated reports, and help to restore trust in global capital markets.
- Exploiting technological change. Technological change is an opportunity to be exploited in investor reporting, not a risk to be avoided. One consistent global reporting framework underpinning investor reporting also provides the impetus for major investments to be made in automating reporting and associated processes, making them more efficient and freeing up scarce resources to be more focused on strategic and value enhancing business activities. Global adoption of a single reporting framework will deliver the critical mass to underpin the required return on investment.

These benefits distinguish IR, when applied according to the <IR> Framework, from all other reporting frameworks being promoted today:

- Its value proposition is broader, and the targeted benefits are greater, deeper and apply globally.

- It offers conceptual rigour, a basis for measuring resulting business improvements, and most importantly, a basis for globally consistent investor reporting, as well as investor stewardship codes.

Continued development of the IIRC and IR

While the IIRC is optimistic that it is continuing on the path projected in 2018, it is aware that the organization itself and IR do not exist in a vacuum, and are subject to the challenges faced by a small organization with a global mission.

The congestion of the corporate reporting landscape and need for rationalization is an increasingly urgent issue and one that requires global leadership. The IIRC is committed to helping to build the solution and will do more to engage with regulators and investors, while pressing for reform of the corporate reporting system itself, including the incentives that encourage a short term focus and negative behaviour in our capital markets.

The IIRC's strategy remains focused on anticipating future global trends and being able to respond to them, to ensure that IR continues to remain relevant to the issues and market needs of today and tomorrow.

The IIRC is also committed to supporting the United Nations and its partners in building a better world in which no one is left behind, not solely for the sake of supporting the **Sustainable Development Goals** (SDGs), but because the <IR> Framework offers individual adopting organizations a framework to demonstrate to investors and other stakeholders why the SDGs are important to their businesses – their what and with – and how the strategy and governance process drive the organization's contribution to society overall.

The short term: Momentum Phase (2018 to 2020)

The current phase in the IIRC's strategic journey, the Momentum Phase, builds on the achievements of the Breakthrough Phase and will popularize the message from the International Federation of Accountants (IFAC) that IR is 'the future of corporate reporting'. The Momentum Phase will accelerate progress towards the goal of integrated thinking and reporting becoming the global norm. It will leverage the support of the IIRC's partners to create the scale and pace needed to deliver the desired step change in adoption.

The Momentum Phase further aims to create impetus and energy across the IIRC's target markets and in key sectors. Greater alignment of the corporate reporting system will be another driver of its future success.

The IIRC's activities will remain focused around six strategic themes between 2018 and 2020:

1. Promote business adoption – the IIRC will engage with greater urgency in key global markets, particularly the USA and China.
2. Mobilize investor demand – the difference between the findings that: 1) 95 per cent of investors surveyed find integrated reports to be 'essential' or 'very useful'; and 2) less than 20 percent of directors and World Business Council for Sustainable Development respondents are producing integrated reports, indicates unmet potential for the IIRC to further harness investor advocacy and support for adoption by directors and WBCSD members.

3. Align the corporate reporting landscape – the work of the IIRC-convened Corporate Reporting Dialogue will continue, particularly through the Better Alignment Project. This project is funded by Bloomberg, and involves key standard setters and framework developers, such as the Global Reporting Initiative, Sustainability Accounting Standards Board, Climate Disclosure Standards Board and CDP. Further information can be found at www.corporatereportingdialogue.com.
4. Facilitate implementation – the IIRC will engage more proactively in the market with technical aids and guidance to make adoption of the <IR> Framework easier.
5. Foster a conducive policy and regulatory environment – the IIRC will seek greater regulatory endorsement of the principles of IR.
6. Maintain a viable and effective organization – the IIRC will continue to work with its council, ambassadors and other stakeholders to maintain the effectiveness of the IIRC.

The Material Matters section of the IIRC's 2018 Integrated Report indicates the current issues that most affect the IIRC's ability to create value. It highlights two particular challenges, discussed further below, that have potential implications for the IIRC's business model and its ability to achieve its mission. These matters will need to be addressed by 2020 if the IIRC and its stakeholders are to be prepared for the next big shift in the IIRC's strategic direction – the launch of its 'Global Adoption Phase' in 2021.

The IIRC also recognizes that it has development work to do on several strategic themes. For instance, it is considering the future development of the IIRC Council, and its interaction with the IIRC Board and IIRC Ambassadors. It should also be clearer and more granular on the path through the Momentum Phase to the Global Adoption Phase, and aim to broaden and deepen its funding base.

Increased focus in response to resource constraints

While the IIRC's income remains stable in the short term, resource constraints continue to limit the work it can reasonably achieve, and an evolution of its fundraising strategy needs to be found. At the same time, the IIRC spreads its reach widely, both geographically and through its relationships. Along with the emerging picture of varied levels of adoption across the globe, the IIRC has narrowed its focus to concentrate on boosting momentum for IR in key markets in order to maximize the IIRC's impact and create a strong foundation for global adoption (see Table 2.4).

Table 2.4 The IIRC's key target markets

2019 Key Market	2019 Objective
USA	Use the New York Council meeting week in November 2019 to make a highly visible impact in the US market
China	Encourage publishing of guidelines on IR or a public commitment to do so by the Chinese Ministry of Finance
Germany	Develop and mobilize a strategy to increase adoption in the German market
ASEAN (Association of Southeast Asian Nations)	Build on existing momentum in the ASEAN market to achieve a 'step-change' in adoption, including through the launch of the ASEAN <IR> Committee and associated reporting awards

The USA, China and Germany have clear economic significance and influence globally, while there is a short-term opportunity to capitalize on good groundwork and momentum building in ASEAN.

This does not mean that the IIRC will cease pursuing progress in other important markets through 2020. By focusing on key markets, the IIRC believes it is more likely to achieve step-change in these markets, providing a solid foundation for the transition to the Global Adoption Phase in 2021.

Proliferation of initiatives

The proliferation of corporate reporting initiatives continues to cause confusion, reporting fatigue and fragmentation in the market. On one level, these allied efforts are welcome, as they represent a broad and mutually reinforcing movement in which IR can play a central role.

However, the convening space created by the IIRC has become a contested one, with the *quantity* of reporting initiatives impeding improvement in reporting *quality*, which is increasingly demanded by the market, and is fundamental to the IIRC's mission. While there is some level of complementarity and shared goals, the competition for funding, support and adopters provides a challenge to the IIRC's mission.

The IIRC is committed to building global agreement about the future of the corporate reporting system in all its dimensions, including a strong and compelling call for greater alignment and, ultimately, harmonization of standards to achieve a simpler and better corporate reporting landscape. A 2019 report by McKinsey & Company, mapping the litany of non-financial reporting initiatives, is informing a review by the IIRC Board of Directors of the current landscape.

The medium to longer term: Global Adoption Phase (2021 to 2025 and beyond)

There is a long journey between now and beyond 2025, through and after the Global Adoption Phase. Perhaps it is too early to speculate on what the path will be, or what the long term journey will deliver. The pathway, or perhaps alternate pathways, will likely become clearer in 2020 as the Momentum Phase continues.

It will be helpful for the IIRC to define and publish the KPIs that it will use to gauge readiness to move to the Global Adoption Phase well before that phase begins. This may involve:

- Requiring a critical mass of adoption in key markets, countries or regions of 'substantive equivalence' of principal investor reporting mechanisms with the <IR> Framework;
- The creation of local IR bodies that are formally connected to the IIRC (e.g., USA, Brazil, Argentina and Germany) in those markets, and which are actively supporting and enabling the implementation of IR.

Other possible developments

Other developments that are likely to begin in the remainder of the Momentum Phase and continue during the Global Adoption Phase follow below. The question for the IIRC in each case will be whether and to what extent it is able to be involved, based on its priorities and resource availability, and assuming all six strategic themes are achieved:

- The emerging trend of assurance of integrated reports. Corporate governance codes in a number of countries recognize assurance of a broad range of corporate reports, in addition to audited financial reports, as a key trust enhancement tool, and this in an environment where integrated reports are becoming the primary source of corporate information. The IIRC Integrated Report 2018 was assured by Crowe UK LLP, Chartered Accountants, with limited assurance obtained. In doing so, the IIRC joined ABN AMRO Bank N.V. as a pioneer in obtaining limited assurance on its 2018 and 2019 Integrated Reports in accordance with the <IR> Framework. Cbus (an Australian pension fund) followed the ABM AMRO and IIRC precedents in having its 2019 integrated report assured in terms of the <IR> Framework. We are not yet aware of any instances of reasonable assurance of an integrated report being prepared in accordance with the <IR> Framework at this stage. The IIRC will consider moving to reasonable assurance in the future.
- Deepening understanding of, and practical implementation experience, in bringing the concept of 'integrated thinking' to life in the context of an IR journey. The work of the Integrated Thinking & Strategy Special Interest Group continues in this area.
- The move to 'IR management systems', including IR automation, to underpin the continued integrity and 'assurability' of integrated reports and processes underlying the preparation of integrated reports. We use the term 'IR management systems' in a broad sense to include reporting strategies that drive integrated reports as the flagship report of an organization's entire corporate reporting portfolio, and associated reporting processes, teams and automation.
- The technology/automation aspect. Again, the question for the IIRC will be whether and to what extent it wants to be involved in this area, including associated assurance, beyond the existing work of the IIRC Technology initiative already underway.
- The potential evolution of the concept of 'Integrated Investment' as IR analysis becomes a core component of investor governance and management processes, and investor stewardship codes further evolve alongside corporate governance codes, including specific reference to IR.
- Questions about standardization associated with the <IR> Framework, and the future direction of the IIRC as an organization, as the <IR> Framework becomes more prominent.

Research opportunities

The <IR> Academic Network is a platform that facilitates the collaboration and sharing of information between academics and others, including reporting organizations, investors, policy-makers and standard setters. The Network also ensures that the IIRC is kept abreast of relevant academic thinking, including further research evidence concerning the business case for IR. While investors are being well served by research from academia, investor groups and organizations such as the Association of Certified Chartered Accountants, research examining the demand for IR by stakeholders other than investors, such as customers, employees, regulators and communities, is needed.

In 2018, the IIRC launched its <IR> Academic Network Oversight Body, which oversees the IIRC's Academic Network. It is a consortium, inaugurally chaired by Deakin University, which aims to stimulate continued research, dialogue and debate in the areas of IR, integrated thinking and broader corporate reporting system reform.

References

Barth, M. E., Cahan, S. F., Chen, L., and Venter, E. R. (2017). The economic consequences associated with integrated report quality: Capital market and real effects. *Accounting, Organizations and Society, 62*, 43–64.

EY. (2018). *Does Your Nonfinancial Reporting Tell Your Value Creation Story?* Available at: www.ey.com/Publication/vwLUAssets/ey-ccass-survey-2018-report/$FILE/ey-ccass-survey-2018-report.pdf (Accessed: 1 August 2019).

IAASB. (2019). *Extended External Reporting Assurance*. Available at: www.ifac.org/publications-resources/consultation-paper-extended-external-reporting-assurance (Accessed: 1 August 2019).

IIRC. (2013). *The International <IR> Framework*. Available at: www.theiirc.org/wp-content/uploads/2013/12/13-12-08-THE-INTERNATIONAL-IR-FRAMEWORK-2-1.pdf (Accessed: 1 August 2019).

IIRC. (2019a). *Building Momentum, IIRC Integrated Report 2018*. Available at: https://integratedreporting.org/integratedreport2018/download/pdf/IIRC_INTEGRATED_REPORT_2018.pdf (Accessed: 1 August 2019).

IIRC. (2019b). *Investor Statement*. Available at: https://integratedreporting.org/resource/investor-statement/ (Accessed: 3 December 2019).

IIRC. (2019c). Journeys into integrated reporting: A view from the IIRC. *The 17th Annual IFRS Masterclass 2019: Implementing and Applying the New IFRS Standards, Crowne Plaza, Auckland, 10 April.*

IIRC. (2019d). *Structure of the IIRC*. Available at: https://integratedreporting.org/the-iirc-2/structure-of-the-iirc/ (Accessed: 18 December 2019).

Zhou, S., Simnett, R., and Green, W. (2017). Does integrated reporting matter to the capital market? *Abacus, 53*(1), 94–132.

3

THE INTEGRATED REPORTING COMMITTEE OF SOUTH AFRICA

On the balance of integrated reporting

Leigh Roberts

International Reporting Committee of South Africa

Wayne van Zijl

University of the Witwatersrand

Dannielle Cerbone

University of the Witwatersrand

Abstract

This chapter examines integrated reporting (IR) from a South African perspective. A brief history is provided, followed by a discussion of the Integrated Reporting Committee of South Africa's ten key considerations for a balanced report. The researchers drew on their existing knowledge of companies' integrated reporting to provide good illustrative examples of the considerations. The examples show that, while many South African listed companies have reputable reporting, assurance of the integrated reports requires attention. Areas for future research include comparing trends in South Africa to those in other jurisdictions where IR has taken hold. This can include investigations on how different governance codes have contributed to variations in IR practice.

Introduction

South Africa (SA) is an interesting setting for examining developments in corporate governance practices and reporting (Malherbe and Segal, 2001; West, 2006; Ntim, 2009; Ntim et al., 2012). It illustrates how corporate practices have evolved in response to economic and societal needs. It also demonstrates how these needs have resulted in SA being considered a leader in corporate governance and integrated reporting (IR) (World Economic Forum, 2018; Eccles et al., 2019).

During the Apartheid[1] regime, SA was systematically excluded from the international capital market, which resulted in an economic slowdown (Rossouw et al., 2002; Armstrong, et al., 2005; De Villiers and van Staden, 2006). By the 1990s, the cost of maintaining Apartheid and the imposed international sanctions bankrupted the government, and corporate practices had fallen far behind international standards (Catchpowle and Cooper, 1999; Malherbe and Segal, 2001).

In this environment, mechanisms for holding companies accountable for their economic, social and environmental performance were limited (Hamann and Kapelus, 2004). Poor corporate governance practices made it difficult for the SA capital market to attract new investors, even after the establishment of a democratic government in 1994 (see De Villiers et al., 2014). At the time the African National Congress (ANC) assumed power in 1994, it:

> inherited an economy which despite being the most vibrant on the continent, with a Gross Domestic Product equal to 75% of that of the rest of sub-Saharan Africa, had a catalogue of problems that would test even the most experienced of economists.
>
> *(Catchpowle and Cooper, 1999, p. 716)*

What was needed was a mechanism to legitimise SA in the international market and to garner much-needed capital investment (see De Villiers et al., 2014). One mechanism SA used was to exploit its strategic location as a gateway into the African continent. In order to mobilise this strategic advantage, SA needed to convince the world that it was ready for investment. Towards this end, the King Committee was convened under the Chairmanship of Professor Mervyn King (IOD, 1994) at the request of the Institute of Directors in Southern Africa (IOD) (Rossouw et al., 2002; Armstrong et al., 2005; West, 2009). The primary purpose of the King Committee was to consider how to promote the highest standards of corporate governance in South Africa (IOD, 1994). The King Committee created King I in 1994 (IOD, 2009). King I was subsequently revised in 2002 (King II), 2009 (King III) and, most recently, in 2016 (King IV). Unlike other corporate governance codes such as Sarbanes-Oxley, the King Code is non-legislative and is based on principles and recommended practices (IOD, 1994, 2002, 2009, 2016). The principles of King I, however, became mandatory for public companies listed on the Johannesburg Stock Exchange (JSE) from 1995 onwards through the JSE Listing Requirements (JSE, 1995, 2012, 2013, 2017).

Another significant milestone in SA's corporate governance landscape was King III's call for an integrated report. King III's adoption by the JSE in 2010 resulted in it becoming the first stock exchange requiring listed companies to prepare an integrated report or explain why they had not (Maroun et al., 2014).

The practice of preparing an integrated report, coupled with the formal adoption of IFRS in 2005 (Ames, 2013), were significant for bolstering, in the eyes of the international investor community, SA's appearance as a legitimate developing economy (Maroun et al., 2014; Atkins and Maroun, 2015). South Africa has been recognised globally for its excellence in this regard, indicating the success of this strategy (Roberts, 2017). While King III recommended that companies publish an integrated report, it did not specify or provide guidance on how to prepare such a report.

Integrated reporting and the Integrated Reporting Committee of South Africa

While King III introduced the integrated report, the inclusion of non-financial information in reports was recommended from the first King Code (IOD, 1994). King I was expanded in King II to include social and environmental considerations (IOD, 2002). King III went further by asking for connected financial and non-financial information in the report. King III defined this as "a holistic and integrated representation of the company's performance in terms of both its finances and its sustainability" (IOD, 2009, p. 108). The report should be succinct and record the effects a company has had on environmental and social issues (IOD, 2009, p. 15).

The implementation of IR presented companies with a challenge, as they were uncertain about how to determine what should or should not be included, how much detail about each issue to provide, and whether items should be discussed separately in sections or holistically throughout the report (Ioana and Adriana, 2013; McNally et al., 2017). Guidance on IR for South African companies was initially provided by the Integrated Reporting Committee of South Africa (IRCSA), which was founded in 2010 (IRCSA, 2011; De Villiers et al., 2014).

The IRCSA published the world's first Discussion Paper (DP) on a framework for IR in 2011 (IRCSA, 2011; Barth et al., 2017). The DP received global acknowledgement and both it and the feedback from public comment were channelled back to the International Integrated Reporting Council (IIRC) in the preparation of its *International <IR> Framework* (IRCSA, 2019d). This DP was very progressive and included a section on possible methods of assuring the integrated report – an issue current researchers are confronting (see Maroun et al., 2014; Maroun, 2017, 2018a). This process set the stage for SA becoming one of the world's leaders on corporate governance and being seen as a legitimate economic partner (Maroun et al., 2014).

The IRCSA aims to provide direction and guidance on IR and integrated thinking in SA through the provision of technical guides, conferences and other supportive activities (IRCSA, 2019a). The founding organisational members of the IRCSA are the Association for Savings and Investment South Africa, the IOD, the JSE Ltd and the South African Institute of Chartered Accountants. The membership of the IRCSA has since grown and currently includes a category for corporate members. Some of these include Ernst and Young, PwC, Liberty Holdings, Eskom Holdings SOC Ltd, Redefine Properties Ltd and Northam Platinum Ltd (IRCSA, 2019a). As the membership of IRCSA has grown significantly, the IRCSA formed a board in 2017, of which Professor Mervyn King is the current chairman and Professor Suresh Kana is the deputy chairman (IRCSA, 2019a).

The inclusion of leading corporate reporting, professional and industry bodies as members enhances the IRCSA's influence, helping them to maintain momentum and drive report quality. This, coupled with their technical guidance, has contributed to the success of the IRCSA as a national body and has established integrated thinking by corporates as the norm (IRCSA, 2019a).

With SA's history, it is not surprising that it is considered a leader in IR. Eccles et al. (2019) recently performed a comparative analysis of integrated reports across ten countries and found that SA's companies scored highest in all metrics.[2] Because of the early inclusion of King III in the JSE Listing Requirements, most JSE listed companies now have over seven years' experience in IR (Eccles et al., 2019), with the result that it has become institutionalised (Ahmed Haji and Anifowose, 2017) and is seen as part of "business-as-usual" (PWC, 2016). This has been complemented by robust support measures from organisations like the IRCSA, which can be adjusted to meet current needs more efficiently than formal legal mechanisms (Eccles et al., 2019). The IRCSA's website, for example, provides many guides on different aspects of preparing an integrated report. Available guidance includes: *Preparing an Integrated Report: A Starter's Guide (Updated)*; *Guidance on Materiality*; *Reporting on Outcomes*; *Disclosure of Governance Information* and many more (IRCSA, 2019c).

Balance in integrated reporting

Sustainable development is defined as "development that meets the needs of the present without compromising the ability of future generations to meet their needs" (United Nations, 1987, p. 8). Integrated thinking is an integral component of sustainable development as it requires a company to take into account the interdependencies among a range of factors that affect its ability to create value over the short, medium and long term (IOD, 2016). A company reporting on its value creation process should not only focus on its ability to create value over time but also ensure that the value is created in a sustainable manner. When reporting on the activities, it is essential that companies provide an objective and balanced report on both positive and negative effects on all six capitals (IOD, 2009). Balanced reporting is critical not only from an ethical point of view but also for accountability: "Balanced reporting is not a choice. It is a part of the governing body's duty of accountability" (Professor King in IRCSA, 2018a). Accountants, auditors and regulators have come under great scrutiny following reports and evidence of numerous corporate scandals. A search on Steinhoff's integrated report shows that their 2016 to 2018 annual reports have been removed/are not published, while their 2015 integrated report is still available but has been annotated with "Information can no longer be relied upon" in bold, red letters on every page (Steinhoff, 2015). Another example is VBS,[3] which has attracted significant attention from those directly affected and the public at large. Corporate failures indicate that, while governance codes exist, their relevance is in their mindful application and leadership's commitment to transparency.

As those charged with governance are ultimately responsible for good corporate governance, the integrated report and its approval, poor IR may pose a reputational risk for such members at the individual level (see Van Zijl and Maroun, 2017). This should serve to encourage those charged with governance to take this duty seriously. Corporate scandals highlight the need for balanced reporting (IRBA, 2018; IRCSA, 2018a). No company is perfect and, while reporting more on the positive aspects of a company may have been the trend in early IR (Carels et al., 2013; Atkins and Maroun, 2015; Ahmed Haji and Anifowose, 2017), this is certainly no longer what society expects (Brown and Dillard, 2014; Flower, 2015). For stakeholders to make well-informed decisions, entities need to be open and transparent about both positive and negative effects of the entity's operations. This balance is crucial during times when a company's (or profession's) legitimacy needs to be repaired (De Villiers and Maroun, 2017; IRBA, 2018; IRCSA, 2018a).

The IRCSA's information paper on preparing a balanced report provides ten key considerations, which facilitate the preparation and publication of balanced integrated reports (IRCSA, 2018a). These are: (1) leadership; (2) planning for a credible integrated report; (3) integrated thinking; (4) determining material matters; (5) assurance over the integrated report; (6) inclusion of both good and bad news; (7) responding to stakeholders' needs; (8) providing forward-looking information to complement historical information; (9) a balance of qualitative and quantitative information; and (10) risks and opportunities. These ten considerations are introduced below to structure the remainder of this chapter.

Leadership

First, those charged with the governance of a company must genuinely commit to balanced reporting and transparency (IRCSA, 2018a). Responsible leadership is considered the cornerstone of good corporate governance and is defined as the exercise of ethical and effective leadership by the governing body aimed at achieving four outcomes: ethical culture, good performance, effective control and legitimacy (IOD, 2016, p. 20).

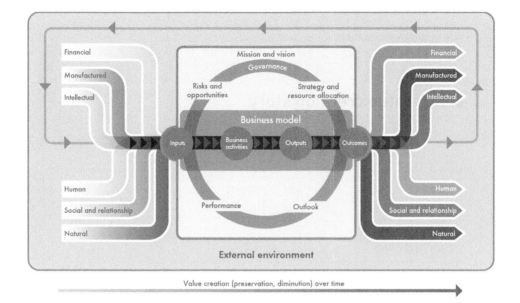

Figure 3.1 Integration among the capitals, value creation and the business model

Source: IIRC (2013). Copyright © December 2013, International Integrated Reporting Council ("the IIRC"). All rights reserved. Used with permission of the International Integrated Reporting Council (IIRC)

A commitment to quality IR can ensure that integrated thinking becomes embedded into all areas of the company – from strategy to the development of key performance indicators, risks and opportunities and allocating sufficient budget and resources to enable the entity to gather, analyse and report in an integrated manner (IRCSA, 2018a).

Leadership takes ultimate responsibility for ensuring that the integrated report is used to communicate a complete description of their value creation process over time (IIRC, 2013; Oliver et al., 2016; Guthrie et al., 2017). The integrated report should present a holistic and complete image of a company's value creation process through its use of, and effects on, financial and non-financial capitals (Casadesus-Masanell and Ricart, 2010; Moolman et al., 2016; Maroun, 2017). Figure 3.1 depicts how the various forms of capital are involved in the value creation process.

The inputs into a company are drawn from the six capitals on which the company is materially dependent. The company's outcomes are its effects on the six capitals now and over time. The six capitals are: financial; manufactured; intellectual; human; social and relationship; and natural capital (IIRC, 2013). Redefine Properties provided a useful illustration of the role and influence of the governing body in the company's value creation process (Figure 3.2).

Planning for a credible integrated report

*Planning is crucial to ensure that credible, balanced reporting is possible (IRCSA, 2018a). Planning will be an iterative process, as companies continue to improve their IR and refine systems to collect and process data on issues material for their company (see also McNally et al.,, 2017). Planning will encourage entities to practise IR throughout the year and not only

▌ Our **value creation story**

Our value creation story illustrates our journey of creating sustained value for all our stakeholders and, within that journey, the various elements we consider and that impact on our ability to achieve our stakeholder goals. By analysing our operating context and stakeholder needs and concerns, we identify risks and opportunities. By considering this, we have determined which matters are most important to Redefine's value creation in the short, medium and long term. We use these as points of reference to guide our strategy and to ensure we only report on those matters that could have a material effect on our ability to deliver stakeholder value.

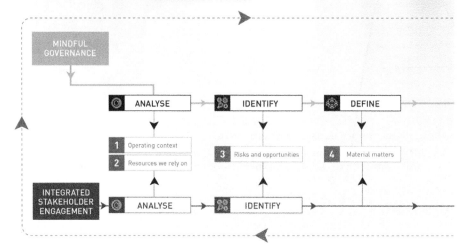

Mindful governance

At Redefine, governance is not simply a matter of compliance. Rather, it is the golden thread that binds all the elements of our value creation story together. Governance is integrated into the way we think and thus the way we operate, ensuring we make choices which are aligned with our values and strategic objectives to enable long-term value creation, while being accountable for our actions. Refer to **page** 45.

Integrated stakeholder engagement

We believe that it is our unique approach to relationships that sets us apart and allows us to deliver sustained value to all our stakeholders. To this end, we integrate stakeholder engagement into every stage of our value creation process, recognising that the nature and quality of these relationships determines the continued success of our business and the growth of our brand. Refer to **page** 19.

▮ Operating context
We analyse our operating context – global, local and property-specific – to determine which risks and opportunities have the greatest impact on our ability to create value in the short, medium and long term. Refer to **page** 15.

▮ Resources we rely on
Our ability to create value depends on our capitals – their availability, how we use them and our impact on them. For more information on our capitals, see our value creation section from **page** 63.

Figure 3.2 Redefine Properties on balanced reporting through leadership

Source: Redefine Properties (2018)

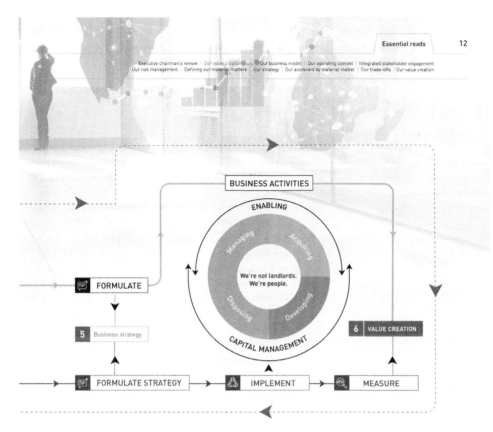

Essential reads 12

Executive chairman's review | Our value creation story | Our business model | Our operating context | Integrated stakeholder engagement
Our risk management | Defining our material matters | Our strategy | Our scorecard by material matter | Our trade-offs | Our value creation

❸ Risks and opportunities

Using our business model, we analyse our operating context, our stakeholder relationships and our dependence on particular resources. From this, we derive our top-of-mind risks and opportunities, which we update throughout the year. Refer to **page** 25.

❹ Material matters

Material matters are issues that will impact on our ability to deliver on our mission – to create sustained value for all our stakeholders. These are identified through a process of analysing the macro-environment, our operating context, the resources we rely on, as well as feedback from our stakeholders, but then also looking inwardly and considering feedback from our business units. We have identified five material matters that form the guiding principles of our strategy. We also use them to measure our success by tracking our performance against them. Refer to **page** 30.

❺ Business strategy

By considering where we are going, we apply our material matters as a compass to formulate our short- to medium-term business plans and long-term business strategies and targets. Refer to **page** 31.

❻ Value creation

Value, for Redefine, means to achieve our stakeholder goals. Refer to **page** 39.

We demonstrate value creation through

❶ Alignment to the sustainable development goals (Refer to **page** 32).
❷ Measurement of the quality of our relationships (Refer to **page** 20). ❸ Delivery on value creation indicators (Refer to **page** 6).

Figure 3.2 (Cont.)

immediately before the report is due (IRCSA, 2018a). Developing internal policies, allocating budgets and responsibilities and setting timelines are vital to support reporting and allowing sufficient time to deal with conflicts, uncertainties and integrating information (IRCSA, 2018a). Table 3.1 summarises the steps needed for effective planning.

Table 3.1 Planning and preparing the integrated report

The governing body has ultimate accountability	It is essential that the organisation's leadership buys in and participates in its integrated report. The governing body owns the report – it gives final approval to the report, and the material matters in it, and oversees its preparation.
The reporting process does not have to be complicated	There is no one-size-fits-all integrated report or integrated reporting process. The reporting process is scalable and may require effort in proportion to the size and structure of the organisation – the process need not be complicated. However, the need for responsibility and early and thorough planning cannot be emphasised enough. The governing body may designate a senior executive to be responsible for the preparation of the report.
Determining materiality is one of the cornerstones of an effective report	Applying materiality means that the organisation reports on all the matters which substantively affect its ability to create value. Material matters cover all aspects of the organisation – strategy, governance, performance, prospects and the six capitals. The integrated report discloses the process for determining materiality and the governing body approves the process and identified material matters.
Reliable information is important for the integrity and credibility of the report	Collecting non-financial data and translating it into an accessible format can be challenging at first. In practising integrated reporting, organisations become better at collecting and integrating this data, a process which can improve their business operations and decision making. The governing body determines the assurance approach for the report, which often includes internal and/or external assurance.
Aim to produce a frank and balanced report	The integrated report should be transparent, accessible and understandable. A good integrated report is clear, concise, easy to understand and uncluttered by detailed information or information which is not material. The report is the organisation's value creation story: additional and detailed information can be housed in supplementary reports, fact sheets or the website. The integrated report should be balanced and transparent, reflecting both good and poor performance and outcomes. Users have said that unbalanced reporting damages an organisation's credibility.

Source: Adapted from: IRCSA (2018b)

Integrated thinking

Integrated thinking should be embedded within all areas of the company (IRCSA, 2018a). This thinking is not unique to the IR regime (although the *International <IR> Framework* has had a positive impact on the adoption of IR (Adams, 2015)). It was pioneered as a business strategy tool under the Novo Nordisk Way of Management (De Villiers et al., 2014). This tool aimed to create a culture of integrating measurement and management and, in so doing, create a cohesive governance structure and environmental, social and economic entity.

Although integrated reports have been prepared for almost a decade in SA, some companies' integrated reports do not illustrate whether they use "integrated thinking" (see EY, 2018). In order to become better integrated thinkers, businesses need to recognise and genuinely believe that the so-called non-financial capitals play a crucial role in the company's success and longevity (IRCSA, 2011; IIRC, 2013). Without this, non-financial effects will not be accepted as legitimate business risks or as providing new opportunities over the medium and long term. Moreover, integrated thinking is an area where *continuous improvement* particularly applies (IOD, 2016). Companies that have adopted IR completely state this has provided a major internal benefit by embedding integrated thinking within their organisations (PWC, 2016; McNally and Maroun, 2018; Dumay et al., 2019).

Research conducted by Black Sun (2014) indicates that some companies are noting improvements in integrated thinking in the form of improved decision making, a better understanding of risks and opportunities, and better collaborative thinking by the board about goals and targets.

On the other hand, some literature suggests that integrated thinking is difficult to achieve in practice because of its ambiguity and a lack of understanding of how it works (Dumay and Dai, 2017; Dumay et al., 2019). The main challenges entities are facing regarding integrated thinking are:

- Understanding what integrated thinking is;
- Identifying and evaluating the connections between all six capitals;
- Connecting information and resources;
- Substantive reshaping of internal practices; and
- Overcoming a compliance approach to the preparation of the integrated report.

Supporting this, and specific to SA, McNally et al. (2017, p. 494) found evidence that "in the absence of integrated thinking, application of codes of best practice do not automatically result in high-quality reporting". Their SA case study company "ticked more boxes than anybody else", but found the entity's reporting to be of low quality, reflecting that IR is about mindful, as opposed to mindless, application (McNally et al., 2017, p. 494).

Determining material matters

Presenting stakeholders with volumes of information reduces their ability to understand the information presented as it makes it difficult for stakeholders to identify key issues. This increases information asymmetry and reduces their ability to make informed decisions (Barth et al., 2017; Zhou et al., 2017). This concept has been embedded in conventional financial reporting logic for decades (see IASC, 1989; IASB, 2018). To be effective, an integrated report should only deal with material information and matters that explain the company's value creation. Determining what is material from all six capitals can be an extensive, subjective exercise in practice. To help with this determination, companies should develop a process to identify, track and report on material matters.

The broad approach followed by the IIRC (2013) when explaining materiality in an IR environment is comparable to that of the Global Reporting Initiative (GRI) (2016) and AccountAbility (2008). According to the IIRC (2013, para 3.18), this involves:

- Identifying relevant matters based on the entity's ability to sustainably affect value creation;
- Evaluating the importance of relevant matters in terms of their known or potential effect on value creation;
- Prioritising the matters based on relative importance and
- Determining the information to disclose as material matters.

This approach avoids a finance-centric conceptualisation of materiality focused primarily on quantitative measures. Materiality should be assessed both quantitatively and qualitatively. This process requires judgement about how each matter affects the company's scope to create value. Importantly, material matters are specific to the organisation itself with the process taking into consideration a company's context, sustainability drivers and effects and stakeholder views (AccountAbility, 2008; Edgley et al., 2015; GRI, 2016). Oceana Group Limited (2018) presents its materiality determination process succinctly and clearly, explaining each material matter's risk, the link to value, the mitigating actions implemented and where more information about the matter can be found (see Figure 3.3).

Just as materiality in a financial reporting context is different from materiality determined in an integrated reporting context, different issues will emerge as being material. Redefine Properties (2018) publishes separate *integrated, sustainability, accountability* and *dependability* reports. Their integrated report focuses on providing a balanced and concise account of the company's value creation from a short-, medium- and long-term perspective, while details about specific issues are provided in other reports. This is frequently called "the octopus approach" to corporate reporting (see Oliver et al., 2016; IRCSA, 2019b).

Assurance over the integrated report

Assurance over financial reporting is well established. As financial reporting has clear standards that must be complied with, assurance can be given that a company's financial report complies with those standards (IAASB, 2009). The IIRC (2013) does not require assurance over the disclosures in the integrated report but states that:

> the reliability of information is affected by its balance and freedom from material error. Reliability (which is often referred to as faithful representation) is enhanced by mechanisms such as robust internal control and reporting systems, stakeholder engagement, internal audit or similar functions, and independent, external assurance
>
> *(IIRC, 2013, p. 21)*

As the IIRC's framework provides only guidance, and much of the reporting may be forward-looking, assuring an integrated report becomes a more complicated process. As a result, there is no assurance over the entire integrated report (Maroun, 2017). Early

	Risk context	Impact on value	Risk mitigation actions
① RESOURCE AVAILABILITY AND ABILITY TO HARVEST	• Reduction in Pilchards and Anchovy (SA and Namibia) beyond normal cyclical fish movements, and SASSI red listing of lobster • Decrease in TAC of certain species where resource appears under pressure • Changes in ecosystem from various environmental factors • Impact of ocean-based mining and seismic surveys	• Loss of revenue and increased marginal costs reducing profitability • Under-utilisation of assets (factories/vessels) • Closure of operations with resulting socio-economic impacts • Reduced market share	• Participate in and exert a positive influence on resource management initiatives with industry, government and scientific working groups in SA and Namibia • Comply with regulations and responsible fishing practices • Utilise own resources to support scientific surveys and provide input to government • Diversify targeted species
② REALLOCATION OF FISHING RIGHTS	• Horse Mackerel (Namibia) rights expire in 2018. Draft policy gives preference to allocating rights to Namibian nationals • BCP Hake Trawl, squid and south coast rock lobster, and Lucky Star pelagic rights up for reallocation in SA in 2020; continuing uncertainty on fishing rights allocation policies and process	• Increased dependency on JV and 3rd party supplier arrangements • Higher costs of contracted quota • Reduced throughput at factories leading to job losses • Under-utilisation of assets (factories/vessels)	• Monitor policy and legislative changes, and engage actively with authorities on the policy and legislative framework • Comply with all relevant legislation and retain credible empowerment and localisation credentials • Engage with government and communities to partner with community co-operatives • Be market leader in production quality and efficiency, ensuring attractive to new quota holders
③ MARKET VOLATILITY	• International market movements • Over leveraged balance sheet • Weakening ZAR vs USD, impact imports of frozen and raw fish • Impact of US / China tariffs on imports to China. • Sensitivity to fishmeal and oil price to global supply and demand dynamics	• Inability to maintain margins • Cost increases and revenue decline • Impede capital raising ability • Trading loss from forex volatility	• Implement hedging policy • Natural business hedge, with both imports and exports • Interest rate swaps and interest rate cap • Strict repayment of debt and covenants
④ PORTFOLIO IMBALANCE	• Concentration of earnings in a particular unit exposes the group to greater earnings volatility	• Increased volatility of earnings	• Business strategy focused on growth and diversification of portfolio • Acquisition of Daybrook and investment in Angola • Business expansion into global aquaculture
⑤ FOOD SAFETY	• Potential deviation from quality or safety standards with own and third-party (local and foreign) producers and suppliers • Mismanagement of non-conforming product by traders • Increase in counterfeit product • Potential sabotage • Possible negative publicity including through social media	• Illness of consumer • Damage to brand and reputation • Loss of market share • Product recall and liability claims • Negative impact on insurance renewal terms, rates and policy limits	• Internal technical department and third-party auditors to ensure compliance with standards • Product recall processes and insurance cover in place • Best practices hygiene and quality practices, with HACCP accreditation • Proactive media engagement strategy

OUR BUSINESS

THE OPERATING CONTEXT

DIVISIONAL PERFORMANCE REVIEWS

GROUP PERFORMANCE AGAINST STRATEGY

SUMMARISED CONDENSED GROUP FINANCIAL STATEMENTS

mimsSHAREHOLDER INFORMATION

Figure 3.3 Oceana Group Limited's materiality determination process

Source: Oceana Group Limited (2018)

Managing our material risks *(continued)*

	Risk context	Impact on value	Risk mitigation actions
6 — BUSINESS INTERRUPTION/ INDUSTRIAL ACTION	• Disruption at own facilities and vessels as a result of: technical breakdown; utilities failure; fire or flooding; political or labour unrest; interruption in IT systems; electrical disruption; inconsistent water pressure/supply • Inability to settle wage negotiations in unionised environment	• Inability to continue operations, resulting in loss of market share and brand • Increase in processing costs and reduced profits • Under-utilisation of labour/loss of earnings • Possible loss of JV & supply partners over the long run • Damage to staff and employee relationships	• Business interruption insurance • Business continuity process complete and in place • Power outage, maintenance and site safety procedures in place and audited • Standard operating procedures in the event of labour unrest • Communications strategy (group/ external) • IT disaster recovery plan
7 — INABILITY TO ACQUIRE FISHING RIGHTS IN SA	• Uncertain policies on reallocation/ extension of rights • Transfer of fishing rights policy requirements not aligned with B-BBEE Act and Codes of Good Practice • Perception by regulators and interested parties of Oceana's market dominance • Incorrect perception that Oceana may divest from Southern Africa • Possible negative impact of implementation of new Codes	• Lack of substantial growth within SA fishing industry • Stagnation of business • Reduced ability to generate and share value	• Maintain active engagement with South African authorities to ensure appropriate alignment on transformation policy • Maintain and develop new JV and supply partnerships to increase volumes • Implement proactive strategy demonstrating transformation efforts, responsible fishing, percentage rights holdings per sector and conversion into value • Diversification of operations and expansion into aquaculture
8 — CASH FLOW MANAGEMENT	• Ineffective projection and management of cash resources • Off-take below sales targets resulting in increased stock levels, and negatively impacting cash • Procurement of large volumes of frozen fish by Lucky Star	• Liquidity strain • Financial loss • Inability to meet financial debt covenants or repay interest and capital on term loans • Delayed creditor payments	• Formalisation of cash flow process and insight into future requirements • Rigorous review of capital and major maintenance expenditures • Timely enforcement of terms with regard to collection of debtors
9 — LEGISLATIVE NON- COMPLIANCE	• Need to maintain systems and skills to track, interpret and ensure effective compliance with often-changing legislative requirements in a highly regulated industry	• Damage to the brand • Fines and penalties • Administrative cost of implementation • Loss of current and future fishing rights	• Comprehensive legislative compliance, monitoring, training and auditing systems in place • Engagement with regulators directly and through industry associations
10 — SCARCITY OF CRITICAL SKILLS/ SUCCESSION PLANNING	• Inadequate pipeline of skills to lead new business opportunities, support current business operation, or replace retiring personnel • Challenges in attracting, developing and retaining best talent	• Inability to sustain current business model and growth strategy • Impact on employment equity targets • Inability to fill key positions	• Policies and guidelines in place for talent and recruitment management, remuneration, skills development and succession planning • Identify opportunity to establish a vehicle to develop required skills for the fishing industry through collaboration with industry and all relevant stakeholders

Figure 3.3 (Cont.)

assurance on integrated reports in SA focused primarily on assuring quantitative metrics that could be easily verified by service providers and external auditors. Examples include CO_2 emissions, water and electricity usage and the number of fatalities or injuries on duty (Dando and Swift, 2003; Junior et al., 2014; Maroun, 2017). A new model for assuring integrated reports is required and SA has contributed much in this regard (see Maroun, 2017, 2018a, 2018b).

Assurance not only adds to the credibility of the integrated report but also serves as a mechanism that those charged with governance may use to ensure that they adequately address their legislative duties[4] (Maroun, 2018a). Most of the current research available explores the determinants of the assurance provider (traditional auditors or expert consultants). Maroun (2018a) developed a diagram illustrating the determinants, assurance models and outcomes in an IR assurance context (see Figure 3.4).

Further work used interviews with expert auditors and preparers to develop three assurance approaches, namely restricted assurance, integrated assurance and Delphi-inspired assurance (Maroun, 2017). Restricted assurance approaches focus on select items of the integrated report (usually the more conventional, verifiable metrics). Integrated assurance approaches "demonstrate how different sources of assurance are used collectively to ensure the reliability" of the integrated report (Maroun, 2017). Finally, a Delphi-inspired approach aims to provide assurance through the use of a panel of independent experts who review the information and processes used to identify, acquire and analyse information used to develop the integrated report. This panel would also consider other qualities of the report, including whether it is balanced, concise and understandable (Maroun, 2017). Nedbank Group (2018) appears to follow an integrated approach in which they present the different types of assurance obtained over different aspects of their integrated report (see Figure 3.5).

Inclusion of both good and bad news

Users are looking for transparency and sincere disclosures. Care is necessary to ensure that a focus on positive outcomes or shared value for stakeholders does not result in an understatement or omission of negative outcomes on the six capitals in the integrated report

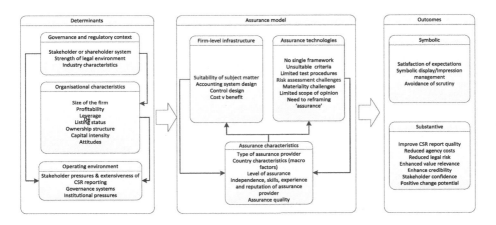

Figure 3.4 CSR assurance model
Source: Maroun (2018a)

Assurance indicators

LA	External limited assurance on selected sustainability information and the application of the FSC and the group's BBBEE status. Related opinions are available at nedbankgroup.co.za.
MO	Management and board oversight through rigorous internal reporting governed by the group's ERMF.
IN	Information sourced from external sources, eg independent surveys.
OV	Independent oversight by regulatory bodies, including SARB, FSCA and various financial sector ombudsman offices.
FS	Financial information extracted from the 2018 Nedbank Group Limited Audited Annual Financial Statements.

2018	2017	2016	Benchmark/Peer average³	Outlook/Target	Assurance
5,91	5,78	5,34	N/A	Continue to increase digital enablement actively	MO LA
1 544	1 474¹	1 368¹	N/A	Continued strong growth as digitally enabled clients start using new innovative digital products	MO LA
114	129	145		Reduce to 60 by 2020	MO
60%	55%	44%	N/A	74% of total outlets converted by 2020	MO
9th (5th bank)	10th (5th bank)	8th (4th bank)	3rd to 9th overall	Top 2 bank brand	IN (Source: Brand Finance)
2,98	2,78	2,78	N/A	Increase in line with our market share	MO LA
13,1%	12,7%	AMPS not done in 2016	18,1% (peer average)	> 15% by 2020	MO LA IN (Source: AMPS 2015 replaced by Consulta in 2017)
18,0%	18,9%	18,7%	20,9% (peer average)	> 19% by 2020	IN (Source: SARB BA900)
14,5%	13,4%	14,3%	24,6% (peer average)	> 16,5% by 2020	IN (Source: SARB BA900)
2,4%	2,0%	2,1%	N/A	> 2% in the medium to long term	MO
82,1%	80,7%	82,9%	75,3% (peer average)	> 85% in the medium to long term	FS
32 971	24 485	18 743	N/A	Reduction of > 45 000 m² by 2020 (revised from > 30 000 m²)	MO
R680m	R238m	N/A	N/A	R1,0bn by 2019 and R1,2bn by 2020	MO
57,2%	58,6%	56,9%	55,7% (peer average)	≤ 53% by 2020	MO FS
2 868	1 695	1 565	N/A	Positive economic profit growth	MO
17,9%	16,4%	16,5%	19,0% (peer average)	≥ 18% by 2020	MO FS
353	336	295	N/A	Increase over time	MO
8 (39 across Africa through ETI)	8 (39 across Africa through ETI)	8	12 across Africa (peer average)	Increase over time to 10	MO
105	85	82	N/A	Increase over time	MO
2	0	0	N/A	Increase over time	MO

³ Peer average consists of the simple average of Absa, FirstRand and Standard Bank.

Figure 3.5 Nedbank Group assurance model
Source: Nedbank Group (2018.)

(IRCSA, 2018a). Acknowledging errors in past judgements and mistakes made, particularly where insufficient improvement has been achieved, can illustrate a company's willingness to be accountable. This can provide a sense of comfort to stakeholders that the report is balanced (IRCSA, 2018a). Including information about how these weaknesses will be addressed is of particular interest to stakeholders, to assess whether management is taking adequate steps to mitigate the risk of future occurrences or is embarking on an impression management campaign (see Flower, 2015).

Being consistent year-on-year with regard to good and bad news also indicates that the report is a balanced report and provides some level of legitimacy to the company (see De Villiers and Maroun, 2017). The use of invalid adjustments and inconsistencies in traditional performance metrics in SA (see Howard et al., 2019) may indicate that this is also prevalent in the less regulated IR context. It is relatively easy for stakeholders to observe and note inconsistencies when comparing prior years' integrated reports to the current year's. Omitting key performance indicators previously presented may lead stakeholders to consider the possibility of impression management and adjust their views of that entity and its integrated report (IRCSA, 2018a).

Liberty Holdings' (2017, 2018) 2017 and 2018 integrated reports reflect consistent reporting, which includes both positive and negative news (see Figure 3.6).

Responding to stakeholders' needs

Stakeholder-centric, as opposed to shareholder-centric, perspectives are becoming mainstream. Maroun (2018a) states that stakeholders have credible interests in a company's operations and companies are deemed legitimate if there is congruence between their actions and social values. The credible interest creates a legitimate "basis for demanding sound social and environmental management" (Maroun, 2018a, p. 17). Additionally, the integrated report provides an opportunity for a company to prepare an integrated report in order to gain legitimacy in the eyes of stakeholders (Deegan and Blomquist, 2006; Brown and Dillard, 2014; Ahmed Haji and Anifowose, 2016).

There is much evidence to suggest that integrated reports are aimed at managing perceptions and persuading stakeholders that companies have shareholders' interests at heart (Dawkins and Ngunjiri, 2008; Solomon and Maroun, 2012a). Stakeholders expect to be heard and their concerns to be considered by management; in order to demonstrate that companies are genuinely addressing stakeholder concerns, integrated reports should address stakeholder concerns raised and explain how these have influenced the identification of risks, strategy, material matters and the company's value creation process, This process should function in an iterative feedback loop (IRCSA, 2018a). Nedbank Group (2017) provides an excellent example of how this can be done (see Figure 3.7).

Providing forward-looking information to complement historical information

Forward-looking information allows users to assess the company's value creation ability in the short, medium and long term (IRCSA, 2018a). Some companies are hesitant to disclose forward-looking information for fear of losing a competitive advantage (Kılıç and Kuzey, 2018). With the high volume of information available, as well as competitors comparing themselves with one another to benchmark themselves and stay relevant, sustainable competitive advantages are unlikely to be given away by forward-looking discloses in an

2017 PERFORMANCE DASHBOARD AND 2018 TARGETS

Figure 3.6 Extract of Liberty Holding's performance for 2017 and 2018

Source: Liberty Holdings (2017, 2018)

2018 performance dashboard and 2019 targets

Metrics	2018			2019
	Actual	Target	Achievement	Target
Combined policyholder persistency performance	Better than actuarial assumption	Actuarial assumption	●	Actuarial assumption
Client net promoter score[1]	n/a	n/a	n/a	> 33%
Net customer cash flows[1]	R10,2 billion	Positive	●	Positive
South African voluntary staff turnover	11,3%	< 14%	●	< 14%
Management control (Diversity at management levels)[1] — Senior management	48%	55%	●	56%
Management control (Diversity at management levels)[1] — Middle management	62%	66%	●	68%
Liberty Group Limited solvency capital requirement cover[2]	1,87 times	1,5 – 2,0 times	●	1,5 – 2,0 times
Risk appetite	Achieved	Manage within risk appetite	●	Manage within risk appetite
Number of adverse findings by industry ombuds and adjudicators[1]	168	n/a	●	< 50
Normalised return on group equity value	3,8%	> 12,0%	●	> 12,0%
Normalised return on IFRS equity	10,1%	15% – 18%	●	15% – 18%
Shareholder Investment Portfolio performance	Below benchmark	Board approved benchmark reference	●	Board approved benchmark reference
Growth in operational profit[1]	+42,1%	n/a	●	n/a
SA Retail new business margin	0,8%	1,0% – 1,5%	●	1,0% – 1,5%
B-BBEE contributor level	2	2	●	2
Corporate social investment spend (South Africa)	R45,6 million	1% of adjusted net operating profit after tax	●	1% of adjusted net operating profit after tax

[1] New metric adopted in 2019
[2] Calculated in terms of the new prudential regulatory regime effective 1 July 2018

● Fully achieved ● Not achieved

Liberty Holdings Limited
Integrated report for the year ended 31 December 2018

Figure 3.6 (Cont.)

THE NEEDS AND EXPECTATIONS OF OUR STAKEHOLDERS

As a financial services provider we are deeply connected to the environment we operate in and the societies we serve. Our ability to deliver value is dependent on our relationships and the contributions and activities of our stakeholders. By providing for their needs and meeting their expectations, we create value for both our stakeholders and Nedbank.

 STAFF

31 887 employees.
29 085 employees in SA businesses.
2 802 employees in non-SA businesses.
62,1% female, **37,9%** male.
78,5% black, **21,5%** white.

24,1% under **29 years of age**.
27,2% with a tenure of more than 10 years.
Staff turnover of **10,6%**.

 CLIENTS

7,9 million clients.

Individuals from **children** to **seniors** and from **entry-level** clients to **high-net-worth** individuals.

Various **legal entities**, such as trusts, non-governmental entities and associations, small businesses, **large corporates** and the **public sector**.

 SHAREHOLDERS

Ordinary and preference shareholders, bondholders and prospective investors.

Retail investors, asset management and retirement funds in SA and increasingly in international markets that invest in Nedbank equity and preference shares as well as funding instruments.

Two credit rating agencies: **Moody's** and **Standard & Poor's**

13 sell-side analysts.

 REGULATORS

SARB – responsible for banking regulation and supervision in SA.
FSB – responsible for overseeing the SA non-banking financial services industry.
NCR – responsible for the regulation for the SA credit industry.

Other: SARS, foreign revenue authorities, various government departments and Chapter 9 institutions, including the Department of Trade and Industry (the dti), Department of Labour, National Treasury, Financial Intelligence Centre (FIC) and the JSE.

We also comply with various regulatory bodies outside SA, including central banks and local financial services regulators of countries in which we have representation or operations.

 SOCIETY

Society represents:

Citizens of the countries in which we operate, comprising individual members of society, non-governmental organisations and suppliers.

The environment on which these citizens depend for their wellbeing.

For more details on how we delivered value to our stakeholders refer to pages 63 to 73.

Figure 3.7 Nedbank's stakeholder needs and expectations
Source: Nedbank (2017)

Their needs and expectations

- Competitive remuneration, effective performance management and recognition.
- Challenging work with opportunities to make a difference.
- Career development and advancement opportunities.
- Employment at a company with a strong brand that is recognised as a good employer.
- An empowering, diverse and enabling environment that embraces diversity and inclusivity.

- Innovative solutions and services, including lending, deposit-taking, transactional and advisory services, global markets, wealth management, asset management and insurance.
- Convenient access to banking (channel of choice), increasingly through digital channels.
- Excellence in client service.
- Value-for-money banking that is competitive and transparent in pricing.
- Responsible banking services and solutions, and a trusted financial partner.

- Shareholder value creation through share price appreciation and an attractive and sustainable dividend stream, enabled by:
  - Growth in net asset value.
  - Sustainable financial returns, with ROE exceeding COE.
  - Attractive and sustainable growth strategy.
  - Sound balance sheet to protect against downside risk.
  - Strong and experienced management.
  - Transparent reporting and disclosure.
  - Sound governance.

- Compliance with all legal and regulatory requirements.
- Being a responsible taxpayer in all jurisdictions where we conduct business.
- Active participation and contribution to industry and regulatory working groups.

- Nedbank providing access to expert advice, products and solutions that help to achieve desired outcomes for individuals, their families, their businesses and their communities.
- Nedbank partnering on common social and environmental issues.
- Nedbank using its resources to promote social, environmental and other common agendas to build a thriving society.
- Embracing transformation through delivery in line with BBBEE legislation.

Creating value for our stakeholders

Our staff are key to making Nedbank a great place to bank and work. Motivated and skilled staff, together with efficient and value-creating solutions, services and operations, offer value to our clients. Staff, as part of society, contribute materially to the communities in which they live and work.

Value is created through

- Employing citizens in the jurisdictions in which we operate.
- Rewarding staff for the value they add.
- Creating job opportunities as we grow.
- Developing our staff to embrace technological changes, further their careers and improve our services and products.
- Transforming to an inclusive society through employment equity and gender equality.
- Motivating and energising our workforce.

Clients remain our largest source of deposits, which enable us to fund lending activities. Gaining more clients results in greater revenue growth, while sustainable banking practices and worldclass risk management mitigate against bad debts.

Value is created through

- Safeguarding deposits, investments and wealth, while growing returns.
- Providing credit that enables wealth creation, sustainable development and job creation.
- Facilitating transactions that are the backbone of economic-value exchange.
- Enabling financial inclusion by providing the previously unbanked with access to affordable products.
- Providing financial education and advice.
- Developing innovative solutions that meet our clients' specific needs.

The financial capital we source from our equity and debt investors and our retained earnings enable business continuity and growth, including strategic investments.

Value is created through

- Increasing net asset value, returns, dividends and share price.
- Maintaining a strong balance sheet to protect against downside risk.

Regulation ensures a sound and stable banking system, which reduces systemic risk and promotes healthy functioning of an economy in which all stakeholders prosper. Good governance and compliance support client confidence in Nedbank and reduce potential for reputational risk. We realise that the tax we pay is an imperative for the economic and social development of the countries in which we operate. We have a responsibility to comply fully with the regulations of the countries in which we operate.

Value is created through

- Embracing sustainable banking practices and regulatory compliance that enable a safe and stable banking system and a thriving society.
- Participation in buying government and public sector bonds.
- Contributing meaningfully to government budgets through our own tax contributions and taxes collected on behalf of SARS and foreign revenue authorities.

We embrace our role in society as an active contributor to building a thriving society and can only do this with engaged communities that have similar values.

Value is created through

- Transforming economies and society positively through our lending and transactional activities, which are increasingly aligned with the SDGs.
- Playing a meaningful role in the broader society as a procurer of goods and services.
- Making a difference through our partnerships and CSI activities.

Figure 3.7 (Cont.)

integrated report (see Porter, 2008). This should not be accepted, or used as a valid reason for excluding useful forward-looking information.

Another factor may be an unwillingness to give specific forward-looking information that may create high expectations and against which management may be held accountable (see McNally et al., 2017; IRCSA, 2018a). This risk may be perceived as being enhanced with quantitative information and reduced with qualitative information (Kadous et al., 2005). This appears to be the case as Kılıç and Kuzey (2018) found that in 2014, integrated reports' forward-looking information was mostly qualitative in nature. The main quantitative disclosures related to environmental targets such as CO_2 emissions, water and electricity consumption, which are metrics for which management may be less concerned with being held to account. Distinguishing between controllable and uncontrollable issues, risks and opportunities within the forward-looking information may help preparers manage stakeholder expectations while providing the forward-looking information demanded by stakeholders (IRCSA, 2018a). Truworths (2018) provides an example of forward-looking information (see Figure 3.8).

A balance of qualitative and quantitative information

Providing a balance of both qualitative and quantitative information allows preparers to provide context for their quantitative information. This improves the ability of users to comprehend what is provided (IRCSA, 2018a). Some areas are more easily reported through qualitative information while others can be reported definitively using quantitative information. Infographics are useful to present industry benchmarks, year-on-year changes and targets in a concise and straightforward format (see IRCSA, 2018a; Kılıç and Kuzey, 2018). Impala Platinum (2018) provides an example of a qualitative and quantitative performance review (see Figure 3.9).

Risks and opportunities

A complete assessment of a company's material risks and opportunities is relevant information to stakeholders and contributes to a balanced report (IRCSA, 2018a). This assessment should include all six capitals (IIRC, 2013; IRCSA, 2018a). Using heat maps allows preparers to reflect risks, their possible impact and likelihood, as well as opportunities, in an easily understood visual. The heat map should clearly reflect the connectivity and linkages among each risk/opportunity, the company's strategy and outlook (IRCSA, 2018a). Royal Bafokeng Platinum (2018) provides a heat map as an example (see Figure 3.10).

Group 5's (2018) integrated report appears to reflect a balanced approach. Early on page 6, Group 5 prominently presents its top six material issues, reflecting a leadership team who acknowledge the group's poor results and challenging circumstances. In doing so, they take ownership and present themselves as willing to engage on important issues and work hard towards improving the company's performance. In presenting a balanced view, companies may also present plans and solutions aimed at addressing those negative issues. These aspects are just as essential to indicate that the leadership has substantively reflected on the negative issues and developed a meaningful plan to address those issues (IRCSA, 2018a).

Balance is not only about providing both good and bad news about a company. In order for an integrated report to be balanced, the report needs to cover the six capitals and have both forward-looking and historical qualitative and quantitative information. These types of

TRUWORTHS

MANAGING THE RISK OF FASHION

Refer to Managing the risk of fashion on page 55 for more detail.

Performance against objectives and targets in 2018

OBJECTIVES AND PLANS FOR 2018	PERFORMANCE AGAINST OBJECTIVES
Ongoing focus on managing the risk of fashion.	Despite the challenging trading conditions, management reduced the level of markdowns on the prior period by managing stock levels, balancing fashion versus core product, managing price points and introducing a wider spread of price points.
Continued consolidation of fabric sourcing and manufacturing to improve value offering for customers.	Achieved better price pointing in merchandise, particularly in core ranges.
	Assisted in stabilising fabric supply during a time of excess demand when several fabric mills in China were relocated and dye houses and laundries faced temporary shutdown or closure due to enforced upgrades.
Leverage the benefits of fabric and supplier sourcing consolidation to improve speed to market.	Increased the volume of fabric purchased locally, thereby enabling the merchandise team to react fast and turn on best-selling styles during the season.
	A major fire at a large local supplier limited the ability to turn on merchandise to the full potential.
Offer merchandise promotions linked to loyalty programme.	Introduced several merchandise promotions linked to the loyalty programme, with varying levels of success.
	Outcomes of experimentation with promotions will be incorporated into enhanced approach to product promotions in the period ahead.
Refocus brand positioning and differentiation between brands offered in the emporium stores.	Strategic project undertaken to review and clarify the brand positioning as well as brand differentiation, and the creation of a DNA statement for each brand.
	Buying teams now use the outcomes of this project to guide decision-making and brand selection.
	Marketing and visual display aligned with the reviewed brand positioning and differentiators.

TARGETS FOR 2018	PERFORMANCE AGAINST TARGETS
Group gross margin 51% – 55%	Gross margin 52.4% (2017: 52.6%)
Truworths gross margin 54% – 57%	Gross margin 55.5% (2017: 55.2%)

Challenges encountered in 2018

- Increase in value-added tax (VAT) rate and the related implications on systems and resources.
- Unusually high level of discounting in the marketplace.
- Pressure on disposable income resulting in customers being more risk averse in their fashion purchases.
- Relocation of fabric mills and temporary shutdown or closure of dye houses and laundries in China has resulted in constrained fabric supply from the region together with inconsistent quality.

GROSS MARGIN
Percentage

2014 2015 2016 2017 2018

RETAIL SALES CONTRIBUTION

- Truworths
- Ladieswear Emporium
- Menswear Emporium
- Ladieswear Designer Emporium
- Kids Emporium
- Identity
- Other

Key risks and mitigation strategies for 2019

DESCRIPTION OF RISK	RISK MITIGATION
Increased international competition.	Monitor impact of the international retailers targeting the Truworths mainstream middle-market customer (most international brands target upper-income customers).
	Constant innovation across sales channels, brands and products, including e-commerce platform, launch of new brand websites and introduction of lay-bys.
Exchange rate volatility creates challenges in managing retail selling prices of imported merchandise.	Forward exchange contracts are used to cover all merchandise imports so price points can be determined at the time of placing orders.
	Continue to seek opportunities for local supply to reduce reliance on imports, including investment in Truworths Manufacturing.
	Improve procurement processes, consolidate fabric sourcing and adjust product ranges to limit product inflation.
	Acquisition of Office has diversified the Group's currency risk which can provide a hedge against the volatile Rand.
Truworths aims to provide quality fashion to customers each season at appropriate margins. This covers buying processes, fashion monitoring, supplier relationships and ensuring Truworths has skilled buying and planning resources.	Apply proven forecasting and design processes and key executive interventions throughout the merchandise life cycle aimed at managing and mitigating the risk of fashion.
	Manage suppliers to ensure risk is spread across the supply chain.
	Balance local and international supply base to take advantage of both quick response and fast fashion.
	Maintain gross margin within target range.
	Execute retention strategies for merchandise buyers and planners.
	Achieve better prices to offer better value by consolidating fabric sourcing across brands while maintaining product quality.
Availability of counterfeit goods devalues the brands.	Substantial work done with counterfeit experts, training of customs officials and numerous raids conducted.
	Appointment of a larger legal team to ensure sufficient attention is devoted to anti-counterfeiting objectives.
	Ongoing assessment and bolstering of counterfeit measures.
	Instituting legal action against perpetrators.

Medium-term opportunities

- Optimise the potential of e-commerce across all brands.
- Grow Loads of Living chain and product offering.
- Improve product mix in Office London to drive sales growth.

Objectives and plans for 2019

- Ongoing focus on managing the risk of fashion.
- Implementation of new brands and product opportunities.
- Implementation of the product life cycle management system.

TARGETS FOR 2019
Group gross margin
51% – 55%
Truworths gross margin
55% – 57%

16

Figure 3.8 Truworth's forward-looking information
Source: Truworths (2018)

Group performance against objectives

Strategy	Operational strategies	KPI performance target for FY2018*
Implats is a focused PGM producer and supplier. Our strategy seeks to sustain optimal levels of production at the lowest possible cost from a diverse and competitive asset portfolio. We seek to position the Company in the lower half of the industry cost curve, and as the industry safety leader, to benefit from future stronger PGM prices and to reward all our stakeholders	Relentlessly drive the safety of our people	Zero fatalities LTIFR <5.5
	Consistently deliver production targets	Refined platinum production of 1.57 – 1.61Moz
	Improve efficiencies through operational excellence	Cost per platinum ounce <R23 100 and stock adjusted unit cost achieved of R22 931 (2017: R22 828)
	Cash conservation	Capital <R4.7 billion
	Maintain our licence to operate	Impala Rustenburg SO_2 at <16tpd Marula community disruptions <10 days Build/sell >230 employee houses

Performance targets and actual performance exclude the associate companies Two Rivers and Mimosa.

Figure 3.9 Impala Platinum's qualitative and quantitative performance review

Source: Impala Platinum (2018)

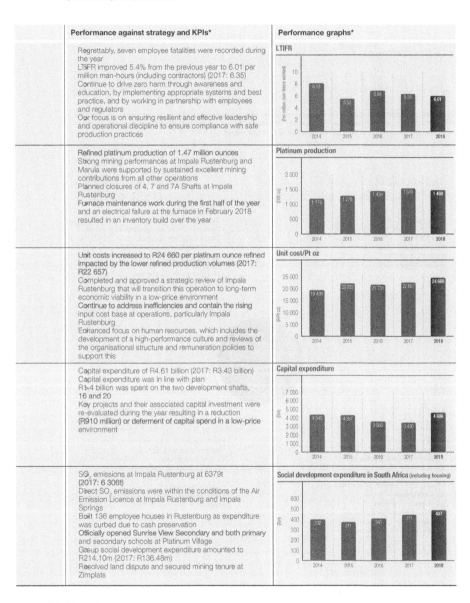

Performance against strategy and KPIs*	Performance graphs*
Regrettably, seven employee fatalities were recorded during the year LTIFR improved 5.4% from the previous year to 6.01 per million man-hours (including contractors) (2017: 6.35) Continue to drive zero harm through awareness and education, by implementing appropriate systems and best practice, and by working in partnership with employees and regulators Our focus is on ensuring resilient and effective leadership and operational discipline to ensure compliance with safe production practices	**LTIFR**
Refined platinum production of 1.47 million ounces Strong mining performances at Impala Rustenburg and Marula were supported by sustained excellent mining contributions from all other operations Planned closures of 4, 7 and 7A Shafts at Impala Rustenburg Furnace maintenance work during the first half of the year and an electrical failure at the furnace in February 2018 resulted in an inventory build over the year	**Platinum production**
Unit costs increased to R24 660 per platinum ounce refined impacted by the lower refined production volumes (2017: R22 657) Completed and approved a strategic review of Impala Rustenburg that will transition this operation to long-term economic viability in a low-price environment Continue to address inefficiencies and contain the rising input cost base at operations, particularly Impala Rustenburg Enhanced focus on human resources, which includes the development of a high-performance culture and reviews of the organisational structure and remuneration policies to support this	**Unit cost/Pt oz**
Capital expenditure of R4.61 billion (2017: R3.43 billion) Capital expenditure was in line with plan R1.4 billion was spent on the two development shafts, 16 and 20 Key projects and their associated capital investment were re-evaluated during the year resulting in a reduction (R910 million) or deferment of capital spend in a low-price environment	**Capital expenditure**
SO₂ emissions at Impala Rustenburg at 6379t (2017: 6 306t) Direct SO₂ emissions were within the conditions of the Air Emission Licence at Impala Rustenburg and Impala Springs Built 136 employee houses in Rustenburg as expenditure was curbed due to cash preservation Officially opened Sunrise View Secondary and both primary and secondary schools at Platinum Village Group social development expenditure amounted to R214.10m (2017: R136.48m) Resolved land dispute and secured mining tenure at Zimplats	**Social development expenditure in South Africa** (including housing)

Figure 3.9 (Cont.)

OUR CHANGING BUSINESS CONTEXT

In this section of our report we:

• review our global and local internal and external environments

• identify the issues that have implications for our business model, their impact or possible impact on value

• provide a brief summary of our strategic response to these issues and guidance as to where you can read more about our response.

We address the risks and opportunities our internal and external environments present, and our responses to them throughout this report. We have provided page references to where this information can be found and an indication as to whether these issues are risks, opportunities or both for RBPlat, on the graphic that follows.

THE MARKETS –
EXTERNAL ISSUES

• Low economic growth
• Socio-political climate
• Uncertain global and local political environment
• Sovereign downgrade risk
• Currency volatility
• PGM market dynamics

External environment

STRATEGIC ISSUES –
EMERGING ISSUES

• Election year in 2019
• **Electrification of powertrains**
• Potential switch from palladium to platinum
• Global emissions legislation
• New Mining Charter requirements
• Retabling of Mineral and Petroleum Resources Development Act (MPRDA)
• Changing stakeholder dynamics
• Regional trade union elections

Known issues

KEY RISKS AND OPPORTUNITIES

New and changing issues

OPERATIONS –
INTERNAL ISSUES

• Safety performance
• Safety stoppages
• **Cost management efficiencies**
• Availability of adequate and appropriate skills
• **Water scarcity and efficiencies**
• **Energy costs, availability and efficiencies**
• Climate change
• Geological complexity
• Trade union branch elections
• Review of closed shop agreement
• Wage agreement negotiations

Internal environment

STRATEGIC CHANGE –
IN EXECUTION

• 100% ownership of our operations – Joint Venture to be dissolved
• Life of mine strategy
• **Processing flexibility and performance**
• Styldrift Mine ramp up to 230ktpm by 2020
• Capital management
• Styldrift moving from capex to opex
• Implementing 24/7 operations at Styldrift Mine

Figure 3.10 Royal Bafokeng Platinum's heat map

Source: Royal Bafokeng Royal Bafokeng Platinum (2018)

Table 3.2 Challenges and contributing factors to preparing an integrated report in South Africa

Challenge	Contributing factors
Lack of commitment to transparency and accountability	• Insufficient governance processes and systems • Doubts about the relevance of integrated thinking and integrated reporting • Managerial attitude not supporting an integrated approach to reporting and based on short-term financial performance
Inadequate processes and systems to support complete and balanced reporting	• Lack of capacity or resources to manage data • Incomplete or insufficient processes for the determination of material matters resulting in difficulty in determining if and when information is material • Inappropriate approaches to assurance
Uncertainty about what to report	• Lack of understanding of the requirements of integrated reporting according to King IV and the <IR> Framework • Insufficient consideration given to the impact of societal and environmental factors
Concerns about potential negative consequences of reporting sub-optimal information	• Fear that reporting will lead to additional scrutiny by regulators • Fear that bad news may result in reputational damage and lower sales • Perceived threat of litigation based on negative information
Over-reliance on consultants.	• Limited managerial participation in the preparation of the report and poor oversight of interpretation

Adapted from: IRCSA (2018a)

information should cover the short-, medium- and long-term perspectives of the company (IRCSA, 2018a).

The IRCSA, summarising work performed by McNally et al. (2017) about the challenges in preparing a balanced integrated report, prepared the helpful information presented in Table 3.2.

Conclusion

As an emerging economy, SA is heavily dependent on foreign capital and relies on internationally aligned codes of best practice to reassure and signal to investors the credibility of the local capital market (Vaughn and Ryan, 2006). The requirement for listed companies to prepare an integrated report has resulted in an improvement of SA's profile as a legitimate developing economy in the eyes of the international investor community (Maroun et al., 2014; Atkins and Maroun, 2015; Roberts, 2017). In a country characterised by social inequality and increasing environmental awareness, stakeholders are paying attention to companies' social and environmental effects. It is essential to adhere to the stakeholder-centric model adopted by the King Codes, the emphasis placed on balancing economic imperatives with sound environmental and social performance, and acknowledge the input of all of a company's resources and relationships.

Results from prior studies indicate that compliance with corporate governance provisions generally improves over time (Patel et al., 2002; Collett and Hrasky, 2005; Barako et al., 2006; Henry, 2008; Ntim et al., 2012). This is confirmed by the reviews conducted by EY and Chartered Secretaries Southern Africa (CSSA), which indicate an overall improvement in the quality of South African integrated reports from 2010 to 2017. In contrast, the reviews also confirm several weaknesses identified by the professional and academic literature. These include, for example, reports that are difficult to read (Du Toit, 2017; Du Toit et al., 2017), repetitive and contain generic disclosure (Solomon and Maroun, 2012b; PWC, 2015) and the need for a more transparent explanation on the link between risk, strategy and financial and non-financial performance (McNally et al., 2017; Naynar et al., 2018)

The benefits of preparing a high-quality integrated report are not limited to better stakeholder relations, improved access to intellectual, financial and human capitals and reduced effects on natural capital. Research indicates that companies with higher quality integrated reports are likely to have more effective processes and systems in place and may also find it easier to identify and manage risks more effectively, implying a high-quality management team (De Villiers and Maroun, 2017; McNally and Maroun, 2018). In addition, high-quality IR decreases information asymmetry and provides relevant information for investors (Barth et al.,2017; Zhou et al., 2017). Finally, there is at least some evidence to suggest that companies that prepare high-quality integrated reports outperform their peers in financial and non-financial terms. This may only be specifically for firms operating in industries with high social and environmental impact, and is noted as an area for future research (see also De Villiers and Maroun, 2017; Guthrie et al., 2017; McNally and Maroun, 2018).

Notes

1 Apartheid was a system of institutionalised racial segregation that existed in South Africa from 1948 until the early 1990s. The National Party legislated a number of laws to propagate Apartheid, namely the Population Registration Act of 1950, the Group Areas Act of 1950, the Prevention of Illegal Squatting Act of 1951, the Prohibition of Mixed Marriages Act of 1949, the Immorality Act of 1950, the Reservation of Separate Amenities Act of 1953, the Suppression of Communism Act of 1950 and the Bantu Education Act of 1953.
2 These include: report quality, materiality, risks and opportunities, strategy and resource allocation, performance and outlook.
3 In 2018, VBS bank collapsed. The collapse of VBS is suspected to be the result of fraud. Investigations were still underway at the time of compiling this chapter. Fraudulent reporting is said to have misled regulators into believing that VBS was in a financially sound position when, in fact, its liabilities exceeded its assets by approximately ZAR180 million, making it insolvent as of 31 March 2017 (Motau, 2018).
4 Those charged with governance are responsible for ensuring a faithfully represented balanced report (IIRC, 2013; IRCSA, 2018b).

References

AccountAbility. (2008). *AA1000APS Accountability Principles Standard 2008*. Available at: www.account ability.org/wp-content/uploads/2016/10/AA1000APS_english.pdf (Accessed: 20 July 2016).
Adams, C. A. (2015). The International Integrated Reporting Council: a call to action. *Critical Perspectives on Accounting*, 27, 23–28.
Ahmed Haji, A., and Anifowose, M. (2016). The trend of integrated reporting practice in South Africa: ceremonial or substantive? *Sustainability Accounting, Management and Policy Journal*, 7(2), 190–224.

Ahmed Haji, A., and Anifowose, M. (2017). Initial trends in corporate disclosures following the introduction of integrated reporting practice in South Africa. *Journal of Intellectual Capital, 18*(2), 373–399.

Ames, D. (2013). IFRS adoption and accounting quality: the case of South Africa. *Journal of Applied Economics and Business Research, 3*(3), 154–165.

Armstrong, P., Segal, N., and Davis, B. (2005). *Corporate Governance: South Africa, a Pioneer in Africa.* Available at: www.africaportal.org/publications/corporate-governance-south-africa-a-pioneer-in-africa/ (Accessed: 25 October 2018).

Atkins, J., and Maroun, W. (2015). Integrated reporting in South Africa in 2012: perspectives from South African institutional investors. *Meditari Accountancy Research, 23*(2), 197–221.

Barako, D. G., Hancock, P., and Izan, H. (2006). Factors influencing voluntary corporate disclosure by Kenyan companies. *Corporate Governance: an International Review, 14*(2), 107–125.

Barth, M. E., Cahan, S. F., Chen, L., and Venter, E. R. (2017). The economic consequences associated with integrated report quality: capital market and real effects. *Accounting, Organizations and Society, 62,* 43–64.

Black Sun. (2014). Realizing the benefits: the impact of Integrated Reporting. Available at: https://integratedreporting.org/wp-content/uploads/2014/09/IIRC.Black_.Sun_.Research.IR_.Impact.Single.pages.18.9.14.pdf (Accessed: 25 October 2018).

Brown, J., and Dillard, J. (2014). Integrated reporting: on the need for broadening out and opening up. *Accounting, Auditing & Accountability Journal, 27*(7), 1120–1156.

Carels, C., Maroun, W., and Padia, N. (2013). Integrated reporting in the South African mining sector. *Corporate Ownership and Control, 11*(1), 991–1005.

Casadesus-Masanell, R., and Ricart, J. E. (2010). From strategy to business models and onto tactics. *Long Range Planning, 43,* 195–215.

Catchpowle, L., and Cooper, C. (1999). No escaping the financial: the economic referent In South Africa. *Critical Perspectives on Accounting, 10,* 711–746.

Collett, P., and Hrasky, S. (2005). Voluntary disclosure of corporate governance practices by listed Australian companies. *Corporate Governance: An International Review, 13*(2), 188–196.

Dando, N., and Swift, T. (2003). Transparency and assurance: minding the credibility gap. *Journal of Business Ethics, 44*(2–3), 195–200.

Dawkins, C., and Ngunjiri, F. W. (2008). Corporate social responsibility reporting in South Africa a descriptive and comparative analysis. *Journal of Business Communication, 45*(3), 286–307.

De Villiers, C., and Maroun, W. (2017). *Sustainability Accounting and Integrated Reporting.* London: Routledge.

De Villiers, C., Rinaldi, L., and Unerman, J. (2014). Integrated reporting: insights, gaps and an agenda for future research. *Accounting, Auditing & Accountability Journal, 27*(7), 1042–1067.

De Villiers, C., and van Staden, C. J. (2006). Can less environmental disclosure have a legitimising effect? Evidence from Africa. *Accounting, Organizations and Society, 31*(8), 763–781.

Deegan, C., and Blomquist, C. (2006). Stakeholder influence on corporate reporting: an exploration of the interaction between WWF-Australia and the Australian minerals industry. *Accounting, Organizations and Society, 31*(4-5), 343–372.

Du Toit, E. (2017). The readability of integrated reports. *Meditari Accountancy Research, 25*(4), 629–653.

Du Toit, E., Van Zyl, R., and Schutte, G. (2017). Integrated reporting by South African companies: a case study. *Meditari Accountancy Research, 25*(4), 654–674.

Dumay, J., and Dai, T. (2017). Integrated thinking as a cultural control? *Meditari Accountancy Research, 25*(4), 574–604.

Dumay, J., La Torre, M., Bernardi, C., and Guthrie, J. (2019). Integrated reporting and integrated thinking: practical challenges. In S. Arvidsson (Ed.), *Challenges in Managing Sustainable Business* (pp. 25–54). Switzerland: Springer.

Eccles, R. G., Krzus, M. P., and Solano, C. (2019). *A Comparative Analysis of Integrated Reporting in Ten Countries.* Available at: https://ssrn.com/abstract=3345590 (Accessed: 4 December 2019).

Edgley, C., Jones, M. J., and Atkins, J. F. (2015). The adoption of the materiality concept in social and environmental reporting assurance: a field study approach. *The British Accounting Review, 47*(1), 1–18.

EY. (2018). *EY's Excellence in Integrated Reporting Awards 2018.* Available at: https://integratedreportingsa.org/ey-excellence-in-integrated-reporting-awards-2018/ (Accessed: 4 December 2019).

Flower, J. (2015). The International Integrated Reporting Council: a story of failure. *Critical Perspectives on Accounting, 27,* 1–17.

GRI. (2016). *Consolidated Set of GRI Sustainability Reporting Standards*. Available at: www.globalreporting. org/standards/gri-standards-download-center/?g=ae2e23b8-4958-455c-a9df-ac372d6ed9a8 (Accessed: 10 February 2017).

GROUP 5. (2018). Group 5 Annual Integrated Report. Available at: www.g5.co.za/ir_latest.php (Accessed: 4 December 2019).

Guthrie, J., Manes-Rossi, F., and Orelli, R. L. (2017). Integrated reporting and integrated thinking in Italian public sector organisations. *Meditari Accountancy Research*, *25*(4), 553–573.

Hamann, R., and Kapelus, P. (2004). Corporate social responsibility in mining in Southern Africa: fair accountability or just greenwash? *Development*, *47*(3), 85–92.

Henry, D. (2008). Corporate governance structure and the valuation of Australian firms: is there value in ticking the boxes? *Journal of Business Finance & Accounting*, *35*(7-8), 912–942.

Howard, M., Maroun, W., and Garnett, R. (2019). Misuse of non-mandatory earnings reporting by companies: evidence from an emerging economy. *Meditari Accountancy Research*, *27*(1), 125–146.

IAASB. (2009). *ISA 200: Overall Objectives of the Independent Auditor and the Conduct of an Audit in Accordance with International Standards on Auditing*. Available at: www.ifac.org/system/files/downloads/ a008-2010-iaasb-handbook-isa-200.pdf (Accessed: 4 December 2019).

IASB. (2018). *Conceptual Framework for Financial Reporting*. IFRS Foundation.

IASC. (1989). *Conceptual Framework*. IASC.

IIRC. (2013). *The International Integrated Reporting Framework*. Available at: www.theiirc.org/wp-con tent/uploads/2013/12/13-12-08-THE-INTERNATIONAL-IR-FRAMEWORK-2-1.pdf (Accessed: 1 October 2013).

Ioana, D., and Adriana, T. (2013). New corporate reporting trends. Analysis on the evolution of integrated reporting. *Annals of the University of Oradea, Economic Science Series*, *22*, 1221–1228.

IOD. (1994). *The King Report on Corporate Governance (King-I)*. Johannesburg, South Africa: Lexis Nexus South Africa.

IOD. (2002). *The King Report on Corporate Governance in South Africa – 2002 (King-II)*. Johannesburg, South Africa: Lexis Nexus South Africa.

IOD. (2009). *The King Code of Governance for South Africa (2009) and King Report on Governance for South Africa (2009)*. Johannesburg, South Africa: Lexis Nexus South Africa.

IOD. (2016). *King IV Report on Corporate Governance in South Africa*. Johannesburg, South Africa: Lexis Nexus South Africa.

IRBA. (2018). *IRBA Integrated Report 2018*. Available at: www.irba.co.za/upload/IRBA%20Integrated% 20Report%202018.pdf (Accessed: 4 December 2019).

IRCSA. (2011). *Framework for Integrated Reporting and the Integrated Report*. South Africa: IRCSA.

IRCSA. (2018a). *Achieving Balance in the Integrated Report*. South Africa: IRCSA.

IRCSA. (2018b). *Preparing an Integrated Report: A Starter's Guide (Updated)*. South Africa: IRCSA.

IRCSA. (2019a). *About the IRC of SA*. Available at: https://integratedreportingsa.org/about/about-the-irc-of-sa/ (Accessed: 23 April 2019).

IRCSA. (2019b). *FAQ: The Octopus Model*. Available at: https://integratedreportingsa.org/faq-the-octo pus-model/ (Accessed: 30 May 2019).

IRCSA. (2019c). *Guidance in South Africa*. Available at: https://integratedreportingsa.org/integrated-reporting/guidance/ (Accessed: 2 May 2019).

IRCSA. (2019d). *Our History*. Available at: https://integratedreportingsa.org/about/our-history/ (Accessed: 3 May 2019).

JSE (1995). *The JSE Handbook*. South Africa: Flesch Financial Publications.

JSE. (2012). *JSE Listing Requirements*. Available at: www.jse.co.za/ (Accessed: 20 February 2015).

JSE. (2013). *JSE Listing Requirements*. Available at: www.jse.co.za/content/JSEEducationItems/Service% 20Issue%2017.pdf (Accessed: 20 February 2015).

JSE. (2017). *JSE Listing Requirements*. Available at: www.jse.co.za/content/JSERulesPoliciesandRegulatio nItems/JSE%20Listings%20Requirements.pdf (Accessed: 18 January 2019).

Junior, R. M., Best, P. J., and Cotter, J. (2014). Sustainability reporting and assurance: a historical analysis on a world-wide phenomenon. *Journal of Business Ethics*, *120*(1), 1–11.

Kadous, K., Koonce, L., and Towry, K. L. (2005). Quantification and persuasion in managerial judgement. *Contemporary Accounting Research*, *22*(3), 643–686.

Kılıç, M., and Kuzey, C. (2018). Determinants of forward-looking disclosures in integrated reporting. *Managerial Auditing Journal*, *33*(1), 115–144.

Liberty Holdings. (2017). *Integrated Report 2017.* Available at: www.libertyholdings.co.za/investor/Docu ments/2017-intergrated-report/LHL_IR2017_IR_Online_Version.pdf (Accessed: 15 May 2019).

Liberty Holdings. (2018). *Integrated Report 2018.* Available at: www.libertyholdings.co.za/investor/liberty-hold ings-limited-integrated-report-2018/Documents/integrated-report2018.pdf (Accessed: 15 May 2019).

Malherbe, S., and Segal, N. (2001). *Corporate Governance in South Africa.* Available at: www.tips.org.za/ files/Corporate_Governance_in_South_Africa.pdf (Accessed: 15 May 2019).

Maroun, W. (2017). Assuring the integrated report: insights and recommendations from auditors and preparers. *The British Accounting Review, 49*(3), 329–346.

Maroun, W. (2018a). A conceptual model for understanding corporate social responsibility assurance practice. *Journal of Business Ethics.* doi:10.1007/s10551-018-3909-z.

Maroun, W. (2018b). Modifying assurance practices to meet the needs of integrated reporting: the case for "interpretive assurance". *Accounting, Auditing & Accountability Journal, 31*(2), 400–427.

Maroun, W., Coldwell, D., and Segal, M. (2014). SOX and the transition from apartheid to democracy: South African auditing developments through the lens of modernity theory. *International Journal of Auditing, 18*(3), 206–212.

McNally, M.-A., Cerbone, D., and Maroun, W. (2017). Exploring the challenges of preparing an integrated report. *Meditari Accountancy Research, 25*(4), 481–504.

McNally, M.-A., and Maroun, W. (2018). It is not always bad news: illustrating the potential of integrated reporting using a case study in the eco-tourism industry. *Accounting, Auditing & Accountability Journal, 31*(5), 1319–1348.

Moolman, J., Oberholzer, M., and Steyn, M. (2016). The effect of integrated reporting on integrated thinking between risk, opportunity and strategy and the disclosure of risks and opportunities. *Southern African Business Review, 20*(1), 600–627.

Motau, A. T. (2018). *VBS Mutual Bank: The Great Bank Heist. Investigator's Report to the Prudential Authority.* Available at: https://uncensoredopinion.co.za/wp-content/uploads/2018/10/VBS-Mutual-Bank-The-Great-Bank-Heist.pdf (Assessed: 4 December 2019).

Naynar, N. R., Ram, A. J., and Maroun, W. (2018). Expectation gap between preparers and stakeholders in integrated reporting. *Meditari Accountancy Research, 26*(2), 241–262.

Nedbank Group Limited. (2017). *Integrated Report 2017.* Available at: www.nedbank.co.za/content/ dam/nedbank/site-assets/AboutUs/Information%20Hub/Integrated%20Report/2017/2017%20Ned bank%20Group%20Integrated%20Report.pdf (Accessed: 2 May 2019).

Nedbank Group Limited. (2018). *Integrated Report 2018.* Available at: www.nedbank.co.za/content/ dam/nedbank/site-assets/AboutUs/Information%20Hub/Integrated%20Report/2018/2018%20Ned bank%20Group%20Integrated%20Report.pdf (Accessed: 2 May 2019).

Ntim, C. G. (2009). *Internal Corporate Governance Structures and Firm Financial Performance: Evidence from South African Listed Firms.* PhD Thesis, University of Glasgow.

Ntim, C. G., Opong, K. K., Danbolt, J., and Thomas, D. A. (2012). Voluntary corporate governance disclosures by post-apartheid South African corporations. *Journal of Applied Accounting Research, 13*(2), 122–144.

Oceana Group Limited. (2018). *Integrated Report 2018.* Available at: http://oceana.co.za/pdf/Integrated% 20Report%202018.pdf (Accessed: 2 May 2019).

Oliver, J., Vesty, G., and Brooks, A. (2016). Conceptualising integrated thinking in practice. *Managerial Auditing Journal, 31*(2), 228–248.

Patel, S. A., Balic, A., and Bwakira, L. (2002). Measuring transparency and disclosure at firm-level in emerging markets. *Emerging Markets Review, 3*(4), 325–337.

Impala Platinum. (2018). *Integrated Report 2018.* Available at: http://implats-reports.co.za/reports/pdf/ 2018/implats-air-2018.pdf (Accessed: 16 May 2019).

Porter, M. (2008). *The Five Competitive Forces That Shape Strategy.* Available at: https://hbr.org/2008/01/ the-five-competitive-forces-that-shape-strategy (Assessed: 4 December 2019).

PWC. (2015). *Integrated Reporting Where to Next?* Available at: www.pwc.co.za/en/assets/pdf/integrated-reporting-survey-2015.pdf (Accessed: 16 February 2016).

PWC. (2016). *Business through a New Lens.* Available at: www.pwc.com/gr/en/publications/assets/sharp ening-the-focus-business-through-a-new-lens.pdf (Assessed: 4 December 2019).

Redefine Properties. (2018). *Redefine Properties Integrated Report.* Available at: www.redefine.co.za/view-file/Redefine-IR_Double-pages.pdf (Accessed: 12 May 2019).

Roberts, L. G. (2017). Integrated reporting: the South African experience. *The CPA Journal, 87,* 10–13.

Rossouw, G. J., Van Der Watt, A., and Rossouw, D. M. (2002). Corporate governance in South Africa. *Journal of Business Ethics*, *37*(3), 289–302.

Royal Bafokeng Platinum. (2018). *Integrated Report 2018*. Available: www.bafokengplatinum.co.za/reports/integrated-report-2018/pdf/full-integrated-final.pdf (Accessed: 16 May 2019).

Solomon, J., and Maroun, W. (2012a). *Integrated Reporting: The Influence of King III on Social, Ethical and Environmental Reporting*. London: ACCA.

Solomon, J., and Maroun, W. (2012b). *Integrated Reporting: The New Face of Social, Ethical and Environmental Reporting in South Africa?* London: ACCA.

Steinhoff. (2015). *Integrated Annual Report*. Available at: www.steinhoffinternational.com/downloads/2018/library/2015/Integrated%20annual%20report%202015.pdf (Accessed: 2 May 2019).

Truworths Limited. (2018). *Integrated Report 2018*. Available at: www.truworthsinternational.com/assets/investor/2018/TRU%20IAR2018-Nov.pdf (Accessed: 16 May 2019).

United Nations. (1987). *Report of the World Commission on Environment and Development: Our Common Future*. Oxford University Press.

Van Zijl, W., and Maroun, W. (2017). Discipline and punish: exploring the application of IFRS 10 and IFRS 12. *Critical Perspectives on Accounting*, *44*, 42–58.

Vaughn, M., and Ryan, L. V. (2006). Corporate governance in South Africa: a bellwether for the continent? *Corporate Governance: An International Review*, *14*(5), 504–512.

West, A. (2006). Theorising South Africa's corporate governance. *Journal of Business Ethics*, *68*(4), 433–448.

West, A. (2009). The ethics of corporate governance: a (South) African perspective. *International Journal of Law and Management*, *51*(1), 10–16.

World Economic Forum. (2018). *The Global Competitiveness Report 2017–2018*. Switzerland: World Economic Forum.

Zhou, S., Simnett, R., and Green, W. (2017). Does integrated reporting matter to the capital market? *Abacus*, *53*(1), 94–132.

4

THE FOURTH WAVE IS INTEGRATED REPORTING

A practitioner's perspective

Michael Bray

KPMG, Deakin University and IIRC

Nick Ridehalgh

KPMG, UNSW and IIRC

Abstract

This chapter traces the evolution of integrated reporting through 'four waves' of business and accounting since the agricultural era. The fourth wave of business is characterised by multi-capitalism, advanced technology and the drive to sustainable development. In 2019 we are in the fourth wave of business and accounting; for accounting, this is integrated reporting. This chapter examines KPMG's involvement in the development of integrated reporting, and how KPMG can continue to develop its integrated reporting advisory and assurance focus through the Momentum (2019–2021) and Adoption (2022–2025) Phases of the International Integrated Reporting Council's strategy, and beyond 2025.

Introduction

This chapter discusses how Integrated Reporting (IR) has developed, how it will further develop in the future, and the consequent implications for company reporting, investors and other stakeholders such as customers, employees, regulators and communities. The chapter approaches IR from a KPMG perspective. It begins by tracing the evolution of KPMG's journey towards IR, which began in the early 1990s. This background is necessary to understand what the future holds for KPMG and its clients in relation to IR, which is analysed toward the end of the chapter. Finally, we identify potential areas of academic research that will benefit integrated reporters, IR advisers and assurers such as KPMG, investors and other stakeholders using integrated reports.

Although the authors have roles with KPMG Australia, they have written this chapter in their personal capacities. The chapter represents neither the views of KPMG Australia nor KPMG globally. Integrated reporting is one of many strategic initiatives that KPMG is focused on.

The evolution of integrated reporting

In a remarkably prescient paper, former KPMG partner Robert Elliott[1] effectively foresaw the creation and development of what we now know as IR in 1992. His paper was titled 'The third wave breaks on the shores of accounting' (Elliott, 1992). Elliott argued that there have been three major waves of business in the last 10,000 years, which have been matched by three subsequent waves of accounting. He mapped the evolution of accounting along with business using the three waves analogy, arguing that by 1992, the third wave of business was already 'breaking on the shores of accounting'. However, the third wave of accounting had not yet occurred. As set out in Table 4.1, Elliott's three waves have now extended to a fourth wave of business (broadly, technology-enabled multi-capitalism), which is being matched by a fourth wave of accounting (IR).

Of the second wave, Elliott wrote, "The agricultural paradigm of wealth creation was dominant for about 10 millennia, until the second great wave of new technology occurred – industry – exploiting the discovery that energy could be harnessed to amplify human labour in the factory" (Elliott, 1992, p. 61). When the second wave arrived ... single-entry accounting was not sufficient. Things began to move faster. However, double-entry bookkeeping had already been codified by Pacioli in 1494. This development preceded the second wave, but double-entry bookkeeping was a necessary (although not sufficient) condition for the industrial revolution.

Another characteristic of a second-wave accounting system is that it focuses on tangible assets, that is, assets of the industrial revolution. These include inventory and fixed assets: for example, coal, iron and steam engines. And these assets are stated at cost. Accordingly, we focus on *costs*, which is the *production* side, rather than the value created, which is the *customer* side.

It is reasonable to assume that the third wave will demand a new accountability technology. However, it has not yet emerged.

Of the third wave, Elliott wrote, "The industrial paradigm was dominant for a much shorter time, until it began to be replaced by the third great wave of change – the information revolution. ... This can be dated to the 1950s ..." (Elliott, 1992, 61–62). He went on to say, 'Information technology is changing everything. It represents a new, post-industrial paradigm of wealth creation and is profoundly changing the way business is done.'

Table 4.1 The parallel paths of business and accounting over the four waves

			The waves of business		The waves of accounting	
	Era	Timespan	*<IR> capitals*			
1st	Agricultural	8000 BC–1650	•	Financial	•	Single Entry Accounting
					•	Double Entry Accounting (1494)
2nd	Industrial	1650-1955	•	Manufactured	•	Financial Reporting (1930)
3rd	Information	1955-'2010'	•	Natural	•	Sustainability Reporting (1980)
			•	Social & Relationship		
4th	Multi-capitalism	2010-Now	•	Human	•	Integrated Reporting (2010)
			•	Intellectual		

Elliott also pinpointed the critical importance of customer satisfaction and relationships to the information era: "Leadership businesses – those that can grasp the potential of IT – use the technology to get closer to their customers. As IT condenses time and space, it literally closes the time and space gaps between customers' demand and enterprises' fulfilment. They use IT to improve quality, in fact, to achieve ever-improving quality" (Elliott, 1992, p. 64). Elliott reminded us that each of the three waves of business have built upon the previous wave. "Just because we are in a post-industrial economy doesn't mean that we can forget the first two waves. People still like to eat (the agricultural wave), and they still like to drive around in automobiles (the industrial wave)" (Elliott, 1992, p. 64). He ventured predictions about third-wave accounting systems characterised by:

- a focus on resources and processes;
- information-based assets such as R&D;
- a need to measure value created for customers;
- enabling the hierarchy rather than locking it in;
- providing real time dials rather than waiting for events to occur to help users who wish to estimate the magnitude, timing and uncertainty of *future* cash flows.

The third wave of accounting that evolved could be broadly referred to as 'sustainability reporting'. It emerged not so much in response to the information era of business, but as a consequence of poor social practices and environmental disasters, which assumed critical importance in the latter half of the 20th century.

The various forms of sustainability reporting (e.g. GRI) do not have a strong focus on the strategic aspects of a business and the metrics measuring the 'what, with, how and why' (explained in KPMG's Business Measurement Process below) of fourth wave businesses. For instance, a GRI-compliant sustainability report need not contain a customer satisfaction metric, although those metrics are critical to contemporary business models and in the context of the trust deficit that exists today. Nor need a metric for the strategic alignment of an organisation's employees be reported, when such alignment is critically important to the ability of an organisation to implement its strategy and when looking at remuneration awarded on so-called non-financial metrics. Therefore, sustainability reporting has not answered the needs of fourth wave businesses.

Elliott envisaged that the third wave of business would evolve based on excellent customer service, enabled by information technology and continuous improvement, but the third wave of accounting did not drive the required business change. The GFC demonstrated that many businesses were not customer-centric.

The fourth wave of business

Accordingly, the fourth wave of business is characterised by the multi-capitalism approach of the <IR> Framework to delivering longer-term value for all stakeholders through innovation and intellectual property, satisfied and strategically aligned customers and employees, and radically enhanced technology.

The six capitals of integrated reporting provide a useful lens through which to distinguish between Elliott's 'third wave of business' of 1992 and today's 'fourth wave of business'. The IIRC's 2018 integrated report provides a useful analysis of the megatrends that have shaped fourth wave business models and a lens through which to view them and the challenges of reporting on them effectively. It explains:

- **Multiple capitalism.** In terms of the <IR> Framework – *financial capital, manufactured capital, natural capital, human capital, social and relationship capital* (which includes customers, who were so important to Elliott's third wave of business) and *intellectual capital* (which includes innovation, intellectual property and R&D, as well as the technology dimension that Elliott emphasised).
- **Technology.** The age of technologically driven data and analytics, robotics, artificial intelligence, the Internet of Things and related connectivity will result in rapid evolution of corporate reporting. These are examples of the *connectivity* guiding principle of integrated reporting. There has been much written and said on these matters, and on their effect on business as well as the future of the accounting profession.
- **Energy and Infrastructure.** The McKinsey Global Institute (2016) estimates that the world needs to invest roughly US $3.3 trillion annually in infrastructure just to support existing expectations of future growth, with 60 per cent of that investment required in emerging economies. KPMG has estimated that around one sixth of the world's population does not have access to reliable supplies of electricity. KPMG asserted that one of the key enablers of investors being able to provide the required capital to close the energy infrastructure gap is better business reporting, particularly IR. Of course, the massive infrastructure gaps in the world today are not confined to energy. The critical issue is that infrastructure gaps in all forms need to be financed if they are to be closed. During the IIRC's participation in the B20 Infrastructure Task Force, the world's major accounting networks identified corporate reporting reform, and specifically the adoption of IR, as important in attracting the required funding to close the gaps, by providing investors with long-term information on risk and opportunity and creating the foundations for sustainable investment. This was reported in a paper by the B20 Panel of Six International Accounting Networks (2014), including KPMG: 'Unlocking investment in infrastructure: is current accounting and reporting a barrier?'
- **Sustainable Development**. Global discussions, which have culminated in the Sustainable Development Goals (SDGs), and the focus on climate change, had already begun in the 1990s (the third wave of business and accounting). The EU Non-Financial Reporting Directive, Paris Climate Change Agreement, the 2016 Financial Stability Board Task Force, the Taskforce for Climate Related Financial Disclosure (TCFD), the Sustainable Development Goals (SDGs) and other global initiatives all set down a challenge to business and capital markets to embed sustainability considerations into mainstream business decision making and reporting.
- **Transparency and Trust**. Another feature of fourth-wave businesses is the world's current trust-deprived environment, as evidenced by the Edelman Trust Barometer of 2018 (Edelman, 2018). Integrated reporting can make a significant contribution to improving transparency and thus help to restore trust.

We are now in the fourth wave of business. Elliott's third wave of business was the 'information era'. Though an artificial dividing line, the fourth wave of business is a further evolution of the third wave, with today's business models and competitive edges dominated by innovation, intellectual property, technology, customer relationship management and satisfaction, and the engagement and strategic alignment of an organisation's people, with technology developments being an enabler of these matters, and in some cases 'doing' them.

The major distinguishing features of fourth wave versus third wave business, in our view, are the combination and integration of multi-capitalism, with this change taking the technology paradigm beyond where Elliott saw it in 1992 (with later innovations, including artificial intelligence, the Internet of Things, and data and analytics).

The fourth wave of accounting

Unfortunately, since the 1980s there has been a divergence between financial and sustainability reporting. Financial and sustainability reporting are both critically important in their own rights, but each has its own limitations in today's business models. The result has been an increase in the volume and complexity of current corporate reporting systems, with an estimated 400-plus reporting frameworks around the world putting great strain on the resources of businesses in preparing the required information, while none are truly dealing with all aspects of the value creation of fourth wave businesses.

The 'new accountability technology' that Elliott predicted in 1992 did not emerge for another 18 years. It emerged, following the global financial crisis (GFC), in 2010 as IR. Specifically, the GFC showed that business practices still prioritised the use of technology and resources to deliver short-term financial performance, but the requirements of businesses' customers, staff and investors had arguably moved beyond the third wave of business (the 'information era' focused on financial performance, as supported by sustainability and technology) to the fourth wave of business.

Integrated Reporting is different to sustainability reporting. It can be used to bring investors and businesses to the table because of its:

*   grounding in integrated thinking, leading to better business practice and decision-making;
*   having investors as the primary audience, but with an aim for integrated reports to be of interest to other stakeholders, including customers, employees, regulators and communities;
*   focus on the customer engagement and satisfaction aspects of social and relationship capital, the strategic alignment aspects of human capital and intellectual capital; and
*   integration of reporting across all six capitals, underpinning its suitability for fourth wave businesses (multi-capitalism), including those most relevant to third wave businesses.

The journey to wave four accounting

It is not surprising that from 1992 it took:

*   18 years for the International Integrated Reporting Council (IIRC) to be formed;
*   over 20 years for its International Integrated Reporting <IR> Framework (<IR> Framework) to be released in 2013; and
*   25 years for the IIRC to declare that its Breakthrough Phase of IR was over and its Momentum Phase had commenced.

The IIRC expects to declare the Momentum Phase over in 2021, when its Global Adoption Phase will commence. By its conclusion in 2025, it will have taken just over 30 years for accounting to catch the fourth wave of business, since Elliott started talking about the 'three waves' in 1992. This is not a long time at all. The 30 years of evolution of IR is a *short* period in the evolution of accounting, as accounting has moved, through its waves, in pursuit of the waves of business during a time span of *over 10,000 years*. Achieving global adoption by 2025 will be remarkably rapid and an incredible achievement.

Through the IR movement, the fourth wave of accounting is now answering the challenge of measuring and reporting on the third and fourth waves of business. Integrated reporting is the answer to the fourth wave of business breaking on the shores of accounting. It is the fourth wave in accounting.

KPMG's involvement in the development of IR

KPMG has been through the evolution of the third and fourth waves of business, and in the context of this book, the third and fourth waves of accounting. It has also been heavily involved in the IIRC and IR since its inception.

There are two key questions for the IIRC:

- Can IR deliver better quality information to investors in support of their investment decision-making, and to other stakeholders to support their approach to decision-making?
- Can technology be used to improve the quality of corporate reporting, particularly its connectivity, timeliness and global consistency?

KPMG has a keen interest in these questions. It has developed the concept of a robust IR management system, to underpin the integrity of the organisation's corporate reports, as defined in Figure 4.1. The reporting strategy is at the centre of the IR management system, which defines:

Corporate Reports Portfolio and Process – Determind through Corporate Reporting Strategy and Implemented Through Integraed Reporting Management System

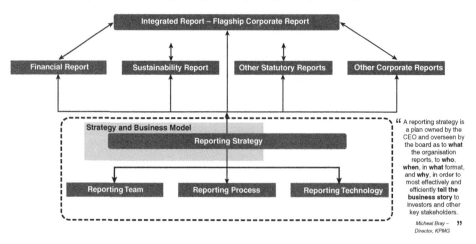

Figure 4.1 Corporate reporting strategy and the use of integrated reporting management systems

- the *what* of an organisation's corporate reporting (its corporate reports portfolio, for which the integrated report is the flagship, and the starting point for navigating to other more detailed reports); as well as
- the *how* (where people, processes and systems are aligned to the effective use of all capitals to create long term value through a reporting strategy). Defining or refining the reporting strategy may lead to further work on the organisation's strategy and business model, or their documentation. This would be an application of integrated thinking through IR.

Today's norm in the fourth wave of business is *multi-capitalism*, with an increased focus on human and intellectual capital. The fourth wave of business is breaking on the shores of accounting, and it requires quality IR management systems, including appropriate technology and integrated assurance as enablers and credibility enhancement techniques, in order to contribute to the restoration of trust.

Chapter 2 in this book deals with where the IIRC and IR are at today, focusing on the IIRC's current agenda and aims. The IIRC recognises that its mission is far from over. The IIRC's goal of achieving global adoption of IR by 2025 is complex and will be challenging. This chapter reports on the role that KPMG has played in the creation and evolution of IR. It explains how KPMG is helping its clients in their IR journeys and is increasingly assuring their IR.

From 1992, KPMG has been 'in the game'. The first real step in KPMG's journey towards IR was not directly about corporate reporting. It was through KPMG developing its financial reporting audit methodology. In the mid-1990s KPMG in the USA began a project known as the Business Measurement Process ^{TM} (BMP). Dealing with the third wave of business had led KPMG to the BMP; and the BMP and the third wave of accounting later led KPMG into IR. Evolution to the fourth wave of business was underway when the BMP commenced.

KPMG's Business Measurement Process

The BMP was essentially a 'front end' to KPMG's audit process, designed to help audit teams to develop the required strategic understanding of their clients' businesses from which the audit could be planned and performed (Bell et al., 1997). The BMP was developed by KPMG globally between 1995 and 1999. Bob Elliott and his 'third wave' thinking provided the innovation on which BMP was built. Elliott found another innovator, KPMG partner Frank Marrs from Texas, to lead KPMG's global BMP development team.

The development and international roll out of BMP was overseen by the KPMG Global BMP Steering Group, on which KPMG Australia was represented. The BMP developed with input from two internationally renowned Harvard professors, Krishna Palepu and Paul Healy. It was rolled out through KPMG's global industry groups and regions.

The industry business models developed then as the tools with which audit teams could implement the BMP methodology still exist today, but are outdated, mainly because of the technological advancements of the last 25 years. However, the core of the BMP methodology holds true for fourth-wave business models.

In IR terms, the BMP was effectively a methodology for *integrated thinking*, and providing audit teams with a better understanding of their clients' businesses, along with the methodologies, tools and training to enable these teams to assure an organisation's integrated thinking as reported in its financial report. Table 4.2 summarises the parallels between the

Table 4.2 Consistency of the BMP with the <IR> Framework

<IR> Framework	The Integrated Report	The BMP phase

• Value creation for the organisation and for others	• Strategy (the *what*)
	  ○ Purpose
	  ○ Strategic objectives
	  ○ Risks and opportunities
		Strategic analysis

• Value Creation Process
• The Capitals
	• Stakeholder information demands
	• Business model and governance (the *how*)
	  ○ Governance process
	  ○ Strategic management process
	  ○ Other key business processes
	  ○ Critical success factors
		Business process analysis

• Value creation for the organisation and for others	• Resources and relationships (the *with*) • Risk management process and critical success factors	Risk assessment

• Value creation Process
• Performance and outlook
	• Reporting process and critical success factors
	• Key performance indicators
	  ○ Achievements (Strategy)
	  ○ Inputs (Resources and relationships)
	  ○ Activities (Critical success factors)
	  ○ Outputs (Products, services and by-products)
	  ○ Outcomes (Resources and relationships)
		Business measurement

• IR is a journey	Continuous improvement	Continuous improvement

<IR> Framework, what an integrated report reflecting integrated thinking would cover, and the phases of the BMP:

Importantly, the BMP was a key enabler in KPMG's development of its interpretation of what has now evolved into the fourth wave of accounting – IR, which is founded on *Integrated Thinking*. KPMG developed a reporting advisory service for its clients based on BMP. The service equivalent to the as yet un-named IR was known as *Performance Insight* between 2000 and 2010.

KPMG's Performance Insight

Performance Insight was developed between 2000 and 2001 because of the leadership of the then Global Head of Audit and Assurance, Hans de Munnik, of KPMG in the Netherlands. Not surprisingly, the members of the global Performance Insight team were previously members of the BMP team.

Most of what was developed for Performance Insight remains relevant in 2020, as it was in reality developed for the third and fourth waves of business and accounting. The issue was that IR had not been invented in 2001! The development needs for accounting today related to the recognition of what fourth wave business models have evolved to, the introduction of the <IR> Framework, and significantly more advanced technology than existed in 1992.

Performance Insight is effectively a service that helps a client to install an IR management system, and to develop quality integrated reports. Performance Insight, supported by the BMP, also helped clients to improve their strategies, business models, risk management and performance measurement, as the basis for reporting in what is now known as an integrated report.

KPMG's Better Business Reporting

Throughout the first decade of the 2000s, KPMG tried to develop a Performance Insight business in an initiative-dense environment. Sarbanes-Oxley in the USA and International Financial Reporting Standards globally were imposing huge compliance challenges on businesses. In addition, rapid developments in technology and related threats (e.g. cyber-crime), the lack of a regulatory mandate for more insightful corporate reporting, and more recently a proliferation of reporting frameworks and initiatives (most of these being forms of 'third-wave' sustainability reporting), significantly constrained further evolution in accounting.

KPMG contributed significantly to the development of IR. The IIRC was formed in 2010, and at the same time KPMG Australia was establishing its Better Business Reporting (BBR) initiative and playing a significant role in the formation and subsequent operation of both the IIRC and the Australian Business Reporting Leaders Forum (BRLF). The BRLF has enjoyed great leadership from prominent Australian company directors, John Stanhope and Steve Vamos. John is also vice-chair of the IIRC and has played a significant role in driving the adoption of IR in almost all of the organisations for which he is a director – AGL, Australia Post and Deakin University.

When the IIRC was formed, KPMG Australia was involved through the contribution of resources, participation in development of the <IR> Framework and associated guidance; and was also watching the contribution from the World Intellectual Capital Initiative (WICI), working with KPMG Japan, which along with the Japanese Ministry of Economy,

Trade & Industry and the AICPA among others, had been instrumental in the formation and operations of WICI. The contribution of WICI to the development and evolution of IR should not be overlooked.

The main contribution of WICI has been in relation to intellectual capital through the provision of:

- an intellectual capital reporting framework;
- a key performance indicator framework, which makes it easier to think through and report on various categories of key performance indicators across all of the IIRC's six capitals; and
- industry key performance indicator libraries for various prominent industries.

The BBR name was chosen by KPMG Australia in 2010, rather than something more explicitly aligned to IR, as:

- the IIRC had only just formed;
- the <IR> Framework was only released later – in 2013; and
- declaration of the IIRC's Momentum Phase was only achieved in 2018.

The BBR branding has since been picked up globally within KPMG and remains in existence today.

The next stage in relation to IR for KPMG – in 2019 and onwards – will evolve as the IIRC works to move to its Global Adoption Phase in 2021, which will essentially be a declaration that IR has started to achieve widespread global adoption. Integrated Reporting should come to be recognised as the global reporting norm when the Global Adoption Phase comes to its conclusion, anticipated by the IIRC to be by 2025.

The future

The IIRC's Momentum Phase (2020–2021)

The aims, objectives and progress of the IIRC in its Momentum Phase are covered in Chapter 2 of this book. That chapter references the IIRC 2018 integrated report for further details. This chapter focuses on a country case study: the adoption of IR in Australia during the IIRC's Momentum Phase.

Case study: IR in Australia in the IIRC's Momentum Phase

KPMG's services relating to IR between 2010 and 2019 have been delivered under the BBR banner. In that period, KPMG has advised clients on:

- 'cutting clutter' in financial reports, remuneration reports, operating and financial reviews, and corporate governance statements;
- business cases – whether IR makes business sense for them based on the return on investment it can bring;
- getting started on an IR journey through benchmarking, facilitation to develop reporting strategies and specific disclosures;
- how to adopt the principles of IR; and

- now, obtaining assurance on integrated reports.

KPMG Australia has done this by adapting the language of the <IR> Framework to language in more common business usage, being the *what, with, how* and *why* of the business. KPMG Australia can further build its BBR advisory and assurance practice by leveraging the early adopter work done by it with clients in the first half of the 2010s, by:

- assisting its clients in creating value in the short, medium and long term by further developing their integrated thinking, IR management systems and reporting on the business clearly, concisely and with integrity; and
- delivering assurance on integrated reports, enhancing their credibility and engendering trust in the organisation. This is the KPMG 'trust through transparency' promise (KPMG, 2019).

In 2019, widespread adoption of IR has not yet been achieved in Australia, but through the great work of the IIRC, BRLF, KPMG and others mentioned in this chapter, the foundations for that have been established. To date:

- Operating and Financial Reviews (OFRs) have not yet been rated as 'substantively equivalent' to integrated reports by the IIRC under current regulatory guidance (the original Regulatory Guide, RG247, 'Effective Disclosure in an Operating & Financial Review', issued by the Australian Securities and Investments Commission in March 2013, prior to the <IR> Framework being issued in December 2013);
- The new 4th Edition ASX Corporate Governance Recommendation 4.3 (p. 20) is not yet effective;
- The IASB and IAASB project teams covering IR and assurance have not yet published guidance, and so nothing has yet been published in Australia by the AASB or AuASB to drive change; however,
- The Australian Financial Reporting Council has published supportive policy statements for IR.

Although Australia does not as yet have a regulatory driver for IR adoption, 4 peer cent of ASX200 companies were found by KPMG Australia to be adopting at least some of the principles of IR as at 30 June 2018. KPMG Australia said in its 2018 report on ASX 200 corporate reporting: 'of organizations surveyed 48% focused their reporting on value creation for shareholders and/or other stakeholders and not just historic financial earnings. (2017: 25%).' In a press release, KPMG Australia said, 'Nearly half of the ASX200 are now leveraging the principles of integrated reporting in the way they communicate long term value creation.' KPMG Australia found that this percentage had risen to 74 per cent at 30 June 2019, confirming this trend, with AGL, Dexus and Transurban issuing their first integrated reports with reference to IR principles.

In addition, the key barriers and challenges relating to IR in Australia have now been largely resolved

- Director Liability. While still cautioning about forward-looking statements in integrated reports, the Australian Institute of Company Directors now has a supportive policy pos- ition on IR, backing that of the Group of 100. In August 2019, the Australian Secur- ities and Investments Commission (ASIC) updated RG247, mainly to provide guidance on climate change disclosures. In the context of director liability, the revision also confirmed that in ASIC's view, the risk of directors being found liable for a misleading or deceptive forward-looking statement in an OFR is minimal, provided:

- the statements are properly framed in the OFR (e.g. being based on information available at the reporting date);
- the statements have a reasonable basis, which includes good governance at board level for signing off on the statements; and
- there is ongoing compliance with continuous disclosure obligations when events or results overtake forward-looking statements in the OFR. If circumstances change after an integrated report is issued, this is not a reporting matter at all – it moves into the realm of continuous disclosure.

In addition, directors from the growing number of organisations now releasing integrated reports are without a doubt satisfied with the integrity of those reports.

- 'Another Report.' It is now well understood that the adoption of IR does not require the creation of a new report. IR principles can be adopted in an existing report, such as in an Operating & Financial Review, or a sustainability report. This was supported by ASIC in a December 2017 Media Release and in 2018 was encouraged by the 4th Edition of the ASX Corporate Governance Council (through Recommendation 4.3) and so is now the developing practice in Australia (ASIC, 2017; ASX Corporate Governance Council, 2019). In 2019 Stockland removed its annual review prepared with reference to the IR principles from its reports portfolio, and prepared its OFR with reference to IR. The work being undertaken internationally by the Corporate Reporting Dialogue, convened by the IIRC, should result in some reduction in the number of competing reporting frameworks in existence today through consolidation, and should result in increased alignment.

The most significant drivers of IR in Australia in 2020 and 2021 are likely to be:

- the new ASX corporate reporting recommendation in the 4th Edition of the ASX Corporate Governance Principles and Recommendations (Recommendation 4.3). Recommendation 4.3 becomes effective in 2020, and will first apply to 31 December 2020, and 31 March, 30 June and 30 September 2021 year end reporting dates. ASX Corporate Governance Principles and Recommendations are implemented and reported on by listed companies using the principle of: 'if not, why not?' A recommendation does not have to be adopted; but if it is not, the Board needs to explain why not. Given that Recommendation 4.3 is about the company having and disclosing its process to ensure the integrity of all of its 'periodic corporate reports', including the OFR, it would be untenable for a Board to contemplate a 'why not' disclosure. Recommendation 4.3 is a mandate for integrity in all corporate reporting, including OFRs. Recommendation 4.3 does not require the adoption of IR. However, it appears to recognise IR as best practice in corporate governance in relation to business reporting to investors. It would be unwise for a Board not to consider the adoption of IR for its OFR when the promoter of Australian best practice in corporate governance is highlighting IR as good practice. The Commentary to Recommendation 4.3 is an in-substance recommendation for IR and its assurance. The ASX and/or ASIC are likely to subject the completeness, accuracy, quality and balance of Recommendation 4.3 disclosures to their surveillance and enforcement regimes under section 777 of the Corporations Act.

- The Australian Accounting Standards Board is likely to release the revised Management Commentary Practice Statement being developed by the International Accounting Standards Board in 2020. It is expected that the IASB Management Commentary guidance will be rated by the IIRC to be 'substantively equivalent' to IR. This will add greater weight to the adoption of IR in Australia, as discussed in the Commentary to Recommendation 4.3.
- The Australian Auditing and Assurance Standards Board is also likely to release guidance on extended external reporting assurance over IR, being developed by the International Auditing and Assurance Standards Board, in 2020. This guidance from the standard-setter will no doubt be recognised as authoritative in relation to the assurance aspects of the supporting Commentary to Recommendation 4.3.

With the effective date of Recommendation 4.3 occurring for individual companies in either 2020 or 2021, and authoritative guidance applicable to integrated reports from the International Accounting Standards Board and International Auditing and Assurance Standards Board imminent being released in 2020, it is expected that the trend towards adoption of IR in Australia will continue in 2020 and 2021.

The BRLF: transition to a formalised IIRC body in Australia?

The BRLF played an important role in the development of corporate reporting in Australia between 2010 and 2019, acting as a discussion forum for those in the Australian corporate reporting system rather than as a decision-making body. Among other things, the BRLF has considered whether IR is right for Australia, and if so, when it should be applied.

To accompany the IIRC's anticipated recognition of Australia's form of management commentary (the Operating & Financial Review) as being 'substantively equivalent' to IR, it is expected that the BRLF will transform to an IR forum aligned with the IIRC. KPMG Australia will not have the leadership role in the ongoing Australian IR body that it has had to date in the BRLF. Of course KPMG Australia will play its role in ensuring the success of that body.

Such a body may build on successful practices in other countries to achieve national consistency in IR practice, and alignment with the IIRC as an institutional approach. These developments can enable national bodies to provide greater local IR implementation support. Possibly the country that has had the most success with such a model to date is Brazil.

The period 2020–2021 will be the time for an Australian-affiliated IIRC body to declare that IR is being widely adopted in Australia, which will be an appropriate time for Australia to play its part in the IIRC moving from its Momentum Phase to its Global Adoption Phase.

Table 4.3 presents a summary of some of the key players in today's Australian Corporate Reporting System. Each of these players is likely to have an important role in an Australian IR body when it is formed.

The IIRC's Adoption Phase (2022–2025)

The aims, objectives and progress of the IIRC in its Adoption Phase are also covered in the IIRC chapter of this book. This chapter focuses on a country case study – on adoption of IR in Australia during the IIRC's Adoption Phase.

Table 4.3 The Australian Corporate Reporting System

Users/stakeholders (or proxies)	Intermediaries	Preparers
Financial Capital – investors and lenders	Regulator • ASIC • APRA	Directors – Australian Institute of Company Directors
Human capital – Australian Human Resources Institute	Standard Setters: • AASB • AuASB • Financial Reporting Council	CEOs – Business Council of Australia
Social & Relationship Capital – World Business Council for Sustainable Development	Investors	CFOs – Group of 100
Natural Capital – World Business Council for Sustainable Development	Investor advocates and advisers, including • Australian Council of Superannuation Investors • Association of Superannuation Funds of Australia • Australian Financial Services Council • Australian Superannuation Funds Association • Australian Shareholders Association	IROs – Australasian Investor Relations Association
Manufactured Capital – Property Council of Australia	Corporate governance leaders • ASX Corporate Governance Council	Company secretaries – Governance Institute of Australia
Intellectual Capital – World Intellectual Capital Initiative	• Financial Reporting Council	General Counsel Law Council of Australia

Analysts, including CFA Institute

The 'IIRC Family' in Australia:

• International Integrated Reporting Council – John Stanhope (Vice-Chair)
• IIRC Board (Pru Bennett, Michael Bray and Louise Davidson)
• IIRC Ambassadors (David Atkin, Merran Kelsall, Gary Lennon, Nick Ridehalgh)
• IIRC Team (Liz Prescott)

Case study: IR in Australia in the IIRC's Adoption Phase

If Australia achieves 'substantive equivalence' with IR in 2020 or 2021, it is likely that progressively more Australian organisations will claim full adoption of the <IR> Framework:

• going beyond claims on adopting some or all of the principles of IR, which is the norm in 2019;

- including a board accountability statement; and
- obtaining independent external assurance on that claim, as effectively envisaged in Recommendation 4.3.

The other key development beyond 2021 (which will be already underway in more progressive organisations in 2020 and 2021) will be the use of *IR Management Systems*, including IR automation. These systems will ensure the integrity of integrated reports (and other corporate reports) for the foreseeable future, after IR becomes the norm. Such systems will provide important evidence for Boards to support the Recommendation 4.3 adoption claims that they will need to make.

The processes, systems and controls relating to IR will be quite different to those operating today in the third wave of accounting – financial and sustainability reporting. This is because:

- IR focuses on **the business** – the *what* (purpose, strategy, risks and opportunities), *with* (resources and relationships), *how* (business model and governance) and *why* (competitive edge delivered through integrated thinking) of the business; and
- achieving conciseness in integrated reports will involve diagrams, pictures and graphs, as well as narratives.

A parallel development with integrated reports becoming the norm, and IR management systems becoming the main defence mechanism of integrity in IR, will be a move to *integrated assurance*. Assurance over the compliance of integrated reports with the <IR> Framework will already have become the norm in 2020–2021. It will be complemented by assurance on the design and operation of IR management systems. The assurance report on the Cbus 2019 annual integrated report was the Australia's first to be expressed in terms of whether the report is 'in accordance with' the <IR> Framework, and among the world's first. We expect that IR advisory and assurance services for KPMG and others will evolve in a complementary fashion over the next five years, with the move to widespread adoption of IR taking place as described above.

There will be less focus on whether IR makes business sense for clients, assisting them with 'cutting clutter' in annual and other reports, getting started on an IR journey and showing them how to adopt the principles of IR. These matters have or will become 'business as usual' for organisations between 2019 and 2021, particularly in an environment where Recommendation 4.3 will soon be effective, and the IASB's Management Commentary Practice Statement and IAASB's extended external reporting assurance guidance will soon be issued.

In the medium term (2022–2025), there is likely to be more focus by KPMG and others on:

- advising clients on their IR management systems, including automation, and/or assuring the design and operating performance of IR management systems. Such advice will require contributions from many parts of KPMG – its Audit, Advisory and Risk Consulting, Management Consulting (technology and change management) and Remuneration Advisory practices in particular; and
- assuring integrated reports. Given the nature of IR, integrated report assurance engagements will also require contributions from many parts of KPMG – the same ones as mentioned above – as strategies, business models, risk management frameworks and key business value drivers, beyond the financials, are assessed and reported on.

On that basis, we believe that IR and IR assurance will be critically important to KPMG's clients as well their key stakeholders, including investors, customers, staff, regulators and the broader community; and accordingly of critical importance to KPMG.

The longer term: 2026 and beyond

Over time, the balance between IR advisory and assurance for the accounting profession is likely to change. Services will be less advisory as organisations make IR a core competency of their own. There will be more demand for integrated assurance. Assurance will extend beyond assurance of integrated reports to assurance on integrated thinking and related business management controls, and IR management systems.

In his 2018 book, the founder of IR and inaugural chair of the IIRC, Professor Mervyn King, posed the question, 'The Auditor – Quo Vadis?' (King and de Beer, 2018). We believe that integrated assurance answers the question posed by Professor King, and is at the heart of the future of the accounting and assurance profession.

Future directions and research opportunities

Robert Elliott was already calling for the changes needed in accounting firms, education and research in 1992 to address the third wave of business. Professor Mervyn King has added to this call regarding **fourth**-wave business through his leadership of the IR movement since 2010 and in relation to IR assurance in his 2018 book.

We call on:

- the accounting profession to meet these needs of their clients, bringing to fruition:

  - the promise of more integrated thinking in the context of implementation of IR, and realising the benefits of doing so by effectively communicating these achievements to all stakeholders in an integrated report; and
  - 'the audit of the future', at first through assurance of integrated reports, and later through integrated assurance.

- academic institutions and academics to have regard to these needs by:

  - broadening research on the benefits to users – beyond a focus on investors to all key stakeholders, including customers, employees, regulators and communities, and all geographies. The research by Professor Mary Barth's team was restricted to investors using integrated reports in the pioneer IR jurisdiction of South Africa (Barth et al., 2017);
  - converting what has been largely anecdotal evidence to date to academic-standard research on the benefits to businesses that come from integrated thinking, the foundation of IR;
  - providing academic-standard research on the true picture of the global state of adoption of IR;
  - assessing the progress and outcomes of the IIRC's ground-breaking work on alignment of the corporate reporting system through mechanisms such as the Global Reporting Dialogue.
  - determining the rigour that will be required of IR management systems.

    ○   increasing academic-standard research into the methodologies used to measure performance in managing and enhancing key capitals (i.e. for intellectual, human and social and relationship capital) as well as determination of levers that will protect/enhance their performance and longer term availability and value.

Note

1 Robert Elliott was a partner in KPMG LLP in New York. He was vice chair of the AICPA Board of Directors for 1998–1999, and served as chairman for 1999–2000. He chaired the AICPA Strategic Planning Committee and Strategic Planning Advisory Subcommittee, and the AICPA Special Committee on Assurance Services ('Elliott Committee') and the Oversight Board of the New York City Elections Project. He served as a member of the AICPA Board of Directors as well as several committees of AICPA. He also served as a vice president of the American Accounting Association and as a member of the SEC Advisory Committee on Capital Formation and Regulatory Processes and the Accounting Education Change Commission. He was a member of the Board of Trustees of the KPMG Foundation and the Big 5 National Steering Committee for Legislative Action. Named as one of 'The 100 Most Influential People in Accounting' by Accounting Today for four consecutive years, Mr Elliott was profiled as a 'Leading Big Six Professional' by *Professional Services Review* in 1995. He is the recipient of numerous awards and honours, including the AICPA Gold Medal Award for Distinguished Service (1997) and the Journal of Accountancy Literary Award (1995). He holds an AB from Harvard University and an MBA from Rutgers University, and is the author or co-author of more than 80 books and articles. Elliott credited Alvin Toffler with the 'third wave' concept. 'He notes, in his book *The Third Wave*, that until about 8000 BC, the dominant mode of life was foraging, fishing, hunting and herding. … But, about 8000 years ago, agriculture was developed, and became the first major new wealth-creating technology.'

References

ASIC. (2017). *ASIC Calls on Preparers to Focus on Financial Report Quality and New Requirements* [Media release]. Available at: https://asic.gov.au/about-asic/news-centre/find-a-media-release/2017-releases/17-423mr-asic-calls-on-preparers-to-focus-on-financial-report-quality-and-new-requirements/ (Accessed: 20 November 2019).

ASX Corporate Governance Council. (2019). *Corporate Governance Principles and Recommendations*. Available at: www.asx.com.au/documents/asx-compliance/cgc-principles-and-recommendations-fourth-edn.pdf (Accessed: 20 November 2019).

B20 Panel of Six International Accounting Networks. (2014). *Unlocking Investment in Infrastructure: Is Current Accounting and Reporting a Barrier?* Available at: https://integratedreporting.org/wp-content/uploads/2014/06/unlocking-investment-in-infrastructure.pdf (Accessed: 20 November 2019).

Barth, M. E., Cahan, S. F., Chen, L., and Venter, E. R. (2017). The economic consequences associated with integrated report quality: Capital market and real effects. *Accounting, Organizations and Society*, 62, 43–64.

Bell, T. B., Marrs, F. O., Solomon, I., and Thomas, H. (1997). *Auditing Organizations Through a Strategic-Systems Lens: The KPMG Business Measurement Process*. Montvale, NJ: KPMG LLP.

Edelman. (2018). *2018 Edelman Trust Barometer*. Available at: www.edelman.com/research/2018-edelman-trust-barometer (Accessed: 29 September 2019).

Elliott, R. K. (1992). The third wave breaks on the shores of accounting. *Accounting Horizons*, 6, 61–85.

King, M., and de Beer, L. (2018). *The Auditor: Quo Vadis?* London: Routledge.

KPMG. (2019). *Rebuilding Trust through Improved Transparency and Insight*. Available at: https://home.kpmg/au/en/home/insights/2018/11/asx-200-corporate-reporting-trends-2018.html (Accessed: 1 December 2019).

McKinsey Global Institute. (2016). *Bridging Global Infrastructure Gaps*. Available at: www.mckinsey.com/industries/capital-projects-and-infrastructure/our-insights/bridging-global-infrastructure-gaps (Accessed: 29 September 2019).

5

INTEGRATED REPORTING

The management accounting perspective of a professional accounting body

Nick Topazio, Rebecca McCaffry, Martin Farrar, Peter Spence,
Peter Simons and Ian Selby

The Chartered Institute of Management Accountants

Abstract

Integrated Reporting (<IR>) is not just an effective corporate reporting tool. Management accountants have identified much commonality between the principles underlying <IR> and effective business decision making and the achievement of strategic goals. This chapter explores <IR> from a management accounting point of view, showing how <IR> helps organizations create value and reach their strategic targets. The Chartered Institute of Management Accountants (CIMA) is both a strong advocate and an early adopter of <IR>; evidence for this is provided in this chapter through its incorporation into our syllabus, research and reporting. The chapter closes with a look at the latest <IR> developments and signposts important steps still to come.

Introduction

The Chartered Institute of Management Accountants (CIMA), founded in 1919, is the world's leading and largest professional body of management accountants. Members and students work in industry, commerce, the public sector and not-for-profit organizations. In January 2017, CIMA and the American Institute of CPAs (AICPA) formed a combined body of professional accountants, the Association of International Certified Professional Accountants ("the Association").

Management accounting evolved as a distinct branch of the accounting profession because financial accounting is insufficient for effective business decision-making. Management accounting has always been about providing a broad range of management information and analysis to inform and guide the management and control cycle; and to ensure that decisions are taken and performance is managed in the interests of the business and its stakeholders.

The Chartered Institute of Management Accountants, and latterly the Association, have been strong advocates of the need for improved corporate reporting for many years. This support started with the work of the AICPA Special Committee on Financial Reporting (the Jenkins Committee) (AICPA, 1994) which was built upon by the Enhanced Business Reporting Consortium (AICPA, 2019) in the US. In the UK, we are active participants in the reform of corporate reporting, starting with the introduction of the Operating and Financial Review (FRC, 2006) and continuing through our membership of the Report Leadership group (PWC, 2016) and the current Financial Reporting Council's Financial Reporting Lab (FRC, 2011).

Our support for enhanced corporate reporting naturally led to our active promotion of the work of the International Integrated Reporting Council (IIRC) since its formation in 2010, and international advocacy for Integrated Reporting (<IR>). For the purposes of this chapter, <IR> refers to the process of corporate reporting in accordance with the IIRC's <IR> Framework, which was published in 2013. The <IR> Framework sets out guiding principles and content elements that govern the overall content of an integrated report, and explains the fundamental concepts that underpin them.

This chapter explains why <IR> is important not just as an effective external reporting process but also as a framework for management decision making. We start by presenting the case for <IR> as an effective corporate reporting mechanism that can benefit both organizations and capital markets. We next explain how the benefits extend to public sector organizations before exploring the linkage between <IR> and global efforts to achieve the UN's Sustainable Development Goals. Following this we explore the touch points between <IR> and effective management accounting, and find much commonality. As well as being a strong supporter and advocate for <IR>, CIMA has "walked the walk". The next section shows how <IR> has been incorporated into our syllabus, research and reporting. Finally we look at the latest <IR> developments and signpost important events to come.

Why <IR>?

Corporate reporting plays an essential role in the effective functioning of the market economy, enabling shareholders and investors to assess the performance of a business across all aspects of its activity, establish its value and exercise effective oversight. To continue to effectively contribute to market efficiency, our financial reporting system must be as dynamic as the financial markets themselves. However, the focus of traditional financial reporting is too narrow. Consider the following change in the nature of the market value of the Standard & Poor's stock market index of the top 500 publicly traded American companies. In the 1970s, over 80 per cent of a company's market value could be traced through to its financial statements. Today, less than 20 per cent of a company's market value can be accounted for by its financial and physical assets (Ocean Tomo, 2015). Other factors, particularly relationships, intellectual and human capital, make up an increasing proportion of a company's value. The financial reporting system has not evolved to adequately reflect this change.

We believe there is a need for enhanced business reporting that provides a more holistic view of corporate performance. While neither traditional financial reporting nor sustainability reporting, on their own, can provide a sufficient view of performance, it is critical for companies to focus on multiple capitals when making decisions. The Chartered Institute of Management Accountants recognizes that a business exists to generate value for its owners. However, there is a growing acceptance that in order to sustain its performance, a business must also generate value for other stakeholders, particularly its customers, suppliers, employees and the society it serves. Furthermore, it must take its impact on the environment and use of finite resources into account to ensure its own sustainability. Such thinking leads to <IR>, which takes the necessary broad view of the interests of the company's stakeholders and its value creation potential.

The work of the IIRC responds to the need for a new reporting paradigm that reflects the rapidly changing business environment. For many businesses, intangible and non-financial assets have become the most important determinants of long-term value creation. This has led to calls for change in the way businesses report and communicate their value creation stories, resonating with the association's key message that it is time to start accounting for the business rather than just the balance sheet.

Research undertaken by CIMA and Tomorrow's Company (CIMA and Tomorrow's Company, 2014, p.5) indicates that <IR> helps an organization:

- create value – by better understanding and connecting the disparate sources and drivers of long-term value to enable better strategy formulation, decision-making and imple-mentation through its business model
- tell its story – of how value is created more effectively, both internally and externally, in a succinct way, in order to win trust and secure reputation by encouraging better relationships with investors, employees and other stakeholders.

As well as directly benefiting organizations, <IR> has been found to contribute to more efficient capital markets. Research indicates a positive association between integrated report quality and both stock liquidity and firm value. Furthermore, evidence suggests that the association between reporting quality and firm value is mainly driven by increasing expected future cash flows. This finding is consistent with investors revising their estimates of future cash flows upward because they have a better understanding of the firm's capitals and business strategy, or that <IR> has led to better decisions being made by managers as a result of integrated thinking (Barth et al., 2016).

Additionally, 12 international institutional investors with US$2 trillion assets under management have recognized the positive impact of adopting <IR> on business decision-making:

> Embedding [<IR> or similar approaches] into the management and reporting of businesses will help to drive improved governance and stewardship practices through more comprehensive identification and management of current and future opportunities and risks. This will help businesses to move the focus on decision-making and capital allocation from the short term to the strategic issues, risks and opportunities that determine future performance in the medium and longer term. This shift will facilitate more sustainable development and stable businesses in the longer term and the growth of more transparent and robust capital markets which will benefit us all.
>
> *(IIRC, 2017, p.3)*

Research by the association in conjunction with the IIRC and stakeholder communications specialist Black Sun highlights the need for a broader view of value. According to a pulse check survey included in a new, brief *Purpose and Profit* (CGMA, 2018c), a majority of the executives surveyed, nearly 9 out of 10, said that organizations need to do a better job at focusing on wider value considerations beyond financial performance. Organizations need to consider further the value created for society and co-created through external relationships.

Benefits to the public sector of adopting <IR>

Historically, funding providers have been the primary users of corporate reports. However, integrated reports will be of benefit to all stakeholders interested in an organization's ability to create value over time. These will include employees, customers, suppliers, business partners, local communities, legislators, regulators and policy-makers. When "value creation" is considered in a non-financial context, these benefits are equally applicable to the public and private sectors.

The emphasis of <IR> on value beyond profit has particular benefits for public sector organizations. Unlike traditional corporate reporting, this more flexible approach enables organizations to focus clearly on how they and their stakeholders define value in the short, medium and long term.

Adopting <IR> helps organizations to embed integrated thinking within their decision-making processes. Integrated thinking promotes a better understanding of the impact of decisions on the value creation process, taking into account the broad range of factors relevant to that process, not just short-term financial considerations. This emphasis encourages better decision-making, greater transparency and a longer-term perspective, all of which are crucial to the sustainability of public services.

A 2014 IIRC survey of public and private sector organizations reporting in accordance with the IIRC <IR> Framework (Black Sun, 2014) found the key benefits to be as follows:

- Breakthroughs in value creation
- Improving what is measured
- Improving management information and decision making
- A new approach to stakeholder relations
- Connecting departments and broadening perspectives

Growing demand for more user-friendly accounting information, which combines financial and non-financial performance to support better decision, making means that public sector organizations need to rethink the way that they present their accounts. Incorporating non-financial information with financial data and determining appropriate key performance indicators can help organizations address these challenges and gain greater understanding of the way in which they create value.

<IR> and the UN's sustainable development goals

On 1 January 2016, the 17 Sustainable Development Goals (SDGs) of the 2030 Agenda for Sustainable Development – adopted by world leaders in September 2015 at an historic UN Summit – officially came into force. Over the next fifteen years, with these new SDGs that universally apply, countries will mobilize efforts to end all forms of poverty, fight inequalities and tackle climate change, while ensuring that no one is left behind.

Corporate reporting has a role to play in these efforts, according to an agreement signed by the United Nations Conference on Trade and Development (UNCTAD) and the IIRC in June 2019. The updated memorandum of understanding reaffirms the commitment of the two organizations to enhance their cooperation to integrate the SDGs into the corporate reporting cycle. This action re-affirms the role of business in helping to achieve the SDGs. In particular, Target 12.6 commits to "integration in corporate reporting" and draws inspiration from Goal 12 (Responsible Consumption and Production) on the need to ensure sustainable consumption and production patterns: "Encourage companies, especially large and transnational companies, to adopt sustainable practices and to integrate sustainability information into their reporting cycle." (UN, 2019). This goal is highly relevant to management accountants. Through cost accounting and management reporting of the organization's operations and financial conditions (including sustainability reporting), management accountants' domain includes management, analysis and insight drawn from financial and non-financial information (CGMA, 2018b, p.17).

Many businesses are already starting to integrate their performance against the SDGs into their mainstream annual reports. The latest findings from the Global Sustainability Index Institute show that only 11 per cent of companies did not refer at least implicitly to the SDGs in their annual report (UNGSII, 2018, p.3).

Integrated Reporting is an effective mechanism for both monitoring the allocation of resources and pursuing the SDGs of the six different "capitals" – human, social and relationship, intellectual, natural, manufacturing and financial. Organizations can apply integrated thinking across strategy-setting, decision-making and managing risk and opportunities. Reporting in accordance with the <IR> Framework can help them better understand and communicate their contribution to the SDGs (CGMA, 2018b, p.18).

Integrated Reporting and management accounting

The role of an organization should be to create value over the short, medium and long term responsibly. This requires understanding the connectivity across a broad range of resources and relationships that an organization uses to create value (i.e., the IIRC's six capitals). This integrated thinking should be extended to how the value created is shared amongst the various stakeholders in terms of dividends, share price appreciation, interest payments, pay, supplier payments, taxes, community initiatives and charitable donations. Integrated Reporting, underpinned by integrated thinking, provides the insight needed across a broader information set with a future orientation, drawing on the organization's business model within the context of its external environment.

This broad view of value creation is shared by the Chartered Global Management Accountant's (CGMA) Business Model Framework (2018a), which is designed to help boards, senior executives and staff quickly and easily gain an understanding of their organization's business model, and shows how board decisions and management actions work together to create value in the context of a wide stakeholder base. This framework recognizes that although shareholder value is key to long term business survival, short-term value creation indicators are not always tangible or financial in nature but can manifest in non-financial or intangible ways, such as through customer satisfaction, reputation, brand loyalty and brand awareness.

Joining the Dots (CIMA, 2016), a major research report, concludes that senior leaders of organizations not displaying the attributes of integrated thinking are struggling to make the right decisions due to bureaucratic decision-making processes, siloed and short-term thinking, intra-organizational breakdowns in trust and collaboration, and difficulty translating ever-expanding volumes of information into relevant knowledge.

Further, the same research identified a group of organizations as "Integrated Thinkers". These organizations have advanced capability in the four Principles to create and preserve value on which the CGMA Global Management Accounting Principles (GMAPs) (CIMA,

2014) focuses – Influence, Relevance, Analysis and Trust – and enjoy a decision-making advantage. Relative to others in their industry, Integrated Thinkers cited better performance, improved strategic execution, fewer failures of strategic initiatives due to delays in decision-making, and reduced susceptibility to delivering flawed information to decision-makers.

The practices of management accounting as described by the GMAPs provide the integrated information required to support integrated thinking and decision-making, taking into account both financial and non-financial performance across multiple timeframes. This integrated information is the foundation for a shared understanding of how an organization creates value through its business model.

Academic research funded by CIMA (Busco et al, 2017) shows how the finance departments in organizations help understand, enhance and report strategies for long-term value creation through integrated thinking and reporting. Based on empirical evidence gathered from a number of international case studies, and conversations with pioneers of integrated thinking as an inclusive approach to planning, measurements and reporting, the research summary sets out ten recommendations to aid the design and management of effective processes of integrated thinking and reporting.

Management accounting that is supported by the GMAPs provides a highly developed, rigorous and fit-for-purpose discipline, and a basis for decision-making and skills development to advance excellence in the practice of integrated thinking and reporting.

As integrated reports become more widespread, we believe it is essential for the protection of investors that such information be reliable. We believe that the credibility and reliability of such information is increased when it is subject to assurance. We further believe that the accountancy profession, given its educational and experience requirements, specialized training and requirements for strict adherence to accountancy laws and professional codes of conduct, is best positioned to provide such assurance services. In July 2017, the AICPA issued a new guide, *Attestation Engagements on Sustainability Information (Including Greenhouse Gas Emissions Information)* (AICPA, 2017), which will assist CPAs with interpreting and applying the AICPA's clarified attestation standards (AICPA, 2016) when performing examination or review engagements on sustainability information. While this guide focuses on sustainability assurance, we ultimately believe it will serve as the foundation for <IR> assurance.

Integrated Reporting at CIMA

Integrated Reporting is particularly important to CIMA, because management accountancy holds that there is more to organizations than just the numbers. Much of the worth of companies comes from intangible factors such as their people, their brand and the partnerships they have with stakeholders – and these factors are best explained in an integrated way.

Integrated Reporting is introduced into the CIMA syllabus at Certificate level – within subject BA3 (Fundamentals of Financial Accounting). Further understanding of the scope, use and benefit of <IR> is developed as candidates progress through the CIMA Professional Qualification syllabus.

Through the CIMA brand, the association sponsors IR-related research such as:

- *Early Evidence on the Economic Consequences Associated with Integrated Reporting Quality* (Barth et al, 2017), which found a positive association between integrated report quality and stock liquidity, firm value and expected future cash flows.

- "Integrated thinking: aligning purpose and the business model to market opportunities and sustainable performance" (Busco et al, 2017), which examines how organizations use integrated thinking techniques to operate in a complex world, characterized by a multitude of internal and external drivers, interdependencies and trade-offs that influence the process of decision-making.

In addition, the association co-sponsored research into how the C-Suite sees long-term value creation. The research, *Purpose Beyond Profit: The Value of Value – Board-Level Insights* (CGMA, 2018c), was launched at the IIRC/ICGN 2018 conference. Results show that the C-Suite, globally, agrees on the increasing benefit of understanding and communicating the value creation potential of organizations to build relationships with stakeholders and improve integrated thinking and strategic decision-making. However, it is also apparent that executives lack the management and reporting information to understand and interpret the future drivers of their business.

The Chartered Institute of Management Accountants has produced five annual integrated reports, with its latest report *Accounting in Extraordinary Times* (CIMA, 2017) eschewing a narrow financial focus in favour of describing how all parts of an organization work together, and how the organization interacts with its external environment. In its inaugural year, the association published its first Integrated Report (Association of International Certified Professional Accountants, 2018). The report is designed to offer information freely while also telling the story of how the organization creates value. Reporting of this kind is a journey. The <IR> Framework as developed by the IIRC can take up to three years to implement fully. The association is dedicated to creating an environment of responsible capital allocation, recognizing the full range of factors that affect value, and supporting integrated thinking and planning.

Latest <IR> developments

In October 2018, the IIRC announced the appointment of Dominic Barton (former Global Managing Partner of McKinsey & Company) as its new chair to build on the immense contribution from Professor Judge Mervyn King, who will continue to undertake global advocacy for <IR> as Chair Emeritus of the council and as a world leader in the field of corporate governance.

One of Barton's first duties as chair was to launch the IIRC's new global strategy, known as the "Momentum Phase". This is aimed at seeing the council increase its efforts for worldwide adoption of integrated thinking as a better way of doing business. Key objectives include promoting integrated thinking as a driver of effective corporate governance, creating a policy and regulatory environment that encourages movement towards <IR>, and among others, pushing for the US and China to adopt <IR>.

While it is true to say that there is a great deal of momentum towards the adoption of <IR> in certain parts of the world (for instance, the UK, where the statutory requirement for a "Strategic Report" is effectively adoption of <IR> principles, as well as more formal adoption in Japan, India and Turkey), there are still significant regions where change is much slower (e.g. in the US and China). One of the often cited reasons for the reluctance of companies to innovate their reporting practices in general is the preponderance of alternative reporting systems and guidelines that they face. With no commonly accepted standard, many managers are reluctant to devote time and resources to moving in one particular direction for fear that the market will take a different course.

Here the work of the Corporate Reporting Dialogue (CRD) is crucial. The CRD was convened by the IIRC to promote greater coherence, consistency and comparability between corporate reporting frameworks, standards and related requirements. The organizations that make up the Corporate Reporting Dialogue are:

- CDP
- Climate Disclosure Standards Board
- Financial Accounting Standards Board (observer)
- Global Reporting Initiative
- International Accounting Standards Board
- International Integrated Reporting Council
- International Organization for Standardization
- Sustainability Accounting Standards Board.

The CRD has set up a Better Alignment Project that is focused on driving better alignment in the corporate reporting landscape, to make it easier for companies to prepare effective and coherent disclosures that meet the information needs of capital markets and society.

Conclusion

Integrated reporting is far more than just another reporting framework. It helps organizations create value, tell their story and contribute to more efficient capital markets. Investors and other stakeholders benefit alongside organizations that adopt <IR>. Investors benefit further when such information has been subject to independent assurance and is thus more credible and reliable.

Barry Melancon, speaking in May 2017, said:

> I would challenge us, as we talk about the different opportunities and the ways that we could help create a different place for business in society, to think in an integrated way. If we're going to have business and employment survive, we have to be truly committed to looking at things in an integrated way.

The work of management accountants, underpinned by the GMAPs, reflects integrated thinking and decision making in practice. The foundation for effective <IR> is integrated thinking, without which the full benefits of <IR> cannot be realized. This shared interest in the concept and practical application of integrated thinking along with the public interest benefit of enhanced corporate reporting is the basis for the association's position as a strong supporter and advocate for <IR>.

References

AICPA. (1994). *Meeting the Information Needs of Investors and Creditors*. Available at: http://3197d6d14b5f19f2f440-5e13d29c4c016cf96cbbfd197c579b45.r81.cf1.rackcdn.com/collection/papers/1990/1994_0101_ReportingJenkins.pdf (Accessed: 23 October 2019).

AICPA. (2016). *Statement on Standards for Attestation Engagements 18*. Available at: www.aicpa.org/content/dam/aicpa/research/standards/auditattest/downloadabledocuments/ssae-no-18.pdf (Accessed: 23 October 2019).

AICPA. (2017). *Attestation Engagements on Sustainability Information Guide (Including Greenhouse Gas Emissions Information)*. USA: AICPA.

AICPA. (2019). *Enhanced Business Reporting Consortium*. Available at: www.aicpa.org/interestareas/frc/accountingfinancialreporting/enhancedbusinessreporting/enhancedbusinessreportingconsortium.html (Accessed: 23 October 2019).

Association of International Certified Professional Accountants. (2018). *2017 Integrated Report*. Available at: www.aicpa-cima.com/content/dam/aicpanas/downloadabledocuments/association-integrated-report-2017.pdf (Accessed 23 October 2019).

Barth, M., Cahan, S., Chen, E., and Venter, E. (2016). *Early Evidence on the Economic Consequences Associated with Integrated Report Quality*. London, UK: CIMA.

Black Sun. (2014). *Realizing the Benefits: The Impact of Integrated Reporting*. Available at: www.blacksunplc.com/en/insights/research/integrated-reporting-benefits-research.html (Accessed 23 October 2019).

Busco, C., Granà, F., and Quattrone, P. (2017). Integrated thinking: aligning purpose and the business model to market opportunities and sustainable performance. *CIMA Research Executive Summary*, *13*(4), 1–27.

CGMA. (2018a). *CGMA Business Model Framework*. Available at: www.cgma.org/resources/reports/practical-guide-business-model-framework.html (Accessed: 23 October 2019).

CGMA. (2018b). *Creating a Sustainable Future: The Role of the Accountant in Implementing the Sustainable Development Goals*. Available at: www.cgma.org/resources/reports/the-role-of-the-accountant-in-implementing-the-sustainable-development-goals.html (Accessed 23 October 2019).

CGMA. (2018c). *Purpose beyond Profit: The Value of Value – Board-Level Insights*. Available at: www.cgma.org/resources/reports/purpose-beyond-profit.html (Accessed: 23 October 2019).

CIMA and Tomorrow's Company. (2014). *Tomorrow's Business Success*. Available at: www.tomorrowscompany.com/publication/tomorrows-business-success/ (Accessed 23 October 2019).

CIMA. (2014). *Global Management Accounting Principles*. Available at: www.cgma.org/resources/reports/downloadabledocuments/global-management-accounting-principles.pdf (Accessed 23 October 2019).

CIMA. (2016). *Joining the Dots: Decision Making for a New Era*. Available at: www.cgma.org/content/dam/cgma/resources/downloadabledocuments/joining-the-dots-report.pdf (Accessed 23 October 2019).

CIMA. (2017). *Integrated Report 2016: Accounting in Extraordinary Times*. Available at: www.cimaglobal.com/Documents/AGM/2016%20Integrated%20Report%20(A4).pdf (Accessed 23 October 2019).

FRC. (2006). *Operating and Financial Review*. Available at: www.frc.org.uk/accountants/accounting-and-reporting-policy/uk-accounting-standards/reporting-statements-in-issue/operating-and-financial-review (Accessed: 23 October 2019).

FRC. (2011). *FRC Financial Reporting Lab*. Available at: www.frc.org.uk/investors/financial-reporting-lab (Accessed: 23 October 2019).

IIRC. (2017). *Investors Support Integrated Reporting as a Route to Better Understanding of Performance*. Available at: http://integratedreporting.org/wp-content/uploads/2017/09/Investor-statement_FinalS.pdf (Accessed 23 October 2019).

IIRC. (2018). *Breaking Through. IIRC Integrated Report 2017*. Available at: https://integratedreporting.org/integratedreport2017/download/pdf/IIRC_INTEGRATED_REPORT_2017.pdf (Accessed: 23 October 2019).

Ocean Tomo. (2015). *Ocean Tomo Releases 2015 Annual Study of Intangible Asset Market Value*. Available at: www.oceantomo.com/blog/2015/03-05-ocean-tomo-2015-intangible-asset-market-value/ (Accessed: 23 October 2019).

PWC. (2016). *Report Leadership: 10 Years on*. Available at: https://pwc.blogs.com/corporatereporting/2016/11/report-leadership-10-years-on.html (Accessed: 23 October 2019).

UNGSII. (2018). *SCR100 SDG Commitment Report*. Available at: http://mediadrawer.gvces.com.br/columbia/original/session-3-3-scr100_20184_2016-2017_comparison_update.pdf (Accessed: 29 October 2019).

United Nations (UN). (2019). *Report of the Secretary-General Special Edition: Progress towards the Sustainable Development Goals*. Available at: https://undocs.org/E/2019/68 (Accessed 23 October 2019).

6

A CASE STUDY ON (AND CASE FOR) INTEGRATED REPORTING AND INTEGRATED THINKING

Relevance to a not-for-profit professional accounting association

John Purcell

Abstract

The principle-based approach adopted in the design of the International Integrated Reporting Framework (<IR> Framework) offers opportunities for experimentation around adaptability to widely differing legal forms of business organization and interactions with constituencies of interest. This case study seeks to reveal opportunities offered by the <IR> Framework relating to strengthening and articulating an organization's reasons for existence to both owners and stakeholders, allowing expression of 'why' and for whose benefit. The case study's not-for-profit professional association setting has broad applications to similar organizations and for-profit organizations. Not-for-profit and for-profit organizations have a vital interest in the evolving character of corporate disclosure, of which the <IR> Framework is both a driver and an example. This chapter canvasses developments in non-financial disclosure, specifically with regard to climate change disclosure, illustrating the importance of effective engagement in public interest-based policy advocacy.

Introduction

This chapter takes as its context a statement made in the Executive Summary of the International Integrated Reporting Council's (IIRC) International Integrated Reporting Framework (<IR> Framework): 'The Framework … [i]s written primarily in the context of the private sector, for profit companies of any size but it can also be applied, adapted as necessary, by public sector and not-for-profit organizations' (IIRC, 2013, p. 4).

The purpose of the chapter is to explore and explain the relevance of the <IR> Framework to CPA Australia, given its distinct legal structure and operating purposes. In particular, emphasis is placed on how integrated reporting (<IR>) can be seen to provide a link between the organization's formal constituent structure and its externally focused activities in policy development and advocacy on behalf of its members.

CPA Australia first produced an integrated report in 2013, combining its financial, sustainability and other annual disclosures into 'one report'. Subsequent reporting years have seen growing sophistication and refinement in preparing reports with reference to the fundamental concepts, guiding principles and content elements of the <IR> Framework. As with many organizations that have embarked on the <IR> 'journey', CPA Australia has a strong background in preparing sustainability reports with reference to the Global Reporting Initiative (GRI).

CPA Australia, through its various antecedent bodies, has a 133-year history and now represents the diverse interests of over 164,000 accounting and finance professionals in 150 regions worldwide. Although formed and headquartered in Australia, CPA Australia operates through a number of overseas branches and representative offices (primarily in Asia, but also in the United Kingdom), serving a substantial membership resident outside of Australia. Based on size of membership, CPA Australia ranks in the top ten professional accounting associations globally. Notwithstanding its nature as a not-for-profit professional association, CPA Australia is of substantial financial size, generating revenues of AUD175.6 million in 2018 and holding total assets of AUD205 million. CPA Australia was recently ranked at 354 in an Australian Financial Review list of the top 500 Australia private companies by revenue.

The first part of this chapter is devoted to an explanation of how, in CPA Australia's circumstances, <IR> can be applied to explain how its operating and legal structure relate to each other. The nature of value creation in a predominantly not-for-profit context is emphasized, with a focus on improving understanding of the need for active engagement on behalf of members in emerging areas of public policy, underpinned by targeted investment in applied academic research. The following two sections of the chapter are illustrative in nature. The first highlights sponsored research into the financial benefits of non-financial performance and disclosure, for which <IR> is now regarded as the leading overarching framework. The second explains the rationale for active engagement in policy development on climate change disclosure that has recently occurred in Australia. The final section of the chapter returns to the theme of governance, with regard to how ideas evident in the development of <IR> might assist understanding of the breadth of emerging governance issues and help to identify the roles that accountants might play.

CPA Australia's legal structure and constitution

This section adopts a formalized approach to particular attributes of governance, explaining how <IR> can guide communication around key elements within the constituent documents of a company. The formal objects of the company, CPA Australia, are analysed as significant authoritative governance statements. Internal application and external communication of these imperatives are presented, as enhanced through respective integrated thinking and <IR>.

Turning to its legal form, CPA Australia is incorporated under the *Corporations Act 2001* (Cth.) as a company limited by guarantee (s. 112). The Corporations Act contains further sections relevant to the form, conduct and governance of companies limited by guarantee, some of which are highly useful in understanding the relevance and value of <IR> to CPA Australia.

First is Section 254SA, which is fundamental to the distinction between a company limited by guarantee and those companies whose shareholder liability is limited by shares:

- Companies limited by guarantee not to pay dividends
- A company limited by guarantee must not pay a dividend to its members.

Given this constraint, it is relevant to consider two further features of the <IR> Framework: the Fundamental Concept of *Value creation* and related matters around the intended audience, and how <IR> is readily adaptable to CPA Australia's approach to both its internal operations and external reporting. The Executive Summary to the <IR> Framework notes in relation to the Fundamental Concepts that: 'The ability of an organization to create value for itself enables **financial returns** to the providers of financial capital' (emphasis added). Further, IIRC (2013) paragraph 2.6, under *Value creation for the organization and for others*, the first of <IR>'s three Fundamental Concepts,[1] states: 'The ability of an organization to create value for itself is linked to the value it creates for others.' We turn now to the intended primary audience of <IR> and the contrast with the parties who might be considered ancillary, though potentially very interested in <IR> disclosures. The following statements are made in the <IR> Framework under *Purpose and users of an integrated report* (Part 1C): 'The primary purpose of an integrated report is to explain to providers of financial capital how an organization creates value over time. It therefore contains relevant information, both financial and other' (IIRC, 2013, para. 1.7). And further: 'An integrated report benefits all stakeholders interest in an organization's ability to create value over time, including employees, customers, suppliers, business partners, local communities, legislators, regulators and policy-makers' (IIRC, 2013, para. 1.8).

It may be tempting to surmise that CPA Australia prepares an integrated report largely on the basis of a sought engagement with a wide base of constituent stakeholders. Considering CPA Australia's legal structure more deeply, while its members provide financial capital, they do not receive financial returns. Rather they receive value across a spectrum of services. Disclosure and communication via the integrated report is not based on the perception that CPA Australia's members comprise varied categories of stakeholder, rather, CPA Australia's members are addressed as having an investment in the value creation attributes of the organization.

The second provision in the Corporations Act specific to companies limited by guarantee, which is relevant to an appreciation of <IR>'s efficacy in enhancing CPA Australia's approach to disclosure, is Section 300B(1), which lies within the numerous statutory rules dealing with corporate financial and director annual reporting (Part 2M.3):

The directors' report for a financial year for a company limited by guarantee must:

(a) contain a description of the short and long term objectives of the entity reported on;
(b) set out the entity's strategy for achieving those objectives;

(c) state the entity's principal activities during the year;

(d) state how those activities assisted in achieving the entity's objectives; and

(e) state how the entity measures its performance, including any key performance indicators used by the entity.

This section, inserted into the Act in 2010, is indicative of recognition that across the spectrum of entities governed by corporate legislation, effective disclosure involves detailed financial information accompanied by narrative analysis. The past decade has seen a growing volume and complexity of non-financial disclosure, accompanied by heightened expectations around quality, relevance and accessibility. The emergence of <IR> is both a reflection of and a response to these challenges. Thus, <IR> is a matter of vital consideration for organizations such as CPA Australia, who are 'stakeholders' in the proper and efficient development of corporate reporting beyond the core traditional components of financial recognition, measurement, presentation and disclosure. CPA Australia's choices around the adoption and presentation of information in an integrated report are more than a demonstration of 'leadership by example', which may have been the primary driver for producing sustainability reports with reference to the GRI reporting guidelines and indicators. <IR> is fundamental to the expression and communication of CPA Australia's corporate purpose and the progress made in the context of its directors' and management's obligations to provide value to members.

What then is the value created by CPA Australia, which enables it in turn to offer value to its members? The following discussion addresses one significant area of value: policy and advocacy undertaken on behalf of, and with input from, members. Within the identified scope for <IR> to address the needs of and to communicate with non-investor stakeholders, is reference to 'legislators, regulators and policy-makers', which, for a professional association, are the primary parties to whom a professional association's policies and advocacy are targeted.

Proactive engagement by CPA Australia in relevant matters of policy and advocacy is not a matter of shifting management discretion. This is best understood with reference to the organization's legal character and characteristics, as defined in both the Corporations Act and its constituent documents. First, two relevant provisions within the Corporations Act:

Section 125 Constitution may limit powers and set out objects

(1) If a company has a constitution, it may contain an express restriction on, or a prohibition of, the company's exercise of any of its powers. The exercise of a power by the company is not invalid merely because it is contrary to an express restriction or prohibition in the company's constitution.

(2) If a company has a constitution, it may set out the company's objects. An act of the company is not invalid merely because it is contrary to or beyond any objects in the company's constitution.

Section 140 Effect of constitution and replaceable rules

(1) A company's constitution (if any) and any replaceable rules that apply to the company have effect as a contract:

(a) between the company and each member;

(b) between the company and each director and company secretary; and

(c) between a member and each other member;

under which each person agrees to observe and perform the constitution and rules so far as they apply to that person.

With regard to the first of these two sections, it is important to reflect on the fact that a company is a legal person, distinct and separate from its shareholders and directors, the latter of whom are vested with powers of management (s. 198A(1)). This common law principle is reflected in modern statute in Section 124, which explains that a company has the legal capacity and powers of an individual. The internal operations of a company (s. 134) are, in turn, governed by the numerous provisions of the Act, along with what are termed the 'replaceable rules' (ss. 135 and 141) and, most significantly for our considerations, by a constitution (s. 136) which, though optional, most companies of any significant size or complexity, will develop and then adopt.

Prior iterations of Australian corporate law required a company to have an objects clause within its constitution, stating the purpose and range of activities in which the company could engage. Given that a company, by virtue of the act of incorporation (s. 119), now has the powers of a natural person, it need not have an objects clause, though subsection 2 of Section 125 makes provision for the adoption of such a statement.

Turning to Section 140, these provisions establish the contractual nature of a company's constitution, bringing with it obligations, rights and the bases of remedy, along with identifying the parties to that contract. The first two limbs of subsection 1 – *between the company and each member* and *between the company and each director* – are significant in understanding the prominence given by CPA Australia to policy and advocacy, and how <IR> generally, along with its underpinning in integrated thinking, drives effectiveness in terms of the <IR> Framework's first Guiding Principle of *Strategic focus and future orientation*.

Of further relevance in the <IR> Framework is Content Element G4, dealing with Governance. Within this complex and vital attribute, disclosure provides key insights into the ability to create value linked to the organization's culture, ethics and values, as reflected in the use of capitals and relationships with key stakeholders. In a traditional and indeed a legal sense, the foundation of governance resides in the formalized purposes contemplated at the time of a company's formation. For this chapter, the relevant capitals are *intellectual, human* and *relationship* applied to the value creation of member interest, linked directly to effective advocacy with policy-makers as a key category of stakeholder.

From this perspective, integrated thinking and <IR> underpin CPA Australia's governance. To elaborate further, CPA Australia (2019a) has, within its Constitution, adopted an objects clause repeated here in full:

The objects of the Company are to **promote excellence, enterprise and integrity amongst Members** and the financial, accounting and business advisory professions generally, to educate Members with respect to their duties and responsibilities as members of the financial, accounting and business advisory professions, and to prescribe the highest standards of ethics and professional conduct for Members. In fulfilling these objects, the Company will:

(a) **take an interest in legislative, economic and social matters affecting the Company's objects**;

(b) affiliate with organisations with similar objects; and

(c) do all such other things incidental or conducive to the attainment of the Company's objects

(emphasis added as these are the aspects of CPA Australia's Constitution most pertinent to the role of, and management's approach to, policy and advocacy)

(CPA Australia (2019a), p. 8)

Interpreting the words in corporate constitutions

It is appropriate to make brief reference to authoritative statements on the construction of corporate constitutions, as their meaning and intention is centred on interpretation of contractual words. This provides a cautious basis for describing how an integrated thinking approach guides CPA Australia's policy and advocacy choices, while being aware of changes in the *external environment* consistent with paragraph 2.21 of the <IR> Framework's Fundamental Concept – *The value creation process*. In CPA Australia's specific operating circumstances, the notion of an *external environment* is the dynamic economic, societal and environmental conditions its members, their clients and stakeholders, and the wider finance profession operate in, and how CPA Australia's integrated report contributes to engagement with members on critical challenges facing the profession. Many of these factors are likely to emerge as key drivers of the profession's relevance and capacity to positively contribute to business, the economy and wider society.

Legal developments in construing the meaning of contractual words outside of corporate constitutions has had a long and occasionally vexed history, though it can now be stated that an objective approach is applied in seeking to give effect to the intentions of the parties in 'reasonable businessperson' terms.[2] Likewise, the challenge to the admissibility of surrounding circumstances[3] to aid interpretation of a contract has been confirmed by the High Court of Australia, though not to such an extent as to contradict the language of the contract when it has a plain meaning.[4]

Returning to corporate constitutions, *Ford's Principles of Corporations Law* (Austin and Ramsay, 2018, pp. 219–223) states that corporate constitutions ought to be treated as business documents, the interpretation of which will be determined objectively to ensure business efficacy. Austin and Ramsay (2018) also acknowledge the trend away from imposing a strict literal interpretation of the meaning of written instruments, and note that, for business efficacy, an enduring effect should be given to instruments of company governance, stating that this 'has led to progressive interpretation like that applied to the Commonwealth Constitution so that sometimes an expression may be read as extending to a new development not envisaged when the constitution was adopted' (Austin and Ramsay, 2018, p. 220). However, they note that this propensity to address the construing of documents in the context of surrounding circumstances, even in the absence of ambiguity, when applied to interpreting the written language of a company constitution, requires caution and is more constrained.

Applying this reasoning to the two highlighted phrases in CPA Australia's constitution objects clause, a reasonable proposition, without of course offering a definitive 'legal opinion', is that integrated thinking may provide a rational and disciplined basis for understanding both the complexity and the interconnected nature of factors affecting the profession into the future, noting the <IR> Framework's future orientation. Given enduring effect of the constitution's reference to 'legislative, economic and social matters', <IR> is a fairly compelling idea that guides proper governance practice, and active and forward-looking engagement in policy and advocacy. It is not unreasonable to conclude that the <IR> Framework's Guiding Principle 3A, dealing with insights about an organization's ability to create value in the short, medium and long term, and Content Element 4G concerning challenges and uncertainties affecting the organization's business model, can be used to guide CPA Australia's advocacy on behalf of members in areas of both traditional and emerging public policy, as reported in its integrated reports.

An understanding of the enduring nature of CPA Australia's objects is based in the 'surrounding circumstances' of the evolving regulatory, economic and social dynamics that affect the attributes of *excellence, enterprise and integrity* amongst members. From this perspective, matters of potential policy and advocacy consideration are not unfettered. They are bound within notions of relevance to the membership. Integrated reporting thus provides a significant platform for communicating and engaging with members on policy and related technical matters that are both currently and potentially relevant.

Members have a contractually supported expectation that CPA Australia, the company, will address matters of both regulatory-based and broader public policy, and that directors, as managers of CPA Australia, are obliged to apply an intent, and by inference resources, to identifying and responding to such matters.

The range of policy and advocacy subject matter covered by CPA Australia is broad. The relative permissiveness evident in CPA Australia's governance documents encourages a view to the future with regard to what will impact the members and the profession generally. Integrated reporting, as a reporting innovation, is an example of developments to which the profession must attend and contribute appropriately. Integrated reporting is a valuable medium for engaging with members, regulators and policy-makers, the latter as key stakeholders, about critical drivers that either transform or create stress in our economic, regulatory and governance systems. The remainder of this chapter examines a number of environmental, social and governance (ESG) issues in which <IR> is playing a role in individual organizations' transformation, serving also as a potential basis for the business community's discourse in international and national regulatory environments.

The maturing of non-financial disclosure

The capacity of an organization to engage in advocacy on critical matters of public policy depends on suitable and sustained levels of investment in applied research; in <IR> Framework terminology this is called *Intellectual capital*. CPA Australia's most recently revised corporate strategy seeks 'to impact policy globally and be active in community advocacy' (CPA Australia, 2019c, p. 1). CPA Australia's 2018 Integrated Report acknowledges that one of the key value created by the accounting profession is through contributing to the stability, efficiency and sustainability of individual companies, financial markets and the economy of countries (CPA Australia, 2019b).

In addressing the challenge of achieving efficient and stable financial markets, a perennial question amongst both practitioners and academics has been whether non-financial information, often described as extended external reporting (EER), contains information valuable to market participants. To support its advocacy for emerging forms of corporate disclosure in parallel with financial reporting, CPA Australia has funded research examining these impacts, including a recent study by the University of Sydney analyzing sustainability information and cost of capital relationships (Jones and Frost, 2017). This study was particularly relevant to the themes of this chapter, in terms of communicating to both members and stakeholders the role of advocacy in shaping good public policy via an integrated thinking-based perspective. The relevant area of public policy is the identification of whether appropriate regulatory and non-regulatory mechanisms for ensuring corporate and wider business reporting remain fit for purpose.

Jones and Frost (2017) add to a substantial literature confirming the favourable relationship between sustainability reporting and internal practices and corporate cost of capital (both debt and equity). The independent variable, against which the dependent variable of cost of capital is measured, is derived from a large-scale sustainability ratings database commonly used by analysts. The study is unusual in its selection of markets – Australia, the United Kingdom and Hong Kong – because most capital markets studies of this type are US-based. The 385 listed companies used in the model are treated in aggregate. The results show that lower sustainability scores (comprising the aggregate of all environmental, social and governance scores scores) are statistically associated with higher cost of capital, after controlling for size (market capitalization), leverage, annual investment returns, a distress risk metric, free cash flow and return on equity. Regression results obtained on cost of capital, where the main independent variable is the total environmental rating, document a negative and statistically significant relationship between total environmental rating and cost of capital. This implies that companies with higher environmental ratings enjoy a lower cost of capital.

In the same study, regression results were also run on cost of capital where the main independent variable was total governance rating, extracted from the sustainability database. There was no significant relationship between the governance rating and cost of capital. This result conflicts with those of prior studies that found a positive relationship between governance and cost of capital. We surmise that given the large amount of attention corporate governance has attracted in recent years, particularly following high-profile corporate scandals and business failures, corporate disclosure practices, especially in larger companies, may have improved significantly. It may be that early adopters gain cost of capital benefits as evidenced in the study's environmental score results. However, as embedding becomes widespread and the norm, the comparative cost of capital gains will dissipate, as evidenced by the study's governance score results. The overall benefit will be better pricing of risk across the whole market, leading to greater stability.

CPA Australia believes these insights bode well for <IR> uptake as a vehicle for communicating recognition and response to environmental and social risks. Looking to the role of the professional accountant, <IR> may provide greater understanding of the complementarity between financial, non-financial and narrative disclosure in market transparency and stability. The next section discusses some aspects of CPA Australia's policy and advocacy activities in the complex areas of climate change, emissions reduction and broader environmental policy.

Climate change disclosures: CPA Australia's policy and advocacy commitment

CPA Australia strives to pursue impartial advocacy on behalf of members and in the public interest. The technical character of much of the organization's advocacy is reflected in detailed, largely publicly available submissions to government, regulators and standards-setters, often supplemented by presentation and questioning in formal public hearings. The subject of engaged public policy has steadily grown, reflecting the realities of regulatory and economic complexity. The need to engage with a broadening agenda of advocacy issues has arisen from the economic and business impact of global 'megatrends', which either challenge the traditional boundaries of accounting activity or compel serious reassessment of accounting's role. Perhaps the most profound and complex of the challenges is climate change. This chapter cannot address the many aspects of climate change and emission policy that CPA Australia legitimately explores (see, Chartered Accountants Australia and New Zealand and CPA Australia, 2019). I concentrate instead on developments in disclosure.

A discussion of CPA Australia's policy and advocacy perspective on climate change disclosure is relevant, given significant aspects within the <IR> Framework dealing with attributes of an organization's interaction and dependency on natural capital and a boundary of consideration, which extends into the external environment. Within that external environment, value over time is assessed variously as created, preserved and diminished. Natural capital is defined in the <IR> Framework as 'all renewable and non-renewable environmental resources and processes that provide goods or services that support the past current or future prosperity of the organization' (IIRC, 2013, para. 2.15), while externalities are seen as being embodied in the 'stock and flow' of assets transformed through the organization's business model.

Addressed through the <IR> Framework's emphasis on connectivity (IIRC, 2013, Part II 3B), both *natural capital* and *reporting boundary* have climate change elements based on an organization's or sector's operating circumstances, which may involve considerations of aspects of finance and accounting. Foremost are specific accounting considerations around interaction with financial capital, along with broader accounting involvement through separate and related governance, oversight and resource allocation considerations.

CPA Australia's business, centred on the services sector, has few direct carbon emissions, wider environmental impact, or dependency. The need for policy and advocacy engagement on climate change policy and business disclosure responses is nevertheless easily justified.

Accounting is embedded in economic and market systems, which cannot be treated in isolation from the natural environment and its complexities. Accounting is an important element in shaping environmentally sensitive business and economic policy. Particularly from an evolving disclosure perspective, accounting is essential to enabling effective wider market-participant responses to climate change. Moreover, accounting as a discipline deals with guiding resource allocation, giving meaningful measurement and disclosure of outcomes, and thus has a role to play in unravelling complexities, both for policy development purposes and to aid the transformation of business and the wider economy. Integrated reporting is one mechanism likely to play a role in meeting investor, market and indeed public expectation of corporate disclosure around critical matters of governance oversight, strategic response and risk management associated with both physical and transition risks (and opportunities) stemming from climate change.

CPA Australia's adoption of the <IR> Framework provides a level of insight and legitimacy in advocating appropriate developments in disclosure and the business/economic transformation imperatives centred on the challenges of climate change.

CPA Australia's legitimacy as an informed and impartial voice for developments in corporate climate-related disclosure is borne out in significant government inquiries, which in turn have played a role in prompting regulator and standard-setter responses. Most relevant is the Senate Economic References Committee inquiry *Carbon risk: a burning issue.* CPA Australia's submission and evidence is quoted extensively in the committee's 2017 report. CPA Australia was among a group of submitters to the inquiry who observed that there were significant opportunities to improve carbon reporting with consequential benefit for business, investors and the community. The submission also emphasized that carbon disclosure should not be undertaken on an exclusively voluntary basis, noting that emission accounting was distinct from the risk arising more broadly in the climate change context. Consequently, the committee's first recommendation was: 'That the Australian Securities and Investments Commission [ASIC] review its guidance to directors to ensure that it provides a proper understanding of the manifestations of carbon risk, and reflects evolving asset measurement implications of carbon risk' (Commonwealth of Australia, 2017, p. 27). The government, in its March 2018 response to this recommendation, agreed in principle, encouraging ASIC to review its relevant guidance material. Subsequently, ASIC issued a number of revisions in August 2019:

- incorporate the types of climate change risk developed by the G20 Financial Stability Board's Taskforce on Climate Related Financial Disclosures (TCFD) into the list of examples of common risks that may need to be disclosed in a prospectus appearing in Table 7 of Regulatory Guide 228 (*Prospectuses: Effective disclosure for retail investors*);
- in Regulatory Guide 247 (*Effective disclosure in an operating and financial review*), highlighting (para. 247.66) climate change as a systemic risk that could impact an entity's financial prospects for future years and that may need to be disclosed in an operating and financial review (OFR)[5];
- further in RG 247, reinforcing that disclosures made outside the OFR (such as under the voluntary TCFD framework or in a sustainability report) should not be inconsistent with disclosures made in the OFR; and
- a minor update to INFO 203 (*Impairment of non-financial assets: Materials for directors*) to highlight climate change and other risks that may be relevant in determining key assumptions that underlie impairment calculations.

ASIC's initiative is symptomatic of wider regulatory trends in Australia around raised expectations placed on companies and directors. It is seen that within duties of care and diligence there is a positive obligation to assess, and where appropriate, disclose the nature and assessed impact of climate change. Noteworthy is Australian Accounting Standards Board/Australian Audit and Assurance Standards Board guidance *Climate-related and other emerging risks disclosures: assessing financial statement materiality using AASB/IASB Practice Statement 2* (April 2019).

A further recommendation from the Senate Economics Committee was that: The Australia Stock Exchange provide guidance regarding the circumstances in which a listed entity's exposure to carbon risk requires disclosure under Recommendation 7.4 of the Australia Stock Exchange Corporate Governance Principles and Recommendations (Commonwealth of Australia, 2017). Around the same time as the Committee's deliberations, the Corporate Governance Council announced steps towards the release of a fourth edition of Principles and Recommendations, noting as the core impetus for revision emerging issues around culture, values and trust, fuelled by recent examples of conduct by some listed entities falling short of community standards and expectations. Recommendation 7.4, within Principle 7 (Recognize and manage risk), now reads:

A listed entity should disclose whether it has any material exposure to environmental and social risks and, if it does, how it manages or intends to manage those risks (ASX Corporate Governance Council, 2019, p. 27).

Recommendation 7.4 is essentially the same as that in the prior third edition except for the omitting of reference to economic risk – this is regarded as self-evident for a commercial enterprise. The material changes to Recommendation 7.4 are in fact in the accompanying Commentary. Aside from the strong encouragement given to entities to reference the TCFD Recommendation (Final Report June 2017), emphasizing potential applicability also to entities falling outside of the obvious mining and fossil fuels sectors, the Commentary identifies reporting made with reference to the <IR> Framework as potentially meeting this governance disclosure by way of cross-referencing.

CPA Australia's involvement in these developments is well supported by reference to its Constitution objects. Matters arising within business and economic activity, in this instance the impact of climate change and the need for markets to respond by both pricing risk and driving transformation, translate into core considerations and implications for the accounting profession, including developments in the frameworks of governance and disclosure, impairment assessments and external audits.

An integrated thinking approach has been very useful to CPA Australia as a basis for determining the legitimate boundaries of policy and advocacy activity. The application of the <IR> Framework provides a way to analyse and communicate these endeavours as attributes of governance responsibility.

Concluding reflections

CPA Australia is not an ASX listed company, required by ASX listing rules to produce a corporate governance statement against the principles and recommendations on an 'if not, why not' basis. It nevertheless has a vital role to play in these developments and surrounding policy debates. Many of CPA Australia's members are employed by listed companies, providing input and advice to their management and boards in relation to governance disclosures. Moreover, the principles and recommendations exist and operate within the broad schematic or architecture of corporate disclosure to which the accounting profession is subject, while also being a custodian of its proper development and application.

The range and complexity of governance developments that have emerged over a relatively short period raise challenges for professional associations and organizations and parties with a legitimate stake in driving best practice. There are practical choices around the scale and focus of engagement with regulators, standard setters and policy-makers. Instruments of soft regulation such as the ASX Corporate Governance Principles and Recommendation capture, in a summary form, deeper and more complex law reforms, and significant challenges to the way in which commercial gain is pursued. Each of these may have practical implications for accountants. Recommendations for dealing with whistle-blower and anti-bribery and corruption policies, along with the strengthened recommendations around the identification and management of environmental and social risk, all influence the way accounting is performed and applied, and raise both risks and opportunities for the profession. Underlying these challenges are shifting expectations and sentiments about the role of corporations and for whose benefit corporations exist, along with challenges to the efficacy of market-based capitalism. As has been the case with initiatives such as the Corporate Reporting Dialogue's Better Alignment Project sponsored by the IIRC, there may be lessons to be learned and opportunities to be gained from a 'systems thinking' approach to governance complexity. The seeds of such developments may already be evident in the IIRC's preparedness to engage in serious discourse on inclusive capitalism, which contains themes not dissimilar to recurring debates in Australia around shareholder primacy and more recently, in the ASX Corporate Governance context, the 'social licence to operate'. That CPA Australia, representing the accounting profession, should have a voice in these profound issues is supported by the constituent document upon which it was formed. Its contribution can be advanced through an integrated thinking approach and illuminated through its integrated report.

Notes

1 The other two being *The capitals* and *The value creation process*.
2 See for example *Electricity Generation Corp v Woodside Energy Ltd* [2014] HCA 7.
3 Events, circumstances and things external though possibly relevant context.
4 Refer *Codelfa Construction Pty Ltd v State Rail Authority* [1982] HCA 24.
5 The related statutory requirement is Section 299A (Annual directors' report – additional general requirement for listed entities) which in subsection 1 requires information that members would reasonably require to make an informed assessment of (a) the operations of the entity reported on, (b) the financial position of the entity reported on and (c) the business strategies, and prospects for future financial years of the entity reported on.

References

ASX Corporate Governance Council. (2019). *Corporate Governance Principles and Recommendations*. Available at: www.asx.com.au/documents/asx-compliance/cgc-principles-and-recommendations-fourth-edn.pdf (Accessed: 3 December 2019).

Austin, R. P., and Ramsay, I. M. (2018). *Ford, Austin and Ramsay's Principles of Corporate Law* (17 ed.). Australia: LexisNexis Butterworths.

Chartered Accountants Australia and New Zealand and CPA Australia. (2019). *Climate Change Authority: Updating the Authority's Previous Advice on Meeting the Paris Agreement*. Available at: www.cpaaustralia.com.au/media/consultations-and-submissions (Accessed: 3 December 2019).

Commonwealth of Australia. (2017). *Carbon Risk: A Burning Issue*. Available at: www.aph.gov.au/Parliamentary_Business/Committees/Senate/Economics/Carbonriskdisclosure45/Report (Accessed: 3 December 2019).

Corporations Act 2001 (Cth). Available at: https://www.legislation.gov.au/Details/C2018C00424 (Accessed: 3 December 2019).

CPA Australia. (2019a). *Constitution*. Available at: www.cpaaustralia.com.au/about-us/our-organisation/our-constitution (Accessed: 3 December 2019).

CPA Australia. (2019b). *CPA Australia Integrated Report 2018*. Available at: www.cpaaustralia.com.au/about-us/our-organisation (Accessed: 3 December 2019).

CPA Australia. (2019c). *CPA Australia Professional Standards Scheme*. Available at: www.cpaaustralia.com.au/about-us/consumer-information (Accessed: 3 December 2019).

IIRC. (2013). *The International Integrated Reporting Framework*. London, UK: IIRC.

Jones, S., and Frost, G. (2017). *Sustainability Information and the Cost of Capital: An Australian, United Kingdom and Hong Kong Listed Company Study*. Australia: CPA Australia.

PART II

Critical reflections on the development of integrated reporting

7

THE <IR> FRAMEWORK

An example of what unfortunately happens when people who fail to comprehend the meaning of 'accountability' take control of an important reporting initiative

Craig Deegan

School of Accounting, RMIT University

Abstract

This chapter adopts a critical perspective to evaluate the International Integrated Reporting Framework (<IR> Framework). Focusing on the notion of 'accountability' and applying a four-step model of accountability, it is argued that the <IR> Framework falls short as a framework that assists or encourages managers and their organizations to demonstrate accountability towards a broad group of stakeholders in respect of various aspects of their social and environmental (and sustainability-related) performance. The lack of focus on accountability, the way materiality is addressed, the nature of the stakeholders being considered, the reporting boundary embraced and the concept of 'capitals' used with the <IR> Framework all act to undermine its suitability as a document to promote meaningful reporting.

Introduction

As is demonstrated in other chapters of this book, *integrated reporting* is a term that has become widely used in larger organizations and industry, particularly over the last decade. Integrated reporting can take a variety of forms and can be defined in a number of ways. Nevertheless, it would generally be perceived as representing the generation of documents or reports that *integrate* or connect information about the social, economic/financial and environmental implications of an organization's operations. This can be contrasted to the common, or *traditional*, practice of providing separate and distinct financial reports and various disconnected sustainability reports. As we also know from other chapters in this book, the International Integrated Reporting Council (IIRC) – formed in August 2010 as a joint initiative of the Prince's Accounting for Sustainability Project (A4S), which in itself was an organization initially established to develop what was then known as 'Connected Reporting', and the Global Reporting Initiative (GRI) – which is a major organization associated with promoting a particular (and not necessarily the best) approach to integrated reporting.

As indicated above, one important issue the IIRC sought to address was the lack of integration between the different reports that organizations typically release. Most larger organizations produce an annual report and various interim financial reports that include a number of financial statements and associated note disclosures, as required by financial accounting standards, corporations law and securities exchange listing requirements. The same organizations often release separate corporate social responsibility or sustainability reports. However, there is typically little or no linkage between the separate reports as they are often prepared by different groups of people who fail to communicate, arguably because they effectively speak different languages. This disconnection has, for many years, led to calls for a form of reporting – which we label integrated reporting – in which various types of information necessary for assessing and evaluating a company's performance are reported in a comprehensive fashion within an integrated report. Such reports would, ideally, show the implications/outcomes of various managerial decisions in terms of the positive and negative social, environmental and economic impacts on a broad group of stakeholders.

As has also been explained in other chapters of this book, the reporting framework developed by the IIRC, hereafter referred to as the <IR> Framework, is a principles-based framework rather than one that stipulates lists of required disclosures. Therefore, it is quite different to, for example, the GRI Sustainability Reporting Standards, which prescribes various social, environmental and economic disclosures. The <IR> Framework provides guiding principles and content elements that are to be used to govern the overall content of an integrated report, and to explain the fundamental concepts that underpin the report. These principles and elements are summarized in Table 7.1. Reading through them, and referring back to the <IR> Framework for further detail, we can probably agree that they

Table 7.1 IIRC Guiding Principles and Content Elements

GUIDING PRINCIPLES

The following Guiding Principles underpin the preparation of an integrated report, informing the content of the report and how information is presented:

Strategic focus and future orientation
Connectivity of information
Stakeholder relationships
Materiality
Conciseness
Reliability and completeness
Consistency and comparability

CONTENT ELEMENTS

An integrated report includes eight Content Elements that are fundamentally linked to each other and are not mutually exclusive:

Organisational overview and external environment
Governance
Business model
Risks and opportunities
Strategy and resource allocation
Performance
Outlook
Basis of preparation and presentation

Source: IIRC, 2013, pp. 16–32

do seem to be logical. If applied properly, the <IR> Framework could perhaps help an organization to produce reports that are useful to some external stakeholders (relative to reports that are prepared without following such principles), although the apparent emphasis within the principles and elements on *value creation* potentially limit the degree to which an organization shall demonstrate accountability.

There is some degree of overlap between these guiding principles and the principles for defining report quality included within the GRI Sustainability Reporting Standards and the Conceptual Framework for Financial Reporting (as well as with other frameworks, such as that of the Water Accounting Standards Board – see www.bom.gov.au/water/standards/wasb/). For example, qualitative characteristics such as conciseness, reliability, consistency and comparability are common to many reporting frameworks. This should not be unexpected, as such principles are generally relevant to increasing the usefulness to users of any information that an organization produces, whether it relates to social, environmental or financial performance. Therefore, so far, perhaps so good. However, a more in-depth review of the <IR> Framework reveals a number of other interesting (and some quite concerning) aspects of the guidelines, some of which are discussed in the following sections.

The notion of accountability: a general discussion

There was much excitement about the A4S project and the subsequent IIRC project in their formative years because it looked as though the projects were leading towards a style of reporting that would encourage increased accountability by organizations to a broader group of stakeholders. There was potential for a broad perspective of performance to be considered, beyond the usual fixation on financial performance, and changes in business or shareholder value.

Across time, there has been much discussion about what information organizations *should* provide in relation to the various facets of their performance. Many arguments are tied to subjective (values-based) opinions about stakeholders' *rights to know* (which, if they are to carry any weight, would seem to require some identification of the stakeholders involved), and associated opinions about the extent of an organization's accountability.

Indeed, once we open a debate about the information that an entity *should* disclose, we are, in effect, entering a debate about the responsibilities and associated accountabilities of organizations. For example, is the sole function of a business organization to generate a profit, or do business organizations have wider responsibilities to the societies in which they operate? Different people will have different views about the accountability that organizations should accept and demonstrate, and therefore will have different views about what information and accounts should be prepared for managerial use and/or distributed to stakeholders. This is reflected in Figure 7.1, which comes from Deegan (2020a). The figure emphasizes in a simplistic but useful way that views about organizational responsibilities affect views about organizational accountabilities, which in turn – in a sequential manner – influence views about the 'accounts' that should be prepared by an organization (that is, views about responsibilities and associated accountabilities influence views about the role of accounting).

There are many views about the responsibilities of business. At one extreme are the views of the famous economist Milton Friedman. In his widely cited book *Capitalism and Freedom*, Friedman rejects the view that corporate managers have any *moral* obligations or responsibilities. He notes that such a view:

Figure 7.1 The relationship between organizational responsibility, accountability and accounts
Source: Deegan, 2020a

> shows a fundamental misconception of the character and nature of a free economy. In such an economy, there is one and only one social responsibility of business [and that is] to use its resources and engage in activities designed to increase its profits as long as it stays within the rules of the game, which is to say, engages in open and free competition, without deception or fraud.
>
> *(Friedman, 1962, p. 133)*

Referring to Figure 7.1, if we believe an organization is responsible *only* for its financial performance and for providing financial returns to its shareholders (and this, unfortunately, does seem to be a view held by many business managers – a view that is often referred to as a Friedmanite view of the world, or a 'shareholder primacy perspective'), then we might accept that there is only a need to produce financial accounts and that it is inappropriate, and indeed wasteful, to produce broader social and environmental performance information/ accounts – unless doing so is expected to enhance the profitability and value of the organization.

At the other end of the responsibility spectrum are those who hold the view that managers should manage the organization for the benefit of *all* stakeholders, not just those (powerful) stakeholders with control over scarce resources (e.g., financial capital providers). Taking a broader perspective of the responsibilities of organizations, an entity's stakeholders have been defined by Freeman and Reed (1983, p. 91) as: any identifiable group or individual who can affect the achievement of an organisation's objectives, or is affected by the achievement of an organisation's objectives. The above definition of stakeholders is a widely used definition by both organizations and by accounting researchers. If we accept that an organization has a responsibility to its stakeholders (beyond its shareholders), then the more broadly an organization defines its stakeholders, the greater the responsibilities and associated accountabilities it will tend to accept, and the broader will be its accounting.

The co-existence of divergent views on the responsibilities of business are nothing new and it is unlikely that there will ever be anything near a universal agreement on how far, and to whom, the social responsibilities of an organization should extend, or relatedly how far the reporting boundaries should extend. Arguably, however, the perspective of organizational responsibilities embraced by the IIRC is far too narrow – as we shall soon discuss.

While to this point we have been discussing accountability, we have not defined it. One commonly accepted definition of accountability used in the social and environmental accounting literature is that provided by Gray et al. (2014, p. 50), which is 'a duty to provide an account (by no means necessarily a financial account) or reckoning of those actions for which one is held responsible'.

As we can see, there is a direct linkage between organizational responsibilities, and the practice of accounting. The above definition of accountability is consistent with the definitions provided by other researchers/organizations; for example:

> Accountability, as we use the term, implies that some actors have the right to hold other actors to a set of standards, to judge whether they have fulfilled their responsibilities in light of these standards, and to impose sanctions if they determine that these responsibilities have not been met.
>
> *(Grant and Keohane, 2005, p. 29)*

> The concept of accountability is a pervasive one ... The notions underlying it are those of accounting for, reporting on, explaining and justifying activities, and accepting responsibility for the outcomes. Accountability involves an obligation to answer for one's decisions and actions when authority to act on behalf of one party (the principal) is transferred to another (the agent) ... Accountability requires openness, transparency and the provision of information, and the acceptance of responsibility for one's actions.
>
> *(Barton, 2006, pp. 257–258)*

> Accountability is a relationship between an actor and a forum, in which the actor has an obligation to explain and to justify his or her conduct, the forum can pose questions and pass judgment, and the actor may face consequences.
>
> *(Bovens, 2010, p. 450)*

> Accountability is acknowledging, assuming responsibility for and being transparent about the impacts of your policies, decisions, actions, products and associated performance.
>
> *(AccountAbility, 2008, p. 6)*

Consistent with the above definitions, according to Gray et al. (2014), accountability involves two responsibilities or duties:

- The responsibility to undertake certain actions (or to refrain from taking certain actions).
- The responsibility to provide an account of those actions.

Accepting the above definitions, we can again see that perceptions of accountability depend on subjective perceptions about the extent of an organization's responsibility, again reflective of Figure 7.1.

As would be expected, social and environmental accounting researchers often link the practice or role of social and environmental accounting/reporting – to which integrated reporting necessarily relates – with the concept of accountability. For example, Gray and Laughlin (2012, p. 240) state:

Social accounting is concerned with exploring how the social and environmental activities undertaken (or not, as the case may be) by different elements of a society can be – and are – expressed. In essence, how they are made speakable – even know-able. So, the process of social accounting then offers a means whereby the non-financial might be created, captured, articulated, and spoken. The analysis of such accounts – and their absence (Choudhury, 1988) – provides a basis through which social accountability can clarify how the relationships which are largely dominated by the economic (Thielemann, 2000) might be renegotiated to accommodate – or even to prioritise – the social and the environmental within these relationships.

Gray et al. (2014, p. 4) further note that the resulting social and environmental 'accounts' that emanate from this form of accounting: may serve a number of purposes but discharge of the organisation's accountability to its stakeholders must be clearly dominant of those reasons and the basis upon which the social account is judged. Having now provided insights into the relationship between corporate responsibility, accountability and accounting (see Figure 7.1), we will now examine what can be considered as a four-step accountability model, which we will soon apply to evaluating the <IR> Framework. As Deegan (2020a) explains, this linkage between responsibilities/values to accountability and ultimately to accounting can be linked to the following four issues:

* *Why* provide an account;
* To *whom* to provide an account;
* *What* to include in an account; and
* *How* to prepare/present an account.

Deegan (2020a, p. 20) provides a simple representation of this sequential relationship, as reproduced as Figure 7.2.

For example, if a judgement is made from a neo-classical economic perspective (e.g., a Friedmanite-type perspective) that accounts of particular aspects of performance *should* be prepared only to the extent that the activity of preparing the accounts increases corporate profitability and therefore the wealth of financial capital providers (the '*why?*' question), then the target audience of those reports might be stakeholders who have the power to influence the economic value of the organization (the '*to whom?*' question) – for example, providers of financial capital (i.e., the stakeholders prioritized within the <IR> Framework). In terms of what aspects of performance should be reflected in the accounts, in this scenario, measures of financial performance or economic value added would likely be prioritized (the '*what to report?*' question). The information would be provided in reports that are compiled with reference to reporting frameworks that emphasize financial measurement of resources and performance, such as those provided by the International Accounting Standards Board (in answer to the final '*how to report?*' question).

By contrast, if a contrary judgement is made that an organization has a responsibility and associated accountability to a broader group of stakeholders in relation to economic, social, and environmental performance and related impacts (the 'why?' report issue), then the audience of the reports would tend to be stakeholders who are most affected (economically, socially and environmentally) by the operations of the entity, or surrogate stakeholders that act in the interests of the affected stakeholders (e.g., NGOs) (the answer to the 'to whom?' question). Issues of stakeholder power would not be particularly pertinent in this view of the world. In terms of the aspects of performance that would be reported within the

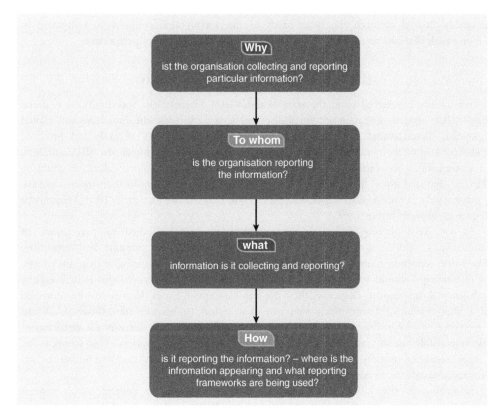

Figure 7.2 A diagrammatic representation of a four-step accountability model
Source: Deegan, 2020a

accounts (the 'what to report?' question), the information would tend to be prioritized in terms of the perceived (subjectively determined) importance of the various social, environmental and economic impacts. The information would be provided by virtue of frameworks beyond financial reporting, which would enable impacts to be reported in a way that promotes further dialogue and improvement in an organization's social and environmental performance (the answer to the 'how to report?' question).

What is being demonstrated here is that although we are applying the same four-step accountability model in both scenarios, and therefore the same four broad steps in our decision-making, we can nevertheless arrive at very different normative prescriptions about how an organization should account for its operations. The differences in the normative prescriptions are a result of the different world views held by those in charge of developing reporting frameworks and requirements.

Therefore, if we are seeking to develop a meaningful reporting framework, it is vital that the people making important decisions about the objective and contents of the framework answer these questions broadly and do not fixate on the interests of a limited group of stakeholders – such as the providers of financial capital. It is the contention of the author of this chapter that those in charge of developing the <IR> Framework embraced an incredibly restricted view of the 'why report?' and 'to whom to report?' questions and this inevitably flowed through the other steps of the accountability model to culminate in a framework that ultimately has limited merit from an accountability perspective.

IIRC's limited focus on accountability

Accountability is referred to at the start of the <IR> Framework. Specifically, it is stated that: <IR> aims to enhance accountability and stewardship for the broad base of capital (financial, manufactured, intellectual, social and relationship, and natural) and promote understanding of their independencies (IIRC, 2013, p. 2). According to the IIRC, there is an accountability for various capitals, but apparently not to stakeholders (albeit, it could be argued – but it is not – that various stakeholders could be caught up in the various capitals). Unfortunately, beyond this, accountability is not defined within the <IR> Framework despite its obvious importance.

As we have already discussed, accountability is directly linked to perceptions of responsibility and is a central and logical component of accounting and reporting. Therefore, reporting frameworks need to be very clear about accountability in terms of *why* an organization should report, *to whom* the organization should report, *what* it shall report, and *how* it should report. Logically, these are key conceptual issues that need to be addressed in a well-developed framework, even one that claims to be principles-focussed. Whilst a reference to responsibility is made in the <IR> Framework, the discussion is restricted to the responsible use of capitals and the responsibility for value creation. This seems to be a very restricted notion of responsibility, particularly given that the responsibilities are directed towards the needs of providers of financial capital.

According to the <IR> Framework, integrated reporting is defined as: A process founded on integrated thinking that results in a periodic integrated report by an organization about value creation over time and related communications regarding aspects of value creation (IIRC, 2013, p. 33). This definition is interesting. The focus of this framework is on reporting information about value creation, rather than about demonstrating meaningful accountability, despite what is said about accountability and stewardship on page 2 of the <IR> Framework. This was of concern to many people who had hoped that the emphasis of integrated reporting as espoused by the IIRC would be to increase the transparency of organizations with regard to a broad group of interested stakeholders, many of whom are not directly interested in value creation *per se*. This is not to say that a focus on value creation is wrong (even though it is rather nebulous). Rather, perhaps the goal of demonstrating a high level of accountability should also be strongly prioritized. It certainly seemed to be a priority at the commencement of the A4S/IIRC project, but along the way the idea of accountability seemed to have been circumvented towards value creation. I leave it to others to determine the underlying motivation behind those responsible for such circumvention.

The application of 'materiality' within the <IR> Framework

The IIRC emphasizes the centrality of materiality to the reporting process. This is important, as assessments of materiality/significance are central to any reporting framework. That is, within any form of organizational report in which discretion is exercised in determining what information to include, it needs to be made very clear to report readers why managers elect to report certain information, but not report other information (often referred to as the 'materiality determination process'). That is, it needs to be clear what the decision rule is for the inclusion, or exclusion, of information in an organizational report.

In terms of the guiding principle of materiality, the <IR> Framework (para. 3.17) states that: An integrated report should disclose information about matters that substantively affect the organization's ability to create value over the short, medium and long term. The <IR> Framework further states (para. 3.20):

> To be most effective, the materiality determination process is integrated into the organization's management processes and includes regular engagement with providers of financial capital and others to ensure the integrated report meets its primary purpose as noted in paragraph 1.7.

This provides a very narrow view of materiality and reflects a very limited approach to stakeholder engagement, and therefore, if applied by managers, it could greatly impede the accountability that organizations might demonstrate. When we then review the <IR> Framework to see the perspective adopted with respect to the primary purpose of an integrated report (or applying Figure 7.2, to determine the apparent answer to the 'why report?' question), we find (para. 1.7): The primary purpose of an integrated report is to explain to providers of financial capital how an organization creates value over time. What such a primary purpose signifies is that there has been an effective shut down in the rights to information of other stakeholders. Those in charge of developing the <IR> Framework have effectively overthrown earlier notions of accountability and broader stakeholder considerations and instilled a shareholder primacy perspective. It is at this point that many people with a concern for the information rights of broader stakeholder groups and broader notions of accountability and sustainability decided that this <IR> Framework probably failed to deliver on its original promise. With this said, it is interesting that the <IR> Framework does refer to stakeholders at various points and emphasizes stakeholder engagement and the need to consider stakeholders' needs and interests. But in doing so, it focuses on stakeholders' interests associated with creating value. Indeed, as we have noted, the whole framework is about value creation. If this was done in a very sophisticated manner with holistic approaches (not necessarily restricted to monetary calculations) to valuing social capital, environmental capital, and so forth and changes therein from the broader stakeholder perspective then this might not be a bad thing – albeit it would be an extremely complicated (but interesting and illuminating) task.

However, as the 'primary purpose of an integrated report is to explain to providers of financial capital how an organization creates value over time' (IIRC, 2013, para. 1.7), and as providers of financial capital invariably care primarily about measures of financial performance, it is very difficult to understand how stakeholders, other than shareholders and lenders/creditors, are really being considered at all. Indeed, there seems to be a lack of logical coherence with respect to how the notion of stakeholders is used throughout the report. Perhaps the reference to stakeholders is to appease people who might be concerned if stakeholders were not, in some way, referred to or defined. However, the reference does seem to be rather tokenistic in nature.

Of interest also is the expectation that disclosure of material information would not be expected if it 'would cause significant commercial harm' (IIRC, 2013, para. 1.17). Even though this is understandable, it nevertheless does again reflect a relegation of accountability to broader stakeholders to a level below the interests of the owners of the organization who would ultimately be financially impacted by the release of commercial information.

The perspective of stakeholders embraced within the framework

If we look at how stakeholders are defined in the <IR> Framework, then we find the following definition:

> Those groups or individuals that can reasonably be expected to be significantly affected by an organization's business activities, outputs or outcomes, or whose actions can reasonably be expected to significantly affect the ability of the organiza-tion to create value over time. Stakeholders may include providers of financial cap-ital, employees, customers, suppliers, business partners, local communities, NGOs, environmental groups, legislators, regulators, and policy makers.
>
> *(IIRC, 2013, p. 33)*

What is interesting is that the first sentence of the above definition of stakeholders is very similar to the definition of stakeholders provided by Freeman and Reed (1983), as referred to earlier in this chapter. However, in contrast with Freeman and Reed (1983), the <IR> Framework seems fixated on the providers of financial capital and so it seems a little bit contradictory/illogical to actually use this definition of stakeholders. I am not sure if those people responsible for the <IR> Framework necessarily understand this apparent contradiction. Further, why would 'those groups or individuals that can reasonably be expected to be significantly affected by an organization's business activities, outputs or outcomes' be concerned with value creation and trade-offs between the values of different capitals? Again, perhaps a very sophisticated approach to identifying and measuring value might be embraced, but this is not clearly the case. Indeed, there is a general lack of guidance on how the whole notion of value creation should be addressed (perhaps consistent with the view this is a principles-based document). If value creation was assessed through widespread engagement with various stakeholders, then this emphasis on value creation might be a good thing – although I do not think that this is what those in charge of developing the framework had in mind. But who really knows?

To many people, the restricted definition of the perceived users of integrated reports is extremely disappointing. This perspective in which providers of financial capital, defined as 'equity and debt holders and others who provide financial capital both existing and potential, including lenders and other creditors' (IIRC, 2013, p. 33), is very similar to the users of financial reports as espoused in the *IASB Conceptual Framework for Financial Reporting*. This again reflects how anchored or influenced the IIRC seems to be by financial reporting frameworks and that the way the focal stakeholders of an organization are identified is consistent with a shareholder primacy perspective. This perspective limits the potential of a reporting framework to provide accountability to broader stakeholder groups beyond shareholders and other providers of financial capital.

What perhaps needed to be accepted, or understood, by the IIRC is that an organization – which operates within society and has effectively been given permission to operate by that society – has a responsibility, and therefore an accountability, to a broad group of stakeholders and not just to those parties that provide financial capital. This is obviously not a new idea, but it is an idea that the IIRC seems to have failed to embrace or grasp. Nevertheless, the restricted view of accountability apparently embraced by the IIRC does reflect the views of many people in business (but not all people!). The pity is that such people, with this heavily restricted view of accountability, seem to have captured the standard-setting processes within the IIRC. This is unfortunate, as the IIRC has established a great deal of support globally. This view is concerning, as once a framework such as the <IR> Framework becomes dominant, it has the potential to become the taken-for-granted approach to reporting and to shape broader reporting practices (Rowbottom and Locke, 2016). Hence, it can effectively become institutionalized. Indeed, the <IR> Framework notes that '[i]t is anticipated that, over time <IR> will become the corporate reporting norm' (IIRC, 2013, p. 2).

Rowbottom and Locke (2016) suggest that a view held by many people active in the development of the <IR> Framework is that if a broader stakeholder perspective had been embraced, as many had hoped, then the resulting reports would be overly long and segmented. Hence, from a pragmatic perspective, focusing on the needs of just the providers of financial capital allowed a less cluttered, less complex and yet more communicative report, albeit that it departed from the original stakeholder perspective. It was apparently all just too hard to look beyond the information needs of the providers of financial capital. However, why it is appropriate that the rights of financial capital providers should dominate in this reporting framework – as they do in many other reporting frameworks – is not at all clear from a broader ethical perspective.

Rowbottom and Locke (2016) further note that 'due to broad philosophical differences between the shareholder and stakeholder perspective, there was a contest to influence the interests inscribed in the IIRC Framework' (p. 101). Those in favour of a shareholder primacy approach ultimately 'won the contest'. In highlighting this extremely narrow 'shareholder primacy' view of accountability embraced during the development of the <IR> Framework, Rowbottom and Locke (2016, p. 101, emphasis added) report:

> The International Corporate Governance Network explicitly set out guidance from a 'shareholder and investor perspective' and warned against a 'wild profusion of *peripheral, trivial or irrelevant measures*'. The UK Financial Reporting Council and Accounting Standards Board also specifically advocated a shareholder-based interpretation by warning that integrated reporting could '*run the risk of being captured by particular stakeholder groups and the reporting of issues that are not material to the needs of long-term investors*' while guarding against 'increasing the length and complexity of the annual report'.

Rowbottom and Locke (2016) also report that there were many alternate views expressed by different participants in the various development phases that called for adoption of a broader stakeholder perspective within the <IR> Framework. However, the broader stakeholder perspectives were over-ridden such that the way the IIRC ultimately identified the key users of integrated reports represented a key detour from early views about what integrated reporting would or should represent. In doing so, this created the potential to alienate the interests of stakeholders who had participated in the integrated reporting project at its inception. Consistent with this view, La Torre et al. (2020, p. 1) comment that:

> The IIRC was born out of a necessity to create a reporting model that can tackle the sustainability challenges of the 21st century. But arguably, the <IR> Framework abandoned the original ideology of its promoters in favour of a capitalist ideology aligned with stock market capitalism.

What a shame! We have all witnessed how a fixation on freely operating markets has created such destruction to environments and societies.

The reporting boundary adopted by the IIRC

All efforts to produce an organizational report initially require clear decisions to be made about the reporting boundary to be applied. Paragraphs 3.30 and 3.31 of the <IR> Framework address the reporting boundary, which is defined as 'the boundary within which matters are considered relevant for inclusion in an organization's integrated report' (IIRC, 2013, p. 33). It is emphasized within these paragraphs that the reporting entity is very much based upon the financial reporting entity – a key concept of financial reporting (often simply referred to as the 'entity concept' or 'entity assumption'). Again, such a decision acts to reinforce a very restricted notion of accountability.

As Deegan (2020a) notes, generally accepted financial accounting principles adopt the entity assumption, which requires an organization to be treated as an entity distinct from its owners, other organizations and other stakeholders. According to this concept, an organization is treated as an *accounting unit* that is quite distinct and separate from the owners, other organizations, and other stakeholders; this acts to define the organization's area of interest in such a way as to limit the events and transactions to be included in the reports. The organization and the stakeholders of that organization are treated as separate accounting entities.

According to the entity assumption, if a transaction or event does not directly affect the entity, the transaction or event is to be ignored for accounting purposes. This means that the externalities caused by reporting entities will typically be ignored, and that performance measures (such as profitability) are incomplete from a broader societal (as opposed to a 'discrete entity') perspective. Therefore, embracing such a principle is very inconsistent with any quest to increase the accountability of an organization from a more stakeholder-oriented/sustainability-oriented perspective. It is not clear that the IIRC understands this apparent contradiction. Indeed, the whole <IR> Framework seems to be lacking coherence and logic on many fronts.

The 'capitals' as used within the <IR> Framework

A particularly interesting aspect of the <IR> Framework is that it refers to six different capitals. However, the shareholder primacy perspective embraced by those who developed the <IR> Framework directly impacts how these capitals are discussed. The <IR> Framework notes that:

> An integrated report aims to provide insight about the resources and relationships used and affected by an organization – these are collectively referred to as 'the capitals' in this Framework. It also seeks to explain how the organization interacts with the external environment and the capitals to create value over the short, medium and long term.
>
> The capitals are stocks of value that are increased, decreased or transformed through the activities and outputs of the organization. They are categorized in this Framework as financial, manufactured, intellectual, human, social and relationship, and natural capital, although organizations preparing an integrated report are not required to adopt this categorization or to structure their report along the lines of the capitals.
>
> *(IIRC, 2013, p. 4)*

Therefore, for the purposes of the <IR> Framework, the value being created by an organization resides in capitals:

2.10 All organizations depend on various forms of capital for their success. In this Framework, the capitals comprise financial, manufactured, intellectual, human, social and relationship, and natural, although as discussed in paragraphs 2.17–2.19, organizations preparing an integrated report are not required to adopt this categorization.

(IIRC, 2013, p. 11)

2.12 The overall stock of capitals is not fixed over time. There is a constant flow between and within the capitals as they are increased, decreased or transformed. For example, when an organization improves its human capital through employee training, the related training costs reduce its financial capital. The effect is that financial capital has been transformed into human capital. Although this example is simple and presented only from the organization's perspective, it demonstrates the continuous interaction and transformation between the capitals, albeit with varying rates and outcomes.

(IIRC, 2013, p. 11)

In relation to changes in capital, it is further stated in the <IR> Framework (para. 2.14):

Although organizations aim to create value overall, this can involve the diminution of value stored in some capitals, resulting in a net decrease to the overall stock of capitals.

As we know, the <IR> Framework suggests six different capitals, of which natural capital is one. IIRC (2013, para. 2.15) defines natural capital (the environment) as:

All renewable and non-renewable environmental resources and processes that pro-vide goods or services that support the past, current or future prosperity of an organization. It includes:

- air, water, land, minerals and forests
- biodiversity and eco-system health.

Again, there are some broader philosophical issues to consider. As we can see from the above definition of 'natural capital', the environment seems to be considered on the basis of how it supports 'the past, current or future prosperity of an organization'. We might question whether the environment should be considered in such an organization-centric and investor-prioritized manner. What about how other stakeholders use or rely upon the capitals? Certainly, there does not seem to be any notion of accountability towards future generations. Is it not the case that the treatment of the environment in an organizational-centric manner is one of the very reasons that the planet currently faces the environmental and social problems that we have created? This also represents a focus on the reporting entity (discussed earlier) rather than a broader systems-focus, which is required for any true attempt to address sustainability. Referring to the environment as part of capital seems to promote a view that it can be drawn down to support growth in other capitals. Again, this view that the environment can justifiably be used and degraded in exchange for economic gains (or gains in other capitals) is a major contributory factor to our current global problems.

The other point to be made here is that given the main audience of integrated reports is deemed to be the providers of financial capital, notions of value will be determined from the investors' perspective. Investors, in general, are notoriously short-term in orientation and tend to focus on near-term financial gains, rather than considering longer-term social and environmental costs and benefits. Therefore, it is difficult from a logical perspective to understand how this focus on value creation from the perspective of providers of financial capital (which has little to do with broader notions of accountability) can guide the long-term sustainability of business operations, or provide any real hope in addressing problems such as climate change. Surely there is a high degree of incompatibility between value creation from the perspective of providers of financial capital, and environmental and social sustainability.

In relation to the various trade-offs, the IIRC (2013, para. 4.56) states:

> It is important, however, that an integrated report disclose the interdependencies that are considered in determining its reporting boundary, and the important trade-offs that influence value creation over time, including trade-offs:
>
> - Between capitals or between components of a capital (e.g., creating employment through an activity that negatively affects the environment)
> - Over time (e.g., choosing one course of action when another course would result in superior capital increment but not until a later period)
> - Between capitals owned by the organization and those owned by others or not at all.

However, it is again emphasized that many people would argue that, when it comes to the environment, there should be no trade-off.

In considering the potential absurdity of this financial capital (or other capitals) versus natural capital tradeoff, reference can be made to various real-life attempts that have been made to place a value on various forms of natural capital. For example, Deegan (2020b) provides an illustration of valuation techniques used by certain government departments within Australia to value a certain species of possum. The rationale for such a valuation was that if the calculated financial value was sufficiently high, then a decision would be made that it would not be appropriate to use their habitat for other purposes such as logging (which would destroy their habitat and kill off the animals). But as Deegan (2020b) notes, should we place a financial value on a possum? As human beings, what rights do we actually have to place economic valuations on other species or on natural capital more generally? Indeed, do issues of economics and nature belong together, particularly when it is used to justify the possible extinction of particular species? Is there a moral justification for such a trade-off? Deegan (2020b) also refers to the famous case in Australia, in which the Australian government undertook a monetary valuation of the Kakadu Conservation Zone in the Northern Territory of Australia to determine how much Australians were willing to pay over the long term to protect the Kakadu area from mining activity. Would a high value really be the only appropriate justification for not allow mining in areas of precious biodiversity?

Returning to the accountability model as detailed in Deegan (2020a) (Figure 7.2), and given the discussion that has followed in this chapter, we can provide some broad answers to each of the four steps of the model, as shown in Table 7.2.

Table 7.2 An application of the accounting model to the <IR> Framework

The four steps of the accountability model	The apparent perspective of the IIRC
Why would the organization collect and report particular information?	To provide information to providers of financial capital about value creation over time
To whom is the organization reporting the information?	The providers of financial capital, meaning that value creation will be measured in a way that ultimately provides information about how shareholder value has increased
What information is the organization collecting and reporting?	Information about changes in the value of designated capitals
How is the organization reporting the information?	Not really clear as there is a noticeable lack of detail about how value is determined (which might be defended because it is a principles-based framework)

Referring to Table 7.2 and the discussion elsewhere in this chapter, do our answers cause us to think that the <IR> Framework is about genuine accountability? I do not think so.

Some strengths of the <IR> Framework

It is not at all clear that the <IR> Framework provides much hope in terms of extending the accountability of organizations with regard to the various non-financial aspects of their operations. However, while a number of negative aspects of the <IR> Framework have been identified, we should also – for balance – acknowledge some of the positive aspects. These include that the <IR> Framework:

- specifically encourages integrated thinking, which is defined as 'the active consideration by an organization of the relationships between its various operating and functional units and the capitals that the organization uses or affects' (IIRC, 2013, p. 33).
- requires consideration of connectivity/interdependencies within an organization. When we consider how different activities within an organization influence one another, this can lead to important changes and cost savings (and costs beyond simply those that are measured in financial terms). For example, we might terminate some products/processes that otherwise looked profitable in isolation. This seems sensible.
- requires explicit consideration of the context within which the organization operates. This is important as information can lack relevance if not enough information is provided about the environment within which an organization operates.
- requires explicit commentary on why particular items are reported – that is why they are material. This arguably improves the credibility and understandability of reports.
- requires explanation of how the reporting boundary has been identified.
- requires explicit consideration of the social, environmental and economic challenges/ risks confronting the organization. Again, at a general level, this makes sense.
- encourages information to be disclosed about how remuneration and incentives are linked to value creation in the short, medium and long term, including how they are linked to the organization's use of, and effects on, the capitals. Knowing how managers

are remunerated in terms of various assigned KPIs is important as it provides insights into what aspects of performance are actually prioritized within an organization, despite corporate rhetoric.
- encourages diagrams of inputs, business activities and outputs, all of which can assist in increasing people's understanding of what is being reported.
- requires answers to 'Where does the organization want to go and how does it intend to get there?'. Such road maps are a valuable addition to reporting.
- requires the identification of significant frameworks and methods used to quantify or evaluate material matters included within the report. Again, this is important for placing the reported information within proper context.
- emphasizes there is no set time dimension for reporting. This is also a useful point as a fixation on short accounting periods can act to create a short-term mindset.
- requires the organization to note how its governance structure supports the organization's ability to create value in the short, medium and long term. While details of the governance structure should extend beyond just their role in creating value, the view that more information about governance is required also has merit.

Concluding comments

My concluding comments start by stressing that the <IR> Framework is just one possible approach to integrated reporting, and one that seems to have numerous limitations. The approach adopted by the IIRC with respect to integrated reporting can be contrasted with the approach taken in some organizations and countries; for example, in South Africa, where for certain organizations, integrated reporting has been required for several years. While not without its limitations, the approach adopted in South Africa embraces a broader stakeholder inclusive approach to integrated reporting. That is, while integrated reporting is mandated for certain organizations within South Africa, there is no requirement that the <IR> Framework must be applied (rather, there is a requirement that information is provided about specific corporate governance principles, which have been identified in what is known as the King IV Report).

There are some possibly useful ideas in the <IR> Framework as noted in the previous section of this chapter. However, the overall contention of this writer is that the <IR> Framework was an initiative that initially showed great promise, but it was captured by certain interests at the formative stages of the project, who then could not see beyond the role of organizations as creating value for providers of financial capital. Such people were wedded to notions of value creation, efficient capital markets, the apparent necessity for ongoing economic growth and the idea that the environment is a resource that can be traded off in the pursuit of increasing the stock of other forms of capital. This is particularly distressing as this has all come at a time when the planet is in crisis and when all of us need to embrace greater accountability for the impacts we are creating for current and future inhabitants of the planet (and beyond just human inhabitants). We clearly need drastic changes in our notions of organizational responsibilities and accountabilities and what the <IR> Framework has done has effectively helped to sustain, and possibly even legitimize, a 'business as usual' approach. The more such a shareholder-focused (possibly obsessed) framework becomes institutionalized, the more damage is done.

References

AccountAbility. (2008). *AA1000 AccountAbility Principles Standard*. Available at: www.accountability.org/standards/ (Accessed: 26 September 2019).

Barton, A. (2006). Public Sector Accountability and Commercial-in-Confidence Outsourcing Contracts. *Accounting, Auditing & Accountability Journal, 19*(2), 256–271.

Bovens, M. (2010). Two Concepts of Accountability: Accountability as a Virtue and as a Mechanism. *West European Politics, 33*(5), 946–967.

Choudhury, N. (1988). The Seeking of Accounting Where it is Not: Towards A Theory of Non-Accounting in Organizational Settings. *Accounting, Organizations and Society, 13*(6), 549–557.

Deegan, C. (2020a). *An Introduction to Accounting: Accountability in Organisations and Society*. Melbourne, Australia: Cengage Learning Australia.

Deegan, C. (2020b). *Financial Accounting*, 9th ed. Sydney, Australia: McGraw Hill Education.

Freeman, R., and Reed, D. (1983). Stockholders and Stakeholders: A New Perspective on Corporate Governance. *Californian Management Review, 25*(2), 88–106.

Friedman, M. (1962). *Capitalism and Freedom*. Chicago: University of Chicago Press.

Grant, R., and Keohane, R. (2005). Accountability and Abuses of Power in World Politics. *American Political Science Review, 99*(1), 29–43.

Gray, R., Adams, C., and Owen, D. (2014). *Accountability, Social Responsibility and Sustainability*. London, UK: Pearson Education.

Gray, R., and Laughlin, R. (2012). It Was 20 Years Ago Today. *Accounting, Auditing and Accountability Journal, 25*(2), 228–255.

IIRC. (2013). *The International <IR> Framework*. Available at: www.theiirc.org (Accessed: 26 September 2019).

La Torre, M., Dumay, J., Rea, M., and Abhayawansa, S. (2020). A Journey towards a Safe Harbor: The Rhetorical Process of the International Integrated Reporting Council. *The British Accounting Review*, forthcoming *52*(2), 1–22.

Rowbottom, N., and Locke, J. (2016). The Emergence of <IR>. *Accounting and Business Research, 46*(1), 83–115.

Thielemann, U. (2000). A Brief Theory of the Market - Ethically Focused. *International Journal of Social Economics, 27*(1), 6–31.

8

THE IIRC'S JOURNEY

From sustainability to investor value

John Flower

Retired, formerly University of Bristol

Abstract

This chapter traces the development of the International Integrated Reporting Council's (IIRC) concept of integrated reporting over the nine years since the organization's foundation. It demonstrates that, over this period, the IIRC's understanding of the objective of integrated reporting underwent a radical transformation – from the reporting of sustainability to the reporting of value for investors. The chapter analyses the reasons for this transformation and perceives two principal motives: that the IIRC required its proposals on integrated reporting to be accepted, and that the IIRC had been captured by the accountancy profession and businesses. The chapter concludes that the substitution of investor value for sustainability may be in the interest of the individual business firm, but it constitutes a disaster for the planet.

Introduction

This chapter traces the evolution of the International Integrated Reporting Council's (IIRC) concept of integrated reporting in the nine years since the organization's foundation in 2010. I argue that, over time, the IIRC's concept underwent a radical transformation, and I seek to find an explanation of this development. Following Rinaldi et al. (2018), I characterize the process as a journey, and I begin with the start of the journey – the IIRC's creation.

The IIRC's creation

The IIRC was created in 2010 at the initiative of the Global Reporting Initiative (GRI) and Accounting for Sustainability (A4S), two bodies that had, over many years, worked hard to promote sustainability reporting. The commitment of A4S to sustainability reporting is obvious from its title. On its website the GRI claims to be '*a leading organization in the sustainability field*' that '*promotes the use of sustainability accounting*'. The two bodies set out the rationale for the creation of the IIRC in a press release, which includes the following paragraph:

The world has never faced greater challenges: over-consumption of finite natural resources, climate change, and the need to provide clean water, food and a better standard of living for a growing global population. Decisions taken in tackling these issues need to be based on clear and comprehensive information; but, as the Prince of Wales[1] has said, we are at present 'battling to meet 21st century challenges with, at best, 20th century decision making and reporting systems'. The IIRC's remit is to create a globally accepted framework for accounting for sustainability ... The intention is to help with the development of more comprehensive and comprehensible information about an organization's total performance, prospective as well as retrospective, to meet the needs of the emerging, more sustainable, global economic model.

(IIRC, 2010, p.1)

This statement bears unmistakable signs of the Prince's idealism: accounting is to be given the task of saving the planet! It is abundantly clear that, according to its founders, the principal task of the new organization was to create a framework for accounting for sustainability that would be globally accepted. I base this claim on two facts: the stated objectives of the founding bodies (A4S and GRI), and the reference in their press release to 'The IIRC's remit ... to create a globally accepted framework for accounting for sustainability.'

Why 'integrated'?

The title of the body created by A4S and the GRI was the IIRC and not the ISRC (International Sustainability Reporting Council), as might have been expected given these bodies' commitment to sustainability. The choice of title can be explained by the way in which social and environmental reporting had evolved in the decades prior to the IIRC's formation in 2010. These decades had witnessed a great expansion in the number and variety of reports on social and environmental matters issued by business firms: reports on such matters as the triple bottom line, and the balanced scorecard. Of particular importance were the sustainability reports based on the GRI's guidelines.

The IIRC analysed the situation in the following terms:

As business has become more complex and gaps in traditional reporting have become prominent, new reporting requirements have been added through a patchwork of laws, regulations, standards, codes, guidance and stock exchange listing requirements ... These developments, led by policy makers, companies and other reporting organizations, investors and civil society, are welcome reactions designed to elicit the information needed in a changing world. However ... many currently perceive a reporting landscape of confusion, clutter and fragmentation.

(IIRC, 2011, p.4)

There was widespread agreement on the need to bring some order into corporate reporting and in particular to bring out more clearly the connections between the different reports. The IIRC's solution was for business firms to issue an integrated report; a single report that would incorporate in one document all the information contained in the profusion of separate reports currently issued by firms. The IIRC (2011, p.6) set out its aim in the following terms: 'a single report that the IIRC anticipates will become an organization's primary report, replacing rather than adding to existing requirements'.

Why did the GRI and A4S accept the principle of integrated reporting? It seems highly unlikely that they originated the idea; the most likely source was Robert Eccles, the Harvard Business School professor, who was a member of the IIRC's original governing body, and who had written one of the first books on integrated reporting (see Eccles and Krzus, 2010).

For A4S and the GRI, the fact that business firms typically issued conventional financial statements (such as balance sheets) and a separate sustainability report had two major negative consequences:

(i) The capital market considered the conventional financial statements to be the more important and more reliable measure of the firm's performance and position. It tended to ignore the other reports as being informal and lacking in authority. Hence, the firm's management, whose position depended on their retaining the confidence of share-holders, generally based their decisions in managing the firm on the impact that their actions would have on the firm's profit as reported in their conventional financial state-ments, and ignored questions of sustainability.

(ii) Hence, the other reports, notably the sustainability report, had little impact on the way that firms were managed. There was a strong feeling that, from the firm's viewpoint, their main function was to present the firm in the best possible light: in other words, they were little more than a public relations tool.

It was felt that both problems would be solved if businesses were obliged to present only one report that combined information on both financial performance and sustainability. In this way, the firm's management in making decisions would be forced to consider the question of sustainability. The Prince of Wales, in particular, was insistent that businesses should not only report on their sustainability but also act sustainably – that, to use the Prince's favourite metaphor, sustainability should be imbedded in the organization's DNA. This would only come about if the organization's primary report (and ultimately its sole report) incorporated information on sustainability.

Integrated reporting also seemed a promising way of dealing with the defects of many of the sustainability reports issued by businesses – that they consisted of a mass of diverse uncoordinated information, with no indication of the relationships between the individual items and with no overall measure of the firm's impact on sustainability (on this point, see Flower, 2017).

I conclude that the aim of A4S and the GRI in founding the IIRC was to promote the reporting of sustainability by businesses through the adoption of a single report, which combined information on sustainability with the financial data of the conventional accounts.

The IIRC's framework

Over the three years following its creation, the IIRC issued a number of documents in which it set out its ideas for the reform of corporate reporting: in 2011, a Discussion Paper; in April 2013, a Consultation Draft of a Framework; and finally, in December 2013, after a period of extensive consultation, the definitive text of its Framework, which sets out the fundamentals of the firm's integrated report. All of these documents are of interest, notably because, in my opinion, they reveal a gradual but significant transformation of the IIRC's thinking. But, in this paper, I concentrate on the Framework, which sets out the IIRC's concept of the form and content of the integrated report of a business.

In the previous section, I claimed that the founders' objective in creating the IIRC was to promote the adoption of sustainability reporting through a single integrated report. The Framework's text in relation to these two matters will now be considered.

The single integrated report

In its Discussion Paper, the IIRC proposed that the integrated report would be an organization's primary report, replacing rather than adding to existing requirements. In the Framework, this proposal is dropped; there is no obligation to present a single integrated report. This represents a highly significant retreat on the IIRC's part; the integrated report loses its status as the organization's primary report; it becomes simply another report, adding to the clutter of reports which the IIRC so graphically condemned in its Discussion Paper.

The significance of this retreat is that the IIRC accepts that firms may issue separate reports on such matters as sustainability. Hence, the need for a firm's integrated report to cover these matters is greatly reduced with far-reaching consequences for the integrated report, as becomes clear when the content of this report is analysed later in this paper. Furthermore, the advantages of combining sustainability information and financial information in the same report are lost.

Sustainability

In the Framework, the IIRC simply ignores sustainability. The word 'sustainability' is mentioned only twice in the Framework's text, in each case it refers to a separate sustainability report, which is not part of the integrated report. In place of sustainability, the IIRC seems to favour the concept of 'value creation'. This seems clear from the Framework's definition of the integrated report: 'An integrated report is a concise communication about how an organization's strategy, governance, performance and prospects, in the context of the external environment, lead to the creation of value over the short, medium and long term' (IIRC, 2013b, para. 1.1).

The IIRC's betrayal of sustainability reporting[2]

There can be no doubt that the objective of the GRI and A4S in founding the IIRC in 2010 was to promote sustainability reporting. This is abundantly clear from the wording of their press release, which mentions 'sustainability' (or a variant) no fewer than 13 times in its three pages. But in the IIRC's Framework, issued some three years later, there are only two references to sustainability, each time to a separate sustainability report (see IIRC, 2013a, para. 1.13 and 4.48). In my opinion the IIRC abandoned sustainability reporting, an action which I characterize as a betrayal (see Flower, 2017).

But the IIRC insists that it is dedicated to the promotion of sustainability accounting. Its website is full of references to sustainability. A possible justification for this claim is that its concept of value creation (defined as increase in the value of capital), combined with a greatly expanded concept of 'capital' to include natural capital (defined as 'all renewable and non-renewable environmental resources') is closely related to the concept of sustainability. If a firm has maintained the value of all its capitals,[3] then it may reasonably claim that it has operated sustainably; for example, if the value of natural capital has been maintained, the firm's activities have not resulted in damage to the environment. Hence, although sustainability is not the Framework's central theme, it can be argued that the IIRC's proposals may cover sustainability without actually using the term. But, for this to be the case, three conditions have to be met:

- The term 'value' should be interpreted very widely, for example as 'value for society'.
- The firm should report comprehensively on all the categories of capital. If all six capitals (valued appropriately) show no decrease resulting from the firm's activities, then one may confidently affirm that sustainability has been achieved.
- But, if one or more capitals shows a decrease, then overall sustainability is only achieved if this decrease in value may be compensated by the increase in the value of other capitals; hence trade-offs between capitals should be permitted.

These conditions are now considered.

Value for whom?

The Framework emphasizes that the principal function of integrated reporting is the reporting of 'value'. Paragraph 1.7 states that 'The primary purpose of an integrated report is to explain to providers of financial capital how an organization creates value over time.'

The crucial point is the meaning given to the word '*value*'; possible alternative interpretations are 'value for society' (which is consistent with social and environmental accounting), 'value for stakeholders' (which is consistent with the stakeholder theory of the firm), and 'value for both present and future generations' (which is consistent with sustainability). The words 'providers of financial capital' in Paragraph 1.7 suggest that the IIRC's focus is 'value for investors'. But the Framework recognizes alternative concepts of value, notably in the following two paragraphs, which, in view of their importance, are quoted in full:

> 2.4 Value created by an organization over time manifests itself in increases, decreases or transformations of the capitals caused by the organization's business activities and outputs. That value has two aspects – value created for:
>
> - The organization itself, which enables financial returns to the providers of financial capital
> - Others (i.e. stakeholders and society at large).
>
> 2.5 Providers of financial capital are interested in the value an organization creates for itself. They are also interested in the value an organization creates for others when it affects the ability of the organization to create value for itself, or relates to a stated objective of the organization (e.g. an explicit social purpose) that affects their assessments
>
> *(IIRC, 2013b, p.10)*

The reference to 'others' in paragraph 2.4 seems to imply that a very wide interpretation is to be given to the word 'value'. However, paragraph 2.5 has the effect of severely limiting 'value for others' as a component of value created by the firm. The primary purpose of an integrated report is to explain the firm's value creation to providers of financial capital and hence '*value*' has to be interpreted according to their interests. Paragraph 2.5 makes clear that the providers of financial capital are primarily interested in the value that an organization creates for itself.

They are interested in the value that an organization creates for others in only two circumstances:

(a)   when this affects the ability of the organization to create value for itself.
(b)   when the creation of value for others is a stated objective of the organization.

Condition (a) is further expounded in the Framework's paragraphs 2.6 to 2.8, which state:

> The ability of an organization to create value for itself is linked to the value that it creates for others … this happens through a wide range of activities, interactions and relationships … for example, the effects of the organization's business activities on customer satisfaction, suppliers' willingness to trade with the organization … When these interactions, activities and relationships are material to the organization's ability to create value for itself, they are included in the integrated report
>
> *(IIRC, 2013b, p.10)*

These paragraphs make clear that the IIRC considers that the integrated report should cover 'value for others' only to the extent that this is 'material to the organization's ability to create value for itself'. Moreover, the reference to the information needs of providers of financial capital reinforces the suspicion that 'value for itself' should be interpreted as 'value for investors'.

Since condition 2(b) above applies to few organizations other than charities, one may confidently conclude that, when the Framework refers to 'value' this should be interpreted as 'value for the firm', and, more precisely, as 'value for investors'. The Framework accepts that providers of capital are principally interested in the monetary benefits that they can expect from the firm (in the form of dividends and other returns on capital), referring in paragraph 2.4 specifically to 'financial returns to the providers of financial capital'. Hence it is reasonable to presume that the investors' principal interest in other capitals is in enabling them to make a better estimate of future cash flows, 'better' in the sense that it is likely to be more accurate in that takes into account such factors as the quality of the workforce, possible future material shortages, and customer relations. Essentially the values of other capitals are assessed solely on their contribution to the firm's profit-making activities. From the firm's viewpoint, other capitals have value only in so far as they contribute to the firm's value.

Investors versus stakeholders

When there is a conflict between meeting the information needs of investors and those of other stakeholders, the IIRC comes down unequivocally in favour of reporting for investors. This abundantly clear from the Framework's most important paragraph: '1.7 The primary purpose of an integrated report is to explain to providers of financial capital how as organization creates value over time' (IIRC, 2013b, p.7). I consider that the Framework adopts an instrumental view of stakeholders other than investors – it may be rational to treat them fairly as this will lead to higher profits in the longer run (for a discussion of instrumental versus normative stakeholder theory, see Flower, 2017). Bearing in mind that the IIRC's concept of 'value' is 'value for investors', the instrumental view is the rationale behind the following extract from paragraph 3.11: '[The Framework] reflects the importance of the relationship with key stakeholders because ... value is not created by or within an organization alone, but is created through relationships with others' (IIRC, 2013b, p.17).

Initially the IIRC gave the impression that it favoured a normative approach to reporting on stakeholders. The Discussion Paper included, as a guiding principle, 'Responsiveness and stakeholder inclusiveness'. The word 'inclusiveness' suggests that the IIRC accepted the principle that stakeholders were part of the coalition that made up the firm – an essential feature of normative stakeholder theory. However, two years later in the Consultation Draft, the principle had become 'Stakeholder responsiveness', and finally, in the Framework, 'Stakeholder relationships', a neutral term which is fully consistent with instrumental stakeholder theory.

In the Framework, the IIRC recognizes the existence of stakeholders, and seeks to give the impression that it takes into account their needs. But it is abundantly clear that the IIRC takes an instrumental view of stakeholders – that, for investors, the relevance of other stakeholders is that the firm's prosperity depends, in part, on their continued cooperation; hence it is important that the firm should treat stakeholders properly because this will result in higher profits for investors. Thus the IIRC (2013b, para. 3.11) states: 'value is not created by or within an organization alone, but is created through relationships with others'. As already noted, in determining the content of the integrated report, priority is given to serving the information needs of capital providers. The IIRC claims that the information will be of benefit to other stakeholders, as they, in common with capital providers, are interested in the organization's ability to create value (ibid, para. 1.8). But there is no obligation on firms to consult with stakeholders on the content of the integrated report (as the GRI requires with respect to its report). The Framework's principal references to stakeholders are in the following texts: '... an integrated report contains qualitative and quantitative information that **may** [emphasis added] include matters such as ... the state of key stakeholder relationships and how the organization has responded to key stakeholders' legitimate needs and interests' (IIRC, 2013b, para. 4.31) '[but] it does not mean that an integrated report should attempt to satisfy the information needs of all stakeholders' (IIRC, 2013b, para. 3.11). The reader is left with the strong impression that the IIRC pays lip-service to the need to consider the interests of other stakeholders, but its primary interest is the needs of investors. The Framework is fundamentally investor oriented; it unashamedly accepts the need to maximize value for investors.

Comprehensive reporting of capitals

The IIRC's concept of different capitals, if applied appropriately, would certainly facilitate the reporting of the firm's impact on society and the environment, and hence on sustainability. This seems to have been the IIRC's original intention, as set out in its 2011 Discussion Paper, which states that:

> The IIRC seeks ... to achieve a reporting framework that ... reflects the use and effect on all the resources and relationships or 'capitals' ... on which the organization and **society** depend for prosperity ... and reflects and communicates the interdependencies between the success of the organization and the value it creates for investors, employees, customers, and, more broadly *society*.
>
> *(IIRC, 2011, p.5, emphasis added)*

However, for the integrated report to cover sustainability, it is essential that the firm should report on *all* the capitals that are affected by its activities, including the capital of society. The Framework's provisions in respect of three of the six categories of capital are now considered.

Manufactured capital: The Framework describes manufactured capital as: 'manufactured physical objects ... that are available to an organization for use in the production of goods or the provision of services, including buildings, equipment, infrastructure (such as roads, ports, bridges, and waste and water treatment plants)' (IIRC, 2013b, para. 2.15). It is clear that manufactured capital includes objects that are not owned by the firm (such as public roads), but only to the extent that they are inputs to the firm's production process. Objects that are not inputs to the firm's production process are excluded; examples of such objects are hospitals and schools. Thus, when these objects are damaged as a result of the firm's operations (say from pollution emanating from the firm), such damage is not reported in the firm's integrated report. Essentially external objects are only reported on if they provide value to the firm.

Human capital: The Framework describes human capital as:

> people's competencies, capabilities and experience, and their motivation to innov-
> ate including their alignment and support for an organization's governance frame-
> work, risk management approach, and ethical values, ability to understand and
> implement an organization's strategy, loyalties and motivations for improving pro-
> cesses, goods and services.
>
> *(IIRC, 2013b, para. 2.15)*

As with manufactured capital, human capital is viewed exclusively from the firm's viewpoint. From the firm's viewpoint, they have no intrinsic value: their value depends exclusively on the contribution that they make to the firm's success. This is a very narrow definition of human capital. It excludes persons who are not inputs to the firm's business model. Consider the example of people living in the local community who are killed by poisonous gases released by the firm. This is a clear example of a decrease in human capital. But, according to the IIRC, this decrease would be reported by the firm only if it had an impact on its future profitability, for example if the people killed were its own employees, if the firm suffered such damage to its reputation that future sales were affected, or if the firm incurred costs in paying compensation or fines. Of course, most firms would feel obliged to cover such a grave event in their reports, because of their need to limit and manage the reputational damage that they would undoubtedly suffer. But this would reporting for the wrong reason – to limit the damage to future profitability and not because the planet has suffered a loss of human capital. If it proved possible to suppress knowledge of the loss of life or of the firm's culpability, then, according to the IIRC's Framework, there would be no obligation for the firm to report the event.

Natural capital: The Framework describes natural capital as: 'all renewable and non-renewable environmental resources and processes that provide goods or services that support the past, current or future prosperity of an organization. It includes air, water, land, minerals and forests, bio-diversity and eco-system health' (IIRC, 2013b, para. 2.15). The important phrase in this description is 'prosperity of an organization'; there is no reference to the prosperity of society as originally envisaged by the IIRC in its 2011 Discussion Paper. The Integrated Report covers natural capital only to the extent that it is an input to the firm's production process. It does not cover the firm's impact on the broader environment. For example, a firm emits large quantities of green-house gases which lead to climate change with a catastrophic impact on the environment, such as a rise in sea-level that inundates many islands. The disappearance of these islands is clearly a loss of natural capital, but the IIRC does not require that it be reported. It would be reported only if the firm depended on these islands; say, for the supply of raw materials.

The fundamental point is that IIRC accepts that the Integrated Report should cover the impact of other capitals on the firm, but ignores the firm's impact on these capitals, except to the extent that this impact rebounds on the firm – for example, when the people killed by the firm's release of poisonous gases include the firm's employees.

The IIRC does accept that a firm may have a wider stewardship responsibility in relation to those elements of capitals that are not inputs to its productive processes. Where such a responsibility is imposed by law, then clearly the firm should report. The Framework states that 'when there is no legal stewardship responsibility, the organization *may* have an ethical responsibility to accept or choose to accept stewardship responsibilities' (IIRC, 2013b, para. 3.16, emphasis added). The significant word is 'may'; there is no obligation to report.

In my opinion, the above analysis makes it abundantly clear that the IIRC requires a firm to report on the effect on its activities on society and on the environment *only* to the extent that there is a material impact on its own operations.

In fact, the Framework acknowledges that there is no requirement for a firm to report comprehensively on its capitals. It states: 'This Framework does not require an integrated report to provide an exhaustive account of all the complex interdependencies between the capitals such that an organization's net impact on the global stock of capitals could be tallied' (IIRC, 2013b, para. 4.56). However, the IIRC is aware of the importance of firms adopting a wider concept of capital than has conventionally been the case. It considers that a firm should report on capitals that it uses, even if they are not owned or controlled by the firm – in flat contradiction of the IASB's definition of an asset. In general the firm is obliged to report on capitals that are inputs to its production process (such as public roads), since the firm's profitability will generally be affected by the condition of these capitals. But it will often be the case that a firm's activities have a negative impact on other capitals but no significant impact on the firm's long-term profitability. In such a case, according to the Framework, there is no requirement to report this negative impact. This conclusion is based on the interpretation of 'value' as 'value for investors'; if the IIRC had adopted a wider concept of value, such as 'value for society' then it would have been necessary for the firm to report on its impact of its activities on all capitals, irrespective of the impact on its profitability.

Trade-offs between capitals

The IIRC accepts that it is appropriate to trade-off a decrease in the value of one category of capital against an increase in another category. For example, the Framework states that 'an integrated report … may also include a discussion of the nature and magnitude of the significant trade-offs that influence the selection of inputs' (IIRC, 2013b, para. 4.16). All trade-offs are problematic in view of the difficulty of measuring the different capitals in consistent and comparable ways. But trade-offs involving natural capital are surely highly unlikely to be in the interests of society as a whole.

The question of whether an increase in one form of capital may compensate for a decline in another form is one of the most hotly disputed topics in the theory of sustainability. For example, the advocates of very strong sustainability claim that no trade-off between natural capital and manufactured capital is permissible, whereas the advocates of weak sustainability accept limited trade-offs (for an analysis of the various grades of sustainability, see Flower, 2017). The Framework ignores the debate between the advocates of the different degrees of sustainability. It simply accepts that firms will make trade-offs. The Framework states that integrated report should disclose 'the important trade-offs that influence value creation' giving as an example 'creating employment through an activity that negatively affects the environment' (IIRC, 2013b, para. 4.56).

I feel that this quotation gives the game away. The IIRC developed the concept of different capitals as a means of enabling firms to justify damaging the environment. Such damage may be justified by an increase in another category of capital, including financial capital.

The abandoning of sustainability

The previous four sections have clearly demonstrated that the three conditions for the IIRC's reporting of capitals to lead to the reporting of sustainability have not been met. In particular the IIRC does not require that firms report on the full impact of their activities on society and the environment. It is evident that the IIRC has abandoned the goal of comprehensive sustainability reporting. The Framework's references to a separate sustainability report suggest that it has assigned this task to other organizations, such as the GRI.

The current (lamentable) state of sustainability reporting

In my opinion, the IIRC has failed to achieve the objectives that its founders, the GRI and A4S, set for it. In particular it has failed comprehensively in respect of two objectives: the realization of the single report and the development of an effective model of sustainability reporting. Yet, paradoxically, the IIRC has had considerable success, for very many enterprises around the world currently issue so-called 'integrated reports' based on the IIRC's Framework.

The IIRC's success

Throughout the world, large MNEs issue conventional financial statements based on the IASB's standards. But they also supplement these accounts with reports providing information on social and environmental matters. The IIRC's Framework (often in combination with the GRI Guidelines and Standards) has become a widely used model for these supplementary reports. This is clear from the IIRC's website, which lists hundreds of companies from around the world that issue integrated reports based on its Framework, including such well-known names as (in alphabetical order) Asahi Group, Astra Zeneca, BHP Billiton, BP, Coca Cola, Diageo, Eni, General Electric, Hyundai, ING, Lloyds Bank, Marks & Spencer, Nestlé, Novo Nordisk, Omron Corporation, Rio Tinto, SAP, Tata Steel, Unilever, Vodafone and the World Bank. These data are confirmed by a survey made by KPMG. (2017), which found that 14 per cent of large businesses throughout the world issued integrated reports.

The principal exception to this general practice is the USA, where the conventional financial statements are based on US GAAP, and the supplementary reports are based on the standards of the Sustainability Accounting Standards Board (SASB). But the SASB does not represent a rival to the IIRC for two reasons: its standards are directed solely at companies listed on an American stock exchange, and its approach is essentially similar to the IIRC's.

Personally, I do not celebrate this wide adoption of integrated reporting, for I consider that the integrated reports, as defined in the IIRC's Framework, suffer from a number of deficiencies that are so serious as to render them a thoroughly inadequate account of sustainability.

Inadequate reporting of damage to the environment and to society

The gravest deficiency in the IIRC's integrated report is its failure to report comprehensively on the damage that the firm's activities have inflicted on the environment and on society. This failure has been comprehensively analysed in previous sections. It is abundantly clear that the integrated report covers only half of the relationship between the firm and the context in which it operates: both the natural environment and the wider society. It covers the impact of these factors on the firm but not the impact of the firm on these factors — the integrated report tells only half of the story and regrettably the less important half.

The sustainability of the firm versus the sustainability of the planet

In much of current sustainability reporting by business firms, there is confusion about *what* is being sustained. Two very different interpretations of the term 'sustainability' are possible: sustainability of the business (the business will continue to exist and flourish in the future) and sustainability of life on the planet. The former seems to be the IIRC's position. Mervyn King, at one time the IIRC's chairman, has claimed of integrated reporting that it 'equips companies to … be better prepared to manage any risks that may compromise the long-term sustainability of the business' (IIRC, 2010). The IIRC's emphasis on the sustainability of the business is confirmed by the stress that it places on 'value for the investor' as demonstrated above.

The IIRC would probably claim that its proposals will lead to firms giving more attention to questions of sustainability than is presently the case. For example, according to the IIRC, firms should consider the impact of their activities on the stocks of natural capital that are inputs to their operations, particularly in the longer run. In doing so, firms may come to appreciate better the danger of future shortages of raw materials and hence adopt a more sustainable method of operating. Firms, in acting so as to assure their own sustainability, are making some contribution to overall sustainability.

But the sustainability of the firm and the sustainability of society and of the planet are not identical, and, in assuring the former, there is no guarantee of achieving the latter.

I conclude that the IIRC abandoned sustainability accounting in favour of creating value for investors, or, to put it more bluntly, it has accepted the aim of promoting investor value.

Value for investors and the role of financial capital

I base my claim that the IIRC has adopted the objective of promoting investor value on the importance that the organization attaches to financial capital. Financial capital is one of the six categories of capital, equal in status to the other five, but it is a very strange form of capital. As Chris Nobes has pointed out, the concept of 'capital' is ambiguous: sometimes it refers to an asset, as in capital gains tax where the word 'capital' refers to an asset that has increased in value, and sometimes it refers to the opposite of an asset – a source of funds, as in share capital (Nobes, 2015). Nobes considers that, because of this ambiguity, the term 'financial capital' in the IIRC's Framework is incoherent. It can be interpreted as referring to three quite different concepts:

• The total capital provided by investors.
• The firm's total assets.
• The firm's financial assets (such as cash and debtors), which are not reported under any other category of capital (such as manufactured capital).

The first concept can be ruled out as it would make financial capital the opposite of the other five capitals, which are all assets.

The second concept can be ruled out, because it would involve double counting of the assets reported under manufactured capital, intellectual capital and so on.

The third concept can be ruled out because it would contradict the rest of the Framework – for example, it would be nonsense to hold that the providers of financial capital mentioned in paragraph 1.7 provide only the funds for financial assets and not for machines and other non-financial assets. Furthermore, a firm's financial assets are not a component of global capital. All financial assets are claims against other persons and firms,[4] with the consequence that, from the view-point of society, their net value is nil.

According to this analysis, the IIRC included in the Framework a category of capital that is incoherent. Why did the IIRC do this? I believe that its principal reason was to demonstrate to investors that it was serious about enhancing the value of their investment.

Why did the IIRC abandon sustainability reporting?

Why did the IIRC abandon sustainability reporting and instead adopt the objective of reporting value for investors? I believe that there were two principal reasons: regulatory capture and the need for acceptance.

Regulatory capture

In my opinion, the IIRC's Framework does not require business firms to provide a full account of their (often negative) impacts on the environment and on society. In fact, the Framework places very few onerous reporting requirements on the business firm (for an analysis, see Flower, 2015). I believe that the reason for this very accommodating attitude is that the IIRC has been captured by business interests. The process started when the IIRC was formally incorporated in August 2010. The IIRC's most remarkable feature at its incorporation was the extraordinarily high-powered character of its governing body, its Council. Among its 40 members were the heads of the IASB,[5] FASB,[6] IFAC[7] and IOSCO,[8] the CEOs of the 'Big Four',[9] the heads of the major British professional accountancy bodies and the CFOs of major multi-nationals, such as Nestlé, Tata and HSBC. The council was dominated by the accountancy profession, preparers and regulators, who made up more than half its members.[10] They outnumbered by far the few representatives of organizations that promoted social and environmental accounting.[11] The strong representation of business interests and conventional accountants[12] sent an ambiguous

Table 8.1 Composition of the IIRC board of directors (September 2019)

Name	Background
Barry Melancon	President and CEO, AICPA
Pru Bennet	Former Managing Director, Blackrock; Principal of Guerdon Associates, a business consultancy
Michael Bray	Director of Better Business Reporting, KPMG
Aron Cramer	President & CEO of BSR*
Helen Brand	Chief Executive ACCA
Richard Sexton	Vice Chairman, Global Assurance, PwC
Louise Davidson	CEO, Australian Council of Superannuation Investors
Izumi Kobayashi	Vice Chair, Japan Association of Corporate Executives
David Nussbaum	Former Chief Executive, WWF-UK; chartered accountant
U.K.Sinha	Chair, Securities & Exchange Board of India

* According to its website, BSR is a global non-profit organization that works with a network of over 250 member companies to build a just and sustainable world.

message: either they were genuinely interested in reforming financial reporting or they were determined to control a new initiative that threatened their established position. Over time it has become clear which interpretation was correct.

The council is instrumental in the appointment of the members of the IIRC's board of directors, the body that oversee the management of the organization. The membership of the current (2019) board is presented in Table 8.1. As shown in Table 8.1, nine of the ten members of the IIRC's board have a background in business management, accountancy or securities regulation. There are no representatives of employees or consumers. Conspicuously absent are NGOs that actively seek to protect the environment, such as Greenpeace, or academics who have adopted a critical attitude towards the destruction of the environment by business, such as Rob Gray, the former director of CSEAR (Centre for Social and Environmental Accounting Research). Rob Gray knows more about accounting for the environment than anyone else on the planet. Why is he not on the IIRC's Board? The answer is obvious. He would articulate the case for the protection of the environment in a way that would embarrass businessmen. The sole member of the board with a background in the environmental movement is David Nussbaum. He has had a very varied career. He qualified as a chartered accountant and worked for fifteen years in business, before becoming the finance director of Oxfam in 1997. Since then he has worked for a number of charities including Transparency International and WWF-UK. I feel (perhaps unfairly) that David Nussbaum, given his background in business, is likely to take a business-friendly approach to the obligations to be required of firms, and, even if I am wrong in this supposition, he would be outnumbered nine to one by the other members of the Board.[13]

The need for acceptance

The IIRC has continually to justify its existence; the most effective way of demonstrating its usefulness is by its proposals being accepted and implemented by business firms. This is very clear from a note by Paul Druckman, the IIRC's then Chief Executive, posted on the IIRC's website. The following extract from the note gives a good impression of its overall message:

A key aspect of our culture is that we have always been market-led. So as we created the Framework it was the 100+ businesses and 30 institutional investors who provided detailed input, rigour and critique to the whole process. As a result of the experimentation and innovation of our pioneers – businesses like Tata, Unilever and Nestlé – we created the conditions for market acceptance. I wanted to apply the same market-led rigour to the IIRC as a team. It surprised some of those I brought into the IIRC when I told them that we were creating an organization that could easily be dismantled if there was an allergic reaction in the market to what we were offering … If the market did not want Integrated Reporting, we would not have pursued our mission.

(IIRC, 2016)

This extract makes abundantly clear that the IIRC's Framework was deliberately designed to appeal to the 'market'. For Paul Druckman, the market was 100+ businesses and 30 institutional investors. At that time (as is still the case today) the management of business firms were obsessed with the need to deliver shareholder value – to maximize (or at least to give the impression of maximizing) the return to shareholders. That would be the preoccupation of the management of the 100+ businesses who contributed to the development of the Framework's text. It would also be the principal concern of the 30 institutional investors. The overriding influence of these parties is clear in the wording of what is arguably the Framework's most important paragraph: '1.7 The primary purpose of an integrated report is to explain to providers of financial capital how an organization creates value over time' (IIRC, 2013b, p.7). The providers of financial capital had to be assured that, in the Framework, their interests were taken fully into account. This was achieved by including financial capital alongside the other five capitals as an element that should be considered in assessing the firm's position and performance. The implicit message is: integrated reporting is completely consistent with the need for the firm's management to maximize the return to providers of financial capital.

The IIRC's journey

The evolution of the concept of integrated reporting from the reporting of sustainability to the reporting of value for investors may be likened to a journey. Rinaldi and colleagues (2018), drawing on the prior research of Perry-Smith and Mannucci (2017), sketch four phases of the journey:

- Generation phase, in which a potentially useful (but untested) idea is chosen for further development, as being (probably) more useful than the others. In the case of the IIRC, this phase was initiated by the GRI and A4S, and culminated in the publication of the Discussion Paper.
- Elaboration phase, in which the idea is further clarified and developed. During this phase, the IIRC consulted very widely, leading to considerable modifications to the initial idea. The output of this phase was the Framework. It is noteworthy that, since its publication, the Framework has not been modified, which suggests that this phase has been successfully completed.
- Championship phase, in which the idea is actively promoted with the aim of achieving general acceptance. This activity occupied much of the IIRC's time and effort during

the five years following the Framework's publication. The wide acceptance of the IIRC's idea of integrated reporting (demonstrated in Section 6.1) suggests that this phase has also been successfully completed.

- Idea implementation phase, in which the idea is implemented in the real world. In the case of the IIRC, this means that businesses actually issue integrated reports, putting into practice the ideas in the Framework. This is the current phase of the IIRC's journey.

This chapter is concerned almost exclusively with the elaboration phase, in which the IIRC subjected the original idea of A4S and GRI to detailed scrutiny and evaluated the chances of success – that it would successfully pass through the remaining phases, ultimately being implemented throughout the world. The IIRC decided that, for this to happen, the original idea needed to be radically changed – from accounting for sustainability to reporting on value for investors.

My conclusions

Some five years ago, I wrote a paper in which I claimed that the IIRC had been a failure (Flower, 2015). On its own terms, it has been a striking success, for, as demonstrated, its concept of integrated reporting has been accepted and is being implemented by businesses throughout the world. However, from the viewpoint of the planet, this is a disaster, as the IIRC's concept of integrated reporting does not require businesses to report fully on the damage that they are inflicting on the environment.

In my opinion the reason that so many business firms issue sustainability reports based on the IIRC's Framework is that it offers them the opportunity of giving the impression that they are serious about sustainability, without revealing anything about the true impact of their activities on sustainability. This enables business firms to continue to harm the environment while giving the impression that they are sustainable.

This contradiction is possible because the IIRC's concept of sustainability is the sustainability of the firm and not the sustainability of the planet. There is no doubt that it is in the interests of the individual firm to take into account many matters external to the firm, notably in relation to the state of the environment and society – such as the reliability of future supplies of raw materials, the need to anticipate future threats arising from climate change, the desirability of having good relations with the local community and so on. In stimulating business firms to consider such matters, the IIRC makes a significant contribution to the continued survival of the individual capitalist firm and hence to the survival of capitalism.

I consider the IIRC's proposals to be an extremely clever way of enabling capitalist firms to carry on 'business as usual'; that is, to continue their present operations with only minimal changes in their mode of operations – essentially only changes that are in their own individual long-term interests. But this does not alter the incontrovertible fact that the present mode of operation of the global capitalist economic system is unsustainable. In the longer run, the system will collapse under the combined impact of the unsustainable operations of the totality of capitalist firms, which, in their sustainability reports, have been deceiving both themselves and the general public into believing that they have been operated in a sustainable fashion.

Notes

1 The Prince of Wales, the next in line to the British throne, had been instrumental in setting up A4S.
2 This section draws heavily on Flower (2017), Chapter 7, Section 4.

3 In addition to natural capital, the Framework lists five other categories of capital: financial capital, manufactured capital, intellectual capital, human capital, and social and relationship capital.

4 Cash (notes and coins) may be considered to be a claim against the Bank of England, and hence is a claim against 'other persons or firms'.

5 The International Accounting Standards Board, the world's independent standard-setting body.

6 The Financial Accounting Standards Board, the USA's standard-setting body.

7 The International Federation of Accountants represents the accountancy profession at the global level.

8 The International Organization of Securities Commissions represents the regulators of securities markets at the global level.

9 'The 'Big Four' are the four largest private accountancy firms: Deloitte, Ernst & Young, KPMG and PriceWaterhouseCoopers.

10 Of the Council's 40 members, 10 represented the accountancy profession (institutes and firms), 10 represented preparers (companies and pension funds) and 8 represented regulators and other public bodies.

11 The only council members who were truly independent of the accountancy profession and big business were, apart from the representatives of A4S and the GRI, John Elkington of the Triple Bottom Line (who soon left), Hugette Labelle of Transparency International and David Nussbaum of WWF. There were no representatives from Greenpeace, Friends of the Earth or radical academic bodies, such as Rob Gray's Centre for Social and Environmental Accounting Research.

12 Exactly half of the council members were qualified accountants.

13 During his tenure as Chief Executive of WWF-UK, David Nussbaum acted more like the head of a large business than a militant protector of the environment. During his last year as Chief Executive, he received a salary of £140,000 for managing a business with income of £71 million, assets of £32 million and a staff of 332. Source: the annual report of WWF-UK available on its web-site.

References

Eccles, R. G., and Krzus, M. P. (2010). *One Report: Integrated Reporting for a Sustainable Strategy.* New York: Wiley.

Flower, J. (2015). The International Integrated Reporting Council: A Story of Failure. *Critical Perspectives on Accounting*, 27, 1–17.

Flower, J. (2017). *The Social Function of Accounts.* London: Routledge.

IIRC. (2010). *Formation of the International Integrated Reporting Committee (IIRC)* [Press release]. 2 August. Available at: https://integratedreporting.org/wp-content/uploads/2011/03/Press-Release1.pdf (Accessed: 17 September 2019).

IIRC. (2011). *Discussion Paper.* London, UK: IIRC.

IIRC. (2013a). *Consultation Draft of the International <IR> Framework.* London, UK: IIRC.

IIRC. (2013b). *International <IR> Framework.* London, UK: IIRC.

IIRC. (2016). *From Narrow Choices to Balanced Decisions.* Available at: https://integratedreporting.org/news/from-narrow-choices-to-balanced-decisions-paul-druckman-reflects-on-five-years-as-a-corporate-reporting-change-maker/ (Accessed: 17 September 2019).

KPMG. (2017). *KPMG Survey of Corporate Social Responsibility 2017.* Available at: https://home.kpmg/xx/en/home/insights/2017/10/the-kpmg-survey-of-corporate-responsibility-reporting-2017.html (Accessed: 17 September 2019).

Nobes, C. (2015). Accounting for Capital. *Accounting and Business Research*, 45(4), 413–441.

Perry-Smith, J., and Mannucci, P. (2017). From Creativity to Innovation. *Academy of Management Review*, 42(1), 53–79.

Rinaldi, L., Unerman, J., and De Villiers, C. (2018). Evaluating the Integrated Reporting Journey. *Accounting, Auditing and Accountability Journal*, 31(5), 1294–1318.

9

INTEGRATED REPORTING

Reflections from a critical dialogic perspective

Judy Brown

Victoria University of Wellington

Sendirella George

Victoria University of Wellington

Jesse Dillard

Victoria University of Wellington, and University of Central Florida

Abstract

We critically assess integrated reporting (IR) with regard to its ability to engage diverse socio-political perspectives on corporate performance. Building on Brown and Dillard (2014), we argue that IR is currently dominated by a business case perspective that privileges financial capital providers and fails to take adequate account of other stakeholder interests. We propose that IR could be broadened out and opened up by applying the multi-perspectival approach of critical dialogic accounting and accountability in assessing and reporting organizational performance. We conclude that accountability should be driving accounting, not the other way around.

Introduction

> [R]esearch in the social and environmental accounting (SEA) literature suggests that an increased level of reporting has not prompted the anticipated increased levels of accountability. Accountability is limited by what is disclosed, and what is disclosed is limited by the extant accounting system (accounting-based accountability). Most current attempts at improving social and environmental accountability by increasing disclosure reflect, at best, incremental changes to the traditional accounting system, a system that has been explicitly designed to meet the needs of financial capital providers.
>
> *(Dillard and Vinnari, 2019, p. 16)*

The scope and scale of the challenges facing contemporary societies regarding climate change, the destruction of natural habitat, biodiversity loss, famine and poverty, stock market collapse, violence, war, and exploitation are unprecedented (Gray et al., 2014, p. 2).

These problems appear to be the direct result of, or exacerbated by, the primacy placed on maximizing economic growth and wealth accumulation at the expense of societal objectives, by the current neoliberal brand of global market capitalism.

Corporations and other business enterprises are being increasingly called upon to limit the current "devastation and injustice" (Gray et al., 2009, p. 550). Business professionals are under pressure to govern their organizations in more ecologically sustainable ways, and to "account" for broader ethical, social, and environmental impacts, rather than prioritizing shareholder wealth maximization. Accountants have also been challenged to help in efforts to address sustainability issues (Gleeson-White, 2014). Business professionals have responded to these pressures by increasingly reporting on their social and environmental impacts.

While some support voluntary reporting and direct their efforts towards the standardization of reports, others are highly critical. The critics argue that in producing social and environmental reports, businesses are primarily motivated by concerns with legitimacy, stakeholder management, and masking conflict. Companies cast themselves in a favourable light rather than seriously addressing their social, environmental and ethical accountability (Gallhofer and Haslam, 2003, p. 124). Thus, "neither traditional financial nor sustainability reporting truly satisfies the information needs of diverse stakeholder groups" (Oll and Rommerskirchen, 2018, p. 19).

Advocates of the International Integrated Reporting Council (IIRC) Framework present integrated reporting (IR) as a reporting mechanism that reflects a holistic view of an organization's value creation and performance (IIRC, 2013a). However, since its inception, IR has proven controversial, with policymakers, businesspeople, academics, and civil society actors divided as to whether it enhances sustainability goals (Brown and Dillard, 2014, p. 1121). Proponents perceive IR as a means of mainstreaming sustainability in businesses and capital markets. Critics argue that IR takes an extremely narrow business case approach to sustainability: adopting the language of financial economics ("capital") and focusing exclusively on "value" creation for investors and profit maximization (Cooper and Senkl, 2016, p. 497). Milne and Gray (2013, p. 20) warn that IR represents "a masterpiece of obfuscation and avoidance of any recognition of the prior 40 years of research and experimentation" and threatens to push us "even further away from any plausible possibility that sustainability might be seriously embraced by any element of business and politics".

We canvass the debates surrounding IR and discuss how the IIRC's current approach to IR is firmly embedded within business case framings of social and environmental reporting that privilege financial capital and fails to adequately account for other stakeholder interests. We argue that this dominance of the business case (which we describe as "monologic") can only be challenged through pluralist approaches to sustainability. Specifically, we explore the potential of critical dialogic accounting and accountability (CDAA) approaches to IR to contribute to a multi-perspective approach to assessing and reporting on financial and non-financial performance. We end the chapter with a brief summary and reflections.

The IIRC's approach to IR

A significant outcome of the so-called social accounting movement (Gray et al., 1996) has been the development and implementation of social and environmental accounting (SEA)[1] research and practice. The SEA project is predicated on the normative argument that businesses have a duty to "discharge information pertaining to their social and environmental interactions to a wider group of constituents than simply financial stakeholders" (Spence, 2009, p. 206). This information will ideally be instrumental in revealing the impacts of business activities – both positive and negative – on the environment and stakeholders, ultimately enhancing organizational accountability in the name of democratic ideals (Gray et al., 2009; Lehman, 1999; Shenkin and Coulson, 2007).

Contemporary development of SEA largely focuses on organization-led social and environmental reporting initiatives, including the use of methods such as triple bottom line reporting, sustainability reporting, and full cost accounting (for an overview, see Molisa and Wittneben, 2008). In preparing these reports, businesses promote their own organizational accountability and effect social change (Gray et al., 1997; Lehman, 1999). In the last three decades there has been a substantial increase worldwide in the quantity of information voluntarily reported by businesses to stakeholders (Stubbs and Higgins, 2014). Initially, these disclosures were primarily made within annual reports. Over time, as their scope expanded, social and environmental disclosures were increasingly separated into formal standalone reports and other media platforms such as websites (De Villiers et al., 2014, p. 1042). At the same time, several groups were developing voluntary reporting standards for organizations. These groups included the Global Reporting Initiative (GRI), the Institute of Social and Ethical Accountability (AccountAbility), the Prince of Wales Accounting for Sustainability (A4S) project, the Carbon Disclosure Project, and the ISO environmental standards (Bellucci and Manetti, 2018; Brown and Dillard, 2014).

The international integrated reporting framework

In response to the growing complexity and length of standalone social and environmental reports, recent efforts have focused on ways of "integrating" social, environmental, and economic information as well as integrating organizational "thinking" and strategy around economic, social, environmental, and governance issues (Bellucci and Manetti, 2018). One outcome is the development of the IIRC Framework. Formed in 2013, the IIRC represents a "global coalition of regulators, investors, companies, standard setters, the accounting profession and NGOs" who share "the view that communication about value creation should be the next step in the evolution of corporate reporting" (IIRC, 2013a, p. 1). The IIRC's long-term vision is "a world in which integrated thinking is embedded within mainstream business practice", and IR becomes the reporting norm (within private and public sectors) (IIRC, 2013a, p. 2). Ultimately, this "cycle of integrated thinking and reporting" is said to result in "efficient and productive capital allocation" and thus "act as a force for financial stability and sustainability" (IIRC, 2013a).

The IIRC Framework represents the foundational document of the IIRC's principles-based guidelines for reporting that offers "concise communication about how an organization's strategy, governance, performance and prospects, in the context of its external environment, lead to the creation of value over the short, medium and long term" (IIRC, 2013a, p. 7). An organization's ability to create value for itself enables financial returns for the providers of financial capital; which in turn is "interrelated with the value the organization creates for stakeholders and society at large", including: "employees, customers, suppliers, business partners, local communities, legislators, regulators and policy-makers" (IIRC, 2013a, pp. 4, 7, 10). By applying the IIRC Framework guidelines, an organization considers and provides insights on: (1) the external environment that affects the organization; (2) the resources and the relationships used and affected by the organization, referred to as the six "capitals" (*financial, manufactured, intellectual, human, social* and *relationship,* and *natural*[2]); and (3) how the organization's interaction with the external environment and the capitals (through business activities and outputs) create value over time (IIRC, 2013a, p. 10). The integrated report looks "beyond the financial reporting boundary" and provides broader explanations of performance (IIRC, 2013a, p. 20, emphasis in original).

Conflicting viewpoints have emerged on the potential of IR to address accountability and sustainability issues (for summaries, see Stubbs et al., 2016; Vesty et al., 2018). The IIRC Framework states that an objective of IR is to enhance "accountability and stewardship" (IIRC, 2013a, p. 2). However, both are narrowly conceived. "Sustainability" is only mentioned three times and only with reference to "sustainability report" (pp. 8, 30) and IR "financial stability and sustainability" (p. 2). Supporters of IR (some academics, many from the business community) argue that IR represents a paradigm shift from a "financial capital market system" to an "inclusive capital market system" (Coulson et al., 2015, p. 293). Moreover, they claim that it broadens "the current shareholder focus and accountability by specifying different forms of capital, associated externalities, and their respective interests" (Vesty et al., 2018, p. 1409). Critics of IR (primarily academics and civil society actors), by contrast, have questioned the ability of IR to meaningfully alter businesses' reporting practices or their accountability for sustainability issues (Brown and Dillard, 2014; Flower, 2015; Stubbs and Higgins, 2014; Thomson, 2015; Tweedie and Martinov-Bennie, 2015). They contend that the IIRC Framework is dominated by a business case approach that reinforces the status quo, by the privileging of economic and financial measures, investors, and wealth maximization. The increasing academic scepticism of IR suggests the need for more research and critical reflection on its "development, articulations, and implications within the contemporary economic, social and political context" (Cooper et al., 2019). Next, we provide a brief critique of the business case approach.

Critique of the business case approach to IR

IR is the most recent in a long line of "top-down" initiatives that attempt to produce perceived "win-wins" for investors and "other" stakeholders (Brown and Fraser, 2006, p. 104); while still privileging the former. The IIRC states the IIRC Framework is "designed by business for business" (2013c, p. 3); puts "businesses in control of explaining how they create value" (IIRC, 2013c); and "has investor needs at its core" (IIRC, 2017). Thus, criticisms of IR can be conceptualized within broader criticisms of the business case framings that dominate mainstream accounting and SEA practice. Integrated reporting has the potential to provide a more holistic view of business activities than traditional financial accounts (Thomson, 2015).

We do not disagree with the idea that businesses and stakeholders can mutually benefit from accountability measures, or that sustainable business practices can have financial value. We argue, however, that business case framings of IR and sustainability issues ignore or subordinate important socioeconomic and political perspectives. Appraisals of organizational performance fail to take multiple values and conflicting perspectives seriously and are neither critical nor holistic. Businesses essentially define their own social and environmental responsibilities, the boundaries of their reports, and how they are evaluated (Burchell and Cook, 2010); justified by the notion that "what is good for business is good for society". As Cooper and Morgan (2013, p. 420) conclude, "a faith in a harmony of interests between capital markets and societal well-being" has been disputed by a wide range of academic research – whether taken from a position of "neo-classical economic theory", "a concern with justice", or "an empirical awareness that capital market health is inversely related to many indicators of societal well-being".

By privileging the interests of investors, the perspectives, values, and accountability needs of other stakeholders[3] are not adequately considered; this is a form of institutional discrimination (Brown and Dillard, 2014, p. 1136). While the IIRC Framework guides organizations to consider how "they respond to key stakeholders' legitimate needs and interests" (IIRC, 2013a, p. 2), there are no indicators or benchmarks of whether, and to what extent, they attempt to identify or engage with divergent/conflicting stakeholder perspectives (Brown and Dillard, 2013, p. 1134; Tweedie and Martinov-Bennie, 2015). The IIRC justifies such an approach by asserting that the interests of investors are "likely to be aligned with the public interest" as "both are focused on the creation of value" (IIRC, 2013b, p. 1). This approach reinforces the highly problematic view of an inherent harmony between market and societal interests.

The privileging of investors is further consummated by the Framework's articulation of "value". The stated objective of IR is the reporting of an organization's "value creation"[4] over time. The notions of value and value creation are "confusing" and "vague" (Humphrey et al., 2017, p. 45). As Flower (2015, p. 5) questions: "value to whom?" Value to stakeholders, society, present and future generations, and/or investors? Each one of these (possibly conflicting) interpretations of value would yield different information and accountability needs, and potentially very different integrated reports and accounting systems. However, the framework leaves little doubt that value is to be considered according to the interests of the providers of financial capital:

> 2.5 Providers of financial capital are interested in the value an organization creates for itself. They are also interested in the value an organization creates for others when it affects the ability of the organization to create value for itself, or relates to a stated objective of the organization (e.g. an explicit social purpose) that affects their assessments.
>
> *(IIRC, 2013a)*

The investor focus is further entrenched in the principle of "materiality" and the disclosure of information around the six capitals. With regards to the former, when deciding whether a matter is material and thus reportable in the integrated report, an organization should disclose "information about matters that substantially affect [its] ability to create value" (IIRC, p. 18), that is, value for investors. With regards to the latter, while the recognition of different capitals has the potential to facilitate the reporting of the organization's impact on society and the environment, reporting around the capitals is "determined by their effects on the organization's ability to create value over time" and "include the factors that affect their availability, quality, and affordability" (IIRC, 2013a, p. 31). Again, this is to be interpreted within the conceptualization of "value for investors". Thus, the IIRC Framework appears to ignore the organization's impacts on these capitals (Flower, 2015, p. 6). For example, an organization does not have to report on the impact of its operations on natural capital (e.g. polluting the environment) if this does not have any "material" impact on its long-term profitability for investors (Flower, 2015, p. 7). As Flower observes, often a firm's activities will "have a negative impact on other capitals but have no significant impact on the firm's long-term profitability". Due to the IIRC Framework's narrow, investor-centric interpretation of value, reporting the negative impact is not required. Given that "the key customer" of the IIRC and the integrated report is identical to that of the International Accounting Standards Board (IASB), "this does not seem to be a brave new world" in organizational reporting and accountability (Alexander and Blum, 2016, p. 246).

The IIRC Framework fails to acknowledge the contestability of sustainability or accountability and continues to "privilege the same interests, perspectives and values undermining mainstream accounting" (Brown and Dillard, 2014, p. 1135). While it promotes a broadening out of the topics accounted for (traditionally ignored as externalities), these are still considered through the narrow lens of investor wealth maximization.

Criticisms of IR's business case approach are further illustrated in analyses of IR in practice. Haji and Hossain (2016) examine the reports of award-winning and highly regarded integrated reporters in South Africa over a four-year period (2011–2014). They find the content is "generic, often vague, and lacks contextual meaning" (p. 439) and that companies continue to use impression management techniques to "exaggerate positive outcomes while underplaying, even dismissing, negative comparisons and trends" (Haji and Hossain, 2016). Stubbs et al. (2016) examine the extent to which IR meets the information needs of stakeholders, through interviews with diverse stakeholders of integrated reports in Australia, concluding that "integrated reporting seems to fall short of what stakeholders need or want" (p. 32). None of the stakeholders interviewed relied on integrated reports as their primary or most valuable source of corporate information; and most found the reporting narratives to be "too general, irrelevant or confected to meet their needs" (Stubbs et al., 2016, p. 32). Interestingly, investors felt very little of the information was new to them and tended to have the least need for integrated reports: "Most institutional investors… have resources that provide them with extensive 'private' information about companies and their performance and are able to directly interrogate management about company disclosures" (Stubbs et al., 2016, p. 32).

Civic and environmental stakeholders felt the reports did not provide a true representation of corporate social and environmental performance. This is especially concerning given these stakeholders "are the least connected and have the least resources for having their information needs met" (Stubbs et al., 2016, p. 32). Stubbs et al. (2016, p. 32) argue this represents "a missed opportunity for companies to communicate effectively to their stakeholders", or even worse "casts considerable doubt on the usefulness of IIRC's integrated reporting framework". They call for a fundamental rethink about the value and desirability of a standalone integrated report that is "static, annual and structured to convey a particular narrative of an organization's position" (Stubbs et al., 2016). Such findings are not confined to IR. Indeed, they are almost identical to similar research on stakeholder perceptions of business case framings of other experiments with social and environmental reporting (see, for example: Azzone et al., 1997; Belal and Roberts, 2010; Diouf and Boiral, 2017; O'Dwyer et al., 2005; Tilt, 2004).

So where does this leave us? In reality, what we have is the traditional reporting logic and investor-centric model with "just a little bit more" tacked on (Dillard and Vinnari, 2019). While IR – as currently approached – may broaden mainstream accounting a little in terms of appraisal "inputs" (e.g. social, human, and environmental capital), the IIRC Framework fails to accommodate perspectives beyond the business case and reinforces the assumptions and logic of the current financial reporting regime (specifically, investor primacy and neoclassical/neoliberal economic logic). Integrated reporting is unlikely to deliver reporting that enables wider debates around organizational accountability and governance and will probably reinforce rather than transform unsustainable organizational practices. Indeed, if IR becomes the primary reporting vehicle for organizations worldwide, we may witness a reduction in social and environmental reporting and, even worse, the continued marginalization of non-shareholder constituencies and publics (Brown and

Dillard, 2014, p. 1137). This "monologism" can and should be challenged and democratized through pluralist approaches to sustainability issues and IR that fundamentally reconsider accounting theory, policy, and practice. In the next section we present one such approach: critical dialogic accounting and accountability (CDAA). Unlike the IIRC, we do not propose this as *the* way forward, nor do we seek to resolve contestability around sustainability and the IIRC Framework. Rather we offer a starting point for critical reflection and "to imagine, develop, and support democratic processes wherein these differences can be recognized and engaged" (Brown and Dillard, 2013, p. 1). Ultimately, this could lead to ongoing dialogue and debate and shared understandings – not necessarily agreement – in the spirit of democratic/agonistic engagement.

(Re)envisioning IR through a CDAA lens

> It has been argued that it is easier to criticize Social Accounting than come up with alternatives ...
>
> *(Cooper et al., 2005, p. 960)*

Having illustrated how the IIRC and its business case approach falls short in meaningfully addressing sustainability issues, we now consider how accounting and accountability systems might be re-envisioned to take social and environmental accountability seriously. Sustainability is often described as involving "post-normal", "unstructured", or "wicked" problems that are difficult to resolve and can only be understood in a context of complexity, uncertainty, and ideologically conflicting perspectives (Block et al., 2018; Dijk et al., 2017; Frame and Brown, 2008). Expert knowledge on how to resolve these problems is often "incomplete, fragmented and uncertain"; and there are significant disagreements on the norms and values at stake and the acceptability of goals and solutions (Block et al., 2018, p. 1424). For example, there is a lack of consensus among businesspersons, policymakers, academics, and civil society groups on whose values and interests should be prioritized when deciding between the importance of economic development and environmental protection; and when considering the relationships between profit-maximization and human wellbeing (Brown and Dillard, 2014, p. 1125).

In line with Gray et al. (2014, p. 4), we argue that one – if not the primary – objective of accounting is to facilitate "accountability" from one party that has the resources and power to act, to another party that holds an interest in (and can be affected by) its actions. Being accountable suggests "accepting or being coerced into, the obligation (demand) to act responsibly toward affected constituencies" (Dillard and Vinnari, 2019, p. 19). Thus, accountability provides a means by which "power and authority can be constrained and legitimized" (Rached, 2016, cited in Dillard and Vinnari, 2019, p. 19). To this end, accounting can play an important role in discharging organizational accountability for economic, social, and environmental impacts to a wider set of affected constituencies; and, thus, addressing sustainability issues. However, for centuries, financial accountability has largely dominated the remits of accounting practitioners and researchers (Tilt, 2009, p. 12). Over time, mainstream accounting has developed into a narrow discipline, with strong neoliberal and capitalist underpinnings; businesses and profit maximization are the focal points for accountability systems, relations, and practices (Shenkin and Coulson, 2007, p. 299). Financial capital providers have emerged as the dominant "affected user" group in organizational accountability relationships and accounting models (Dillard and Vinnari,

2019, p. 21). Their criteria for evaluating an entity's performance and potential have been codified into laws, regulations, and mainstream accounting standards/systems, for example the financial reporting standards developed by the IASB/FASB and now the IIRC Framework. Indeed, the usefulness of accounting systems and resulting reporting/disclosures has almost entirely been determined by their accountability and decision-making needs (Dillard and Vinnari, 2019). Even when accounting models are applied to assessing sustainability issues, they are based on the same positivistic and quantitative techniques used in financial and economic analyses: for example, cost-benefit analysis (CBA), probabilistic risk assessment, and discounting (Brown and Dillard, 2014, p. 1126). Proponents of these methods in academic, public policy, and standard-setting spheres misleadingly portray them as apolitical and capable of supporting rational decision-making that addresses a diverse range of issues and interests (Brown and Dillard, 2014.). They fail to acknowledge that these technologies – as conventionally practiced – are captured by and applied within a narrow business case/neoliberal economic lens that privileges dominant elites by, for example, "ignoring or de-valuing common property, non-market based livelihoods or the rights of indigenous peoples"; and – as in the case of discounting – implying "that costs and benefits impacting future generations are less important than those in the present" (Brown and Dillard, 2014, p. 1126). Critical accounting researchers have for many decades challenged this monologism of the business case/neoliberalism in mainstream accounting and SEA practice, arguing it has denied the plurality of (often critical) perspectives and interests in organizational accountability; and significantly narrowed and limited what information is reported, how it is reported, who the reporting is for, how the reporting is used, and even who does the reporting.

For these reasons, we contend that mainstream accounting is woefully ill-equipped to deal with sustainability issues, as its techniques, models, and methods serve the interests of dominant elites and frame the issues at stake in a way that privileges their perspectives. However, we argue that there is nothing inherent about accounting that requires that it be approached and practiced in such narrow and reductionist ways: "Depending on which methods are selected, how they are applied and the form in which results are presented, appraisal can help to 'broaden out' and 'open up' sustainability assessment in ways that support democratic interrogation of divergent perspectives" (Brown and Dillard, 2014, p. 1127).

So how could accountability and accounting be approached differently? How could IR be developed beyond a business case conceptualization to meaningfully address sustainability issues; and hold powerful actors accountable for "all their actions, not just those that affect powerful constituencies or those that can be represented through financial or consumer market transactions"? (Dillard and Vinnari, 2019, p. 28).

Critical dialogic accounting and accountability seeks to "democratize" accounting by engaging with citizens and stakeholder groups to enable them to develop accountings that accord with their own philosophical and political standpoints. Moreover, it recognizes and takes seriously the unequal power relations between organizations and their constituencies (and the role monologic accounting practices play in perpetuating these power imbalances) (Brown and Dillard, 2015, p. 2). Critical dialogic accounting and accountability refuses to privilege capital markets and financial capital providers, and rejects the idea of a "universal narrative" (Brown, 2009, p. 317). Instead, it views societies as "contests of narratives" (Brown, 2009, p. 317) with multiple constituencies that have different accountability needs, interests, values, and power. Under CDAA, accountability "takes as its starting point the rights and responsibilities of the constellation of constituencies, human or non-human, affected by an account provider's actions" (Dillard and Vinnari, 2019, p. 18). Accounting then gains its relevance through its relationship with accountability, with accounting systems explicitly designed to meet the information needs relevant to the evaluation criteria specified by the diverse constituencies (Dillard and Vinnari, 2019). Thus, CDAA systems provide the "action space" wherein powerholders' actions, as accounted for in the critical dialogic accounts, are assessed against the evaluation criteria designed by the various constituencies (Dillard and Vinnari, 2019, p. 22).

> A pluralistic environment would probably contain multiple accountability systems comprised of multiple evaluation criteria sets, and multiple, though not necessarily mutually exclusive, accounting systems. Such a perspective changes the question from "What can accounting hold someone accountable for?" (accounting-based accountability) to "What accounting is needed for a specific accountability system?" (accountability-based accounting).
>
> *(Dillard and Vinnari, 2019, p. 22)*

Informed by an agonistic approach to democracy, CDAA also recognizes that if pluralism is to be taken seriously, democratic designs need to recognize and accept "ongoing ideological contestation between plural social groups" (Brown and Dillard, 2013, p. 8) and the impossibility of "achieving a fully inclusive rational consensus" (Mouffe, 2000, p. 1). Conflicts and antagonisms are neither "disturbances that unfortunately cannot be eliminated" nor impediments to the realization of an ideal harmony (Laclau and Mouffe, 2001, p. xvii). Instead, they sustain democracy (Brown, 2009, p. 320). Indeed, the impetus for a final resolution or consensus implies the destruction of the "political", and thus puts democracy at risk (Brown, 2009, p. 321). At the same time, CDAA recognizes that choices and decisions need to be (and are) made. Individuals and groups do often reach at least a "temporary consensus" and this may involve deliberative practices and majoritarian procedures (Brown, 2009, p. 323). However, political (dis)agreements are rarely, if ever, settled definitively (Brown, 2009).

Brown (2009, pp. 324–328) and Dillard and Brown (2012) propose a set of eight principles that could underpin the design, implementation, and evaluation of CDAA systems: (1) recognizing multiple ideological orientations; (2) avoiding monetary reductionism; (3) being open about the subjective and contestable nature of calculations; (4) enabling access for non-experts; (5) ensuring effective participatory processes; (6) addressing power relations; (7) recognizing the transformative potential of CDAA; and (8) resisting new forms of monologism.

We now turn to IR and how it might be re-envisioned through a CDAA lens. As Thomson (2015, p. 20) argues, if IR is to be an authentic attempt at improving the capacity of businesses to make more sustainable decisions, then in addition to being "mandatory, plausible, understandable, truthful, and reliable"; it must "embrace and meet the urgent challenges posed by our unsustainable world". In accordance with CDAA, consideration must be given to what a sustainable world looks like (fully acknowledging the ideological and conflictual compromises made to achieve it), the limits within which businesses can operate in this world, and the vast and divergent constituencies they must discharge responsibility for/ accountability to in doing so. Then, the information needs of these "responsibility networks" (Dillard and Vinnari, 2019) can be ascertained: so they are able to evaluate whether or not businesses (the "powerholders") are performing in what the constituencies have characterized as sustainable actions and outcomes. Thus, IR should offer disclosures that render such actions and outcomes transparent by accounting "for all the unsustainable consequences of [corporations'] actions and intentions" (Thomson, 2015, p. 21).

Following the first principle of CDAA, individuals and groups with different socio-political perspectives will conceptualize "sustainability" and "value(s)" differently. Thus, they will seek to "account" for them differently – for different things and in different ways (Brown, 2009, p. 324) – and might have different information needs, claims, and expectations (Dillard and Vinnari, 2019). Under CDAA, IR cannot privilege business case perspectives above all others; and must open up the definition of "value" beyond "value for investors". Instead, IR should engage with a diversity of viewpoints and consider, for example, "value(s)" for the environment, current and future generations, indigenous communities, and the wider citizenry. This entails the establishment of a broad stakeholder base and the recognition that, because of power asymmetries, some voices cannot "command a seat at the table" (Brown, 2009, p. 324). However, CDAA does not embrace a "total pluralism" (Brown, 2009, p. 324). To address power relations, totalitarian positions or those based on the subordination of minority groups are excluded. Diversity without such limits threatens democratization.

An integrated report should inform constituencies "how (or whether) the organization is contributing towards sustainable transformation by making visible the interrelationships and consequences of that entity's actions and intentions on social, ecological and economic systems" (Brown, 2009, p. 324). This requires, for example, information on the "six capitals" that is not limited to how they affect the organization's value creation for investors; and instead considers how the organization affects (positively and negatively) the "value" of these six capitals – as defined by various constituencies in both quantitative and qualitative terms. This would also require opening up "materiality" assessments beyond currently techno-rational understandings that attempt to unify stakeholder concerns while obscuring possible contradictions (Puroila and Mäkelä, 2019, pp. 1062–1063). Materiality needs to be redefined in relation to information that is of "material value" (for various decision-making and accountability needs) to a range of constituencies.

The second and third principles of CDAA warn against the exclusive reliance on reductionist (quantitative, especially monetary) valuations as "optimal" representations that are meaningful for all stakeholders (Brown, 2009, p. 324). Moreover, they reaffirm the subjectivity and contestability of all calculations, definitions, and decision rules that "too often imply a false sense of objectivity, precision and legitimacy" (Dillard and Brown, 2012, p. 9). In line with its rejection of universalizing top-down narratives, CDAA rejects the notion of an objective accounting reality that can be observed, measured, and reported in a neutral apolitical manner that is meaningful for all stakeholders (Brown, 2009, pp. 324–325). Instead, CDAA recognizes that accountants, standard-setters, and policymakers subjectively choose what to include in their calculus and appraisal methods, and whose perspectives to take (Brown, 2009, p. 25). It argues that individuals and groups engaged in dialogic exchanges must be transparent about the subjective and inherently contestable nature of the values and assumptions on which their accountings are based so they may be open to challenging and reconstruction (Brown, 2009). As Brown and Dillard (2013, p. 1142) propose, this requires the development of "technologies of humility" (Jasanoff, 2003) that admit important knowledge gaps, recognize the importance of ongoing and critically reflexive learning, and adopt a more precautionary approach to decision-making. How could these principles be applied to IR? While the IIRC Framework states that both quantitative and qualitative/"other" information could be reported, this information is only deemed "material" and reportable insofar as it "represents the organization's ability to create value" for investors over time (IIRC, 2013a, pp. 16–17). There is no recognition of the inherently subjective nature of this information and the technologies used to convey it, nor the knowledge gaps (on (un)sustainable organizational practices) that it perpetuates. Instead, integrated reports should include a combination of "scientific, economic, financial, statistic [sic], ethical and aesthetic narratives which enable reflexive engagements involving different stakeholders representing a plurality of interests, epistemological and ontological perspectives" (Thomson, 2015, p. 21). A CDAA approach would argue for the provision of a range of financial/non-financial information and technologies in integrated reports; for example, based on different definitions of value and sustainability, and for different user groups, while acknowledging the impossibility of a fully inclusive, complete, and objective account. Affected constituencies could thus see, for themselves, the diverse effects of business activities (sustainable and unsustainable), and make their own judgements about "monetization, incommensurability and the extent to which they are prepared to make trade-offs" (Brown, 2009, p. 325). When making decisions and appraising their own performance, integrated reporters will need to engage in a critical and reflexive process that allows for ongoing adaptation, and shifting knowledges, values, and priorities (Leach et al., 2010, pp. 115–116, cited in Brown and Dillard, 2014, p. 1124).

Ultimately, this re-envisioning of IR would require reopening dialogue between the IIRC, IR practitioners and preparers, and these constituencies (many of whom withdrew from the debates long ago when their concerns were no longer being heard) (Oll and Rommerskirchen, 2018, p. 32). However, such dialogue would have to take place within meaningful and effective participatory processes, where power dynamics are explicitly recognized (the sixth and seventh principles of CDAA). This would require consideration of issues such as accessibility, rights to information and participation, engagement processes, and the ethics of dialogue (Brown and Dillard, 2014, p. 1142). The fifth principle of CDAA argues that participatory processes can only be successful if they enable individuals and groups to "speak and press their claims in their own voices"; and engage in ongoing and robust democratic debates (Dillard and Brown, 2012, p. 10). Given our conceptualization of CDAA as being predicated on the accountability needs of constituencies, they must be involved from the beginning in "engagement" processes (e.g. in redeveloping the IIRC Framework, and the preparation of integrated reports). Procedural rules must also be developed and adhered to and dialogic entitlements (by way of legal and/or authoritative information rights) given, so there is a "more even playing field" ensuring that different constituencies can speak and be heard (Brown, 2009, p. 317). If such changes are to be successful, they also require broader societal and structural reforms (Brown, 2009, p. 326). Here, we emphasize the importance of collective action against powerful elites, such as the production of counter-accounts by social movements. Counter-accounts are often used by social movement actors to contest and counter financial and other calculative models such as cost-benefit analyses and valuation methodologies; to reject monetization and valuation in certain contexts; and to offer alternative representations of "reality" to that presented by organizations.

Summary and reflections

In this chapter, we have drawn on the SEA and CDAA literatures to offer a critical assessment of IR and its potential to address sustainability issues. We argue that, as it stands, the IIRC Framework is dominated by business case perspectives of SEA, accountability, and sustainability that ignore and obscure other possible and legitimate perspectives. Flower (2015, p. 15) suggests this is due to a division in the IIRC between the "idealists (advocates of social and environmental accounting)" and the "realists (representatives of the accountancy profession, preparers … and regulators)". The latter, he contends, have won – making up the majority of the IIRC and securing the acceptance of their preferred proposals (Flower, 2015, p. 15). Whether Flower (2015) is correct, and/or the business case monologism is because of a lack of understanding or awareness of alternative perspectives, the practical effect is the further reinforcement and institutionalization of neoclassical-neoliberal-capitalist ideology in accounting. Integrated reporting dangerously supports the existing systems that have caused or exacerbated the present global sustainability issues, listed at the beginning of this chapter, that we are confronting and trying to find solutions for. This is even more concerning given the IIRC's self-portrayal as an authoritative thought leader (IIRC, 2012, p. 20), with the aim of developing "a global consensus on the direction in which reporting needs to evolve" (IIRC, 2011, p. 1).

However, we do not view such developments from a perspective of doom and gloom. In line with Thomson (2015, p. 21) we agree that IR appears to be a well-intentioned initiative, based on a pragmatic desire to contribute towards sustainable business practices. However, this potential is severely limited if it is "too deeply rooted in the business case for sustainability rather than the sustainability case for business" (Thomson, 2015, p. 21). Thus, in this chapter we have advocated for accounting initiatives like IR to be re-envisioned using a CDAA lens that engages with the plurality of perspectives in relation to accountability and sustainability; takes ideological conflicts seriously; and addresses power dynamics explicitly. A CDAA approach to IR should not only broaden the inputs of accounting (in terms of the issues addressed and socio-political perspectives recognized), but also open up organizational practices to democratic contestation. We have shown how IR could be redeveloped in a critical dialogic way by re-envisioning concepts such as "value" and "materiality"; prioritizing and understanding the viewpoints and values of non-investor constituencies and addressing their (quantitative and qualitative) information and accountability needs; and establishing effective participatory processes and rules of engagement that empower marginalized communities, and enable their voices to be incorporated into the IIRC Framework and integrated reports. We are under no illusions that these actions will not involve significant implementation barriers. Nor do we assume they will address all of the sustainability challenges modern societies face. However, we believe CDAA and its application to IR offers promising avenues for social change in and beyond accounting.

Notes

1 SEA has been referred to by many names: social accounting; social disclosure; social reporting; sustainability accounting; social responsibility disclosure; social, environmental, and ethical reporting. These terms are often used interchangeably: we use SEA to encompass them all.
2 Organizations are not required to adopt this categorization or to structure their report along the lines of the capitals (IIRC, 2013a, p. 12).
3 These include, but are not limited to, consumers, employees, suppliers, local communities, NGOs, labour unions, social movements, governments, indigenous communities, developing countries, and future generations.
4 Mentioned over 50 times in the IIRC Framework's 168 paragraphs.

References

Alexander, D., and Blum, V. (2016). Ecological economics: A Luhmannian analysis of integrated reporting. *Ecological Economics*, *129*, 241–251.
Azzone, G., Brophy, M., Noci, G., Welford, R., and Young, W. (1997). A stakeholders' view of environmental reporting. *Long Range Planning*, *30*(5), 699–709.
Belal, A. R., and Roberts, R. W. (2010). Stakeholders' perceptions of corporate social reporting in Bangladesh. *Journal of Business Ethics*, *97*(2), 311–324.

Bellucci, M., and Manetti, G. (2018). *Stakeholder engagement and sustainability reporting*. London, UK: Routledge.

Block, T., Goeminne, G., and Van Poeck, K. (2018). Balancing the urgency and wickedness of sustainability challenges: Three maxims for post-normal education. *Environmental Education Research*, 24(9), 1424–1439.

Brown, J. (2009). Democracy, sustainability and dialogic accounting technologies: Taking pluralism seriously. *Critical Perspectives on Accounting*, 20(3), 313–342.

Brown, J., and Dillard, J. (2013). Agonizing over engagement: SEA and the "death of environmentalism" debates. *Critical Perspectives on Accounting*, 24(1), 1–18.

Brown, J., and Dillard, J. (2014). Integrated reporting: On the need for broadening out and opening up. *Accounting, Auditing & Accountability Journal*, 27(7), 1120–1156.

Brown, J., and Dillard, J. (2015). Opening accounting to critical scrutiny: Towards dialogic accounting for policy analysis and democracy. *Journal of Comparative Policy Analysis*, 17(3), 247–268.

Brown, J., and Fraser, M. (2006). Approaches and perspectives in social and environmental accounting: An overview of the conceptual landscape. *Business Strategy and the Environment*, 15(2), 103–117.

Burchell, J., and Cook, J. (2010). Approaching corporate social responsibility from beyond the confines of the business case. *International Journal of Sociology and Social Policy*, 30, 11/12.

Cooper, C., Rodrigue, M., and Tregidga, H. (2019). *Special issue: Critical perspectives on integrated reporting*. Available at: www.journals.elsevier.com/critical-perspectives-on-accounting/call-for-papers/special-issue-critical-perspectives-on-integrated-reporting. (Accessed: 18 July 2019).

Cooper, C., and Senkl, D. (2016). An(other) truth: A feminist perspective on KPMG's true value. *Sustainability Accounting, Management and Policy Journal*, 7(4), 494–516.

Cooper, C., Taylor, P., Smith, N., and Catchpowle, L. (2005). A discussion of the political potential of social accounting. *Critical Perspectives on Accounting*, 16(7), 951–974.

Cooper, D. J., and Morgan, W. (2013). Meeting the evolving corporate reporting needs of government and society: Arguments for a deliberative approach to accounting rule making. *Accounting and Business Research*, 43(4), 418–441.

Coulson, A. B., Adams, C., Nugent, M., and Haynes, K. (2015). Exploring metaphors of capitals and the framing of multiple capitals: Challenges and opportunities for IR. *Sustainability Accounting, Management and Policy Journal*, 6(3), 290–314.

De Villiers, C., Rinaldi, L., and Unerman, J. (2014). Integrated reporting: Insights, gaps and an agenda for future research. *Accounting, Auditing & Accountability Journal*, 27(1), 1042–1067.

Dijk, M., de Kraker, J., van Zeijl-rozema, A., van Lente, H., Beumer, C., Beemsterboer, S., and Valkering, P. (2017). Sustainability assessment as problem structuring: Three typical ways. *Sustainability Science*, 12(2), 305–317.

Dillard, J., and Brown, J. (2012). Agonistic pluralism and imagining CSEAR into the future. *Social and Environmental Accountability Journal*, 32(1), 3–16.

Dillard, J., and Vinnari, E. (2019). Critical dialogical accountability: From accounting-based accountability to accountability-based accounting. *Critical Perspectives on Accounting*, 62, 16–38.

Diouf, D., and Boiral, O. (2017). The quality of sustainability reports and impression management: A stakeholder perspective. *Accounting, Auditing & Accountability Journal*, 30(3), 643–667.

Flower, J. (2015). The International Integrated Reporting Council: A story of failure. *Critical Perspectives on Accounting*, 27, 1–17.

Frame, B., and Brown, J. (2008). Developing post-normal technologies for sustainability. *Ecological Economics*, 65(2), 225–241.

Gallhofer, S., and Haslam, J. (2003). *Accounting and emancipation*. London: Routledge.

Gleeson-White, J. (2014). *Six capitals: The revolution capitalism has to have – Or can accountants save the planet?* Sydney: Allen & Unwin.

Gray, R., Adams, C. A., and Owen, D. (2014). *Accountability, social responsibility and sustainability: Accounting for society and the environment*. Harlow: Pearson Education Limited.

Gray, R., Dey, C., Owen, D., Evans, R., and Zadek, S. (1997). Struggling with the praxis of social accounting: Stakeholders, accountability, audits and procedures. *Accounting, Auditing and Accountability Journal*, 10(3), 325–364.

Gray, R., Dillard, J., and Spence, C. (2009). Social accounting research as if the world matters: An essay in postalgia and a new absurdism. *Public Management Review*, 11(5), 545–573.

Gray, R., Owen, D., and Adams, C. (1996). *Accounting & accountability: Changes and challenges in corporate social and environmental reporting*. London: Prentice Hall.

Haji, A. A., and Hossain, D. M. (2016). Exploring the implications of integrated reporting on organisational reporting practice: Evidence from highly regarded integrated reporters. *Qualitative Research in Accounting & Management, 13*(4), 415–444.

Humphrey, C., O'Dwyer, B., and Unerman, J. (2017). Re-theorizing the configuration of organizational fields: The IIRC and the pursuit of 'enlightened' corporate reporting. *Accounting and Business Research, 47*(1), 30–63.

IIRC. (2011). *Towards integrated reporting: Communicating value in the 21st century.* London: IIRC.

IIRC. (2012). *Understanding transformation: Building the business case for integrated reporting.* London: IIRC.

IIRC. (2013a). *The International <IR> Framework.* London: IIRC.

IIRC. (2013b). *Materiality: Background briefing paper.* London: IIRC.

IIRC. (2013c). *Business leaders: What you need to know.* London: IIRC.

IIRC. (2017). *Creating value: Benefits to investors.* London: IIRC.

Jasanoff, S. (2003). Technologies of humility: Citizen participation in governing science. *Minerva, 41*(3), 223–244.

Laclau, E., and Mouffe, C. (2001). *Hegemony and socialist strategy: Towards a radical democratic politics* (2nd ed.). London: Verso.

Leach, M., Scoones, I., and Stirling, A. (2010). *Dynamic sustainabilities: Technology, environment, social justice.* London: Earthscan.

Lehman, G. (1999). Disclosing new worlds: A role for social and environmental accounting and auditing. *Accounting, Organizations and Society, 24*(3), 217–241.

Milne, M. J., and Gray, R. (2013). W(h)ither ecology? The triple bottom line, the global reporting initiative, and corporate sustainability reporting. *Journal of Business Ethics, 118*(1), 13–29.

Molisa, P., and Wittneben, B. (2008). Sustainable development, the clean development mechanism and business accounting. In B. Hansjüergens, and R. Antes (Eds.), *Economics and management of climate change: Risks, mitigation and adaptation.* Berlin: Springer Verlag, pp. 175–192.

Mouffe, C. (2000). *Deliberative democracy or agonistic pluralism* (vol. 72). Vienna: Institute for Advanced Studies.

O'Dwyer, B., Unerman, J., and Hession, E. (2005). User needs in sustainability reporting: Perspectives of stakeholders in Ireland. *European Accounting Review, 14*(4), 759–787.

Oll, J., and Rommerskirchen, S. (2018). What's wrong with integrated reporting? A systematic review. *Sustainability Management Forum, 26*(1–4), 19–34.

Puroila, J., and Mäkelä, H. (2019). Matter of opinion: Exploring the socio-political nature of materiality disclosures in sustainability reporting. *Accounting, Auditing & Accountability Journal, 32*(4), 1043–1072.

Rached, D. (2016). The concept(s) of accountability: Form in search of substance. *Leiden Journal of International Law, 29*(2), 317–342.

Shenkin, M., and Coulson, A. B. (2007). Accountability through activism: Learning from Bourdieu. *Accounting, Auditing & Accountability Journal, 20*(2), 297–317.

Spence, C. (2009). Social accounting's emancipatory potential: A Gramscian critique. *Critical Perspectives on Accounting, 20*(2), 205–227.

Stubbs, W., and Higgins, C. (2014). Integrated reporting and internal mechanisms of change. *Accounting, Auditing & Accountability Journal, 27*(7), 1068–1089.

Stubbs, W., Higgins, C., and Milne, M. (2016). *An exploration of the information needs of selected stakeholders of integrated reporting.* Available at: www.cpaaustralia.com.au/~/media/corporate/allfiles/document/professional-resources/sustainability/report-exploration-stakeholder-needs-integrated-reporting.pdf. (Accessed: 9 July 2019).

Thomson, I. (2015). 'But does sustainability need capitalism or an integrated report' a commentary on 'The International Integrated Reporting Council: A story of failure' by Flower, J. *Critical Perspectives on Accounting, 27*, 18–22.

Tilt, A. (2009). Corporate responsibility, accounting and accountants. In S. O. Idowu, and W. L. Filho (Eds.), *Professionals' perspectives of corporate social responsibility.* Berlin, Heidelberg: Springer, pp. 11–32.

Tilt, C. A. (2004). Corporate social disclosure: The influence of lobby groups. *Journal of the Asia Pacific Centre for Environmental Accountability, 10*(2), 3–6.

Tweedie, D., and Martinov-Bennie, N. (2015). Entitlements and time: Integrated reporting's double-edged agenda. *Social and Environmental Accountability Journal, 35*(1), 49–61.

Vesty, G. M., Ren, C., and Ji, S. (2018). Integrated reporting as a test of worth: A conversation with the chairman of an integrated reporting pilot organisation. *Accounting, Auditing & Accountability Journal, 31*(5), 1406–1434.

10

ARE INTEGRATED REPORTING AND IFRS COMPETING FRAMEWORKS?

Richard Barker

Saïd School of Business, Oxford University

Alan Teixeira

Deloitte LLP and Department of Accounting and Finance, The University of Auckland

Abstract

Although integrated reporting emphasizes the contemporaneous relationship between financial and non-financial capitals, its primary purpose is to explain how an organization creates value over time. This is similar to the purpose of management commentary, which is part of a general-purpose financial report. We compare and contrast the information requirements of an integrated report with the type of information that supplements the primary financial information in general purpose financial reports, prepared in accordance with International Financial Reporting Standards (IFRS). We examine whether the information in those reports is intended to be forward-looking and predictive, whether non-financial capitals can (and should) be monetized in order to facilitate integration, and whether the reporting boundary should be drawn in different ways to serve different purposes. We find that the International Integrated Reporting Framework and IFRS do not serve different purposes or apply different approaches, but that – in essence – they are competing frameworks. While IFRS has highly developed standards for reporting financial capital, neither has a well-developed approach for reporting any other capital.

Introduction

The International Integrated Reporting Framework (denoted in this chapter as the "<IR> Framework" or "<IR>") has emerged in recent years as a credible reporting framework. The International Financial Reporting Standards (IFRS) are more firmly established. The IFRS Foundation states that "144 (87%) of jurisdictions require IFRS Standards for most domestically accountable companies" (IFRS Foundation, 2019). Although those standards focus mainly on financial information, some standards require entities to disclose

Table 10.1 Comparison of content elements

<IR> Framework	Management commentary
Organizational overview and external environment	Nature of the business
Governance	Objectives and strategies
Business model	Resources, risks and relationships
Risks and opportunities	Results and prospects
Strategy and resource allocation	Performance measures and indicators
Performance	
Outlook	
Basis of preparation and presentation	

information not directly related to amounts reported in the financial statements. Furthermore, the International Accounting Standards Board (IASB), the standard-setting body of the IFRS Foundation, has published guidance on producing management commentary to supplement and complement the financial statements.[1] In this chapter we assess similarities and differences between <IR> and the IASB's requirements and guidance.

Our central question is the following: are the <IR> Framework and IFRS competing frameworks, or do they serve different purposes?

<IR> and general purpose financial reporting

An integrated report is a "concise communication about how an organization's strategy, governance, performance and prospects, in the context of its external environment, lead to the creation of value in the short, medium and long term" (International Integrated Reporting Council (IIRC, 2013, p. 7)). It looks beyond the reporting boundary of the financial statements by focusing on those risks, opportunities and outcomes that have a significant effect on the ability of the financial reporting entity to create value (IIRC, 2013, p. 20).

A General Purpose Financial Report (GPFR): "provides financial information about the reporting entity's economic resources, claims against the entity and changes in those economic resources and claims that is useful to primary users in making decisions relating to providing resources to the entity" (IASB, 2018).

A GPFR includes general purpose financial statements and could include management commentary.[2] General purpose financial statements are a "particular form of general purpose financial reports that provide information about the reporting entity's assets, liabilities, equity, income and expenses" (IASB, 2018, para. 1.2, 1.12 and 3.2). Management commentary provides information about matters that could affect those elements. Management commentary: "complements and supplements the financial statements by communicating integrated information about the entity's resources and the claims against the entity and its resources, and the transactions and other events that change them" (IASB, 2010, para. 10).

Table 10.1 lists the elements of an integrated report set out in the <IR> Framework, alongside the elements of management commentary set out in the practice statement. Apart from some examples of the type of information that might be consistent with these elements, neither the <IR> Framework nor the IASB's practice statement set out specific metrics.

At first sight, it is not immediately obvious from Table 10.1 whether these two approaches are fundamentally different from one another, or if instead they differ in language but not in substance.

<IR> framework

The IIRC has a Framework to "establish Guiding Principles and Content Elements that govern the overall content of an integrated report, and to explain the fundamental concepts that underpin them" (IIRC, 2013, p. 7). The objectives of the <IR> Framework are anchored on the financial capital of an entity and the information needs of investors. To that end, the <IR> Framework sets out the six capitals that are intended to capture a complete picture of an entity: financial; manufactured; intellectual; human; social and relationship; and natural. We use the following notations to refer to these capitals:

$$(F, \ M, \ I, \ H, \ S, \ N)$$

where F = financial, M = manufactured, I = intellectual, H = human, S =s ocial and relationship and N = natural.

An integrated report should provide information about these capitals, and the relationships and interactions between them. It is intended to be more than a summary of information in other communications (e.g., financial statements, a sustainability report, analyst calls, or website content); rather, it makes explicit the connectivity of information to communicate how value is created over time (IIRC, 2013, p. 8).

The <IR> Framework is written to provide requirements and guidance for the preparation of an integrated report. The IIRC has not issued any standards on recognition or measurement principles for the six capitals. However, there are many bodies that develop standards related to non-financial capitals – such as the Sustainability Accounting Standards Board (environmental, social and governance), Global Reporting Initiative (sustainability) and the World Intellectual Capital/Assets Initiative (industry-specific key performance indicators (KPIs)). The IASB has standards for measuring and reporting financial capital. The <IR> Framework does not refer to any of these financial or non-financial standards.

IFRS framework and standards

The IFRS Framework sets out the objectives and qualitative characteristics of a GPFR, which apply to financial statements and management commentary.[3] The IFRS Framework also discusses information specific to the financial statements.[4] Similar to the <IR> Framework, the anchor is the financial capital of an entity and the information needs of investors.

The IFRS Framework is written mainly to help the IASB develop IFRS Standards that are based on consistent concepts. Although it is also intended to help preparers develop consistent accounting policies, that is limited to when no standard applies to a particular transaction or event or a standard provides a choice of accounting policies (IASB, 2010, SP1.1).

Financial statements

The IASB defines a complete set of financial statements as comprising the primary financial statements (financial position, profit or loss and other comprehensive income, changes in equity and cash flows) and the notes as "comprising significant accounting policies and other explanatory information" (IASB, 2019a, para. 1.10).[5]

Financial statements convey information about an entity's assets, liabilities and equity, and changes in them (income and expenses). The IASB publishes Standards and Interpretations setting out how entities are required to recognize and measure these elements, and what information needs to be disclosed about individual elements. There are 42 Standards, 20 Interpretations and two Practice Statements currently in effect.

Most IFRS Standards include disclosure requirements. Some standards specify that a particular element must be shown on a separate line in the primary financial statements, such as total property, plant and equipment. Many standards require that the notes include a disaggregation of an element in the primary financial statement, such as the property, plant and equipment disaggregated into classes or the timing of the repayments of a non-current liability.

Some IFRS Standards require the disclosure of financial information about recognized assets or liabilities that supplements the recognized amounts. For example, IAS 40 *Investment Properties* requires entities that use the cost model to also disclose the fair value of investment properties. Similarly, IAS 16 *Property, Plant and Equipment* requires entities that use the fair value model to also disclose the amounts that would be reported under the cost model. For those entities using the cost model, IAS 16 encourages the disclosure of the fair value of the property, plant and equipment when this is materially different from its carrying amount.

Some of the disclosures relate to assets and liabilities that are not recognized, such as assets that have been fully depreciated but are still being used (IAS 16), contingent assets and liabilities (IAS 37 *Provisions, Contingent Liabilities and Contingent Assets*) and synergies and intangibles that do not qualify for separate recognition when a new business is acquired (IFRS 3 *Business Combinations*). IAS 38 *Intangible Assets* requires an entity to provide a description of significant intangible assets that it controls but does not recognize as assets because they have not met the recognition criteria in IAS 38. The IASB plans to use its revision of the Management Commentary Practice Statement to consider what additional information about intangible assets should be presented in the management commentary because "[t]rying to capture the value of intangibles is a hugely subjective exercise and would pose enormous recognition and measurement challenges" (Hoogervorst, 2019b).

Entities are required to provide information about the composition of the reporting entity (group), whether some owners have interests in only parts of that group and the nature of restrictions the structure imposes on the ability to use assets, settle liabilities or use cash held in one part of the group (IFRS 12 *Disclosure of Interests in other Entities* and IAS 7 *Statement of Cash Flows*). Changes to the reporting entity, such as when it acquires a material new business, must be disclosed, including information such as the primary reason for the acquisition (IFRS 3).

The IFRS Standards include several requirements about risks to which the entity is exposed. These include requirements to disclose information about the nature of, and changes to, risks associated with consolidated and unconsolidated structured entities (IFRS 12), how liquidity risk is managed (IFRS 7 *Financial Instruments: Disclosures*), and an explanation of demand risk and regulatory risk in relation to regulatory assets (IFRS 14 *Regulatory Deferral Accounts*).

Some of the disclosures relate to how the risks are managed, such as descriptions of collateral and credit enhancements. Entities are required to explain how their activities are organized. This helps users understand how management operates the business, by reporting information that is consistent with that segmentation (IFRS 8 *Operating Segments*) and that sets out how the entity manages its net assets and its financial capital (IAS 1 *Presentation of Financial Statements*).

The accounting policies used to recognize and measure the elements must be disclosed (IAS 1), as well as changes to them and the effects of new IFRS requirements not yet applied (IAS 8 *Accounting Policies, Changes in Accounting Estimates and Errors*). Information about uncertainties associated with some elements such as inputs that are sensitive to a fair value measure must be disclosed (IFRS 13 *Fair Value Measurement*).

There is a range of other disclosure requirements for information that is not reflected in the carrying amounts in the primary financial statements, such as the characteristics of pension plans (IAS 19 *Employee Benefits*), related party information (IAS 24 *Related Party Disclosures*), unfulfilled conditions on government grants (IAS 41 *Agriculture*) and a description of non-adjusting events outside of the reporting period (IAS 10 *Events after the Reporting Period*).

Overall, while the <IR> Framework calls simply for the reporting of financial capital, the requirements of IFRS set out – in comprehensive detail – precisely what financial capital means in practice. While there are some grey areas here, in that some disclosures go beyond the reporting of amounts recognized in the financial statements, there is nevertheless a high level of structure, consistency and clarity imposed on the reporting of financial capital. Moreover, this is done in a way that suggests no obvious difference between the meaning of financial capital in <IR> and in IFRS.

Management commentary

The IASB has a Practice Statement that sets out guidance on management commentary. The Practice Statement is being revised to "help investors better understand the financial impact of aspects of business performance that cannot be adequately captured in the financial statements" (Hoogervorst, 2019b). The project to revise the Management Commentary Practice Statement focuses on information that supplements the primary financial statements by providing information about matters that could affect those elements:

(a) the reporting entity's business model, strategy, risks and operating environment that explains the entity's current financial performance and financial position and provides insights into the entity's long-term prospects;
(b) activities that could affect the entity's future financial statements, such as intangible resources and relationships not recognized in the financial statements or information about environmental matters important for the entity's long-term success;
(c) non-financial performance metrics; and
(d) forward-looking information, such as forecasts and targets.

(IASB, 2019b)

The IASB states that this information is sometimes referred to as "non-financial information" or "pre-financial information". In materials developed so far, the staff have used the term "operational information" but are still considering whether that is the best label to use.

Although management commentary is part of a GPFR, IFRS Standards apply only to the financial statements. Some of the information required by IFRS Standards, such as how an entity manages risk, seems to be more consistent with the objective of management commentary than financial statements. The IASB seems to acknowledge this by allowing some supplementary information to be presented in management commentary and incorporated into the financial statements by cross-reference. However, this constraint limits how the IASB can develop disclosure requirements for supplementary information.

While the IASB does not refer directly to non-financial capitals, there are clearly links between natural capital and 'environmental matters important for the entity's long-term success', and between intellectual, human, social and relationship capitals and "intangible resources and relationships not recognised in the financial statements". Such links are also evident in calls by investors for "non-financial performance metrics". While these links are not specific, there is no obvious inconsistency here between the concepts in <IR> and IFRS.

Non-IFRS information

A distinct issue arising in an IFRS context is that many IFRS-compliant entities include, within their financial statements and management commentary, what is variously referred to as non-GAAP or non-IFRS information, or "alternative performance measures".

Alternative performance measures have become the subject of increased focus by securities regulators. A non-GAAP financial measure is defined by IOSCO as "a numerical measure of an issuer's current, historical or future financial performance, financial position or cash flow that is not a GAAP measure" (IOSCO, 2016). The European Securities and Markets Regulator published guidelines on reporting alternative performance measures in 2015 and the US Securities and Exchange Commission updated its guidance in 2016. Many securities regulators place constraints on the presentation of non-IFRS information. For example, they typically require that they: are not given more prominence than IFRS measures; have clear and unbiased labels; include explanations of why the measures are useful; provide a clear explanation of the basis of calculation; be used consistently; and be reconciled to IFRS measures. The IASB Chairman has also discussed concerns about non-IFRS information, which the IASB has discussed in its Disclosure Initiative projects (Hoogervorst, 2015, 2016).

There is a wide range of supplementary information reported, such as alternative measures of profit, per-store sales, customer churn rates, oil and gas reserves, and environmental information. The information about non-financial capitals anticipated by the <IR> Framework would be considered non-IFRS information. Some of the non-IFRS information is disclosed because regulators in some jurisdictions require that a company disclose the information in its annual report, such as a European requirement for companies to list all of their subsidiaries, associates and some other investments (EU Accounting Directive SI 2015/980).

While such information is "non-IFRS", this means only that it stands outside the formal recognition and measurement criteria required in the financial statements. It is not inconsistent with being included in the management commentary. It is therefore not a source of difference between financial reporting and integrated reporting, but instead an issue specifically concerned with the financial statements.

Reporting <IR> capitals within the IFRS Framework

One way to classify information consistently between <IR> and IFRS is to anchor on financial information that is recognized in the primary financial statements. Such information would include material in the notes which disaggregates information in the primary financial statements, such as a list of operating expenses, a reconciliation showing the movements in property, plant and equipment or a schedule separating lease liabilities into time bands. We define this as *primary financial information*. Disclosures that are not primary financial information are *supplementary information*.

Given the structure of the statement of financial position in IFRS, it is clear that there is not just a generally accepted measurement of financial capital, but also partial measurement of other capitals, to the extent that they are controlled by the reporting entity. Indeed, financial capital is measured indirectly, as a claim on these (net) assets (Nobes, 2015). As represented in Figure 10.1, these are likely to include manufactured capital, along with partial recognition of intellectual capital (typically through acquisition), and partial (most likely rather limited) recognition of natural capital (for example, land or biological assets).

To the extent that intellectual capital and natural capital are not recognized, because they are not controlled or perhaps not measurable, they can be reported on in the management commentary. So, too, can human capital or social and relationship capital, neither of which meets the definitional test of an asset in IFRS, yet both of which are relevant in helping investors understand the financial impact of aspects of business performance.

Figure 10.1 links the <IR> capitals with the structure of an IFRS general-purpose financial report. The question raised by this structure is whether <IR> and IFRS are aligned, or whether there are fundamental differences not evident in the presentation in Figure 10.1. An answer to this question would provide two main insights. The first, on the main question in this chapter, concerns whether there is conflict or complementarity between <IR> and IFRS. The second, on the structure of IFRS, concerns why the IASB requires the disclosure of particular supplementary information. On the second of these questions, it is not always clear why some supplementary information is required. For example, the Basis for Conclusions that accompanies IAS 16 does not explain why the International Accounting Standards Committee (IASC)

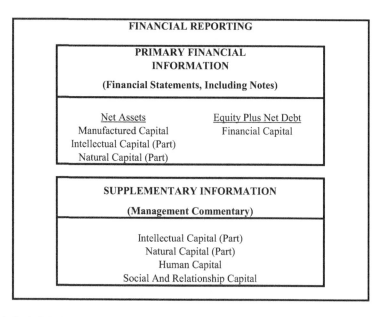

Figure 10.1 Capitals in IFRS

decided to include a requirement for entities measuring property, plant and equipment at fair value to also disclose the carrying amount that would have been recognized if they had applied the cost model.[6] It could be that the supplementary disclosures are required to improve cross-entity comparability, because of the choice of measurement model in these cases, or because of concerns about relevance or reliability of fair value.[7] The IASB has indicated that some of the disclosure requirements it is currently considering could be to help users of the financial statements assess future financial performance.

Differences between the frameworks

On the main question of conflict or complementarity, subsequent sections of this chapter will explore three possible candidates for differences between <IR> and IFRS. In brief, these differences concern whether reporting is intended to be forward-looking and predictive, as opposed to providing additional contemporaneous information (such as the variation in an estimate); whether capitals can (and should) be monetized in order to facilitate integration; and whether the reporting boundary should be drawn in different ways to serve different purposes.

Contemporaneous and predictive information

The first guiding principle in the <IR> Framework is that an integrated report should have a "strategic focus and future orientation" (IIRC, 2013, p. 16). In contrast, the IASB perceives financial statements to be "essentially backward-looking" and to contain "limited forward-looking information" (Hoogervorst, 2019a). However, the IASB sees its management commentary as the primary vehicle for providing more forward-looking information.

The IASB's characterization of the financial statements as backward-looking understates the importance of forward-oriented estimates in the recognition and measurement of assets and liabilities. The IFRS Standards require that the carrying amount of every asset reflect an assessment of its recoverability. This is achieved by either measuring the asset at fair value or assessing each asset for impairment. Fair value and impairment assessments both require estimation and consideration of future cash flows. Even simple depreciation and amortization calculations require an assessment of the expected life of the asset and its expected residual value.

The IFRS Standards also anticipate future cash outflows for liabilities. The cost of restoring an asset must be recognized when an entity's activities create that future obligation. For some activities this obligation arises when the entity begins the activity that is causing the damage to the land and results in a liability being recognized at the commencement of that activity. The IASB's recognition criteria make the reporting entity responsible for restoring the natural or manufactured capital of another entity, and recognizing it when it measures financial capital.

The Chairman of the IASB has suggested that the carrying value of assets recognized in relation to mineral resources, such as property, plant and equipment and assets, could be overstated if the impact of climate-related risks is not properly taken into account (Hoogervorst, 2019a). If this is the case either there is a problem with how the standards are written or with how they are applied.

Although primary financial information incorporates forward-looking information, there are practical reasons why there could be significant estimation uncertainty associated with some assets and liabilities. Using climate change as an example, it is likely to be challenging for many entities to estimate the cash flow consequences of climate-related activities. The cash flow consequences could be beyond the normal forecast horizon of an entity, or even if an entity is able to estimate the cash flows those outflows might occur in periods so far into the future that the present value is not material to the current period financial statements. In many cases the assets will have completed their contribution to the entity before the effects of climate change have an effect on their recoverability.[8] These considerations arise simply from time and uncertainty and so they are practical constraints for both <IR> and IFRS, as opposed to being a difference in principle between the two approaches.

In general, the objectives of the <IR> Framework seem to be broadly aligned with the IASB's Conceptual Framework and its Management Commentary Practice Statement. In particular, the <IR> Framework's explanation of the relationship between financial information and risks, opportunities and outcomes is consistent with the IASB's description of pre-financial information. The IASB states that one of the objectives of management commentary is to set out the potential impact the company's strategy will have on financial performance, which may not have yet been captured by the financial statements. The IASB uses the term "other financial information" rather than non-financial information to convey that this "other information" is a precursor to future financial performance. Management commentary:

> should provide users of financial statements with *integrated* information that … explains management's view not only about what has happened, including both positive and negative circumstances, but also why it has happened and *what the implications are for the entity's future.*
>
> *(IASB, 2010, para. 9, emphasis added)*

The discussion here suggests that, through both an <IR> and IFRS lens, future financial capital is a function of, at least some, current supplementary information, as well as current primary financial information. Using the <IR> capitals, this can be expressed as follows.

$$F_{t+n} = f(F_t, \; M_t, \; I_t, \; H_t, \; S_t, \; N_t)$$

The change in financial capital is a potential independent variable. The primary source of predictive information in the financial statements is the income statement. Importantly, while the balance sheet categorizes capitals independently of one another, the flow data in the income statement are implicitly integrated, the product of all of the capitals being deployed jointly (Penman, 2009; Barker and Penman, 2018). For example, the level of revenue achieved for a technology company is a function of at least financial, manufacturing, intellectual and human capitals, whether these are recognized or not.

This "model" could be used to examine the relationship between other information and financial capital in future periods. Some entities disclose information about their customer relationships, their employees or their relationship with the environment. Presumably they choose to provide this information because they consider that those relationships have an effect on future financial performance. An entity might consider that better (worse) environmental performance attracts (discourages) customers and therefore affects future sales. This approach could also be used to assess whether supplementary information required by an IFRS Standard or regulation has predictive qualities. A positive (negative) change in future financial capital could be consistent with the actions in relation to a capital being perceived as increasing (decreasing) future cash flows – such as a change in investment in human capital increasing (decreasing) sales, a switch to more (fewer) sustainable supplies, or an increase (decrease) in social capital affecting the award of approval to build in a neighbourhood.

It might be possible to assess whether "good corporate citizens" within a sector experience a wealth transfer (i.e., between entities) when they present evidence of a shift in their non-financial capitals. For example, does a positive action in relation to a capital by one entity lead to improved future financial performance by taking market share off another entity that has not taken the equivalent steps to "improve" that capital (e.g., improved social responsibility of one entity relative to another)?

Integration, a monetary unit and changes in capitals

A feature of the <IR> Framework is that the six capitals are characterized as being contemporaneously integrated – that is, it is the integration, trade-offs and relationships between them that are important. The question arises whether, and how, trade-offs can be evaluated if the capitals themselves are either difficult to measure or incommensurable.

The <IR> Framework describes integrated thinking as:

> the active consideration by an organization of the relationships between its various operating and functional units and the capitals that the organization uses or affects … that takes into account the connectivity and interdependencies between … the capitals that the organization uses or affects … including trade-offs, between them.
>
> *(IIRC, 2013, p. 33)*

The <IR> Framework states that an integrated report is designed to show a holistic picture of the combination, interrelatedness and dependencies between the factors that affect the organization's ability to create value over time. However, while the <IR> Framework offers visual ways to convey the integration, it does not provide a basis for assessing changes in capitals, either individually or collectively. The <IR> Framework does not explain how to assess trade-offs between capitals. For example, is creating employment through an activity that negatively affects the environment a positive or negative outcome? How can these effects be measured? How should externalities be interpreted, for example if aggregate capital is unchanged, yet employment benefits the entity while environmental damage imposes external costs (outside the financial boundary of the reporting entity)? The answer in the <IR> Framework appears to be that the reason for looking beyond financial capital is to focus on the risks, opportunities and outcomes that have a significant effect on the ability of an entity to create value (IIRC, 2013, p. 20). In this case, the approach is not directly concerned with the capitals themselves, but only with an entity's dependence on those capitals, which is an approach entirely in line with that of IFRS.

Mechanisms for evaluating the integration of the capitals – that is, how a change in one capital affects other capitals – would differentiate <IR> from earlier approaches to assessing multiple aspects of performance, such as triple-bottom line and the balanced scorecard.

Current practice, however, suggests a "relatively low" depth of integration (Gibassier et al., 2019). This same problem is, of course, shared with the management commentary. The difference is that the <IR> Framework emphasizes that the contemporaneous relationship between the capitals is important. While <IR> appears to promise more, neither actually delivers.

The <IR> Framework states that the "capitals are stocks of value that are increased, decreased or transformed through the activities and outputs of the organization" (IIRC, 2013, p. 11). The <IR> Framework includes the example of an organization improving its human capital through employee training, with the related training costs reducing its financial capital. It also refers to the possible relationships between capitals over time, stating that maximizing "financial capital … at the expense of human capital (e.g., through inappropriate human resource policies and practices) is unlikely to maximize value for the organization in the longer term" (IIRC, 2013, p. 11). This is consistent with the idea that current activities related to the non-financial capitals can affect future financial capital.

The IFRS Framework includes elements that recognize and measure changes in financial capital (income and expenses) that provide a measure of financial performance (income).[9] Positive (negative) income reflects an increase (decrease) in financial capital. Although the <IR> Framework refers to changes in capitals, it does not provide an equivalent to income for any of the non-financial capitals.

The elements recognized in financial statements are quantified in monetary terms. A monetary unit provides a unifying measure. The IFRS Standards therefore provide a basis for presenting a stock of financial capital at a given point in time.[10] Importantly, the IFRS Standards already partially capture an entity's relationships with its staff, customers and intellectual property: employees (IAS 19), customers (IFRS 15 *Revenue for Contracts with Customers*); intellectual property (IAS 38). In most cases, the recognition requirements result in these activities being captured in the income statement, rather than capitals. The information is limited, in that the flows in the income statement are typically not related to corresponding capitals, as (for example) in the case of expenditure on training (human capital) or the consumption of natural resources (natural capital).

There is no equivalent to the monetary unit for measuring the <IR> Framework's non-financial capitals. This makes comparing capitals, changes in capitals and trade-offs between them difficult, if not impossible. The <IR> Framework notes that recognizing non-financial capital "may also include monetizing certain effects on the capitals (e.g., carbon emissions and water use)" (IIRC, 2013, p. 28) but only as an example of a quantified KPI.

Overall, there appears to be no difference in substance between <IR> and IFRS with respect to whether capitals can (and should) be monetized in order to facilitate integration. There is only one, unambiguous, monetized capital in either framework, which is financial capital.

The reporting entity and reporting boundary

The IFRS Framework defines a reporting entity as "an entity that is required, or chooses, to prepare financial statements". A reporting entity does not need to be a legal entity. It can be a portion of an entity or can comprise more than one entity (combining two or more entities). This definition is a relatively new addition to the IFRS Framework, having been added in the 2018 revision.

The boundaries of a financial report can be inferred from the IFRS Framework's recognition criteria, which are anchored on a control model. Once the reporting entity has been identified, or specified, the entity reports the assets it controls and the liabilities for which it is responsible, and changes to those assets and liabilities. As well as control over individual assets it includes the assets and liabilities controlled by the subsidiaries of the reporting entity.

The <IR> Framework notes that the financial reporting entity is determined according to applicable financial reporting standards, which revolve around the concepts of control or significant influence.[11] As illustrated in Figure 10.2, the boundary for an integrated report is determined by the financial reporting entity (the boundary used for financial reporting purposes) *plus* risks, opportunities and outcomes attributable to or associated with other entities/stakeholders, beyond the financial reporting entity, that have a significant effect on the ability of the financial reporting entity to create value (IIRC, 2013, p. 19). The <IR> Framework includes an example of the labour practices of suppliers, suggesting that an integrated report is intended to capture, when it is material, activities of the supply and customer chain as well as those of the entity itself. This seems to suggest a fundamental difference between <IR> and IFRS.

The <IR> Framework could lead to the same factors being reported by more than one entity in the same supply chain. For example, an energy company might report its emissions along with emissions caused by its product. Corporate users of that product might also report the emissions related to that product. In a similar manner, emissions caused by a transportation company might be reported by that company as well as by users of its services. In contrast, the control criteria underlying IFRS financial statements should lead to a specific element being reported by only one entity.[12]

It is not clear how the <IR> Framework reconciles this broader reporting of risks and opportunities with the reporting of non-financial capitals, particularly given the lack of recognition criteria in the <IR> Framework. A reporting entity does not control the public goods it uses, the community in which it operates or its customers, nor its employees or

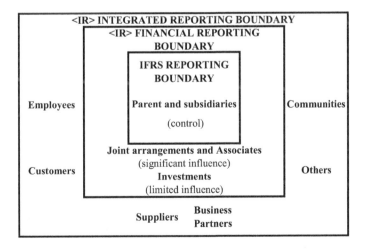

Figure 10.2 The reporting boundary

suppliers. In contrast, and as illustrated in Figure 10.2, IFRS makes a clear distinction between capitals controlled by the reporting entity and those that lie outside the financial reporting boundary but are material to it.

Based on the discussion in the previous section on trade-offs and commensurability, it does not seem realistic to measure all six capitals; nor is it consistent with the overall objective in <IR> that focuses on the informational needs of the providers of an entity's financial capital. Hence, an apparent fundamental difference in reporting boundary between <IR> and IFRS is not really a difference at all. The relevant comparison is between <IR> and GPFR, not just the financial statements. The IASB's notion of control does not guide the inclusion of information in the management commentary, any more than it does the content of integrated reports. In both domains, information is relevant, and should be included, whether or not it concerns capitals that are controlled by the reporting entity. The overall purpose of the two approaches is not different; therefore, neither is the information that should ideally be included in each.

Summary

We have asked whether <IR> and IFRS are competing frameworks. Our answer is "yes". There is nothing in <IR> that differs in substance from IFRS financial reporting.

The objectives of the <IR> and IFRS Frameworks are both anchored on the financial capital of an entity and the information needs of investors. The IASB acknowledges, and the IIRC emphasizes, the importance of information beyond the financial capitals.

The <IR> Framework expects an integrated report to include information about the six capitals including the interdependencies and trade-offs between them as well as how changes in their availability, quality and affordability affect the ability of the organization to create value (IIRC, 2013, p. 31). However, this expectation is effectively given no more substance than in the IASB's management commentary, which is also intended to provide supplementary information for the benefit of investors.

With respect to primary financial information, the IASB's financial statement reporting requirements are supported by 42 Standards, 20 Interpretations and a Practice Statement.[13] In contrast, for supplementary information, the IASB provides only the Management Commentary Practice Statement. <IR> does not have any Standards. Although there are third-party standards and guidance that address some aspects of the non-financial capitals in the <IR> Framework, none are as yet globally accepted as a basis for <IR>. There are also no standards to guide entities on the integration of these capitals.

The interest in <IR> suggests that there is at least some dissatisfaction with corporate reporting that focuses solely on financial information. The question remains as to whether <IR> can mature into a credible reporting model or whether its ideas should instead influence the IASB's GPFR requirements, and the management commentary in particular.

The IASB's Management Commentary Practice Statement already states that the information it provides should be integrated. The IASB has never explicitly acknowledged non-financial capitals, and in this regard <IR> provides a stimulus and a call to action. The IASB's project on management commentary provides an opportunity for the IASB to incorporate these aspects of the <IR> Framework principles in its Practice Statement. It also gives the IASB an opportunity to rationalize its own requirements for information supporting the financial statements, in terms of setting out principles for when supplementary information should be required and whether it should be in a management commentary or as a note to the financial statements. The Chairman of the IASB does not think the IASB is equipped to enter the field of sustainability reporting directly, because "setting sustainability reporting standards requires expertise that we simply do not have" (Hoogervorst, 2019a). However, the IASB could rely upon other bodies to develop standardized requirements for use in the management commentary. In this respect, the implication of this chapter is that <IR> does not have a role distinct from that which the IASB ought to subsume within the management commentary. The valuable role of the IIRC has been to shake up the world of corporate reporting and standard-setting, extending its scope to embrace multiple capitals. If the IASB acts to improve the Management Commentary Practice Statement to incorporate integrated thinking, it would make <IR> redundant.

Notes

1 The guidance is in the *IFRS Practice Statement Management Commentary A framework for presentation* (IASB, 2010). The IASB uses the term "management commentary". Other names for this part of an annual report include narrative report, Director's report and management's discussion and analysis (MD&A).
2 The IASB considers management commentary to be part of General Purpose Financial Reporting (IASB, 2019b).
3 We use the terms Financial Report and Financial Statements in the remainder of this chapter.
4 Those chapters discuss Financial Statements and the Reporting Entity, The Elements of Financial Statements, Recognition and Derecognition, Measurement, Presentation and Disclosure and Concepts of Capital and Capital Maintenance.
5 IAS 1 *Financial Statement Presentation*. All references in this chapter to individual standards are drawn from the (IASB, 2019a).
6 IAS 16 and IAS 40 were developed by the IASC, the predecessor to the IASB. The disclosure requirements were in the versions adopted by the IASB. The IASC did not publish a basis for conclusions with IAS 16. The basis that accompanies IAS 16 was published by the IASB and relates only to amendments it made to the standard.
7 The disclosure requirements in IAS 16 and IAS 40 were developed when the IFRS Framework had the qualitative characteristics of relevance and reliability. The revised Framework replaced reliability with faithful representation.
8 There are examples of entities providing information about risks associated with climate change. For example the New Zealand company Watercare Services Limited (2018, 2019) includes in its 2018 and 2019 Annual Reports case studies that explain how it is assessing risks such as those to assets that would be more at risk if sea levels rise or are exposed to more flooding. The reports also discuss how more extreme weather such as longer droughts and greater rainfall periods could affect the supply and demand for water and could require changes to the material used in underground pipes.
9 The IFRS Framework has concepts of "profit or loss" and "other comprehensive income" that measure "Total comprehensive income".
10 The IFRS Standards have different measurement bases, some using current fair value with others basing the accounting on the transaction price. Although the usefulness of net financial capital that aggregates mixed measures might raise some issues about usefulness, it is nevertheless a valid aggregation.
11 Despite its reference to applicable financial reporting standards, the <IR> Framework mischaracterizes the IASB's definition of the reporting entity. The <IR> Framework definition states that joint ventures and associates are part of the reporting entity, The IASB's reporting entity is based on a control model and therefore does not include joint ventures or associates. The IASB's reporting entity presents the net investments in joint ventures and associates, but the elements (assets, liabilities, income and expenses) of the joint ventures and associates are not the elements of the reporting entity.
12 This will not always be the case. Because there is some judgement involved, it is possible that some assets will be recognized by more than one entity. There are also specific examples where the IFRS Standards cause a single asset to be recognized by two entities, such as when a lessor classifies a lease as an operating lease and the lessee recognizes a right-of-use asset.
13 The IASB has two practice statements. One addresses materiality and therefore relates to primary financial information. The second relates to management commentary.

References

Barker, R., and Penman, S. (2018). Moving the conceptual framework forward: accounting for uncertainty. *Contemporary Accounting Research*, forthcoming 10.1111/1911-3846.12585.

EU Accounting Directive SI 2015/980. The companies, partnerships and groups (accounts and reports) regulations 2015. Available at: http://www.legislation.gov.uk/uksi/2015/980/contents/made.

Gibassier, D., Adams, C., and Jérôme, T. (2019). *Integrated Reporting and the Capitals' Diffusion*. Available at: www.researchgate.net/publication/334805728_Integrated_reporting_and_the_capitals'_diffu sion_-Gibassier_Adams_and_Jerome_-20191Integrated_Reporting_and_the_Capitals'_Diffusion (Accessed: 21 November 2019).

Hoogervorst, H. (2015). *Mind the Gap (between non-GAAP and GAAP)*. Available at: www.ifrs.org/-/media/ feature/news/speeches/2015/hans-hoogervorst-korea-march-2015.pdf (Accessed: 21 November 2019).

Hoogervorst, H. (2016). *International Accounting Standards Board (2016). Performance reporting and the pitfalls of non-GAAP metrics*. Available at: www.ifrs.org/-/media/feature/news/speeches/2016/hans-hooger vorst-eaa-annual-conference-may-2016.pdf (Accessed: 21 November 2019).

Hoogervorst, H. (2019a). *IASB Chair on What Sustainability Reporting Can and Cannot Achieve*. Available at: www.ifrs.org/news-and-events/2019/04/speech-iasb-chair-on-sustainability-reporting/ (Accessed: 21 November 2019).

Hoogervorst, H. (2019b). *Strengthening the Relevance of Financial Reporting*. Available at: www.ifrs.org/news- and-events/2019/06/strengthening-the-relevance-of-financial-reporting/ (Accessed: 21 November 2019).

IASB. (2010). *IFRS Practice Statement: Management Commentary. A Framework for Presentation*. London: IFRS Foundation.

IASB. (2018). *Conceptual Framework for Financial Reporting*. London: IFRS Foundation.

IASB. (2019a). *IFRS Standards, Bound Volume*. London: IFRS Foundation.

IASB. (2019b). *Agenda Paper 15, IASB Meeting May 2019*. Available at: www.ifrs.org/-/media/feature/ meetings/2019/may/iasb/ap15-management-commentary.pdf (Accessed: 21 November 2019).

IFRS Foundation. (2019). *Who Uses IFRS Standards?* Available at: www.ifrs.org/use-around-the-world/ use-of-ifrs-standards-by-jurisdiction/#analysis (Accessed: 21 November 2019).

IIRC. (2013). *The International <IR> Framework*. London: IIRC.

IOSCO. (2016). *Statement on NON-GAAP Financial Measures*. Available at: www.iosco.org/library/pub docs/pdf/IOSCOPD532.pdf (Accessed: 21 November 2019).

Nobes, C. (2015). Accounting for capital: the evolution of an idea. *Accounting and Business Research*, 45(4), 413–441.

Penman, S. (2009). Accounting for intangible assets: there is also an income statement. *Abacus*, 45(3), 359–371.

Watercare Services Limited. (2018). *Annual Report 2018*. Available at: https://wslpwstoreprd.blob.core. windows.net/kentico-media-libraries-prod/watercarepublicweb/media/watercare-media-library/ reports-and-publications/annual_report_2018.pdf (Accessed: 21 November 2019).

Watercare Services Limited. (2019). *Annual Report 2019*. Available at: https://watercareannualreport.co. nz/ (Accessed: 21 November 2019).

11

FROM SKANDIA AND THE CHURCH OF INTELLECTUAL CAPITAL TO THE MYTHICAL CHURCH OF THE INTERNATIONAL INTEGRATED REPORTING COUNCIL

John Dumay

Macquarie University

Abstract

Organizational myths abound, and we argue that intellectual capital (IC) and integrated reporting (IR) are based on similar mythical foundations. These myths have given rise to the creation of what I call the Church of Intellectual Capital and the Church of the International Integrated Reporting Council. However, as members of a Church, organizations have not always been on their best behaviours, some of which is dishonest and hidden behind corporate reporting facades. However, these facades threaten the ability of the International Integrated Reporting Council to deliver on its Momentum Phase strategy and spread the word of IR beyond its current reach.

Introduction

In its heyday in the 1990s, intellectual capital (IC) helped to explain and report how economic value was being created in the knowledge economy. However, along with creating economic value comes the opportunity to harvest it. We explore how IC reporting failed because there was too much harvesting of economic value and protecting value creation from competitors. The harvesting caused dismay among IC's proponents, whom I describe as members of the Church of Intellectual Capital. Intellectual capital reporting was declared dead in 2012 (Dumay, 2016).

There is a potential for IC reporting resurrection because human, relational and intellectual (structural) capitals are now part of the International Integrated Reporting Council's (IIRC) integrated reporting framework (De Villiers and Hsiao, 2018). I argue that the Church of the International Integrated Reporting Council also exists because the IIRC and IR are founded on the same myths of IC's creation, and is God-like in its existence.

The myths are closely related to questionable roots in accounting for sustainability (Flower, 2015). The assumption that integrated reporting (IR) has proven benefits, and the myths reinforce corporate façades reporting good behaviours, while hiding dishonest behaviours (Dumay et al., 2019). Unfortunately, citizens and integrated report users have no power to change corporate behaviour (Thomson, 2015). Similarly, IR and the IIRC have no power to change corrupt or ethical corporate cultures, deeply rooted in organizational myths.

Establishing the IC Church

In 2012, I interviewed Leif Edvinsson, one of the grandfathers of IC research and the former Director of Intellectual Capital at the Swedish insurer Skandia in the 1990s. Even though Skandia became famous for its IC statements in the early 1990s, by the new millennium, it had all but abandoned IC statements (Dumay, 2012). I wanted to know why.

> **Leif Edvinsson:** Because … coming in [was] a new management team who were focused on the harvesting of the organization … So, they looked at the balance sheet and saw that "Wow, we can sell off!" … then they stripped the organization of its velocity. But, it's like sailing. If you make your tack on the wrong side …

I remembered that Professor Aino Kianto had recently emailed me, saying " I find [IC] not being practised by managers … as much as it is being preached by as academics … ". I then realised that as academics, we were preachers in the IC church. I identified Leif and the other IC professors as the cardinals and priests, PhD students as deacons, and the remaining attendees from businesses and practice as the congregation. It seemed IC was part of a belief system and the professors were struggling to understand why the uptake of IC reporting by companies was less than they had hoped it would be. At that time, more than 20 years after the introduction of IC, the high priests of the Church of Intellectual Capital were still preaching the same message, to no avail.

I realised that IC reporting seemed to have had its heyday and was well and truly in decline. When I investigated further and found no publicly available IC reports from any listed company for 2012, I realised that IC reporting had died. I included the slide shown in Figure 11.1 in my next presentation declaring that IC reporting lived from 1994, the first year that Skandia issued an IC statement, and was gone by 2012.

What is the future for IC reporting?

> Where we are heading is not going to solve anything. It is a dead end. It has actually been a dead end for quite some time.
>
> (Karl-Erik Sveiby, Interview, September 2012)

Figure 11.1 Intellectual Capital Reporting: RIP

In assessing the future for IC reporting, we need to ask what has changed since 2012. According to Schaper (2016), companies realised that IC reports didn't add any value to the company, and possibly reduced their value. Value reduction occurs because IC reports should tell a value creation story. However, if that story reveals a company's competitive advantage, then its competitors will understand the value creation process as well. Thus, many companies realised that the main benefits did not come from reporting, but from managing IC and improving internal processes. This finding echoes the original research on the development of IC statements in Denmark; Mouritsen et al. (2001) discovered that the companies participating in the research project were producing IC statements to gain internal benefits, rather than disclosing information to lenders or other providers of capital.

The providers of financial capital were viewed negatively when the world economy, in 2008 and 2009, suffered its worst setback since the 1930s' Depression, with the advent of the global financial crisis (GFC). The GFC is important because it marked a major changing point for accounting. It was accounting that allowed the valuation of financial instruments to expand until the bubble burst. Arguably, accounting and performance have become too myopic and now investors and the accounting profession take a longer-term view. Additionally, the GFC coincided with continuing calls for companies to consider their social and environmental sustainability (IIRC, 2013a).

It was against the backdrop of renewed interest in social and environmental sustainability and the impacts of the GFC that that the International Integrated Reporting Committee (later Council) was formed by representatives of the Global Reporting Initiative (GRI) and The Prince's Accounting for Sustainability Project (A4S) (Gleeson-White, 2014). In their initial joint press release the GRI and A4S declared that "The IIRC's remit is to create a globally accepted framework for accounting for sustainability" (GRI and A4S, 2010). Thus, the initial vision for integrated reporting (IR) was to promote social and environmental sustainability, which in turn, should promote economic sustainability.

For the proponents of IC reporting, the advent of IR signalled some new hope that IC would be back on the agenda of major companies, and there might be a resurrection of IC reporting. As Dumay (2016) outlines:

> The IC wealth-creation myth believers are heartened because the [International Integrated Reporting Framework (IIRC Framework)] includes six capitals. When you take away the physical capitals of financial, manufactured and natural capital, the remaining three intangible capitals broadly align with IC's three capitals: human capital with human capital; social and relational capital with relational capital; and IC with structural capital. This has ushered in a new era of hope for the IC reporting faithful that IC reporting is firmly back on the agenda of companies, especially large listed companies, which are the target of the IIRC and IR.

However, the evidence at that time did not support this hope. According to Dumay et al. (2017), few companies were making use of the capitals in the integrated reports published. In support of their argument, Dumay et al. (2017) use evidence from the corporateregister. com website, which classifies integrated reports on two levels:

Level 1: The IIRC and/or the IIRC Framework are referenced in the report.
Level 2: The IIRC and/or the IIRC Framework are referenced in the report, and the report includes information about at least two of the capitals as defined in the IIRC Framework.

According to Dumay et al. (2017) in 2017, corporateregister.com identified 1,426 integrated reports of which 866 were level 1 (60.7 per cent) and 560 (39.3 per cent) were Level 2. However, as at 26 September 2019, corporateregister.com had identified 2660 integrated reports, with 1,277 (48 per cent) Level 1 reports, and 1383 (52 per cent) Level 2 reports. Thus, it has taken more than nine years, with some more take-up between 2017–19, for some evidence of an IC reporting resurrection to take place, keeping in mind the threshold for being classified as a Level 2 report is only two of the six capitals, and these two capitals might not be related to the three intellectual capitals identified above.

Even though there is evidence of increasing compliance with the IIRC Framework (IIRC, 2013b), some scholars question the relevance and usefulness of integrated reports for external users. For example, Abhayawansa et al. (2019) found that many sell-side analysts were not even aware that one of the companies they were analysing issued an integrated report, and also questioned the veracity of an integrated report, to the extent that even if they were aware of such a report that would likely not use it in their analysis. Thus, IR today suffers from the same maladies that eventually caused the demise of IC reporting. Thus, while there are some signs that interest in IC reporting is growing through IR, the future is still rather bleak. Thus we need to have a critical assessment of IR's future (De Villiers and Sharma, 2018).

Does IR have a future?

To answer this question, we need to look more deeply at IR. Arguably, IR has not changed since the IIRC (2013b) issued its initial framework. Even after a consultation process in 2017 to get feedback on IR implementation, the IIRC concluded that the IIRC Framework was fit for purpose (IIRC, 2017), and thus to date the framework remains unchanged. However, in more recent documents provided by the IIRC, there is evidence that IR is beginning to morph back towards a social and environmental sustainability agenda, alongside "financial stability and sustainability" (IIRC, 2013b). For example, the IIRC (2018) is now talking about helping to develop sustainable finance as part of the application of IIRC Framework. Additionally, the IIRC is undergoing significant changes in the board and management, with the recent appointment of Dominic Barton as chairman, and the resignation of Richard Howitt as CEO (IIRC, 2019a). Not only is IR evolving in practice, but the IIRC itself is evolving. Thus in considering whether IR has a future we need to understand its roots and current practice.

Questionable roots in accounting for sustainability

Considering that IR started out as an accounting for sustainability framework and that sustainability is a key issue on the agenda of many companies, investors and consumers, is IR the answer to providing sustainability information to users? Arguably not, because IR seems to have suffered from deep capture; the economic interests of stock market capitalism overtook the initial intent to develop an accounting for sustainability reporting framework (La Torre et al., 2020). Thus, the roots of IR's purpose are questionable.

The questionable roots of IR are also found in the early academic commentaries written while the IIRC was developing the IIRC Framework. Early criticism of IR is found in Milne and Gray's (2013) article critiquing sustainability reporting. As Milne and Gray (2013, p. 20) outline, there was no evidence of sustainability accounting in the then proposed IIRC Framework:

> The IIRC's discussion paper, Towards Integrated Reporting is a masterpiece of obfuscation and avoidance of any recognition of the prior 40 years of research and experimentation. Despite its claims for sustainable development and sustainability, it is exclusively investor focused and it has virtually nothing—and certainly nothing substantive—to say about either accountability or sustainability. Should IR take over from GRI and the TBL as the focus of choice, then we will be heading even further away from any plausible possibility that sustainability might be seriously embraced by any element of business and politics.

When the final IIRC Framework was released, there was substantial disappointment among scholars that any mention of sustainability was removed, despite its founders being the GRI and A4S (Flower, 2015).

The disappointment among scholars surrounding the lack of sustainability accounting in the IIRC Framework is found initially in Flower's (2015) paper where he brands IR a "failure". Flower's (2015) main criticism is that "the IIRC has abandoned sustainability accounting", and he proposes two arguments. First, "the IIRC's concept of value is 'value for investors' and not 'value for society'", and second, "the IIRC places no obligation on firms to report harm inflicted on entities outside the firm" (ibid). The main reason for abandoning sustainability is that the IIRC was captured by the accounting profession and big business, leaving the GRI and A4S behind (La Torre et al., 2020). Further evidence of the capture by a capitalist ideology is seen in Howitt and Thurm's (2018) argument that IR represents a shift from "monocapitalism to multicapitalism" and considering Howitt was still then the CEO of the IIRC, it is ample evidence to support Flower's arguments.

While Flower (2015) is a vocal IR critic, many other scholars have been IR supporters from the outset. As Dumay et al. (2016) point out in their seminal IR literature review, there is evidence that there was considerable practitioner and academic support for research to promote IR through the Association of Chartered Certified Accountants (ACCA) and the International Association for Accounting Education and Research (IAAER). Additionally, several academics openly declared their support for IR; most notable is Adams' (2015) "call to action" in response to Flower's (2015) criticism. Specifically, Adams (2015) argues for "integrated reporting and its potential to change the thinking of corporate actors leading to the further integration of sustainability actions and impacts into corporate strategic planning and decision making". Since then Adams has gone onto publish several other academic articles (e.g. Adams et al., 2016) and position papers (e.g. Adams, 2017) in support of IR and the IIRC from a social and environmental sustainability perspective.

To balance Flower's (2015) critique and Adams' (2015) call to action, Thomson's (2015) commentary paper asks whether "sustainability needs capitalism or an integrated report". In answering the question Thomson (2015) supports Flower's "criticisms and conclusions [...] and provides some additional insights into the possible impact of Integrated Reporting". One insight worth elaborating is Thomson's critique of how IR is supposed to transform corporate behaviour towards a more sustainable path.

The grand theory about integrated and other forms of voluntary corporate reporting is that powerful citizens use the reports as a tool to inform themselves of corporate behaviour. If corporations do not perform the way that these citizens expect, then these citizens can use their economic power against the corporation by exercising their power as "an employee, a good neighbour, voting in a democratic country, through the choices they make when consuming and their savings and pensions" Thomson (2015). However, as Thomson (2015, p. 20) rightly laments:

> Sadly, on Planet Earth citizens with steady employment, savings, a pension, substantial consumer choice, reasonable levels of disposable income, able to participate in free and fair elections in countries make up a very small percentage of world citizens. Only 11.3% of the world's population live in full democratic state, 48% of the world are in vulnerable employment [...], half the adult population do not have a bank account and 22% use it for savings, only 30% of Middle Class Americans have a pension plan and what purchasing power do 3 billion of our fellow citizens have with their daily income of $2.50 [or less].

Further complicating the situation is that IR's intended audience are the "providers of financial capital to enable a more efficient and productive allocation of capital" and not to make the planet more sustainable (IIRC, 2013b). As Dumay et al. (2019) argue, if the interests of the providers of financial capital are aligned with managers' desire to earn bonuses, then this encourages dishonest behaviours as in the Skandia case, and as recently observed by the Australian banking Royal Commission into misconduct in Australian financial institutions. In one instance, bank employees motivated by bonus contracts were discovered to have been charging the accounts of deceased customers for financial advice they obviously could not use (Dumay et al., 2019). Therefore, if the interests of the providers of financial capital are aligned with the desire of citizens to create more wealth for themselves at the expense of society and the environment, then all IR will do is reinforce dishonest behaviour.

As Thomson (2015) argues, the IIRC's discourses about the providers of financial capital (investors) and how IR works is "mythical". There is no evidence to show how the claims made by the IIRC provide are true, otherwise we would expect that after more than nine years, IR would already be the corporate reporting norm. However, IR still seeks to break into key markets such as China and the US (IIRC, 2019a). If IR is as good as it claims, then breaking into these markets should be easy, and yet the IIRC has had little success, especially in the neo-liberal and capitalistic US setting (Adams, 2018). It does seem that IR is somewhat mythical.

The IR myth and the IIRC

Our world abounds in myth. Since the beginning of civilization people have needed to tell stories about people, events and natural phenomenon that may have no reasonable explanation. Modern day myths are narratives used to promote "an unproved or false collective belief that is used to justify a social institution".[1] IR appears to be a myth because the IIRC has been continually using pathos-based rhetoric to promote IR and itself. According to La Torre et al. (2020, p. 11) the "IIRC's myths are based on highly institutionalised and taken-for-granted concepts and paradigms, such as knowledge, knowledge-based intangibles, and international harmonization. The IIRC connects itself with these myths to justify its action". The evidence that IR and the IIRC are justified is the IIRC's lead role in forming the "Corporate Reporting Dialogue, to bring greater consistency, coherence and clarity to the corporate reporting landscape, a major objective of our strategy during this Momentum Phase" (IIRC, 2019a, p. 5). The Corporate Reporting Dialogue seeks to converge and align the different reporting frameworks and is at the heart of the IR myth.

It is through the Corporate Reporting Dialogue that the IIRC promotes a myth as it seeks to position itself as the corporate reporting norm and the leader in all forms of corporate reporting. The Corporate Reporting Dialogue is an initiative designed to respond to market calls for greater coherence, consistency and comparability between corporate reporting frameworks, standards and related requirements. Considering that IR seeks to become the "corporate reporting norm", the converging that the IIRC seeks is integrating the other competing reporting frameworks with IR, rather than IR integrating towards the other frameworks. Evidence in support of the IIRC considering IR to be the dominant framework is seen on the webpage entitled "The Landscape Map", where the purpose, scope and content of the competing frameworks and standards are compared against IR as a benchmark as shown in Figure 11.2. Thus, the way that the IIRC controls the Corporate Reporting Dialogue and then displays that it believes that all other frameworks are inadequate in comparison perpetuates the IR myth that positions IR as the superior framework. I am not sure the proponents of the other frameworks and standards would agree with such a mythical comparison, considering the IIRC shows that their content is less than half of IR's.

While the IIRC promotes its mythical qualities, the mythical nature of IR allows reporters to embrace the myth and thus IR becomes malleable to organizational needs. As a respondent noted in Gibassier et al.'s (2018) study of IR implementation, "IR is like God – no one has met Him but everybody talks about Him". However, Gibassier et al. (2018, p. 1350) conclude that IR's mythical nature allowed the company to acknowledge IR as:

> aspirational and praised this imaginary feature. Multiple participants reflected on the nature of IR and developed collective conceptualizations and reconceptualizations of the innovation. Throughout this journey, individuals connected these concep-tions to the foundational socio-economic vision of the company.

Corporate Reporting Dialogue

| | About | Better Alignment Project | Publications | Events | News | Contact | 🔍 |

Purpose | Scope | **Content**

● = Full coverage　◖ = Partial coverage
Click on each button for more information

Content of standard or framework through the lens of ‹IR›

Initiative	Organisational overview and external environment ⓘ	Governance ⓘ	Business model ⓘ	Risks and opportunities ⓘ	Strategy and resource allocation ⓘ	Performance ⓘ	Outlook ⓘ
CDP Questionnaires	◖	◖	◖	◖	◖	◖	◖
CDSB Framework	◖	◖		◖	◖	◖	◖
FASB Accounting Standards	◖		◖	◖	◖	◖	
GRI Sustainability Reporting Standards	◖	◖	◖	◖		◖	◖
International Financial Reporting Standards	◖		◖	◖	◖	◖	
ISO 26000 – Social responsibility	◖	◖				◖	◖
Sustainability Accounting Standards	◖	◖	◖	◖		◖	◖

Figure 11.2 The dominant position of IR against other frameworks
Source: IIRC, 2019b.

Thus, the IR myth can connect to the company's myth(s) and connect to social and environmental sustainability, even though no discourse about social and environmental sustainability is present in the IIRC Framework (Flower, 2015). Integrated reporting then becomes a façade (Cho et al, 2015).

That IR becomes a façade is more evidence of its mythical nature. A prime example is an Australian bank, which was a founding member the Integrated Reporting Corporate Network, and yet was singled out for dishonest behaviour in the Australian Government Royal Commission enquiry into misconduct in the Australian financial system (Royal Commission, 2018). As Casonato et al. (2019) report, the bank's reporting practices had an investor and stakeholder focus to repair lost legitimacy after a 2004 scandal. By 2010 the bank seemed to have regained the trust of investors and stakeholders. However, despite producing integrated reports since 2010 the bank once again faced significant scandals. Thus, implementing IR only affected the bank's public façade, while its unchanging organizational culture helped perpetuate the scandals. Once again, there is evidence that IR does not change corporate behaviour, and the IR myth reinforces dishonest behaviour (Dumay et al, 2019).

Conclusion

To conclude this chapter, I refer to the Church of Intellectual Capital. It seems that IR is caught in the same hype and belief systems that now constitute the Church of the International Integrated Reporting Council, because like any religion, IR is founded on the very myths of its creation, and is God-like in its existence (Gibassier et al, 2018). So long as the Church of International Integrated Reporting Council remains with its priests and followers, we will continue to see companies issue integrated reports until the point comes when the myth underlying the Church can no longer be supported by reality. As La Torre et al. (2020) outline, there still is "insufficient evidence of its benefits, a controversial shift in its underpinning ideology, and a lack of traditional sources of regulatory power and legitimation". If the IIRC does not *spread the word* and use its Momentum Phase strategy to break into key markets such as the US, China, Germany and Asia, which were key markets identified in its previous Breakthrough Phase strategy (IIRC, 2014), then the Church is at risk of failing or being confined to specific jurisdictions where it has made some inroads such as South Africa and Japan (IIRC, 2019a).

What seems to be missing from the IIRC's Momentum Phase strategy is how to ensure that IR is not a mere façade of corporations to report on their good behaviours, while behind the scenes the culture driving dishonest behaviours survives because the process of constructing an integrated report does not cause the employees to reflect on their past and change behaviour. The IIRC (2019a, p. 16) is even concerned that the credibility of integrated reports is a material risk because poor quality integrated reports and data within them may "fail to meet investors' information needs and undermine the benefits and concept of integrated reporting". However, the IIRC has no power to enforce any reporting quality standard, or prevent companies from using IR as corporate reporting façade. As Thomson (2015) rightly laments, even citizens have little or no power to change corporate behaviour, just as IR and the IIRC have little power to change corrupt corporate cultures, or even ethical corporate cultures that are deeply rooted in organization myths (see Dumay and Dai, 2017).

As the Skandia case shows, even a company that has a strong corporate culture based on IC, and who are believers and upstanding members of the Church of Intellectual Capital's congregation can stray from the flock. As the IIRC continues its Momentum Phase strategy, it too is worried about companies leaving the congregation as the number of participating companies fell from 95 in 2017 to 90 in 2018 (IIRC, 2019a). So, the danger is that ethical companies will look towards other reporting frameworks and thus challenge the IIRC's self-imposed myth of primacy as outlined on the Corporate Reporting Dialogue website. Maintaining the congregation is important for the IIRC because like any church, they are reliant on the contributions of their believers, and if these numbers continue to dwindle then so too will the IIRC's ability to engage with their followers, and preach the word to new markets in the US, China, Germany and Asia.

Note

1 https://www.dictionary.com/browse/myth, accessed 27 September 2019.

References

Abhayawansa, S., Elijido-Ten, E., and Dumay, J. (2019) A practice theoretical analysis of the irrelevance of integrated reporting to mainstream sell-side analysts. *Accounting & Finance*, *59*(3), 1621–1653.

Adams, C. (2017). *The Sustainable Development Goals, integrated thinking and the integrated report*. London: IIRC.

Adams, C. A. (2015) The International Integrated Reporting Council: a call to action. *Critical Perspectives on Accounting*, *27*(1), 23–28.

Adams, C. A., Potter, B., Singh, P. J., and York, J. (2016) Exploring the implications of integrated reporting for social investment (disclosures). *The British Accounting Review*, *48*(3), 283–296.

Adams, M. (2018). Emerging integrated reporting practices in the United States. In J. Guthrie, J. Dumay, F. Ricceri, and C. Nielsen (Eds.), *The Routledge companion to intellectual capital: frontiers of research, practice and knowledge* (pp. 365–379). London: Routledge.

Casonato, F., Farneti, F., and Dumay, J. (2019). From sustainability to integrated reporting: how the IIRC framework affected disclosures by a financial institution. In S. O. Idowu, and M. Del Baldo (Eds.), *Integrated reporting: antecedents, perspectives and outlook for organizations and stakeholders* (pp. 125–140). Amsterdam: Springer.

Cho, C. H., Laine, M., Roberts, R. W., and Rodrigue, M. (2015) Organized hypocrisy, organizational façades, and sustainability reporting. *Accounting, Organizations and Society*, *40*, 78–94.

De Villiers, C., and Hsiao, P.-C. (2018). Integrated reporting and the connections between integrated reporting and intellectual capital. In J. Guthrie, J. Dumay, F. Ricceri, and C. Nielsen (Eds.), *The Routledge companion to intellectual capital: frontiers of research, practice and knowledge* (pp. 483–491). London: Routledge.

De Villiers, C., and Sharma, U. (2018). A critical reflection on the future of financial, intellectual capital, sustainability and integrated reporting. *Critical Perspectives on Accounting* [In press]. 10.1016/j.cpa.2017.05.003.

Dumay, J. (2012) Grand theories as barriers to using IC concepts. *Journal of Intellectual Capital*, *13*(1), 4–15.

Dumay, J. (2016) A critical reflection on the future of intellectual capital: from reporting to disclosure. *Journal of Intellectual Capital*, *17*(1), 168–184.

Dumay, J., Bernardi, C., Guthrie, J., and Demartini, P. (2016) Integrated reporting: a structured literature review. *Accounting Forum*, *40*(3), 166–185.

Dumay, J., Bernardi, C., Guthrie, J., and La Torre, M. (2017) Barriers to implementing the International Integrated Reporting Framework: a contemporary academic perspective. *Meditari Accountancy Research*, *25*(4), 461–480.

Dumay, J., and Dai, T. (2017) Integrated thinking as a cultural control? *Meditari Accountancy Research*, *25*(4), 574–604.

Dumay, J., La Torre, M., and Farneti, F. (2019) Developing trust through stewardship. *Journal of Intellectual Capital*, *20*(1), 11–39.

Flower, J. (2015) The International Integrated Reporting Council: a story of failure. *Critical Perspectives on Accounting*, *27*(1), 1–17.

Gibassier, D., Rodrigue, M., and Arjaliès, D.-L. (2018) "Integrated reporting is like God: no one has met Him, but everybody talks about Him": the power of myths in the adoption of management innovations. *Accounting, Auditing & Accountability Journal*, *31*(5), 1349–1380.

Gleeson-White, J. (2014). *Six capitals: the revolution capitalism has to have—or can accountants save the planet?* Sydney: Allen & Unwin.

Howitt, R., and Thurm, R. (2018). *From monocapitalism to multicapitalism: 21st century system value creation.* Available at: https://blogs.thomsonreuters.com/sustainability/2018/06/07/executive-perspective-from-monocapitalism-to-multicapitalism-21st-century-system-value-creation/ (Assessed: 7 June 2018).

IIRC (2013a). *Basis for conclusions – International <IR> Framework.* London: IIRC.

IIRC (2013b). *The International <IR> framework.* London: IIRC.

IIRC (2014). *Strategy: the breakthrough phase 2014–17.* London: IIRC.

IIRC (2017). *International <IR> Framework implementation feedback: summary report.* London: IIRC.

IIRC (2018). *International Integrated Reporting Council reacts to High Level Expert Group on Sustainable Finance call for greater integration.* Available at: http://integratedreporting.org/news/international-integrated-reporting-council-reacts-to-high-level-expert-group-on-sustainable-finance-call-for-greater-integration/ (Accessed: 5 October 2018).

IIRC (2019a). *Building momentum: IIRC intergrated report 2018.* London: IIRC.

IIRC (2019b). *The landscape map.* Available at: https://corporatereportingdialogue.com/landscape-map/ (Accessed: 27 September 2019).

La Torre, M., Dumay, J., Rea, M. A., and Abhayawansa, S. (2020). A "journey" toward a safe harbor: the rhetorical process of the International Integrated Reporting Council. *The British Accounting Review*, *52*(2), 1–22. [In press].

Milne, M. J., and Gray, R. (2013) W(h)ither ecology? The triple bottom line, the global reporting initiative, and corporate sustainability reporting. *Journal of Business Ethics*, *118*(1), 13–29.

Mouritsen, J., Larsen, H. T., and Bukh, P. N. D. (2001) Intellectual capital and the 'capable firm': narrating, visualising and numbering for managing knowledge. *Accounting, Organizations and Society*, *26*(7-8), 735–762.

The Prince's Accounting for Sustainability Project (A4S) and Global Reporting Initiative (GRI). (2010). *Formation of the International Integrated Reporting Committee (IIRC)* [Press Release]. Available at: www. theiirc.org/wp-content/uploads/2011/03/Press-Release1.pdf (Accessed: 17 March 2013).

Royal Commission (2018). *Royal commission into misconduct in the banking superannuation and financial service industry. First round of public hearings: consumer lending.* Canberra: Australian Government.

Schaper, S. (2016) Contemplating the usefulness of intellectual capital reporting: reasons behind the demise of IC disclosures in Denmark. *Journal of Intellectual Capital, 17*(1), 52–82.

Thomson, I. (2015) 'But does sustainability need capitalism or an integrated report' a commentary on 'The International Integrated Reporting Council: a story of failure' by Flower, J. *Critical Perspectives on Accounting, 27,* 18–22.

PART III

Current integrated reporting knowledge and future research opportunities

12

ARCHIVAL RESEARCH INFORMING THE DUAL OBJECTIVE OF INTEGRATED REPORTING

Mary E. Barth

Stanford University

Steven F. Cahan

University of Auckland

Li Chen

University of Auckland

Elmar R. Venter

University of Pretoria

Abstract

The International Integrated Reporting Framework (IIRC Framework) of the International Integrated Reporting Council (IIRC) has determined that the objective of integrated reporting is twofold: improved information for outside providers of financial capital and better internal decision-making by management. We refer to the first objective as the capital market channel of the benefits of integrated reporting and the second objective as the real effects channel. We review the literature using archival research methods to determine the extent of evidence supporting the dual objective of integrated reporting. Overall, additional academic research on both channels will be useful to standard setters, regulators, managers, and users of corporate reports in evaluating the benefits of integrated reporting.

Introduction

The International Integrated Reporting Framework (IIRC Framework) of the International Integrated Reporting Council (IIRC) sets out a dual objective for integrated reporting. The first

183

objective is improving the information available to outside providers of financial capital to enable more efficient capital allocation. The second objective is to support integrated internal thinking, decision-making, and actions that focus on value creation for the firm. Hence, the IIRC foresees that the effective implementation of integrated reporting will result in both external and internal benefits for a firm.

Academic researchers are equipped to provide independent and objective evidence on whether integrated reporting achieves its dual objective in practice. Academic research is based on theory and the scientific method, which results in inferences that are conceptually sound and internally consistent (Barth, 2018). Academic research follows rigorous thinking and analyses that are subject to extensive review; it is not opinion or advocacy (Barth, 2018).

Academic researchers can use a range of methods to gather evidence, including archival, analytical, and experimental approaches. Our interest was in the archival evidence on the dual objective of integrated reporting. Archival researchers collect data from third party repositories or hand collect data to examine associations and systematic changes between variables of interest using econometric techniques. We searched the most pertinent journals in accounting and finance to identify articles that address the dual objective of integrated reporting. We discuss these articles and provide insights on the current state and future direction of this literature.

The remainder of this chapter presents: the background on integrated reporting; the selection of articles reviewed; a discussion of the first objective of integrated reporting, namely improved external information; a discussion of the second objective of integrated reporting, namely better internal decisions; and concluding comments.

Integrated reporting

Advocates of integrated reports believe that such reports address the shortcomings of conventional corporate reporting. These deficiencies include the backward-looking nature of financial accounting; the omission of a substantial component of firms' value encapsulated in intangible assets; the disconnection of various reports firms provide, such as annual reports and stand-alone sustainability reports; the lack of connectivity between financial reports and the firm's strategy and value creation process; the absence of non-financial performance indicators; and the failure to recognize a firm's wider obligations to society and the environment (e.g., EY, 2014). Paul Druckman, former CEO of the IIRC, states that an integrated report is "where an organisation explains how it is going to create value," and explains:

> It is a concise communication of value. It explains how a company will be a viable thriving entity in the short, medium and long term. It is not just about financial profit. Companies cannot think of themselves as apart from society – they are part of it. And that needs to come through in their communication on value.
>
> *(Druckman, 2013)*

The IIRC was established in 2010 following the global financial crisis. With the support of the Accounting for Sustainability (A4S) initiative fronted by HRH The Prince of Wales and the Global Reporting Initiative, the IIRC's mandate is to develop and promote a framework for integrated reporting. Issued in 2013, the IIRC Framework is principles-based and does not provide a standard format for integrated reports or specify particular disclosure requirements. Instead, the IIRC Framework sets out seven guiding principles and eight content elements for an integrated report. These principles and elements relate to six capitals that the organization uses to create value, which allows managers to provide a narrative to explain how the firm creates value.[1]

Because integrated reports include financial and non-financial information, they are broader in scope than conventional corporate reports. For example, whereas financial statements address financial capital, they only partially cover manufactured, intellectual, human, social, and natural capitals (IIRC, 2016). Integrated reports are supposed to deal with all resources and relationships that materially affect the value-creation activities of the firm (Cohen and Simnett, 2015). Also, integrated reports focus on long-term future-oriented information, whereas traditional corporate reports typically focus on short-term historical performance.

A key feature that distinguishes integrated reporting from other reporting formats is that information about the six capitals is to be presented in an integrated manner to support the first objective of integrated reporting, namely improved external information. As a result, the connectivity of information is perhaps the most important principle of an integrated report, as it is intended to reveal to providers of financial capital how the firm will generate value over the long term. The IIRC Framework defines connectivity of information as an integrated report showing "a holistic picture of the combination, interrelatedness and dependencies between the factors that affect the organization's ability to create value over time" (IIRC, 2013, p. 5). As such, simply combining a traditional financial and corporate social responsibility (CSR) report will not meet the requirements of the IIRC Framework, because the information will not be connected.

Connectivity of information also supports the second objective of integrated reporting, namely better internal decisions. The IIRC (2013, p. 2) defines integrated thinking as "the active consideration by an organization of the relationships between its various operating and functional units and the capitals that the organization uses or affects". The IIRC (2013, p. 2) contends that "integrated thinking leads to integrated decision-making and actions that consider the creation of value". As such, integrated reporting intends to equip management to understand a firm's business better, thereby improving managerial decision-making and external reporting.

If archival researchers want to contribute evidence on the effectiveness of integrated reporting, it is important for them to understand what an integrated report is according to the IIRC Framework. Archival researchers have the challenging task of operationalizing the integrated reporting construct, that is, measuring how well firms' integrated reports meet the guiding principles and content elements of the IIRC Framework. A natural inclination for researchers will be to base their proxies for integrated reporting on the vast literature on CSR reporting. The danger of such an approach is that CSR reporting quality generally does not capture the connectivity of information – the key principle of integrated reporting. In addition, measuring the quality of integrated reports cannot be done by merely completing a disclosure checklist. Because the IIRC Framework is principle-based, it requires an experienced reader to evaluate the quality of an integrated report against the objectives, guiding principles, and content elements of the IIRC Framework.

Method

We searched all B – or higher rated – journals on the 2016 Australian Business Deans Council list in the "accounting" and "finance" fields of research.[2] We excluded actuarial, mathematical, and statistical journals. We added the *Journal of Business Ethics*, *Strategic Management Journal*, and *Management Science* from the "business" field of research to our search because these journals have historically published articles on CSR. In total, we searched 159 journals for articles containing "integrated reporting", "integrated report", "integrated reports", or "integrated thinking" in their titles. We identified 95 articles, of which one was analytical, 17 were archival, two were experimental, and 61 were qualitative; the remaining articles included commentaries, editorials, and literature reviews.

Our interest was in the 17 archival articles. We read the abstracts of these articles to identify those that provided evidence on one or both of the objectives of integrated reporting. Of the 17 articles, nine provided evidence on the objectives of integrated reporting, whereas the remaining articles focused mainly on the determinants of integrated reporting adoption or quality and issues specific to intellectual capital disclosures in integrated reports. In the next two sections, we discuss the nine articles that provided evidence on the objectives of integrated reporting.

Improved external information

A number of articles investigated whether the economic consequences of integrated reporting were consistent with improved information for external providers of financial capital. These articles built on a well-established literature that links disclosure with economic outcomes through the capital market channel, such as firm value, liquidity, and cost of capital. We commence this section by discussing agency and non-agency theories that could explain how integrated reporting affects economic outcomes. Thereafter, we discuss the archival evidence in the literature.

Agency theory

Agency theory posits that information asymmetry exists between managers with superior information and information-disadvantaged outsiders, such as investors. This agency problem can lead to adverse selection, which increases the price of shares, reduces liquidity, and increases the cost of capital because investors demand a premium as compensation for risk (e.g., Francis et al, 2008; Gietzmann and Ireland, 2005). Disclosure is a mechanism that managers can use to reduce information asymmetry and thereby decrease investors' monitoring cost by levelling the playing field among investors (Verrecchia, 2001). However, high-quality disclosure is not costless because disclosure involves preparation costs, litigation risk, and proprietary costs (Leuz and Wysocki, 2016). A firm's disclosure quality represents the outcome of trading off these costs and benefits.

Prior literature finds support for the agency theory discussed in the previous paragraph, but primarily for voluntary disclosure (for overviews of this literature, see Healy and Palepu (2001) and Leuz and Wysocki (2016)). However, voluntary disclosure is subject to selection bias associated with incentives for voluntary disclosure. By voluntarily disclosing private information, managers reveal that the benefits of the disclosure are greater than the cost. Because it is difficult to correct for self-selection bias, empirical tests of the relationship between voluntary disclosure quality and economic consequences are likely to find expected benefits (Larcker and Rusticus, 2010). As a result, the recent literature has examined disclosure quality and agency theory in the context of mandatory disclosure. Most of these studies focus on the global adoption of IFRS (e.g., Daske et al, 2008, 2013).

Extending agency theory to mandatory disclosure settings helps avoid confounded inferences resulting from self-selection associated with firms' decisions about whether to provide the disclosure. Because mandatory disclosers could be compelled into a second-best reporting alternative, inferences based on mandatory settings establish a lower limit for economic consequences of disclosure quality. However, as Leuz and Wysocki (2016) note, mandatory reporting standards also afford managers discretion because the disclosures are intended to elicit managers' private information, and thus involve the manager making subjective assessments.

Because integrated reporting is mandatory in South Africa, many of the archival studies use South African data. The South African setting provides integrated reports for a sizeable number of firms not affected by self-selection, as is the case in voluntary settings.

Integrated reporting has the potential to reduce information asymmetry about the capitals that affect value. Zhou et al. (2017) reason that integrated reports can contain new value-relevant information, but these reports also can present previously disclosed information more concisely and usefully. As mentioned before, the IIRC Framework requires managers to report on a broader set of capitals than those contained in conventional financial reports. Although voluntary CSR reports may address some of the capitals not addressed by financial reports, CSR reports are criticized for being disconnected from the firm's strategy, business model, and financial performance (e.g., Serafeim, 2015). Consequently, providers of financial capital obtain a partial and incoherent representation of the firm's ability to create value over the short, medium, and long term.

Firm value is affected by a firm's expected future cash flows and the riskiness of those cash flows, that is, its cost of capital. Proponents of integrated reporting state that these reports can improve investors' ability to estimate future cash flows by improving the quality, range, and connectivity of data being produced (e.g., Black Sun, 2014; RobecoSAM, 2015).

With regard to the cost of capital, Leuz and Wysocki (2016) explain that the theoretical link between disclosure quality and stock liquidity may extend to the cost of capital because illiquidity imposes trading costs on investors for which they require compensation. In addition, because investors require compensation for risk, the IIRC Framework maintains that integrated reporting can explain a firm's exposure to risks and how its strategy and business model address those risks.

A firm's cost of capital is the sum of the risk-free return and the risk premium. A well-established literature links disclosure and the cost of equity capital. There is a link between disclosure and cost of equity if disclosure affects a firm's non-diversifiable risk. Lambert et al. (2007) posit that accounting information can influence the cost of capital directly through the market's assessment of the riskiness of future cash flows.

There are at least three channels through which disclosure can affect a firm's cost of equity capital. First, disclosure is a mechanism that managers can use to reduce information asymmetry. As mentioned above, integrated reporting improves and expands the information available to capital market participants, which may reduce information asymmetry.

Second, disclosure can improve investors' awareness of non-financial aspects of the firm, which results in a larger investor base with increased risk sharing amongst investors (Merton, 1987). Merton's (1987) capital market equilibrium model allows for incomplete information. In that setting, investors only purchase shares in firms that they know about because gathering and processing information about a firm is costly. By providing an inexpensive, but complete, overview of a firm's activities, integrated reports can help the firm expand its investor base, and thereby lead to a lower cost of capital.

Third, investors do not know the firm's true expected return. Disclosure reduces parameter uncertainty and estimation risk, parts of which are non-diversifiable (Hail and Leuz, 2006). Integrated reporting can reduce parameter uncertainty and estimation risk because it can explain in a concise manner to providers of financial capital how a firm creates value over time, by creating a holistic picture of the interrelatedness of the six capitals on which a firm depends. The strategic focus and future orientation guiding principle of integrated reporting and the content elements relating to the business model, risks and opportunities, strategy and resource allocation, and outlook may be useful to investors in reducing parameter uncertainty and estimation risk.

Non-agency theory

To the degree that disclosure increases liquidity, there also are non-agency-based theories that tie liquidity to firm value (Barth et al, 2017). Liquidity promotes the entry of informed investors into the market for the firm's shares, which results in higher and more informative prices (Khanna and Sonti, 2004). Higher prices provide feedback to management and affect their decisions. In turn, the improved managerial decisions result in better performance and higher firm value. With knowledge of these effects, informed traders trade even more aggressively, which results in a positive cascade whereby good news leads to more good news. Consistent with this theory, Fang et al. (2009) find that liquidity is positively associated with firm value and that the effect is greater for firms with high business uncertainty. Because integrated reports contain information on capitals that are difficult to measure and contain uncertain forward-looking information, integrated reporting may affect liquidity by stimulating informed investors to trade more.

Analysts

Zhou et al. (2017) and Bernardi and Stark (2018) examine the effect of integrated reporting by South African firms on financial analysts. Zhou et al. (2017) use a self-developed measure of integrated report quality that captures the alignment between the firm's integrated report and the 2012 draft Framework. Using data from 2009–2012, Zhou et al. (2017) report a negative association between changes in integrated report quality and subsequent changes in analyst earnings forecast error, but not changes in forecast dispersion. They also find a negative association between changes in integrated report quality and subsequent changes in firms' cost of equity capital for firms with low analyst followings. Their evidence suggests that analysts find integrated reporting useful in assessing the future financial performance of firms. In addition, when firms have a weak information environment, investors are willing to accept a lower return if the firms have higher integrated report quality. This suggests that integrated reporting is associated with reduced information asymmetry between investors and management.

For 40 South African firms, Bernardi and Stark (2018) find that Bloomberg's environmental, social, and governance (ESG) scores were negatively associated with analyst forecast accuracy after integrated reporting became mandatory, but not before. Their evidence is consistent with integrated reporting making ESG disclosures more useful for analysts to predict future financial performance. However, Bernardi and Stark's (2018) findings are attributable to environment-related disclosures, which leads them to suggest that some industries, such as financial services, may not benefit from integrated reporting.

Value relevance of accounting numbers

Baboukardos and Rimmel (2016) investigate the effect of the mandatory adoption of integrated reporting in South Africa on the value relevance of accounting numbers. They find an increase in the value relevance of earnings following the adoption of integrated reporting. This evidence is consistent with the value relevance of earnings increasing as a result of connecting firms' financial information with the range of capitals required by the IIRC Framework. In addition, Baboukardos and Rimmel (2016) find a decrease in the value relevance of book value of equity following the adoption of integrated reporting. They infer that this is consistent with integrated reporting identifying liabilities not recognized for financial statement purposes (e.g., environmental liabilities). An extension of their findings would imply that the unrecognized liabilities evident from an integrated report exceed, on average, the unrecognized assets.

Firm value and its components

Barth et al. (2017) investigate both capital market and real effects associated with integrated report quality in South Africa. In this section, we discuss the capital market effects and in the next section we address the real effects. Barth et al. (2017) extend the work of Lee and Yeo (2016), which finds a positive association between integrated report quality and firm value. Barth et al. (2017) investigate the channels through which this association occurs. An increase in firm value may be attributable to an increase in liquidity, an increase in expected future cash flows, and/or a decrease in the discount rate. The liquidity and discount rate channels represent capital market effects, whereas the expected future cash flow channel may be capital market or real effects.

Barth et al. (2017) find that integrated report quality is negatively associated with the bid-ask spread, which is an inverse proxy for liquidity. This evidence suggests that high-quality integrated reports are associated with decreased information asymmetry between investors and management. With regard to the discount rate channel, Barth et al. (2017) find no association between integrated report quality and cost of capital. At face value, this finding may appear inconsistent with Zhou et al. (2017). However, Zhou et al. (2017) find a negative association between integrated report quality and cost of capital mainly for firms with a weak information environment. Because Barth et al.'s (2017) sample is based on the 100 largest firms on the JSE, which arguably have a strong information environment, the findings of these two studies are not necessarily inconsistent.

Finally, Barth et al. (2017) investigate the expected future cash flow channel. They find a positive association between integrated report quality and analysts' estimates of expected future share prices, which is a proxy for expected future cash flows. This channel could include a capital market or a real effect. With regard to the capital market effect, expected future cash flows could increase if investors are able to predict future cash flows more accurately with the information presented in the integrated report. However, Barth et al. (2017) find no association between integrated report quality and analysts' target price forecast accuracy. This evidence suggests that integrated report quality does not help sophisticated investors to predict expected future cash flows more accurately.

Based on agency theory, liquidity influences firm value by decreasing the cost of capital. Because Barth et al. (2017) find a significant association for liquidity, but not cost of capital, their evidence is more consistent with non-agency-based reasons.

Investor clientele

Because integrated reporting intends to reduce managerial myopia, a situation in which managers focus on short-term performance to the satisfaction of short-term oriented investors, Serafeim (2015) investigates whether United States firms that practice integrated reporting attract investors with a longer time horizon. Serafeim (2015) finds a positive association between firms' tendency to practice integrated reporting and long-term investors.

Improved internal decisions

Although the real effects literature relating to integrated reporting is sparse compared to the capital market literature, real effects are not foreign to the accounting literature. Leuz and Wysocki (2016, p. 545) define real effects as situations in which the firm "changes its behaviour in the real economy (e.g., investment, use of resources, consumption) as a result of the disclosure mandate". A key aspect of the IIRC Framework is that the IIRC envisions that the process of preparing an integrated report will affect managerial decision-making. In particular, the IIRC Framework states that such decision-making will focus on the creation of value over the short, medium, and long term.

Integrated reporting can influence internal decision-making in various ways. Indeed, one of the proposed benefits of integrated reporting is that it fosters integrated thinking and integrated decision-making. Because the information required for an integrated report is multi-disciplinary, integrated reporting has the potential to break down internal silos. Combined with integrated reporting's long-term focus, these factors could result in better real decisions and enhanced firm value (Eccles and Serafeim, 2015; Simnett and Huggins, 2015).

Company reports also are used by shareholders to monitor managers (Lambert, 2001). Thus, higher quality reports should improve shareholders' monitoring ability and reduce the amount of firm cash that managers misappropriate. As a result, integrated reports can provide a more holistic understanding of firm value and can improve monitoring of managers' decisions. In addition, disclosure about the six capitals can be informative to stakeholders, such as customers and employees, who associate with firms that are socially responsible. This could lead to increased sales and financial performance (Plumlee et al, 2015).

Collectively, these mechanisms could result in management obtaining a better understanding of a firm's value drivers and identifying previously unrecognized risks and opportunities, which in turn could affect decisions and strategies.

To date the archival evidence on the effect of integrated reporting on improved internal decision-making is sparse. This is probably because finding empirical proxies that measure the decision-making effect encapsulated by the IIRC Framework is more challenging than measuring economic consequences.

A proxy that indirectly captures the effect of managerial decisions is operating cash flow. Operating cash flows can be affected directly by integrated reporting by out-of-pocket costs associated with preparing integrated reports, which can be substantial for small firms (ACCA, 2014), and by real decisions made by the firm to the extent that such decisions are different from the decisions that would be made in the absence of integrated reporting.

As mentioned previously, Barth et al. (2017) find that integrated reporting is positively associated with expected future cash flows, which could be attributable to investors estimating expected future cash flows accurately (a capital market effect) or to higher future cash flows arising from improved internal decisions (a real effect). Barth et al. (2017) present two pieces of evidence that are consistent with the real effect channel. First, integrated report quality is positively associated with one-year- and two-year-ahead operating cash flows. Second, integrated report quality is positively associated with investment efficiency.

Maniora (2017) compares integrated reporters with firms that have no ESG reporting (non-reporters), firms that issue a stand-alone ESG report (stand-alone reporters), and firms that include ESG information in their annual report (annual reporters). Maniora (2017) finds that integrated reporters have higher levels of integrated thinking than non-reporters, but lower levels than stand-alone reporters, and that there is no difference in the levels of integrated thinking between integrated reporters and annual reporters.

In addition, Maniora (2017) compares the economic, ESG, and combined performance of integrated reporters to those of the other three types of reporters (non-reporters, stand-alone reporters, and annual reporters). Maniora (2017) finds that integrated reporters have higher ESG and overall performance than non-reporters, but lower performance than stand-alone reporters, and there is no difference in these performance measures between integrated reporters and annual reporters. With regard to economic performance, Maniora (2017) finds that integrated reporters are superior to non-reporters, but there are no differences between integrated reporters and stand-alone reporters or annual reporters.

At face value, Maniora's (2017) evidence suggests that integrated reporting is not successful at stimulating integrated thinking beyond other ESG reporting formats, and that in some cases it may even be detrimental. However, the study's findings should be considered in the context of its research design. As De Villiers et al. (2017) point out, relabelling an annual report as an "integrated report" is not sufficient evidence that a firm has prepared an integrated report that meets the objectives, principles, and content elements of the IIRC Framework. At the other extreme, firms may not relabel their annual report as integrated, but may apply the IIRC Framework very effectively. Because Maniora's (2017) research design does not take into account the extent to which the integrated reporters included in the study's sample comply with the IIRC Framework, the inferences are confounded by those reporters that have adopted integrated reporting in form, but not in substance. In addition, the control group of annual reporters may include firms that have adopted integrated reporting in substance, but have not relabelled their report as "integrated".

In summary, there is a dearth of research on the real effects of integrated reporting. Does integrated reporting lead to improved managerial decision-making that focuses on value creation over the short, medium, and long term? This is an area in which academic research can extend our understanding of the benefits of integrated reporting.

Conclusion

Academic researchers are able to provide independent and rigorous evidence on issues of interest to standard setters and regulators. Since the release of the IIRC Framework in 2013, integrated reporting has emerged as an alternative to traditional corporate reporting that could potentially transform existing reporting practices. In particular, the IIRC (2013) contends that integrated reports that meet the objectives, guiding principles and content elements of the IIRC Framework are able to improve the information available to external providers of capital, resulting in more efficient allocation of capital, and to improve internal decisions by management that are focused on value creation. We surveyed the existing archival literature that provides evidence on these two objectives of integrated reporting.

With regards to the first objective of the IIRC Framework, which is improved external information, the literature provides evidence that high-quality integrated reports are associated with higher firm value, higher liquidity, lower analysts' forecast errors, lower cost of capital for firms with a weak information environment, and more long-term focused investors. Despite this evidence, this literature is emerging and many research opportunities remain. For example, thus far, this literature focuses exclusively on equity investors. Because the objective of the IIRC Framework is to provide improved information for all external providers of capital, evidence on whether integrated reporting is useful to other types of capital providers can advance this literature. In addition, the extant literature largely provides average effects for large samples of firms. Limited evidence exists on settings or firms for which the effect of integrated reporting on economic outcomes is more or less pronounced.

With regard to the second objective of the IIRC Framework, which relates to better internal decisions, archival evidence is sparse. There is some evidence that integrated report quality is positively associated with *ex post* operating cash flows and investment efficiency. This evidence is consistent with integrated reporting leading to better internal decisions. However, more evidence is needed on whether integrated reporting achieves this objective of the IIRC Framework. The limited observability of internal decision-making makes finding suitable proxies a challenge to advancing this literature.

Notes

1 The seven guiding principles are: strategic focus and future orientation; connectivity of information; stakeholder relationships; materiality; conciseness; reliability and completeness; and consistency and comparability. The eight content elements are: organizational overview and external environment; governance; business model; risks and opportunities; strategy and resource allocation; performance; outlook, and basis of preparation. The six capitals are: financial, manufacturing, human, intellectual, social and relationship, and natural. See IIRC (2013).
2 See www.abdc.edu.au.

References

Association of Chartered Certified Accountants (ACCA). (2014). *Understanding investors: The changing corporate perspective*. London, UK: ACCA.

Baboukardos, D., and Rimmel, G. (2016). Value relevance of accounting information under an integrated reporting approach: A research note. *Journal of Accounting and Public Policy, 35*(4), 437–452.

Barth, M. E. (2018). How international accounting research influences policy and standard setting. *Journal of International Accounting Research, 17*(2), 1–11.

Barth, M. E., Cahan, S. F., Chen, L., and Venter, E. R. (2017). The economic consequences associated with integrated report quality: Capital market and real effects. *Accounting, Organizations and Society, 62*, 43–64.

Bernardi, C., and Stark, A. W. (2018). Environmental, social and governance disclosure, integrated reporting, and the accuracy of analyst forecasts. *British Accounting Review, 50*(1), 16–31.

Black Sun. (2014). *Realizing the benefits: The impact of integrated reporting*. Available at: www.blacksunplc.com/en/insights/research/integrated-reporting-benefits-research.html (Accessed: 17 June 2019).

Cohen, J. R., and Simnett, R. (2015). CSR and assurance services: A research agenda. *Auditing: A Journal of Practice & Theory, 34*(1), 59–74.

Daske, H., Hail, L., Leuz, C., and Verdi, R. (2008). Mandatory IFRS reporting around the world: Early evidence on the economic consequences. *Journal of Accounting Research, 46*(5), 1085–1142.

Daske, H., Hail, L., and Verdi, R. (2013). Adopting a label: Heterogeneity in the economic consequences around IAS/IFRS adoptions. *Journal of Accounting Research, 51*(3), 495–547.

De Villiers, C., Venter, E. R., and Hsiao, P.-C. K. (2017). Integrated reporting: Background, measurement issues, approaches and an agenda for future research. *Accounting & Finance, 57*(4), 937–959.

Druckman, P. (2013). *Integrated reporting – What it is – And is not: An interview with Paul Druckman*. Available at: http://drcaroladams.net/integrated-reporting-what-it-is-and-is-not-an-interview-with-paul-druckman/ (Accessed: 17 June 2019).

Eccles, R. G., and Serafeim, G. (2015). Corporate and integrated reporting: A functional perspective. In E. Lawler, S. Mohrman, and J. O'Toole (Eds.), *Corporate stewardship: Achieving sustainable effectiveness* (pp. 156–172). New York: Routledge.

EY. (2014). *Integrated reporting: Elevating value*. London, UK: EY.

Fang, V. W., Noe, T. H., and Tice, S. (2009). Stock market liquidity and firm value. *Journal of Financial Economics*, *94*(1), 150–169.

Francis, J., Nanda, D., and Olsson, P. (2008). Voluntary disclosure, earnings quality, and cost of capital. *Journal of Accounting Research*, *46*(1), 53–99.

Gietzmann, M., and Ireland, J. (2005). Cost of capital, strategic disclosures and accounting choice. *Journal of Business Finance & Accounting*, *32*(3-4), 599–634.

Hail, L., and Leuz, C. (2006). International differences in the cost of equity capital: Do legal institutions and securities regulation matter? *Journal of Accounting Research*, *44*(3), 485–531.

Healy, P. M., and Palepu, K. G. (2001). Information asymmetry, corporate disclosure, and the capital markets: A review of the empirical disclosure literature. *Journal of Accounting and Economics*, *31*(1-3), 405–440.

International Integrated Reporting Council (IIRC). (2013). *The international integrated reporting framework*. London, UK: IIRC.

International Integrated Reporting Council (IIRC). (2016). *Navigating the corporate reporting landscape*. London, UK: IIRC.

Khanna, N., and Sonti, R. (2004). Value creating stock manipulation: Feedback effect of stock prices on firm value. *Journal of Financial Markets*, *7*(3), 237–270.

Lambert, R. (2001). Contracting theory and accounting. *Journal of Accounting and Economics*, *32*(1-3), 3–87.

Lambert, R., Leuz, C., and Verrecchia, R. E. (2007). Accounting information, disclosure, and the cost of capital. *Journal of Accounting Research*, *45*(2), 385–420.

Larcker, D. F., and Rusticus, T. O. (2010). On the use of instrumental variables in accounting research. *Journal of Accounting and Economic*, *49*(3), 186–205.

Lee, K., and Yeo, G. H. (2016). The association between integrated reporting and firm valuation. *Review of Quantitative Finance and Accounting*, *47*(4), 1221–1250.

Leuz, C., and Wysocki, P. D. (2016). The economics of disclosure and financial reporting regulation: Evidence and suggestions for future research. *Journal of Accounting Research*, *54*(2), 525–622.

Maniora, J. (2017). Is integrated reporting really the superior mechanism for the integration of ethics into the core business model? An empirical analysis. *Journal of Business Ethics*, *140*(4), 755–786.

Merton, R. C. (1987). A simple model of capital equilibrium with incomplete information. *The Journal of Finance*, *42*(3), 483–510.

Plumlee, M., Brown, D., Hayes, R. M., and Marshall, R. S. (2015). Voluntary environmental disclosure quality and firm value: Further evidence. *Journal of Accounting and Public Policy*, *34*(4), 336–361.

RobecoSAM. (2015). *The sustainability yearbook 2015*. Zurich, Switzerland: RobecoSAM.

Serafeim, G. (2015). Integrated reporting and investor clientele. *Journal of Applied Corporate Finance*, *27*(2), 34–51.

Simnett, R., and Huggins, L. (2015). Integrated reporting and assurance: Where can research add value? *Sustainability Accounting, Management and Policy Journal*, *6*(1), 29–53.

Verrecchia, R. E. (2001). Essays on disclosure. *Journal of Accounting and Economics*, *32*(1-3), 97–180.

Zhou, S., Simnett, R., and Green, W. (2017). Does integrated reporting matter to the capital market? *Abacus*, *53*(1), 94–132.

13

INTEGRATED REPORTING ASSURANCE

State of the art, current issues, future challenges and research opportunities

Adriana Rossi

Department of Business and Management, LUISS Guido Carli

Mercedes Luque-Vilchez

Finance and Accounting Area, Faculty of Law and Business Sciences, University of Córdoba

Cristiano Busco

Roehampton Business School, Roehampton University, and Department of Business and Management, LUISS Guido Carli

Abstract

Academia, the International Integrated Reporting Council (IIRC) and the International Auditing and Assurance Standards Board (IAASB) have revealed that making the integrated report subject to an assurance engagement is necessary to satisfy stakeholders' demands for credible and reliable documents, which will guarantee market stability and support organizations in a sustainable way to improve their operational performance. Even though the proportion of integrated reports that are assured remains low, the procedures followed for their assurance have swiftly gained prominence. In both academic and professional sectors, these assurance procedures are now considered one of the auditing innovations of recent decades. However, there are several issues that concern researchers, standard setters, and practitioners. This chapter will provide insight into this emerging field, by analysing the state of play of assurance practices, current issues, and future challenges and research opportunities.

Introduction

Over the past few decades, increasing numbers of companies have started to communicate their sustainability performance alongside their mandatory financial reporting in response to stakeholders' attention to environmental, social, and ethical issues. Voluntary stand-alone

Corporate Social Responsibility (CSR) reports (e.g. Sustainability Reports, Triple Bottom Line Reports, Environmental and Social Reports) have swiftly gained remarkable prominence, to the point that they are now considered a reporting norm (KPMG, 2017).

The overall balance of the reporting content has been questioned, despite the success in terms of the reliability and accuracy of the information that is disclosed, its diffusion, and the veracity of the actions reported by organizations to implement a sustainable strategy, and to resolve externalities associated with their operations (Boiral, 2013). What has emerged is that CSR reports rarely provide a reliable, complete, and balanced overall communication between companies and stakeholders with regard to companies' overall performances.

Assurance services for CSR reports are intended to serve as an external and independent control mechanism conducted by a qualified third party, accompanying the function provided by the financial audit. They are now perceived as a necessary mechanism to give reports credibility (Park and Brorson, 2005) and thus discharge companies' social and environmental responsibilities (Larrinaga et al., 2018). It is hardly surprising that worldwide growth in assurance reports has more than doubled among the G250[1] over the last 12 years, to the extent that it is now accepted standard practice (KPMG, 2017). The most rapid growth has been in countries such as Japan, Taiwan, and the USA, where high rates of CSR reporting have been achieved (KPMG, 2017).

Numerous benefits appear to be associated with the adoption of assurance services: they help to create greater stakeholder confidence in the accuracy and transparency of the information that is provided (Hodge et al., 2009; Kolk and Perego, 2010); help to provide stability to markets and their operations (Kend, 2015); and provide a comprehensive understanding of emergent issues (Zadek et al., 2004), among others. External sustainability assurance represents the next stage of development in CSR reporting, as methodological approaches become more developed and the demands of report users more sophisticated.

Integrated reporting (IR) represents the latest development in corporate sustainability accounting, combining financial and non-financial information in one report. It is the most relevant innovation designed to communicate a comprehensive organizational description, in terms of value creation and impacts from an economic, social, and environmental point of view (Busco et al., 2013; De Villiers et al., 2014, 2017; Dumay et al., 2016; Eccles and Krzus, 2010).

The Integrated Reporting Framework (IR Framework), promoted by the International Integrated Reporting Council (IIRC), through a principles-based approach, is intended to show how an organization's strategy, governance, performance, and operations lead to the development of sustainable value in the short, medium, and long term. The IIRC Framework has set itself an ambitious goal: "enhance accountability and stewardship for the broad base of capitals (financial, manufactured, intellectual, human, social and relationship, and natural) and promote understanding of their interdependencies" (IIRC, 2013, p. 2), providing insight into the way that an organization's purpose and business model can be aligned with market opportunities and sustainable performance (Busco et al., 2018).

The success of the IR instrument also appears to depend on two recent normative innovations that highlight the demand to rethink the whole corporate accounting system within a wider prospective, combining financial and non-financial information to offer an integrated perspective: (i) European Directive 2014/95/EU,[2] which requires some large companies, especially financial groups, to insert environmental and social statements in their management reports; and (ii) the Sustainable Development Goals (SDGs) promoted by the United Nations, which define global aspirations for 2030, relying on the critical role of business organizations to deliver on the promise of sustainable and inclusive growth (Busco et al., 2018).

Although CSR reports and integrated reports differ in content, aim, and final addressees, both provide non-financial and qualitative information. Therefore, previous issues raised by research about CSR assurance provide a basis for examining the relatively new process of IR assurance (Corrado et al., 2019). The IR Framework is an attempt to overcome the actual separation between financial and CSR reporting models, which has made them incapable of exchanging meaningful information, and often far too long-winded and complex, without providing responses to broader societal, environmental, and economic questions beyond those that address immediate stakeholder interests (Monciardini et al., 2016). The practical difficulties in constructing a new, holistic, yet concise reporting model have led numerous parties to question the quality, usefulness, reliability, and accuracy of those documents. The main criticisms to emerge are related to the fact that many of the component parts of an integrated report are subjective: the definition of a business model; the approach to risk management and its practice; and the commentary on business actions. The discretionary power of managers throughout the reporting process and the perception that IR could become yet another "greenwashing" tool or marketing instrument are two aspects that erode the trust of actual and potential users (i.e., Corrado et al., 2019; Dumay et al., 2016; Simnett and Huggins, 2015).

The IIRC is aware of the importance of this issue, and states that the reliability of information can be enhanced "by mechanisms such as robust internal control and reporting systems, stakeholder engagement, internal audit (or similar functions) and independent, external assurance" (IIRC, 2013, p. 21). Findings from the engagement of the IIRC with stakeholders (IIRC, 2014a, 2014b, 2015) and the most recent consultation document published by the International Auditing and Assurance Standards Board (IAASB) (IAASB, 2019), reiterate the importance of assurance mechanisms. Such instruments can give credibility to the information disclosed by integrated reports, reducing the informational asymmetries between organizations and their stakeholders (Reimsbach et al., 2017). Academia is unanimous in recognizing the relevance of IR assurance in enhancing the trust of users (Hay, 2015; Maroun, 2018; Simnett et al., 2016). However, the connection between IR and the assurance of sustainability information is a new scenario in corporate practice that is characterized by a paucity of practical guidance (Cohen and Simnett, 2015; Demartini and Trucco, 2017; Maroun, 2017).

In the following section, an overview of IR assurance trends is presented. Then both the standards used for the assurance process of IR and the main technical challenges and methodological issues related with this process are analysed, followed by a synthesis of the main IR assurance issues analysed in the literature. The final section sets out the future challenges of IR assurance and the research opportunities that are associated with it.

IR assurance services: trends

Currently, the Global Reporting Initiative (GRI) Framework is the most widespread framework for the preparation of sustainability reports, with "63 percent of N100[3] reports and 75 percent of G250 reports applying it" (KPMG, 2017). In an evolutionary process in which sustainability issues on the international agenda are assuming relevance, the recent innovation that is the Integrated Report (IR) (IIRC, 2013) is gaining prominence and the *"number of companies that specifically label their reports as integrated"* is slowly and steadily increasing (KPMG, 2017, p. 24). During 2017, 14 per cent of companies among both the G250 and the N100 published an integrated corporate report and around two thirds declared that they follow the IIRC Framework, particularly in countries such as Japan and Spain where the increase has been more significant (KPMG, 2017).

While GRI standards are mostly focused on disclosing environmental, social, and governance (ESG) information through a set of specific Key Performance Indicators (KPIs), often as addenda to financial reporting (Jensen and Berg, 2012), IR attempts to overcome "silo vision", in order to interlink information in real time. Moreover, while GRI reporting is retrospective, IR places the focus on strategy, and prospective risks and opportunities for business: the IIRC Framework (IIRC, 2013) has a strategic and long-term vision that deals with questions concerning "where" the company intends to move and "how" it will deploy its future plans. Thus, IR presents a more holistic image of the company, which is meant to link the present with the future, as well as financial and non-financial information and measures. In line with the function that assurance brings to sustainability reporting (Larrinaga et al., 2018; Park and Brorson, 2005), third-party assurance has become a necessary mechanism that gives integrated reports greater credibility.

Progressive growth in the IR assurance market is expected (Cohen and Simnett, 2015; Green and Cheng, 2019), as mentioned above, due to the increased production of integrated reports and the demand for credible information worldwide (Birkey et al., 2016; Simnett and Huggins, 2015). In that respect, Serafeim (2015) found that the likelihood of "external assurance for the whole report is 45% higher for integrated reports" (p. 38) among companies preparing integrated or sustainability reports in keeping with the GRI guidelines. Consistent with those results, Miller et al. (2017, p. 8) found that the proportion of companies in the USA receiving external assurance on their reports, between 2013 and 2014, increased by 5 per cent. These results are surprising, considering that the adoption of IR assurance is voluntary in most countries, and that there are no guidelines offering detailed explanations on its implementation (e.g., Demartini and Trucco, 2017). All of this leads us to conclude that companies want to follow the latest reporting trends; despite all the difficulties that may imply.

Considering the countries that are leading the adoption of IR assurance, such as in the case of CSR assurance (Miller et al., 2017; Perego and Kolk, 2012), Kılıç (2018) pointed to Europe and South Africa. As Kılıç (2018) explained, it is not surprising in the case of South Africa, where IR assurance adoption is mandatory.

In the European context, Spain is an example of how the adoption of external verification for non-financial and diversity information in the integrated report has been reinforced by national legislation. Law 11/2018,[4] which transposes Directive 2014/95/EU on non-financial information into the Spanish legal system, states that non-financial information must be verified by an independent assurance provider, unlike some other European countries. The provision of assurance is not obligatory in the directive. Thus, Directive 2014/95/EU makes clear, with regard to the verification of the reports, that:

> statutory auditors and audit firms should only check that the non-financial state-ment or the separate report has been provided. In addition, it should be possible for Member States to require that the information included in the non-financial statement or in the separate report be verified by an independent assurance services provider.
>
> *(European Commission, 2014, p. 330/3)*

Given the obligation to provide assurance in Spain, it is hardly surprising that, according to the EY (2019), most Spanish listed companies, in 2018, referred to the IIRC in their reports, and 100 per cent of those companies had had their reports verified. As early as 2016, eight Spanish companies, all of which were listed companies, were participating in the

IR adoption pilot plan (Rodríguez-Gutiérrez et al., 2019), and all provided external assurance to their integrated reports. The Spanish case suggests that the largest companies are fully aware of the relevance of considering IR in their reporting practices.

With regard to the type of industry leading the adoption of IR assurance, the financial industry, as with sustainability reporting, leads the adoption of IR assurance (Miller et al., 2017).

Most IR assurance engagements are not conducted on the whole report but only on some areas, and are carried out "by accounting firms in compliance with International Standards on Assurance Engagements 3000 (ISAE 3000), and provided with a limited level and narrow scope" (Kılıç, 2018, p. 38). It is also interesting to note that Kılıç (2018) found that social information was assured relatively rarely (it was more common to verify environmental information), in line with our findings with reference to the Spanish listed companies that participated in the IR adoption pilot plan in 2016.

Suitable standards for the IR assurance process

ISAE 3000 and AA1000 AS

Currently, the frameworks used as references for the IR assurance process are the ISAE 3000 standard and the AA1000 AS framework (Ackers and Eccles, 2015; Corrado et al., 2019; Maroun, 2017), already widely adopted for assurance on sustainability reporting and recognized as the main international assurance standards (e.g. Larrinaga et al., 2018). These frameworks are designed to provide assurance on readily identifiable subject matter, following precisely defined criteria such as the GRI Standards (Jones and Solomon, 2010; Maroun, 2017).

The ISAE 3000, a widely recognized international standard, is published by the International Auditing and Assurance Standards Board (IAASB), an independent international standard setting body, which develops frameworks for auditing and assurance, facilitating their adoption and implementation. The IAASB issues International Standards on Auditing (ISAs) used for financial audits and is therefore strongly accounting-oriented. ISAE 3000 identifies two different engagement levels; "reasonable assurance engagement" and "limited review engagement".

The first (reasonable assurance) requires that the assurance provider should reduce the engagement risk to an acceptably low level in the circumstances of the engagement, as the basis for a positively phrased statement ("we found the content of the report to be reliable") in the conclusions from the practitioner (IAASB, 2005). The aim of the second (limited assurance engagement) is the reduction of the assurance engagement risk to a level that is acceptable under the circumstances of the engagement, but where that risk is greater than it would be for a reasonable assurance engagement, leading to a negatively phrased statement of approval from the practitioner (IAASB, 2005) (i.e. "nothing has come to our attention suggesting that the content of the report is not reliable"). In that sense, the practitioner's conclusion in a limited assurance engagement will assume a highly cautious tone. Overall, the generic quality of ISAE 3000 is applied to a wide range of non-financial assurance exercises, rather than exclusively concerning itself with the provision of sustainability assurance.

AccountAbility, an international consulting and standard organization that helps firms to improve their responsible business practices and long-term performance, promotes AA1000S. It issued the AA1000 standard series as a set of interrelated frameworks: AA1000AS is the specific assurance standard published in 2003 and revised in 2008, which was also enriched with an

Addendum in 2018, to support organizational users and assurance providers. The AA1000AS is a standard based on four principles: inclusivity, materiality, responsiveness, and the new Impact principles that expect that companies "should monitor, measure and be accountable for how their actions affect their broader ecosystems" (AccountAbility, 2008, p. 8).

Standard AA1000AS provides two types of assurance engagement: type 1 and type 2. In type 1, the assurance provider is expected to "*evaluate the nature and the extent*" of adherence by the organization to all four AA1000 AccountAbility Principles Standards (see Larrinaga et al., 2018, Appendix 2). It must provide an assurance on how an organization manages sustainability performance and communicates them in a CSR or IR system, without verifying the reliability of the information (AccountAbility, 2008). A Type 2 assurance engagement goes a step further by evaluating the reliability of the specific sustainability information that is reported, as agreed in the scope of the engagement and selected on the basis of the materiality determination. Moreover, the type 2 assurance engagement may be conducted by providing a high or a moderate level of assurance. With a high level of assurance, the risk of an error in any conclusion is reduced to "*very low*", which will enhance user confidence, but not to a "*high level*", and it will merely require evidence gathering at a limited depth.

A key element of this framework is connected with the provision of final recommendations on reporting quality and the underlying organizational processes, as well as on the systems and the methodologies that are applied. The guidance also requires the provision of publicly available information concerning the assurance provider and its independence, impartiality and competencies. In this sense, AA1000AS "most closely aligns itself with the stakeholder accountability perspective" (O'Dwyer and Owen, 2005, p. 212). A detailed description of the main aspects described in an assurance statement that distinguish between the two standards can be found in Table 13.1.

What can be seen in Table 13.1 is that both frameworks lack the capacity to express an opinion on data of both a financial and a non-financial nature. As highlighted by Maroun (2017), these traditional methodologies "do not necessarily provide a suitable framework for supporting a formal opinion on an integrated report" (Maroun, 2017, p. 343), because they were not designed for a multi-dimensional document that aims to communicate a concise overview of an organization, integrating and connecting both quantitative and qualitative data. In this sense, IIRC suggested that:

> innovation is needed to overcome perceived inadequacies in meeting emerging needs with current practices or because premature assumptions about what assurance on <IR> should look like could actually inhibit innovation, not only in assurance on <IR> but also in the nature and quality of Integrated Reporting itself.
>
> *(IIRC, 2015 p. 14)*

Technical challenges and methodological issues

In response to this need for innovation, IIRC (2015) and IAASB (2019), through the involvement of a significant group of stakeholders (e.g. internal auditors; assurance practitioners; educators and trainers; professional bodies and related standard-setters), asked for contributions in facilitating: "the convergence of international and national auditing and assurance standards, thereby enhancing the quality and consistency of practice throughout the world and strengthening public confidence in

Table 13.1 Assurance standards framework comparison

Assurance engagement elements	AA1000AS	ISAE3000
Assurance practitioner characteristics		
Independence	✓	✓
Impartiality	✓	
Competence	✓	✓
Responsibility	□□□✓	✓
Criteria	Inclusivity; Materiality; Responsiveness; Impact	Relevance; Completeness; Reliability; Neutrality; Understandability
Nature and extent of the process	✓	
Scope		
Standard to be used	✓	✓
Stakeholder engagement	✓	
Objectives	✓	✓
Tasks and activities carried out	✓	✓
Sufficient and appropriate evidence	✓	✓
Assurance level and associated form	*Reasonable (positive form)/limited (negative form)*	*Type1/Type 2 Positive form*
Possibility to provide different levels for different subject matter	✓	✓
Formal requirements		
Title	✓	✓
Addressee	✓	✓
Date and place of the document	✓	✓
Name of the assuror and signature	✓	✓
Conclusions		
Evaluation of the system, processes, information, and data used to support sustainability performance disclosure on the issues agreed	✓	
Evaluation of the quality of the public disclosure and the underlying system, processes, information, and data	✓	

the global auditing and assurance profession" (IAASB, 2019 p. 2). The IIRC Framework has attempted to provide some level of standardization, to facilitate the application of assurance services to integrated reports (Miller et al., 2017, p. 5). However, the IIRC has provided no specific guidelines, explaining that it "does not aspire to be a leader in assurance" (IIRC, 2015, p. 6), and limiting the scope of its actions to researchers and practitioners, by encouraging them to experiment and to improve IR assurance practices. In this regard, the document "Assurance on <IR>. Overview of feedback and call to action" published in July 2015, summarizes significant matters raised in the previous consultation paper "Assurance on <IR>: Introduction to the discussion" (2014b) and identifies steps to ensure the debate continues and leads to effective solutions.

The international consultation paper on Extended External Reporting (EER) Assurance (IAASB, 2019) faces a range of technical challenges, and aims to stimulate discussion about specific (key) challenges in assurance engagements and to provide guidance that may support assurance users and providers. The results of this first phase include guidance for practitioners applying ISAE 3000 to the IR assurance process, showing awareness of the effort involved for companies in learning new practices, and for that reason, opting for a model grounded in existing audit practice.

A shared view expressed by respondents (and supported by academia, see for example Maroun, 2017) is that the complexity of IR has obliged professional practitioners to apply a broader, mixed approach to enhance credibility and confidence. Assurance is only one of a range of mechanisms that organizations can implement. Figure 13.1 represents the "Mixed approach to IR assurance".

This innovative "mixed approach to IR assurance" is based on four pillars: (1) internal audit; (2) governance and senior management; (3) stakeholder consultation; and (4) external assurance. The system of internal control (pillars 1 and 2) should establish whether the preconditions for an assurance engagement are present and support the external assurance process. However, IAASB highlights how governance and internal control over the reporting process often lack maturity, causing engagement acceptance issues. Finally, it is crucial to take into account the opinions of different stakeholders in the identification of material aspects.

When conducting an assurance engagement on an integrated report, the difficulty is to define the extent and the nature of the subject matter in a document that, by its nature, is interpretively constructed, dynamic and context-dependent. The considerable "variation in the interpretation of the IIRC's principles" permits organizations to explain how they are generating sustainable returns using different approaches (De Villiers et al., 2014, p. 1049). This causes uncertainty for assurance practitioners, because of the insecurity felt over the appropriateness of the report in terms of completeness, materiality and content "which should be subject to test procedures" (Maroun, 2017, p. 332; see also Maroun and Atkins, 2015).

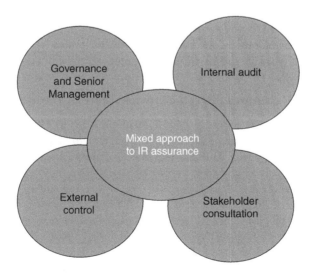

Figure 13.1 Mixed approach to IR assurance

Numerical and financial information are tested by assurors, adopting an approach based on specific test and criteria, in order to objectively verify data and processes without considering the extent to which business management is evidenced (Maroun and Atkins, 2015). If data are historical and factual, qualitative sections of an IR can be included in the subject matter of an assurance engagement (Maroun, 2017). To that end, those charged with governance must explain how they have relied on different forms of "security", in order to issue a statement on the reliability and the completeness of an IR.

Materiality is maybe the most important (and debated) guiding principle proposed by the IIRC. The materiality concept, widely proposed in both the financial reporting and CSR reporting systems, considers information to be "material" when its omission or misstatement would influence decisions made by the report's users, which according to the IIRC "requires a high degree of judgment and involves numerous strategic considerations". The manner in which material information is defined and then selected throughout the assurance engagement process represents a crucial and challenging issue for practitioners, given the complexity of assessing quantitative thresholds for non-financial information (Mio, 2013).

Numerous respondents emphasize that in the absence of standards that can be applied to examine and test the materiality of the information in an integrated report, any references to materiality are of little value. The strategy of "unpacking" IR using different standards and methodologies for different sections now appears to be the most efficient approach. For example, this view assumes that the financial information will be audited with reference to ISAE 3000, and that non-financial information will be secured (in part) following AA1000 (or even some other additional standard such as ISAE 3410, which is used for dealing with greenhouse gas statements in conjunction with ISAE 3000).

Consequently, issues related to the level of assurance that can reasonably be provided; the examination of different types of capitals (and their interconnections); and how to assure additional narrative and future-oriented information (i.e., Maroun, 2017; Maroun and Atkins, 2015; Simnett and Huggins, 2015) represent challenges and technical issues that will be have to be negotiated.

One further critical area is connected with the range of skills and expertise necessary to carry out an IR assurance engagement. In particular, a comprehensive skill called "integrated business analysis" (IAASB, 2019 p. 18) that consists of a holistic understanding of how value is generated and distributed across the full range of capitals includes ethical values; industry-specific expertise; professional scepticism and judgment; using a risk-based approach; assessing the work of specialists; and evaluating the appropriateness of evidence.

IR assurance literature review: state of the art

In this section, we present an analysis of the most recent academic studies on IR assurance services. Although the IIRC encourages research as a tool to improve the quality of IR assurance practices (Corrado et al., 2019), studies that have explored the content, the processes, and the methodologies of IR assurance services are scarce (Dumay et al., 2016; Green and Cheng, 2019). Most studies on IR assurance are conceptual and theoretical (i.e., Cheng et al., 2014; De Villiers et al., 2014; Dumay et al., 2016; Simnett and Huggins, 2015; Stubbs and Higgins, 2014) and published empirical studies are mainly restricted to specific contexts (see Caglio et al., 2019; Maroun and Atkins, 2015; Maroun, 2017, 2018, 2019 on South Africa; Briem and Wald, 2018 for Germany; Miller et al., 2017 on the USA).

An initial line of research focused its attention on the effects of an external IR assurance mechanism (Caglio et al., 2019; De Villiers et al., 2014; Dumay et al., 2016;

Mio, 2013; Simnett and Huggins, 2015; Simnett et al., 2016; Stubbs and Higgins, 2014). These studies highlighted several critical aspects and methodological challenges: among others, the use of appropriated assurance models and their appropriateness for the IR; and the need for complex skills to administer IR assurance – requiring multidisciplinary assurance teams (e.g. Simnett and Huggins, 2015; Simnett et al., 2016; Stubbs and Higgins, 2014). Simnett et al. (2016) highlighted

> a number of technical challenges outstanding in the IR assurance process, such as identifying materiality levels, the level of assurance that can reasonably be provided on aspects of the integrated report, and how to assure more discursive and future-oriented information.
>
> *(p. 271)*

Caglio et al. (2019) analysed the difficulty of reading integrated reports, highlighting that the lack of clarity of the text is less problematic when the integrated report is assured. Therefore, the provision of assurance potentiates the creation of firms' economic value.

Despite the growth of IR assurance, apart from some exceptions (Briem and Wald, 2018; Maroun, 2019), little is known of the determinants of IR assurance adoption (De Villiers et al., 2014, 2017; Rinaldi et al., 2018). Briem and Wald (2018) presented the first empirical evidence on the factors that determine IR assurance. Specifically, Briem and Wald (2018) examined the question using the insights offered by institutional theory and the diffusion of innovations theory. Their analysis looked at the influence of the motivation that exists within a company and the role that auditors play in the implementation of IR assurance and the development of IR assurance processes. They found that coercive pressures from company stakeholders motivated the provision of IR assurance. Interestingly, the authors underlined the dangers of IR assurance turning into a new ceremonial response to satisfy increasingly stringent market pressures, arguing that auditors are needed for proper guidance of the implementation of the IR assurance process. They likewise warned that an understanding of company motivation and the auditor's task of implementing the IR assurance process would also require an understanding of investor participation, due to the significant role of investors and their influence.

Maroun (2019) used framing theory to study the same issue and complemented the Briem and Wald's (2018) results, finding that coercive pressures are not the only motivation for the provision of IR assurance, as normative and mimetic forces also drive the adoption of IR assurance. Moreover, Maroun (2019) explained that the provision of external IR assurance is influenced by the relevance of IR for the organization (and that factors such as firm size and type of industry are by no means the main determinants). The conclusions that Maroun (2019) offered were consistent with those of Larrinaga et al. (2018) in the case of sustainability reporting, which demonstrated that corporate characteristics (e.g., size or listed status) cannot in themselves account for the adoption of sustainability assurance.

A further line of research has explored both the internal and the external approaches that organizations employ to assure an integrated report (Maroun, 2017, 2018; Maroun and Atkins, 2015). Maroun and Atkins (2015) conducted an exploratory study in which audit experts were interviewed in South Africa, to suggest a short-term solution for achieving an IR assurance model/approach, so that practitioners can:

develop a set of guidelines which recommend those parts of the integrated report that should be the subject of an assurance engagement and offer a basis for describing how assurance is provided over the material components of the integrated report.

(Maroun and Atkins, 2015, p. 5)

Maroun (2017) developed a potential approach based on interviews with auditors and practitioners in South Africa, complemented by principles from existing assurance frameworks used in ISAs and ISAE. The insight from that study formed the basis of three assurance models: "restricted, integrated and Delphi-inspired assurance" (p. 329). These three models are associated with three levels of assurance over the integrated report. The restricted level focuses on the examination of the financial information and possible inconsistencies in the integrated report; the integrated model provides assurance to some parts of the integrated report; and the Delphi model provides assurance to the whole report. This last model requires a highly qualified team and a panel of experts. Broader and more complex subject matter such as providing assurance to the entire integrated report requires a multidisciplinary team, with a consequent increase in costs. To enhance the value of the assurance process, assurors must have adequate knowledge and heterogeneous skills and expertise (IIRC, 2015).

In a subsequent study, Maroun (2018) added to his earlier work (Maroun, 2017), by proposing a framework for the IR assurance process through which the "initial elements of an interpretive assurance model" (p. 400) could be identified. These elements are:

an examination of the completeness of the explanation of the value creation process provided in an integrated report; the methods used to support management discussion and analysis; and the reasonability of the review process used to ensure the reliability of qualitative, subjective and forward-looking representations contained in an integrated report.

(Maroun, 2018, p. 400)

As Kılıç (2018) explained, the framework that Maroun (2018) proposed is a useful one, because quantitative items are mainly assured, despite the substantial quantity of qualitative information that can be assured in an IR. In that sense, the interpretive assurance model that Maroun (2018) advanced is fundamental for the analysis of the qualitative, subjective, and forward-looking information that is disclosed.

Table 13.2 summarizes the main aspects that the literature explores, showing associated findings and issues that remain open.

Future challenges and research opportunities

Despite the considerable prominence that integrated reports have gained among the audit innovations of the past decade, several challenges persist that will only be answered over time.

In order to define and construct assurance practice, it is first necessary to understand the content and extent of integrated thinking (Stubbs and Higgins, 2014). To that end, time must be allowed for organizations that are going through the learning process to introduce this new framework, as the existing literature has made clear (e.g., Adams, 2015). The adoption of this new framework requires, among other things, changes in decision-making and communication processes (Adams, 2014).

A further challenge is related to the role of government in promoting IR assurance quality. The South African and Spanish cases offer examples of state regulations that

Table 13.2 Summary of the main IR assurance issues analysed by the literature

IR assurances issues	Main studies	Main findings	Some concerns
The role of IR assurance	Corrado et al. (2019); De Villiers et al. (2014); Maroun and Atkins (2015); Reimsbach et al. (2017); Simnett and Huggins (2015)	– Increase in both the production of integrated reports and the demand for credible information worldwide. – Lack of independence of assurance practitioners, which can affect the objectivity and robustness of the whole assurance process. – High level of heterogeneity in the concept of IR assurance.	– IR assurance as a managerial tool to improve investors' perceptions. – Ambiguity and heterogeneity surrounding IR assurance.
Factors explaining the adoption of an external IR assurance.	Briem and Wald (2018); Maroun (2019)	– Coercive pressures + normative and mimetic forces driving the adoption of IR assurance. – Adoption of external IR assurance is influenced by the relevance of IR for the organization (factors such as firm size and type of industry are not the main determinants).	– IR assurance risks turning into a new ceremonial response to increasingly stringent market pressures. – Need for changes to existing assurance practices.
Trends during the adoption of IR assurance.	Kılıç (2018); Miller et al. (2017)	– Increase in the percentage of integrated reports with external assurance. – IR assurance is voluntary in most countries. – Regarding the adoption of IR assurance:	– Absence of any detailed guidelines that explain implementation procedures.

(Continued)

Table 13.2 (Cont.)

IR assurances issues	Main studies	Main findings	Some concerns
		– Europe and South Africa are at present the global leaders. – The financial industry is the leading sector.	
Effects of IR assurance adoption	De Villiers et al. (2014); Dumay et al. (2016); Mio (2013); Simnett and Huggins (2015); Caglio et al. (2019)	• In terms of the effects of the adoption of an external IR assurance mechanism for improving the credibility several methodological challenges need to be overcome. • In terms of the economic consequences of the adoption of IR assurance	• Doubts over its appropriateness compared to its perceived benefits.
Materiality and completeness of the IR.	Green and Cheng (2019); Maroun and Atkins (2015); Mio (2013); Simnett and Huggins (2015)	• Materiality and completeness, crucial technical challenges outstanding. For example, the importance of how qualitative factors affect the determination of materiality and, in general, the difficulty over the definition of the material information for its selection.	• Lack of guidance over the definition of material aspects.
Potential (external and internal) approaches to the IR assurance process.	Maroun and Atkins (2015); Maroun (2017, 2018); Simnett et al. (2016)	Interpretative assurance models (e.g. restricted, integrated and Delphi-inspired assurance) appear to be more appropriate when analysing the qualitative information included in the IR.	• Lack of global regulation and specific standards.

encourage companies to adopt an IR framework (in the South African case) and to provide assurance using an external provider (in the Spanish case).

Integrated reporting assurance also opens the door to significant employment opportunities. Assurors wishing to enhance the value of the assurance process require proper knowledge, heterogeneous skills, and expertise (IIRC, 2015), in response to the rising demand for higher quality assurance providers. Integrated reporting assurance practice still appears to be at an initial stage, in which practices and processes have yet to be consolidated, and the traditional Big-4 accounting firms are still the market leaders. Nevertheless, even the Big-4 companies have been observed to limit their work to specified sections of the reports, partly because they lack the heterogeneous competences needed to negotiate an assurance engagement that covers the entire integrated report.

Future academic studies could attempt to find deeper explanations for the construction of rules and routines and their configuration throughout the IR assurance process. An understanding of IR assurance practice requires an examination of the content of an assured integrated report that refers to its characteristics (see Larrinaga et al., 2018, on sustainability reporting assurance). Despite the relevance of understanding the practice itself, little is known about the configuration of IR assurance practice. An exploration of the emergence of IR assurance in relation to the role of the assurors, such as institutional entrepreneurship or/and carriers (Sahlin-Andersson and Engwall, 2002), would also represent an important contribution in this investigative area. A deeper explanation of the possible motivations that lead companies to adopt IR assurance, and the role of external IR assurance providers, as well as investor involvement in IR and the assurance process, would be potential areas of exploration in the future.

Finally, we would like to stress that the nature of IR is forward-looking, strategically focused and should communicate the interconnections between different types of resources and capitals (financial and manufacturing, intellectual, human, social, relational, and natural), as well as organizational strategy, risk assessment, and business operations. Thus, explanations could also be sought in future studies relating to the management of stakeholder relations and the generation of sustainable returns (Maroun, 2017). In that sense, the journey is just beginning and the extent of the information communicated to stakeholders and its content and quality is still in an embryonic state (Busco et al., 2013; Corrado et al., 2019).

Notes

1 "The G250 refers to the world's 250 largest companies by revenue, based on the Fortune 500 ranking of 2016" (KPMG, 2017, p. 3).
2 Directive 2014/95/EU of the European Parliament and of the Council of 22 October 2014.
3 "The N100 refers to a worldwide sample of 4,900 companies comprising the top 100 companies by revenue" (KPMG, 2017, p. 3).
4 Law 11/2018, of the Spanish Official State Bulletin, 28 December 2018.

References

AccountAbility. (2008). *AA1000AS Assurance Standard*. London: AccountAbility.
Ackers, B., and Eccles, N. S. (2015). Mandatory corporate social responsibility assurance practices: The case of King III in South Africa. *Accounting, Auditing & Accountability Journal, 28*(4), 515–550.
Adams, C. A. (2014). *The assurance of integrated reports: Let's get some perspective before we get technical*. Available at: https://drcaroladams.net/the-assurance-of-integrated-reports-lets-get-some-perspective-before-we-get-technical/ (Accessed: 9 October 2019).
Adams, C. A. (2015). The International Integrated Reporting Council: A call to action'. *Critical Perspectives on Accounting, 27*, 23–28.

Birkey, R. N., Michelon, G., Patten, D. M., and Sankara, J. (2016). Does assurance on CSR reporting enhance environmental reputation? An examination in the U. S. context. *Accounting Forum, 40*, 143–152.

Boiral, O. (2013). Sustainability reports as simulacra? A counter-account of A and A+ GRI reports. *Accounting, Auditing & Accountability Journal, 26*(7), 1036–1071.

Briem, C. R., and Wald, A. (2018). Implementing third-party assurance in integrated reporting: Companies' motivation and auditors' role. *Accounting, Auditing & Accountability Journal, 31*(5), 1461–1485.

Busco, C., Frigo, M. L., Riccaboni, A., and Quattrone, P. (2013). *Integrated reporting. Concepts and cases that redefine corporate accountability.* Switzerland: Springer.

Busco, C., Granà, F., and Izzo, M. F. (2018). *Sustainable development goals and integrated reporting.* London: Routledge.

Caglio, A., Melloni, G., and Perego, P. (2019). Informational content and assurance of textual disclosures: Evidence on integrated reporting. *European Accounting Review.* doi:10.1080/09638180.2019.1677486.

Cheng, M., Green, W., Conradie, P., Konishi, N., and Romi, A. (2014). The international integrated reporting framework: Key issues and future research opportunities. *Journal of International Financial Management & Accounting, 25*(1), 90–119.

Cohen, J. R., and Simnett, R. (2015). CSR and assurance services: A research agenda. *Auditing: A Journal of Practice & Theory, 34*(1), 59–74.

Corrado, M., Demartini, P., and Dumay, J. (2019). Assurance on integrated reporting: A critical perspective. In S. O. Idowu, and M. del Baldo (Eds.), *Integrated reporting* (pp. 199–217). Cham: Springer.

De Villiers, C., Rinaldi, L., and Unerman, J. (2014). Integrated reporting: Insights, gaps and an agenda for future research. *Accounting, Auditing & Accountability Journal, 27*(7), 1042–1067.

De Villiers, C., Venter, E. R., and Hsiao, P.-C. K. (2017). Integrated reporting: Background, measurement issues, approaches and an agenda for future research. *Accounting & Finance, 57*(4), 937–959.

Demartini, C., and Trucco, S. (2017). Integrated reporting. In C. Demartini, and S. Trucco (Eds.), *Integrated reporting and audit quality* (pp. 9–35). Cham: Springer.

Dumay, J., Bernardi, C., Guthrie, J., and Demartini, P. (2016). Integrated reporting: A structured literature review. *Accounting Forum, 40*(3), 166–185.

Eccles, R. G., and Krzus, M. (2010). *One report: Integrated reporting for a sustainable strategy.* Hoboken, NJ: Wiley.

European Commission. (2014). *Directive 2014/95/EU of the European Parliament and of the Council of 22 October 2014 amending directive 2013/34/EU as regards disclosure of non-financial and diversity information by certain large undertakings and groups.* Available at: https://eur-lex.europa.eu/legal-con tent/EN/TXT/?uri=CELEX%3A32014L0095 (Accessed: 9 October 2019).

EY. (2019). *Rethinking sustainability. Estudio Comparativo de los Estados de Información No Financiera (EINF) del IBEX 35.* Available at: www.ey.com/Publication/vwLUAssets/ey-rethinking-sustainability-estu dio-comparativo-de-los-estados-de-informacion-no-financiera-del-ibex-35/$FILE/ey-rethinking-sus tainability-estudio-comparativo-de-los-estados-de-informacion-no-financiera-del-ibex-35.pdf (Accessed: 9 October 2019).

Green, W. J., and Cheng, M. M. (2019). Materiality judgments in an integrated reporting setting: The effect of strategic relevance and strategy map. *Accounting, Organizations and Society, 73*, 1–14.

Hay, D. (2015). The frontiers of auditing research. *Meditari Accountancy Research, 23*, 158–174.

Hodge, K., Subramaniam, N., and Stewart, J. (2009). Assurance of sustainability reports: Impact on report users' confidence and perceptions of information credibility. *Australian Accounting Review, 19*(3), 178–194.

IAASB. (2005). *Handbook of international auditing, assurance, and ethics pronouncements 2005 edition.* Available at: www.mas-business.com/docs/2005_IAASB_HandBook.pdf (Accessed: 9 October 2019).

IAASB. (2019). *Extended External Reporting (EER) assurance IAASB consultation paper.* Available at: www. ifac.org/system/files/publications/files/EER-Consultation-Paper.pdf (Accessed: 9 October 2019).

IIRC. (2013). *The international integrated reporting framework.* London, UK: IIRC.

IIRC. (2014a). *Assurance on <IR>. An explanation of issues.* London, UK: IIRC.

IIRC. (2014b). *Assurance on <IR>. An introduction to the discussion.* London, UK: IIRC.

IIRC. (2015). *Assurance on <IR>. Overview of feedback and call to action.* Available at: http://integrate dreporting.org/wp-content/uploads/2015/07/IIRC-Assurance-Overview-July-2015.pdf (Accessed: 9 October 2019).

Jensen, J. C., and Berg, N. (2012). Determinants of traditional sustainability reporting versus integrated reporting. An institutionalist approach. *Business Strategy and the Environment, 21*(5), 299–316.

Jones, M. J., and Solomon, J. F. (2010). Social and environmental report assurance: Some interview evidence. *Accounting Forum, 34*(1), 20–31.

Kend, M. (2015). Governance, firm-level characteristics and their impact on the client's voluntary sustainability disclosures and assurance decisions. *Sustainability Accounting, Management and Policy Journal, 6*(1), 54–78.

Kılıç, M. (2018). *Assurance of integrated reports: Evidence from early adopters*, 3rd International Trakya Accounting Finance and Auditing Symposium, 1–4 October 2018, Trakya University.

Kolk, A., and Perego, P. (2010). Determinants of the adoption of sustainability assurance statements: An international investigation. *Business Strategy and the Environment, 19*(3), 182–198.

KPMG. (2017). *KPMG International survey of corporate responsibility reporting 2017*. Amsterdam: KPMG International.

Larrinaga, C., Rossi, A., Luque-Vilchez, M., and Núñez-Nickel, M. (2018). Institutionalization of the contents of sustainability assurance services: A comparison between Italy and United States. *Journal of Business Ethics*, 1–17. doi:10.1007/s10551-018-4014-z.

Maroun, W. (2017). Assuring the integrated report: Insights and recommendations from auditors and preparers. *The British Accounting Review, 49*(3), 329–346.

Maroun, W. (2018). Modifying assurance practices to meet the needs of integrated reporting: The case for "interpretive assurance". *Accounting, Auditing & Accountability Journal, 31*(2), 400–427.

Maroun, W. (2019). Exploring the rationale for integrated report assurance. *Accounting, Auditing & Accountability Journal, 32*(6), 1826–1854.

Maroun, W., and Atkins, J. (2015). *The challenges of assuring integrated reports: Views from the South African auditing community*. London: The Association of Chartered Certified Accountants.

Miller, K. C., Fink, L., and Proctor, T. Y. (2017). Current trends and future expectations in external assurance for integrated corporate sustainability reporting. *Journal of Legal, Ethical and Regulatory Issues, 20*(1), 1–17.

Mio, C. (2013). Materiality and assurance: Building the link. In C. Busco, M. L. Frigo, A. Riccaboni, and P. Quattrone (Eds.), *Integrated reporting* (pp. 79–94). Cham: Springer.

Monciardini, D., Dumay, J., and Biondi, L. (2016). *Integrated reporting and EU law. Competing, converging or complementary regulatory frameworks?* SMART conference "Life-cycle based management and reporting for sustainable business", University of Oslo, Norway.

O'Dwyer, B., and Owen, D. L. (2005). Assurance statement practice in environmental, social and sustainability reporting: A critical evaluation. *The British Accounting Review, 37*(2), 205–229.

Park, J., and Brorson, T. (2005). Experiences of and views on third-party assurance of corporate environmental and sustainability reports. *Journal of Cleaner Production, 13*(10–11), 1095–1106.

Perego, P., and Kolk, A. (2012). Multinationals' accountability on sustainability: The evolution of third-party assurance of sustainability reports. *Journal of Business Ethics, 110*(2), 173–190.

Reimsbach, D., Hahn, R., and Gürtürk, A. (2017). Integrated reporting and assurance of sustainability information: An experimental study on professional investors' information processing. *European Accounting Review, 27*(3), 559–581.

Rinaldi, L., Unerman, J., and De Villiers, C. (2018). Evaluating the integrated reporting journey: Insights gaps and agendas for future research. *Accounting, Auditing & Accountability Journal, 3*(5), 1294–1318.

Rodríguez-Gutiérrez, P., Correa, C., and Larrinaga, C. (2019). Is integrated reporting transformative? An exploratory study of non-financial reporting archetypes. *Sustainability Accounting, Management and Policy Journal, 10*(3), 617–644.

Sahlin-Andersson, K., and Engwall, L. (2002). Carriers, flows, and sources of management knowledge. In K. Sahlin-Andersson, and L. Engwall (Eds.), *The Expansion of management knowledge* (pp. 9–28). Stanford, California: Stanford University Press.

Serafeim, G. (2015). Integrated reporting and investor clientele. *Journal of Applied Corporate Finance, 27*(2), 34–51.

Simnett, R., and Huggins, A. L. (2015). Integrated reporting and assurance: Where can research add value? *Sustainability Accounting, Management and Policy Journal, 6*(1), 29–53.

Simnett, R., Zhou, S., and Hoang, H. (2016). Assurance and other credibility enhancing mechanisms for integrated reporting. In C. Mio (Ed.), *Integrated reporting* (pp. 269–286). London: Palgrave Macmillan.

Stubbs, W., and Higgins, C. (2014). Integrated reporting and internal mechanisms of change. *Accounting, Auditing & Accountability Journal, 27*(7), 1068–1089.

Zadek, S., Raynard, P., Forstater, M., and Oelschlaegel, J. (2004). *The future of sustainability assurance*. London: Certified Accountants Educational Trust.

14

THE IMPACT OF GOVERNANCE ON INTEGRATED REPORTING

A literature review

Patrick Velte and Jannik Gerwanski

Institute of Management, Accounting & Finance (IMAF), Leuphana University Lueneburg

Abstract

In line with the increasing relevance of integrated reporting (IR) in recent years, a growing body of research has emerged investigating various determinants of IR implementation and quality. Corporate governance potentially affects IR practices; prior studies have documented their influence on sustainability reporting and other forms of voluntary disclosure. This chapter provides a systematic literature review of empirical quantitative studies that analyse the relationship between specific governance factors and IR. Building on stakeholder-agency theory, our literature review describes the effect of both firm-specific and country-specific governance factors on IR. The subsequent discussion of key implications and recommendations for further research offers valuable insights for academia, practice and regulators.

Introduction

Integrated reporting (IR) is intended to summarize a firm's value creation over time by combining all material financial and nonfinancial information into one concise business report (IIRC, 2013). This new reporting medium has two goals: putting an end to the disconnected and heterogeneous corporate reporting environment, and delivering decision-useful information to a firm's various stakeholder groups (Eccles and Krzus, 2010, 2015). As stated in the International Integrated Reporting Council's (IIRC) Framework, one major content element in IR is governance. Although IR is increasingly gaining momentum in practice and academia (De Villiers et al., 2014, 2017a, 2017b; De Villiers and Sharma, 2017), empirical quantitative research on the impact of governance variables on IR is rare in comparison to research on sustainability reporting. The following literature review identifies, organizes and condenses the prevailing literature on firm-specific and country-related governance factors, and reveals factors that drive the decision to implement IR and affect IR quality. Subsequently, we stress the main limitations of current research and provide useful recommendations for future research.

Theoretical foundation and IR research framework

According to the IIRC Framework, IR aims to give a concise presentation of the firm's value creation over time for 'all stakeholders interested in an organization' (IIRC, 2013, p.4). In line with the intention to provide decision-useful information by combining all *material* financial and nonfinancial information in one report, the underlying integrated thinking approach implies that integrated reports also contain all *material* information related to a firm's governance structure (e.g. De Villiers et al., 2014; Lai et al., 2016; Gerwanski et al., 2019).

Stakeholder-agency theory (Hill and Jones, 1992) has a central role in IR research (e.g., Frias-Aceituno et al., 2014; Gianfelici et al., 2018). The theory posits that the information disclosed in integrated reports should decrease information asymmetries and alleviate conflicts of interest between managers and different stakeholder groups (Eccles and Krzus, 2015). In order to conduct effective IR procedures, firms need appropriate internal and external CG systems. Hence, different *internal CG mechanisms*, such as the composition of the board of directors and its committees, should reduce agency costs and increase the likelihood of compiling a (high quality) integrated report. Nevertheless, in the light of its narrative nature and the lack of specific guidelines, prior research has shown that the preparation of an integrated report is characterized by managerial discretion (Beattie, 2014; Higgins et al., 2014; Lai et al., 2018), which paves the way for corporate greenwashing and impression management. These circumstances emphasize the relevance of different *external CG institutions* (e.g., institutional investors, blockholders or an external IR assurer), which monitor management's sustainability-related activities and contribute to the credibility of integrated reports. Further, *country-specific governance factors* that relate to a firm's operating environment may influence its willingness to implement IR and disclose its value creation process to investors and other stakeholders. Factors such as a country's investor protection laws, degree of legal enforcement, legal origin and culture may affect IR preparation and presentation of information.

Despite governance factors being highly relevant to IR, and extensive consideration of governance in related literature reviews on corporate social responsibility (CSR) reporting (e.g., Velte, 2017), extant IR literature reviews do not focus on governance factors (e.g., De Villiers et al., 2014, 2017a, 2017b; De Villiers and Sharma, 2017). For this reason, the following review structures the existing IR literature according to firm-specific (internal and external CG) and country-specific governance factors, as shown in Figure 14.1. Specifically, with respect to the firm-specific dimension, we differentiate between a variety of board composition variables (e.g., diversity, independence, size and expertise) as well as shareholder and assurance-related variables (e.g., assurance of the integrated or CSR report). Regarding country-specific governance factors, we distinguish between investor protection, legal enforcement, legal origin and culture.

Method

Using a keyword search for 'integrated reporting', we searched multiple bibliographic databases, including Web of Science, Google Scholar, SSRN, EBSCO and Science Direct, for studies investigating IR in a CG context. Our selection was not limited to a specific country or time frame, but focused only on multivariate archival studies published in peer-reviewed literature, which were analysed using vote counting (Light and Smith, 1971). We deliberately discarded studies without an international journal ranking (ABS, Scimago, VHB Jourqual), to ensure the quality of the studies. In total, we identified 16 studies matching

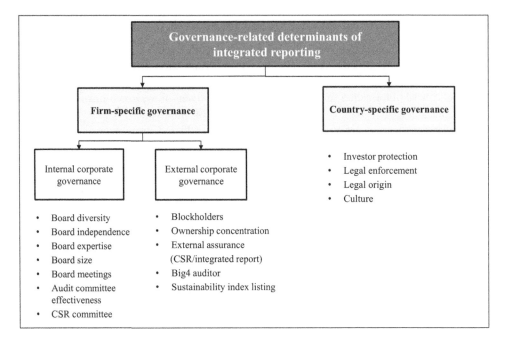

Figure 14.1 Governance-related determinants of IR

our sampling criteria. Table 14.1 provides an overview of the selected studies, arranged by publication year, region, journal and content.

The selection of studies shows an increasing number of publications in high-ranked empirical literature over time, which is reflective of the accelerating awareness of IR in academic research. All but one study refer to an international setting. Overall, studies on the determinants of publishing an integrated report have investigated both firm-specific and country-specific factors, whereas the determinants for IR quality are predominantly analysed from a firm-specific angle. Table 14.2 summarizes the key results.

Firm-specific governance factors (CG)

In line with the expected relevance of a firm's CG to IR, Lai et al. (2016) and Melloni et al. (2017) used the Bloomberg governance scores to investigate the effect of a firm's governance performance on publishing integrated reports and IR quality, respectively. While Melloni et al. (2017) came to the conclusion that governance performance is not related to IR quality, Lai et al. (2016) showed that firms with higher governance performance are more likely to release an integrated report. The results indicate that governance performance seems to drive the likelihood of engaging in IR, but does not lead to differences in quality. The following sections present the results of our review, concentrating on internal and external firm-specific CG determinants on IR.

Internal corporate governance

The board of directors is not only responsible for representing stakeholders' interests, but also has the duty of controlling management and overseeing CG practices (Ben-Amar and

Table 14.1 Selection of studies

Firm-specific governance factors		Country-specific governance factors	
Panel A: Publication year			
Total: 16	• 2019: 2	• 2019: 1	
	• 2018: 3	• 2018: 1	
	• 2017: 3	• 2017: 2	
	• 2016: 4	• 2016: 1	
	• 2015: 1	• 2013: 2	
	• 2013: 1		
Panel B: Region			
Total: 16	• International: 13	• International: 7	
	• South Africa: 1		
Panel C: Journal			
Total: 16	• Australian Accounting Review (1)	• Australian Accounting Review (1)	
	• Business Ethics (1)	• Business Ethics (1)	
	• Business Strategy and the Environment (3)	• Business Strategy and the Environment (1)	
	• Corporate Social Responsibility and Environmental Management (3)	• Corporate Social Responsibility and Environmental Management (1)	
	• Journal of Accounting and Public Policy (1)	• International Business Review (1)	
	• Journal of Cleaner Production (1)	• Journal of Cleaner Production (1)	
	• Managerial Auditing Journal (2)	• Social Responsibility Journal (1)	
	• Problems and Perspectives in Management (1)		
	• Social Responsibility Journal (1)		
Panel D: Content			
Total: 16	• Publication of an integrated report: 6	• Publication of an integrated report: 5	
	• Integrated reporting quality: 7	• Integrated reporting quality: 2	

McIlkenny, 2015). Accordingly, different board characteristics that contribute to board efficiency and affect management's decision to both compile an integrated report and determine IR quality have been identified (Gerwanski et al., 2019). Since prior research has found that board diversity enriches corporate decisions with respect to financial and CSR reporting (e.g., Rupley et al., 2012; McGuinness et al., 2017), prior studies have investigated the effect of *gender diversity* (Frias-Aceituno et al., 2013b; Fasan and Mio, 2017; Garcia-Sanchez and Noguera-Gamez, 2018; Kilic and Kuzey, 2018; Gerwanski et al., 2019) and *foreign diversity* (Frias-Aceituno et al., 2013b) on IR practices. Given that female representation is argued to enrich corporate board decisions through different perspectives,

Table 14.2 Key results of archival research on the impact of firm-specific and country-specific governance variables on IR

Year	Author(s)	Reference	Country Sample size Period	Independent variable(s)	Dependent variable(s)	Significant results
2019	Garcia-Sanchez et al.	Corporate Social Responsibility and Environmental Management	• International • 6,442 firm-year observations • 2006–2014	• Board characteristics factor (independence, gender diversity, experience, expertise, external consultants) • Investor protection factor (anti-self-dealing index, creditor protection and capital market development) • Country transparency index (index of corruption perception)	• Publication of an integrated report	• Board as control mechanism (+) • Investor protection as control mechanism (+) • Country transparency (+) • Munificence * Board (+) • Munificence * Investor protection (+) • Munificence * Country transparency (+)
2019	Gerwanski et al.	Business Strategy and the Environment	• International • 359 firm-year observations • 2013–2016	• Board gender diversity • IR assurance • Dow Jones Sustainability Index (DJSI) listing	• IR quality (materiality disclosure quality)	• Board gender diversity (+) • IR assurance (+)

2018	Garcia-Sanchez and Noguera-Gamez	Australian Accounting Review	• International
			• 3,294 firm-year observations
			• 2009–2013
				• Board size
				• Board gender diversity
				• Investor protection:
				  • Common/civil law
				  • Anti-director rights
				  • Country's judicial efficiency
				  • Country's index of law and order
					• Publication of an integrated report	• Country's judicial efficiency (+)
						• Country's index of law and order (+)

Year	Author	Journal	Sample	Independent variables	Dependent variables	Results
2018	Kilic and Kuzey	Managerial Auditing Journal	International 55 firm-year observations 2014	• Board size • Board independence • Board gender diversity	• IR quality (forward-looking disclosure index)	• Board gender diversity (+)
2018	Velte	Problems and Perspectives in Management	International 215 firm-year observations 2014–2016	• Audit committee financial expertise • Audit committee sustainability expertise	• IR quality (readability)	• Audit committee financial expertise (+) • Audit committee sustainability expertise (+) • Audit committee financial expertise * sustainability expertise (+)
2017	Fasan and Mio	Business Strategy and the Environment	International 65 IIRC pilot programme members 2012–2013	• Board size • Board independence • Board meetings • Board gender diversity • Legal origin	• IR quality (materiality disclosure quality)	• Board size (−) • Board gender diversity (−)
2017	Melloni et al.	Journal of Accounting and Public Policy	International 104 firm-year observations 2013–2014	• Governance performance	• IR quality: Conciseness (length, readability) • Completeness (ESG score) • Balance (tone)	• No effect (±)
2017	Rivera-Arrubla et al.	Social Responsibility Journal	International 91 firm-year observations 2011	• Legal origin (code/case law) • Big four firm for financial audit • External assurance of the IR	• IR quality (disclosure index)	• External assurance (+)

(Continued)

Table 14.2 (Cont.)

Year	Author (s)	Reference	Country / Sample size / Period	Independent variable(s)	Dependent variable(s)	Significant results
2016	Haji and Anifowose	Managerial Auditing Journal	• South Africa • 246 firm-year observations • 2011–2013	• Overall audit committee effectiveness • Audit committee size • Audit committee meetings • Audit committee independence • Audit committee financial expertise • Audit committee authority • Sustainability committee • Ownership concentration • Governance performance	• IR Quality: • Extent of IR • Quality of IR (based on the IIRC's <IR> Framework guiding principles)	Extent of IR/IR Quality • Overall audit committee effectiveness (+) • Audit committee meetings (+) • Audit committee authority (+) • Sustainability committee (+) • Ownership concentration (+)
2016	Lai et al.	Business Strategy and the Environment	• International • 309 (matched) firm-year observations • 2009–2011	• Governance performance	• Publication of an integrated report	• Governance performance (+)
2016	Stacchezzini et al.	Journal of Cleaner Production	• International • 54 firm-year observations • 2011–2013	• Board independence	• IR quality (sustainability action disclosure)	• Board independence (–)
2016	Vaz et al.	Business Ethics: A European Review	• International • 1,449 firm-year observations • 2012	• Legal origin (code/case law) • Investor protection • Collectivism (Hofstede) • Feminism (Hofstede) • IR assurance	• Publication of an integrated report	• Collectivism (+)
2015	Sierra-Garcia et al.	Corporate Social Responsibility and Environmental Management	• International • 7,344 firm-year observations • 2009–2011	• CSR assurance • Audit firm as CSR assurer	• Publication of an integrated report	• CSR assurance (+)

	Author	Journal	Sample	Independent variables	Dependent variable	Findings
2013a	Frias-Aceituno et al.	Journal of Cleaner Production	International 2,129 firm-year observations firms 2008–2010	• Legal origin (code/case law) • Legal enforcement (efficiency of the legal system, index of law and order)	• Publication of an integrated report	• Code law (+) • Legal enforcement (+)
2013b	Frias-Aceituno et al.	Corporate Social Responsibility and Environmental Management	International 1,575 firm-year observations 2008–2010	• Board size • Board independence • Board meetings • Board gender diversity • Board foreign diversity	• Publication of an integrated report	• Board size (+) • Board gender diversity (+)
2013	Garcia-Sanchez et al.	International Business Review	International 3,042 firm-year observations 2008–2010	• Collectivism (Hofstede) • Feminism (Hofstede) • Tolerance of uncertainty (Hofstede) • Power distance (Hofstede) • Country's long-term orientation (Hofstede)	• Publication of an integrated report	• Collectivism (+) • Feminism (+)

skills, values and beliefs, Gerwanski et al. (2019) and Kilic and Kuzey (2018) found that gender diversity positively affects IR quality. Arguing that boards with higher female representation tend to show a higher willingness to adhere to ethics, transparency and sustainability, Frias-Aceituno et al. (2013b) expected and concluded that board diversity increases a firm's likelihood of compiling an integrated report. Fasan and Mio (2017) were surprised to find the opposite effect, which they described as 'apparently counter-intuitive' (p. 302). In line with legitimacy theory, the authors surmise that difficulties in implementing IR may lead to employing higher board diversity as a signal to markets, which is not followed by the expected actions.

Several studies investigate the effect of *board independence* on IR practices (Frias-Aceituno et al., 2013b; Stacchezzini et al., 2016; Fasan and Mio, 2017; Kilic and Kuzey, 2018). Stacchezzini et al. (2016) found a negative association between board independence and IR quality, which they argued to be related to managerial discretion in the preparation of the integrated report facilitating opportunistic behaviour. In line with this reasoning, Garcia-Sanchez et al. (2019) showed that the board of directors constitutes a relevant control mechanism, which constrains managers to prepare an integrated report.

Building upon the reasoning that a larger board size and higher meeting frequency are associated with better exchange of views, more discourse and thus better decision quality, several scholars investigated whether *board size* (Frias-Aceituno et al., 2013b; Fasan and Mio, 2017; Garcia-Sanchez and Noguera-Gamez, 2018; Kilic and Kuzey, 2018) and *board meeting frequency* (Frias-Aceituno et al., 2013b; Fasan and Mio, 2017) affect corporate engagement in IR or IR quality. Although board meeting frequency seems not to affect IR, two studies found statistically significant results with respect to board size. Frias-Aceituno et al. (2013b) showed that firms with larger boards are more likely to issue an integrated report, Fasan and Mio (2017) showed that board size impairs IR quality. While the higher plurality of opinions in larger boards seems to be beneficial for the implementation of IR, many different views may lead to lower reporting quality.

The audit committee oversees the firm's IR process and is in charge of monitoring managers and the external auditor (Klein, 2002; Haji and Anifowose, 2016). Since an effective audit committee should incentivize management to implement IR that provides decision-useful information to addressees, it is assumed to play a central role in IR implementation and quality. Despite its relevance, only two studies focused on the audit committee in an IR context. Velte (2018) showed that both *audit committees' financial* and *sustainability expertise*, as well as their interaction, increase the readability and thereby quality of integrated reports. In a similar vein, Haji and Anifowose (2016) investigated whether *audit committee effectiveness, size, meeting frequency, independence, expertise* and *authority* contribute to IR quality. Their results indicate that audit committee effectiveness, meeting frequency and authority leverage the quality of integrated reports. Haji and Anifowose (2016) further argued that, if present, the sustainability committee has an essential role by supporting the audit committee in overseeing sustainability disclosures in the integrated report and thus should lead to higher IR quality. The results confirm this reasoning and reveal that firms with a sustainability committee show a higher quality of reporting.

External corporate governance

As well as the aforementioned internal governance factors, the extant literature has also investigated the effect of different *external CG* variables on IR preparation and quality. Given that IR allows a large degree of managerial discretion in the reporting process

(Garcia-Sanchez et al., 2019; Gerwanski et al., 2019), an external IR assurer in its gatekeeper function can mitigate conflicts of interest between management and stakeholders (e.g., Velte and Stawinoga, 2017a, 2017b). Moreover, management's decision to have its CSR or integrated report assured should signal quality and transparency to stakeholders (Simnett and Huggins, 2015). Building on this consideration, Vaz et al. (2016) and Sierra-Garcia et al. (2015) investigated the effect of an *external assurance of the CSR report* on the firm's likelihood of compiling an integrated report. The idea behind this reasoning is as follows: first, firms that are willing to spend money for the assurance of their CSR report might be likewise willing to spend money for IR. Second, firms that have their CSR report assured attach importance to the credibility of their reporting, and thus might have a higher propensity to engage in IR that aims to provide transparent and decision-useful information to a firm's different stakeholders. Third, assurers of the CSR report might also recommend engagement in IR to increase overall reporting quality to stakeholders. While Sierra-Garcia et al. (2015) identified such an association, Vaz et al. (2016) could not confirm their hypothesis. Moreover, Gerwanski et al. (2019) and Rivera-Arrubla et al. (2017) found that an *IR assurance* (IRA) positively affects IR quality. Staying with the assurance/audit dimension, Rivera-Arrubla et al. (2017) evaluated whether the appointment of a *Big4 auditor* for the financial audit has an impact on a firm's IR quality, but found no significant association. In sum, the assurance-specific results are quite inconclusive with regard to their effect on IR preparation and quality.

Assuming that blockholders have both an increased information demand for IR as well as high bargaining power, a firm's ownership concentration may have an effect on either the preparation or the quality of integrated reports. The only corresponding study was conducted by Haji and Anifowose (2016), who found a positive effect of *ownership concentration* on IR quality. Staying with the ownership focus, and elaborating on Serafeim (2015), who showed that IR firms have less transient investors, Gerwanski et al. (2019) assumed that more sustainable firms have more socially responsible investors (SRI), who exert (sustainable) shareholder pressure on IR quality. Specifically, the authors investigated whether firms listed in the *Dow Jones Sustainability Index* (DJSI) compiled integrated reports of superior quality, but found no significant effect.

Country-specific governance factors

The impact of *country-specific governance* factors on either the publication or quality of an integrated report has also received academic attention. Assuming that a country's level of *investor protection* might lead to a higher managerial willingness to fulfil the information demand of their stakeholders, this may increase a firm's likelihood of preparing an integrated report. This possible association has been investigated by several scholars (Frias-Aceituno et al., 2013a; Vaz et al., 2016; Garcia-Sanchez and Noguera-Gamez, 2018; Garcia-Sanchez et al., 2019). Garcia-Sanchez et al. (2019) found that the level of investor protection (measured using a factorial analysis composed of an anti-self-dealing index, creditor rights index and market development) lowers munificence and increases the likelihood of preparing an integrated report. Further, they showed that the country's level of transparency enhances the likelihood to engage in IR. In a similar vein, Garcia-Sanchez and Noguera-Gamez (2018) found that the level of a country's judicial efficiency and index of law and order encourage IR, while Frias-Aceituno et al. (2013a) indicated that legal enforcement (i.e. efficiency of the legal system and an index of law and order) drives the publication of an integrated report.

Unlike Garcia-Sanchez and Noguera-Gamez (2018), who classified a country's orientation towards common or civil law as an element of investor protection, several studies have applied the civil/common law variable to measure the effect of a country's *legal origin* (Frias-Aceituno et al., 2013a; Vaz et al., 2016; Fasan and Mio, 2017; Rivera-Arrubla et al., 2017). While case law regimes have a strong focus on shareholders, code law regimes are more oriented towards stakeholders. Despite Frias-Aceituno et al.'s (2013a) finding that firms operating in code law regimes are more likely to compile an integrated report, all other studies ubiquitously failed to achieve statistical significance.

With another country-specific focus, two studies investigated the effect of Hofstede's *cultural dimensions* on IR (Garcia-Sanchez et al., 2013; Vaz et al., 2016), assuming that a country's culture affects not only individuals, but also corporations, and determines their behaviour. Specifically, Vaz et al. (2016) and Garcia-Sanchez et al. (2013) came to the conclusion that integrated reports are more likely to be compiled in countries with a higher degree of collectivism, while Garcia-Sanchez et al. (2013) also identified firms operating in more feminist countries to be more likely to prepare an integrated report.

Implications and recommendations

What is integrated reporting (quality)?

Earlier research in the domain of IR critically invoked the absence of IR-specific guidance in the presence of high managerial discretion (e.g., definition, assessment and information of the firm's 'capitals' or the materiality of information (Gerwanski et al., 2019)). This absence leads to reporting heterogeneity and entails the risk of managerial greenwashing and impression management through 'rebranding' the annual report as an integrated report (Haji and Hossain, 2016; Rivera-Arrubla et al., 2017). In response to this lack of clarity, most studies defined different criteria; for example, IR-specific principles or adherence to the IIRC Framework (Gerwanski et al., 2019) in order to qualify whether the underlying report was a 'real' *integrated report* or not. Building on this consideration, future research should refine existing ways to identify a 'real' integrated report. This could be done, for example, through the application of an IR scoring scheme, which should take into account both IR content elements (such as the focus on capitals or a firm's stakeholder dialogue (e.g., Lee and Yeo, 2016; Haji and Anifowose, 2016)), and guiding principles (e.g., materiality, conciseness and connectivity).

Further, the academic approaches applied to operationalize the abstract term IR *quality* lead to the basic question: how is IR quality defined and what distinguishes a high-quality integrated report from one of inferior quality? While outside the CG context, several studies operationalized IR quality by means of the 'EY Excellence in Integrated Reporting Awards' score (e.g., Barth et al., 2017), three within the scope of our review (Lai et al., 2017; Fasan and Mio, 2017; Gerwanski et al., 2019) proxied IR quality based on a firm's *materiality disclosure*, which has a central role in IR.

In line with the intention of the narrative reporting medium to apply 'plain language over the use of jargon or highly technical terminology' (IIRC, 2013, p.21; Beattie, 2014; Higgins et al., 2014; Lai et al., 2018), scholars referred to the *readability* of the integrated report to assess its quality (Melloni et al., 2017; du Toit, 2017; Velte, 2018). In the light of the various measures of IR quality, future research should develop further measures to evaluate IR quality. For example, in line with the basic idea of IR, future studies might proxy IR quality with a score that captures the degree of interconnection of the firm's capitals, which would simultaneously allow a differentiation from managerial impression management.

Internal CG perspective

Starting with the *internal CG perspective*, there should be more research specific to the board of directors as a key player in the further process of IR, as it decides on both the voluntary implementation of IR and its quality. Given that extant studies provide contrasting results (e.g., gender diversity, board size, board meeting frequency), the diverse findings might be driven by hitherto unobserved effects, which should be investigated in future research. Building on different studies in the domain of *behavioural accounting*, which show that managers' educations and professional backgrounds (Lewis et al., 2014), along with personality and preferences (Gibbins et al., 1990) and sustainability-related attitudes (Helfaya and Moussa, 2017), drive their voluntary disclosure behaviour, it should be investigated how far different CEO and CFO demographics (e.g., gender, age, experience, education) or behavioural characteristics (e.g., altruism, narcissism, overconfidence) affect engagement in IR. Moreover, in line with the increasing relevance of non-financial components in a firm's *management compensation* (e.g., Davila and Venkatachalam, 2004; O'Connell and O'Sullivan, 2014), there should be specific research on whether sustainability goals or long-term incentives, such as stock options, increase willingness to compile high-quality integrated reports.

While Haji and Anifowose (2016) and Velte (2018) focused on the effect of several characteristics specific to the composition of the *audit committee* (e.g., effectiveness, size, expertise and independence) on IR quality, many questions about the association between the audit committee and IR remain unanswered and should be addressed in further research. These include how the audit committee addresses technical challenges arising during the internal assurance of the IR and how, in practice, a sufficient degree of quality is ensured in the absence of corporate IR experience and the lack of IR-specific guidelines (IIRC, 2015). Further, following Feng et al. (2017) who argued that IR-applying 'organizations intend to improve the reporting process year by year by learning from prior year experiences' (p. 347), future research should consider a) how far *learning effects* affect the work performed by the audit committee; b) how these learning effects are themselves affected by the audit committee; and c) the effect of the audit committee on IR quality, which should be re-assessed over time.

External CG perspective

Similarly, the *external CG perspective* offers various opportunities for further research. Unlike the audit committee, which focuses on internal assurance, there are numerous academic calls for research on the as yet under-investigated *external IRA*, which is quite common in the related domain of CSR assurance (e.g., De Villiers et al., 2014; Casey and Grenier, 2015; Simnett and Huggins, 2015) and led to, in parts, inconclusive results in our review. In parallel with the discussion about the choice of the assurer for the corporate social responsibility assurance (CSRA), future studies should assess whether appointing a Big 4 auditor rather than a specialized consultant (or vice versa) leads to differences in IR quality. Specifically, while Big 4 auditors refer to international auditing and assurance standards and are governed by different quality mechanisms, specialized consultants are frequently assumed to possess superior subject-specific knowledge (Simnett et al., 2009). Moreover, we know very little about the effects of the assurance level on IR quality. Since a higher assurance level is often argued to accompany a higher reliability for report users and thus presumably coincides with higher reporting quality (Hasan et al., 2003; Fuhrmann et al., 2017), the underlying assurance level might affect IR quality. Nevertheless, assurers' lack of IR-related experience and firms' insufficient implementation of adequate IR reporting infrastructures in the absence of an IRA-specific standard may impair the value of an IRA and reinforce the discussion about the necessity of such a standard (De Villiers et al., 2014; Maroun, 2017).

Although there is a strong emphasis on investors in the concept of IR (IIRC, 2013; Flower, 2015) and different scholars have shown its capital market relevance (e.g., Lee and Yeo, 2016; Barth et al., 2017; Zhou et al., 2017), so far, there is little evidence on the association between investors and the publication of an integrated report, or its quality, respectively. Assuming that IR alleviates information asymmetries and discloses relevant information to investors, outside investor pressure may convince management to compile an integrated report of high quality. Accordingly, different measures of shareholder activism may affect the preparation and quality of an integrated report and need to be investigated (e.g., Gillan and Starks, 2000). Specifically, future studies should examine factors such as foreign investors, government investors and managerial ownership, and re-assess the effect of concentrated ownership on IR reporting and quality. Despite the increasing importance of sustainable investors to corporations (Renneboog et al., 2008) and the assumption that *SRI investors* are more engaged in a firm's (sustainability) monitoring, only one study has investigated the effect of sustainable index listing (Dow Jones Sustainability Index) on IR quality, but the results did not achieve statistical significance (Gerwanski et al., 2019). In the light of the low research density, future studies should re-assess the effect of SRI investors or examine whether there is an association between firms' signing of the Principles for Sustainable Investors (PRI) and the publication of an integrated report.

Country-specific governance factors

Shifting from the firm-specific to a macro perspective, there are also several *country-specific governance factors*, which remain under-investigated in an IR context. Specifically, so far, no study discriminates between one-tier (e.g., UK) and two-tier (e.g., Germany) regimes. Given that two-tier systems are supposed to limit managerial leeway and thus provide higher independence (e.g., Maassen and van den Bosch, 1999), and are related to the degree of information asymmetry (Belot et al., 2014), it would be worth investigating the implications of the system on IR (e.g., in France where legislation allows firms to choose between a one-tier and a two-tier system). Further, while most of the recent studies have focused on an international sample in order to increase the sample size of IR adopters, there is also a need to conduct empirical studies on the impact of CG on IR on a national level or region, for example, in South Africa (where IR is mandatory) or a special regime like the EU (as IR and non-financial reporting is especially relevant there). This would allow exploration of whether determinants and implications vary between countries; cross-country studies show only aggregated effects which may hide off-setting or opposing effects. Future studies should expand the range of factors in the country's legal system beyond those already investigated (e.g., case and common law, indices of judicial efficiency and law and order) to include regulatory and legal aspects that may affect the diffusion and implementation of IR. For instance, an event study in a *European* context could assess the effect of the recent EU directive (2014/95/EU), which obliges large capital-market oriented firms to disclose non-financial information in either their management report or a separate (integrated) report, and thereby may encourage IR in Europe.

Methodological issues

From a *methodological* point of view, future studies should cover several shortcomings in extant studies. While on the one hand, further research should address potential *endogeneity* concerns (e.g., reversed causality), on the other hand, it is presumable that an optimal level, rather than a maximum, of governance will lead to increased IR implementation and IR quality; this potentially indicates that the association might be non-linear (indicating a U-shape or inverted U-shaped curve). Different analytical approaches, including dynamic regression models (GMM estimation), instrumental variable approaches (2SLS or 3SLS) or simultaneous equations models (SEM), should be applied in future research. Further, while many studies measure the *publication* of an integrated report with a dummy variable, we encourage the usage of individual disclosure scores, which account for both IR quantity *and* quality, and thus should have more explanatory power. Besides, as is common for cross-country samples and country-specific research, the comparability of the studies may be limited due to differing underlying contextual factors (Adhariani and De Villiers, 2018). Further, organizations are likely to be at different stages with regard to their IR implementation (Beck et al., 2015), which may lead to differing applications of the integrated thinking process and IR (summary report versus 'one report'). Staying with the firm-specific perspective, further factors such as organizational complexity (Lee and Yeo, 2016) or corporate culture, which have not yet been included in CG-related studies, should be a part of future research. Moreover, returning to the assumption that an effective CG structure should lower the incentives for *earnings management* (Garcia-Sanchez et al., 2019; Gerwanski et al., 2019), the association between IR and earnings quality should be reassessed not only by using the commonly applied accruals models, but also while accounting for differing reporting policies by measuring real earnings management (Roychowdhury, 2006).

Conclusion

As a firm's CG reporting is part and parcel of IR and governance mechanisms are indispensable to both the success and quality of IR, we have provided a systematic literature review on the association between governance and IR. By examining the existing academic literature on the topic, we aimed to reveal the underlying trends, thereby identifying and addressing prevailing research gaps for future studies. During the course of this investigation, we identified different firm-specific (internal and external factors) and country-specific governance determinants for the implementation and quality of IR. With regard to internal CG determinants, we identified a distinct academic focus on board composition, and we recommend more studies to focus on the role of its committees, particularly the audit and sustainability committees. With regard to external CG factors, the effect of an external CSR assurance or IRA has been investigated by several studies, which came to mixed conclusions. Further, investor-specific factors (e.g., institutional investors) are very scarce in the research so far. With respect to country-specific governance determinants, as yet, the scope of the prevailing studies is limited to investor protection, legal origins and a country's culture. Building upon our analysis of the extant literature, at the core of our review, we discussed various recommendations for future studies.

References

Adhariani, D., and De Villiers, C. (2018). Integrated reporting: Perspectives of corporate report preparers and other stakeholders. *Sustainability Accounting, Management and Policy Journal, 10*(1), 126–156.

Barth, M. E., Cahan, S. F., Chen, L., and Venter, E. R. (2017). The economic consequences associated with integrated report quality: Capital market and real effects. *Accounting, Organizations and Society, 62*, 43–64.

Beattie, V. (2014). Accounting narratives and the narrative turn in accounting research: Issues, theory, methodology, methods and a research framework. *The British Accounting Review, 46*(2), 111–134.

Beck, C., Dumay, J., and Frost, G. (2015). In pursuit of a 'single source of truth': From threatened legitimacy to integrated reporting. *Journal of Business Ethics, 141*(1), 191–205.

Belot, F., Ginglinger, E., Slovin, M. B., and Sushka, M. E. (2014). Freedom of choice between unitary and two-tier boards: An empirical analysis. *Journal of Financial Economics, 112*(3), 364–385.

Ben-Amar, W., and McIlkenny, P. (2015). Board effectiveness and the voluntary disclosure of climate change information. *Business Strategy and the Environment, 24*(8), 704–719.

Casey, R. J., and Grenier, J. H. (2015). Understanding and contributing to the enigma of corporate social responsibility (CSR) assurance in the United States. *Auditing: A Journal of Practice & Theory, 34*(1), 97–130.

Davila, A., and Venkatachalam, M. (2004). The relevance of non-financial performance measures for CEO compensation: Evidence from the airline industry. *Review of Accounting Studies, 9*(4), 443–464.

De Villiers, C., Hsiao, P.-C. K., and Maroun, W. (2017a). developing a conceptual model of influences around integrated reporting. New insights and directions for future research. *Meditari Accountancy Research, 25*(4), 450–460.

De Villiers, C., Rinaldi, L., and Unerman, J. (2014). Integrated reporting: Insights, gaps and an agenda for future research. *Accounting, Auditing & Accountability Journal, 27*(7), 1042–1067.

De Villiers, C., and Sharma, U. (2017). A critical reflection on the future of financial, intellectual capital, sustainability and integrated reporting. *Critical Perspectives on Accounting*, [Online first]. doi:10.1016/j.cpa.2017.05.003.

De Villiers, C., Venter, E. R., and Hsiao, P.-C. K. (2017b). Integrated reporting: Background, measurement issues, approaches and an agenda for future research. *Accounting & Finance, 57*(4), 937–959.

Du Toit, E. (2017). The readability of integrated reports. *Meditari Accountancy Research, 25*(4), 629–653.

Eccles, R. G., and Krzus, M. P. (2010). *One Report: Integrated Reporting for a Sustainable Strategy*. New Jersey: Wiley.

Eccles, R. G., and Krzus, M. P. (2015). *The Integrated Reporting Movement. Meaning, Momentum, Motives, and Materiality*. New Jersey: Wiley.

Fasan, M., and Mio, C. (2017). Fostering stakeholder engagement: The role of materiality disclosure in integrated reporting. *Business Strategy and the Environment, 26*(3), 288–307.

Feng, T., Cummings, L., and Tweedie, D. (2017). Exploring integrated thinking in integrated reporting – An exploratory study in Australia. *Journal of Intellectual Capital, 18*(2), 330–353.

Flower, J. (2015). The International Integrated Reporting Council: A story of failure. *Critical Perspectives on Accounting, 27*, 1–17.

Frias-Aceituno, J. V., Rodriguez-Ariza, L., and Garcia-Sanchez, I. M. (2013a). Is integrated reporting determined by a country's legal system? An exploratory study. *Journal of Cleaner Production, 44*, 45–55.

Frias-Aceituno, J. V., Rodriguez-Ariza, L., and Garcia-Sanchez, I. M. (2013b). The role of the board in the dissemination of integrated corporate social reporting. *Corporate Social Responsibility and Environmental Management, 20*(4), 219–233.

Frias-Aceituno, J. V., Rodriguez-Ariza, L., and Garcia-Sanchez, I. M. (2014). Explanatory factors of integrated sustainability and financial reporting. *Business Strategy and the Environment, 23*(1), 56–72.

Fuhrmann, S., Ott, C., Looks, E., and Guenther, T. W. (2017). The components of assurance statements for sustainability reports and information asymmetry. *Accounting and Business Research, 47*(4), 369–400.

Garcia-Sanchez, I.-M., Martinez-Ferrero, J., and Garcia-Benau, M.-A. (2019). Integrated reporting: The mediating role of the board of directors and investor protection on managerial discretion in munificent environments. *Corporate Social Responsibility and Environmental Management, 26*(1), 29–45.

Garcia-Sanchez, I.-M., and Noguera-Gamez, L. (2018). Institutional investor protection pressures versus firm incentives in the disclosure of integrated reporting. *Australian Accounting Review*, 28(2), 199–219.

Garcia-Sanchez, I.-M., Rodriguez-Ariza, L., and Frias-Aceituno, J. V. (2013). The cultural system and integrated reporting. *International Business Review*, 22(5), 828–838.

Gerwanski, J., Kordsachia, O., and Velte, P. (2019). Determinants of materiality disclosure quality in integrated reporting: International evidence. *Business Strategy and the Environment*, 28(5), 750–770.

Gianfelici, C., Casadei, A., and Cembali, F. (2018). The relevance of nationality and industry for stakeholder salience: An investigation through integrated reports. *Journal of Business Ethics*, 150(2), 541–558.

Gibbins, M., Richardson, A., and Waterhouse, J. (1990). The management of corporate financial disclosure: Opportunism, ritualism, policies, and processes. *Journal of Accounting Research*, 28(1), 121–143.

Gillan, S. L., and Starks, L. T. (2000). Corporate governance proposals and shareholder activism: The role of institutional investors. *Journal of Financial Economics*, 57(2), 275–305.

Haji, A. A., and Anifowose, M. (2016). Audit committee and integrated reporting practice: Does internal assurance matter? *Managerial Auditing Journal*, 31(8/9), 915–948.

Haji, A. A., and Hossain, D. M. (2016). Exploring the implications of integrated reporting on organisational reporting practice: Evidence from highly regarded integrated reporters. *Qualitative Research in Accounting & Management*, 13(4), 415–444.

Hasan, M., Roebuck, P., and Simnett, R. (2003). An investigation of alternative report formats for communicating moderate levels of assurance. *Auditing: A Journal of Practice & Theory*, 22(2), 171–187.

Helfaya, A., and Moussa, T. (2017). Do board's corporate social responsibility strategy and orientation influence environmental sustainability disclosure? UK evidence. *Business Strategy and the Environment*, 26(8), 1061–1077.

Higgins, C., Stubbs, W., and Love, T. (2014). Walking the talk(s): Organisational narratives of integrated reporting. *Accounting, Auditing & Accountability Journal*, 27(7), 1090–1119.

Hill, C. W. L., and Jones, T. M. (1992). Stakeholder-agency theory. *Journal of Management Studies*, 29(2), 131–154.

IIRC. (2013). *The International <IR> Framework*. Available at: https://integratedreporting.org/wp-con tent/uploads/2013/12/13-12-08-THE-INTERNATIONAL-IR-FRAMEWORK-2-1.pdf (Accessed: 1 February 2019).

IIRC. (2015). *Assurance on <IR>. Overview of Feedback and Call to Action*. Available at: http://integratedre porting.org/wp-content/uploads/2015/07/IIRC-Assurance-Overview-July-2015.pdf (Accessed: 16 January 2019).

Kilic, M., and Kuzey, C. (2018). Determinants of forward-looking disclosures in integrated reports. *Managerial Auditing Journal*, 33(1), 115–144.

Klein, A. (2002). Audit committee, board of director characteristics, and earnings management. *Journal of Accounting and Economics*, 33(3), 375–400.

Lai, A., Melloni, G., and Stacchezzini, R. (2016). Corporate sustainable development: Is 'integrated reporting' a legitimation strategy? *Business Strategy and the Environment*, 25(3), 165–177.

Lai, A., Melloni, G., and Stacchezzini, R. (2017). What does materiality mean to integrated reporting preparers? An empirical exploration. *Meditari Accountancy Research*, 25(4), 533–552.

Lai, A., Melloni, G., and Stacchezzini, R. (2018). Integrated reporting and narrative accountability: The role of preparers. *Accounting, Auditing & Accountability Journal*, 31(5), 1381–1405.

Lee, K. W., and Yeo, G. H. H. (2016). The association between integrated reporting and firm valuation. *Review of Quantitative Finance and Accounting*, 47(4), 1221–1250.

Lewis, B. W., Walls, J. L., and Dowell, G. W. S. (2014). Difference in degrees: CEO characteristics and firm environmental disclosure. *Strategic Management Journal*, 35(5), 712–722.

Light, R. J., and Smith, P. V. (1971). Accumulating evidence: Procedures for resolving contradictions among different research studies. *Harvard Educational Review*, 41(4), 429–471.

Maassen, G., and van den Bosch, F. (1999). On the supposed independence of two-tier boards: Formal structure and reality in the Netherlands. *Corporate Governance: An International Review*, 7(1), 31–37.

Maroun, W. (2017). Assuring the integrated report: Insights and recommendations from auditors and preparers. *The British Accounting Review*, 49(3), 329–346.

McGuinness, P. B., Vieito, J. P., and Wang, M. (2017). The role of board gender and foreign ownership in the CSR performance of Chinese listed firms. *Journal of Corporate Finance*, 42, 75–99.

Melloni, G., Caglio, A., and Perego, P. (2017). Saying more with less? Disclosure conciseness, completeness and balance in integrated reports. *Journal of Accounting and Public Policy, 36*(3), 220–238.

O'Connell, V., and O'Sullivan, D. (2014). The influence of lead indicator strength on the use of nonfinancial measures in performance management: Evidence from CEO compensation schemes. *Strategic Management Journal, 35*(6), 826–844.

Renneboog, L., Ter Horst, J., and Zhang, C. (2008). Socially responsible investments: Institutional aspects, performance, and investor behavior. *Journal of Banking & Finance, 32*(9), 1723–1742.

Rivera-Arrubla, Y. A., Zorio-Grima, A., and Garcia-Benau, M. A. (2017). Integrated reports: Disclosure level and explanatory factors. *Social Responsibility Journal, 13*(1), 155–176.

Roychowdhury, S. (2006). Earnings management through real activities manipulation. *Journal of Accounting and Economics, 42*(3), 335–370.

Rupley, K. H., Brown, D., and Marshall, S. (2012). Governance, media and the quality of environmental disclosure. *Journal of Accounting and Public Policy, 31*(6), 610–640.

Serafeim, G. (2015). Integrated reporting and investor clientele. *Journal of Applied Corporate Finance, 27*(2), 34–51.

Sierra-Garcia, L., Zorio-Grima, A., and Garcia-Benau, M. A. (2015). Stakeholder engagement, corporate social responsibility and integrated reporting: An exploratory study. *Corporate Social Responsibility and Environmental Management, 22*(5), 286–304.

Simnett, R., and Huggins, A. L. (2015). Integrated reporting and assurance: Where can research add value? *Sustainability Accounting, Management and Policy Journal, 6*(1), 29–53.

Simnett, R., Vanstraelen, A., and Chua, W. F. (2009). Assurance on sustainability reports: An international comparison. *The Accounting Review, 84*(3), 937–967.

Stacchezzini, R., Melloni, G., and Lai, A. (2016). Sustainability management and reporting: The role of integrated reporting for communicating corporate sustainability management. *Journal of Cleaner Production, 136*(Part A), 102–110.

Vaz, N., Fernandez-Feijoo, B., and Ruiz, S. (2016). Integrated reporting: An international overview. *Business Ethics: A European Review, 25*(4), 577–591.

Velte, P. (2017). Does board composition have an impact on CSR reporting? *Problems and Perspectives in Management, 15*, 19–35.

Velte, P. (2018). Is audit committee expertise connected with increased readability of integrated reports. *Problems and Perspectives in Management, 16*, 23–41.

Velte, P., and Stawinoga, M. (2017a). Integrated reporting: The current state of empirical research, limitations and future research implications. *Journal of Management Control, 28*(3), 275–320.

Velte, P., and Stawinoga, M. (2017b). Empirical research on corporate social responsibility assurance (CSRA): A literature review. *Journal of Business Economics, 87*(8), 1017–1066.

Zhou, S., Simnett, R., and Green, W. (2017). Does integrated reporting matter to the capital market? *Abacus, 53*(1), 94–132.

15

INTEGRATED REPORTING IN THE PUBLIC SECTOR

Sumit Lodhia

Centre for Sustainability Governance, School of Commerce, University of South Australia

Amanpreet Kaur

Centre for Sustainability Governance, School of Commerce, University of South Australia

Belinda Williams

College of Business & Economics, University of Tasmania

Abstract

This chapter discusses the potential of integrated reporting for public sector organizations. It emphasizes that the public sector is a useful context for exploring integrated reporting, given its societal and sustainability focus. Initially, the focus is on sustainability reporting and the evolution from this form of reporting to integrated reporting. The current status of integrated reporting in the public sector is then discussed. Further studies on integrated reporting and thinking in the public sector are needed to expand our knowledge and understanding of this mechanism and accordingly, the final section outlines future research opportunities.

Introduction

Sustainability is one of the most crucial issues being faced by communities worldwide, and it demands collaborative thinking and action. The concept of sustainability emerged in the 1960s because of substantial environmental degradation caused by imbalanced industrial growth, population growth and poor resource management (Kopnina and Shoreman-Ouimet, 2015). This has led to increasing concerns and awareness about environmental and social impacts of organizational activities including the public sector. There are several critical sustainability issues that are affecting people and the planet, such as climate change, environmental degradation, loss of biodiversity, freshwater scarcity, waste, income inequality, unemployment, fairness and justice, health and safety and poverty (Diesendorf, 2000; OECD, 2001; Schaltegger et al., 2006; Hopwood et al., 2010; UN, 2015). All these issues have drawn social and political attention, and calls have been made to advance the notion of sustainable development.

Consequently, private and public sector organizations are expected to identify and address sustainability issues. Although both of these sectors are equally accountable for their impact on the environment and society, the role and potential of public sector organizations (PSOs) in advancing the notion of sustainable development has been emphasized because they primarily exist to deliver public policy and to promote social welfare (Broadbent and Guthrie, 1992; Ball and Grubnic, 2007; Lewis, 2008; Ball et al., 2014). Ball and Grubnic (2007) recognize 'an affinity between a public sector ethos and the notion of community and fair resource distribution inherent in sustainable development' (p.252). The Global Reporting Initiative's (GRI) Public Sector Supplement asserts that PSOs:

> have a civic responsibility to properly manage public goods, resources, and/or facilities in a way that supports sustainable development objectives and promotes the public interest. Public agencies are expected to be open and transparent in their management of public funds and assets. As significant employers, providers of services, and consumers of resources, public agencies also have a major impact on national and global progress towards sustainable development. Given their size and influence, public agencies are expected to lead by example in reporting publicly and transparently on their activities to promote sustainability.
>
> *(GRI, 2005, pp. 7–8)*

This implies that the public sector has not only a major role in advancing sustainable development but is also expected to lead by example in relation to transparency and reporting.

In the last two decades, both practitioners and academics have proposed, examined and discussed the emergence of innovative reporting tools in the public sector for enhancing transparency and accountability on sustainability issues (Biondi and Bracci, 2018). The prominent reporting tools that have transformed reporting practices in the public sector include social and environmental reporting, sustainability reporting (SR) and more recently integrated reporting (IR) as it brings thinking, planning and reporting together.

Integrated extends the potential of sustainability reporting and aims to change the mindset of leaders by encouraging them to create value over the short, medium and long term. Moreover, it offers a framework that can enable organizations to manage complex interconnections between people, ideas, finance and the natural environment (CIPFA, 2016). This aim of this chapter is to establish the need for and scope of IR in the public sector. To address this, the notion of sustainability reporting in the public sector is first discussed. We then present an overview of the uptake of IR practice in the public sector through a critical review of existing studies on IR and the final section envisions future research opportunities on IR in the public sector.

Sustainability reporting in the public sector

Although this chapter focuses on IR practice, this section outlines the state and drivers of sustainability reporting in the public sector as this reporting tool offers the foundation for the emergence of IR. The sustainability reporting mechanisms provide readily available back-end systems, controls and assurance processes, which are critical to support the development of an integrated report, such as, for example, gathering robust 'non-financial' data (CIPFA, 2016). Therefore, before reviewing the state of IR practice, it is important to recognize those practices that have led to the adoption of IR.

In the public sector, sustainability reporting is regarded as: 'A public account of an organisation's sustainability performance achieved through a combination of: leadership;

strategic partnering; stakeholder engagement; policy outcomes; and the management of the organisation's impacts on the local environment, social well-being and economic prosperity' (Ball, 2005, p. 4). Sustainability reporting processes and practices have enabled PSOs to systematically identify and interlink the economic, social and environmental costs and benefits of organizational strategies and actions (Lewis, 2008). The use of effective sustainability reporting mechanisms drives organizational changes for sustainability in the public sector (Domingues et al., 2017) and enables organizations to communicate their contribution to sustainable development (Lamprinidi and Kubo, 2008).

The existing literature indicates that sustainability reporting in the public sector is driven by a variety of internal and external factors. Dickinson et al. (2005), in their global study, found PSOs largely produce sustainability reporting to monitor their performance, demonstrate their progress towards sustainability principles, meet stakeholder information demands, comply with regulatory requirements and manage public relations. Additionally, local context-based studies have provided in-depth insights into regional and cultural drivers of sustainability reporting. For instance, Marcuccio and Steccolini (2005) highlighted that socio-psychological forces (such as willingness to adopt innovative and progressive management techniques) and techno-economic forces (for example, the search for improved financial and non-financial performance through better accountability, reporting and management system) together shape sustainability reporting in Italian local governments.

Most of the extant research indicates that internal influences such as leadership and accountability drive sustainability reporting practices in the public sector. Lodhia et al. (2012), in their study of 19 Australian PSOs, revealed that internal policy requirements and internal stakeholders drove the reporting practices in these agencies. Similarly, Farneti and Guthrie (2009), Bellringer et al. (2011), Lodhia and Jacobs (2013), and Domingues et al. (2017) reported that sustainability reporting practices in the public sector are internally driven. They generally concluded that the internal organizational practices and internal stakeholders provide a more powerful reasoning for sustainability reporting in comparison to adhering to external legitimacy.

Prior literature has also investigated the nature, role, and drivers of stakeholder engagement in sustainability reporting in the public sector (Imoniana et al., 2012; Kaur and Lodhia, 2014, 2016, 2017, 2018, 2019; Greco et al., 2015). Greco et al. (2015) assessed the level of engagement achieved by 11 Italian local councils using the AccountAbility (2011) framework. They found that stakeholder engagement was limited to informing. In contrast, Kaur and Lodhia (2017, 2018) found evidence of effective stakeholder engagement in the sustainability accounting and reporting processes. Similarly, Imoniana et al. (2012) showcased stakeholder involvement in the budgeting process of Brazilian municipalities. The authors found that stakeholders played an important role in monitoring the sustainability indicators of Brazilian municipalities to evaluate their performance.

To communicate sustainability performance to internal and external stakeholders, PSOs use a range of communication media including annual reports, social reports, environmental reports, sustainability reports, web-based reporting, strategy documents, operational plans, council minutes and publicly available scorecards (Marcuccio and Steccolini, 2005; Farneti and Guthrie, 2009; Williams et al., 2011). However, some of these media, including strategy documents, operational plans and council minutes, have limited value for external stakeholders (Farneti and Guthrie, 2009). Moreover, there is a lack of consistency in terms of the use of formal or informal reporting approaches (Williams, 2015).

The use of GRI sustainability reporting guidelines by PSOs has been contested by some researchers. Guthrie and Farneti (2008) explored social and environmental disclosures in Australian PSOs including federal, state and local government bodies. The study revealed that these organizations 'cherry picked' the GRI indicators they wished to disclose, and their reports lacked complete disclosure on the social, environmental and economic impacts of organizational activities. Similar findings were reported by Leeson et al. (2005), Guthrie and Farneti (2008), Tort (2010), Marx and Van-Dyk (2011), Lodhia et al. (2012) and Domingues et al. (2017). The usefulness of the GRI guidelines for PSOs has been questioned as they fail to recognise the importance of specific issues addressed by the public sector, such as educational awareness, which is crucial to many government departments (Guthrie and Farneti, 2008; Lodhia et al., 2012).

Although sustainability reporting in the past has encouraged PSOs to identify and report on their sustainability issues, it has not been very successful in promoting integrated thinking, which is critical in linking thinking, planning and reporting processes. Hence, as discussed earlier, IR has emerged as a response to these issues and to transform existing reporting practices. It offers a more comprehensive reporting framework that can instigate collaborative thinking and action on sustainability, and communicate how sustainability norms and principles are embedded, operationalized and delivered by the public sector. The next section presents the need for and state of IR in the public sector.

Integrated reporting in the public sector

Movement to and benefits of integrated reporting in the public sector

IR and the associated International Integrated Reporting Framework (IIRC Framework) is a new form of reporting that has seen growing interest from PSOs. It is more than simply another report that summarizes information contained in other reports (e.g. the financial report, or the sustainability report). Rather, it seeks to explain how an organization creates value over time by enhancing accountability and stewardship, and promoting understanding of the interdependencies between the organization's capital sources (IIRC, 2013). Although the IIRC Framework was initially seen as being primarily focused on the private sector, the International Integrated Reporting Council (IIRC) considers its applicability to be wider: 'it can also be applied, adapted as necessary, by public sector and not-for-profit organizations' (IIRC, 2013, p.4). The literature supports this statement, arguing that there is great potential in broadening the focus of IR initiatives beyond the private sector (Adams and Simnett, 2011; Bartocci and Picciaia, 2013; Lodhia, 2015).

The literature has examined potential advantages IR could offer the public sector. These advantages include the opportunity for public sector organizations to move beyond historical reporting practices through the recognition and reporting of diverse forms of capital in value creation (Bartocci and Picciaia, 2013; Veltri and Silvestri, 2015; Cohen and Karatzimas, 2015; Katsikas et al., 2017; Montecalvo et al., 2018; Manes-Rossi and Orelli, 2019; Farneti et al., 2019). This could potentially lead to a more inter-connected view of sustainability for the public sector (Guthrie et al., 2017; Montecalvo et al., 2018; Manes-Rossi, 2018). Integrated reporting also provides the ability and discretion for public sector organizations to tailor the principles-based IIRC Framework to tell their individual stories through reporting orientated towards organizational ends (Veltri and Silvestri, 2015; Lodhia, 2015; Oprisor et al., 2016). However, it needs to be noted that the IIRC Framework is not just about IR; it is about organizational thinking in an integrated manner, decision-making and actions leading to more integrated processes, and a movement away from silo thinking, often noted in public sector organizations (Bartocci and Picciaia, 2013; Macnab, 2015; Guthrie et al., 2017; Katsikas et al., 2017, 2017; Manes-Rossi, 2018).

With the public sector having a broad base of stakeholders, the application of the IIRC Framework also has potential through its focus on stakeholder engagement as a guiding principle, specifically:

> An integrated report should provide insight into the nature and quality of the organization's relationships with its key stakeholders, including how and to what extent the organization understands, takes into account and responds to their legitimate needs and interests.
>
> *(IIRC, 2013, p. 5)*

By having a stronger focus on stakeholder engagement, the integrated approach could potentially lead to improved provision of useful information to stakeholders and improved accountability outcomes for the public sector (Wild, 2011; Bartocci and Picciaia, 2013; Oprisor et al., 2016; Katsikas et al., 2017; Guthrie et al., 2017; Manes-Rossi, 2018; Montecalvo et al., 2018; Manes-Rossi and Orelli, 2019).

Potential challenges to implementing integrated reporting in the public sector

Notwithstanding the potential advantages IR can bring to the public sector, it is important to also consider potential challenges discussed in the literature. For example, as the IIRC Framework does not specify measures and metrics, this could potentially lead to inconsistency and lack of comparability between public sector entities, with some arguing for the continued usage of the GRI in preparing integrated reports (Manes-Rossi, 2018). However, without support and agreement by key actors (e.g. public sector organizations, standard setters, professional organizations) (Oprisor et al., 2016), issues of consistency and comparability could potentially occur across all sectors, pointing to the need for an agreed approach towards IR in the public sector.

Others have raised concerns about the private sector focus of the IIRC Framework development, noting that the level of adaptation required for the public sector is an area that requires further exploration (Oprisor et al., 2016; Manes-Rossi and Orelli, 2019). Guthrie et al. (2017) noted that the public sector is often resistant to change, causing the possible adoption of any new reporting framework to be little more than a cosmetic change to internal management processes. Others have questioned the relevance of reporting against all six capitals in the public sector, arguing for a simplified reporting approach using a combination of IR and popular reporting, but this approach is yet to be examined (Cohen and Karatzimas, 2015).

Potential resources available for the public sector

In recognition of the implementation challenges facing IR in the public sector, resources have been developed to help explain why and how the public sector should adopt IR. These include the establishment of the Public Sector Pioneer Network[1] by the IIRC in 2014, in partnership with the Chartered Institute of Public Finance and Accountancy (CIPFA). Resources provided by the network include access to webinars, network meetings, expert insights, resources and shared learning on interpreting the applicability of IR to the public sector. In 2016, the network published a public sector guide specifically focusing on helping leaders understand how integrated thinking and reporting can assist the public sector, through the provision of five case study organizations and their experiences in implementing IR. Other publicly available resources that focus on the benefits of IR KMPG (2012), PwC (2015), Deloitte (2015), CIMA (2016) and EY (2018).

Review of integrated reporting literature in the public sector

Studies have noted the importance and the need for research in the public sector, but research examining IR practice is currently lacking (Montecalvo et al., 2018; Dumay et al., 2016; Guthrie et al., 2017). Given the size and influence of the public sector (GRI, 2005), this is an important gap in the literature that requires addressing. An overview of the current empirical contributions to the literature is discussed below, providing insights into the current state of IR in the public sector.

Few studies have examined types and levels of disclosure in accordance with the IIRC Framework. Two studies (Montecalvo et al., 2018; Farneti et al., 2019) analyzed IR reporting from a state-owned enterprise (SOE) perspective, specifically focusing on New Zealand Post (NZP), a participant in the IIRC's pilot programme. Montecalvo et al. (2018), in applying an institutional theory perspective, examined the influence of IR on sustainability disclosures over the period 2001–2015 in NZP. With adoption of the IIRC Framework in 2012, the study found that IR positively impacted the balance and content of sustainability disclosures, leading to the conclusion that IR enhances sustainability reporting and is a useful accounting technology. Farneti et al. (2019) examined how social disclosures by NZP were influenced by the adoption of the IIRF Framework specifically focusing on intellectual, human, and social and relationship capitals. Through the lens of stakeholder theory, the study found that the IR process led to more meaningful stakeholder engagement, resulting in an increase in more relevant social disclosures. Both studies noted the positive impact IR brought to external reporting at NZP and the potential this may have for SOEs and the public sector in general. However, Montecalvo et al. (2018) raised questions as to whether the IIRF Framework provides a comprehensive framework for all aspects of sustainability, calling for further research in this area.

Other disclosure studies have also examined levels of adherence with the IIRC Framework, noting that prior application of reporting standards and guidelines such as the GRI places organizations in a privileged position in preparing integrated reports (Katsikas et al., 2017). Guthrie et al. (2017) noted how IR can penetrate into public sector organizations through internal levels of change, while Katsikas et al. (2017) found progressive adoption of integrated thinking through management commitment, development of communication channels, provision of professional training and support developed across time. Veltri and Silvestri (2015), in analysing the integrated report of a South African public university, found the level of adherence to the IIRC Framework to be variable, noting a higher focus was required on integrated thinking and more responsiveness to stakeholders. In a further study, Manes-Rossi and Orelli (2019), who examined the IR approaches of three local government councils (Johannesburg, Melbourne and Warsaw), concluded that disclosures were heavily influenced by pressure from main actors, differing across locations in terms of principles and focus adopted.

A small number of public sector studies have examined the extent to which IR focuses on stakeholder engagement. Farneti et al. (2019), noted more meaningful stakeholder processes occurred following the implementation of IR, as did Katsikas et al. (2017). However, Katsikas et al. (2017) highlighted the need for deeper engagement with all stakeholders, arguing that if stakeholders had an improved comprehension of the linkages between financial and non-financial activities, this would help in alleviating conflicting stakeholder expectations and provide a better understanding of the organization as a whole. Similarly, Manes-Rossi (2018), investigating stakeholder engagement across six public sector 'IR early adopters', found varying levels of engagement, while noting its importance.

In drawing this section to a close, it is clear there is potential for IR in the public sector but further exploration and research is required to overcome a number of challenges presented in this section. This is discussed in the next section.

Future research opportunities on integrated reporting in the public sector

The studies discussed above have extended the literature on IR in the public sector. They are a useful start but there is much more that could be explored within this sector. The emphasis in this section is on identifying future research opportunities in relation to IR. The context for such studies, comparisons with corporate entities, developments in theorizing, and a focus on integrated thinking (rather than merely reporting) are some areas that could be developed further in relation to IR in the public sector. Furthermore, developments in IR through the auspices of the IIRC, and the link between IR and sustainable development goals, provide a basis for exploring their relevance to public-sector entities. The role of information and communication technologies, assurance, regulation and stakeholder perceptions of IR in the public sector also provide considerable scope for future research.

Our overview of the existing studies on IR indicates that the focus is on Australian, New Zealand, South African and Italian research contexts. Other contexts will need to be investigated. This could include public sector agencies in developing countries, comparing the situation in these contexts to that of entities in the developed world. Country-specific studies are needed to gain an in-depth understanding of the current status of public sector integrated thinking and reporting on a global scale. Integrated reporting and integrated thinking studies at various tiers of the public sector could also provide specific context-based information. For instance, the Australian Commonwealth Sector (Lodhia et al., 2012; Lodhia and Jacobs, 2013), states and local councils (Goswami and Lodhia, 2014) could be studied for IR practices.

Comparisons between public sector entities and companies would also be useful in understanding whether their organizational motives have a role in IR. Corporations have profitability and shareholder wealth maximization as their underlying goal, leading to criticism about whether they are really committed to sustainability issues (Gray, 2001; Milne and Gray, 2014). This is of particular concern for IR as some authors claim that the sustainability focus has been replaced by the value focus in recent times (De Villiers et al., 2014). However, with public sector entities, the goal of benefiting the entire society provides scope for a greater focus on sustainability in the IR process.

The theoretical insights informing IR in the public sector also need to be developed further. Theories at different levels (Llewelyn, 2003) will provide a lens to explore the empirical data in public sector settings. Research methods used for these studies can also be expanded, with approaches such as focus groups, action research, surveys and quantitative methods accompanying the commonly used interviews and content analysis mechanisms.

There is a need for further studies like that of Guthrie et al. (2017), which explore the integrated thinking process in the public sector. A mere focus on reporting is not sufficient in establishing how IR is embedded into organization processes and established as a practice (Lodhia, 2015). Of particular interest is the role of the various organizational participants in integrated thinking, given that this mechanism attempts to break down organizational silos. For instance, what role do accountants have in facilitating integrated thinking in public sector agencies? Who are the other participants in integrated thinking and reporting in organizations? It would also be worthwhile exploring whether integrated thinking is effectively practised in the public sector, the key factors in the success of this process, and the challenges to it.

The various developments in IR facilitated by the IIRC could be assessed within a public sector context in order to gain empirical evidence of actual practices. As an example, the six capitals approach advocated by the IIRC could be used to extend performance management, governance and accountability in the public sector. The use of the IIRC Framework in public sector entities could also be investigated. Public sector entities involved in the IIRC pilot project could also be studied, extending the studies that looked at New Zealand Post (Montecalvo et al., 2018; Farneti et al., 2019).

The 2030 Agenda for Sustainable Development, commonly referred to as Sustainable Development Goals (SDGs), established by the United Nations, will impact organizations, governments and society in general. The public sector will certainly be impacted by these goals and it would be useful to assess the linkage between the SDGs and IR (Adams, 2017) for the public sector. Given that the goal of the public sector is to serve the public interest, the integration of SDGs into public sector systems and processes will be of interest and a useful research endeavour.

Information and communication technologies, especially social media, have transformed corporate communications (Lodhia, 2018) and they also provide potential for IR (Lodhia and Stone, 2017). It would be interesting to observe, for example, the role of social media as a communication tool for IR information and to analyse whether it enhances the effectiveness of IR in the public sector. Issues such as the use of Big Data and the Internet of Things to facilitate integrated thinking and reporting could also be explored.

The assurance of integrated information within the public sector is another issue that could be explored. Such information has to be credible and there is a lack of evidence on the auditing processes involved in this process. Key issues such as who audits such information, the type of assurance statements that are produced and their role in enhancing the credibility of integrated information could be investigated. Internal audits in relation to integrated information could also be studied in future research, given the prevalence of mechanisms such as environmental performance audits in the public sector (Rika and Jacobs, 2019).

Some studies have explored stakeholder perceptions of IR in the public sector (Manes-Rossi, 2018; Manes-Rossi and Orelli, 2019). Further studies are needed to complement these and similar work in the sustainability accounting and reporting area (Kaur and Lodhia, 2014, 2016, 2017, 2018, 2019). The regulatory aspect of IR in the public sector also needs to be explored. A critical issue that needs addressing is whether this practice should remain voluntary or whether mandatory requirements are needed. An analysis of the views of the various participants in IR is needed to explore this matter. Such studies would provide insights into the effectiveness of voluntary IR and the future of public sector IR regulation.

Note

1 https://integratedreporting.org/ir-networks/public-sector-pioneer-network/

References

AccountAbility. (2011). *Stakeholder engagement standard: Final exposure draft*. London, UK: AccountAbility.

Adams, C. A. (2017). *The sustainable development goals: Integrated thinking and the integrated report*. IIRC and ICAS.

Adams, S., and Simnett, R. (2011). Integrated reporting: An opportunity for Australia not-for-profit sector. *Australian Accounting Review, 21*(3), 292–301.

Ball, A. (2005). *Advancing sustainability reporting: An agenda for public service organisations: A discussion paper*. London: Chartered Institute of Public Finance and Accountancy.

Ball, A., and Grubnic, S. (2007). Sustainability accounting and accountability in the public sector. In J. Unerman, J. Bebbington, and B. O'Dwyer (Eds.), *Sustainability accounting and accountability* (pp. 243–265). London: Routledge.

Ball, A., Grubnic, S., and Birchall, J. (2014). Sustainability accounting and accountability in the public sector. In J. Beggington, J. Unerman, and B. O'Dwyer (Eds.), *Sustainability accounting and accountability* (pp. 176–196). London: Routledge.

Bartocci, L., and Picciaia, F. (2013). Towards integrated reporting in the public sector. In C. Busco, M. L. Frigo, A. Riccaboni, and P. Quattrone (Eds.), *Integrated reporting: Concepts and cases that redefine corporate accountability* (pp. 191–204). Cham, Switzerland: Springer.

Bellringer, A., Ball, A., and Craig, R. (2011). Reasons for sustainability reporting by New Zealand local governments. *Sustainability Accounting, Management and Policy Journal, 2*(1), 126–138.

Biondi, L., and Bracci, E. (2018). Sustainability, popular and integrated reporting in the public sector: A fad and fashion perspective. *Sustainability, 10*(9), 3112.

Broadbent, J., and Guthrie, J. (1992). Changes in the public sector: A review of recent "alternative" accounting research. *Accounting, Auditing & Accountability Journal, 5*(2), 3–31.

Chartered Institute of Chartered Accountants (CIMA). (2016). *Integrated reporting in the public sector*. Available at: https://integratedreporting.org/resource/cima-integrated-reporting-in-the-public-sector/ (Accessed: 22 May 2019).

Chartered Institute of Public Finance and Accountancy (CIPFA). (2016). *Integrated thinking and reporting: Focusing on value creation in the public sector: An introduction for leaders*. Available at: https://integratedreporting.org/wp-content/uploads/2016/09/Focusing-on-value-creation-in-the-public-sector-_vFINAL.pdf (Accessed: 23 October 2019).

Cohen, S., and Karatzimas, S. (2015). Tracing the future of reporting in the public sector: Introducing integrated popular reporting. *International Journal of Public Sector Management, 28*(6), 449–460.

De Villiers, C., Rinaldi, L., and Unerman, J. (2014). Integrated reporting: Insights, gaps and an agenda for future research. *Accounting, Auditing & Accountability Journal, 27*(7), 1042–1067.

Deloitte. (2015). *Integrated reporting as a driver for integrated thinking?* Available at: www2.deloitte.com/content/dam/Deloitte/nl/Documents/risk/deloitte-nl-risk-integrated-reporting-a-driver-for-integratedthinking.pdf (Accessed: 23 May 2019).

Dickinson, D., Leeson, R., Ivers, J., and Karic, J. (2005). *Sustainability reporting by public agencies: International uptake, forms and practice*. Victoria, Australia: The Centre for Public Agency Sustainability Reporting.

Diesendorf, M. (2000). Sustainability and sustainable development. In D. Dunphy, J. Benveniste, A. Griffiths, and P. Sutton (Eds.), *Sustainability: The corporate challenge of the 21st century* (pp. 19–37). Sydney: Allen & Unwin.

Domingues, A. R., Lozano, R., Ceulemans, K., and Ramos, T. B. (2017). Sustainability reporting in public sector organisations: Exploring the relation between the reporting process and organisational change management for sustainability. *Journal of Environmental Management, 192*, 292–301.

Dumay, J., Bernardi, C., Guthrie, J., and Demartini, P. (2016). Integrated reporting: A structured literature review. *Accounting Forum, 40*(3), 166–185.

EY. (2018). *EY's excellence in integrated reporting awards: A survey of the integrated reports of South Africa's top 10 state-owned entities*. Available at: https://integratedreportingsa.org/ey-excellence-in-integrated-reporting-awards-2018/ (Accessed: 22 May 2019).

Farneti, F., Casonato, F., Montecalvo, M., and De Villiers, C. (2019). The influence of integrated reporting and stakeholder information needs on the disclosure of social information in a state-owned enterprise. *Meditari Accountancy Research, 27*(4), 556–579.

Farneti, F., and Guthrie, J. (2009). Sustainability reporting by Australian public sector organizations: Why they report. *Accounting Forum, 33*(2), 89–98.

Global Reporting Initiative (GRI). (2005). *Sector supplement for public agencies*. Amsterdam: GRI.

Goswami, K., and Lodhia, S. (2014). Sustainability disclosure patterns of South Australian local councils: A case study. *Public Money & Management, 34*(4), 273–280.

Gray, R. H. (2001). *Accounting for the environment*. London: Sage Publications.

Greco, G., Sciulli, N., and D'Onza, G. (2015). The influence of stakeholder engagement on sustainability reporting: Evidence from Italian local councils. *Public Management Review, 17*(4), 465–488.

Guthrie, J., and Farneti, F. (2008). GRI sustainability reporting by Australian public sector organizations. *Public Money & Management, 28*(6), 361–366.

Guthrie, J., Manes-Rossi, F., and Orelli, R. L. (2017). Integrated reporting and integrated thinking in Italian public sector organisations. *Meditari Accountancy Research, 25*(4), 553–573.

Hopwood, A., Unerman, J., and Fries, J. (2010). Introduction to the accounting for sustainability case studies. In A. Hopwood, and J. Unerman (Eds.), *Accounting for sustainability: Practical insights* (pp. 1–28). London: Routledge.

IIRC. (2013). *The International <IR> Framework*. Available at: http://integratedreporting.org/resource/international-ir-framework/ (Accessed: 15 May 2019).

Imoniana, J. O., Domingos, L. C., Soares, R. R., and Tinoco, J. E. P. (2012). Stakeholders' engagement in sustainability development and reporting: Evidence from Brazil. *African Journal of Business Management, 6*(42), 10634–10644.

Katsikas, E., Manes-Rossi, F., and Orelli, R. (2017). *Towards integrated reporting: Accounting change in the public sector*. Switzerland: Springer.

Kaur, A., and Lodhia, S. (2014). The state of disclosures on stakeholder engagement in sustainability reporting in Australian local councils. *Pacific Accounting Review, 26*(1/2), 54–74.

Kaur, A., and Lodhia, S. (2016). Influences on stakeholder engagement in sustainability accounting and reporting: A study of Australian local councils. *Corporate Responsibility & Stakeholding, 10*, 105–129.

Kaur, A., and Lodhia, S. (2017). The extent of stakeholder engagement in sustainability accounting and reporting: Does empowerment of stakeholders really exist? *Modern Organisational Governance, 12*, 129–145.

Kaur, A., and Lodhia, S. (2018). Stakeholder engagement in sustainability accounting and reporting: A study of Australian local councils. *Accounting, Auditing & Accountability Journal, 31*(1), 338–368.

Kaur, A., and Lodhia, S. (2019). Key issues and challenges in stakeholder engagement in sustainability reporting: A study of Australian local councils. *Pacific Accounting Review, 31*(1), 2–18.

Kopnina, H., and Shoreman-Ouimet, E. (2015). Introduction: The emergence and development of sustainability. In H. Kopnina, and E. Shoreman-Ouimet (Eds.), *Sustainability: Key issues* (pp. 3–24). London: Routledge.

KPMG. (2012). *Integrated reporting. Performance insight through better business reporting*. Available at: www.kpmg.com/AU/en/IssuesAndInsights/ArticlesPublications/Better-Business-Reporting/Documents/integrated-reporting-issue-2.pdf (Accessed: 22 May 2019).

Lamprinidi, S., and Kubo, N. (2008). Debate: The global reporting initiative and public agencies. *Public Money & Management, 28*, 326–329.

Leeson, R., Ivers, J., and Dickinson, D. (2005). Sustainability reporting by the public sector: Momentum changes in the practice, uptake and form of reporting by public agencies. *Accountability Forum, 8*, 12–21.

Lewis, T. (2008). Debate: Public sector sustainability reporting: Implications for accountants. *Public Money & Management, 28*(6), 329–331.

Llewelyn, S. (2003). What counts as 'theory' in qualitative management and accounting research? Introducing five levels of theorizing. *Accounting, Auditing & Accountability Journal, 16*(4), 662–708.

Lodhia, S. (2015). Exploring the transition to integrated reporting through a practice lens: An Australian customer owned bank perspective. *Journal of Business Ethics, 129*(3), 585–598.

Lodhia, S. (2018). Is the medium the message? Advancing the research agenda on the role of communication media in sustainability reporting. *Meditari Accountancy Research, 26*(1), 2–12.

Lodhia, S., and Jacobs, K. (2013). The practice turn in environmental reporting: A study into current practices in two Australian commonwealth departments. *Accounting, Auditing & Accountability Journal, 26*(4), 595–615.

Lodhia, S., Jacobs, K., and Park, Y. J. (2012). Driving public sector environmental reporting: The disclosure practices of Australian Commonwealth departments. *Public Management Review*, *14*(5), 631–647.

Lodhia, S., and Stone, G. (2017). Integrated reporting in a social media and internet communication environment: Conceptual insights. *Australian Accounting Review*, *27*(1), 17–33.

Macnab, A. (2015). Debate: Would outcome costing and integrated reporting link resources to strategy in the public sector? *Public Money & Management*, *35*(6), 399–400.

Manes-Rossi, F. (2018). Is integrated reporting a new challenge for public sector entities? *African Journal of Business Management*, *12*(7), 172–187.

Manes-Rossi, F., and Orelli, R. L. (2019). New frontiers for local government reporting: Learning by pioneers. In M. S. Chiucchi, and P. Demartini (Eds.), *Qualitative research in intangibles, intellectual capital and integrated reporting practices: Opportunities, criticalities and future perspectives* (pp. 13–40). Roma, Marzo: RomaTre Press.

Marcuccio, M., and Steccolini, I. (2005). Social and environmental reporting in local authorities: A new Italian fashion? *Public Management Review*, *7*(2), 155–176.

Marx, B., and Van-Dyk, V. (2011). Sustainability reporting at large public sector entities in South Africa. *South African Journal of Accounting Research*, *25*(1), 103–127.

Milne, M. J., and Gray, R. H. (2014). W(h)ither ecology? The triple bottom line, the global reporting initiative, and corporate sustainability reporting. *Journal of Business Ethics*, *118*(1), 13–29.

Montecalvo, M., Farneti, F., and De Villiers, C. (2018). The potential of integrated reporting to enhance sustainability reporting in the public sector. *Public Money & Management*, *38*(5), 365–374.

Oprisor, T., Tudor, A. T., and Silvia, N. C. (2016). The integrated reporting system: A new accountability enhancement tool for public sector entities. *Audit Financiar*, *7*(139), 749–762.

Organisation for Economic Cooperation and Development (OECD). (2001). *Sustainable development: Critical issues*. Paris: OECD Publishing.

PricewaterhouseCoopers (PwC). (2015). Implementing integrated reporting. Available at: www.pwc. com/gx/en/auditservices/publications/assets/pwc-ir-practical-guide.pdf (Accessed: 22 May 2019).

Rika, N., and Jacobs, K. (2019). Reputational risk and environmental performance auditing: A study in the Australian commonwealth public sector. *Financial Accountability & Management*, *35*(2), 182–198.

Schaltegger, S., Bennett, M., and Burritt, R. (2006). Sustainability accounting and reporting: Development, linkages and reflection – an introduction. In S. Schaltegger, M. Bennett, and R. Burritt (Eds.), *Sustainability Accounting and Reporting* (pp. 1–33). Dordrecht, The Netherlands: Springer.

Tort, L. E. (2010). *GRI reporting in public agencies*. Amsterdam, The Netherlands: Global Reporting Initiative.

United Nations (UN). (2015). *Transforming our world: The 2030 agenda for sustainable development*. United Nations.

Veltri, S., and Silvestri, A. (2015). The Free State University integrated reporting: A critical consideration. *Journal of Intellectual Capital*, *16*(2), 443–462.

Wild, S. (2011). Public sector accountability for cultural assets: An integrated reporting approach. *International Journal of Environmental, Cultural, Economic and Social Sustainability*, *7*(5), 379–390.

Williams, B. R. (2015). Reporting on sustainability by Australian councils: A communication perspective. *Asian Review of Accounting*, *23*(2), 186–203.

Williams, B. R., Wilmshurst, T., and Clift, R. (2011). Sustainability reporting by local government in Australia: Current and future prospects. *Accounting Forum*, *35*(3), 176–186.

PART IV

Implementation of IT and IR

16

INTEGRATED THINKING OR INTEGRATED REPORTING, WHICH COMES FIRST?

Caroline M. Bridges

The University of Auckland

Mark Yeoman

Corporate executive involved with Integrated Reporting since 2011

Julie Harrison

The University of Auckland

Abstract

The International Integrated Reporting Council (IIRC) published a framework on integrated reporting in December 2013 that guides the preparation of an integrated report. The integrated report is intended to be a true reflection of the value creation process of an organization. The IIRC advocates the adoption of integrated thinking within an organization prior to the production of the first integrated report. In this chapter, we examine two businesses in New Zealand that embarked on the adoption of integrated reporting in opposite ways, one by producing an integrated report first and the other by developing integrated thinking before attempting to produce an integrated report. By comparing their experiences, we evaluate which should come first.

Introduction

The International Integrated Reporting Council (IIRC) published the International Integrated Reporting Framework (IIRC Framework) in 2013 (IIRC, 2013). The IIRC promotes a "cycle" of integrated thinking and reporting (IIRC, 2013, p.2). This suggests that both elements are required in order to fully implement the requirements of the IIRC Framework. Further, integrated thinking "leads to better integration of the information systems that support internal and external reporting and communication, including

241

preparation of the integrated report" (IIRC, 2013, p.2). Accordingly, the IIRC Framework promotes the implementation of integrated thinking as a precursor to an organization preparing an integrated report. However, an organization can choose one of two options: start with integrated reporting (IR) and then develop integrated thinking to support the reporting process or, alternatively, develop integrated thinking processes and then report the consequences of that decision in an integrated report. For an organization considering adopting IR there may be compelling reasons to consider either option.

The publication of an integrated report signals that an organization is committed to being held accountable for the information contained within it, even if the internal processes for the report are immature. It would seem logical to implement integrated thinking within the organization first, so that the value creation proposition is well understood before attempting to articulate the outcomes of that thinking. If integrated thinking is embedded within the organization then the resulting integrated report is more likely to be of higher quality (Esch et al., 2019). However, implementing integrated thinking across an organization may not be the best way to start the IR process if homogenization stifles innovation (Dumay and Dai, 2017) and the challenges of bringing together business segments in a cohesive fashion threaten to derail progress on preparing the first integrated report.

In this chapter the experiences of two organizations that chose different starting points to adopt IR are examined. Ultimately, there is no perfect way to adopt IR. The reality is that it requires a nudge to ensure that once a company adopts IR, its journey is sustained. Committing to IR is the nudge that is required. Without articulating the results of integrated thinking in a report, ongoing improvement can be stifled. The IIRC has stated that producing an integrated report is a learning process and an organization will improve its reporting year on year. The experiences of the two organizations discussed in this chapter can help other organizations that are contemplating embracing IR to select an optimum pathway to implementing it and help the IIRC as it collects the experiences of organizations as they adopt IR.

This chapter proceeds as follows. First, the concept of integrated thinking is introduced to explain why it is important to the process of IR. Second, the key parts of the IIRC Framework are explained to suggest challenges that the two organizations are likely to have encountered when preparing an integrated report and to identify some of the reasons they adopted IR. Third, we detail the experiences of the two organizations examined as they developed integrated thinking and reporting. Finally, some of the lessons learned along the way are shared.

Integrated thinking

The IIRC Framework states that integrated thinking and IR are *both* required in order to achieve the goals set by the IIRC. But although integrated thinking can lead to IR, they can both exist independently and it is not necessary or required for them to co-exist (Al-Htaybat and von Alberti-alhtaybat, 2018). This is surprising, given the statements in the IIRC Framework. Accordingly, there is the potential for the adoption of the IIRC Framework to lead to outcomes that were unexpected by the IIRC.

The IIRC framework defines integrated thinking as follows:

> Integrated thinking is the active consideration by an organization of the relationships between its various operating and functional units and the capitals that the organization uses or affects. Integrated thinking leads to integrated decision-making and actions that consider the creation of value over the short, medium and long term
>
> *(IIRC, 2013, p.2)*

However, there is no detailed guidance on how integrated thinking should be implemented, so the concept can be difficult for any organization adopting IR. Therefore, it can be adopted in an idiosyncratic way (Feng et al., 2017).

Further, the IIRC Framework (IIRC, 2013, p. 2) emphasizes the importance of "connectivity and dependencies" between the factors that affect an organization's value creation processes. These factors are defined to include the organization's six capitals (financial, manufactured, intellectual, human, social and relationship and natural) in the past, present and future; its ability to respond to stakeholders' needs and concerns; and its response to the external environment.

Long-term support is required by senior executives in the management team of any organization to ensure that the concept of integrated thinking will be fully articulated and successfully embedded in that organization. The concept of connectivity of information through integrated thinking is also a challenge for organizations, although experience can improve understanding (La Torre et al., 2019).There is little guidance given on how to establish integrated thinking and it relies on interpretation by management. Establishing what integrated thinking is and developing the internal systems to apply it takes time and effort (CIMA, 2017) and the understanding of integrated thinking is likely to change over time. For an organization embarking on a journey into IR, this can be a challenge, as it relies on a sustained commitment by management to establish a road map for success. Changing management structures and personnel can reduce the commitment to successfully embedding IR and therefore the commitment to IR needs to be incorporated into an organization's long-term plans.

An organization will be receptive to the adoption of integrated thinking to create more value in the short, medium and long term if there is a perceived lack of, or weaknesses in, its internal management reporting processes, as this inevitably leads to information being put in silos. In that case the concept of integrated thinking is seen as an improvement from siloed decision-making because value within an organization will be assessed in a more holistic way (Dumay and Dai, 2017). If existing management practices are already seen as efficient, then adopting integrated thinking will be less likely to be seen as a positive move, as the perceived benefit may not outweigh the cost of implementation. In addition, a significant barrier to adopting an integrated thinking approach relates to getting managers in siloed organizations to recognise the equivalence of broader organizational goals with their own divisional performance objectives.

Integrated thinking is broader than IR and is of particular importance to investment decision-making and prioritization where organizations are considering the impact and trade-offs across a multi-dimensional scope encapsulated by the six capitals. While integrated thinking is not necessary for this multi-dimensional approach, the IIRC Framework provides a common language and scaffold on which managers can base more productive discussions on these issues.

Benefits from viewing the business more holistically have been reported despite the lack of detailed guidance on integrated thinking. Improvements from adopting IR have been reported as a result of "changes in the decision-making processes" or integrated thinking (IIRC, 2017). That is, there can be a change to internal decision-making from the adoption of IR (Barth et al., 2017). United Utilities reported that integrated thinking is similar to systems thinking and they viewed their network of assets as one big system (ACCA, 2018). Dutch bank FMO reported that integrated thinking added value because the concept of considering how the organization created value through the business model was beneficial (ACCA, 2018). Accordingly, a different way of thinking can provide benefits in developing new accounting tools and improved decision-making (Guthrie et al., 2017).

The IIRC framework

The IIRC published the IIRC Framework in 2013 with the objectives of improving the quality of corporate reporting and increasing trust between organizations and their stakeholders. In addition, IR was designed to enable investors to make better decisions and, in particular, more effective capital allocation decisions. The purpose of the cycle of integrated thinking and reporting is to ensure a more effective distribution of capital.

For any individual organization, its motivation for the adoption of IR may extend beyond lowering the cost of capital. An increase in the voluntary disclosure of non-financial information can be motivated by legitimacy concerns (Beck et al., 2015) or to respond to the concerns of particular stakeholders (De Villiers et al., 2014), as well as to reduce agency costs (De Villiers and Hsiao, 2018). Adopting IR can also be used to help an organization as it attempts to achieve some of the United Nations Sustainable Development Goals (UNSDG) (Adams, 2017). Therefore, the objective of lowering the cost of capital may not be the primary motive for adopting IR and other motivations may also encourage an organization to consider adoption.

The IIRC Framework sets out the requirements for an integrated report. However, an organization can publish and label any report as an integrated report even though it may simply reflect a summary of financial and non-financial information and not comply with the IIRC Framework. Initially, the information contained in integrated reports was not highly regarded by users and only used in conjunction with other, more familiar information sources to evaluate the performance and prospects of an organization (Reimsbach et al., 2018). That is, there is a learning process for stakeholders and for preparers. Prior experience of preparing sustainability reports can be adapted to assist with an integrated report compared to organizations that have not previously prepared sustainability information (Massingham et al., 2019). However, IR should focus on material issues and activities that drive progress towards strategic objectives within the six capitals and not all information included within sustainability reports will be relevant. Each integrated report produced by an organization will build on previous reports and comparability between reports and between organizations can be compromised by shifting presentation styles. This potentially limits the usefulness of an integrated report.

The two key parts (or fundamental concepts) of the IIRC Framework are the "capitals" and the value creation process. The capitals are defined as "stocks of value that are increased or decreased or transformed through the activities and outputs of the organization" (IIRC, 2013, p.11). The six capitals identified in the IIRC Framework are financial, manufactured, intellectual, human, social and relationship and natural capital. An integrated report should consider how the stocks of capital are changed and "provide insight" (IIRC, 2013, p.10) about how they create value. This can be problematic for preparers of integrated reports (ACCA, 2019) as it requires considering the business and the business model from a novel and holistic perspective. For an organization considering adopting IR, there needs to be a shared understanding of the capitals of the business. The capitals are also linked to both the purpose of the business and the strategic objectives. Consideration of how the capitals interact with each other requires integrated thinking and can be undertaken once the links are understood.

The capitals of an organization are important not only to develop integrated thinking, but also to link the thinking to strategy and strategy development, which requires introducing novel ideas. Reporting on strategy in an integrated report with reference to capitals is, therefore, difficult both for preparers and users who are unused to the new terminology. This requires educating stakeholders, both internally and externally, to explain the capitals and how they link to the value creation process and the strategic objectives of the organization.

The benefits of adopting IR are less about the benefits to external stakeholders, and more about developing a better internal understanding of the business model and identifying where value is created (ACCA, 2019). The commitment to IR empowers an organization to think beyond business-as-usual to develop a stronger intellectual framework that is relevant to stakeholders beyond the investment community. The IIRC developed IR as a way to report to providers of financial capital, but for many organizations other stakeholders are just as important.

Preparing an integrated report is both a challenge for preparers in establishing the report in terms of the IIRC Framework and a challenge in terms of communicating a new report to stakeholders and educating them on the contents. The IIRC has talked about a learning process, and noted that preparers will improve the quality with each new integrated report. For many organizations, the idea that a document is published that is not of the highest standard can be challenging and may deter preparers from proceeding with a published report until a high standard can be achieved. Further, reporting negative news or a lack of progress against a key performance indicator may be confronting for organizations more comfortable with the traditional "feel good" qualitative commentary. However, providing notice of the intention to publish an integrated report gives a signal to stakeholders of a change to the reporting priorities. If an organization then does not go ahead and produce a report this can have an adverse effect on any other legitimizing behaviour. Accordingly, it may be preferable for an organization to publish a report, even if stakeholders face challenges in evaluating that report.

Integrated thinking and reporting in practice

Organization Alpha

Organization Alpha was an established business operating in New Zealand that was suffering a serious decline in revenue and needed to reinvent itself, as it was losing legitimacy as a relevant business. Alpha was a State-Owned Enterprise (SOE) and owned by the Government of New Zealand. The threat to its business required innovative strategy initiatives to maintain its relevance economically within New Zealand. Alpha had diversified its business operations prior to adopting IR and had devised a strategy to maintain its reputation as a business with a future relevant to all New Zealanders. Although government-owned, Alpha had links to market effects as a result of issuing listed debt securities. Alpha was not a target for IR adoption by the IIRC as it was not a listed company, but its prior experience issuing sustainability reports using the Global Reporting Initiative made it an appropriate business to trial the principles of IR. Alpha joined the pilot programme of the IIRC, which consisted of a group of organizations interested in improving corporate reporting. Alpha committed to adopting IR in 2013.

Once the decision to prepare an IR had been taken, Alpha started with a blank piece of paper, although the business had some experience with the Global Reporting Initiative guidelines and other alternative approaches to reporting. A team of managers was brought together as a steering group to help create the report. This group of individuals represented different areas of the business and as a result of the collaboration they learned more about each other's business units. This resulted in each member appreciating the business as a whole rather than as siloed business units. Some members of the steering group interviewed were from Head Office and pre-disposed to support the initiative, but every member of the group reported a positive experience. The holistic view meant that all those concerned with preparing the integrated report felt more connected to the business as a whole. This experience helped later reports as it was easier for them to construct a narrative of the business as a whole, rather than as disparate business units.

At the time of adoption there was no understanding of the importance of integrated thinking and the first report used information that was previously reported in the sustainability report and annual report, piecing the information together using the capitals as the frame of the report. There was little in the way of new information, but the introduction of the capitals was a new innovation. The first report in 2013 introduced the concept of IR as a signal of an innovation in reporting, along with a new focus. The changes were to external reporting only. That is, there was no active program to drive the IR concepts into internal decision making or make changes to procedures or align with strategic objectives. Rather, the focus was to produce an innovative report that demonstrated that Alpha was a business with a future. The narrative of the report was an opportunity to tell the unique story of the organization.

The adoption of IR was a novel idea for the senior management of Alpha. There were challenges in establishing the required tools in order to discover relics of value to include in the integrated report. Previously, there were elements of the organization that were not articulated in corporate reports and yet were important components of the value creation process. The journey to considering and articulating the capitals was viewed as painful but a fruitful education to reveal important drivers of value.

The adoption of IR was a signal of a new approach to corporate reporting and "this [integrated report] provides a deeper and more comprehensive assessment of our activities, beyond traditional financial and narrative reporting" (Alpha Annual Review, 2013, p.6). Once the board had taken the decision to produce an integrated report, there was no going back. Any reversal of the reporting information would have resulted in a negative signal to stakeholders.

The board of Alpha demonstrated courage in adopting IR, as the implications of adoption were not apparent at the start. Alpha was an early adopter of IR and there was limited evidence of the implications of adopting IR beyond the aspirational statements by the IIRC. The IIRC Framework was in flux and Alpha started with limited guidance. The board required education to be persuaded of the potential advantages of adoption. Commitment to adoption by the board was required to ensure the initiative was continued.

Despite red ink appearing on the profit and loss statement of Alpha, other aspects of the business were able to be discussed. The integrated report was used to articulate the story of the organization, about where the business had been and where it was going, and to present stories of the organization that were previously not highlighted.

Materiality in an integrated report is important for determining what information should be included. Alpha specifically discussed materiality in its 2019 integrated report. Stakeholders were consulted and the material issues for each group of stakeholders were reported. The material issues were defined by Alpha as: 'A material issue is a risk or an opportunity as determined by our stakeholders (internal and external) that could significantly impact our business performance over the medium and long term' (Alpha Integrated Report, 2019, p.64). The adoption of IR became a way for Alpha to articulate the many positive aspects of its business that may have been less visible than the emerging negative ones. That is, it was able to describe its story or the narrative of the business by considering *all* activities of the business. The integrated report applied a different lens to uncover aspects of the business that were previously not reported.

Organization Beta

Beta was a successful retail organization that was a listed company on the New Zealand stock exchange (NZX) and, therefore, faced scrutiny from analysts. The business was also facing challenges in a competitive sector and from the introduction of online sales technology. Beta had previously promoted sustainability issues and prepared separate sustainability reports. Beta considered adopting IR from 2015.

Beta adopted integrated thinking in 2015 to ensure that the company's different business units were aligned and to focus on integrated thinking to better understand how the business was managed. The time taken to prepare the first report was not as important as understanding the business. Beta produced its first integrated report in 2018: 'We have not moved formally into the integrated reporting world; first we are embedding the principles of integrated thinking through the business so that the reporting step comes as a natural extension of what we do' (Beta Annual Report, 2018, p.30). By the time Beta considered adopting IR its Board was already aware of the principles of IR and did not require substantial persuasion to adopt, although the timetable to produce an integrated report was not defined.

Beta incorporated a risk matrix in its first integrated report and explained that materiality was relative to each strategy and capital. Beta used materiality to determine what was reported in its integrated report. Five groups of stakeholders were identified and the difficulty in measuring the strength of each relationship was acknowledged. The report highlighted this was an area that Beta planned to focus on in the future. There is some indication that materiality was developed considering stakeholders' views.

Integrated reporting aims to provide information about the value creation process over the short, medium and long term. Beta had a short shorter operating cycle and the longer-term focus of IR was a challenge. With such intense pressure on Beta's short-term key performance measures, viewing any long-term objectives seemed less useful. However, the process of aligning measurement systems with strategic objectives provided benefits unforeseen at the outset. The 2019 report states that:

> Our commitment to a fully integrated report this year recognises that not every-thing we do is about financial value and we want to keep our stakeholders informed about the many non-financial initiatives we are undertaking and the pro-gress we are making.
>
> *(Beta Integrated Report, 2019, p.16)*

Comparison of approaches

As both Alpha and Beta had experience in reporting on sustainability in a separate sustainability report they were, therefore, well placed to consider a general view of business value beyond financial statements. In general, the decision to adopt a new reporting framework incorporating non-financial measures is motivated by different reasons, but legitimacy in one form or another is the most common. An organization will respond where the social contract has changed, either as a result of the organization losing legitimacy relative to societal expectations, or where societal expectations have changed and the organization has not responded. Alpha's and Beta's legitimacy challenges related to changes in the business environment caused by digital disruption and the need to transform their businesses to respond to changing societal demands.

The adoption of IR requires a business case to be articulated and supported by a champion within the business to persuade the board to support the adoption of IR and to educate them on the advantages of adoption. The champion is required to maintain momentum while the organization progresses with IR adoption. The notion of multiple capitals beyond purely financial was a new concept for both Alpha and Beta and education in considering and articulating non-financial value was required. In both cases there were champions among the executive officers who were able to convince the boards to adopt IR. Without a champion or champions there is the potential for the initiative to fade away and not be sustained when there are changes in personnel or corporate structure with potentially different priorities.

The development of integrated thinking in Beta allowed it to align its reporting and strategy for both the short term and longer term. This allowed IR to be a natural output of the integrated thinking process, thus embedding both integrated thinking and reporting in the organization. In contrast, without integrated thinking being a fast follower of reporting in Alpha, the ability to sustain IR may have been limited. The amount of effort in translating business activities that had been managed in non-integrated ways into the integrated report presented a significant overhead of cost and effort, which was reliant on non-systemic processes usually performed by a small number of individuals. Consequently, without integrated thinking, the reporting side was likely to have declined or failed to evolve at Alpha as those individuals involved in developing the integrated report left the organization.

As a result of the adoption of integrated thinking, both Alpha and Beta changed their internal investment decision-making processes by adding non-financial strategic investment decision criteria. For example, at Beta they found that incorporating non-financial information assisted decision makers where the financial information alone was found to be inadequate and "it is a reflection of the integrated way we are addressing our strategic priorities: integrating our capitals to give us a holistic view of our vulnerabilities and opportunities" (Beta Integrated Report, 2019, p.16). Prior to integrated thinking, if a project was not financially viable but was strategically important, decision makers would be forced to either minimize financial risk or create quasi-financial terms to support a project. After implementing integrated thinking, if a project was not financially viable but delivered against other key strategic performance indicators in relation to one or more of the six capitals, these could be used to justify the project. The addition of the capitals helped guide the strategic information required to make better decisions.

There was an unexpected benefit in the preparation of the integrated report and the articulation of integrated thinking within both organizations, which was the level of employee engagement. For example, divisional management at Alpha felt more connected to Head Office decision-making following their participation in the integrated report preparation process. The opportunity to reflect on the operations of the business and the full range of activities that were happening was only available as a result of the adoption of IR and the establishment of integrated thinking for both Alpha and Beta.

The challenges for any organization adopting IR are considerable. There needs to be a key person who is senior enough to maintain the momentum in ensuring adoption continues beyond the first flush of enthusiasm. There also needs to be a team responsible across business segments for the preparation of integrated reports and for reviewing internal processes within the organization that can affect change in new processes. Any organization that has any degree of complexity will face challenges in assessing material issues and identifying common key performance indicators that can be used in an integrated report. Materiality is one of the key guiding principles of IR and it affects what will be reported. Without evidence of stakeholder engagement, there can be little assurance that material matters are being reported. There will be non-financial issues that cannot be quantified and consistent measurement bases to be agreed that require cooperation; this can be a challenge without buy-in from managers.

Conclusion

Adopting IR does not occur in a vacuum and success in any new initiative within an organization depends on prior experience in adopting new frameworks. A champion is required with influence over the board and senior management to ensure that any new programme is enthusiastically adopted and the momentum for change is maintained. Prior experience with IR by at least one senior manager was helpful for Beta, whereas Alpha relied on its sustainability manager to research information and maintain momentum. Both organizations demonstrated that integrated thinking does not have to be perfect for it to be successful. However, it must align the key performance indicators linked to the strategies driving value in the capitals to the organization's day-to-day management focus and decision-making.

The decision to adopt IR is separate from the decision regarding whether to commence with the reporting or the thinking first. The logical first step is to embed integrated thinking within the organization and ensure measurement systems are in place to provide useful information in the subsequent integrated report. However, given the newness of this form of corporate reporting, there is leeway for organizations to develop integrated thinking in tandem with developing IR. Accordingly, the integrated report provides an opportunity to communicate new and innovative directions taken by an organization on a shorter timeline than is required to develop integrated thinking prior to publishing the first integrated report. The information in an integrated report is not likely to provide useful additional content without a review of internal systems to ensure they align with the strategic objectives of an organization. However, the decision to commence reporting using the IIRC Framework drives change as it provides both a signal that an organization is changing and a nudge for it to do so. This ensures that progress is made towards embedding IR within an organization.

Adopting integrated thinking or IR is ultimately a matter of choice and the decision will be made to suit the organization. Where legitimacy has been threatened, adopting IR acts as a signal of change. Where strategic legitimacy is less important than organizational legitimacy, then adopting integrated thinking and embedding that within the organization first may be a more successful strategy.

References

ACCA. (2018). *Insights into integrated reporting 2.0: Walking the talk.* London: ACCA.

ACCA. (2019). *Insights into integrated reporting 3.0: The drive for authenticity.* London: ACCA.

Adams, C. (2017). *The Sustainable Development Goals, integrated thinking and the integrated report.* London: IIRC and ICAS.

Al-Htaybat, K., and von Alberti-alhtaybat, L. (2018). Integrated thinking leading to integrated reporting: Case study insights from a global player. *Accounting, Auditing & Accountability Journal, 31*(5), 1435–1460.

Barth, M. E., Cahan, S. F., Chen, L., and Venter, E. R. (2017). The economic consequences associated with integrated report quality: Capital market and real effects. *Accounting, Organizations and Society*, *62*, 43–64.

Beck, C., Dumay, J., and Frost, G. (2015). In pursuit of a 'single source of truth': From threatened legitimacy to integrated reporting. *Journal of Business Ethics*. 10.1007/s 10551-014-2423-1

CIMA. (2017). *Research executive summary Vol. 13 Issue 3: Integrated thinking*. Available from: www.cima global.com/Documents/Research%20and%20Insight/Integrated%20Thinking%20Report%20vol% 2013%20issue%203.pdf (Accessed: 15 October 2019).

De Villiers, C., and Hsiao, P. C. K. (2018). Why organizations voluntarily report: Agency theory. In: C. De Villiers, and W. Maroun (Eds.), *Sustainability accounting and integrated reporting* (pp. 49–56). London: Routledge.

De Villiers, C., Rinaldi, L., and Unerman, J. (2014). Integrated reporting: Insights, gaps and an agenda for future research. *Accounting, Auditing & Accountability Journal*, *27*(7), 1042–1067.

Dumay, J., and Dai, T. (2017). Integrated thinking as a cultural control? *Meditari Accountancy Research*, *25* (4), 574–604.

Esch, M., Schnellbächer, B., and Wald, A. (2019). Does integrated reporting information influence internal decision making? An experimental study of investment behavior. *Business Strategy and the Environment*, *28*(4), 599–610.

Feng, T., Cummings, L., and Tweedie, D. (2017). Exploring integrated thinking in integrated reporting: An exploratory study in Australia. *Journal of Intellectual Capital*, *18*(2), 330–353.

Guthrie, J., Manes-Rossi, F., and Orelli, R. L. (2017). Integrated reporting and integrated thinking in Italian public sector organizations. *Meditari Accountancy Research*, *25*(4), 553–573.

IIRC. (2013). *The international integrated reporting framework*. London, UK: IIRC.

IIRC. (2017). *Creating value: The cyclical power of integrated thinking and reporting*. London: IIRC.

La Torre, M., Bernardi, C., Guthrie, J., and Dumay, J. (2019). Integrated reporting and integrating thinking: Practical challenges. In: S. Arvidsson (Ed.), *Challenges in managing sustainable business* (pp. 25–54). Cham: Palgrave Macmillan.

Massingham, R., Massingham, P. R., and Dumay, J. (2019). Improving integrated reporting: A new learning and growth perspective for the balanced scorecard. *Journal of Intellectual Capital*, *20*(1), 60–82.

Reimsbach, D., Hahn, R., and Gürtürk, A. (2018). Integrated reporting and assurance of sustainability information: An experimental study on professional investors' information processing. *European Accounting Review*, *27*(3), 559–581.

17

MANAGING AND MEASURING SOCIAL IMPACT THROUGH INTEGRATED THINKING AND REPORTING

The case of a European university

Cristiano Busco

Roehampton University of London, and LUISS Guido Carli

Fabrizio Granà

ESCP Business School

Giulia Achilli

Royal Holloway University of London

Abstract

Contemporary organizations face the critical need to identify valuable accounting and reporting practices that represent and communicate their impacts on the environment and on society. However, no widely accepted scientific approach to impact measurement exists, and the relationship between organizational impacts and the resources (capitals) used throughout the value creation process is unclear. This chapter illustrates the design of an impact assessment tool in a public organization. The chapter draws upon the experience of a European university to show the potential of combining Integrated Thinking and Reporting (IT&R) with two widely used impact assessment tools (the Social Return on Investment (SROI) and the Total Impact Measurement Model (TIMM)) to better understand and assess organizations' impacts according to the different capitals exploited to create value for stakeholders.

Introduction

Contemporary organizations face the critical need to identify valuable accounting and reporting practices that represent and communicate their impacts on the environment and the society, thus supporting a comprehensive decision-making process for sustainable value creation. Despite the increase in the number of accounting and reporting practices that attempt to model organizations' value creation process (Adams, 2015, 2017; Adams and Simnett, 2011; Churet and Eccles, 2015; Deloitte, 2016; Eccles and Krzus, 2014, 2010; PwC, 2018), no widely accepted scientific approach to impact measurement exists. On one hand, this is due to the lack of a shared definition of 'social impact' (Maas and Liket, 2011; Vanclay et al., 2015). On the other, the concept of value creation is still strictly related to the increase, decrease or transformations of the resources (inputs) used by the organization's business activities to generate outputs, thus overlooking the impacts generated by them (Maas and Liket, 2011). As a consequence, current reporting approaches are mainly focused on communicating to stakeholders how organizations create value, instead of measuring and representing the impact generated.

Recent accounting studies have emphasized the role of Integrated Thinking and Reporting (IT&R) in re-determining how organizations conceive and create value, moving towards the integration of social, human, environmental and economic dimensions, instead of considering them separately (Adams, 2015; Busco et al., 2013, 2018; De Villiers et al., 2014; Eccles and Krzus, 2014; Eccles and Spiesshofer, 2015; Simnett and Huggins, 2015; Terblanche and De Villiers, 2019). In particular, these studies argue that IT&R enable organizations to overcome a 'silo' approach by fostering interactions among departments and top managers to identify the main capitals that affect organizations' value creation.

In this context, public organizations are facing increasing external pressures to review their business models and become more 'business-like' entities. However, considering the primary objective of most public organizations – to deliver services to the public, rather than make profits and generate a return on equity for investors – their performance can only be partially evaluated by examining their financial position. Therefore, public organizations need to develop robust decision-making mechanisms to understand the trade-off between the limited resources available and their intended and unintended impacts on the community.

As civic-oriented organizations, universities are primarily asked to educate and prepare current and future generations of employees, leaders and citizens who may contribute positively to societal challenges. To this end, universities are expected to define and measure their impacts on the society, ensuring that the activities pursued are sustainable and viable in the short, medium and long term (Adams, 2018; BUFDG, 2016, 2017). For these reasons, universities, as public institutions, represent an interesting case for the purpose of this chapter.

By drawing on the experience of a European university named Athena (this is a pseudonym for confidentiality), this chapter aims to illustrate and discuss the design of an impact assessment tool in a public organization. In particular, we show the potential of combining IT&R with two widely used impact assessment tools (the Social Return on Investment – SROI, and the Total Impact Measurement Model – TIMM) (Maas and Liket, 2011; Millar and Hall, 2013; WBCSD, 2019) to better understand and assess organizations' impacts according to the different capitals exploited throughout the value creation process.

The chapter is structured as follows. The next section reviews the literature on social impact and its relation with the emerging IT&R approach. The following section illustrates the issues public organizations, and particularly universities, face when measuring their impacts. Thereafter, we discuss the experience of Athena, which has recently designed an impact assessment tool, and the final section summarizes and concludes our chapter.

Social impact, integrated thinking and reporting

Social impact has been defined as

> something that is experienced or felt in either a perceptual (cognitive) or a corporeal (bodily, physical) sense, at any level, for example at the level of an individual person, an economic unit (family/household), a social group (circle of friends), a workplace (a company or government agency), or by community/society generally.
>
> *(Vanclay et al., 2015 p. 2)*

As 'social impact' basically refers to anything linked to stakeholders' perceptions, almost anything can potentially have a social impact as long as it is valued by a specific group of stakeholders (Maas and Liket, 2011; Vanclay et al., 2015).

Given the ambiguity of the notion of social impact, measuring it remains a challenge for organizations. As argued by Maas and Liket (2011), social impact is difficult to quantify because of its qualitative nature. Further, organizations can have a positive or negative impact on society along several dimensions (environmental, economic and social), which makes it hard to attach an objective value to the impact.

The first attempt to measure organizations' social impact arose in the 1970s alongside economic and environmental impact assessment. Traditionally, the three impact assessments have been used separately, emphasizing economic returns over the social and environmental dimensions, thus affecting the ways in which companies see their value creation process.

Organizations often find difficulties in determining the cause-effect relationships between their core business activities, the outputs produced and the impacts these generate on society. These difficulties derive from the definition of value creation, which has barely changed since the days of Luca Pacioli. In fact, value creation is often perceived as strictly related to the increase or decrease in resources (i.e. inputs) used by organizations through their core business activities and production of outputs (Kolodinsky et al., 2006; Maas and Liket, 2011). While outputs are related to organizations and represent what they can measure or assess directly, impacts refer to the portion of the total outcome that results from organizations' activities, above and beyond what would have happened anyway (Clark et al., 2004, p. 7). It is important to consider intended as well as unintended, negative as well as positive, and both long-term and short-term effects. Ideally, evaluation of the impact should inform strategic planning, thus rendering the assessment process recursive (see Figure 17.1).

However, organizations still have difficulty integrating impacts in their strategic planning. This may be due to the lack of suitable accounting and reporting systems to support strategy execution and fully reflect the extensive variety of 'capitals' that are used and affected by organizations' value creation processes (De Villiers et al., 2014; Dumay et al., 2016; Gray, 2010; Owen, 2013). The evolving regulation on corporate disclosure (see, for example, European directive 2014/95), as well as stakeholders' growing information requirements (Adams and Narayanan, 2007; Yongvanich and Guthrie, 2006), have led organizations to

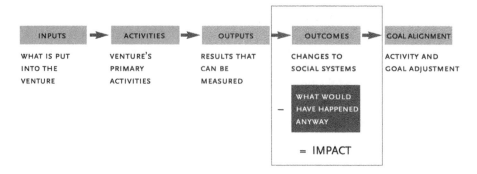

Figure 17.1 Impact Value chain
Source: Clark et al. (2004, p. 7)

move to a more encompassing and integrated approach to value creation. Corporate reports such as CSR reports and sustainability reports have been used to inform stakeholders how organizations align their strategies and business models with market opportunities and sustainable performance.

Positioned at the centre of this debate, Integrated Reporting (IR) has rapidly gained considerable prominence as one of the main management and accounting innovations of the last decade (Busco et al., 2018; De Villiers et al., 2014; Eccles and Krzus, 2014). Integrated Reporting requires a continuous interaction between an organization's departments and top managers to determine how value is created and what drivers affect stakeholders' perception of organizational initiatives and activities. As mentioned by the International Integrated Reporting Framework (International Integrated Reporting Council, 2013), organizations depend on six different types of capitals, which are stores of value that, in one form or another, become inputs to an organization's business model. In particular, the capitals identified by the International Integrated Reporting Council (IIRC) are: financial, manufactured, intellectual, human, social and relationship, and natural capital.

The multi-capital approach has been also embraced in the literature on social impact (Vanclay et al., 2015), according to which all community resources or assets can be represented as a set of capitals that needs to be considered while assessing overall community wellbeing. In order to evaluate the impact organizations have on their stakeholders and society, the environment and the economy in general, both the IR and social impact literature suggests all these capitals should be considered in a holistic manner. In particular, IR relies on integrated thinking as an approach that encourages organizations to actively reconsider the relationships between the capitals that they use and affect, and their various operating and functional units (IIRC, 2013). Integrated thinking involves identifying, executing and monitoring business decisions and strategies for long-term value creation (Busco et al., 2018; Dumay and Dai, 2017; Guthrie et al., 2017). This approach enables mediation across a number of trade-offs, such as:

- the way in which different forms of capital impact the value creation process;
- environmental, social and governance (ESG) performance with financial and economic results;
- lagging and leading measures of performance;

- different types of reports (e.g., financial, social and environmental reports) and over-coming the logic of 'siloed' communication;
- short-term and long-term objectives;
- the multiple needs of a variety of stakeholders;
- the analysis of the multiple organizational functions and expertise that contribute to the value creation process; and
- the value creation for the business (which concerns shareholders, employees and investors) and for other stakeholders.

Thus, IT&R guidelines help organizations to determine what capitals affect and are affected by their value creation process, and help them assess their impact on society. The next section focuses on how public organizations, particularly universities, attempt to assess their social impacts.

Universities and social impact

Measuring the social and economic impact of public services has gained momentum in the last decade, as public organizations are required to increase their quality of service while respecting governments' cost-cutting requirements. Around one third of global gross domestic product (GDP) comes from the public sector, comprising investment in infrastructure, educational opportunities and health care (IIRC, 2016). Due to time and resource constraints, public sector organizations need ways of broadening the conversation about the services they deliver and the impact they generate in meeting short- and long-term demands. However, there is a lack of agreement about what is to be measured, and how to measure the impact of public services. Considering the active contribution of public organizations in improving local services within the community, their performance cannot be evaluated only by examining financial ratios and cash flows (IIRC, 2016). Although there are areas, such as health care, where non-financial measurement systems are universally used to assess social well-being, there is still variation in the types of measures applied within public organizations. The reasons behind this 'lack of agreement' lie in the long-term effects of public organizations' initiatives, which often require complex sets of interventions and massive project financing decisions. These factors make any attempt to assess social impact time consuming, costly and complex to validate using an external auditor.[1]

As civic-oriented organizations, universities influence human impacts on society and the environment, as they conduct research in some of the most relevant disciplines such as medicine, geology, business and law. Further, they work in collaboration with national and multinational organizations and engage with individuals and groups across society, while driving economic growth and improving the efficiency and effectiveness of their activities. Moreover, with teaching and research as their core activities, universities are fundamentally required to educate and prepare current and future generations of employees, leaders and citizens who may contribute positively to societal challenges (Adams, 2018; BUFDG, 2017).

Currently, universities are changing their traditional operations and acting as more business-like entities. For this reason, they are under scrutiny by stakeholder groups, particularly politicians, commentators, local municipalities and citizens (BUFDG, 2016). Further, the increased number of digital educational institutions or alternative providers of higher education has made students more selective in their choice of where to study. The evolving competitiveness of the educational sector has greatly increased the pressure for universities to demonstrate the benefits that their activities create for the local community in which they operate (BUFDG, 2017).

To deal with these challenges, universities need to address two key priorities (Adams, 2018). On one hand, they need to be as transparent as possible when explaining to a variety of stakeholders their pricing decisions on courses and the use they make of students' fees and other financial sources. On the other hand, universities also need to communicate how they transform the lives of individuals and local communities, and make a global impact (Adams, 2018). While universities are currently working towards the achievement of these priorities, their business models and accounting and reporting practices fail to capture their impact on the environment and on society as a whole. Conventional reporting only provides stakeholders with poor and disconnected information about how universities can manage the challenges ahead, deliver services and support communities.

Increasing numbers of universities are addressing these limitations by implementing IT&R (BUFDG, 2017). As highlighted by the IIRC, IR helps public entities to embed integrated thinking and encourage closer working relationships across departments by: stimulating a more cohesive approach to decision-making that focuses on value creation in the short, medium and long term; formulating integrated and robust strategies and objectives; providing better strategic perspectives and a wider view of risks and opportunities; deepening organizations' understanding of their business processes; and making internal and external communication more connected (IIRC, 2016).

As emphasized by the Chair of the British Universities Finance Directors Group (BUFDG, 2016, p. 2):

> [the] Integrated Reporting framework offers an opportunity for universities to develop their annual reports from unremarkable repositories of financial information into engaging, enlightening, and even surprising tales of a university's hopes, successes, failures, and values [...] an Integrated Report can find an audience beyond just regulators or governors, and become a useful tool for a wider range of stakeholders to gain a deeper understanding of a university's performance, plans, and prospects.

The next section illustrates the case of a European university – named Athena, also referred to as 'the University' – to explain how IT&R have contributed to the development of an innovative social impact assessment tool.

The case of Athena

Athena was founded in the sixteenth century and is one of the oldest universities in Europe. The University receives approximately 60,000 applications every year, making it one of the most popular universities in Europe in terms of volume of applications. In 2019, Athena was ranked as one of the top ten European universities by the US News' Best Global Universities Ranking,[2] and among the top thirty universities in the world according to the Times Higher Education Ranking.[3]

Athena was also one of the first universities in Europe to adopt the IT&R approach. In 2018, the University was recognized as a benchmark for the public sector due to its experience in developing and publishing integrated reports. As emphasized in Athena's integrated report 2017/2018, the multi-capital approach suggested by the IIRC helps to explain the impacts generated by the University (p. 2):

our value model explains how the University draws on multiple capitals and helps to demonstrate an overall net positive impact for the University, its specific stakeholders, society in general and the natural environment in which we operate. Our objective is to make the world a better place by delivering a positive impact through our graduates and our staff.

This statement is coherent with both the vision of the University, which is to 'deliver impact for society' and its mission, which aims (Athena's integrated report 2017/2018, p. 9):

to provide the highest quality research-led teaching and learning; challenge the boundaries of knowledge, research and disciplines; enable graduates and staff to be exceptional individuals equipped to address global challenges; promote good health, economic growth, cultural understanding and social wellbeing.

To fulfil its vision and mission, Athena has set two specific strategic objectives: Leadership in learning, and Leadership in research. To be a leader in learning, the University aims to equip students with the knowledge, skills and experiences to be successful graduates who contribute to society. To be a leader in research, Athena commits to conducting research of the highest standard across a broad spectrum of disciplines. To offer an overview of the key areas related to the strategic objectives, Athena has identified four development themes, specifically: Influencing globally; Contributing locally; Partnerships with industry; and Digital transformation and data (See Figure 17.2).

To succeed as a leader in learning and teaching, the University considers all resources (financial and non-financial) that contribute to value creation, as well as the risks, opportunities and outcomes that could affect its ability to create value over time. The University's Value Creation Model is a fundamental part of the 2017/2018 Integrated Annual Report. The Model shows how Athena uses its capitals to create and sustain value for stakeholders. The Value Creation Model illustrates the overall strategic objectives (Leadership in learning, and Leadership in research) of the University at its centre, surrounded by the four development themes (Influencing globally; Contributing locally;

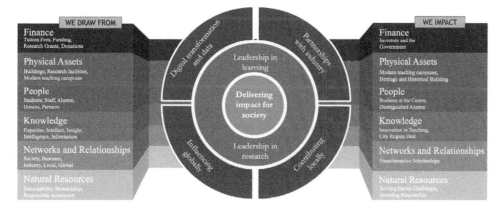

Figure 17.2 Strategy and Value Model
Adapted from: Athena's integrated report (2017/2018)

Partnerships with industry; Digital transformation and data). To achieve its mission Athena draws from and impacts on the following capitals: Finance; Physical Assets; People; Knowledge; Networks and Relationships; Natural Resources (see Figure 17.2).

To measure its impact on the different capitals, in 2018 Athena has developed an assessment tool drawing on two of the most widely used impact measurement systems: the SROI and the TIMM. These methodologies provide a framework to better assess, both qualitatively and quantitatively, how organizations affect the community and the society in which they operate.

The Social Return on Investment

The SROI provides a framework to identify and measure how organizations affect society. It involves reviewing the inputs, outputs, outcomes and impacts made and experienced by stakeholders in relation to the activities of an organization (SROI Guidelines, 2012).

The SROI approach aims to assign a monetary value to the social, economic and environmental benefits and costs created by an organization. The impact estimation; that is, the value created, relates to the investments made and is expressed as a ratio, which shows the organization's impact on society as a portion of the investment made. For instance, an SROI ratio of 3:1 means that for every euro invested, the organization generates 3 euros of social value (SROI Guidelines, 2012).

To analyse organizations' impact on society, the SROI approach involves six stages:

1. **Establishing scope and identifying key stakeholders**. This first stage sets the boundaries about what the SROI analysis will cover, who will be involved in the process and how. In order to establish the scope, the following questions may be useful: *What is the purpose of the SROI? Who is it for? What is the background? What resources do you have available? Who will undertake the SROI? What activities will you focus on? What period of delivery will your analysis cover? Is the analysis a forecast, a comparison against a forecast or an evaluation?* (SROI Guidelines, 2012, p. 20). Once the scope of the analysis is clear, the next step is to identify and involve stakeholders. To do so, organizations are required to list all stakeholders who might affect or be affected by the activities within the scope, whether the effect is positive or negative, intentional or unintentional. This emphasis on involving stakeholders is a distinctive feature of SROI. However, not all stakeholders are necessarily equally affected by organizations' initiatives. For this reason, the SROI framework suggests that managers carefully classify the stakeholders impacted in terms of the main objectives of the investment made.
2. **Mapping inputs, outputs and outcomes**. This stage involves defining inputs, outputs and outcomes. In particular, the 'map' details the resources (inputs) used within organizations to deliver activities (measured as outputs) which result in outcomes for stakeholders. In mapping the *inputs* of a certain activity, organizations are required to provide financial values to the resources sacrificed for its achievement. On the contrary, *outputs* represent a quantitative summary of an activity. However, defining just inputs and outputs is not the main objective of SROI. As an outcomes-based measurement tool, SROI aims at monitoring the changes that are taking place for stakeholders.
3. **Evidencing outcomes and giving them a value**. The third stage involves developing outcome indicators to collect evidence on the outcomes that are occurring, and assessing their relative importance by valuing them.

4. **Establishing impact**. This section assesses whether the outcomes analysed result from organizations' activities. In particular, this assessment estimates how much of the outcome would have happened anyway (i.e. regardless of the actions of the organization) and what proportion of the outcome can be determined to have been added by organizations' activities (impact). Establishing impact is important as it reduces the risk of over-claiming and helps identify stakeholders that have not been considered during the determination of the scope of the analysis. To measure the impact, organizations have to deduct the outcomes that could have happened even if the activity had not taken place. These outcomes are generally called *deadweight* and are calculated as a percentage of the total quantity of the outcome initially evaluated.

5. **Calculating the SROI**. This stage summarizes the financial information recorded in the previous stages. In particular, it calculates the ratio between the financial value of the investment and the financial value of the social costs and benefits.

6. **Reporting, using and embedding**. This last step involves reporting to stakeholders, communicating and embedding the SROI analysis within the organization's decision-making process.

Table 17.1 summarizes the main benefits and criticisms of the SROI methodology.

Table 17.1 Benefits and criticisms of the SROI model

Benefits	Criticisms
• Promotes better communication and engagement between different stakeholders;	• The choice of indicators is underpinned by assumptions and preferences on how the impact can be achieved;
• Provides a tool for impact evaluation;	• Little debate on which stakeholders are involved, whose voices are heard and who is marginalized;
• Impact mapping is fundamental to align the vision with the organization's resources and performance, and to improve the management of relationships and expectations between stakeholders;	• The highlight of the relationships between inputs, outputs and outcome/impact is often a secondary element behind the strong emphasis on the overall SROI ratio;
• Sustained improvement in the quality of data that can be used as evidence for impact assessment.	• Weak basis for understanding how and why impacts occur;
	• Focus on inputs and outputs without considering the initiatives;
	• Focus on collecting data on quantitative measures, which represents a risk of overlooking what actual activities are being carried out;
	• *Deadweight* is not clear and is determined on the base of assumptions;
	• Challenges in attributing monetary values to outcomes and impacts. These do not capture the social value in terms of improvement of personal utility (i.e. quality of life), as these values do not result in actual financial savings.

Cristiano Busco et al.

Total Impact Measurement Model

The TIMM supports organizations in understanding and measuring how different activities contribute to the economy, the environment and society. It provides an assessment of how value is generated (or potentially destroyed) in both the short and long term, helping decision makers to consider and communicate the net impact of their actions, beyond financial results (PwC, 2013). In this regard, the TIMM is an impact assessment tool that enables managers to compare strategies and make business decisions, while evaluating the trade-offs between different options. In so doing, the TIMM aims to provide managers with comprehensive knowledge of the overall impact generated by their decisions and a better understanding of which stakeholders will be affected by them (PwC, 2013).

The TIMM, see Figure 17.3, can be represented as a 'wheel', showing the organization's activities at its centre, surrounded by the stakeholders who are affected by its operations (the second circle). Each of the impacts is then represented around the outside of the 'wheel' (social, environmental, tax and economic). The four key dimensions of impact considered in the TIMM are:

- Social impact: it measures and values the consequences of business activities on societal outcomes such as health, education and community cohesion.
- Environmental impact: it measures emissions to air, land and water, and the use of natural resources.
- Tax impact: it identifies and measures a business's overall tax contribution.
- Economic impact: it measures the effect of a business activity on the economy in a given area and changes in economic growth (output or value added) and associated changes in employment.

Figure 17.3 Total Impact Measurement Model
Adapted from: PwC (2013, p. 17)

260

Table 17.2 Benefits and criticisms of the TIMM model

Benefits	Criticisms
• Promote better communication and engagement between different stakeholders; • Attempt to assess the cause–effect and trade-off relations between multiple variables; • Visualize negative and positive effects of certain performances for a single project; • Involve a multiple number of stakeholders in the evaluation of impact; • Focus on taxation; • Suitable for comparison (e.g. make or buy); • The impact evaluation system is closer to the idea of Integrated Reporting.	• Focus on effects more than quantitative impacts; • No tools available for the assessment of impact (i.e. impact mapping of SROI); • Focus on measuring the effects of implementing a single project rather than looking at the organization value chain; • Further improvements are needed to understand how and why impacts occur (focus on inputs and outputs not on initiatives).

The TIMM is applied through a four-step process:

1. **Define the scope**: The first step is about defining the scope of the impacts (for example the timeframe, the geography, the areas of business and the relevant parts of the value chain) that need to be assessed to determine the right investment choices and demonstrate the value created for stakeholders;
2. **Determine the impact**: The second step maps the total impacts among each dimension, which means determining the social, economic, environmental and tax impacts, how they arise, what methodologies can and should be used to assess them and what data need to be collected;
3. **Collect and analyse data**: This stage requires the collection of a significant amount of information in areas such as employment, tax paid and resources used. Any necessary additional information can be sourced externally;
4. **Attribute a value**: The final stage quantifies outcomes and impacts, giving them a financial value and tracking them over time. This may require techniques such as economic and process modelling to estimate impacts and valuation techniques to monetize them.

Table 17.2 summarizes the main benefits and criticisms of the TIMM model.

The design of Athena's impact assessment tool

To develop its impact assessment tool, Athena integrated the SROI with the TIMM. The integration of the two tools was decided following analysis of their analogies with the IIRC Framework. In particular, four analogies were considered relevant: the focus on value creation, and on strategic development, materiality and stakeholders' relationships.

The new impact assessment tool has been designed using a recursive four-step process:

1. Determine the scope and strategic objectives;
2. Identify the key inputs (capitals), initiatives and outputs and collect data accordingly;

3. Identify the outcomes and measure them through adequate key performance indicators (KPIs);
4. Evaluate the impacts and review the strategic objectives.

The four stages described above were applied in a pilot analysis to assess the impacts generated by the University for the 'Contributing locally' development theme (see Figure 17.2).

Generally speaking, the development theme 'Contributing locally' refers to Athena's commitment to making a positive impact in its local area and contributing directly to the health and wellbeing of the community through its training and research programmes. For instance, in 2017, the University launched an initiative to strengthen relationships with local communities, putting research and teaching at their service, and increasing access to its buildings and facilities. As a result, a growing number of students have been trained to work in the community and enhance digital literacy. Further, the University is currently supporting the establishment of a Centre for Homeless People in the local area, and a Student Employability Programme to generate a sustainable pipeline of talent, providing access to the right tools, and giving individuals the resources they need to excel.

Tables 17.3 and 17.4 show the design of the new impact assessment tool developed by Athena. In Table 17.3, the first three columns refer to the definition of the scope. At this stage, the tool requires the identification of the development theme selected for the analysis; in this case, 'Contributing locally', and the strategic aims associated with that development theme. In our example, this is 'Improving the quality of University's teaching by involving the community in it.' The third column identifies the six capitals potentially used to achieve the strategic objective.

In the second stage, the key inputs, initiatives and outputs are identified according to the different capitals. For instance, the key inputs related to the capital 'Finance' have been identified as the investments made by the University in social activities, and particularly the cost of organizing a number of events to involve the community in the University's teaching (strategic aim). The columns 'Initiatives' and 'Outputs' respectively identify all the activities organized by the University and the corresponding income and associated in-kind community benefits generated (See Table 17.3).

Table 17.4 illustrates stages three and four of the impact assessment process. In particular, stage three identifies the potential outcomes generated by the University's initiatives. Outcomes are assessed by collecting opinions and responses from all the stakeholders involved (e.g. students, families, universities and other public institutions, local authorities, voluntary groups) and then measured according to adequate key performance indicators per capital.

Stage four evaluates the impacts generated according to the four dimensions of the TIMM model (Economic, Social, Environmental and Tax) for each capital employed. Once the impact is assessed, the tool attempts to financially value it and assess the potential contribution of each capital employed and affected by the University's initiatives in the achievement of the Sustainable Development Goals (SDGs) (See Table 17.4).

The impact assessment tool described above is still in its early stages. In future years, Athena is planning to improve it by extending its analysis to all the other development themes. The result of the analysis will enable the University's top management to reflect upon all the strategic initiatives that positively impact its stakeholders, society in general and the natural environment in which it operates.

Table 17.3 Stages one and two

Stage 1 – Define the scope			Stage 2 – Measure the initiatives and performance		
Development themes	Strategic aims	Capitals	Inputs	Initiatives	Outputs
The development themes give an overview of key areas for development over the period of our Strategic Plan.	i.e. Community engagement programme	What kind of capitals do you employ?	What kind of resources are employed?	What kind of activies and initiatives have been pursued?	What is the KPI associated with the capital per Initiative (*only enter numbers*) Summary of activity in numbers. Key performances achieved?
Contributing Locally	**Improving the quality of University's teaching by involving communities in it**	FINANCE	Investments made	– Cost of organizing a number of events – Contribution made	These activities have brought us to … – New income and associated in-kind community benefits generated.
		PHYSICAL ASSETS	Buildings and or infrastructures used	– Space or building rented and cost of them	These activities have brought us to …
		PEOPLE	wages and time of staff	– Staff and student volunteers active; – Cost of staff and volunteers involved;	These activities have brought us to … % of internal and external staff
		KNOWLEDGE	Investments in research or Publications or intellectual property		These activities have brought us to …

(Continued)

Table 17.3 (Cont.)

	Stage 1 – Define the scope			Stage 2 – Measure the initiatives and performance		
Development themes	Strategic aims	Capitals	Inputs		Initiatives	Outputs
		SOCIAL & RELATIONAL	Network of institutes and people that cooperate with the University	– % of events delivered in Partnership with state school; – % of events delivered in Partnership with primary and secondary schools; – % of events delivered with other Universities;	These activities have brought us to …	– people reached by projects and activities delivered under the community engagement programme.
		NATURAL RESOURCES	Land water or energy used	– CO_2 Consumed according to lights turned on per hour, Heating per m3, flights, car use, etc.	These activities have brought us to …	

Source: Adapted from: Athena's impact assessment tool.

Table 17.4 Stages three and four

	Stage 3 – Measuring the outcome			Stage 4 – Valuing the impact		
	The outcomes (what changes) DIRECT					
Stakeholders	Description	Indicator	TIMM model dimensions		Financial proxy	Sustainable Development Goals impacted
			Economic: Payroll, Profits, investments, exports, intangibles	*Social:* Livelihoods, Health, Education, Empowerment, Community cohesion *Environmental:* GHGs and other air emissions; Water pollution; Waste; Land use; Water use. *Tax:* Profit taxes, people taxes, production taxes, property taxes, environmental taxes		
Where did you get the information from? What kind of stakeholders have been impacted?	How would the stakeholder describe the changes?	How would you measure it?			What proxy would you use to value the change?	Contribution to the achievement of SDGs
– **Students** – **Families** – **Universities and other public institutions** – **local authorities,** – **Voluntary Groups**	How much of this income has been used to improve Local Area performance or students' educational experience within the University? Has the income been reinvested?	N/A	% of economic impact		N/A % of tax impact	
		N/A	% of economic impact		N/A % of tax impact	

(*Continued*)

Table 17.4 (Cont.)

Stage 3 – Measuring the outcome			Stage 4 – Valuing the impact				
The outcomes (what changes) DIRECT							
Stakeholders	Description	Indicator	TIMM model dimensions			Financial proxy	Sustainable Development Goals impacted
	Have families and students gained support from the University initiatives?	N/A	% of economic impact	% of social impact		% of tax impact	N/A — 17 PARTNERSHIP FOR THE GOALS; 8 DECENT WORK AND ECONOMIC GROWTH
		N/A	% of economic impact	% of social impact		% of tax impact	N/A — 9 INDUSTRY, INNOVATION AND INFRASTRUCTURE
	Has this affected the number of families or students taking part in learning and teaching experiments?	N/A		% of social impact		% of tax impact	N/A — 17 PARTNERSHIP FOR THE GOALS; 16 PEACE, JUSTICE AND STRONG INSTITUTIONS
	Considering the reduced consumption of resources and the average number of events, we can assume that …	N/A			weight of environmental impact	% of tax impact	N/A — 7 AFFORDABLE AND CLEAN ENERGY; 12 RESPONSIBLE CONSUMPTION AND PRODUCTION

Adapted from: Athena's impact assessment tool

Conclusions

By drawing on the experience of a European university, Athena, this chapter has illustrated the design of an impact assessment tool in a public organization. In particular, we have showed the potential of the integration of IT&R with SROI and TIMM to improve the assessment of organizations' impacts.

As discussed in the previous sections, Athena developed a new impact assessment tool that helps to classify inputs and outputs according to the main initiatives, while showing their relationships with the different capitals involved. The tool also provides an overview of the various dimensions of impact in accordance with the TIMM model, thus improving the University's performance measurement and reporting process. Also, the new tool contributes to creating engagement between different departments, thus improving data collection and fostering discussion and reflection upon those strategic initiatives that have a positive impact on society.

Being in its infancy, the tool requires significant commitment and a clear allocation of responsibility among the employees involved in its implementation. The University is also planning to involve a broader spectrum of stakeholders (for example through questionnaires, surveys and focus groups) to improve the impact assessment process and better allocate the resources employed (capitals) in accordance with short-, medium- and long-term strategic objectives.

Notes

1 www.theguardian.com/public-leaders-network/2012/mar/27/measuring-impact-public-services.
2 '10 Best global universities in Europe'. U.S. News. https://www.usnews.com/education/best-global-universities/slideshows/10-best-global-universities-in-europe.
3 'Best universities 2019'. Times Higher Education. www.timeshighereducation.com/world-university-rankings/2019/world-ranking#!/page/0/length/25/sort_by/rank/sort_order/asc/cols/stats.

References

Athena's Integrated Report 2017/2018.
Adams, C., and Narayanan, V. (2007). The 'standardization' of sustainability reporting. In: J. Unerman, J. Bebbington, and B. O'Dwyer (Eds.), *Sustainability accounting and accountability* (pp. 70–85). New York: Routledge.
Adams, C. A. (2015). The international integrated reporting council: A call to action. *Critical Perspectives on Accounting*, 27, 23–28.
Adams, C. A. (2017). Conceptualising the contemporary corporate value creation process. *Accounting, Auditing & Accountability Journal*, 30(4), 906–931.
Adams, C. A. (2018). *Let's talk value: How universities create value for society*. London: Advance HE.
Adams, S., and Simnett, R. (2011). Integrated reporting: An opportunity for Australia's not-for-profit sector. *Australian Accounting Review*, 21(3), 292–301.
BUFDG. (2016). *Integrated reporting in HE: Helping Universities tell their stories better*. Available at: www.efficiencyexchange.ac.uk/wp-content/uploads/Integrated-Reporting-IR-in-HE-Web-v3-5.pdf (Accessed: 23 August 2019).
BUFDG. (2017). *Integrated reporting in four British universities*. Available at: www.bufdg.ac.uk/ir/ (Accessed: 23 August 2019).
Busco, C., Frigo, M. L., Quattrone, P., and Riccaboni, A. (2013). *Towards integrated reporting: Concepts, elements and principles*. London, UK: Springer.
Busco, C., Granà, F., and Quattrone, P. (2018). Integrated thinking: Aligning purpose and the business model to market opportunities and sustainable performance. *CIMA*, 13(3), 1–27.
Churet, C., and Eccles, R. G. (2015). Integrated reporting, quality of management, and financial performance. *Journal of Applied Corporate Finance*, 26(1), 8–16.

Clark, C., Rosenzweig, W., Long, D., and Olsen, S. (2004). *Double bottom line project report: Assessing social impact in double bottom line ventures.* Available at: https://community-wealth.org/sites/clone.community-wealth.org/files/downloads/paper-rosenzweig.pdf (Accessed: 23 August 2019).

De Villiers, C., Rinaldi, L., and Unerman, J. (2014). Integrated reporting: Insights, gaps and an agenda for future research. *Accounting, Auditing & Accountability Journal, 27*(7), 1042–1067.

Deloitte. (2016). *Social purpose and value creation: The business returns of social impact.* Available at: www2.deloitte.com/by/en/pages/risk/articles/2017/social-purpose-and-value-creation.html (Accessed: 23 August 2019).

Dumay, J., Bernardi, C., Guthrie, J., and Demartini, P. (2016). Integrated reporting: A structured literature review. *Accounting Forum, 40*(3), 166–185.

Dumay, J., and Dai, T. (2017). Integrated thinking as a cultural control? *Meditari Accountancy Research, 25*(4), 574–604.

Eccles, R., and Krzus, M. P. (2014). *The integrated reporting movement.* Hoboken, NJ: John Wiley.

Eccles, R. G., and Krzus, M. P. (2010). *One report: Integrated reporting for a sustainable strategy.* Hoboken, NJ: John Wiley.

Eccles, R. G., and Spiesshofer, B. (2015). *Integrated Reporting for a Re-Imagined Capitalism.* Available at: www.hbs.edu/faculty/Publication%20Files/16-032_3860cfaa-ebd3-4d7e-ac9a-53272ca8cc2d.pdf (Accessed: 23 August 2019).

Gray, R. (2010). Is accounting for sustainability actually accounting for sustainability.and how would we know? An exploration of narratives of organisations and the planet. *Accounting, Organizations and Society, 35*(1), 47–62.

Guthrie, J., Manes-Rossi, F., and Orelli, R. L. (2017). Integrated reporting and integrated thinking in Italian public sector organisations. *Meditari Accountancy Research, 25*(4), 553–573.

IIRC. (2013). *International <IR> Framework.* London: IIRC.

IIRC. (2016). *Integrated thinking and reporting: Focusing on the value creation in the public sector.* Available at: https://integratedreporting.org/resource/focusing-on-value-creation-in-the-public-sector/ (Accessed: 23 August 2019).

Kolodinsky, J., Stewart, C., and Bullard, A. (2006). Measuring economic and social impacts of membership in a community development financial institution. *Journal of Family and Economic Issues, 27*(1), 27–47.

Maas, K., and Liket, K. (2011). Social impact measurement: Classification of methods. In: R. L. Burritt, et al. (Ed.), *Environmental management accounting, supply chain management, and corporate responsibility accounting* (pp. 171–202). New York: Springer.

Millar, R., and Hall, K. (2013). Social return on investment (SROI) and performance measurement. *Public Management Review, 15*(6), 923–941.

Owen, G. (2013). Integrated reporting: A review of developments and their implications for the accounting curriculum. *Accounting Education, 22*(4), 340–356.

PwC. (2013). *Measuring and managing total impact: A new language for business decisions.* Available at: www.pwc.com/gx/en/sustainability/publications/total-impact-measurement-management/assets/pwc-timm-report.pdf (Accessed: 23 August 2019).

PwC. (2018). *Integrated Reporting: What's your value creation story?* Available at: www.pwc.com/my/en/assets/publications/2018/ir-report-2018-final-web.pdf (Accessed: 23 August 2019).

Simnett, R., and Huggins, A. L. (2015). Integrated reporting and assurance: Where can research add value? *Sustainability Accounting, Management and Policy Journal, 6*(1), 29–53.

SROI. (2012). *A guide to social return on investment.* Available at: www.socialvalueuk.org/app/uploads/2016/03/The%20Guide%20to%20Social%20Return%20on%20Investment%202015.pdf (Accessed: 23 August 2019).

Terblanche, W., and De Villiers, C. (2019). The influence of integrated reporting and internationalisation on intellectual capital disclosures. *Journal of Intellectual Capital, 20*(1), 40–59.

Vanclay, F., Esteves, A. M., Aucamp, I., and Franks, D. (2015). *Social impact assessment: Guidance for assessing and managing the social impacts of projects.* Fargo, ND: International Association for Impact Assessment.

World Business Council for Sustainable Development (WBCSD). (2019). *PwC: Total impact analysis.* Available at: https://www.wbcsd.org/Programs/Redefining-Value/Business-Decision-Making/Assess-and-Manage-Performance/Measuring-and-valuing-impact-business-examples/PwC-Total-impact-analysis (Accessed: 23 August 2019).

Yongvanich, K., and Guthrie, J. (2006). An extended performance reporting framework for social and environmental accounting. *Business Strategy and Development, 15*(5), 309–321.

18

INTEGRATED REPORTING PREPARERS

Mode of cognition, stakeholder salience and integrated thinking in action

Riccardo Stacchezzini

Department of Business Administration, University of Verona

Alessandro Lai

Department of Business Administration, University of Verona

Abstract

The chapter outlines an Integrated Report taxonomy based on integrated reporting (IR) preparers' conceptions of this innovative form of reporting. It emphasizes that report preparation relies on preparers' cognitive modes and their perception of stakeholder salience. Since several actors may participate as IR preparers, the design of an Integrated Report cannot be taken for granted. However, integrated thinking can facilitate integration between preparers' different cognitive modes and a balanced prioritization of stakeholders. The taxonomy can help practitioners understand their positioning and help them to prepare Integrated Reports based on integrated thinking. The taxonomy also unveils research opportunities for exploring preparers' roles in the IR process.

Introduction

The chapter explores organizational actors' roles in the Integrated Report preparation process. First, it highlights that several actors may be involved, directly or indirectly, as integrated reporting (IR) preparers. Based on case insights from prior studies on the IR process, the chapter explains these actors' roles in shaping the Integrated Report. In particular, it emphasizes that the content and language of an Integrated Report emerge from preparers' cognitive modes and their perceptions of stakeholder salience. A narrative cognitive mode facilitates a storytelling IR approach, whereas a paradigmatic mode supports argumentation based on value creation processes. Further, who the preparers prioritize while developing the materiality determination process informs their selection of the material issues to be reported.

The chapter also outlines an Integrated Report taxonomy based on interactions between preparers' cognitive modes and stakeholder salience and shows that integrated thinking can facilitate integration between their different cognitive modes and a balanced prioritization of stakeholders, thus providing useful information for both financial and nonfinancial stakeholders. Practitioners may use the taxonomy to ascertain the IR views established and those missing in their organization, and fill the gaps in knowledge needed to develop Integrated Reports based on integrated thinking. Scholars may use the taxonomy to empirically determine prevalent views on Integrated Reports among IR adopters and the evolution of such views according to IR preparation and the involvement of (additional) different actors as preparers. The chapter concludes by outlining further research opportunities related to preparers' roles in the IR process.

Who are the IR preparers and what do they do?

'Who is responsible for the overarching reporting process?'; 'Who will contribute information?'; 'Who will collect/collate the information?'; 'Who will write the Integrated Report?'; 'Which senior manager will review the report before it is submitted to the executive team?'; 'Which governing body committee, if any, will approve the final report before it is submitted to the governing body?'; 'Who is the audience of the various reports included in the reporting suite?'; and 'Who will design, typeset and publish the Integrated Report?' The Integrated Reporting Committee of South Africa (2018) suggests that these are just some of the questions to be addressed in preparing an Integrated Report. The International Integrated Reporting Council (IIRC, 2013) does not define who the preparers must be in its International Integrated Reporting Framework (hereafter, IIRC Framework). However, it requires the inclusion of a statement from 'those charged with governance' to explain their responsibility to ensure IR integrity, the application of their 'collective mind' in preparing and presenting the report and their opinion about whether it is developed in accordance with the IIRC Framework or the steps taken to achieve this goal (IIRC, 2013, p. 9, § 1.20).

Although these questions lack predetermined answers, the board of directors is the governance body that may naturally take this responsibility, in line with its responsibility for financial reports. Simultaneously, we can expect that the actual Integrated Report preparation (i.e. collecting information and writing the report) will be delegated to organizational staff or to external advisors. As field studies on the IR process demonstrate (Al-Htaybat and von Alberti-alhtaybat, 2018; Busco et al., 2018; Lai et al., 2018; Vesty et al., 2018), Integrated Report preparation involves several actors. The department charged with financial report preparation can also be the one more directly involved in Integrated Report preparation (Lai et al., 2018). However, the communication department or the sustainability department may lead such preparation. A dedicated team—or even a new unit —can be created (Stacchezzini et al., 2019). This team may comprise actors from the same or different departments.

Along with the department(s) directly involved in Integrated Report writing, several other actors, both internal and external, may participate indirectly in the preparation process. Internal actors may be managers and employees of departments, who are not in charge of Integrated Report preparation, but who must provide narrative sections or calculate indicators related to the activity and performance of a single department or business unit. For instance, the risk management department may support the explanation of the risks and opportunities content by providing information on the company's risk management approach, policies and risk metrics (Stacchezzini et al., 2019). Some departments may provide feedback collected within the corporate reporting environment. For instance, the investor relationship department head may provide feedback about the evolution of investors' information needs (Stacchezzini et al., 2019) and about IR effects on investor behaviour (Lai et al., 2017a, 2018).

The department(s) directly involved in report writing may require support from external experts, such as advisors, audit firms, communication agencies and academics. Companies may need advice in the IR initiation phase, when they lack the necessary expertise, and may request external support from audit firms or experienced academics to understand the fundamental concepts and core processes behind Integrated Report preparation. Communication agencies may play a key role by helping companies to define the general document design and by providing typographic solutions (Lai et al., 2018).

All these actors, who have varying responsibilities, roles and expertise, must make many discretionary choices. Since it has a principle-based approach (IIRC, 2013, p. 7, § 1D), the IIRC Framework does not provide detailed recommendations about report content, although it identifies 'fundamental concepts' related to value creation processes and eight 'content elements' and lists pertinent questions to be addressed (IIRC, 2013, p. 24). The Framework also leaves room for choosing '[q]uantitative indicators, such as KPIs and monetized metrics' to be disclosed and the appropriate 'context' for disclosing these indicators (IIRC, 2013, p. 8, § 1.11). The form of an Integrated Report can vary. It may be 'either a standalone report or be included as a distinguishable, prominent and accessible part of another report or communication' (IIRC, 2013, p. 8, § 1.15). For instance, it may constitute the prominent part of the management commentary provided with the consolidated financial statement or a significant part of a sustainability report. As a stand-alone report, it may act as an 'entry point' (IIRC, 2013, p. 8, § 1.16) to more detailed information in other types of reports (e.g. sustainability and corporate governance reports).

Further, although the primary recipients of an Integrated Report are the financial capital providers (i.e. shareholders and debtholders), several other stakeholders are expected to be interested, including 'employees, customers, suppliers, business partners, local communities, legislators, regulators and policy-makers' (IIRC, 2013, p. 7, § 1.8). With regard to the 'purpose and users of IR', '[t]he primary purpose of an integrated report is to explain to providers of financial capital how an organization creates value over time' (IIRC, 2013, p. 7, § 1.7). However, the stakeholders to whom the company plans to address its Integrated Report cannot be taken for granted (Eccles and Krzus, 2014).

Moreover, the IIRC recognizes that the organization must exercise judgement in applying, individually and collectively, the seven 'guiding principles' in the IIRC Framework (IIRC, 2013, p. 16, § 3.2). Another discretionary aspect is related to the reporting unit: the Integrated Report can be prepared at single entity or group level. Some companies may choose to prepare it at department level. This is the case for the 'internal Integrated Report' (Mio et al., 2016), which is usually initiated by the department in charge of preparing the external Integrated Report, but can be extended to other departments.

Considering these discretionary choices and the judgements associated with such choices, Integrated Report preparers—namely, all individuals and bodies directly or indirectly involved in writing, assisting in writing, collecting information, providing comments and reviewing and taking responsibility for the IR—play a fundamental role in determining the content and language of an Integrated Report. Given the flexibility of the IIRC Framework and the discretionary choices and judgement associated with report preparation, preparers' conceptions about the Integrated Report influence its preparation.

This chapter therefore highlights the ways in which report preparation is influenced both by preparers' cognitive modes and their perception of stakeholder salience; that is, the degree to which they establish priority among competing stakeholders' claims (Mitchell et al., 1997). Cognitive modes, which psychologists divide into narrative and calculative/paradigmatic (Bruner, 1986, 1990), result in the assignment of different accountability functions to the Integrated Report (Lai et al., 2018). Conversely, 'stakeholder salience' influences the materiality determination process, by which preparers differentiate material issues from those that are not material in the IR context (Eccles and Krzus, 2014). The next section develops these arguments theoretically and presents pertinent case insights from articles published in accounting journals.

How preparers conceive of the integrated report

Preparers' cognitive modes and the functions assigned to the integrated report

According to Bruner (1986, 1990), people draw on two different modes of cognition to interpret the world and their experiences, as well as to engage with other individuals. One mode, the *paradigmatic* or *logico-scientific* one (also named as *calculative* within the accounting literature—see Boland and Schultze, 1996),

> attempts to fulfil the ideal of a formal, mathematical system of description and explanation. It employs categorization or conceptualization and the operations by which categories are established, instantiated, idealized, and related to one another to form a system
>
> *(Bruner, 1986, p. 12)*

The paradigmatic mode, namely, the mode of science, is used to classify the world logically. The aim of thought grounded in this mode is to explain inter-relationships underlying sets of observable variables. This mode functions to offer predictions, since it establishes and tests hypotheses about the nature of reality (Adler, 2008).

Conversely, the *narrative* mode of cognition is 'concerned with the meaning that is ascribed to experiences through stories' (Adler, 2008, p. 423). It organizes the complex—often ambiguous—world of human intention and action into a meaningful structure. Bruner (1990) states that the role of a narrative is to explain noncanonical (i.e. unanticipated or atypical) events, by recasting these in a story-based format, which makes these experiences appear safer or more familiar. Thus, the narrative solves issues and decreases tensions (Bruner, 1990).

Similarly, Boland and Schultze (1996) maintain that the construction of corporate accountability is dependent on the cognitive mode of the individual who must discharge accountability. Thus, the paradigmatic cognitive mode, which is based on argumentation and computation, is expected to yield hierarchical/individualizing types of accountability, and create a distance between those expecting and those discharging accountability (Roberts, 1991). Conversely, the narrative cognitive mode (Bruner, 1986) is the primary source for socializing types of accountability, because the narrator builds meaningful dialogues, mutual understanding and trust with addressees. That is, '[N]arration as a mode of cognition is the principle occasion for socially constructing an accountable self and a world in which accountability is expected' (Boland and Schultze, 1996, p. 65).

Inspired by Boland and Schultze (1996), recent accounting research (Lai et al., 2018) reveals that socializing effects associated with IR are strongly influenced by the narrative cognitive mode used by IR preparers. The company Lai et al. (2018) analysed in their case study did not support evolving from the calculative form of accountability to one closer to the narrative form merely through the addition of a new report (the Integrated Report) to existing financial and sustainability reports. Rather, it altered the 'traditional' management commentary of the financial report into an Integrated Report and made it the first part of the financial report. It used the Integrated Report specifically to narrate its value creation story, based on its new strategy and business model disclosure. From this perspective, the Integrated Report is not used to complement accounting data; instead, accounting data are used to support descriptions of the process used to implement the new strategy. Thus, the Integrated Report, constructed as a storytelling tool, served to highlight socializing accountability effects: it successfully tackled accountability tensions that the preparers experienced. These tensions diminished because of storytelling that offered narrative explanations of how this company could implement its new strategy, which resulted in significant achievements. In this regard, Bruner (1990) predicts that based on preparers' cognitive modes, Integrated Report narratives enable readers to understand noncanonical events; in this case a contingent change in corporate strategy and the intrinsic complexity of the business model of the insurance sector.

Stakeholder salience and materiality determination process

Integrated Report preparation is connected closely to the implementation of the materiality principle of the IIRC. However, materiality is a 'malleable' concept (Edgley, 2014, p. 255) and the method of implementing it in practice cannot be defined *ex ante*, since it relies on preparers' judgement (Eccles and Krzus, 2014). Eccles and Krzus (2014, p. 121) argued that the selection of material issues relies on *to whom* an Integrated Report is addressed and on who, within the company, actively participates in the materiality determination process. Thus, the prioritization of financial stakeholders (i.e. shareholders and debtholders, rating agencies, financial analysts and, more generally, the financial community) rather than nonfinancial ones (e.g. customers, suppliers and local communities) is expected to influence the selection in various ways.

Recent accounting research (Lai et al., 2017b) has empirically tested the Eccles and Krzus (2014) argument by showing that the selection of material issues to be inserted in an Integrated Report is strictly connected to the audience its preparers have decided to address. In the company studied by Lai et al. (2017b), the preparers decided to focus on some issues (i.e. corporate strategy and business model) and to overlook others (i.e. the capital and sustainability effects) because they prioritized investors (shareholders and debtholders) and other financial stakeholders (rating agencies and financial analysts). Preparers also believe that nonfinancial stakeholders gain important benefits by reading Integrated Reports. However, financial stakeholders are the primary report recipients, given the aim of the IIRC to explain to 'providers of financial capital how an organization creates value over time' (IIRC, 2013, p. 7). Such conformity leads to the possibility that an Integrated Report can fulfil nonfinancial stakeholders' expectations and enhance a dialogue with them, albeit to the extent that their expectations diverge from those of financial stakeholders (Rowbottom and Locke, 2016; De Villiers et al., 2017). Both types of stakeholders probably hold basic, convergent expectations about company strategy and its effects. For instance, those interviewed for Lai et al.'s (2017b) study believe that all stakeholders expect broader content (e.g. strategic considerations and business model disclosures). Conversely, their expectations about more specific issues, such as understanding the effects of company strategy on the six types of capital depicted by the IIRC Framework (IIRC, 2013), are unlikely to converge.

The resulting integrated report: a taxonomy

This chapter argues that the preparation process of an Integrated Report relies on preparers' cognitive modes and their opinions on stakeholder salience. Empirical insights show how these two aspects can actually inform the preparation. The interaction of these aspects allows the creation of an Integrated Report taxonomy.

Typically, different actors participate in the reporting process (e.g. board of directors, operational managers, employees, external advisors and different departments), which implies that the report is a combination of different cognitive modes and perceptions of stakeholder salience. The combination results in two possible situations: in one, a company office is committed to using the information provided by many company staff and departments to write the Integrated Report, and this office will directly influence report characteristics in terms of cognitive mode and stakeholder salience. In the other, the information provided by many staff is merely merged and partially adapted by the report writers: the resulting Integrated Report can be qualified in one quadrant or another of the matrix, according to the final document features. However, the governance body charged with approving this report plays a major role in selecting and orienting the work of the staff and departments designated to prepare the report.

In any case, the taxonomy reflects the prevalent process, considering that although an Integrated Report (unlike other types of reports) must rely on both financial and nonfinancial information (otherwise, it is not 'integrated'), we cannot expect it to present a story without any numbers or an argumentation without any narrative. The mixture of cognitive modes and stakeholder salience in an Integrated Report does not reduce the significance of the proposed taxonomy, but it helps the writer be aware of their own positioning.

In the first quadrant of the proposed matrix (Table 18.1), the report emerges as a storytelling of financial achievements and relies on preparers' ability to write narratives about company financial results. Many preparers develop this aptitude by writing management commentaries in financial reports. The International Accounting Standard Board project on management commentary and similar initiatives clearly

Table 18.1 An Integrated Report taxonomy based on interactions between preparers' cognition mode and stakeholder salience

		Stakeholder salience	
		Financial stakeholders	*Nonfinancial stakeholders*
Mode of cognition	Narrative	1 Storytelling of financial achievements	2 Storytelling of sustainability achievements
	Calculative/ Paradigmatic	3 Computation and argumentation of financial achievements	4 Computation and argumentation of sustainability achievements

reveals 'increasing reliance on narratives in the business reporting package' (Beattie, 2014, p. 121).

These types of Integrated Reports are usually devoted to:

- highlighting challenging market conditions in the overall economy or the industry to which the company belongs, to justify results obtained through management efforts, when results are weak;
- enthusiastically extolling company results, when satisfactory, and comparing them with competitors' results; and
- attempting to excuse insufficient/bad results, promising recovery to a more acceptable situation and hypothesizing a timeframe acceptable to investors.

Integrated Report preparers can apply their ability to write narratives about the main, essential report content, such as analysing business models and effects on development of diverse types of capital. These reports are moulded according to such perspectives when the organization's attention to sustainability issues is yet to develop sufficiently (as in some real-world cases; see Lai et al., 2018) because the main purpose is to address investors' requirements.

Integrated Reports based on narratives aimed at addressing nonfinancial stakeholders' expectations—particularly sustainability achievements—are represented in the second quadrant in Table 18.1. Typically, companies provide this report type based on experience gained following their extensive reports on social and environmental aspects, which they prepare in addition to traditional financial reports. Companies provide descriptive documents, mainly to satisfy nonfinancial stakeholders (and usually present these in the general shareholders' meetings as well). Regardless of whether they prepare such reports after shifting focus to increasing their socio-environmental attention, or before it (to gain greater legitimation about sustainability themes), this cognitive mode is useful in writing an Integrated Report: preparers learn to describe social/environmental topics, which were not previously common knowledge among them. Therefore, they become aware that they must carefully assess, combine and organize such information in successfully telling convincing stories.

Reports in the third quadrant depict situations in which preparers are interested mainly in dealing with financial subjects; here, calculation and argumentation support disclosure on related achievements. These reports rely on a tradition traceable not only to larger companies, but also to smaller ones, whose reports offer limited narrative and focus on accounting data. As companies expand, they preserve and improve these capabilities, even adding elaborated accounting summaries and key performance indicators, to satisfy shareholders' needs for quick summaries. Financial analysts, rating agencies, accounting firms and external professionals supporting investors prefer easier readability of company results and easier comparisons with the past or with competitors. Hence, this approach to financial reports is useful in preparing effective Integrated Reports because it is instrumental in making exposures more precise and catching reader attention. Further, it facilitates providing relevant information concisely and supporting the company story with easily read data that effectively depict the main business model features and related results.

Occasionally, preparers are willing to also address nonfinancial stakeholders by using a calculative cognitive mode (see the fourth quadrant, Table 18.1). This happens when the writers are more able to provide data than to explain the business model, because the latter is very simple and does not require a broad narration. This type of presentation is appropriate in some situations; for instance:

- when the company's social and environmental issues are huge and need to be treated in a strictly technical way, through data disclosure of organizational improvements obtained, based on an engineering vision of such issues and consequently of the reports; and
- when the company has progressed substantially towards enriching social and environmental disclosures with key performance indicators, supported by data collection systems that provide preparers with these types of information.

Most companies lack the ability to prepare this type of Integrated Report. Such reports allow them to illustrate their story using measures and accounting evidence instead of telling a generic story. The availability of coherent, reliable data on sustainability achievements is among the first requests from consultants helping companies to prepare Integrated Reports, because such data support business model explanations and other information provided.

The different combinations in the matrix show how opposite modes of cognition and varied stakeholder salience characterize the building of coherent Integrated Reports. Although the taxonomy in Table 18.1 demonstrates the contrasts between the quadrants, we are convinced that a balance between the two directions would allow preparers to successfully consider:

- enriching narratives with data and key performance indicators that support the storytelling or, conversely, that explain stories underlying data; and
- addressing the expectations of different types of stakeholders.

Thus, the final extended meaning of the proposed taxonomy is to widen awareness about the choices preparers must make: if they are able to balance narratives and calculative expositions, they can build interesting stories about the business and related value creation, enriched by data and performance indicators that make these stories more credible to every reader. If they are able to embrace the interests of investors and other stakeholders, they may be able to prepare Integrated Reports that overcome the separation between different types of business reporting. This avoids returning to unwanted forms of 'silo reporting' and fulfils the purpose of combining financial and sustainability issues. In our view, this is the main way to increase the diffusion of an Integrated Report and ensure its credibility as an instrument able to progressively replace traditional forms of reporting for every user.

To improve preparers' abilities to combine different stakeholders' salience, we have to consider another issue, which must be seen as a further result of Integrated Report preparation (year after year), rather than an *a priori* characteristic of management commitment: the effort to promote integrated thinking inside the company.

Preparers' integrated thinking

The IIRC and the World Intellectual Capital/Assets Initiative (WICI, 2013) developed a background paper on connectivity, which conceptualizes integrated thinking in terms of linkages between strategy, governance, past performance and future prospects, as well as across functional departments. The Chartered Institute of Management Accountants (2017) suggests ways to 'make integrated thinking happen' (p. 18) based on IR pioneers' experiences. In particular, it suggests that organizations should create cross-functional groups for business planning, measuring and reporting, and for identifying drivers and activities that support the implementation of corporate business models. Feng et al. (2017) identify active boards, management involvement and cross-organizational teams for IR preparation as channels through which integrated thinking emerges. Further, De Villiers et al. (2017, p. 454) consider 'breaking down the barriers between departments and stimulating strategic dialogue between financial and non-financial teams' as relevant aspects in their argument that IR requires managers to engage in integrated thinking.

Based on case insights from recent articles on IR implementation (Corbella et al., 2019; Stacchezzini et al., 2019), this chapter highlights how integrated thinking might shape IR by encouraging interactions among preparers with different cognitive modes and different views on stakeholder salience. We argue that integrated thinking can facilitate integration between these different cognitive modes and a balanced prioritization of stakeholders, to provide useful information for financial and nonfinancial stakeholders.

Case insights also show that integrated thinking emerges from interactions among departments and the constitution of cross-functional groups. This interaction allows Integrated Reports to contain calculative as well as narrative features. Indeed, an Integrated Report is not entirely influenced by the cognitive mode of the department that 'owns' the IR process (i.e. accounting and finance). Other departments, such as the sustainability, investor relations and risk management departments, play a substantial role in defining the contribution of the types of capital to value creation. The sustainability department provides pertinent KPIs, as well as detailed narratives on actions related to sustainability projects, for corporate strategy implementation. The resulting Integrated Report is influenced by both the predominantly calculative cognitive mode of the staff of the accounting and finance, investor relations and risk management departments, and the more narrative approach of the sustainability department staff.

In contrast, preparers' willingness to define the connections between types of capital and corporate strategy, business model and performance—which constitutes another important component of integrated thinking (WICI, 2013)—encourages balanced prioritization of the requirements of financial and nonfinancial stakeholders. This results from preparers' understanding of the hidden connections among different forms of capitals, sustainable actions and corporate financial performance. Such involvement causes preparers to consider the company's impact on all capital types and on related stakeholders, beyond the more traditional focus on financial capital and financial stakeholders. A dedicated value creation table is useful in this regard, since it allows preparers to communicate how the company creates value(s) for itself and different stakeholders, with detailed disclosure of the cause-and-effect relationships between different forms of capital and value creation.

In summary, integrated thinking can stimulate both integration between different cognition modes and a more balanced prioritization of stakeholders. Integrated Reports may emerge as something more than a storytelling or an argumentation of the value creation for a single class of stakeholders. Probably, this is the true worth of an 'enlightened' corporate report (Humphrey et al., 2017) based on integrated thinking.

Research opportunities

This chapter sought to demonstrate the role of preparers in shaping the content and language of an Integrated Report. In particular, it focused on demonstrating that preparers' cognitive modes and their perceptions of stakeholder salience are not neutral when choices must be made in drafting these reports. Integrated thinking is another relevant feature of preparers' mindsets, because it can help to merge different approaches to corporate reporting (storytelling vs. computational) and facilitate accountability to a broad range of stakeholders (both financial and nonfinancial).

Because the aforementioned features are only some among several that inform preparers' ways of reasoning and acting, we believe that further explorations of preparers' mindsets and behaviour might enhance understanding of the practical potential of IR (De Villiers et al., 2016, 2017; Rinaldi et al., 2018). We see potential in exploring how preparers approach IR in relation to discourses that emerge in organizations or in the corporate reporting environment (Higgins et al., 2014; Humphrey et al., 2017). Indeed, how preparers see Integrated Reports may change over time, as a result of external pressures and internal considerations of these reports' utility. To enhance our understanding of the emergence of IR (Rowbottom and Locke, 2016), studies may investigate IR institutionalization processes at the micro level, by focusing more on 'interactions between single preparers or small groups in implementing or understanding the IR idea' (Rinaldi et al., 2018, p. 1294).

In addition, further research on IR preparers may involve a more detailed focus on the corporate governance implications of IR preparation, in line with some of the questions posed by the Integrated Reporting Committee (IRC) of South Africa (2018). For instance, researchers could explore whether IR implementation relies on a board decision or a management-level decision, and how this choice influences IR effects on employees' engagement with this type of report. Investigations could also focus on the 'functioning' of dedicated bodies formally charged with the responsibility for Integrated Report preparation. Studies could also explore CEO and board engagement during the preparation process, their conceptions of the Integrated Report and their individual or collective roles in supporting the organization's IR project. Studies might also be developed with reference to where and how integrated thinking arises and expands through the company's hierarchy with the support of dedicated governance mechanisms. Opportunities continue to be available for conducting critical and interpretative studies on IR preparers.

References

Adler, J. M. (2008). Two modes of thought: The narrative/paradigmatic disconnect in the Bailey book Tax controversy. *Archives of Sexual Behavior, 37*(3), 422–425.

Al-Htaybat, K., and von Alberti-alhtaybat, L. (2018). Integrated thinking leading to integrated reporting: Case study insights from a global player. *Accounting, Auditing & Accountability Journal, 31*(5), 1435–1460.

Beattie, V. (2014). Accounting narratives and the narrative turn in accounting research: Issues, theory, methodology, methods and a research framework. *The British Accounting Review, 46*(2), 111–134.

Boland, R., and Schultze, V. (1996). Narrating accountability: Cognition and the production of the accountable self. In: R. Munro, and J. Mouritsen (Eds.), *Accountability: Power, ethos and the technologies of managing* (pp. 62–82). London, UK: International Thomson Business Press.

Bruner, J. (1986). *Actual Minds, Possible Worlds.* Harvard, MA: Harvard University Press.

Bruner, J. (1990). *Acts of Meaning.* Harvard, MA: Harvard University Press.

Busco, C., Giovannoni, E., Granà, F., and Izzo, M. (2018). Making sustainability meaningful: Aspirations, discourses and reporting practices. *Accounting, Auditing & Accountability Journal, 31*(8), 2218–2246.

CIMA (Chartered Institute of Management Accountants). (2017). Integrated thinking: Aligning purpose and the business model to market opportunities and sustainable performance. Available at www.cima global.com/Documents/Research%20and%20Insight/Integrated%20Thinking%20Report%20vol% 2013%20issue%203.pdf (Accessed: 30 July 2019).

Corbella, S., Florio, C., Sproviero, A. F., and Stacchezzini, R. (2019). Integrated reporting and the performativity of intellectual capital. *Journal of Management and Governance, 23*(2), 459–483.

De Villiers, C., Hsiao, P. C. K., and Maroun, W. (2017). Developing a Conceptual Model of influences around Integrated Reporting, New Insights, and Directions for Future Research. *Meditari Accountancy Research, 25*(4), 450–460.

De Villiers, C., Venter, E. R., and Hsiao, P. C. K. (2016). Integrated reporting: Background, measurement issues, approaches and an agenda for future research. *Accounting & Finance, 57*(4), 937–959.

Eccles, R. G., and Krzus, M. P. (2014). *The Integrated Reporting Movement: Meaning, Momentum, Motives, and Materiality*. New York: John Wiley.

Edgley, C. (2014). A genealogy of accounting materiality. *Critical Perspectives on Accounting, 25*(3), 255–271.

Feng, T., Cummings, L., and Tweedie, D. (2017). Exploring integrated thinking in integrated reporting–an exploratory study in Australia. *Journal of Intellectual Capital, 18*(2), 330–353.

Higgins, C., Stubbs, W., and Love, T. (2014). Walking the talk(s): Organisational narratives of integrated reporting. *Accounting, Auditing & Accountability Journal, 17*(7), 1090–1119.

Humphrey, C., O'Dwyer, B., and Unerman, J. (2017). Re-theorizing the configuration of organizational fields: The IIRC and the pursuit of "Enlightened" corporate reporting. *Accounting and Business Research, 47*(1), 30–63.

Integrated Reporting Committee (IRC) of South Africa. (2018). Preparing an integrated report – A starter's guide (Updated). Available at: http://integratedreportingsa.org/ircsa/wp-content/uploads/2018/12/IRC-Achieving-Balance-Paper-web.pdf (Accessed: 30 July 2019).

International Integrated Reporting Council (IIRC). (2013). International integrated reporting framework. Available at: http://integratedreporting.org/wp-content/uploads/2015/03/13-12-08-THE-INTERNATIONAL-IR-FRAMEWORK-2-1.pdf (Accessed: 30 July 2019).

Lai, A., Melloni, G., and Stacchezzini, R. (2017a). Integrated reporting and preparers' accountability: A matter of context. In D. Vrontis, Y. Weber, and E. Tsoukatos (Eds.), *8th Annual Conference of the EuroMed Academy of Business – Global and national business theories and practice: Bridging the past with the future* (pp. 782–787). Valetta, Malta: Euromed Press.

Lai, A., Melloni, G., and Stacchezzini, R. (2017b). What does materiality mean to integrated reporting preparers? An empirical exploration. *Meditari Accountancy Research, 25*(4), 533–552.

Lai, A., Melloni, G., and Stacchezzini, R. (2018). Integrated reporting and narrative accountability: The role of preparers. *Accounting, Auditing & Accountability Journal, 31*(5), 1381–1405.

Mio, C., Fasan, M., and Pauluzzo, R. (2016). Internal application of IR principles: Generali's internal integrated reporting. *Journal of Cleaner Production, 139*, 204–218.

Mitchell, R. K., Agle, B. R., and Wood, D. J. (1997). Toward a theory of stakeholder identification and salience: Defining the principle of who and what really counts. *Academy of Management Review, 22*(4), 853–886.

Rinaldi, L., Unerman, J., and De Villiers, C. (2018). Evaluating the integrated reporting journey: Insights, gaps and agendas for future research. *Accounting, Auditing & Accountability Journal, 31*(5), 1294–1318.

Roberts, J. (1991). The possibilities of accountability. *Accounting, Organizations and Society, 16*(4), 355–368.

Rowbottom, N., and Locke, J. (2016). The emergence of <IR>. *Accounting and Business Research, 46*(1), 83–115.

Stacchezzini, R., Florio, C., Sproviero, A. F., and Corbella, S. (2019). An intellectual capital ontology in an integrated reporting context. *Journal of Intellectual Capital, 20*(1), 83–99.

Vesty, G., Ren, C., and Ji, S. (2018). Integrated reporting as a test of worth. *Accounting, Auditing & Accountability Journal, 31*(5), 1406–1434.

WICI (World Intellectual Capital/Assets Initiative). (2013). Connectivity background paper for <IR>. Available at: http://integratedreporting.org/wp-content/uploads/2013/07/IR-Background-Paper-Connectivity.pdf (Accessed: 30 July 2019).

19

INTEGRATED THINKING FOR STAKEHOLDER ENGAGEMENT

A processing model for judgments and choice in situations of cognitive complexity

Leonardo Rinaldi

Centre for Critical and Historical Research on Organisation and Society (CHRONOS),
Centre for Research into Sustainability (CRIS), Accounting and Financial Management Department,
School of Business and Management, Royal Holloway University of London

Abstract

How is "Integrated Thinking" implicated in stakeholder engagement? Framing engagement programmes poses serious dilemmas for decision-makers who, on the one hand, are increasingly asked to involve stakeholders in the development or implementation of corporate plans, but on the other, fall back on intuitive judgment (and its major biases) when it comes to making decisions. This chapter argues that integrated thinking can be thought of as a dynamic process in which judgments and choices are influenced by heuristics and biases constantly (re-)negotiated through active exchange with stakeholders. Drawing on Daniel Kahneman's (2012) work on decision-making, the chapter proposes a process model for judgments and choice that helps illustrate how integrated thinking can contribute more effectively to contemporary stakeholder engagement struggles.

Introduction

The development of Integrated Reporting (IR) embodies a new approach to management reasoning; one based on the concept of integrated thinking. The International Integrated Reporting Council (IIRC) (2013) promotes integrated thinking as an approach aimed at helping companies address pressing social, environmental and governance issues in ways that enable them to create value over the short, medium and long term (IIRC, 2013). According to the IIRC, the ability of an organization to create value is strongly interrelated with its capacity to respond to stakeholders' legitimate needs and interests through a wide range of activities, interactions and relationships. A guiding principle that underpins the implementation of IR practice focuses on stakeholder relationships. This principle reflects the importance of stakeholder engagement because "value is not created by or within an organization, alone but is created through relationships with others" (IIRC, 2013, p. 17). Thus, integrated thinking provides a rationale for a "stakeholder engagement perspective" to be instilled within organizations, which will also enrich organizations' relational capital.

As IR practices have become more widely adopted, a growing body of literature has begun investigating IR practice (De Villiers et al., 2017, for a review of the rapidly emergent IR academic literature; De Villiers et al., 2014, 2017; Dumay et al., 2016; Velte and Stawinoga, 2017), and an increasing number of studies have started to examine integrated thinking (Al-Htaybat and von Alberti-alhtaybat, 2018; Dumay and Dai, 2017; Guthrie et al., 2017; Venter et al., 2017). This latter body of research has studied the practical challenges of implementing integrated thinking (La Torre et al., 2019) or its links with intellectual capital (Stacchezzini et al., 2018) and the broader value creation process (Adams, 2017), but has paid scant attention to the role of integrated thinking in framing the relationships between organizations and stakeholders.

The framing of engagement initiatives poses serious dilemmas for organizations. Decision-makers are increasingly asked to involve a wide range of stakeholders, such as employees, customers, suppliers, debt and equity providers, and governments, in the development or implementation of corporate programmes. These individuals often use highly complex methods for gathering information about problems and for formulating answers. However, when it comes to making decisions, they typically fall back on intuition (Martin, 2009). The quality of their intuition sets an upper limit on the quality of the entire engagement and decision-making process.

The purpose of this chapter is to explore the role that the cognitive study of decision processes can play in fostering an integrated form of thinking and, in doing so, improve stakeholder engagement. A common theme in academic scholarship is that stakeholder engagement increases accountability (Bebbington et al., 2014). Indeed, several authors have evaluated and critiqued existing practices to structure an understanding of how specific engagement initiatives are effective in shaping an organization's accountability (Adams and Frost, 2006; Barone et al., 2013; Boesso and Kumar, 2009a; Brown and Dillard, 2013a; Gray, 2002). However, little is known about how decision-makers mobilize modes of thinking to frame engagement practices among stakeholders. This has recently led to a call for more research into the development of new theoretical models, seeking to provide novel understandings of the stakeholder engagement processes in the emerging field of IR (Rinaldi et al., 2018). This chapter explores this call by linking the notion of Integrated Thinking with organizational Stakeholder Engagement and Dialogue initiatives. We argue that integrated thinking can be thought of as the property of a dynamic process in which judgments and choice are influenced by heuristics and biases constantly (re-)negotiated through dynamic exchange with stakeholders. Drawing on Daniel Kahneman's (2012) work on decision-making, this chapter proposes a process model for judgments and choice that helps illustrate how integrated thinking can contribute more effectively to contemporary stakeholder engagement struggles.

To make the argument, the chapter proceeds as follows. First, we (briefly) examine existing research on stakeholder engagement and introduce a theoretical approach to decision-making by drawing on Kahneman's (2012) dual processing framework. The chapter then develops a process model conceptualizing how integrated thinking in situations of cognitive complexity can be achieved. Finally, we discuss the contribution and implications for the study, while proposing future lines of research.

Literature review and research gap

This section elucidates the notion of stakeholder engagement by clarifying its function, underlying mechanisms and key characteristics. It discusses the existing studies on SE in IR and clarifies the gap in the literature.

> Stakeholder engagement is the process used by an organisation to engage relevant stakeholders for a clear purpose to achieve agreed outcomes. It is now also recognised as a fundamental accountability mechanism since it obliges an organisation to involve stakeholders in identifying, understanding and responding to sustainability issues and concerns, and to report, explain and answer to stakeholders for decisions, actions and performance
>
> *(AccountAbility, 2015, p. 12)*

The above quotation encapsulates what makes stakeholder engagement a crucial element of the sustainability accounting and accountability process within organizations. Engaging with stakeholders is increasingly regarded as an important part of corporate social, environmental, economic and ethical governance and accountability mechanisms (Archel et al., 2011; Barone et al., 2013; Brown and Dillard, 2013b; Deegan and Unerman, 2011; O'Dwyer et al., 2011). The relevance of stakeholder interaction is that only by consulting with potential stakeholders can organizations develop knowledge and understanding of their needs and expectations. Addressing these expectations should be the aim of "good" corporate governance and accountability (Bebbington et al., 2007; Thomson and Bebbington, 2005; Unerman and Bennett, 2004).

Nonetheless, it is argued that for stakeholder engagement to lead to meaningful corporate accountability, mechanisms whereby stakeholder views can feed into the decision-making process have to be created, while techniques to hold management to account need to be established. Otherwise, organizations' stakeholder engagement and dialogue "risks representing only an exercise of power over non-financial stakeholders who are disadvantaged by means of a more or less sophisticated management tool" (Owen et al., 2001).

Organizations use a vast and heterogeneous set of channels to engage with their stakeholders, ranging from conversations to the written exchange of ideas and physical meetings (Burchell and Cook, 2008; Freedman and Jaggi, 2006). Some of these techniques focus on principles and mechanisms directed towards designing or implementing frameworks to engage with the various constituency groups (AccountAbility, 2015; Bebbington et al., 2007; Belal and Roberts, 2010; Boesso and Kumar, 2009b; Brown, 2009; UNEP, 2005), while other research has examined, evaluated and assessed the quality of such engagement (Freedman and Jaggi, 2006; Manetti, 2011).

These studies provided important insights into the process of developing and promoting stakeholder engagement. Given the centrality of stakeholder engagement for an organization's sustainability and accountability, it is important to understand the difference between high-grade and low-grade engagement. One of the key points that qualifies an engagement process as meaningful is the integration of stakeholder engagement into organizational governance and decision-making (Brown and Dillard, 2013a; Gray, 2002). However, as is the case with addressing the dimension of corporate governance in sustainability accounting and accountability processes more generally, there has been little if any debate in the academic literature regarding the decision-making process that shapes high-grade stakeholder engagement and dialogue. Specifically, little is known about how decision-makers mobilize modes of thinking to frame engagement practices with stakeholders.

The rapid evolution of Integrated Reporting (IR) has promoted a novel approach to management reasoning, based on the concept of integrated thinking. Integrated thinking is defined by the IIRC as *"the active consideration by an organization of the relationships between its various operating and functional units and the capitals that the organization uses or affects"* (IIRC, 2013, p. 2). The aim of integrated thinking is to promote integrated decision-making and actions that consider the creation of value over the short, medium, and long term. "The more integrated thinking is embedded in the business, the more likely it is that a fuller consideration of key stakeholders' legitimate needs and interests is incorporated as an ordinary part of conducting business" (IIRC, 2013, p. 18). Given the complexities of today's social context, organizations' existing forms of accountability seem overly simplistic and unrealistic to an increasing number of scholars (Messner, 2009). At the same time, creativity, innovation, and invention have become central topics for organizations scholars (Adler and Chen, 2011; Perry-Smith and Mannucci, 2017). This newer work emphasizes the importance of understanding how individuals, groups, and organizations cognize the social context (Paisey and Paisey, 2011), enter situations where neither means nor ends are understood (Alvarez and Barney, 2005), and make judgments and choices in situations of cognitive complexity (Tversky and Kahneman, 1974, 1981). Understanding change, innovation, and entrepreneurship requires the ability to identify and understand the processes of judgment and choice, not just accountability. With this in mind, the following section presents the theoretical framing that has been used to inform the analysis in this paper.

Kahneman's dual processing framework

Integrated thinking has been conceptualized as the conditions and procedures that are conducive to an inclusive process of decision-making, which has a material effect on an organization's ability to create value over time (Busco et al., 2017; Guthrie et al., 2017). Integral to this managerial approach are two components. The first connects beliefs and attitudes: organizational values, strategy, and performance. The second connects departments; the relationships between an organization's internal units, processes, and individuals, and their interactions (Dumay and Dai, 2017). This process requires resisting the simplicity and certainty that comes with conventional thinking and implies a continuous process of integrating intuition, reason, and imagination, with a view to developing a holistic range of strategy, tactics, action, and assessment (Martin, 2009).

This section introduces Daniel Kahneman's dual processing framework to show that this approach can offer innovative ideas to inform management reasoning and develop organizations' relational capital through ground-breaking stakeholder engagement practices. Daniel Kahneman is a psychologist and economist, notable for his work on the psychology of judgment and decision-making (Tversky and Kahneman, 1974). He was awarded the 2002 Nobel Memorial Prize in Economic Sciences for his pioneering work on the integration of psychological research into economic science. His research aimed to increase the understanding of how people make economic decisions, particularly the mental processes used in forming judgments and making choices. In contrast with previous research indicating that people's decisions are determined by the expected gains from each possible future scenario multiplied by its probability of occurring, Kahneman's work demonstrated that irrational choices, based on giving more weight to some scenarios than to others (such as, for example, complex situations when the future consequences are uncertain), lead to decisions that are different from those predicted by traditional

˙economic theory (Tversky and Kahneman, 1981). In these circumstances, Kahneman's experiments challenged the prevailing theory that people are rational actors, showing that only a few evaluated the underlying probability of complex scenarios, while most people relied on heuristic shortcuts (Kahneman, 2012).

Through his analysis of models of thought, Kahneman provided key insights into peoples' ways of thinking, arguing that there are two approaches that social actors use to think. This is "dual processing theory" and postulates that judgment and choice occur via two very different ways of processing information that operate at the same time: the intuitive and the deliberative systems (Morewedge and Kahneman, 2010; Tversky and Kahneman, 1974).

The intuitive system is always active, operating automatically and quickly, "with little or no effort and no sense of voluntary control" (Kahneman, 2012, p. 20). The intuitive system relies on innate skills that individuals are born with to perceive the world around them, such as the ability to recognize objects, to orient attention and avoid losses. This system also depends on learned associations between ideas (e.g. revenues-minus-costs-equals-profit) and skills such as reading and understanding the nuances of social situations (e.g. detecting hostility or friendliness). This knowledge is stored in memory and accessed without intention and without effort, while other mental activities become fast and automatic through prolonged practice.

The operation of the deliberative system, in contrast, needs intentional activation. It is often associated with the subjective experience of agency, choice, and concentration. This system assigns attention to the effortful mental activities that require rational and logical responses, such as the assessment of complex situations. To do that, the deliberative system needs considerable energy in the form of focus and attention. Thus, it tires easily and cannot be maintained for long periods of time. A common feature of the diverse operations of the deliberative system is that they require attention and stop when attention is drawn away (Kahneman, 2012).

While different in nature, the intuitive and the deliberative systems are profoundly related and constantly interact with each other. As Kahneman (2012, p. 24) argues:

> [intuitive and the deliberative systems] are both active whenever we are awake. [The intuitive system] runs automatically and [the deliberative system] is normally in a comfortable low-effort mode, in which only a fraction of its capacity is engaged. [The intuitive system] continuously generates suggestions for [the deliberative system]: impressions, intuitions, intentions, and feelings. If endorsed by [the deliberative system], impressions and intuitions turn into beliefs, and impulses turn into voluntary actions. When all goes smoothly, which is most of the time, [the deliberative system] adopts the suggestions of [the intuitive system] with little or no modification.

At the same time, the deliberative system has some ability to change the way the intuitive system operates, by instructing the typically instinctive functions of attention and memory. This happens, for instance, when individuals are required to do something˙ that does not come naturally to them, finding that its continuation requires effort. Building on Kahneman's insights, the next section develops a process model conceptualizing how integrated thinking in situations of cognitive complexity can be understood and framed.

Cognitive heuristics and biases: towards a processing model of stakeholder engagement

Mainstreaming stakeholder engagement into decision-making is a pressing challenge in achieving transparent organizational processes with greater input from stakeholders, and in obtaining their support for the decisions that are taken (Brown and Dillard, 2013a; Owen et al., 2001; Rinaldi et al., 2014). Building on Kahneman's dual processing framework, this chapter develops a process model of how stakeholder engagement can be co-achieved with relevant stakeholders, which gives rise to different responses. Figure 19.1 summarizes the combined institutional and organizational factors central to the model.

Organizations have access to a wide range of capabilities and practices. The organizational environment represents the forces within an organization that affect performance, operations, and resources (Felin et al., 2012). However, organizations are also exposed to stakeholder scrutiny. The stakeholder environment represents the set of institutional pressures that create canons of accountability and enforce legitimacy norms for organizational practices (Edelman and Stryker, 2005). These environments are reciprocally tied to each other and to the social context. Organizations operating in this arena, therefore, need to consider the adoption of engagement practices congruent with the dissimilar knowledge and expertise available in the field in order to promote cross-fertilization, innovation and, ultimately, high-quality group decisions. The objective is to stimulate the exchange and elaboration of information among decision-makers in order to minimize the evaluation and discussion biases that can steer the process away from the engagement goals. Evaluation bias addresses the individual level of information processing, and discussion bias addresses the group level of collective information processing during group discussion (Brodbeck et al., 2007). Both phases of the decision-making process are prone to being influenced by a range of heuristics and biases related to the complexity of cognitive processes possessed by the social actors involved. Building on Kahneman's work, this chapter suggests that stakeholder engagement can use cognitive ease, associative activation, and repeated experience as forms of integrated thinking.

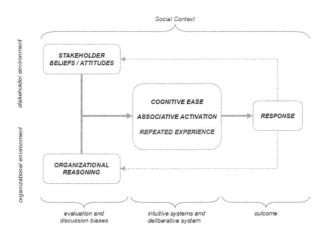

Figure 19.1 Stakeholder engagement processing model for judgments and choice in situations of cognitive complexity

Engaging through cognitive ease

Cognitive ease is a process in the intuitive system that assesses the extent to which the deliberative system needs to operate. Kahneman (2012) argues that cognitive ease ranges along a continuum comprised of two extremes: easy and strained. *Easy* is the sign that there is no need to redirect cognitive attention towards pressures or problems. In contrast, *strained* indicates a situation requiring increased mobilization of complex cognitive tasks such as control and computation. Kahneman (2012) found that the cognitive state has an important influence on decision-making. When subjects are in a state of cognitive ease, they tend to trust their intuition and believe what they see and experience. They are also casual and perfunctory in their thinking. When they feel strained, they are more likely to be alert, sceptical and invest more effort in what they are doing, yet be less intuitive and creative in this process (Tversky and Kahneman, 1981).

One way to engage with stakeholders is by implementing forms of thinking that integrate the key characteristics of the dual mental systems used in forming judgments and making choices: intuition, reason, and imagination. The intuitive system appears to have a special aptitude for the construction and interpretation of stories about *active agents*; that is, agents who have personalities, habits, and abilities. For example, if one quickly forms a good (or bad) opinion of a stakeholder, one would expect a good (or bad) attitude towards them. The deliberative system, instead, can follow rules, compare objects against several attributes and make deliberate choices between options. The intuitive system does not have this capability as it can only detect simple relations, such as basic similarities and differences. While the intuitive system is very good at integrating information about a single topic, it does not deal with multiple distinct topics at once and is not proficient in using purely quantitative information.

A crucial capability of the deliberative system is *executive control*, which consists of the adoption of *task sets* through which it can program memory to follow instructions that override routine responses (Kahneman, 2012). In the context of stakeholder engagement, consider the following: an organization is involved in a consultation process in order to be able to construct an account of its corporate social and environmental impact. The process is aimed at obtaining a better understanding of which stakeholder seems to be most affected by the organization's actions and how responsibility within the company could be allocated to alleviate that impact. Setting up for this exercise can be challenging. Nonetheless, the organization improves over time with practice and structure. However, with this newly acquired tendency to focus on stakeholders, more intellectual resources – in the form of deliberative thought – will be required by decision-makers to perform it. Research has demonstrated that when the deliberative system is busy, the intuitive system has more influence on behaviour (Tversky and Kahneman, 1981). Consequently, decision-makers who are cognitively busy are also likely to make superficial judgments in social situations. For example, performance-focused stakeholder engagement initiatives that place too much emphasis on how organizations are doing in specific phases of the engagement process have the potential to disrupt results by loading decision-makers' cognitive systems with futile, anxious considerations.

How can organizations deal with cognitive ease within stakeholder engagement programmes? Kahneman's work (Kahneman, 2012) showed that one way of minimizing the bias in decision-making and addressing complex issues is to promote *intellectual engagement*. When social actors believe a conclusion is true, they are also very likely to believe arguments that appear to support it, even when those arguments are unsound. Difficult problems can be solved when decision-makers are not tempted to accept (or offer) superficially plausible answers that come readily to mind. More alert and intellectually active decision-makers, who are less willing to be satisfied with superficially attractive answers and are more sceptical about their intuition, are more likely to think through the problem rather than turn to standard operating procedures.

Research on cognitive strain has shown that there are severe limitations on peoples' ability to process sensory signals, and subjects who experience "cognitive strain" try to reduce it using simplification strategies (Slovic et al., 2014) such as associative activation and repeated experience. The following sections will explore these two forms of integrated thinking in more detail.

Engaging through associative activation

Another way to engage with stakeholders, arising from situations of cognitive complexity, is by taking into account the cognitive phenomenon known as associative activation. Associative activation is a process in which ideas that have been evoked trigger other ideas in a spreading cascade of activities that occur cognitively (Morewedge and Kahneman, 2010). The main feature of this set of events is *coherence*: each element is connected and supports and strengthens the others. This process happens rapidly and simultaneously, producing a self-reinforcing pattern of cognitive, emotional and physical responses that is associatively coherent. Social cognition studies have long researched the subtle and unanticipated effects of people's social environments on their thoughts and behaviours (Jacoby et al., 1989). These studies have shown that mere exposure to socially relevant stimuli can facilitate, or *prime*, a host of impressions, judgments, goals, and actions, often even outside of people's intentions or awareness (Molden, 2014). The *priming effect* is the influence on an action of an idea. If an idea is currently on someone's mind (whether or not the individual is conscious of it) they will be quicker than usual to recognize a multitude of related ideas when they are presented. Primed ideas have the ability to prime other ideas, although in a weaker fashion. The activation of the primed idea spreads though a small part of a network of associated ideas.

Research has shown that the priming effect can occur in different stages (Carroll and Payne, 2014). For example, a set of words can prime thoughts of a phenomenon, which in turn primes behaviour associated with this phenomenon, without any conscious awareness. This particular form of associative activation, which consists of the reciprocal priming of an action and an idea, is known as the *ideomotor effect*. Reciprocal priming effects tend to produce coherent judgments and choices, and carry two important implications for corporate accountability studies. First, priming is not restricted to concepts and words but also comprises attitudes, behaviour, thoughts, actions and emotions. Second, actions and emotions can be primed by events that we are not consciously aware of. Research findings of priming studies suggest that living in a culture that surrounds us with reminders of cooperation and mutual understanding may shape behaviour and attitudes in ways that could reduce the level of conflict between organizations and their various political, social, and economic stakeholders (Molden, 2014).

How can organizations promote associative activation with their stakeholders? Decision-makers who are serious about stakeholder engagement can embrace cognitive stances that prime cooperation and dialogue rather than those that promote counterproductive associative activations. Some organizations, for instance, provide a frequent reminder of the need for respect though value systems strategically located in the premises of the organization or published in the organizational disclosure; others prompt collegiality, conveying the feeling of shared responsibility, aiming to increase the appeal of democratic ideas. Kahneman's work (Kahneman, 2012; Morewedge and Kahneman, 2010; Tversky and Kahneman, 1981) showed that the effects of priming can reach quite far into social actors' lives. For example, just as money primed people to become more independent than they would be without the associative trigger (Kahneman, 2012), participation can be expected to prime shareholder behaviour and decision-making by associatively promoting collaborative work and dialogic forms of consensus, achieving actions (Barone et al., 2013; Brown, 2009; Brown and Dillard, 2013b; Thomson and Bebbington, 2005; Unerman and Bennett, 2004).

Engaging though the halo effect

The tendency to admire (or despise) everything about a situation or a person, including circumstances that have not been witnessed, is known as the "*halo effect*". The halo effect depends on the intuitive system, which provides our conscious self with a representation of the world that is deliberately simpler and more coherent than the underlying reality. In the context of stakeholder engagement, consider the following example: an organization meets for the first time with several stakeholder groups to arrange and structure a consultation process. Most of the group representatives are pleasant and easy to talk to. During these meetings, one of these representatives is someone whose group is required to make major compromises to facilitate the pursuit of a long-term goal. What do decision-makers know about the propensity of this participant to compromise? There is little reason to believe that people who are personable in social situations are also prone to compromise in the context of a dispute. But the group representatives are cherished, like cooperation itself, and cooperating with people more broadly. While concrete evidence of the ability to compromise and the tendency towards cooperation is missing from this example, this association (halo effect) has the potential to bias our model of judgment and choice, leading us to believe that personable people are also easy to compromise with. Evidence accumulates gradually, but its interpretation is shaped by the emotions attached to first impressions (Clark et al., 2014).

While the halo effect has the potential to influence decision-makers by reducing the total value of the information provided to them, it can be tamed by minimizing the effects associated with the reciprocal influence of the subjects involved in the process (Kahneman, 2012). This principle, known as *independent judgment*, aims not only at reducing collusion but also at preventing each source of information from influencing the others. The principle of independent judgement has immediate application for the conduct of stakeholder engagement initiatives, activities in which organizations and managers invest significant physical and intellectual resources. The standard practice of open discussion, for example, gives weight to the opinions of those who speak early and emphatically, increasing the potential for others to line up with them. For instance, before an issue is discussed, the different parties involved in the process could be asked to give a very brief summary of their position, independently from each other. In doing so, the diversity of knowledge and opinion in the group is valued and redundancy in the various sources of information is reduced. If engagement programmes are to derive the most useful information from a pluralistic environment and promote high-quality group decisions, they should try to make each source uncorrelated.

Contributions

As IR practices have become more widely adopted and a growing body of literature is investigating IR practice, more needs to be done to understand the role of integrated thinking in framing the relationships between organizations and stakeholders. The aim of this chapter was to explore the role that the cognitive study of decision-making processes can play in fostering an integrated form of thinking and, in so doing, improve stakeholder engagement. While existing research has criticized the extent to which stakeholder engagement practices are effective in shaping an organization's accountability, little is known about how decision-makers mobilize modes of thinking to frame engagement practices with stakeholders. Drawing on Daniel Kahneman's (2012) work on decision-making, we proposed a stakeholder engagement processing model for judgments and choice that helps illustrate how integrated thinking can contribute more effectively to contemporary stakeholder engagement struggles.

This chapter contributes to the integrated reporting literature in two ways. First, we extend existing studies of organizational accountability (Adams and McNicholas, 2007; Ahrens, 1996; O'Dwyer and Boomsma, 2015; Parker, 2005). In particular, we contribute to the debate around the somewhat neglected topic of organizational micro-foundations (Felin et al., 2012; Felin et al., 2015; Power, 2019) by suggesting that integrated thinking is a dynamic set of micro-processes in which judgments and choice are influenced by heuristics and biases, constantly (re-)negotiated through dynamic exchange with stakeholders. This has important implications for understanding how aspects of institutional complexity are framed. Rather than a universal approach to integrated thinking, the process of stakeholder engagement is multidimensional and contingent on different types of audiences, each of which requires different types of approach to decision-making.

Second, while prior work on integrated thinking remained silent on what constitutes the force of integration and assumed the notion of agreement, this chapter offers a systematic account of how organizations can formulate and take decisions while contemplating the multiple cognitive schemes of the types of audiences involved. That is, we bring together various elements of Kahneman's framework in a dynamic process model that distinguishes three types of reasoning that result from the interaction between the intuitive and deliberative system, each leading to different responses to stakeholder engagement.

In the following paragraphs, a set of integrated thinking/stakeholder engagement areas for which a cognitive approach can be particularly fruitful are identified and briefly discussed. While this agenda is not exhaustive, the extent of the empirical and theoretical challenges that surround the impact of integrated thinking, the scope of the research avenues, and the research questions indicated below, show that academic research still has much potential.

First, Kahneman's dual-processing framework is a way to focus on the understanding of how psychological attributes and biases affect strategic choices, an aspect that has been somewhat neglected in prior accountability research. More specifically, there is a need for future research into the foundations of integrated thinking in organizations.

Second, dialogic accountability has been an influential concept in explaining the organizational approach to stakeholder engagement (Unerman and Bennett, 2004; Bebbington et al., 2007; Burchell and Cook, 2008; van Huijstee and Glasbergen, 2008; Brown, 2009). However, most research on stakeholder engagement has overlooked the cognitive mechanisms behind dialogic engagement. In the emerging practice of integrated thinking, there is a need to advance the understanding of how specific biases and heuristics affect dialogic engagement, and the effect of such biases in organizations' accountability contexts.

Finally, stakeholder engagement research seems to assume that once the process is defined, a successful execution follows. However, more needs to be known about the conditions leading organizational actors and decision-makers to execute engagement with stakeholders. For example, future research could focus on the micro-level processes of organizational actors, the structures they are embedded in, and how the interactions between them influence the activities required to engage with stakeholders.

The more integrated thinking is embedded in organizations, the more likely it is that a fuller consideration of key stakeholders' legitimate needs and interests is incorporated as an ordinary part of conducting business. Future research could provide insight into these matters.

References

AccountAbility. (2015). *AA1000 Stakeholder Engagement Standard 2015.* Available at: www.accountabil ity.org/images/content/8/7/875/AA1000SES%202015.pdf (Accessed: 5 September 2019).

Adams, C. A. (2017). Conceptualising the contemporary corporate value creation process. *Accounting, Auditing & Accountability Journal, 30*(4), 906–931.

Adams, C. A., and Frost, G. R. (2006). The internet and change in corporate stakeholder engagement and communication strategies on social and environmental performance. *Journal of Accounting & Organizational Change, 2*(3), 281–303.

Adams, C. A., and McNicholas, P. (2007). Making a difference: Sustainability reporting, accountability and organisational change. *Accounting, Auditing & Accountability Journal, 20*(3), 382–402.

Adler, P. S., and Chen, C. X. (2011). Combining creativity and control: Understanding individual motivation in large-scale collaborative creativity. *Accounting, Organizations and Society, 36*(2), 63–85.

Ahrens, T. (1996). Styles of accountability. *Accounting, Organizations and Society, 21*(2/3), 139–173.

Al-Htaybat, K., and von Alberti-alhtaybat, L. (2018). Integrated thinking leading to integrated reporting: Case study insights from a global player. *Accounting, Auditing & Accountability Journal, 31*(5), 1435–1460.

Alvarez, S. A., and Barney, J. B. (2005). How do entrepreneurs organize firms under conditions of uncertainty? *Journal of Management, 31*, 776–793.

Archel, P., Husillos, J., and Crawford, S. (2011). The institutionalisation of unaccountability: Loading the dice of Corporate Social Responsibility discourse. *Journal: Accounting, Organizations and Society, 36*(6), 327–343.

Barone, E., Ranamagar, N., and Solomon, J. F. (2013). A Habermasian model of stakeholder (non) engagement and corporate (ir)responsibility reporting. *Accounting Forum, 37*(3), 163–181.

Bebbington, J., Brown, J., Frame, B., and Thomson, I. (2007). Theorizing engagement: The potential of a critical dialogic approach. *Accounting, Auditing & Accountability Journal, 20*(3), 356–381.

Bebbington, J., Unerman, J., and O'Dwyer, B. (2014). *Sustainability Accounting and Accountability* (2nd ed.). London: Routledge.

Belal, A. R., and Roberts, R. W. (2010). Stakeholders' perceptions of corporate social reporting in Bangladesh. *Journal of Business Ethics, 97*(2), 311–324.

Boesso, G., and Kumar, K. (2009a). An investigation of stakeholder prioritization and engagement: Who or what really counts. *Journal of Accounting & Organizational Change, 5*(1), 62–80.

Boesso, G., and Kumar, K. (2009b). Stakeholder prioritization and reporting: Evidence from Italy and the US. *Accounting Forum, 33*(2), 162–175.

Brodbeck, F. C., Kerschreiter, R., Mojzisch, A., and Schulz-Hardt, S. (2007). Group decision making under conditions of distributed knowledge: The information asymmetries model. *The Academy of Management Review, 32*(2), 459–479.

Brown, J. (2009). Democracy, sustainability and dialogic accounting technologies: Taking pluralism seriously. *Critical Perspectives on Accounting, 20*(3), 313–342.

Brown, J., and Dillard, J. (2013a). Agonizing over engagement: SEA and the "death of environmentalism" debates. *Critical Perspectives on Accounting, 24*(1), 1–18.

Brown, J., and Dillard, J. (2013b). Critical accounting and communicative action: On the limits of consensual deliberation. *Critical Perspectives on Accounting, 24*(3), 176–190.

Burchell, J., and Cook, J. (2008). Stakeholder dialogue and organisational learning: Changing relationships between companies and NGOs. *Business Ethics: A European Review, 17*(1), 35–46.

Busco, C., Granà, F., and Quattrone, P. (2017). *Integrated Thinking. Aligning Purpose and the Business Model to Market Opportunities and Sustainable Performance.* Available at: www.cimaglobal.com (Accessed: 30 August 2019).

Carroll, J. S., and Payne, J. W. (2014). *Cognition and Social Behavior.* London: Routledge.

Clark, K., Quigley, N., and Stumpf, S. (2014). The influence of decision frames and vision priming on decision outcomes in work groups: Motivating stakeholder considerations. *Journal of Business Ethics, 120*(1), 27–38.

Deegan, C., and Unerman, J. (2011). *Financial Accounting Theory* (2nd European ed.). Maidenhead: McGraw-Hill.

De Villiers, C., Hsiao, P. C. K., and Maroun, W. (2017). Developing a conceptual model of influences around integrated reporting, new insights and directions for future research. *Meditari Accountancy Research, 25*(4), 450–460.

De Villiers, C., Unerman, J., and Rinaldi, L. (2014). Integrated Reporting: Insights, gaps and an agenda for future research. *Journal: Accounting, Auditing & Accountability Journal, 27*(7), 1042–1067.

De Villiers, C., Venter, E. R., and Hsiao, P. C. K. (2017). Integrated reporting: Background, measurement issues, approaches and an agenda for future research. *Accounting & Finance, 57*(4), 937–959.

Dumay, J., Bernardi, C., Guthrie, J., and Demartini, P. (2016). Integrated reporting: A structured literature review. *Accounting Forum, 40*(3), 166–185.

Dumay, J., and Dai, T. (2017). Integrated thinking as a cultural control? *Meditari Accountancy Research, 25* (4), 574–604.

Edelman, L. B., and Stryker, R. (2005). A sociological approach to law and the economy. In: R. Swedberg, and N. Smelser (Eds.), *The Handbook of Economic Sociology* (pp. 527–553). Princeton, NJ: Princeton University Press.

Felin, T., Foss, N. J., Heimeriks, K. H., and Madsen, T. L. (2012). Microfoundations of routines and capabilities: Individuals, processes, and structure. *Journal of Management Studies, 49*(8), 1351–1374.

Felin, T., Foss, N. J., and Ployhart, R. E. (2015). The microfoundations movement in strategy and organization theory. *The Academy of Management Annals, 9*(1), 575–632.

Freedman, M., and Jaggi, B. (2006). *Environmental Accounting: Commitment or Propaganda.* Oxford: JAI Press.

Gray, R. (2002). The social accounting project and accounting organizations and society privileging engagement, imaginings, new accountings and pragmatism over critique? *Accounting, Organizations and Society, 27*(7), 687–708.

Guthrie, J., Manes-Rossi, F., and Orelli, R. L. (2017). Integrated reporting and integrated thinking in Italian public sector organisations. *Meditari Accountancy Research, 25*(4), 553–573.

IIRC. (2013). *The International <IR> Framework.* Available at: www.theiirc.org/wp-content/uploads/2013/12/13-12-08-THE-INTERNATIONAL-IR-FRAMEWORK-2-1.pdf (Accessed: 29 March 2019).

Jacoby, L. L., Kelley, C., Brown, J., and Jasechko, J. (1989). Becoming famous overnight: Limits on the ability to avoid unconscious influences of the past. *Journal of Personality and Social Psychology Journal of Personality and Social Psychology, 56*(3), 326–338.

Kahneman, D. (2012). *Thinking, Fast and Slow.* New York: Penguin.

La Torre, M., Bernardi, C., Guthrie, J., and Dumay, J. (2019). Integrated reporting and integrating thinking: Practical Challenges. In: S. Arvidsson (Ed.), *Challenges in Managing Sustainable Business: Reporting, Taxation, Ethics and Governance* (pp. 25–54). Cham: Springer.

Manetti, G. (2011). The quality of stakeholder engagement in sustainability reporting: Empirical evidence and critical points. *Corporate Social Responsibility and Environmental Management, 18*(2), 110–122.

Martin, R. L. (2009). *The Opposable Mind: How Successful Leaders Win Through Integrative Thinking.* Boston, MA: Harvard Business Review Press.

Messner, M. (2009). The limits of accountability. *Accounting, Organizations and Society, 4*(8), 918–938.

Molden, D. C. (2014). Understanding priming effects in social psychology: What is "Social Priming" and How does it Occur? *Social Cognition, 32*(Supplement), 1–11.

Morewedge, C. K., and Kahneman, D. (2010). Associative processes in intuitive judgment. *Trends in Cognitive Sciences, 14*(10), 435–440.

O'Dwyer, B., and Boomsma, R. (2015). The co-construction of NGO accountability. *Accounting, Auditing & Accountability Journal, 28*(1), 36–68.

O'Dwyer, B., Owen, D., and Unerman, J. (2011). Seeking legitimacy for new assurance forms: The case of assurance on sustainability reporting. *Journal: Accounting, Organizations and Society, 36*(1), 31–52.

Owen, D. L., Swift, T., and Hunt, K. (2001). Questioning the role of stakeholder engagement in social and ethical accounting, auditing and reporting. *Accounting Forum, 25*(3), 264–282.

Paisey, C., and Paisey, N. J. (2011). Visibility, governance and social context. Financial management in the Pre-reformation Scottish church. *Accounting, Auditing & Accountability Journal*, *24*(5), 587–621.

Parker, L. D. (2005). Social and environmental accountability research: A view from the commentary box. *Accounting, Auditing & Accountability Journal*, *18*(6), 842–860.

Perry-Smith, J. E., and Mannucci, P. V. (2017). From creativity to innovation: The social network drivers of the four phases of the idea journey. *Academy of Management Review*, *42*(1), 53–79.

Power, M. (2019). Modelling the microfoundations of the audit society: Organizations and the logic of the audit trail. *Academy of Management Review*, Available online: doi: 10.5465/amr.2017.0212.

Rinaldi, L., Unerman, J., and De Villiers, C. (2018). Evaluating the integrated reporting journey: Insights, gaps and agendas for future research. *Accounting, Auditing & Accountability Journal*, *31*(5), 1294–1318.

Rinaldi, L., Unerman, J., and Tilt, C. (2014). The role of stakeholder engagement and dialogue within the sustainability accounting and reporting process. In: J. Bebbington, J. Unerman, and B. O'Dwyer (Eds.), *Sustainability Accounting and Accountability* (pp. 86–107). London: Routledge.

Slovic, P., Fischhoff, B., and Lichtenstein, S. (2014). Cognitive processes and societal risk taking. In: J. S. Carroll, and J. W. Payne (Eds.), *Cognition and Social Behavior* (pp. 165–184). Hove, UK: Taylor & Francis.

Stacchezzini, R., Florio, C., Sproviero, A. F., and Corbella, S. (2018). An intellectual capital ontology in an integrated reporting context. *Journal of Intellectual Capital*, *20*(1), 83–99.

Thomson, I., and Bebbington, J. (2005). Social and environmental reporting in the UK: A pedagogic evaluation. *Critical Perspectives on Accounting*, *16*(5), 507–533.

Tversky, A., and Kahneman, D. (1974). Judgment under uncertainty: Heuristics and biases. *Science*, *185*, 1124–1131.

Tversky, A., and Kahneman, D. (1981). The framing of decisions and the psychology of choice. *Science*, *211*, 453–458.

UNEP. (2005). *The Stakeholder Engagement Manual. Volume 1: The Guide to Practitioners' Perspectives on Stakeholder Engagement*. Available at: www.mas-business.com/docs/Vol%201%20Stakeholder% 20Engagement%20Practitioners%20Perspectives.pdf (Accessed: 3 December 2019).

Unerman, J., and Bennett, M. (2004). Increased stakeholder dialogue and the internet: Towards greater corporate accountability or reinforcing capitalist hegemony? *Accounting, Organizations and Society*, *29*(7), 685–707.

van Huijstee, M., and Glasbergen, P. (2008). The practice of stakeholder dialogue between multinationals and NGOs. *Corporate Social Responsibility and Environmental Management*, *15*(5), 298–310.

Velte, P., and Stawinoga, M. (2017). Integrated reporting: The current state of empirical research, limitations and future research implications. *Journal of Management Control*, *28*(3), 275–320.

Venter, E. R., Stiglingh, M., and Smit, A. R. (2017). Integrated thinking and the transparency of tax disclosures in the corporate reports of firms. *Journal of International Financial Management & Accounting*, *28*(3), 394–427.

PART V

The content of integrated reports

20

INTEGRATED REPORTING ADOPTION WITH NO SUBSTANTIAL CHANGES

A case study of a large chemical producer

James Guthrie

Macquarie University

Matteo La Torre

University "G. d'Annunzio" of Chieti-Pescara

Abstract

This study investigates how companies adopt the International Integrated Reporting Framework (IIRC Framework). It takes a case study approach using content analysis of a large company's social and environmental disclosures. Despite claiming to produce an integrated report, the findings indicate that the company does not follow the IIRC Framework. This study provides evidence that, when subject to external regulatory pressure, companies may not change their past practices with a new reporting framework. Instead, they may rely on their established internal practices and other guidelines to construct their reports. The study's findings have implications for both academics and practitioners seeking to develop integrated reporting.

Introduction

Since 2017, over 6,000 large European entities have had to choose which reporting framework to use to comply with the newly introduced regulation on disclosing non-financial information, EU Directive 2014/95. The European regulation allows companies to select a reporting framework, making the reasons companies adopt a particular reporting framework a topic of interest for researchers. Bartels et al. (2016) identified 383 non-financial "reporting instruments" in 64 countries that companies can use to disclose their sustainability-related information. Given the wide-ranging options available to companies seeking to comply with the EU Directive, La Torre et al. (2018) called for research investigating why and how companies adopt specific reporting frameworks.

Over the past decade, the emergence of integrated reporting (IR) has sparked interest in investigating the factors behind non-financial reporting adoption. Prior research has focused on the external pressures and determinants of IR adoption. However, Rinaldi et al. (2018, p. 1304) noted that "a key insight is that IR's development strongly depends on its (yet to be demonstrated) capacity to affect organizations' internal processes".

This study investigates the adoption of IR by a large German chemical company. Through a case study, using archival and content analysis, we investigate the company's reporting practices to develop insights into the reporting changes underpinning the adoption of IR. Our findings demonstrate that, despite claiming engagement with the principles of IR, the company's reporting approach does not follow the International Integrated Reporting Framework (IIRC Framework). The company described its report as an "Integrated Report", but there was no substantial change from its previous GRI-based economic, environmental, and social performance reports. This finding suggests that companies are reluctant to adopt current reporting frameworks when they have established information and disclosure practices.

Previous relevant research

This study is positioned in the literature on non-financial reporting. Different terms have been used to indicate the practice of non-financial reporting. These include social accounting (SA), social and environmental reporting (SER), social reports, sustainability reporting (SR), corporate social responsibility (CSR) reporting, and IR. Thus, researchers have relied on a broad set of definitions to conduct empirical studies of non-financial disclosures (Fifka, 2012). For instance, Gray (2002, p. 687) uses social accounting to summarize in one:

> generic term for convenience … all forms of 'accounts which go beyond the eco-
> nomic' and … all the different labels under which it appears – social responsibility
> accounting, social audits, corporate social reporting, employee and employment
> reporting, stakeholder dialogue reporting as well as environmental accounting and
> reporting.

Also, KPMG, which has published yearly international surveys since 1993 to report on global trends in SR, has adopted the term "corporate responsibility reporting" (KPMG, 2017).

Non-financial reporting frameworks: the global reporting initiative and The International Integrated Reporting Council

Over the last five decades, SEA and SR practices have been continuously changing, and the changes have resulted in new terminology and new practices (Fifka, 2012). After about 2010, with increased awareness of global warming, social inequalities, and the power of global corporations, SR entered a regulatory stage. The United Nations Sustainable Development Goals for 2030 is an overarching framework of goals to which a number of countries have agreed (United Nations, 2015).

Other regulatory initiatives include the EU Directive regarding the disclosure of non-financial information by large organizations adopted by the European Parliament (Dumay et al., 2017). The EU Directive requires public-interest entities with more than 500 employees to issue non-financial disclosures, which should include environmental, social, and employee-related, human rights and anti-corruption information as well as a description of the business model, due diligence policies, and non-financial KPIs. The EU Directive, while mandating the disclosures to report, leaves companies free to choose the framework and methods to prepare their non-financial disclosures. However, as La Torre et al. (2018) pointed out, there are over 30 contemporary frameworks for SR that companies can adopt. This regulatory initiative poses both practical challenges and further questions for future research (La Torre et al., 2018).

Of the various corporate reporting frameworks and guidelines used to provide companies with a method for reporting their sustainability performance, the two most commonly used are the Global Reporting Initiative (GRI) and the IIRC Framework. The GRI sustainability reporting framework is used by the world's largest companies, with 75 per cent of the G250 using the framework (KPMG, 2017). The GRI was founded in 1997 as an international not-for-profit organization fostering the use of SR. The framework supports organizations in reporting on economic, environmental, and social performance. The SR guidelines were developed through a stakeholder-based approach with contributions by experts from various organizations and industries. They include specific guidelines for several sectors (GRI, 2013). One advantage of such a reporting framework is the increased credibility of sustainability reports that result from the use of GRI and standardization (De Villiers et al., 2014).

More recently, the IIRC Framework has emerged as another approach to corporate reporting. The International Integrated Reporting Committee (IIRC) was founded in August 2010 by the Prince's Accounting for Sustainability Project (A4S) and the GRI to create a globally accepted framework for accounting for sustainability (GRI and Prince's Accounting for Sustainability Project, 2010). The IIRC Framework itself is limited to general principles. It sets content elements that should be covered in an integrated report and gives guiding principles that specify how the report content should be determined and presented. It relies on the concept of "capitals", which are stocks of value (i.e., resources and relationships that can grow, diminish and be converted during the organization's business operations). The IIRC Framework's six capitals are financial, manufactured, intellectual, human, social and relationship, and natural capital (IIRC, 2013b).

Research into IR adoption

Prior research has investigated why companies adopt the IIRC Framework. For instance, Lai et al. (2016) investigated whether the decision to adopt IR stems from the need to address legitimacy, finding that the adoption decision is neither a legitimation strategy nor a response to external legitimacy pressures. The authors note that IR adopters already have higher ESG disclosure ratings compared to non-adopters (Lai et al., 2016) and that they already have external legitimacy. Thus, external and institutional forces do not explain IR adoption; rather there is a range of studies from performative research investigating internal changes underpinning adoption (e.g., Haji and Hossain, 2016; Du Toit et al., 2016; Guthrie et al., 2017; La Torre et al., 2019a).

Rinaldi et al. (2018) pointed out that the integrated report's ability to shape organizations' internal processes is a significant focus for research investigating adoption and implementation (e.g., McNally et al., 2017; Stubbs and Higgins, 2014). Lodhia (2015) concludes that IR adoption results from the organization's intention to build its strategic position. Thus, the transition to IR is not merely about a response to external forces but is shaped by the change in the values and beliefs underpinning the reporting's internal processes (Lodhia, 2015).

Prior research has also been interested in investigating the implications of IR for internal process and changes. For instance, Beck et al. (2017, p. 191) found that the adoption of external guidelines "has evolved from pragmatic adoption as a means of seeking external legitimation to the present position where those that prepare external reports are informed by the organization's strategic positioning and not constrained by the promulgation of voluntary guidelines". A further understanding of the internal changes as a result of IR is provided by Guthrie et al. (2017), who investigated the internal mechanisms of change that can lead organizations adopting IR to pursue integrated thinking in the context of a public sector organization. Gibassier et al. (2018, p. 1349) demonstrated how the abstractness in the IIRC Framework concepts allows companies to embrace, translate, and reconceptualize IR at the organizational level so that individuals can embrace the "mythical" dimension of IR. Gibassier et al. (2018, p. 1369) argued that:

> the aspirational nature of IR meant that they would need to invent certain elements. The foundational myth of the organization, referred to as the "dual project," instilled confidence among organizational actors that the IR myth could be embraced and ultimately incarnated.

Rinaldi et al. (2018) complemented Gibassier et al.'s (2018) findings by arguing that realizing the full potential of IR lies in aligning its aspirational features "with the company's foundational (or current) socio-economic vision" (p. 1307). However, this emphasizes that the IIRC Framework is malleable to several interpretations that can challenge the IIRC's capitalist vision in practice (Flower, 2015). Gibassier et al. (2018, p. 1349) concluded their study with the view that translating the organization's aspiration into the adoption of IR challenges "the vision of IR suggested by the IIRC to stay true to its conceptualization of IR". This positioning of IR as malleable informs our research question: what are the changes in reporting practices occurring with the adoption of IR?

Research method

In this chapter, we present a case study of integrated reports produced by the world's largest chemical company. PWC (2013, p. 32) outlined how "good reporting" can be developed and introduced some illustrations of "best practices". Our case study organization was cited as an example of "what good reporting looks like" by PWC. The company's actions have also been applauded by several other institutions. As a so-called "best practice" organization, it is an appropriate choice of organization for our study. Additionally, our case study organization joined the IIRC pilot program at its inception.

We analyzed the company's reporting practice in 2013, the first year of reporting according to the IIRC Framework, and the subsequent progression in its reports until 2019.[1] The company's 2013 report was described as an Integrated Report, and thus we expected the corporate reporting practice in 2013 to be an experiment in early adoption of the IIRC Framework.

We undertook an archival and interpretative analysis of the company's public documents and communications to provide evidence of how IR was shaped and constructed within the organization. We analyzed the archival data through content analysis. According to Guthrie and Abeysekera (2006, p. 115), content analysis "is a technique for gathering data that uses a set of procedures to make valid inferences from the text" and "involves codifying qualitative and quantitative information into pre-defined categories to derive patterns in the presentation and reporting of information". Content analysis has to meet specific requirements (Guthrie et al., 2004; Guthrie and Abeysekera, 2006): while there is little consensus on the most suitable unit of analysis, the main element is that the "categories of classification must be clearly and operationally defined".

Since we were interested in investigating IR adoption in practice, we classified our data into three framing devices, which reflect the most evident elements of a reporting practice. According to Michelon et al. (2015), stand-alone CSR or sustainability reports, the reporting guidelines used, and the reports' assurance represent the three main components of "CSR reporting practice", which despite their symbolic function remain the most visible artefacts of companies' SR practice. Therefore, to analyse the reporting practice, we adapted this for IR and collected and analyzed our data and evidence according to the following framing devices, which represent the main constituent and symbolic elements of a reporting practice:

- the report, as the final artefact of reporting practice;
- the reporting guidelines; and
- the assurance of reports.

By focusing on a case study involving a single organization, we took a performativity approach and developed an understanding of practices and their contingencies. Lounsbury and Crumley (2007) highlighted the benefits of performativity in examining new practices, innovations, and organizational procedures. They argued that the notion of performativity "assumes that individual performances of practice play a key role in both reproducing and altering a given practice through variation in its enactment" as its ontological position lies in the assumption that innovations are continually produced (Lounsbury and Crumley, 2007, p. 996).

Results: a case study on the adoption of IR

The story of the company and its previous reporting practices

Our case study organization is one of the world's largest chemical producers by sales, excluding formulated products such as pharmaceutical drugs and coatings. In 2014, sales amounted to about US$950 billion. Approximately 100,000 employees work for the company globally. Its corporate mission is "We create chemistry for a sustainable future", and the following statement "We combine economic success, social responsibility, and environmental protection" suggests a commitment to the pursuit of a sustainable corporate strategy and to the evaluation of its performance not solely in financial terms.

The company's efforts towards sustainable development are globally recognized. For instance, it is in the Dow Jones Sustainability World Index (DJSI World) due to, among other reasons, its risk management and human capital development. Furthermore, the company is listed in the CDP Global 500 Climate Disclosure Leadership Index (CDLI). The CDP is a non-profit organization representing over 700 institutional investors. Those include awards on a national level, such as the German Diversity Prize in 2011 and the award for the best German sustainability report in 2009, as well as international prizes.

The company's commitment to SR has its roots in the late 1980s. Having published its first environmental report in 1988, the first report depicting its economic, environmental, and social aspects was in 2003. The company next reported on environmental and social information in addition to financial performance in 2007. It has continuously presented itself as a pioneer in the practice of SR (Moutchnik, 2013). As such, it has contributed to the emergence of an increased public expectation for more corporate transparency with regard to social and environmental activities and, ultimately, to the establishment of SR as the norm (Wolf and Schwindenhammer, 2011). Additionally, the company has been involved in the further development of the GRI guidelines as an organizational stakeholder since 2005 and it joined the IIRC pilot program business network to contribute to developing the IIRC Framework (IIRC, 2013a). Table 20.1 provides a brief historical outline of the changing nature of the company's sustainability reports.

Table 20.1 History of sustainability and corporate reports

Date	Name report(s)	Type of reporting	Pages
2000	Environment, safety, and health 2000;		60
	Social responsibility 2000		68
2001	Environment, safety, and health 2001;	Separated thematic sustainability reports	12
	Social responsibility 2001		76
2002	Environment, safety, and health 2002;		12
	Social responsibility 2002		68
2003	Corporate report 2003	Sustainability reports including economic, environmental, and social aspects	76
2004	Corporate report 2004		84
2005	Corporate report 2005		100
2006	Corporate report 2006		92
2007	Report 2007		228
2008	Report 2008: Economic, environmental, and social performance		258
2009	Report 2009: Economic, environmental, and social performance	Reporting combining financial and sustainability reporting (since 2008 named and acknowledged as integrated report within the reports)	224
2010	Report 2010: Economic, environmental, and social performance		232
2011	Report 2011: Economic, environmental, and social performance		240
2012	Report 2012: Economic, environmental, and social performance		244
2013	Report 2013: Economic, environmental, and social performance		252
2014	Online corporate integrated report 2014: Economic, environmental, and social performance		
2015	Online corporate integrated report 2015: Economic, environmental and social performance		
2016	Online corporate integrated report 2016: Economic, environmental and social performance	Online reports named and acknowledged as integrated reports	
2017	Online corporate integrated report 2017: Economic, environmental and social performance		
2018	Online corporate integrated report 2018: Economic, environmental and social performance		

Since 2000, the company has continuously published a social and environmental report, despite changes in the nature and labelling of its reports. This shows a development of SR practices over time, shifting from reporting social and environmental information separately toward a more IR approach, by combining various financial and social and environmental reports into one report from 2008. That is, the company started to explore an integrated approach for corporate reporting many years before the emergence of the IIRC and the development of the IIRC Framework. Therefore, the company embraced an IR concept that differs from that of the IIRC Framework and is closer to the idea of "One Report" (Dumay et al., 2017). Furthermore, it started to publish an online integrated report from 2014 to improve users' navigation experience of its annual reports.

The company's reporting practice: a snapshot in 2013

In this section, we present the results of the company's reporting practice in 2013. We analyzed the company's reporting approach in 2013 because it was the first business year after the issue of the IIRC Framework. Additionally, as the company joined the IR pilot program on its inception in order to develop IR and the IIRC Framework in practice, the corporate reporting practice in 2013 should have resulted in early adoption and experimentation with the IIRC Framework. The following sub-sections discuss the results according to the elements framing a reporting practice that was outlined above.

The company report for 2013

The report for the business year 2013 was published in 2014 and is titled "Report 2013: Economic, environmental and social performance" – hereafter "the Report". It comprises financial and social and environmental information and is structured according to the sections described in Table 20.2.

In the section "About this report", the Report is described as an "integrated report which documents … economic, environmental and social performance" and it is further stated that the "report integrates financial and sustainability reporting". Also, the Report highlights how value is created for "our employees, shareholders, business partners, neighbours and the public". Throughout the Report, the company constructs a communication for a wider audience, not just for shareholders and investors. Thus, despite the IIRC Framework stating that investors and financial capitals providers should be the privileged audience of integrated reports, this company adopts a stakeholder-oriented approach (see, Abeysekera, 2013; Dumay et al., 2017).

The Report describes the financial year 2013 (i.e., the calendar year 2013), deploying different forms of communication such as narratives, numbers, pictures, graphs, figures, and tables. Also, many sections of the report refer to the content elements of the IIRC Framework, such as business model, strategy, opportunities and risks, and corporate governance. There is also extensive coverage of topics related to sustainability and social and environmental performance. The sections dedicated to sustainability are placed prominently after the description of the group and its strategy and before the innovation and business model sections. However, there are further sections dedicated to social and environmental aspects of the business, such as: "Working at the company", "Social commitment", "Responsibility along the value chain", "Supply chain management", "Raw materials", "Responsible Care Management System", "Safety, security and health", "Environment". Thus, if we exclude the mandatory and financial contents (e.g., financial statement, corporate governance report), social and environmental issues are dominant in the

Table 20.2 Contents of the Report 2013: Economic, environmental and social performance

Sections of the Report (same order as in report)	Number of pages
Cover	13
About this report	3
1. To Our Shareholders	10
2. Management's Report	
The Group	3
Our strategy	6
Sustainability	3
Innovation	6
Investments and acquisitions	2
Business models and customer relations	1
Working at the company	6
Social commitment	1
The business year	44
Responsibility along the value chain	
Supply chain management	1
Raw materials	2
Responsible Care Management System	1
Safety, security and health	5
Environment	7
Forecast	
Opportunities and risk report	9
Economic environment in 2014	3
Outlook 2014	3
3. Corporate Governance	20
4. Consolidated Financial Statements	74
5. Supplementary Information on the Oil & Gas Segment	10
6. Overviews	16
Total pages	*249*

company's report. The materiality matrix in the Report shows the material topics visualized on a plane indicating the relevance attached to each issue both by the company and by external stakeholders. Items shown in the right upper corner have the highest importance from an internal and external perspective. The materiality matrix shows that the company's disclosures go further than what is prescribed by the GRI.

In an initiative of "self-reporting", the company groups the 38 material topics identified into eight action fields. Those aggregated categories of important sustainability-related matters are: "employment and employability", "energy and climate", "food", "operational excellence", "responsible partnering", "products and solutions", "resources and ecosystems", and "water". They are also reported using different forms of communication (e.g., narratives, numbers, pictures, graphs, figures, and tables).

Reporting guidelines used

Although we expected an early adoption of the IIRC Framework, the Report uses version G3.1 of the GRI guidelines and an application-level A+. Although the expression "integrated" is used, a first impression is that the Report brings together previously separated disclosures on financial and social and environmental matters. However, the company omits to mention its participation in the IIRC pilot program business network; instead it refers to its contribution to other organizations such as the United Nations Global Compact and the GRI. In addition to following the GRI G3.1 guidelines, the United Nations Global Compact's ten principles and the Blueprint for Corporate Sustainability Leadership by the Global Compact LEAD platform are implemented.

Comparing the GRI guidelines to the IIRC Framework, the GRI aims at a change towards a sustainable global economy and is not addressing primarily one particular group of stakeholders, while the IIRC Framework is aimed at capital markets. As mentioned above, the IIRC Framework seeks to increase the quality of financial information investors have at their disposal to make better decisions for their capital allocation. Nevertheless, SR, as promoted by the GRI, and IR are connected since SR provides foundations for the compilation of an integrated report and, therefore, is one essential component (GRI, 2016). Also, the difference in focus between the two approaches becomes noticeable when considering the investor network of the IR pilot program, which demonstrates that the IIRC explicitly values the opinion and concerns of the investing community. Therefore, while the GRI and the IIRC Framework could appear complementary, they are essentially competing frameworks.

As De Villiers et al. (2014, pp. 1049–1050) noted, the IIRC's perspective of sustainability relates to value creation over the short, mid, and long term, which can be accomplished through efficient use of all capitals, including non-financial capitals. However, the emphasis is on financial value, particularly from an investor's point of view (De Villiers et al., 2014, p. 1049). As IR is primarily for financial capitals providers, the conception of value creation underpinning the IIRC Framework means value for investors. The IIRC Framework reflects and embeds a capitalist ideology (Flower, 2015), which pursues the interest of capital markets and economic value (La Torre et al., 2019), and is not motivated by purely social and environmental aims (Brown and Fraser, 2006; Milne and Gray, 2013).

The GRI G3.1 reporting guidelines, which have been applied in the Report, outline how an organization should define the items to be included in an SR. The reporting principles suggested by the GRI for defining the Report content are: "stakeholder inclusiveness"; "sustainability context"; "materiality"; and "completeness" (GRI, 2011). The GRI describes a process comprising four steps: identification, prioritization, validation, and review of topics. While taking into account the reporting principles outlined above, to determine their SR content, organizations should follow a process though which potentially relevant topics are identified, prioritized according to their ascertained materiality, and validated (GRI, 2011). The output is a schedule of material topics (as shown in the previous section) and performance indicators on which to report. The process, which recurs for each reporting period, concludes with a review of the report just finalized (GRI, 2011, p. 184).

Sustainability reporting assurance

To increase the credibility of their sustainability disclosures, companies mandate third parties to assure their disclosures (Dando and Swift, 2003). Although this is not compulsory, the number of firms having their sustainability data externally assured has been continuously increasing since 2002 (KPMG, 2017). This widespread adoption of SR assurance is also due to the recommendations by many SR guidelines that assurance practices be adopted to improve the reliability of sustainability information and increases users' confidence (La Torre et al., 2018).

The GRI promotes the use of external assurance in its G3.1 and G4 guidelines (GRI, 2011, p. 41; GRI, 2013, p. 85). Companies that have had their sustainability disclosures reviewed by a third party can add a "+" to their respective application level (GRI, 2011, p. 5). This mechanism should motivate companies to have their sustainability reports assured. Despite that, several studies raise concerns about the symbolic use of assurance (Boiral, 2013; Boiral et al., 2019a, 2019b).

With regard to our case study, the German Sustainability Code does not prescribe external assurance but points out that it enhances credibility (RNE, 2012, p. 3, 2014). The sustainability data in the "Management's Report", which represents an integral part of the 2013 report, was audited by KPMG AG Wirtschaftsprüfungsgesellschaft. The assurance report is not included in the print version of the 2013 report, but is available online, where it states that the respective parts of the 2013 report were reviewed to provide a limited level of assurance, as opposed to a reasonable one. Any further information on sustainability issues available on the website and cross-referenced in the print version of the 2013 report was assured.

Obtaining limited rather than reasonable assurance has become a common practice (KPMG, 2017, p. 33). Thus, the third party declaring that corporate disclosures are in accordance with the respective reporting criteria will phrase its conclusion in a negative form, as in the case of our organization: "nothing has come to our attention to indicate that the sustainability performance information for the business year 2013 in the Report is not, in all material respects, presented fairly in accordance with the reporting criteria".

The assurance was carried out in line with the International Standard for Assurance Engagements (ISAE) 3000 and 3410 and completed with the confirmation that nothing material had been noted by KPMG that was not presented fairly in the Report. These auditing standards are published by the International Auditing and Assurance Standards Board (IAASB), a standard-setting entity belonging to the global organization for the accountancy profession, IFAC. While ISAE 3000 establishes rules for assurance engagements other than audits or reviews of historical financial information in general, ISAE 3410 provides details for the assurance of greenhouse gas statements. As explained in ISAE 3000, a limited assurance engagement – as obtained by our organization – reduces the assurance engagement risk to an acceptable level. The adoption of ISAE standards for assurance corroborates the accounting sustainability assurance providers' preference for ISAE 3000, in contrast to the AA1000 standards preferred by non-accounting providers (Farooq and De Villiers, 2019). In using ISAE 3000, external assurance providers undertake an audit and review process that is more similar to financial audit and less flexible than AA1000 (Farooq and De Villiers, 2019).

For our company, the external assurance by KPMG and the self-attested application level A+ of the Report indicate a comprehensive implementation of the GRI guidelines. Fulfilling the GRI G3.1 guideline conforms to the German Sustainability Code. Thus, to provide credibility and a reliable appearance for its sustainability information, the company adopts institutionalized external assurance practices, which result from and are influenced by the assurance providers' established routines. There is no reference to IR and the IIRC Framework in relation to external assurance. This is interesting in light of the debate on innovative and flexible assurance methodologies for IR and SR (Farooq and De Villiers, 2019; Maroun, 2018).

Discussion and conclusion

This study was motivated by contemporary regulatory pressures for adopting corporate reporting frameworks and guidelines for SR in the context of the new European regulation on non-financial reporting. We investigated the adoption of IR by a large German chemical company to explore the reporting changes underpinning its adoption of IR and to understand how companies adapt their reporting practices according to a new reporting framework like the IIRC Framework. Our case study demonstrates that despite external forces supporting the adoption of the IIRC Framework, the company's reporting approach does not follow the IIRC Framework and instead continues to abide by its previous corporate reporting practices, by continuing to use the GRI guidelines. There is no substantial change from its previous GRI-informed economic, environmental, and social disclosure and, despite naming its reports "integrated reports", the company's whole corporate reporting approach remains anchored to its previous reporting practices.

While it can be assumed that companies calling their corporate reports "integrated reports" may be a strategic response to a new fashion, in our case, the company embraced an IR concept many years before the IIRC's emergence. However, its approach is closer to the multi-stakeholder model in the idea of "One Report" than that prescribed by the IIRC. Dumay et al. (2017) outline that, while the IIRC has attempted to dominate and control the concept and practice of IR, there are other models of IR. One such model is that proposed by Eccles and Krzus (2010) in their book *One Report*, which differs from the IIRC Framework because it is aimed at a wide range of stakeholders and seeks to foster the links between financial and non-financial information with no prescriptions; the IIRC Framework, on the other hand, is mainly for investors and relies on set principles and guidelines.

The findings of our exploration of one company's adoption of IR suggest that the voluntary adoption of non-financial reporting frameworks is not only driven by a need for legitimacy but is also translated through internal organizational elements and behaviours (Guthrie and Parker, 1989). It also demonstrates that IR is a practice that is open to different interpretations and adaptations when adopted into organizations (Busco et al., 2018; Gibassier et al., 2018; Rinaldi et al., 2018). While the IIRC's rhetoric leveraged an increasing trend toward integrating financial and non-financial information into companies' annual reports (La Torre et al., 2019b), the way IR operates in practice raises some questions about the IIRC's ability to maximize this opportunity and meet companies' needs in practice.

Our research provides regulators and standard setters for non-financial disclosure with some practical implications regarding the adoption of reporting frameworks. First, it helps us to understand the rationales and barriers that can obstruct implementation of the IIRC Framework in practice. Our results provide evidence that when companies' previous reporting practices are well-established internally, new reporting frameworks, like the IIRC Framework, are likely to be difficult to adopt in practice. Second, when an accounting artefact, like the IIRC Framework, is not adopted, we need to reflect on what makes accounting tools relevant/irrelevant for companies. Organizations may choose to adapt their reports in a way that responds to external pressures to adopt a new practice, but without shifting significantly from their previous reporting practices.

Like all studies, ours is subject to limitations. Principally, as a case study of a single company, the findings should be generalized with caution. Thus, we call for further performative research aimed at unveiling the multiple factors that shape the internal processes behind adoption of the IIRC Framework.

Note

1 This chapter uses some empirical evidence from Janek (2014), "Sustainability and Integrated Reporting: A Case Study on the 2013 Report", Master's thesis, Bologna University.

References

Abeysekera, I. (2013). A Template for Integrated Reporting. *Journal of Intellectual Capital*, *14*(2), 227–245.

Bartels, W., Fogerlberg, T., Hoballah, A., and der Lugt, C. V. (2016). *Carrots & Sticks: Global Trends in Sustainability Reporting Regulation and Policy*. Amsterdam: KPMG; Global Reporting Initiative (GRI); United Nations Environment Programme; Centre for Corporate Governance in South Africa.

Beck, C., Dumay, J., and Frost, G. (2017). In Pursuit of a 'Single Source of Truth': From Threatened Legitimacy to Integrated Reporting. *Journal of Business Ethics*, *141*(1), 191–205.

Boiral, O. (2013). Sustainability Reports as Simulacra? A Counter-Account of A and A+ GRI Reports. *Accounting, Auditing & Accountability Journal*, *26*(7), 1036–1071.

Boiral, O., Heras-Saizarbitoria, I., and Brotherton, M. C. (2019a). Assessing and Improving the Quality of Sustainability Reports: The Auditors' Perspective. *Journal of Business Ethics*, *155*(3), 1–19.

Boiral, O., Heras-Saizarbitoria, I., Brotherton, M. C., and Bernard, J. (2019b). Ethical Issues in the Assurance of Sustainability Reports: Perspectives from Assurance Providers. *Journal of Business Ethics*, *159*(4), 1–15.

Brown, J., and Fraser, M. (2006). Approaches and Perspectives in Social and Environmental Accounting: An Overview of the Conceptual Landscape. *Business Strategy and the Environment*, *15*(2), 103–117.

Busco, C., Giovannoni, E., Granà, F., and Federica Izzo, M. (2018). Making Sustainability Meaningful: Aspirations, Discourses and Reporting Practices. *Accounting, Auditing and Accountability Journal*, *31*(8), 2218–2246.

Dando, N., and Swift, T. (2003). Transparency and Assurance: Minding the Credibility Gap. *Journal of Business Ethics*, *44*(2–3), 195–200.

De Villiers, C., Rinaldi, L., and Unerman, J. (2014). Integrated Reporting: Insights, Gaps and an Agenda for Future Research. *Accounting, Auditing & Accountability Journal*, *27*(7), 1042–1067.

Du Toit, E., van Zyl, R., and Schutte, G. (2016). Integrated Reporting by South African Companies: A Case Study. *Meditari Accountancy Research*, *25*(4), 654–674.

Dumay, J., Bernardi, C., Guthrie, J., and La Torre, M. (2017). Barriers to Implementing the International Integrated Reporting Framework. *Meditari Accountancy Research*, *25*(4), 461–480.

Eccles, R. G., and Krzus, M. P. (2010). *One Report: Integrated Reporting for a Sustainable Strategy*. Hoboken, NJ: John Wiley.

Farooq, M. B., and De Villiers, C. (2019). The Shaping of Sustainability Assurance through the Competition between Accounting and Non-Accounting Providers. *Accounting, Auditing & Accountability Journal*, *32*(1), 307–336.

Fifka, M. (2012). The Development and State of Research on Social and Environmental Reporting in Global Comparison. *Journal Für Betriebswirtschaft*, *62*(1), 45–84.

Flower, J. (2015). The International Integrated Reporting Council: A Story of Failure. *Critical Perspectives on Accounting*, *27*, 1–17.

German Council for Sustainable Development (RNE). (2012). *The German Sustainability Code (GSC): Recommendations of the German Council for Sustainable Development*. Berlin: German Council for Sustainable Development (RNE).

German Council for Sustainable Development (RNE). (2014). *Frequently Asked Questions*. Available at: www. nachhaltigkeitsrat.de/en/topical/testseite-dnk/faq/?size=veludpckmnfzxu (Accessed: 8 July 2014).

Gibassier, D., Rodrigue, M., and Diane-laure, A. (2018). Integrated Reporting Is like God: No One Has Met Him, but Everybody Talks about Him. *Accounting, Auditing & Accountability Journal*, *31*(5), 1349–1380.

Global Reporting Initiative (GRI). (2011). *Sustainability Reporting Guidelines Version 3.1*. Amsterdam: GRI.

Global Reporting Initiative (GRI). (2013). *G4 Sustainability Reporting Guidelines: Reporting Priciples and Standard Disclosures*. Amsterdam: GRI.

Global Reporting Initiative (GRI). (2016). *Forging a Path to Integrated Reporting: Insights from the GRI Corporate Leadership Group on Integrated Reporting*. Amsterdam: GRI.

Global Reporting Initiative (GRI) and Prince's Accounting for Sustainability Project. (2010). *Formation of the International Integrated Reporting Committee (IIRC)* [Press Release]. Available at: http://integratedre porting.org/wp-content/uploads/2011/03/Press-Release1.pdf (Accessed: 31 August 2018).

Gray, R. (2002). The Social Accounting Project and Accounting Organizations and Society Privileging Engagement, Imaginings, New Accountings and Pragmatism over Critique? *Accounting, Organizations and Society*, *27*(7), 687–708.

Guthrie, J., and Abeysekera, I. (2006). Content Analysis of Social, Environmental Reporting: What Is New? *Journal of Human Resource Costing & Accounting*, *10*(2), 114–126.

Guthrie, J., Manes-Rossi, F., and Orelli, R. L. (2017). Integrated Reporting and Integrated Thinking in Italian Public Sector Organisations. *Meditari Accountancy Research*, *25*(4), 553–573.

Guthrie, J., and Parker, L. D. (1989). Corporate Social Reporting: A Rebuttal of Legitimacy Theory. *Accounting and Business Research*, *19*(76), 343–352.

Guthrie, J., Petty, R., Yongvanich, K., and Ricceri, F. (2004). Using Content Analysis as a Research Method to Inquire into Intellectual Capital Reporting. *Journal of Intellectual Capital*, *5*(2), 282–293.

Haji, A. A., and Hossain, D. M. (2016). Exploring the Implications of Integrated Reporting on Organisational Reporting Practice. *Qualitative Research in Accounting & Management*, *13*(4), 415–444.

IIRC. (2013a). *IIRC Pilot Programme Yearbook 2013. Business and Investors Explore the Sustainability Perspective of Integrated Reporting*. London, UK: IIRC.

IIRC. (2013b). *The International Integrated Reporting Framework*. London, UK: IIRC.

Janek, C. (2014). *Sustainability and Integrated Reporting: A Case Study on the 2013 Report*. Master's thesis, Bologna University.

KPMG. (2017). *The KPMG Survey of Corporate Responsibility Reporting 2017*. London, UK: KPMG.

La Torre, M., Bernardi, C., Guthrie, J., and Dumay, J. (2019a). Integrated Reporting and Integrated Thinking: Practical Challenges. In: S. Arvidsson (Ed.), *Challenges in Managing Sustainable Business Reporting, Taxation, Ethics and Governance* (pp. 25–54). Switzerland: Palgrave Macmillan.

La Torre, M., Dumay, J., Antonio Rea, M., and Abhayawansa, S. (2019b). A Journey Towards a Safe Harbour: The Rhetorical Process of the International Integrated Reporting Council. *The British Accounting Review*, Available online: 10.1016/j.bar.2019.100836.

La Torre, M., Sabelfeld, S., Blomkvist, M., Tarquinio, L., and Dumay, J. (2018). Harmonising Non-Financial Reporting Regulation in Europe: Practical Forces and Projections for Future Research. *Meditari Accountancy Research*, *26*(4), 598–621.

Lai, A., Melloni, G., and Stacchezzini, R. (2016). Corporate Sustainable Development: Is 'Integrated Reporting' a Legitimation Strategy? *Business Strategy and the Environment*, *25*(3), 165–177.

Lodhia, S. (2015). Exploring the Transition to Integrated Reporting Through a Practice Lens: An Australian Customer Owned Bank Perspective. *Journal of Business Ethics*, *129*(3), 585–598.

Lounsbury, M., and Crumley, E. T. (2007). New Practice Creation: An Institutional Perspective on Innovation. *Organization Studies*, *28*(7), 993–1012.

Maroun, W. (2018). Modifying Assurance Practices to Meet the Needs of Integrated Reporting: The Case for 'Interpretive Assurance'. *Accounting, Auditing & Accountability Journal*, *31*(2), 400–427.

McNally, M. A., Cerbone, D., and Maroun, W. (2017). Exploring the Challenges of Preparing an Integrated Report. *Meditari Accountancy Research*, *25*(4), 481–504.

Michelon, G., Pilonato, S., and Ricceri, F. (2015). CSR Reporting Practices and the Quality of Disclosure: An Empirical Analysis. *Critical Perspectives on Accounting*, *33*, 59–78.

Milne, M. J., and Gray, R. (2013). W(h)ither Ecology? The Triple Bottom Line, the Global Reporting Initiative, and Corporate Sustainability Reporting. *Journal of Business Ethics*, *118*(1), 13–29.

Moutchnik, A. (2013). Im Glaslabyrinth Der Kommunikation. Der Dialog Mit Stakeholdern Über Umwelt, Nachhaltigkeit Und CSR in Social Media. *Uwf UmweltWirtschaftsForum*, *21*(1), 19–37.

PricewaterhouseCoopers AG (PWC). (2013). *Integrated Reporting in Germany: The DAX 30 Benchmark Survey 2013*. Frankfurt am Main: PwC.

Rinaldi, L., Unerman, J., and De Villiers, C. (2018). Evaluating the Integrated Reporting Journey: Insights, Gaps and Agendas for Future Research. *Accounting, Auditing & Accountability Journal*, *31*(5), 1294–1318.

Stubbs, W., and Higgins, C. (2014). Integrated Reporting and Internal Mechanisms of Change. *Accounting, Auditing & Accountability Journal*, *27*(7), 1068–1089.

United Nations. (2015). *United Nations Summit on Sustainable Development 2015 – 70th Session of the General Assembly*. New York: United Nations.

Wolf, K. D., and Schwindenhammer, S. (2011). Vom Business Case Zum Public Case? Der Beitrag Privater Selbstregulierung Zu Global Governance. *Zeitschrift Für Wirtschafts- Und Unternehmensethik*, *12*(1), 10–28.

21

IS THE INTEGRATED REPORT A POTENTIAL SOURCE OF INFORMATION ON SUSTAINABLE VALUE CREATION?

Elisabeth Albertini

IAE Paris, Université Paris 1 Panthéon Sorbonne

Charles H. Cho

Schulich School of Business, York University

Abstract

The International Integrated Reporting Framework, issued by the International Integrated Reporting Council in 2013, has been subject to much controversy. Despite its potential to provide information of sustainable value creation, controversies have arisen because of its misleading concept of "value", which focuses on value creation for financial stakeholders, rather than society, and its lack of obligation to report on environmental damages (De Villiers et al., 2017; Flower, 2015; Thomson, 2015). Therefore, we investigate the type of information disclosed on sustainable value creation in a sample of international integrated reports.

Introduction

There is a growing recognition that intangible assets form a significant part of an organization's business value, which are not reflected in the financial statements (Graham et al., 2005). While physical and financial assets explained 83 per cent of market value in 1975, they explained only 19 per cent of this value in 2009 (IIRC, 2011). Indeed, the current financial reporting system struggles to handle the economic properties of intangible assets since value can no longer be measured solely on the basis of financial outcomes (Guthrie et al., 2012; Powell, 2003). There are prominent issues with traditional reporting, as it no longer reflects the increasing complexity of business models and how companies create value over the short, medium and long term (Barth, 2015; Lassini et al., 2016). There is an increasing demand from investors for information about the risks and the opportunities that companies are facing (Frias-Aceituno et al., 2014). Hence, companies are encouraged to disclose financial information as well as environmental, social and governance information (Bagnoli and Redigolo, 2016).

An essential concept in the value creation process is that companies should expand their reporting to include all the resources they use as inputs to their business activities (Melloni et al., 2016; Robertson and Samy, 2015). Although financial statements prepared in accordance with the International Financial Reporting Standards (IFRS) play a significant role in capital markets and the decision-making of market participants, regulators and key organizational stakeholders increasingly recognize the need for relevant non-financial information not contained in the financial annual statements (IFAC, 2013). Accordingly, the demand for reporting on sustainability performance has significantly increased (Jensen and Berg, 2012; Pistoni et al., 2016). In this context, IR can address these needs since

> [it] brings together material information about an organization's strategy, govern-ance, performance and prospects in a way that reflects the commercial, social and environmental context within which it operates [and] provides a clear and concise representation of how an organization can demonstrates stewardship and how it creates and sustains value.
>
> *(IIRC, 2011, p. 2)*

In recent years, the complexity of the business world has led to growing demands for companies to provide information about their financial performance, corporate governance and contribution to sustainability (Frias-Aceituno et al., 2014; Pistoni et al., 2016). In addition, there is an increasing need for investors to obtain more information about the value creation process, since financial reporting systems imperfectly account for most intangible assets generated or controlled by companies (IIRC, 2017). From a multiple capitals perspective, integrated reporting (IR) can be a powerful means to reduce information asymmetry by providing information on sustainable value creation processes (Adams, 2015; IIRC, 2017).

In 2013 the International Integrated Reporting Council (IIRC) issued the International Integrated Reporting Framework (IIRC Framework), which defines IR as "a concise communication about how an organization's strategy, governance, performance and prospects, in the context of its external environment, lead to the creation of value over a short, medium and long term" (IIRC, 2013, p. 7). At the heart of the IIRC Framework is the notion that companies should expand their reporting to include all the resources they use as inputs for their business activities. The IIRC uses the term "capital" to denote these various resources and identifies six forms of capitals: "financial", "manufacturing", "intellectual", "human", "social and relationship" and "natural" (IIRC, 2013). In addition, high quality information about environmental, social and governance topics signals that potentially significant business risks are being effectively managed, lowering the cost of equity from a shareholder perspective (De Villiers and van Staden, 2011).

However, the IIRC Framework has triggered a great deal of controversy. Flower (2015) argues that, to some extent, the IIRC has abandoned the concept of sustainability reporting since the concept of value focuses on "value for investors" rather than "value for society" (pp. 5–6), and the IIRC imposes no obligation to report damages inflicted on the environment. Indeed, although individuals in the social and environmental sustainability sphere played an important role in founding the IIRC, the IIRC Framework emphasizes future value creation for financial stakeholders (De Villiers et al., 2017). Thomson (2015) argues that "IR reduces sustainability into five sources of corporate value, but sources of value that need to be better managed in order to increase the wealth of individual investors not society's prosperity" (p. 19). Therefore, this current debate leads us to investigate the type of information disclosed on sustainable value creation in integrated reports.

Literature review

Issues with the IIRC Framework

The aim of the IIRC Framework is to improve the quality of information available to financial capital providers to enable more efficient and productive capital allocation (Dumay et al., 2016). Researchers and practitioners now seek to bring together information about strategy, governance, performance, and social and environmental impacts in the narrative section of financial reports (Melloni et al., 2016). These capitals are enhanced, consumed, modified, destroyed or otherwise affected through the activities and outputs of the company (IIRC, 2013). However, some issues regarding the purpose of IR can be highlighted.

First, although IR is viewed as an essential requirement to achieve a more sustainable economy, and greater accountability and transparency at a corporate level (Adams, 2015; Eccles and Krus, 2010; King and Roberts, 2013), several academics consider the IIRC Framework to be exclusively investor-focused, with little to say about sustainability (Brown and Dillard, 2014; Cheng et al., 2014; Flower, 2015; Milne and Gray, 2013). Indeed, De Villiers et al. (2014) underline that the IIRC's framing of sustainability can create conflicts between economic and social/environmental outcomes. For example, while sales of goods and services contribute to value creation, they can also have negative environmental outcomes in terms of pollution. Moreover, since the primary purpose of IR is to explain firm value creation to providers of financial capital, value has to be interpreted according to their interests (Flower, 2015; Melloni et al., 2016).

Second, the IIRC requires a firm to report on the effect of its activities on stakeholders, on society and on the natural environment only to the extent that there is a material impact on its own operations (Flower, 2015). Indeed, a company's integrated report should indicate how the firm, through its activities, has created value measured by the increase in the value of the capitals identified by the IIRC. This poses a problem as some capitals are external to the company, such as natural capital and some components of manufactured capital, such as road infrastructures, airports and port installations (Flower, 2015). Since natural capital does not belong to an organization, stakeholders other than investors support the costs of a net decrease in natural capital (Cheng et al., 2014). Moreover, the IIRC Framework states that: "where a stewardship responsibility is not imposed by law or regulation, the organization may nonetheless accept stewardship responsibilities in accordance with growing stakeholder expectations" (IIRC, 2013, p. 18).

Third, while the IIRC (2013) recognizes that trade-offs between social, economic and environmental objectives exist and should be reported, it does not acknowledge the need to combine different, desirable, but often incompatible forms of sustainability (Coulson et al., 2015; Robertson and Samy, 2015). The question of whether one form of capital can be substituted by another lies at the heart of the distinction between weak and strong sustainability (Van den Bergh, 2010). Weak sustainability assumes unconditional substitution between various capitals, while advocates of strong sustainability argue that capitals are complementary but not necessarily interchangeable (Ekins et al., 2003). The weak sustainability criterion is based on a near-perfect substitutability between man-made capital and natural resources (Figge, 2005). According to the strong sustainability view, natural capital is non-substitutable and should be maintained at or above some threshold levels (De Groot et al., 2003; Ekins et al., 2003). In the IIRC Framework, some components of natural capitals reported are renewable (flora and fauna), while the main part of the natural capital (air, water, land and fossil fuels) is not renewable and thus cannot be replaced by man-made capital. Therefore, this implies that, to some extent, the IIRC supports a weak sustainability perspective.

Signalling theory

Signalling theory is fundamentally concerned with reducing information asymmetry between two parties (Spence, 2002). At the core of signalling theory are signallers; insiders such as executives or managers who obtain information about an individual (Spence, 1973), a product (Kirmani and Rao, 2000), or an organization, which is not available to outsiders such as investors or customers (Connelly et al., 2011). According to signalling theory, voluntary disclosure is a signal conveyed to the market in order to reduce information asymmetries, optimize financing costs and increase the value of the firm (Baiman and Verrecchia, 1996). The claim that communications act as market signals has its roots in earlier research on finance and accounting. Discretionary disclosure beyond regulatory obligations has been considered as firms signalling their stock quality with the aim of influencing market prices (Zerbini, 2017). Externalities caused by the business activity may be positive or negative in the sense that they can increase or reduce the value embodied in the capitals (including the natural capital), and thus increase or reduce value created for the organization (Villalonga, 2004). Hence, providers of financial capital need information about material externalities to assess their effects and allocate resources accordingly (Beattie and Smith, 2013).

Stiglitz (2000) has highlighted two broad types of information where asymmetry is particularly problematic – information about quality and intent. Information asymmetry about the quality of an organization is particularly important when one party is not fully aware of the other party's characteristics. Information asymmetry is also important when one party is concerned about the other party's behaviour or behavioural intentions. According to signalling theory (Spence, 1973, 2002), signals disclosed by these companies can be classified in three categories – intent, camouflage and need (Connelly et al., 2011). Intent signals indicate possible future actions, camouflage signals disguise a possible liability, while need signals communicate the company's requirements to the receivers of the signal (Connelly et al., 2011). In this context, some issues can be raised about the ability of integrated reports to effectively reduce information asymmetry when reporting on multiple capitals.

First, the principles-based approach to the IIRC framework makes it difficult to compare companies. The lack of mandatory reporting allows companies to disclose either their value creation process or the impact their activities have on various capitals, in either an integrated report or a stand-alone report (Flower, 2015). While the principle-based approach recognizes the wide variation in different organizations' circumstances (IIRC, 2013), this flexibility may limit the degree of comparability across organizations. Furthermore, the obligations of those preparing integrated reports are couched in very broad terms and in cases of non-disclosure of information for these reasons, companies can simply explain why this information has been omitted, emphasizing the IIRC's lack of compulsoriness (Flower, 2015).

Second, the lack of compulsory key performance indicators (KPI) increases the complexity of the integrated reports as it allows companies to freely decide what kind of information to disclose about their value creation process (Coulson et al., 2015; Melloni et al., 2016). Indeed, the IIRC Framework acknowledges that "quantitative indicators such as KPIs and monetized metrics [...] can be very helpful in explaining how an organization creates value and how it uses and affects various capitals"; however, it explicitly states that "It is not the purpose of integrated reporting to quantify or monetise the value of the organization at a point of time, the value it creates over a period, or its uses of or effects on all capitals" (IIRC, 2013, p. 8). Moreover, the IIRC Framework accepts that it is appropriate to trade-off a decrease in the value of one category of capital against an increase in another category (IIRC, 2013). Apart from the fact that this assumption clearly refers to weak sustainability, the lack of guidance from the IIRC on how to measure the use of various capitals may greatly enhance the complexity of IR for those preparing it. Indeed, the lack of KPIs may specifically increase the complexity of the capital measurement concept and the impact adoption of IR practices (Robertson and Samy, 2015). In this context, the question is raised whether more companies, some for the first time, will consider and report on the direct and indirect negative impacts that their operations have on human, social and environmental capitals, thus reducing information asymmetry (De Villiers et al., 2017).

Third, the comprehensive reporting of capitals may reduce the comparability of information disclosed over time and between companies. The IIRC Framework does not require managers to adopt the categories it identifies or to structure their reports along the lines of the capitals (Simnett and Huggins, 2015). Hence, it could be difficult to report the use of these capitals in consistent or comparable ways (Brooking, 1996; Melloni et al., 2016). Moreover, the *comply or explain* approach by which organizations should disclose the reason they consider any capital as immaterial, and thus exclude it from the integrated report, may reduce the comparability of information between companies (Flower, 2015).

Thus, from the signalling theory perspective and drawing upon the current debates, it can be questioned whether IR can effectively reduce the information asymmetry reporting on multiple capitals.

Methodology

First, some broad descriptive and qualitative analyses were conducted on the 1,367 stand-alone integrated reports issued by different international companies in 2017 (based on fiscal year 2016) and examined by Gibassier et al. (2018).[1] Second, to gain deeper knowledge on the information disclosed in integrated reports, we conducted a qualitative content analysis of 11 integrated reports published between 2013 and 2016 by French companies. Qualitative content analysis is defined as "the process by which segments of data are identified as relating to, or being an example of a more general idea, instance, theme or category" (Lewins and Silver, 2007, p. 81). We used the QSR NVivo software to carry out the administrative task of organizing the data efficiently (Welsh, 2002). NVivo facilitates data management, coding, text retrieval and theory testing, and has become a widely used tool in qualitative research (Crowley et al., 2002). After this first reading, we started coding the IR published by the companies of our sample using *ex ante* constructed coding nodes derived from the literature from the IIRC framework for the typology of capitals (Financial Capital, Manufactured Capital, Intellectual Capital, Social and Relational Capital, Natural Capital, Human Capital) and from the Flower (2015) classification (internal or external capital, owned or not owned capital, renewable or not renewable capital) that offers capital subdivisions allowing a more in-depth analysis from a signalling theory perspective. During our analysis, new coding nodes emerged, following the process of open coding with respect to our research question, such as "CSR", "Value for society", "Value for shareholders", "Purpose of the IR" adding important new factors into our theoretical framework (Krippendorff, 2013; Yin, 2009).

Findings

Trends in IR adoption worldwide

The worldwide geographical distribution of companies that have published an IR is as follows (we only list those represented as 3 per cent or more): 25 per cent in South Africa; 18 per cent in Japan; 6 per cent in the United Kingdom; 5 per cent in the Netherlands; 4 per cent in Spain; 3 per cent in Switzerland, Australia and Finland. We note that 8 countries account for more than 65 per cent of the final sample, with South Africa and Japan accounting for 43 per cent of the sample. Hence, the diffusion of IR remains quite heavily concentrated in a few countries.

Companies that publish an integrated report mainly operate in the services sector (28 per cent of the sample). This is followed by machinery, equipment, furniture and recycling (11 per cent of the sample). The number of companies with more than 5,000 employees represented only 58 per cent of the total sample, while medium-sized enterprises represented 28 per cent and small enterprises 14 per cent. Finally, two thirds of the companies that published an integrated report are listed. As for the capitals, we note that the vast majority of companies described between 4 and 6 capitals. The first two capitals mentioned were human capital (present in 97 per cent of the reports) and social/relational capital (95 per cent). Natural capital was mentioned in fourth position behind financial capital. The last two capitals were intellectual capital (58 per cent) and manufactured capital (43 per cent).

Trends in IR adoption in Europe

From a European perspective, the companies issuing an integrated report were mainly listed (63 per cent of the sample) and the average number of employees was 29,426 over 313 firms. Regarding the capitals detailed, European companies focused mainly on four capitals: human, social, intellectual and natural. For human capital, companies mentioned mainly the number of employees (93 per cent of the sample); the total amount of money spent on employees (55 per cent); the percentage of employees covered by collective agreements (38 per cent); employee satisfaction/engagement (47 per cent); average hours of training provided per year and per employee (41 per cent); and new employee hires (46 per cent).

With regard to social capital, European companies disclosed information about their stakeholder relationships, focusing mainly on NGOs and academia (48 per cent); legislators, regulators and policy makers (45 per cent); customers (42 per cent); shareholders (38 per cent); employees (38 per cent); competitors (29 per cent); lenders (7 per cent); and distribution channels (4 per cent). When reporting about customers, European companies often presented this topic in a separate section in order to highlight customer satisfaction, new products, and health and safety issues.

When reporting on intellectual capital, European companies disclosed information about their ISO9000 and similar quality systems (41 per cent); brands (40 per cent); corporate culture (26 per cent); company reputation (24 per cent); organizational structure (20 per cent); patents (14 per cent); corporate image (8 per cent); management philosophy

(7 per cent); trademarks (3 per cent); computer software (3 per cent); licensing agreements (2 per cent); and franchises (1 per cent).

For natural capital, European companies disclosed information about their natural capital strategy and actions plans (40 per cent); environmentally related management systems, policies and standards (38 per cent); climate change strategy and action plans (21 per cent); natural capital partners (16 per cent); percentage of ISO14001 certified sites corporates (11 per cent); and water strategy and action plans (11 per cent).

To conclude, despite a call to look for long-term value creation, targets were often absent in European company integrated reports and if they were present, they demonstrated mid-term outlooks. Moreover, companies did not elaborate on some capitals extensively, even if they presented the capitals as key inputs in their business models. This was notably the case for intellectual and manufactured capitals, leading us to conclude that there may be a disconnection between recognizing the importance of capitals in the value creation process and being able to account for it to stakeholders. Finally, while climate change, waste, energy and water are growing challenges, many were not well reported and accounted for in the integrated reports of European companies.

Results from the qualitative content analysis

In a more detailed, qualitative content analysis of French companies' integrated reports, we were able to detail the capitals used as inputs to or outcomes of the value creation process. According to the IIRC Framework, "an organization's business model is its system of transforming inputs, through its business activities, into outputs and outcomes that aims to fulfil the organization's strategic purposes and create value over the short, medium and long term" (IIRC, 2013, p. 25). All companies referred to the six forms of capitals mentioned by the IIRC as inputs in their value creation process. The most cited capitals were social and relational capitals, far ahead of the financial, human, manufactured, intellectual capitals, with natural capital far behind.

When mentioning their social and relational capital, companies almost exclusively described *externally* owned social capital, presenting their key relationships with their suppliers, consumers, shareholders, local authorities and NGOs as key partners. This implies that companies mainly disclose information about their externally owned social capital as a meaningful way of creating value from a long-term perspective. When referring to their *internally* owned social capital, companies frequently mentioned their brands, reputation, shared norms, common values or behaviours as meaningful ways of building a strong capital that the company could rely on in its value creation process.

For financial capital, all companies presented it as a significant input in their value creation process, in a very positive tone and from a very stable perspective over the examined period. Companies suggested that they had no difficulty obtaining cash from investors or loans from banks in a rather long-term perspective. Moreover, almost all companies detailed how they generated adequate cash-flow to finance the implementation of their strategy.

When referring to human capital, companies mentioned either the number of employees and employees' turnover, their human resource management, their training programmes or their job policy. It should be stressed that companies discussed human capital in considerable detail, disclosing information about employees' skills, employability, motivation and ability to work together to implement the company's strategies.

For manufacturing capital, it is worth highlighting that companies never mentioned external manufacturing capital such as roads, infrastructure or water and waste treatment plants as inputs in their value creation process over the period studied; they mainly described their internal manufacturing capital, which played a significant role in their value creation process.

When describing intellectual capital, companies gave equal emphasis to their owned (patents, copyrights, software) and non-owned capitals (tacit knowledge, procedures or protocol) in their integrated reports over the period. Some companies referred to their intellectual capital in very generic terms, without disclosing specific details.

Finally, for natural capital, companies mentioned their energy consumption, giving details about the type of energy used, and their water consumption. Most of the companies disclosed the pollution for which they were responsible for during their manufacturing processes, while none quantified their consumption of natural capital. All companies mentioned their use of natural capital in very generic terms. The word "natural" was mostly associated with some programs implemented by companies in order to preserve the environment and not merely with the concept of capitals or resources. Overall, there was very little information regarding the natural capital used by companies other than consumption of water and energy.

The IIRC Framework (IIRC, 2013) refers to outcomes as the "internal or external consequences (positive or negative) for the capitals as a result of an organization's business activities and outputs" (IIRC, 2013, p. 14). A positive outcome is a net increase in the capitals, reflecting the creation of value, while a negative outcome is a net reduction in the capitals, reflecting the destruction of value. Companies disclosed much more about their internal outcomes than about their external ones, and it is not surprising that they considered they had created more value than they had destroyed. For the external outcomes, companies mainly mentioned the benefits of their socially responsible activities. They also described the impact of their environmental practices in terms of reduction of energy or water consumed during the manufacturing process. There were many references to external outcomes, such as customer satisfaction, commercial success or customer retention. Companies often mentioned surveys that had been implemented to monitor customer satisfaction rates over time, without disclosing much about the survey results. Only one company mentioned its tax commitment as an outcome, without specifying the amount of tax paid. As for internal outcomes, companies mainly referred to their financial results, presenting financial KPIs usually used in their balance sheets and income statements. Hence, the most cited internal outcome was their cash and earned revenue. Finally, companies often mentioned employee satisfaction surveys, yet very few provided the results of these surveys; they more frequently disclosed the decreasing rate of labour accidents.

As mentioned earlier, companies disclosed much more detail about their positive than their negative outcomes and presented the positive consequences of their business activities on the various capitals. When referring to social and relational capitals, companies might describe an increase in a brand preference. Companies disclosed increases in their internal manufacturing capital by describing new plants. Increase in financial capital was reported using traditional financial KPIs. Finally, only one company detailed an increase in natural capital by describing environmental activities, and one company referred to a negative outcome in financial capital because it had faced some significant financial difficulties.

We must emphasize that the value creation described by the French companies mainly benefited shareholders, since all companies disclosed details about the dividends they paid. Indeed, the information disclosed by companies about the capitals used or produced in their business model was primarily related to the financial dimension. Few companies referred to value creation for *stakeholders*, associating this specific value creation with non-financial objectives such as CSR activities. Companies did not present much of their socially responsible activities, and when they did so, the disclosed information was very general and not contextualized, leading us to question the sincerity of these activities.

Discussion

The objective of this chapter was to investigate what kind of information is disclosed by companies in their integrated reports. Our findings showed some interesting issues.

First, from a signalling theory perspective, companies do not disclose negative information about the capitals they use during their manufacturing and selling processes. Only one company disclosed a reduction in financial capital, having been through significant financial difficulties. No other company reported any decrease in any of the capitals. They only disclosed increases in capital or positive information, as though their business models were only creating value, without reducing any capitals. This is somewhat surprising since companies' business models are based on the consumption of some capitals to produce others, at least in terms of natural capital. Our results therefore confirm that from a signalling theory perspective, actions taken by insiders are driven by the objective to intentionally communicate the positive aspects of the company. However, not all the positive information disclosed is useful as signal(s), since insiders may inundate outsiders with unobservable actions that cannot be verified.

Second, from a multiple capital perspective, only four capitals out of six were really mentioned by companies. According to Flower (2015), companies have disclosed much information about their internal capitals, such as financial capital when detailing their equity and their fundraising; internal manufactured capital when referring to their plants; and human capital when discussing their workforce. Information about human capital is not difficult to present in an integrated report since French companies already disclose it in various mandatory reports such as "NRE" or "Grenelle 2". The social relational capital is the only external capital that is significantly cited, since companies rely on it to succeed in their strategic goal of gaining competitive advantage from their partnerships. These collaborations are measured and managed by companies from a return on investment perspective. Hence, information about this external capital is not difficult to report, since companies depend on it from a long-term perspective. The other external capitals – manufacturing capital (public infrastructure) and natural capital – are not mentioned, implying that companies do not consider public goods important in the value creation process. Hence, companies consume these public goods without considering their reduction or replacement.

Third, it should be noted that companies have issued very different integrated reports in terms of either the content or the form. This reduces the comparability of the information disclosed from either the multi-capitals perspective or the sustainability perspective. Indeed, the lack of compulsory reporting allows companies to present information in a way that emphasizes the positive aspects of their business model, while negative aspects such as the reduction in natural capital are concealed, confirming findings reported by Chauvey et al. (2015). When analysing our findings, it was notable that intellectual capital – considered to be the basis of the knowledge-based economy and a key resource for gaining sustained competitive advantage (Dean and Kretschmer, 2007) – was the second least-cited capital, either as an input or an outcome, rating only above natural capital. Intellectual capital, such as operations, procedures and processes, has a positive effect on the financial performance of companies since organizations are increasingly employing advanced technologies to compete in today's economy. There is no doubt that companies rely on their intellectual capital as a significant part of their competitive advantage. However, the examined companies reported little about this capital, either because they did not want to disclose information to competitors about the role of intellectual capital in their value creation process, or because this kind of capital is very difficult to measure as an input or as output. Accounting frameworks were developed in an era dominated by tangible assets, and firms' reporting systems have mirrored this approach. This finding shows that companies are not comfortable with intellectual capital reporting, and both financial and non-financial indicators led to the conclusion that there is no reduction of information asymmetry in this strategic field (Bagnoli and Redigolo, 2016).

From our findings, signals disclosed by these companies can be classified into three categories (Connelly et al., 2011) – intent, camouflage and need signals, as mentioned above and which we elaborate on below.

Intent signals refer to the future strategies of companies. From that perspective, companies describe in detail the associations and partnerships implemented (or those about to be) in order to be more competitive either by offering a differentiation advantage or an effect size advantage. These signals are mainly composed of information about social and relational capital and the expected positive consequences either for the social capital field or from a financial perspective.

Camouflage signals refer to information disclosed by companies to distract the recipients' attention from the real consequences of the company's business model. Companies did not disclose any information about the destruction of the natural capital they were responsible for, while disclosing much information about the reduction of pollution. The fact that companies detail the positive consequences of their CSR activities or proactive environmental strategies as external outcomes while failing to mention the destruction of natural capital is a camouflage signal. This signal is mainly composed of information that presents the positive consequences of practices rather than negative information about the reduction of the relevant capital.

Need signals refer to the requirements companies send to information recipients in order to influence their decisions about resource allocation. Companies seek financial resources from shareholders as much as they seek legitimacy and licence to operate from their other stakeholders. Hence, companies that disclose significant information about the dividends they distributed to shareholders send a signal encouraging them to maintain their financial support. Furthermore, when a company refers to the value it has created for society as a whole it sends a signal to stakeholders to maintain its legitimacy to operate as a company serving the interests of society. Thus, information about value creation can be considered as providing need signals.

We must also note that there is some confusion between *CSR* and *IR* – indeed, several examined companies stopped publishing a stand-alone CSR report from the moment they issued an integrated report, thus considering the integrated report as an adequate medium to disclose their CSR activities. This confusion shows that companies may not fully understand the concepts of sustainability on one hand, and multi-capitals concepts in relation to the value creation process on the other. Moreover, the confusion between CSR and IR decreases the credibility of both reporting systems. From the CSR perspective, companies may find that the operationalization of CSR principles is difficult to elaborate since there is no standardized definition of CSR (Montiel and Delgado-Ceballos, 2014). Moreover, the implementation and management of CSR practices is becoming more complex because of companies' extended responsibilities towards numerous and varied stakeholders (Pistoni et al., 2016). From the IR perspective, companies may have considered integrated reports as a new way of disclosing qualitative information about their CSR activities without presenting the entire list of quantitative indicators requested in French regulations. The question may arise to what extent the specific context of France's regulation prevents listed companies from implementing IR since they already have to comply with extended and certified CSR reporting in their annual reports. The introduction of mandatory reporting in France had a significant impact on the uptake of sustainability disclosure, as shown by the increasing number of CSR reports in the three years after its mandate (Stubbs and Higgins, 2018). The transposition of the directive 2014/95/EU into French law has influenced nonfinancial reporting practices for large French companies.

Finally, for the sustainability academic field, the integrated reports disclosed by companies describe a very weak sustainability perspective. Natural capital is the least-cited capital, suggesting that it is not consumed through manufacturing or value creation processes. No company mentioned any reduction in this capital. For these companies, it seems that natural capital is either unnecessary to their business model, or that these companies do not consider the consumption of natural capital while producing their goods or selling their services. Unsurprisingly, it must be pointed out that no companies presented negative outcomes regarding natural capital, apparently trying to convince us that they either replaced the natural capital they consumed or did not consume any natural capital in their manufacturing process. While companies disclosed their pollution reduction through multiple quantitative indicators indicating the evolution over time, they never mentioned the reduction of natural capital. Again, this finding leads to the conclusion that companies still do not recognize the negative externalities their activities have on natural capital, maybe because they do not "pay" for it. From the companies' perspective, natural capital, which is hardly ever mentioned, is perfectly substituted by one of the other capitals, leading to the conclusion that business models of the sample companies are clearly based on a weak sustainability perspective. In that context, we wonder whether their business models are going to create value from a long-term perspective.

Conclusion

As documented and discussed above, the information disclosed by companies through integrated reports remains clearly incomplete, leading to the conclusion that asymmetries of information are not reduced. Indeed, from a multiple capital perspective, only four capitals out of six are really mentioned by companies. The other capitals are significantly less cited, leading us to conclude that companies did not succeed in presenting a concise multiple capitals perspective. At this stage, there is a need for debate about the possibility of harmonization. Harmonization may depend on the creation of international communities of practices, which bring together practitioners, policy makers and leaders from all over the world (Dumay et al., 2016). Given the IR framework's emphasis on disclosing how a firm's strategy is reflected in its business model, managers and boards of directors should change their views and start to see the business and its long-term perspective in a different light, thus echoing the concept of "integrated thinking".

From a signalling theory perspective, empirical studies are needed on whether investors or analysts change their capital allocation, decisions or recommendations in response to various formats of IR and the information provided in them. From a managerial perspective, more qualitative research is needed to explore how and to what extent IR processes truly alter management control systems, top management thinking, strategy or business models.

Note

1 In their analysis, Gibassier et al. (2018) comprehensively examined and coded each IR using a list of 20 items such as governance, risks and opportunities, strategy and resource allocation, performance, financial capital, manufactured capital, social and relationship capital, human capital, natural capital. The different capitals were coded from the definitions provided by the IIRC framework.

References

Adams, C. A. (2015). The International Integrated Reporting Council: A Call to Action. *Critical Perspectives on Accounting*, 27(March), 23–28.

Bagnoli, C., and Redigolo, G. (2016). Business Model in IPO Prospectuses: Insights from Italian Innovation Companies. *Journal of Management & Governance*, 20(2), 261–294.

Baiman, S., and Verrecchia, R. (1996). The Relation among Capital Markets, Financial Disclosure, Production Efficiency, and Insider Trading. *Journal of Accounting*, 34(1), 1–22.

Barth, M. E. (2015). Financial Accounting Research, Practices, and Financial Accountability. *Abacus*, 51(4), 499–510.

Beattie, V., and Smith, S. J. (2013). Value Creation and Business Models: Refocusing the Intellectual Capital. *British Accounting Review*, 45(4), 243–254.

Brooking, A. (1996). *Intellectual Capital. Core Asset for the Third Millenium Enterprise*. London: International Thomson Business Press.

Brown, J., and Dillard, J. (2014). Integrated Reporting: On the Need for Broadening Out and Opening Up. *Accounting, Auditing & Accountability Journal*, 27(7), 1120–1156.

Chauvey, J. N., Giordano-Spring, S., Cho, C., and Patten, D. M. (2015). The Normativity and Legitimacy of CSR Disclosure: Evidence from France. *Journal of Business Ethics*, 130(4), 789–803.

Cheng, B., Ioannou, I., and Serafeim, G. (2014). Corporate Social Responsibility and Access to Finance. *Strategic Management Journal*, 35(1), 1–23.

Connelly, B. L., Certo, S. T., Ireland, R. D., and Reutzel, C. R. (2011). Signaling Theory: A Review and Assessment. *Journal of Management*, 37(1), 39–67.

Coulson, A., Adams, C., Nugent, M., and Haynes, K. (2015). Exploring Metaphors of Capitals and the Framing of Multiple Capitals: Challenges and Opportunities for IR. *Sustainability Accounting, Management & Policy Journal*, 6(3), 290–314.

Crowley, C., Harre, R., and Tagg, C. (2002). Qualitative research and computing: methodological issues and practices in using QSR NVivo and NUD*IST. *International Journal of Social Research Methodology*, 5(3), 193–197.

De Groot, R., Van der Perk, J., Chiesura, A., and Van Vliet, A. (2003). Importance and Threats as Determining Factors for Criticality of Natural Capital. *Ecological Economics*, 44(2), 187–204.

De Villiers, C., Rinaldi, L., and Unerman, J. (2014). Integrated Reporting: Insights, Gaps, and an Agenda for Future Research. *Accounting, Auditing & Accountability Journal*, 27(7), 1042–1067.

De Villiers, C., and van Staden, C. J. (2011). Where Firms Choose to Disclose Voluntary Environmental Information. *Journal of Accounting and Public Policy*, 30(6), 504–525.

De Villiers, C., Venter, E., and Hsiao, P. C. K. (2017). Integrated Reporting: Background, Measurement Issues, Approaches and an Agenda for Future Research. *Accounting & Finance*, 57(4), 937–959.

Dean, A., and Kretschmer, M. (2007). Can Ideas be Capital? Factors of Production in the Postindustrial Economy: A Review and Critique. *Academy of Management Review*, 32(2), 573–594.

Dumay, J., Bernardi, C., Guthrie, J., and Demartini, P. (2016). Integrated Reporting: A Structured Literature Review. *Accounting Forum*, 40(3), 166–185.

Eccles, R. G., and Krus, M. P. (2010). *One Report: Integrated Reporting for a Sustainable Strategy*. New York: John Wiley.

Ekins, P., Simon, S., Deutsch, L., Folke, C., and De Groot, R. (2003). A Framework for the Practical Application of the Concepts of Critical Natural Capital and Strong Sustainability. *Ecological Economics*, 44(2–3), 165–185.

Figge, F. (2005). Capital Substitutability and Weak Sustainability Revisited: The Conditions for Capital Substitution in the Presence of Risk. *Environmental Values*, 14(2), 185–201.

Flower, J. (2015). The International Integrated Reporting Council: A Story of Failure. *Critical Perspectives on Accounting*, 27(March), 1–17.

Frias-Aceituno, J. V., Rodriguez-Ariza, L., and Garcia-Sanchez, I. M. (2014). Explanatory Factors of Integrated Sustainability and Financial Reporting. *Business Strategy and the Environment*, *23*(1), 56–72.

Gibassier, D., Adams, C., and Jérôme, T. (2018). *Integrated Reporting and the Capitals' Diffusion*. Présenté à 8ème Etats Généraux de la Recherche Comptable, Paris.

Graham, J. R., Harvey, C. R., and Rajgopal, S. (2005). The Economic Implications of Corporate Financial Reporting. *Journal of Accounting and Economics*, *40*(1/3), 3–73.

Guthrie, J., Ricceri, F., and Dumay, J. (2012). Reflections and Projections: A Decade of Intellectual Capital Accounting Research. *The British Accounting Review*, *44*(2), 68–82.

IFAC. (2013). *Enhancing Organizational Reporting*. Available at: www.ifac.org/publications-resources/enhancing-organizational-reporting-integrated-reporting-key-1 (Accessed: 25 November 2019).

IIRC. (2011). Towards Integrated Reporting: Communicating Value in the 21st Century. London, UK: IIRC.

IIRC. (2013). *The International <IR> Framework*. Available at: www.theiirc.org/international-ir-framework (Accessed: 25 November 2019).

IIRC. (2017). *Journey to Breakthrough: IIRC Integrated Report 2016*. London, UK: IIRC.

Jensen, J. C., and Berg, N. (2012). Determinants of Traditional Sustainability Reporting Versus Integrated Reporting. An Institutionalist Approach. *Business Strategy and the Environment*, *21*(5), 299–316.

King, M., and Roberts, L. (2013). *Integrate, Doing Business in the 21st Century*. Claremont, SA: Juta.

Kirmani, A., and Rao, A. R. (2000). No Pain, No Gain: A Critical Review of the Literature on Signaling Unobservable Product Quality. *Journal of Marketing*, *64*(2), 66–79.

Krippendorff, K. (2013). *Content analysis: An introduction to its methodology* (3rd ed.). Thousand Oaks, CA: Sage.

Lassini, U., Lionzo, A., and Rossignoli, F. (2016). Does Business Model Affect Accounting Choice? An Empirical Analysis of European Listed Companies. *Journal of Management & Governance*, *20*(2), 229–260.

Lewins, A., and Silver, C. (2007). *Using Software for Qualitative Data Analysis: A Step by Step Guide*. London: Sage Publications.

Melloni, G., Stacchezzini, R., and Lai, A. (2016). The Tone of Business Model Disclosure: An Impression Management Analysis of Integrated Reports. *Journal of Management & Governance*, *20*(2), 295–320.

Milne, M., and Gray, R. (2013). W(h)ither Ecology? The Triple Bottom Line, the Global Reporting Initiative, and Corporate Sustainability Reporting. *Journal of Business Ethics*, *118*(1), 13–29.

Montiel, I., and Delgado-Ceballos, J. (2014). Defining and Measuring Corporate Sustainability: Are We There Yet? *Organization & Environment*, *27*(2), 113–139.

Pistoni, A., Songini, L., and Perrone, O. (2016). The How and Why of a Firm's Approach to CSR and Sustainability: A Case Study of a Large European Company. *Journal of Management & Governance*, *20* (3), 655–685.

Powell, S. (2003). Accounting for Intangible Assets: Current Requirements, Key Players and Future Directions. *European Accounting Review*, *12*(4), 797–811.

Robertson, F. A., and Samy, M. (2015). Factors Affecting the Diffusion of Integrated Reporting: UK FTS 100 Perspective. *Sustainability Accounting, Management & Policy Journal*, *6*(2), 190–223.

Simnett, R., and Huggins, A. L. (2015). Integrated Reporting and Assurance: Where can Research Add Value? *Sustainability Accounting, Management & Policy Journal*, *6*(1), 29–53.

Spence, M. (1973). Job Market Signaling. *Quarterly Journal of Economics*, *87*(3), 353–374.

Spence, M. (2002). Signaling in Retrospect and the Informational Structure of Markets. *American Economic Review*, *92*(3), 434–459.

Stiglitz, J. E. (2000). The Contributions of the Economics of Information to Twentieth Century Economics. *Quarterly Journal of Economics*, *115*(4), 1441–1478.

Stubbs, W., and Higgins, C. (2018). Stakeholders' Perspectives on the Role of Regulatory Reform in Integrated Reporting. *Journal of Business Ethics*, *147*(3), 489–508.

Thomson, I. (2015). "But Does Sustainability Need Capitalism or an Integrated Report" A Commentary on "The International Integrated Reporting Council: A Story of Failure" by Flower, J. *Critical Perspectives on Accounting*, *27*(March), 18–22.

Van den Bergh, J. C. (2010). Externality or Sustainability Economics? *Ecological Economics*, *69*(11), 2047–2052.

Villalonga, B. (2004). Intangible Resources, Tobin's q, and Sustainability of Performance Differences. *Journal of Economic Behavior & Organization, 54*(2), 205–230.

Welsh, E. (2002). Dealing with data: Using NVivo in the qualitative data analysis process. *Forum: Qualitative Social Research, 3*(2), Article 26. http://www.qualitative-research.net/index.php/fqs/article/view/865/1881.

Yin, R. K. (2009). *Case study research: design and methods* (4th ed.). Thousand Oaks, CA: Sage.

Zerbini, F. (2017). CSR Initiatives as Market Signals: A Review and Research Agenda. *Journal of Business Ethics, 146*(1), 1–23.

22

INTEGRATED REPORTING IN PRACTICE

Practical insights into implementing integrated reporting

Yvette Lange

PwC South Africa

Abstract

Integrated reporting (IR) has gained momentum since being adopted; however there are still questions around the progress and impact of IR for South African companies who prepare integrated reports and how these address the needs of stakeholders for value-relevant information. While it is recognized that companies have invested much time and effort into incrementally improving their IR efforts over the past years, there is also recognition that these same companies need to continue maturing in certain aspects of their reporting. A desktop qualitative survey of eight South African listed companies' integrated reports, considering 31 factors across the reported areas of governance, business model outcomes and key performance indicators, was performed. The factors used were derived from PwC's IR model and the IIRC's International <IR> Framework. The study revealed insights for each of the three focus areas identified and confirmed the need for further enhancement in reporting by companies of governance aspects, business model outcomes and key performance indicators as a way to show strategic progress. Insights from the study are presented together with reflections on findings and practical reporting considerations for companies as they continue on their journey to report in a meaningful, transparent and succinct way.

Has progress been made since South African companies initiated their integrated reporting efforts?

> Why should I improve my integrated report? My board doesn't see the value in spending the time and none of my investors ever ask about it? What I really focus on is the results announcement and presentation.

The question posed above seems to be a reasonable ask: it's the communications around the results that move the share price, not the integrated report – at least in the short term. And in today's technologically driven, data-fuelled, interconnected world, a paper-based, backward-looking document that comes out months after the year-end can seem increasingly irrelevant. Companies say they don't get any reaction to their reporting so they don't make the effort, while investors say reports are boilerplate and lacking in information value. There can be pressures from boards to stay within the pack and not differentiate the company's reporting, or to keep reporting minimalist as part of the corporate image or culture.

From our point of view and based on the global investor research performed, the integrated report does seem to remain an important source of information for investors. PricewaterhouseCoopers has always seen the ability to produce a good annual report as a sign of good reporting discipline within a company generally, and have certainly always believed that the unique mix of content (strategic, governance and performance) and oversight and assurance (executive, board and auditor) means the integrated report still plays a key confirmatory role in a company's year-round reporting strategy.

Producing an integrated report should be part of a company's broader strategic communication and stakeholder engagement strategy. In other words, a company should at all times understand what the information needs of their stakeholders are (including investors) so that they are able to respond in a meaningful, impactful and timely way. In this way, maximum value will be derived from producing external reports of any kind by the company.

We are often told that bigger companies have more resources available when producing an integrated report and therefore their disclosures will be better, but our experience suggests that this isn't necessarily the case. What really seems to matter is that those involved have the support of the board in putting transparency first; that they look beyond the numbers; and that they take the opportunity to communicate their story with both the highs and the lows, making it both engaging and useful to all their stakeholders.

To confirm some of these views regarding the importance of IR for investors, extracts from the 'Global Investor Survey on Corporate Reporting' (PwC, 2017) are provided in Figures 22.1 to 22.3.

Looking back over the years of our IR surveys on the Top 40 Johannesburg Stock Exchange (JSE) listed companies, we recognize the hard work that many companies continue to put into their reporting, and comparing most reports with their equivalents from five or more years back, they would be chalk and cheese. But, after many years of this steady progress, we recognize that companies need to continue maturing in their reporting. Based on a desktop survey we have performed on eight reports, we have confirmed three key themes, each corresponding to what investors find important, as seen in the extracts on the previous page, and thus where companies need to pay attention to derive value from the aims and benefits of IR:

- **Governance:** Investors are interested in the quality of management and governance within a company and look to an integrated report to glean a sense of 'governance in action' within a company and how it contributes towards value creation. Furthermore, governance remains an important area of focus in the South African landscape, given the King IV Report on Corporate Governance for South Africa 2016 and companies listed on the JSE seeking to apply the principles of the code in a way that contributes to the achievement of the King IV's stated governance outcomes, as well as application of the code to meet the JSE listings requirements.
- **Business model outcomes**: In the investor survey, less than 50 per cent felt that companies do a good job of explaining their business model and how they make their money, as well as how they create value for themselves, their shareholders and other stakeholders.

Figure 22.1 Global Investor Survey on Corporate Reporting (Extract 1)
Source: PwC (2017)

Figure 22.2 Global Investor Survey on Corporate Reporting (Extract 2)
Source: PwC (2017)

Defining value creation and specifically articulating the outcomes of a company's business activities shifts the focus from inputs into the business model to a more substantive view of how the company manages the different capitals to ensure they generate sustainable returns and benefits for all of the different stakeholders for the company.

- **Performance with a focus on Key Performance Indicators (KPIs)**: Investors do not show much trust in the transparency of companies with regard to the metrics they use internally to plan and manage their business. Investors can thus be sceptical around the performance results presented and their consistency over a specific time period. Furthermore, it is important for companies to set indicators that will support their monitoring of the implementation of their strategy, and use meaningfully determined key performance indicators with corresponding targets to more accurately, transparently and convincingly report their value creation story to investors and other stakeholders.

I believe management is sufficiently transparent about the metrics they use internally to plan and manage their business.

African investors are less positive with **17%** *thinking that companies are sufficiently transparent about the metrics they use internally, whereas* **39%** *of Asia Pacific investors agree with the statement.*

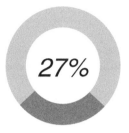

27%

Figure 22.3 Global Investor Survey on Corporate Reporting (Extract 3)
Source: PwC (2017)

For each area, we provide insights from our research, together with our reflections on practical reporting considerations for companies as they continue on their journey to report in a meaningful, transparent and succinct way.

Research methodology

The top eight companies listed on the JSE top 40 (by market capitalization as at 19 August 2019), which prepare integrated reports, were identified and their most recent integrated reports available were used for the purposes of this research. A list of these companies is provided in Appendix A. For each of the companies selected, a detailed assessment of 31 factors was performed across the three areas of governance, business model outcomes and key performance indicators for each of the selected integrated reports. The assessment of these focus areas was informed by PwC's IR model and the IIRC's International <IR> Framework (IIRC, 2013).

Focus areas, emerging findings, reflections and considerations

Theme 1: Governance

The companies assessed seem comfortable reporting on basic summarized governance disclosures. Although a significant improvement was noted, we continued to see 'boilerplate' disclosures in the corporate governance section, which do not adequately reflect what those charged with governance have actually done in adding value to the company.

Very few reports clearly linked the section on governance to the rest of the integrated report – 13per cent of the reports surveyed showed clear opportunities for improvement in this regard. There are significant opportunities to integrate the reporting of the actions and the responsibilities of those charged with governance of the operations and strategies of the company, to provide a holistic view of governance.

Only a quarter of the companies surveyed clearly described their company's culture and values and how these drive governance and the overall tone from the top.

An area of great improvement was the provision of some description of the actual activities undertaken by the board, which was effectively communicated by 63 per cent of reports surveyed. However, 25 per cent of the reports were identified as still requiring some improvement in this regard.

In terms of providing more than basic disclosures in their review of board effectiveness, only 13 per cent of the reports examined were assessed as having achieved good reporting. These reports included disclosure on the logistics and processes undertaken in assessing the effectiveness of the board, as well as extensive disclosure of the outcomes of the review and the follow-up actions planned in future.

Only two companies surveyed provided effective disclosure about board succession planning, while a further four of the companies surveyed made some reference to board succession and rotation.

Gender and race are important factors to consider in achieving board diversity. In assessing the organization's leadership structure, we reviewed integrated reports to determine whether policies and targets for board diversity were disclosed. No mention of a policy or a target for board diversity could be found in 75 per cent of the reports; however, all of the reports surveyed made some reference to supporting policies on broader organizational diversity and related statistics on this for the reporting period.

Reflections and considerations

Within the South African context, reporting is a fundamental part of the King IV Report on Corporate Governance for South Africa 2016 (the 'King IV Report') (King Committee, 2016). It is through appropriate reporting of governance that companies earn the right to the flexibility that a principles-based framework, such as the King IV Report, allows. However, governance reporting also has a wider role to play in building investor confidence and encouraging the taking of a long-term view. Governance is not just about confidence in the financial statements; it is about confidence in the company in general. It is about showing how the company's business model, strategy and objectives, risks, performance and rewards are governed.

Governance reporting is a real opportunity to reap the benefits of the good practice that exists within companies, and to build the confidence of investors and other stakeholders and therefore company value. Few companies currently use this opportunity successfully.

Going beyond compliance – starting to take the communication opportunity

- **Don't just report on processes.** Meaningful governance reporting does not just report governance processes. It reports how governance activities have been applied to the integrated thinking process and the 'backbone' of the integrated report. Useful tips include:

  o Don't just list what the board and its committees are responsible for; explain what they actually did
  o Give real-life examples of what they did; mini case-studies can work well
  o Explain how governance was applied to key challenges or events in the year. Do this particularly where there has been controversy; readers will not be impressed by silence on subjects they expect to see covered.

- **Go beyond the bare facts.** To take one example, in order to comply with the King IV Report, every company has to give information about the roles of directors and the composition of the board and its committees. The biographies of directors generally show that they are well-qualified and experienced individuals. Companies can go beyond these bare facts by:

o explaining the directors' most relevant skills or experience for the particular board
o showing how the skills and experience of the directors complement each other
o when reporting on the board evaluation, explaining why a particular conclusion was reached and what actions arose; not just setting out the process and reporting the overall conclusion.

All of this can make a real contribution to building the confidence of stakeholders in the robustness and effectiveness of the board.

- **Communicate what makes the company distinctive**. The business model is part of what makes a company distinctive; it should capture the essence of the commercial proposition. Establishing the business model is very much part of governance. Companies should also ensure also that specific challenges and issues in particular industries are addressed; too many governance reports could be picked up from one annual report and dropped into the report of another company in a different industry.
- **Focus on the key messages and use structure to help with this.** To start with, decide on a small number of key messages for the reader to 'take away' and ensure that they are clearly communicated. To help do this, think about how the report can be structured. Consider communicating key messages separately from the other required disclosures and 'standing data'. This can be done simply by 'boxing out' information from the rest of the text. Increasingly, these messages are introduced in the chairman's personal report rather than in the main body of the governance report.

Theme 2: Business outcomes

Defining the inputs, processes, outputs and outcomes of the organization's business model enables an organization to explain how it creates value. An organization's business model is the perfect tool with which to explain exactly what the organization does, and therefore how it makes money and thus creates value. An organization's business model illustrates how it uses various capitals, including relationships and resources as inputs to its business activities to produce outputs in the form of products, service, material by-product or waste.

Outcomes represent the internal and external outputs, both positive and negative, of the organization's business activities, with regard to the capitals. Internal outcomes could include employee morale, organizational reputation, revenue and cash flows. External outcomes on the other hand include customer satisfaction, tax payments, brand loyalty, and social and environmental effects of the organization itself or of its broader value chain. It is easy for an organization to focus on positive outcomes while negative outcomes and trade-offs that diminish value are often not discussed. Based on our survey, 13 per cent of the companies we examined require significant improvement with regard to the discussion of the impact of their activities on external non-financial capitals, while the remaining 87 per cent achieved this to varying extents.

After internalizing the value proposition of the organization into its strategy and business model, the organization should develop an integrated dashboard to monitor the relevant input, output and impact indicators.

Integration of financial and non-financial capital outcomes is a key element of the integrated dashboard. Only 13 per cent of companies successfully integrate the management of their non-financial capitals into their core strategic business priorities.

Even though quantification of impacts is not a requirement of the IIRC Framework, this is an area where companies can show innovation in reporting. Currently only 25 per cent of companies make any attempt to link management of non-financial capital with financial performance.

Reflections and considerations

The need for companies to clearly articulate their business model is undeniable. However, in our complex and dynamic modern world, many companies struggle to articulate their purpose, and to demonstrate how they create value, their resilience to change, and the quality and sustainability of the business and its performance.

In December 2015, the Integrated Reporting Committee of South Africa (2015) issued an information paper on outcomes-based reporting titled 'Reporting on Outcomes: An Information Paper'. The paper highlights the same reporting challenges that we have identified in our past and current surveys. Professor Mervyn King reiterates in the foreword of this paper that investors use information disclosed in the integrated report to conclude whether, in their view, management have identified, and managed, all the capitals relevant to their business. He also highlights that transparent disclosure in the integrated report is an opportunity for an organization to re-establish trust with its stakeholders. The paper points out that identifying outcomes should be part of the organization's existing decision-making processes rather than something undertaken only to prepare the integrated report. The paper also reiterates that outcomes cannot be identified without a clear understanding of the organization's business model, strategy, and capital inputs and outputs, as well as the legitimate needs of its stakeholders.

The following should be considered when attempting to explain value creation:

- Discuss outcomes that materially impact on the organization's ability to create value in the short as well as the long term. Companies should define value for themselves and articulate this in the integrated report.
- Disclose information in a balanced way, covering both positive and negative outcomes, and discuss mitigating measures for negative outcomes.
- Consider outcomes specific to the organization, whether within its control or not, and put outcomes in context through integration with other elements of the integrated report, such as the business model.
- Discuss outcomes in the context of the organization's business activities. This includes outcomes up or down the supply or value chains.
- Disaggregate outcomes if this will provide more useful information.
- Consider comparability over time, and comment on outcomes not yet addressed.
- Consider unintended outcomes and how they may impact on the organization's risk management processes.
- Discuss how one outcome may simultaneously impact on one or more capitals, positively and/or negatively, and discuss management's trade-off decisions.
- Consider the cost/benefit of reporting quantitatively and whether methodologies are available.

Creating an integrated dashboard

As referred to in the findings, the organization should develop an integrated dashboard to monitor the relevant input, output and impact indicators. The integrated dashboard is a tailor-made, organization-specific tool developed by PwC (2015) to monitor stakeholder value with a set of relevant management information. As illustrated in Figure 22.4, we set out four steps for developing an integrated dashboard.

The benefits of developing a connectivity matrix and integrated dashboard include:

* Assisting in engagement with investors and other stakeholders by explaining the value creation process in an insightful and intuitive manner;
* The outcomes shown (even without impacts) may provide important insights for decision-makers using the tool; and
* The board and other decision-makers can gain improved insights into the value created for stakeholders.

Theme 3: Key performance indicators

The efforts that organizations make in developing a resilient business model and comprehensive strategy can only be evaluated when performance is measured against strategy on an ongoing basis, using indicators that truly reflect the key areas of an organization's performance. Measuring the success of an organization's strategy is dependent on identifying the right performance indicators – the key indicators that inform strategy. This sounds simple, but it can be challenging to align your strategy firstly to value drivers, and then to KPIs appropriate for providing management information.

Steps to take for developing the intergrated dashboard

	1 Assess available information	**2** Design the connectivity	**3** Construct dashboard	**4** Implement in interanal/external reporting
steps				
Activities	• Define purpose, scope and (integrated) team • Assess current dashboards in place • Discuss user needs and (functional) requirments • Assess available information on all elements and add to dashboard format	• Determine the correlations between the elements • Consider establishing existence of potential connections using data analytics • Analyse the gaps and determine project plan to overcome gaps	• Determine final look and feel of integrated dashboard • Make data logistics connections to source systems • Establish integrated dashboard	• Implement instruction usage and adapt reporting manual • Use integrated dashboard as foundation for board meetings • Use the connectivity matrix in your external reporting • Review and adapt
Deliverables	Baseline assessment	Connectivity matrix	Integrated dashboard	Integrated decision making and reporting

Figure 22.4 Integrated Reporting: Where to Next? (Extract 1)

Source: PwC (2015)

Over half (63 per cent) of the reports surveyed clearly identified the performance measures that were selected to monitor progress against strategy. The remaining reports demonstrated deficiencies in identifying key measures of success.

Companies have room for improvement in contextualizing performance measures. None of the reports surveyed clearly defined each KPI and the rationale for its use, and targets for future performance were only provided in 63 per cent of reports surveyed. This information is crucial in contextualizing how the company monitors performance, yet appears to be a luxury when producing an integrated report.

On average, 19 KPIs were included in the reports – with 25 per cent of these being financial KPIs and the balance being others, including those indicating sustainability performance. Only 13 per cent of the reports surveyed demonstrated clear alignment of KPIs with remuneration policies, while a further 63 per cent demonstrated some alignment. This is an important aspect in creating the right culture to ensure strategy is achieved across both financial and non-financial aspects. It indicates an area of improvement for companies wishing to incentivize appropriate behaviours to create value for all stakeholders in the long term.

The link between remuneration and incentives and value creation is often thought to be one of the true measures of an organization's commitment to integrated thinking. Performance measures in isolation, without a clear link to the reward of those tasked with implementing an organization's strategy, are often not a fair reflection of what actually drives underlying value.

Very few reports provided a clear link between key performance indicators and remuneration policies for executive directors and key management. Most remuneration scheme disclosures included narratives about fixed and variable remuneration, with a statement that these were aligned with the company's strategy.

However, it is not clear how the objectives set for management relate to the company's objectives and key value drivers.

Reflections and considerations

Business performance is under ever-increasing scrutiny as regulations drive companies to consider accountability to stakeholders, executive pay continues to rise, and trust in business remains low. Key performance indicators (KPIs), both financial and non-financial, have long been seen as an important component of the information needed to explain a company's progress towards its stated goals. However, while most companies now identify KPIs, questions remain over the relevance of the measures highlighted. In short, are the KPIs presented really the key to measuring business success?

Tips for transparent disclosure

We believe that a few small, basic changes make this one area of reporting that can easily produce a quick win in improving the overall quality of the integrated report:

* **Linkage**. Explicitly align your KPIs to your strategic priorities, and where relevant, demonstrate linkage to executive remuneration measures. This can be done using symbols, numbers or other icons.
* **Relevance**. Explain why the measures you have chosen are right for your strategy. Make these reasons specific for your company. Investors and stakeholders are looking to understand the choices you make; they don't want to read generic statements.

- **Performance data and rationale**. Give an insight into what the performance data shows, what factors have driven the change and whether this is in line with expectations. Don't just reiterate what an accompanying graph already shows.
- **Targets**. Clearly identify the desired performance of each KPI and when management believe that target can be achieved. Remember to report overall performance in the context of this journey, not just the yearly achievements.
- **Define your KPIs**. Be clear about how you are calculating your measures. Allow investors and other stakeholders to understand what has and hasn't been included in your calculation. This could be done in a separate glossary at the end of the report, as long as it is referenced on the KPI page.

In order to translate your strategy into relevant management information (KPIs), Figure 22.5 outlines a number of steps to complete:

1. Objectives: Clearly understand your organization's strategic objectives
2. Value drivers: Consider what activities the business model should excel at to deliver on its strategic objectives
3. KPIs: Think about how much you want to measure – and whether it can be measured. Remember your aim; selecting metrics that are aligned to strategic goals and tell you what is really happening in the business. Therefore it is important to:

   - Have a clear view of the strategic goals and how these can be measured
   - Find a balance between financial and non-financial KPIs
   - Use leading (forecast) and lagging (past performance) KPIs and
   - Make sure your KPIs provide intelligent, connected information that is still easily understandable and relevant for people throughout the organization

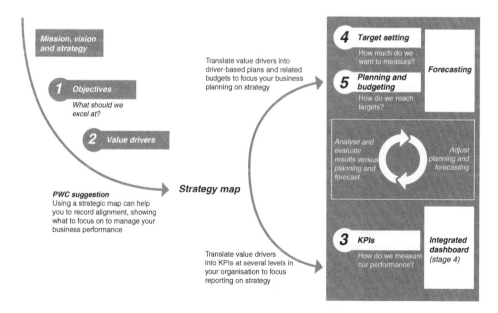

Figure 22.5 Integrated Reporting: Where to Next? (Extract 2)
Source: PwC (2015)

4. Target setting: Your KPIs are also used to set targets and objectives for teams and individuals, against which performance is measured

5. Planning and budgeting: In order to achieve its targets, the organization should develop and implement action plans.

*   **What is key?** The starting point for choosing which performance indicators are key to a particular company should be those that the board uses to manage its business. In our experience, many boards tend to receive financial performance indicators, even though they may be communicating strategies such as maximizing customer experience, or attracting and retaining the best and brightest people.

*   A challenge is whether the KPIs currently presented to the board are those that allow them to assess progress against stated strategies, and when reported externally, allow readers to make a similar assessment. If not, is this because information is simply not available or because it has not yet been escalated to the board, but may instead be assessed by management or individual business units?

*   In addition, the KPIs will, to a degree, be conditioned by the industry in which a company operates. For example, a company in the retail industry might use customer satisfaction as a KPI whereas an oil and gas company might opt for a measure of exploration success, such as the value of new reserves. However, management should not feel compelled to create KPIs to match those reported by peers. The overriding need is for the KPIs to be relevant to that particular company. Management should explain their choices in the context of the chosen strategies and objectives and provide sufficient details on measurement methods to allow readers to make comparisons with other companies' choices, should they want to.

*   **How many KPIs?** Giving the reader multiple performance measures without explaining which ones are key to managing the business does not aid transparency. As noted previously, the choice of which ones are key is unique to each company and its strategy; it is therefore impossible to specify how many KPIs a company should have. However, our experience suggests that between four and ten measures are likely to be appropriate for most types of company.

*   **How rigid is the choice of KPIs?** Management should reflect on whether the KPIs continue to be relevant over time. Strategies and objectives develop over time, making it inappropriate to continue reporting on the same KPIs as in previous periods. Also, more information may become available to management, facilitating reporting on new KPIs that provide a deeper understanding of the business, or changing how an existing KPI is calculated. The choice of KPIs is not set in stone for all time, but the reason for, and nature of, change in KPIs and how they are measured and reported should be clearly explained.

*   **Alignment of KPIs with remuneration policies**. Probably the most popular metric traditionally used to set executive remuneration is to ensure the company is generating returns above its cost of capital. This is meant to give shareholders comfort regarding the investment they have made, and ensure a sustainable return.

*   Social and economic criteria, such as employment diversity, have now become more meaningful metrics, particularly in the South African context. These criteria cover a broader spectrum of non-financial measurements that are hidden from day-to-day accounting but have a direct and significant effect on the well-being of the company. Some commentators have labelled these measures 'soft' KPIs, but since they will

ultimately determine the future of the company, they should become measurements that directly influence remuneration and incentives paid to executive directors.

- Customer service is a reasonably easy measure, but issues such as climate change and the carbon footprint produced by an organization's day-to-day operations are far more challenging to manage and measure. This is a complex subject that requires deep intro- spection at board level. The most useful insights will not come from the kinds of high- level metrics executives use to assess a business's value creation potential, such as return on invested capital, economic profit and top-line growth. Although necessary, such metrics do not reflect the underlying causes of value creation in the long term, but should be viewed as financial indicators supporting the sustainability of the business.

- Finding the right metrics to apply to directors' remuneration is therefore an item that should begin to appear on the agenda in every boardroom. Remuneration committees, acting on behalf of the board, will in the future be tasked with the responsibility to measure directors and management on a new dual basis: financial and sustainability per- formance. Some companies have already embarked on serious policy revision to guide the remuneration committee to include, for example, environmental KPIs, when delib- erating executive remuneration.

Conclusion

With any new concept, attention is often focused on the intended output. In the case of IR, this can result in a disproportionate focus of energies on the end product – the 'integrated report' – without similar time and resources being spent on assessing and improving more holistic business management approaches – sometimes also referred to as 'integrated thinking'.

While many organizations have improved the quality of their reporting, a communication gap still exists between reporter and investors and other stakeholders. We believe every organization will reach its own 'tipping point' – a stage where further improvement requires fundamental change. Simply redesigning the reporting structure or adding some new content won't be enough.

To rebuild stakeholder trust, information communicated in an integrated report and other parts of the company's strategic communications will need to be comprehensive, display the right tone and present a consistent, coherent and aligned picture across all key stakeholders and channels of communication. Corporate reporting, including IR, will only deliver true value for a company if it is robust and meets stakeholder expectations.

Questions for consideration for building trust in your reporting

- What does your reporting say about you?
- Do the messages you convey reflect the reality of your company internally?
- Are the messages you give to all your stakeholder groups aligned?

Boards can enhance the credibility of integrated reports by

- having people on the board who understand a broad range of risks
- including on the board people who can think in an integrated way
- governing internal controls over non-financial and qualitative data
- drawing on the skills of experts to guide and critique
- linking strategy development with the IR process
- engaging external assurers, paying particular attention to the scope of the engagement

Five stages of integrated reporting:

PricewaterhouseCooper's IR approach proposes five stages in the IR journey (Figures 22.6 and 22.7). The proposed stages and steps shouldn't be read as a set of prescriptive tasks; nor should achieving the benefits of IR and thinking be approached as a compliance exercise. Each organization will need to tailor these five stages to its specific situation and remain focused on its own assessment of value and its value creation process.

Each stage is centered on a number of guiding questions, designed to structure and stimulate the thinking process for management teams. This approach supports a continuous improvement process and promises concrete benefits, not only at the end of the road, but also at the end of each stage.

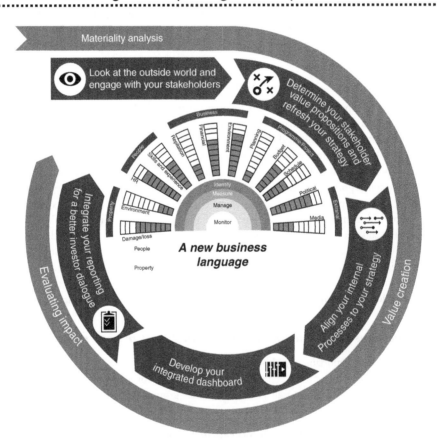

Figure 22.6 Integrated Reporting: Where to Next? (Extract 3)

Source: PwC (2015)

Figure 22.7 Integrated Reporting: Where to Next? (Extract 4)

Stages on the journey	Guiding questions	The cumulative benefits to your reporting
Stage 1 Look at the outside world and engage with your stakeholders	• Have you identified and prioritised your stakeholders and assessed how you engage with them? • Have you considered the business opportunities and risks arising from megatrends? • How well do you understand your competitive position in the market? • How do you assess materiality?	• Stakeholder engagement process • Value chain map • Analysis of operational context and competitors • Materiality matrix
Stage 2 Determine your stakeholder value proposition and refresh your strategy	• How do you define value for your stakeholders? • How do you create value for your stakeholders? • Is your strategy resilient for the short, medium and long term? • Should you refresh your strategy and goals to reflect all your material issues?	• Definition of value • Improved risk reporting • Value creation process
Stage 3 Align your internal processes to your strategy	• How does your organizational culture and behaviour support delivery of your strategic objectives? • Is your integrated management information enabled by systems and processes? • Can you link your strategic objectives to your suite of management information?	• Value drivers • Qualitative disclosures of connectivity • Insight into cultural alignment • Relevant KPIs The first three stages enable reporting disclosures as highlighted as well as contributing to the overall operational benefits listed below.

(*Continued*)

Figure 22.7 (Cont.)

Stages on the journey	Guiding questions	The cumulative benefits to your reporting
Stage 4 Develop your integrated dashboard	• Can you communicate to the rest of your organization how your strategy delivers value to stakeholders? • Can you ensure that your management information provides holistic insight to the board and other decision makers? • Do you make decisions based on holistic management information? • Do you have the right data to drive your decisions? • How do you evaluate your impact and is it incorporated into your dashboard?	• Connected insights into (predictive) relationships between stakeholder value and impact • The integrated dashboard breaks down silos between different departments, clarifying how each department contributes to business benefits • Reduced reporting burden as the integrated dashboard combines several (pre-existing) reports into one overarching report with factual (vs. intuitional) stakeholder value • Communication tool (internal and external) on how the organization creates the value that stakeholders are looking for • Aligned internal and external reporting, improving the efficiency of external reporting processes at the end of the year • Measurement of impact: Total Impact Measurement and Management

www.pwc.com/totalimpact

Stage 5

Integrate your reporting for a better investor dialogue

- Within your existing reporting process, have you nominated a multidisciplinary steering group?
- Has the board provided the steering group with a clear vision? What story is to be told?
- Have you nominated one responsible writer?
- Have you started on a blank page and determined the scope and boundaries?
- Are you using the connectivity matrix (see figure 12) as the storyline?
- Is there a clear communication plan for how to improve the use of the annual report within your investor dialogue?

- External reporting becomes more valuable for your investor dialogue, and for the dialogue with other stakeholders
- Your external reporting becomes the solid basis for continuous and fundamental improvement of your reporting and alignment of internal and external reporting

Figure 22.7 (Cont.)
Source: PwC (2015)

References

IIRC. (2013). *The International Integrated Reporting Framework*. Available at: https://integratedreporting. org/wp-content/uploads/2013/12/13-12-08-THE-INTERNATIONAL-IR-FRAMEWORK-2-1. pdf (Accessed: 14 October 2019).

The Integrated Reporting Committee of South Africa (IRC). (2015). *Reporting on Outcomes: An Information Paper*. Available at: www.integratedreporting.org (Accessed: 14 October 2019).

King Committee. (2016). *King IV Report on Corporate Governance for South Africa*. Available at: www. iodsa.co.za/general/custom.asp?page=KingIVReport&DGPCrPg=1&DGPCrSrt=6A (Accessed: 14 October 2019).

PwC. (2015). *Integrated Reporting: Where to Next?* Available at: www.pwc.co.za/en/assets/pdf/integrated-reporting-survey-2015.pdf (Accessed: 14 October 2019).

PwC. (2017). *Global Investor Survey on Corporate Reporting*. Available at: www.pwc.com/gx/en/corpor ate-reporting/assets/cr-survey-global-final.pdf (Accessed: 14 October 2019).

Appendix A: Companies surveyed

1. Naspers – 2019 report
2. Anglo American – 2018 report
3. FirstRand – 2018 report
4. Standard Bank Group – 2o18 report
5. Anglo Platinum – 2018 report
6. Vodacom – 2019 report
7. MTN – 2019 report
8. Sasol – 2018 report

23

INTEGRATED REPORTING AND CONNECTIVITY

Exploring connectiveness

Eleonora Masiero, Carlo Bagnoli, Chiara Mio
and Maurizio Massaro

Department of Management, Ca' Foscari University of Venice

Abstract

Corporate communication has increasingly attracted researchers' interest, with an increase in research traditions and theories adopted. Among the different principles and theories through which integrated reporting (IR) can be explored, the present chapter focuses on the principle of connectivity. As a central principle that shapes IR, connectivity of information is reinterpreted in this chapter through a tripartite approach. Since our approach differs from the definition provided within the International Integrated Reporting Framework (IIRC Framework), in this chapter, connectivity is renamed "connectiveness". This chapter illustrates how organizations can strengthen their communication by putting into practice one of the six "IIRC Framework" guiding principles, connectivity of information, and by integrating their IR approach with other forms of stakeholder interaction.

Introduction

In 2013, the International Integrated Reporting Council (IIRC) anticipated that the future of corporate reporting was about to move from different and disconnected forms of communication to an integrated form of disclosure, driven, among other principles, by connectivity of information, which "is one of the six principles guiding the content and presentation of the integrated report" (World International Capital Initiative, 2013, p. 1). Within the integrated reporting (IR) context the concept of connectivity is defined as follows: "An integrated report should show, as a comprehensive value creation story, the combination, inter- relatedness and dependencies between the components that are material to the organization's ability to create value over time" (World International Capital Initiative, 2013, p. 1). As explained in the International Integrated Reporting Framework ("IIRC Framework"), connectivity improves when an integrated report follows a logical structure, adopts an appropriate, clear form of communication, and uses navigation tools enabling linking of sections and cross-referencing (IIRC, 2013). Acknowledging that communication technology and digital transformation represent essential tools for improving connectivity, the IIRC illustrates the benefits of adopting digital reports over "static papers and PDF documents" and describes how icons (placed in the report) can be adapted to accompany the reader through the website (World International Capital Initiative, 2013, p. 11).

Illustrating what constitutes an effective communication from a different angle, Brennan and Merkl-Davies (2018, p. 557) adopt a dialogic and interactive model of corporate communication, arguing that the overall communication process "can be improved by offering audiences the opportunity to provide feedback, to query information, and to arrive at a mutual understanding of an issue". Within this framework, Brennan and Merkl-Davies (2018) introduce the concept of connectivity as a key feature of communication effectiveness, but their definition of connectivity diverges from that provided in the IIRC Framework. Using the communication studies literature, Brennan and Merkl-Davies (2018, p. 553) conceptualize connectivity through three elements: "the ability to connect different sections of a text (textual connectivity), to connect texts of different time periods or different genres (intertextual connectivity), and to connect firms with their audiences (relational connectivity)".

Referring specifically to IR, Brennan and Merkl-Davies (2018, p. 564) observe that the principle of connectivity of information provided by the IIRC is "used in a different but complementary manner to the concept of connectivity in communication" literature upon which their paper relies. Building on Brennan and Merkl-Davies' (2018) work, Masiero et al. (2019, p. 13) show that, given the increasingly relevant role played by civil society in asking organizations to account for their actions and statements, organizations should increase their communication effectiveness by integrating "digital media with newspapers' public dialogue and with continuous, face-to-face dialogic interactions".

Taking these perspectives into account, the purpose of this chapter is to illustrate how organizations can strengthen their communication by integrating their IR approach with other forms of interaction with stakeholders. As an illustration, this chapter presents a case study of Generali S.p.A. (hereafter Generali), a global insurance company based in Italy. By relying on and extending Brennan and Merkl-Davies' (2018) conceptualization of connectivity, this study illustrates how Generali achieved effective communication by integrating the IIRC Framework's connectivity of information concept with other forms of relational connectivity. The case study focuses on Generali because it has been an Italian pioneer in adopting the IIRC Framework and because it was awarded the Business International Finance Awards 2018 in the category "Financial Reporting, Integrated Reporting, Non-Financial Informational". Therefore, Generali represents a "best practice" example because its method of connecting information provides insights that other firms can consider when attempting to improve stakeholder engagement. Given the large amount of information potentially available, the focus in this chapter is on exploring the environmental and climate-related information provided by Generali.

Acknowledging that in this chapter the idea of connectivity is conceptualized and explored in a different way than in the IIRC Framework, we decided to use the word "connectiveness" instead of "connectivity" when presenting and discussing the findings. Our findings show that it is the interconnection between different communication channels that enables effective communication. Furthermore, this research indicates that despite supporting the adoption of digital channels and hyperlinks, to reach the wider society, the IIRC Framework's connectivity of information has to be intertwined with up-to-date communications with stakeholders that occur through newspapers and face-to-face interaction. To effectively enhance stakeholder engagement, the information provided by the IIRC Framework should be integrated with a broader spectrum of communication channels.

Voluntary disclosure and effective communication

Corporate communication has increasingly attracted researchers' interest, with an increase in research traditions and theories adopted (Merkl-Davies and Brennan, 2017). For instance, reviewing the accounting disclosure research field, Parker (2013, in Merkl-Davies and Brennan, 2017, p. 434) notes the following theoretical lenses: "agency theory, signalling theory, legitimacy theory, stakeholder theory, institutional theory, media richness theory, mass communication theory, visual culture, and critical theory". Similarly, when focusing on the rationale behind organizations' decision to voluntarily communicate with external stakeholders, most of the same theoretical frameworks apply. Common theories adopted by researchers include agency theory, signalling theory, capital need theory, legitimacy theory (Shehata, 2014), stakeholder theory (Agudo-Valiente et al., 2015) and theoretical concepts such as organizational façade and organized hypocrisy (Cho et al., 2015). As Merkl-Davies and Brennan (2017, p. 437) observed, different theories should be simultaneously adopted to explain the rationale behind corporate communication.

Recognizing that "there is no single theory of communication, which encompasses all aspects of communication" but a dialogue among different theories, Merkl-Davies and Brennan (2017, p. 437, 452) observe that "[a]ccounting communication is interactive", especially in "external communication via social media, which enables organizations to engage in a dialogue with their audiences". In this regard, changes related to technology and social media are driving companies to communicate through different means than the traditional financial statement, thus increasing and speeding up information transmission and changing audience involvement (Hobson et al., 2018). The relevance of an active dialogue is also underlined by Ferraro and Beunza (2018, p. 31), who developed a model showing how stakeholder engagement results from companies actively engaging in a dialogue to respond to "reputational threats", thus enabling mutual understanding with stakeholders. As Ferraro and Beunza (2018, p. 32) explain, "dialogue is a communicative approach that involves deliberation aimed at achieving a common understanding of issues, and determining the best actions to address them."

Communication developments through digital technology

Recent studies have illustrated how digital media have changed communications between organizations and their stakeholders. As Massaro et al. (2017) observe, digital communication presents a new touchstone for the whole literature on corporate disclosure, offering new research opportunities. For instance, Dumay and Guthrie (2017, p. 30) underline that new digital communication technologies had not only enabled the production of more information, but also facilitated its flow and sharing and allowed the dissemination of data not directly produced or controlled by organizations. Digital communication channels, such as Web 2.0 technologies, are changing the way people communicate and exchange information (Massaro et al., 2017; Zhang, 2016), reorganizing "the way in which organizations collect information", redefining "stakeholders' expectations" (Bellucci and Manetti, 2017, p. 874) and providing "new ways to audit, access, evaluate and trade on that information" (Dumay and Guthrie, 2017, p. 30). Thus, the firms–stakeholders connection is changed because of social media applications that allow stakeholders "to receive real-time feedback about organizational announcements and engage in conversations" (Bellucci and Manetti, 2017, p. 874).

As observed by Agudo-Valiente et al. (2015, p. 24) "[o]rganisations need to be aware of the importance of interacting and establishing channels of communication with different stakeholders to identify both their demands and expectations, developing specific socially responsible strategies." Similarly, Brown (2009, p. 325) addresses the need for communication providers to adopt a transparent attitude to enable receivers to "challenge and reconstruct them" In line with Brennan and Merkl-Davies (2018, p. 554), these studies show that the advent of digital communication and social media require providers to acknowledge and adopt new communicative approaches, using alternative communication channels to reach a "wider range of stakeholders" and to increase firm–stakeholder dialogues.

Connectivity: a conceptual model of effective communication

Merkl-Davies and Brennan (2017, p. 433) distinguish between two broad research perspectives: functionalist-behavioral transmission and symbolic interpretive narrative. The latter, named the transactional model, focuses on interactive dialogical communication. In the transactional model, "communication is viewed as a dynamic and interactive process by a reciprocally linked sender and receiver situated in a specific communicative context" (Merkl-Davies and Brennan, 2017, p. 439). Building on this previous work, and especially on the dialogic model of communication, Brennan and Merkl-Davies (2018, p. 557) "argue that corporate communication can be improved by offering audiences the opportunity to provide feedback, to query information, and to arrive at a mutual understanding of an issue." To define what constitutes communication effectiveness, Brennan and Merkl-Davies (2018) introduce the concept of connectivity. Different from the principle of connectivity of information developed in the IIRC Framework, Brennan and Merkl-Davies' connectivity occurs in a two-way symmetrical communication process driven by a dialogue strategy and by a mutual understanding between firms and stakeholders. Acknowledging this different approach to the concept of connectivity, Brennan and Merkl-Davies (2018, p. 564) observe that the principle of connectivity of information provided by the IIRC is "used in a different but complementary manner to the concept of connectivity in communication" literature upon which their paper relies.

Brennan and Merkl-Davies (2018, p. 553) conceptualize connectivity through three elements: "the ability to connect different sections of a text (textual connectivity), to connect texts of different time periods or different genres (intertextual connectivity), and to connect firms with their audiences (relational connectivity)". Textual connectivity is achieved through two main features: "cohesion" and "coherence". The former concerns "the way surface features of the text […] are linked to each other grammatically, to organize text, using signposts to hold together the writing, so it is easy to understand", whereas the latter is related to "the way concepts introduced in the text are linked to each other in meaningful ways, so readers can understand the way the ideas are organized" (Brennan and Merkl-Davies, 2018, p. 562). While cohesion and coherence are means of textual connectivity, intertextual connectivity is supported by digital communications platforms, such as hyperlinks on a web page and social media, tags and cross-referencing tools. Similarly, the use of digital media platforms and social media enables relational connectivity to be achieved through report customization, webcasting and web conferences, online participation meetings, glossaries and feedback loops (Brennan and Merkl-Davies, 2018). Relational connectivity should enhance companies' ability "to respond to stakeholder needs, interests, or expectations" (Brennan and Merkl-Davies, 2018).

Building on Brennan and Merkl-Davies (2018), Masiero et al. (2019) illustrate the benefits of integrating web platforms with other forms of communication. More specifically, Masiero et al. (2019, p. 13) explain that "given the key role played by civil society, to effectively communicate with a broad range of stakeholders, organizations should integrate digital media with newspapers' public dialogue and with continuous, face-to-face dialogic interactions". Drawing on Brennan and Merkl-Davies (2018), this chapter examines how connectivity is understood by the IIRC, and illustrates, through the case study of Generali, how effective communication is resulting from the interconnections between the different forms through which connectivity is enacted.

Integrated reporting

IR: an inclusive response to a demand for clearer information

Voluntarily adopted, the IIRC Framework enables organizations to provide a concise and comprehensive communication of how they create value in the short, medium and long term for themselves and for the societies in which they operate (IIRC and IFAC, 2015). The primary aim of an integrated report "is to explain to providers of financial capital how an organization creates value over time" (IIRC, 2013, p. 4), improving "the quality of information" and thus enabling "a more efficient and productive allocation of capital" (IIRC, 2013, p. 2, 2017). The adoption of IR enables organizations to narrate their value creation to a much wider range of stakeholders "including employees, customers, suppliers, business partners, local communities, legislators, regulators and policy-makers" (IIRC, 2013, p. 4).

Among the academic studies, Beck et al. (2017, p. 192) provide evidence that despite the "IIRC's narrow identification of target stakeholders", organizations' adoption of IR is aimed at responding to a broad stakeholders' group, which exceeds the providers of financial capital. Similarly, Barth et al. (2017, p. 46) underline that "[c]ommunication with investors and stakeholders is fundamental to integrated reporting". In recent years, the shift towards IR has emerged in response to stakeholders and society displaying an increasing demand for companies' financial, governance and sustainability information (Frias-Aceituno et al., 2014). This need resulted, among other factors, from the changing business context subsequent to the global financial crisis and from increasing social and environmental issues (Hanks and Gardiner, 2012; Higgins et al., 2014; IIRC, 2015). However, investors and other stakeholders' calls for clearer corporate reporting and better information already existed in the 1990s (IIRC, 2017), with the growth of non-financial forms of disclosure and a search for increasing report comparability (Adams, 2015; Beck et al., 2017), the need to integrate financial and non-financial information, and to provide an all-inclusive and complete picture of businesses' activities (Adams and Frost, 2008; Beck et al., 2017). Addressing the "missing linkages and lack of connectivity of previous reports" the IR enables organizations to integrate financial and non-financial information in a single document (Beck et al., 2017, p. 194; Manes-Rossi et al., 2018, p. 2). Mio et al. (2016, p. 216) emphasize that the internal implementation of IR can advance management control systems by increasing the "connection with strategy and organizational culture", increasing the "usage of non-financial indicators" and enabling a "better understanding of cause-effect relationships". Another perspective emerges in Lai et al. (2018, p. 1381) illustrating how IR "preparers' narrative mode of cognition facilitates dialogue with integrated report users".

IR: connectivity of information

The IIRC Framework, which leads and supports organizations' preparation of their integrated reports, provides companies with guiding principles and content elements with which to shape their communication content. Since its first development, hopes for the IIRC Framework were high, as shown in the following statement:

> It is anticipated that, over time, <IR> will become the corporate reporting norm. No longer will an organization produce numerous, disconnected, and static communications. This will be delivered by the process of integrated thinking, and the application of principles such as connectivity of information.
>
> *(IIRC, 2013, p. 2)*

Interestingly, within the IIRC Framework, the guiding principle of "connectivity of information" represents "[a] key feature of integrated reports that distinguishes integrated reporting from other reporting formats" (Barth et al., 2017, p. 45). Through this principle, the IIRC Framework supports organizations' connection of their "strategy, governance, performance and prospects" to best communicate their "value creation story" (IIRC and IFAC, 2015, p. 2). The guiding principle, "connectivity of information" states: "An integrated report should show a holistic picture of the combination, interrelatedness and dependencies between the factors that affect the organization's ability to create value over time" (IIRC, 2013, p. 5). Integrated reporting relies on the concept of "integrated thinking", which entails discerning "what" and "how" in connecting "strategy, governance, past performance and future prospects" (World International Capital Initiative, 2013, p. 1). An important feature of connectivity is the connection between qualitative and quantitative information. While numerical information "can lend a level of objectivity and reliability to the integrated report", its integration with narrative information enables the organization to provide additional, important data to enhance readers' understanding about the specifics of the context (World International Capital Initiative, 2013, p. 21). In addition to connecting financial with non-financial information, organizations' material matters, past achievements and future expectations or opportunities, the concept of connectivity involves presenting a coherent value creation story about the organization "in a concise, coherent and logical manner" (World International Capital Initiative, 2013, p. 19). Thus, connectivity has an important role in "establishing the big picture, connecting time horizons and developing a consistent message". As World International Capital Initiative (2013, p. 1) explains: "Connectivity is enhanced when the integrated report features a logical structure, linked sections, cross-referencing and navigation devices such as icons, colour coding or other tools." The World International Capital Initiative (2013, p. 1) highlights the relevant role played by information technology (IT), which, through digital reporting platforms, web-based applications, customized information provision and technology-based feedback loops, is improving organizations' connectivity with stakeholders. In fact, using these tools, IT enables organizations to better respond to stakeholders' needs and interests. In this regard, it should be noticed that "Stakeholder Responsiveness" is another IR principle. Hence, connectivity is also enhanced by the organization's ability to use IT, especially web-based applications and social media, for the provision of timely, accessible, reliable and useful information, enabling stakeholders to provide effective feedback (World International Capital Initiative, 2013, p. 11).

Methodology

This study presents the case of Generali, a multinational insurance company based in Italy. This study adopts Brennan and Merkl-Davies (2018) concept of connectivity, exploring, disentangling and illustrating Generali's communication through the three forms; textual connectivity, intertextual connectivity and relational connectivity. Given that the connectivity lens used to explore corporate communication differs from the one informing the preparation of the integrated report, "connectivity" will be replaced with "connectiveness".

Generali provides an interesting research context for exploring how connectiveness is operationalized, because of its active involvement in developing the IIRC Framework. Between 2012 and 2014 this insurance company participated in the IIRC Pilot Programme, helping to test and develop the IIRC Framework and to launch the <IR> Insurance Network.[1] In 2018, Generali was awarded the Business International Finance Awards 2018 in the category "Financial Reporting, IR, Non-Financial Informational".[2] Also in 2018, Generali was included in the international stock exchange index for Corporate Social Responsibility: Dow Jones World Sustainability Index.[3] Generali considers dialogue with its stakeholders as a relevant activity, as specifically reported on the company's website.[4] In 2015, Generali launched a program for obtaining external feedback about materiality analyses conducted the year before.[5] Accordingly, in 2016, Generali participated in the "Italian National Dialogue on Sustainable Development" aimed at preparing a paper about activities to combat climate change.

The data collected for this study comprises different documents (web pages, videos, reports and brochures) and social media (LinkedIn, Twitter and YouTube), available through Generali's website. On Generali's website, the section "Our responsibility" provides, through various links and archived reports, explanations about how Generali's reporting has evolved over the years, how Generali is reporting now and information about the stakeholders with whom the organization is communicating. The same section also lists the stakeholders with whom Generali aims to communicate. These are employees, clients, agents and distributors, contractual partners, the financial community and the community in general. While Generali's reports are accessible through different links, the "Media"[6] section presents the range of communication and social media used by Generali.

Given the large amount of information potentially available, we focus on a specific topic, exploring the environmental and climate-related information provided by Generali. This choice enables comparison and integration of the data emerging from this exploration with the findings of Masiero et al. (2019).

Given Brennan and Merkl-Davies (2018) concept of connectivity, our data analysis consisted of different phases. To explore textual connectiveness, we assessed the structure of the "Annual Integrated Report 2017", focusing our attention on how the information was disclosed, and searching for the textual features described by the World International Capital Initiative (2013) and by Brennan and Merkl-Davies (2018). A number of techniques were used to explore intertextual connectiveness. First, a webpage analyzer[7] was adopted and used to explore the structure of the website section "Our Responsibility"[8] where the reports are provided. Second, we explored all the connections, selecting a page randomly in the "Annual Integrated Report 2017", relating to environmental and climate-related information. In doing so, we started from the hyperlink on page 23 of the "Annual

Integrated Report 2017". Third, we developed a qualitative content analysis (Kohlbacher, 2006), considering single sentences as the unit of analysis. Every sentence was manually searched in other documents, starting with the sentences available on page 23 of the "Annual Integrated Report 2017". Initially, we explored those documents that were connected through hyperlinks (in the text of the webpages) to the second level of connection. Later, we considered those documents that emerged by browsing through the website. Finally, to explore relational connectiveness, we explored the social media available through the website, taking into consideration the availability of feedback loops on the webpages. The findings section illustrates the different forms of connectiveness, providing explanatory examples.

Findings

This section presents the main findings derived from our analysis, distinguishing between textual, intertextual and relational connectiveness.

Textual connectiveness

Pages 4 and 5 of the "Annual Integrated Report 2017" (hereafter "AIR 2017") provide an overview of Generali's reports and explanations about how the document is structured. Pages 80–81 explain how the non-financial information is disclosed, and how readers can spot non-financial topics using infographic images posted at the margin of the text. A Glossary is provided (pages 98–103), which can also be found via other website pages.[9] After the Index, which introduces the content, on each page, information is presented using short texts that are clearly distinguished one from the other by the colours allocated to titles, subtitles, sentences and the background of each section; by the presence of bullet points and interspaces; and finally by the text style. Additionally, integrative information is provided using notes in the margins of the pages. A case in point is the explanation of the concept "Core&More" provided on page 4 of "AIR 2017".

The use of pictures enriches narrative and numerical texts, integrating information about results, facts, people, places and relevant historical and current events. Pictures provide documents (e.g., the overview of Generali's reports provided on pages 4–5), locations (e.g., pages 12–13) and people (e.g., pages 36–37). With regard to cross-references and navigation devices, "AIR 2017" presents icons (corroborated with brief explanations or page numbers), hyperlinks and infographics placed at the margins of texts. For instance, the icon of an open book followed by a page number and by the infographic "NFS" serves to inform the reader that at a certain page further explanation is available about how non-financial information is disclosed.

Intertextual connectiveness

Infographics and hyperlinks not only allow users to connect different sections of the text within the same report but also redirect readers to external documents or online sections providing further related information. For example, on page 3 of "AIR 2017", the image of a laptop followed by a brief description redirects the reader to Generali's website where the on-line report is available. A further example is the laptop icon placed at the top of page 27, which, followed by a brief text, redirects the reader's attention to the "Annual Integrated Report and Consolidated Financial Statement 2017" for integrative information. Analyzing

Generali's webpage "Our Responsibilities"[10] shows that this website section is connected to 482 internal links, nine external links and has a Link Juice[11] of 98.2 per cent. In this regard, each of Generali's web pages provides, on the left side, connections to all the other web pages available in that section. Also, the webpage text can contain specific hyperlinks leading readers to other documents.

To provide a broader illustration of how intertextual connectiveness takes place on the Generali website, we explored the environmental and climate-related information, progressively moving from "AIR 2017" to other media. Using the hyperlinks on the webpages (excluding the connections provided on the left side of the page), readers can access other documents. For instance, on pages 22 and 23, "AIR 2017" and the "Annual Integrated Report and Consolidated Financial Statements 2017" both discuss the group's policy on Environment and Climate-related topics. Through the hyperlink placed at the bottom left of page 23, the reader has access to a webpage providing similar information plus additional, related material. In turn, again excluding the connections provided on the left side of the page, this page gives access to a series of other documents, such as a press release document, a PDF technical note and other related content. Each of these supplementary materials enlarges upon previous information provided through "AIR 2017" and adds additional data by exploring other specific themes. Starting from "AIR 2017" and exploring the content of each document through to the second level of connection shows that specific environmental and climate-related information is traceable through other documents and has been updated over time both before and after the publication of "AIR 2017". Also, on navigating through Generali's website, it is apparent that part of the "AIR 2017" environmental and climate-related information is also available as videos and interviews. For instance, the same information is accessible through the section "Media".[12]

Relational connectiveness

Simultaneously with Generali's full-year results release, the group was also active on social networks, uploading posts on Twitter and LinkedIn and receiving feedback from stakeholders on these channels. Looking at the differences between Twitter and LinkedIn, the former reports a post from Ansa English News and a CNBCJ interview to the Group CEO. The latter provides a link to YouTube, making available different interviews. In this regard, browsing on YouTube, information about the full year 2017 results and climate change policy is retraceable again in a video which obtained 1,418 views (www.youtube.com/user/GruppoGenerali?reload=9 – accessed 09/07/2019).

With regard to feedback loops, Generali uses a variety of strategies. For instance, to collect feedback about the 2018 report, Generali invites readers to submit their comments to integratedreporting@generali.com.[13] Furthermore, at the bottom of each page of Generali's[14] website page there is an icon offering readers the opportunity to take a two-minute surve. By clicking on the virtual red button, the reader has access to a window explaining and providing an anonymous survey structured in three parts. The first section asks the reader to identify him/herself given a range of stakeholder possibilities (client, job seeker, employee, analyst, investor, shareholder, media/journalist, blogger, media rep, CSR/SR professional, NGO representative, suppliers). The second part asks the reader to evaluate, on a scale of 1 to 5, seven topics related to the website. These are Usability, Graphics, Contents, Technical Performance, Mobile Optimization, Interactive Tools, Accessibility. Finally, there is the opportunity for the reader to add a comment of up to 500 words.

Integrating these findings with the results of Masiero et al. (2019), this chapter illustrates how Generali integrates information obtained from a range of sources. Specifically, Masiero et al. (2019, p. 7) explain how Generali's communication with stakeholders (throughout 2018) consisted of a continuous dialogue, which by going beyond the information provided in "AIR 2017", aimed at responding to the stakeholders' needs and expectations by continuously considering their feedback and replying with additional information and explanations "through different means (public and private meetings, interviews, round table, formal documents)" tailored to the different stakeholders. Using longitudinal analysis Masiero et al. (2019) show how dialogue with stakeholders to achieve a common understanding and approach to critical topics led the more sceptical stakeholders to progressively change their opinions, from negative to positive, about Generali's approach to critical matters. Based on Masiero et al.'s (2019, p. 7) findings illustrates how the dialogue led to a common understanding between the organization and its stakeholders.

Discussion and conclusion

Among the different approaches and theories via which external communication can be explored, this chapter selected connectivity, as conceptualized by Brennan and Merkl-Davies (2018) and renamed it connectiveness to distinguish it from the definition of connectivity of information shaping the integrated report. Brennan and Merkl-Davies (2018) describe connectiveness as connecting "different sections of a text (textual connectiveness)", "texts of different periods or different genres (intertextual connectiveness)" and, finally, as connecting "firms and their audiences (relational connectiveness)" (Brennan and Merkl-Davies, 2018, pp. 553–554). Adopting this tripartite approach, this chapter illustrates how organizations can strengthen their communication by putting into practice one of the six IIRC guiding principles, connectivity of information and by integrating their IR approach with other forms of interaction with stakeholders.

Acknowledging that communication technology and digital transformation represent essential tools for improving connectiveness, the IR guidelines illustrate the benefits of adopting digital reports and describe how icons placed in the report can be used to guide the reader through the website (World International Capital Initiative, 2013). Despite not entering in the specifics of IR structure, Brennan and Merkl-Davies (2018, p. 564) emphasized that the concept of connectivity of information as conceptualized by IIRC is "used in a different but complementary manner to the concept of connectivity in communication" developed in their paper. The recent study by Masiero et al. (2019, p. 13) adds to Brennan and Merkl-Davies (2018) seminal research by showing that "to effectively communicate with a broad range of stakeholders, organizations should integrate digital media with newspapers' public dialogue and with continuous, face-to-face dialogic interactions". To illustrate how this integration is enacted, this chapter presents a case study of Generali, a global insurance company based in Italy. Generali was selected because it was among the Italian pioneers adopting IR, and because it has recently been awarded the "Business International Finance Awards 2018 in the category Financial Reporting, Integrated Reporting, NonFinancial Informational".

Starting by showing how textual connectiveness is enacted in Generali's integrated report, our findings show that Generali's "AIR 2017" facilitates readers' connection with relevant concepts in two ways. "AIR 2017" dedicates some pages, at the beginning and the end of the report, to an explanation of how and where information is reported and clarifies the meaning of the infographics used. The report also differentiates and highlights texts and headings. In this regard, in each page, text comprehension and content connection are facilitated not only by the use of icons and infographics, but also through the adoption of different colours for the background and for the text, the size of the text, adding notes at the margins of the pages, and communicating using short paragraphs and colourful images.

The communication technique adopted by Generali in its "AIR 2017" is in line with the principle of connectivity described by the World International Capital Initiative (2013, p. 19) thus avoiding repetitions and enhancing transparency. Generali's communication is aligned also with Brennan and Merkl-Davies' (2018, p. 562) description of textual connectiveness where the "cohesion" of the writing and the "coherence" of the concepts' presentation represent two key aspects for enabling textual connectiveness. In this regard, Generali's approach increases stakeholders' understanding and engagement, while reducing the level of complexity as described in a recent paper by Lai et al. (2018), illustrating how dialogue with stakeholders is enhanced through IR narratives.

Exploring intertextual connectiveness, we found that Generali supports its readers by providing cross-referencing tools and navigation devices. Infographics and hyperlinks in the margins of the text serve not only to connect different sections of the report but also to redirect readers to a range of external documents, thus deepening the focus on specific themes, or updating, over time, the information provided in the report. The application of these communication techniques is in line with the World International Capital Initiative (2013, p. 19) document on applying the principle of connectivity of information and it is also aligned with the definition and implementation of intertextual connectiveness as presented by Brennan and Merkl-Davies (2018, p. 566).

Additionally, Generali's adoption and connection of a range of digital communication channels demonstrates on one hand how the Group's commitment to interacting with stakeholders is put into practice, and on the other hand provides a further example of how digital technologies support communication and customization (Agudo-Valiente et al., 2015; Massaro et al., 2017; World International Capital Initiative, 2013; Zhang, 2016). Our findings illustrate that in addition to interconnecting different corporate media, Generali corroborates its external communication with videos and interviews available on its website multimedia gallery.

Following Brennan and Merkl-Davies' (2018, p. 566) description of relational connectiveness, Generali emerges as proactive in organizing, presenting and enhancing the understanding of the information provided to a broad spectrum of stakeholders, thus fostering "accessibility". For instance, the glossaries in "AIR 2017" and the website enable non-expert readers to understand the meaning of specific or technical information. Another important feature of relational connectiveness achieved by Generali is the way in which Generali enables "stakeholder responsiveness" (World International Capital Initiative, 2013). In addition to connecting with different media, Generali enriches communication by providing videos and interviews, making them available on the website and social media. Similarly, Generali incentivizes stakeholders' feedback through a variety of methods.

More importantly, Generali updates the information provided over time and makes it accessible, thus enhancing "informativity" (Brennan and Merkl-Davies, 2018, p. 566). As the findings of Masiero et al. (2019) show, Generali's commitment to achieving an effective dialogue with a broader spectrum of stakeholders has led the organization to adopt the use of digital media, integrating digital media and newspapers' public dialogues with direct face-to-face continuous dialogue. The findings show how dialogue improves mutual understanding. The connectiveness provided through the IR becomes the starting point for integrated multimedia communication, which expands into a real-time, fruitful dialogue.

Considering the observations by Bellucci and Manetti (2017)that social media have changed firm–stakeholder connections by facilitating the diffusion of updated information and supporting stakeholders' ability to provide feedback, this chapter provides an example of how organizations' awareness of the relevance of adopting a broad connectiveness approach can effectively enable them to enhance fruitful, continuous dialogue. This chapter adds to previous studies of Generali that explored integrated report-related matters, showing how the internal implementation of an IR can advance Management Control Systems (Mio et al., 2016) and illustrating how dialogue with stakeholders is enhanced through IR narratives (Lai et al., 2018). Furthermore, this chapter integrates the work by Masiero et al. (2019) by focusing on how Generali intertwined the three forms of connectiveness conceptualized by Brennan and Merkl-Davies (2018) to enable a constant dialogue with stakeholders using a variety of techniques.

Notes

1 See: http://integratedreporting.org/profile/generali-group/
2 See: www.generali.com/media/News/Assicurazioni-Generali-won-at-the-2018-Business-Inter national-Finance-Awards
3 See: www.generali.com/media/press-releases/all/2018/Generali-has-been-included-in-the-Dow-Jones-Sustainability-World-Index
4 See: www.generali.com/our-responsibilities/responsible-investments
5 See: www.generali.com/our-responsibilities/responsible-business/Materiality-Matrix
6 See: www.generali.com/media
7 See: www.seowebpageanalyzer.com/
8 See: www.generali.com/our-responsibilities
9 See: www.generali.com/info/glossary, and www.generali.com/media/press-releases/all/2018/Finan cial-Information-at-30-September-2018-Press-Release
10 See: www.generali.com/our-responsibilities
11 See: www.searchmetrics.com/glossary/link-juice/
12 See: www.generali.com/media/multimedia-gallery/video/interviews
13 See: http://integratedreporting.org/profile/generali-group/
14 See: www.generali.com/

References

Adams, C. A. (2015). Critical perspectives on accounting the international integrated reporting council: A call to action. *Critical Perspectives on Accounting, 27*, 23–28.

Adams, C. A., and Frost, G. R. (2008). Managing social and environmental performance: Do companies have adequate information? *Australian Accounting Review, 17*(43), 2–11.

Agudo-Valiente, J. M., Garcés-Ayerbe, C., and Salvador-Figueras, M. (2015). Corporate social performance and stakeholder dialogue management. *Corporate Social Responsibility and Environmental Management, 22*, 13–31.

Barth, M. E., Cahan, S. F., Chen, L., and Venter, E. R. (2017). The economic consequences associated with integrated report quality: Capital market and real effects. *Accounting, Organizations and Society, 62*, 43–64.

Beck, C., Dumay, J., and Frost, G. (2017). In pursuit of a 'single source of truth': From threatened legitimacy to integrated reporting. *Journal of Business Ethics, 141*(1), 191–205.

Bellucci, M., and Manetti, G. (2017). Facebook as a tool for supporting dialogic accounting? Evidence from large philanthropic foundations in the United States. *Accounting, Auditing & Accountability Journal, 30*(4), 874–905.

Brennan, N. M., and Merkl-Davies, D. M. (2018). Do firms effectively communicate with financial stakeholders? A conceptual model of corporate communication in a capital market context. *Accounting and Business Research, 48*(5), 553–577.

Brown, J. (2009). Democracy, sustainability and dialogic accounting technologies: Taking pluralism seriously. *Critical Perspectives on Accounting, 20*(3), 313–342.

Cho, C. H., Laine, M., Roberts, R. W., and Rodrigue, M. (2015). Organized hypocrisy, organizational façades, and sustainability reporting. *Accounting, Organizations and Society, 40*, 78–94.

Dumay, J., and Guthrie, J. (2017). Involuntary disclosure of intellectual capital: Is it relevant? *Journal of Intellectual Capital, 18*(1), 29–44.

Ferraro, F., and Beunza, D. (2018). Creating common ground: A communicative action model of dialogue in shareholder engagement. *Organization Science, 29*(6), 989–1236.

Frias-Aceituno, J. V., Rodríguez-Ariza, L., and Garcia-Sánchez, I. M. (2014). Explanatory factors of integrated sustainability and financial reporting. *Business Strategy and the Environment, 23*(1), 56–72.

Hanks, J., and Gardiner, L. (2012). *Integrated Reporting: Lessons from the South African Experience.* Washington, DC: IFC.

Higgins, C., Stubbs, W., and Love, T. (2014). Walking the talk(s): Organisational narratives of integrated reporting. *Accounting, Auditing and Accountability Journal, 27*(7), 1090–1119.

Hobson, J., Libby, R., and Tan, H. T. (2018). New corporate disclosures and new methods. *Accounting, Organizations and Society, 68–69*, v–vii.

IIRC. (2013). *The International <IR> Framework.* Available at: https://integratedreporting.org/resource/international-ir-framework/ (Accessed: 7 December 2019).

IIRC. (2015). *Progress Through Reporting IIRC Integrated Report 2015.* Available at: https://integratedreporting.org/wp-content/uploads/2014/12/IIRC-Integrated-Report-2015.pdf (Accessed: 7 December 2019).

IIRC. (2017). *Creating Value. Benefits to Investors.* Available at: https://integratedreporting.org/resource/creating-value-benefits-to-investors/ (Accessed: 7 December 2019).

IIRC and IFAC. (2015). *Materiality in <IR> Guidance for the Preparation of Integrated Reports.* Available at: https://integratedreporting.org/wp-content/uploads/2015/11/1315_MaterialityinIR_Doc_4a_Interactive.pdf (Accessed: 7 December 2019).

Kohlbacher, F. (2006). The use of qualitative content analysis in case study research. *Forum Qualitative Sozialforschung/Forum: Qualitative Social Research, 7*(1), 1–30.

Lai, A., Melloni, G., and Stacchezzini, R. (2018). Integrated reporting and narrative accountability: The role of preparers. *Accounting, Auditing and Accountability Journal, 31*(5), 1381–1405.

Manes-Rossi, F., Tiron-Tudor, A., Nicolò, G., and Zanellato, G. (2018). Ensuring more sustainable reporting in europe using non-financial disclosure—De Facto and De Jure evidence. *Sustainability, 10*, 1–20.

Masiero, E., Arkhipova, D., Massaro, M., and Bagnoli, C. (2019). Corporate accountability and stakeholder connectivity. A case study. *Meditari Accountancy Research.* doi:10.1108/MEDAR-03-2019-0463

Massaro, M., Dumay, J., and Bagnoli, C. (2017). When the investors speak. Intellectual capital disclosure and the web 2.0. *Management Decision, 55*(9), 1888–1904.

Merkl-Davies, D. M., and Brennan, N. M. (2017). A theoretical framework of external accounting communication: Research perspectives, traditions, and theories. *Accounting, Auditing and Accountability Journal, 30*(2), 433–469.

Mio, C., Marco, F., and Pauluzzo, R. (2016). Internal application of IR principles: Generali's internal integrated reporting. *Journal of Cleaner Production, 139*, 204–218.

Parker, L. D. (2013). The accounting communication research landscape. In: L. Jack, J. Davison, and R. Craig (Eds.), *The Routledge Companion to Accounting Communication* (pp. 7–25). London: Routledge.

Shehata, N. F. (2014). Theories and determinants of voluntary disclosure. *Accounting and Finance Research, 3*(1), 18–26.

World International Capital Initiative. (2013). *Connectivity. Background Paper for <IR>.* London, UK: IIRC.

Zhang, Y. (2016). *Stock Message Boards: A Quantitative Approach to Measuring Investor Sentiment.* New York, USA: Palgrave Macmillan.

PART VI

Assurance and investors' perspectives on integrated reporting

24

THE JOURNEY TO INTEGRATED REPORT ASSURANCE

Different pathways to add credibility and trust to an integrated report

Shan Zhou

The University of Sydney

Roger Simnett

UNSW Sydney

Michael Bray

KPMG, Deakin University and IIRC

Abstract

The demand for assurance on integrated reporting (IR) is increasing as this form of reporting becomes more widespread. The different nature of information contained in an integrated report, compared to traditional financial and sustainability reports, gives rise to significant challenges and opportunities associated with assurance engagements on IR. The International Integrated Reporting Council (IIRC) is working closely with the International Auditing and Assurance Standards Board (IAASB), which is currently developing guidance for practitioners when undertaking an Extended External Reporting (EER) assurance engagement in accordance with the International Standard on Assurance Engagements (ISAE) 3000. In the current vacuum of regulatory guidance, a range of credibility-enhancing approaches to IR is emerging, including two approaches under the current IAASB remit (the ISAE 3000 approach and the ISA 720 approach), and two innovative approaches currently outside the IAASB remit: the combined assurance approach; and what we are describing as the integrated report assurance approach, which aligns with the International Integrated Reporting Framework (<IR> Framework) principles, and overcomes a number of the identified challenges associated with other assurance approaches. The diversity of credibility-enhancing approaches to IR and the non-mandatory nature of such services provide opportunities for academics to inform practitioners and regulators on the current state, the demand for, and the consequences of these various assurance approaches to IR.

Introduction

The principles-based approach underpinning the International Integrated Reporting Framework (<IR> Framework) gives rise to a variety of formats for the presentation of integrated reports. For example, an integrated report can be a stand-alone document or included as a distinguishable, prominent and accessible part of another report or communication, including the organization's annual report.

With a variety of possible formats, enhancing the credibility of integrated reporting (IR) requires some versatility. In this chapter, we first examine the demand for credibility-enhancing approaches for IR, including independent external assurance, and the response from regulators/standard setters in this area. We then discuss different pathways by which credibility and trust in the information contained in an integrated report can be built and evolve. Finally, we identify potential areas for future research.

The demand for credibility and trust in extended external reporting and IR assurance

Public trust in the contribution, accountability and integrity of business has been declining (Edelman, 2018). More transparent and informative corporate disclosure through Extended External Reporting (EER)[1] should be a way to regain public trust, as information users are increasingly looking beyond items currently recognized in the financial statements and sustainability reports for their decision making. EER, in particular IR, can play a significant role in rebuilding trust through its role in catalysing corporate focus and disclosure of business-centric matters such as the strategy, business model and governance, on matters material to the stakeholders of the business and by providing a framework for greater transparency on material non-financial matters (KPMG, 2018a).

Figure 24.1 shows the importance and role of credible EER in trust building. As this figure shows, all three stages are important for trust to be built, and any additional reporting under stage 2 will only be beneficial if it is seen to be credible.

The demand for credibility-enhancing techniques in EER is likely to come from both internal management and external stakeholders. Internally, the value of credibility-enhancing techniques may manifest at different stages. In the early stages, companies can seek credibility enhancing techniques in EER in response to external pressures, such as compliance with legislative requirements for GHG emissions in Europe under the EU Emissions Trading Scheme or as a requirement to meet industry-specific expectations. As companies progress along their IR journey, they may actively seek ways to enhance performance for their own benefit, instead of merely in response to external pressure. They may use credibility-enhancing techniques to generate greater confidence in the accuracy and reliability of key data that informs their internal business decisions. Companies may also look to gain a competitive advantage through strategic differentiation by enhancing transparency and reliability through assurance (WBCSD, 2016).

External demand for credibility-enhancing techniques can come from investors, including those using Socially Responsible Investing (SRI) indices, which are placing increasing reliance on using non-financial disclosures in making investment decisions. Credibility-

Figure 24.1 The importance and role of credible EER in trust building

enhancing techniques provide investors with greater confidence in the information they use, which allow them to have greater confidence in their investment decisions, and thus create value. Ratings agencies also acknowledge the value added by external assurance and incorporate the use of external assurance into their scoring process. Reporting standard setters and framework developers often recognize the importance of obtaining external assurance on reports. For example, reporters can claim that their corporate social responsibility (CSR) reports are of a higher level of quality according to the Global Reporting Initiative (GRI) guideline if their reports are externally assured. The Sustainability Accounting Standards Board (SASB) also perceives benefit from external assurance and is creating its standards to enable companies to have their data externally assured if they voluntarily seek to do so (WBCSD, 2016).

The various reporting formats available for producing an integrated report have resulted in challenges to traditional assurance practices, and created new credibility-enhancement techniques and opportunities. Most organizations have a regulated/mandated financial statement audit, and have made the decision, mainly voluntarily, to separately purchase assurance for non-financial information. While these siloed assurance practices can still improve the credibility of some of the additional information included in an integrated report, it is difficult to see these practices achieving all of the concepts that underpin an integrated report, in particular connectivity. This has therefore given rise to the development of other innovative assurance practices, including those outside of professional services, to add credibility and trustworthiness to integrated reports.

The traditional assurance approach to EER is outlined in the International Standard on Assurance Engagements 3000 (ISAE 3000), which is similar in methodology and procedure to a financial statement audit, with the major difference being the subject matter being assured and the attention paid to the various challenges that this subject matter poses to these assurance engagements. Compared to the reporting of financial information, non-financial information contained in EER is more diverse, more qualitative and can be more forward-looking in nature. In addition, in relation to IR, business-centric information (e.g., strategy), often in diagrammatic or graphical forms, is important. These characteristics have led to challenges in undertaking assurance engagements on this type of information, including whether traditional assurance models will be an appropriate fit for IR. In addition, the broader subject matter means that under a traditional (ISAE 3000) assurance approach, there is increased complexity in the subject matter information being assured and a potential broadening of the skill set required by the assurance team, leading to the increased likelihood of requiring multidisciplinary assurance teams. These challenges raise the issue as to whether the cost of assurance on an integrated report will be disproportionate to the perceived benefits (Simnett et al., 2016).

A range of professional services and business practices could help to enhance the credibility of and trust in EER. These professional services can extend beyond assurance engagements and include agreed-upon procedural engagements, compilation engagements, assurance readiness engagements, certifications, expert insight reports, consultancy (advisory) engagements, maturity assessments and the use of internal audits. Business practices include the development of systems and processes for the collection of the underlying subject matter, and other processes by which those responsible for the subject matter develop confidence that the underlying information is credible.

However, as outlined in Figure 24.1, enhancement of credibility and trust will not be realized unless the characteristics, processes and results of these professional services and business practices are effectively communicated to users. For example, transparency about the competence of those performing the professional service, a summary of the work performed and an explicit reference to national or international standards for quality control of the practitioner's firm, as well as to relevant ethical requirements, may help add credibility to the EER (IAASB, 2018a). Also, a signing off by those responsible for the subject matter, and a statement as to why they are confident in the subject matter, can increase the credibility and trust of report users in the underlying information.

The international integrated reporting council and its approach to credibility-enhancing techniques

In this section we trace the development and discussion of credibility-enhancing techniques associated with the development of the <IR> Framework. As we outline, at all stages the International Integrated Reporting Council (IIRC) has considered not only the reporting framework, but also the associated credibility of the information.

A significant majority of respondents to the draft <IR> Framework released for comment by the IIRC in April 2013 agreed that an integrated report needs to be credible and that independent, external assurance is a fundamental mechanism for ensuring reliability and enhancing credibility (Hoang and Simnett, 2013; IIRC, 2013a). However, in view of the practical challenges and the costs of assuring integrated reports, it was recognized that external assurance is not necessarily the only way to increase the credibility and usefulness of the information contained in the integrated report. In response to this consultation, the <IR> Framework released in December 2013 did not require the integrated report to be externally assured, but acknowledged that the reliability of reported information can be enhanced by mechanisms such as external assurance, robust internal control and reporting systems, stakeholder engagement, internal audit and responsibility statements by those charged with governance (IIRC, 2013b).

In order to follow up further on the assurance issues outstanding after the approval of the <IR> Framework in December 2013, in July 2014 the IIRC released two discussion papers to explore assurance issues on IR. These discussion papers clarified that the IIRC was not, and did not aspire to become, a key player in the assurance field. However, the IIRC did seek to promote robust assurance, along with other mechanisms that build the credibility of, and trust in, IR. There was some contention about whether assurance standards at the time were appropriate, and whether specific assurance standards should be developed (IIRC, 2014a, 2014b).

The IIRC released a response document to the consultation process entitled "Assurance on <IR>: Overview of feedback and call to action" (IIRC, 2015), which summarized significant matters raised in the debate on the discussion papers. The majority (84.1 per cent) of the respondents agreed that assurance should be a priority, depending on the reporting stages, reporting entities' needs and the importance of other credibility-enhancing mechanisms.

The IIRC identified the IAASB as the key assurance standard-setter contributing to the IR assurance journey, as it sets auditing and assurance standards in the public interest, including standards that could be applied to assurance on IR (ISAE 3000). The IIRC acknowledged that the IAASB had set up an Integrated Reporting Working Group (IRWG) and was reviewing responses to the technical challenges raised by the IIRC. We discuss the initiatives from the IAASB in the following section.

The IAASB and the development of international assurance standards

The IAASB's mission is to serve the public interest by setting independent, high-quality standards on quality control, auditing, review and other assurance, and related professional services (IAASB, n.d.). The IAASB's work is highly influenced by the international environment in which it operates. The IIRC's issuance of the <IR> Framework was referred to as one of the important global developments that the IAASB needed to consider in achieving its strategic objectives (IAASB, 2014). This continues to be an important strategic objective for the IAASB, as evidenced by the fact that one of their strategic objectives for 2017–2021 is to "influence initiatives to develop (assurance) standards and guidance that meet user needs for external reporting beyond financial reporting" (IAASB, 2016, 2018a, 2018b).

In September 2014, the IAASB (2018a) established an IRWG to:

* Monitor developing interest in EER and related demand for assurance over EER; and
* Develop initial thinking on the nature of such engagements, the scope of the subject matter information and the suitability of criteria, and other matters related to assurance, including how the IAASB's existing assurance standards could be applied.

The IAASB issued a series of publications on assurance on IR. In July 2015, it issued a publication entitled "Exploring Assurance on Integrated Reporting and Other Emerging Developments in External Reporting" (IAASB, 2015a). The publication was intended to inform stakeholders of the ongoing work undertaken by the IAASB to explore issues on the assurance of IR that were highlighted by the IIRC's discussion papers and feedback, including the nature of assurance, the suitability of the <IR>

Framework as criteria for assurance, and the necessary competence and capability of assurance practitioners (IAASB, 2014).

In 2016, the IAASB released for public comment a Discussion Paper, "Supporting Credibility and Trust in Emerging Forms of External Reporting: Ten Key Challenges for Assurance Engagements". The discussion paper set out the principal findings from research and outreach regarding developments in emerging forms of EER frameworks and professional services (IAASB, 2016). Thirty-nine responses were received on the discussion paper. The following paragraphs summarize the main issues highlighted in the discussion paper and the corresponding responses to these issues (IAASB, 2017a, 2017b).

The principal findings from the IRWG's research and outreach to date

Extended External Reporting is still evolving to meet the emerging needs of a variety of stakeholders for wider information about the entity. There is demand for actions to support credibility and trust, but this is not limited to calls for professional services. Various types of professional services engagements are performed in relation to EER, but these are primarily advisory and assurance engagements. There is a need for flexibility in the nature of professional services as reporting frameworks evolve, to enable the delivery of credibility and trust in an appropriate manner.

The factors that enhance credibility and trust in EER for stakeholders

Four key factors are identified in the discussion paper to enhance user credibility and trust: a sound reporting framework; strong governance; consistent wider information; and external professional services reports. One possible additional factor identified from the respondents is the experience and education of users with respect to EER assurance.

How the characteristics of such services can support enhancing credibility and trust

The following characteristics were identified in the discussion paper:

- Competence that is demonstrated or generally well known
- Objectivity and independence
- Quality of the performance of the engagement
- Quality control, where applicable, at the engagement and firm level by the practitioner and firm that perform the engagement
- Clarity of reporting, including a summary of the work performed

Ten key challenges in relation to EER assurance engagements and how they could be addressed

The challenges identified were:

- Scoping EER assurance engagements
- Suitability of criteria

- Materiality
- Building assertions in planning and performing the engagement
- Maturity of governance and internal control processes
- Narrative information
- Future-oriented information
- Professional skepticism and professional judgement
- Competence of practitioners performing the engagement
- Form of the assurance report

The respondents rated the highest priority challenges to be suitability of criteria, materiality and the form of the assurance report, while noting the inter-relatedness of the challenges and suggesting that they may need to be addressed together. While the discussion paper suggested that the Ten Key Challenges are currently barriers to more widespread use of assurance engagements in relation to EER, many respondents suggested that the current low demand was more related to the immaturity of the reporting frameworks and regulatory requirements of EER itself, rather than the key challenges of assurance engagements being the principal barrier. Cost of assurance was also seen as another key barrier for some.

How are the IAASB's current international standards being applied and what more might be needed?

The majority of respondents supported the development of more non-authoritative guidance on existing international assurance standards (i.e., ISAE 3000), but not a new assurance standard introducing mandatory requirements at this time, although the IAASB recognized that the latter may be appropriate in the future. Caution was expressed that the IAASB should develop guidance in a manner that does not stifle innovation in EER and related assurance engagements.

To what extent is EER information covered in a financial statement audit?

When EER information is included in an annual report, the auditor is required to read the EER and consider whether there is a material inconsistency between that information and the financial statements, as well as the auditor's knowledge obtained during the audit. This requirement is contained in ISA 720 (Revised), *The Auditor's Responsibilities Relating to Other Information*, for purposes of the audit of the financial statements (IAASB, 2015b). It does not constitute a separate assurance engagement on the EER. Several respondents thought user credibility and trust engendered by the work of financial statement auditors under ISA 720 (Revised) was not sufficient when EER was included in the annual report and could give rise to an expectation gap.

There is potentially demand for assurance beyond ISA 720 to enhance credibility and trust in EER information contained in the annual report, and this may increase in the future. The general consensus from the responses was that the extent of assurance over EER information in the annual report should be decided by the market (e.g., investors, those charged with governance, regulators and other stakeholders). An ISA 720 approach to enhancing the credibility of EER information is contained later in this chapter.

In response to the comments received on the 2016 discussion paper, in October 2017 the IAASB approved an EER assurance project proposal and established the EER Task Force. The key objective of the project is to enable more consistent and appropriate application of ISAE 3000 (Revised) to EER assurance engagements and greater trust in the resulting assurance reports by users of EER. The scope of the project is the development of non-authoritative IAASB EER guidance, rather than new or modified IAASB standards.

The IAASB plans to progress with the project through activities in three areas:

- Developing non-authoritative guidance in applying the IAASB assurance standards to EER, in particular ISAE 3000 (Revised)
- Continuing to provide thought leadership on assurance issues in relation to EER
- Coordinating the work of the project with related initiatives of other relevant international organizations, including the Corporate Reporting Dialogue, the IIRC, the World Business Council for Sustainable Development (WBCSD) and the Principles for Responsible Investment (PRI).

The project is being undertaken in two phases. The first phase aims at providing guidance relating to five of the Ten Key Challenges:

- Making materiality judgements;
- The maturity of governance and internal control over EER processes;
- Evaluating the suitability of criteria;
- Building assertions; and
- Working with narrative and future-oriented information.

In February 2019, the IAASB issued for comment a Consultation Paper entitled "Extended External Reporting Assurance", which is an exposure draft providing guidance on the above five Key Challenges (IAASB, 2018a, 2019a). In general, the respondents were supportive of the guidance. However, there was a common concern that the guidance was too long and technical, and hence not very accessible. Guidance addressing the remaining Ten Key Challenges is currently being developed during the second phase, with the guidance from both phases being expected to be published together in early 2020. The draft guidance is intended to be "framework-neutral", such that it can be applied to assurance engagements over EER reports that are prepared using any EER framework, or entity-developed criteria, including integrated reports (IAASB, 2018b, 2019b).

Different pathways to IR assurance in practice

One of the challenges when undertaking an assurance engagement on EER, especially in the development of assurance guidance, standards or methodology, originates from the multiple reporting forms of IR, which are commonly at various stages of evolution and adoption. For example, companies with a history of producing stand-alone sustainability reports may progress to producing integrated reports by integrating material information from annual reports and sustainability reports, and adding information about the strategy, business model, governance and intellectual capital (among other matters), in accordance with the <IR> Framework principles. Examples of where this approach has been commonly observed in practice include listed companies on the Johannesburg Stock Exchange (JSE) in South Africa, where the corporate governance code (King Code), incorporating the principles of IR was developed, mainly from a history of companies producing stand-alone sustainability reports.

Other companies may have a system of augmenting their mainstream corporate filings with a separate section that incorporates the additional information content required by the <IR> Framework, such as strategy, risks and opportunities, business model, governance and prospects. Examples of this approach include the Operating and Financial Review (OFR) in Australia (ASIC, 2013), the Strategic Report in the UK (FRC, 2018), the Management Commentary at the IASB and the Management Discussion & Analyses (MD&A) in the US.

In addition to reporting format variation, the level of adoption varies across organizations. For example, some organizations may find it more appropriate at early stages of their IR journey to stop short of asserting full adoption of the <IR> Framework, and instead apply various principles of the framework, explaining the extent to which the full <IR> Framework has been applied in the Basis of Preparation (Deakin University, 2019).

Depending on the stage of the reporting journey towards IR, different assurance approaches may be applied to different types of IR reports. In the following paragraphs, we discuss four alternative assurance approaches that can be applied to an integrated report; that is, the ISAE 3000 approach, the ISA 720 approach, the combined assurance approach and the integrated report assurance approach. A summary of the benefits and challenges associated with these approaches can be found in Table 24.1. We discuss these approaches under current IAASB and emerging approaches.

Table 24.1 Benefits and challenges associated with different assurance approaches on IR

IR pathways	Assurance approach	Main benefits and challenges associated with the assurance approach	
Combining the sustainability report with the management commentary or the full annual report	ISAE 3000	Benefits	Clearly defined subject-matter dealing with information other than traditional financial statements
		Challenges	Not sufficient to address the integration of strategic business information
Modifying an existing report such as a governance document or strategic report or management commentary/ discussion and analysis by tailoring it in accordance with the Guiding Principles and Content Elements of the <IR> Framework	ISA 720	Benefits	Applicable to the IR pathway when non-financial information is integrated into mainstream corporate filing
		Challenges	Does not provide assurance, and therefore may not be sufficient to address user demand.
Combining the sustainability report with the annual report or modifying an existing report with the Guiding Principles and Content Elements of the <IR> Framework	Combined assurance approach	Benefits	Cost-effective and easy to implement; can be applied to multiple IR pathways
		Challenges	Does not provide assurance, and therefore may not be sufficient to address user demand.
Adopting IR internally to underpin management information by exploring how existing reporting systems may be adapted to accommodate an IR approach	Integrated report assurance approach	Benefits	Designed for IR hence the relevance and value to users is high; the level of assurance is high; potentially does not place as high a requirement on assurance practitioner expertise in the subject matter of each of the capitals as the other assurance approaches.
		Challenges	In the development stage and may take time to mature before widespread application

Current IAASB assurance approaches

The IAASB assurance standards are divided into two main groups: the ISA standards and the ISAE standards. The ISA standards establish requirements and provide applications and other explanatory material on the responsibilities of an auditor when engaged to undertake an audit of financial statements. The ISAE standards establish requirements and provide applications and other explanatory material on the responsibilities of an assurance provider when undertaking and reporting on assurance engagements other than audits or reviews of historical financial information. This categorization is problematic for IR assurance engagements, as the subject matter covers both financial and non-financial information. We discuss firstly the ISAE 3000 approach and then the ISA 720 approach.

The ISAE 3000 approach

Many companies had developed systems of producing stand-alone sustainability reports before the IR trend. These companies naturally progressed into IR by combining material aspects of their annual report and sustainability report, while adopting the principles of the <IR> Framework. For these types of integrated reports, the ISAE 3000 approach, with its focus on assurance of sustainability reports as a separate assurance engagement, would likely be part of the IR assurance journey. Companies listed on the JSE in South Africa, which were required to produce an integrated report from 2011 onwards, are examples of those adopting this approach (Wang et al., 2019). This commonly creates challenges in implementing the principles of the <IR> Framework, particularly in the areas of "connectivity" and "conciseness". In practice, we commonly observe the inclusion of two audit/assurance reports, on financial statements and sustainability reports respectively, in the annual reports of JSE listed companies (Zhou et al., 2017).

Traditionally the reporting criterion against which a sustainability report has been assured has been the GRI. The information in the sustainability report has then been added to the annual report and over time has become more integrated or connected. The assurance approach most frequently used in practice has been to assure the sustainability information against the GRI framework, using ISAE 3000 as the assurance standard. Very seldom has the <IR> Framework been the reporting framework for assurance engagements. Recently there has been an example of an integrated report assured under ISAE 3000 in accordance with the <IR> Framework. EY Amsterdam conducted a review for the Integrated Annual Review for the 2018 and 2019 years of ABN AMRO Group N.V. using the <IR> Framework as the reporting criteria. The assurance engagement was performed in accordance with Dutch Standard 3810N, which is a specific Dutch standard based on ISAE 3000.

The ISA 720 approach

An alternative development of IR starts from augmenting an integral part of an annual report, usually the Directors' Report, with the <IR> Framework content elements, such as strategy, business model and prospects. Examples of this approach include the Strategic Report in the UK and the OFR in Australia.

The UK has been adopting the Enhanced Business Review (EBR) as part of the Directors' Report since 2007. In the first few years of its operation, market participants criticized the fact that important and relevant information was obscured in a morass of superfluous detail (Kay, 2012). Since 2013, UK companies have been required to provide a separate Strategic Report (to replace the former EBR section), which is a separate section at the front of an annual report (as opposed to being part of the Directors' Report).

The Strategic Report in the UK aims to bring together all of the most relevant information in a cohesive, clear manner, i.e., to tell a "joined up story" that enables shareholders to assess how well the directors have discharged their duty to promote the long-term success of the company (FRC, 2014). In developing the Guidance on the Strategic Report, the UK FRC was mindful of developments in IR, so that the <IR> Framework and the Guidance on the Strategic Report encourage similar qualitative characteristics and content (FRC, 2014).

Since the Strategic Report forms part of the annual report, it falls under the financial statement auditors' responsibility to read and consider other information under ISA 720. The revision of ISA 720 by the IAASB in 2015 led to amendments to the UK Companies Act 2006 for financial years commencing on or after 1 January 2016. It requires auditors, based on the work undertaken in the course of the audit, to state the following in their report: (a) whether the information given in the Strategic Report for which the accounts are prepared is consistent with those accounts; (b) whether the Strategic Report has been prepared in accordance with applicable legal requirements; and (c) whether, in light of the knowledge and understanding of the company and its environment, the auditor has identified material misstatements in the Strategic Report.

In Australia, listed companies have been including an OFR as part of the Directors' Report since 2013. The OFR is one of the key sources of information about entities and plays an important role in promoting the accountability of boards, similar in principle to the EBR in the UK. The objectives of the OFR requirements are to provide shareholders with a narrative and analysis to supplement the financial report and assist shareholders in understanding the operations, financial position, business strategies and prospects of an entity (ASIC, 2013). In this way, it encourages similar principles to those of the <IR> Framework and is heralded as a useful stepping stone to IR. It is suggested that applying the <IR> Framework as a guide for OFR content will allow companies to meet their statutory reporting obligations (ASIC, 2017; ASX, 2019). In the meantime, the concept of IR is gaining traction in Australia. The KPMG survey reveals that 48 per cent of the ASX listed companies adopted at least some of the principles of <IR> in 2018, compared to 25 per cent in 2017 (KPMG, 2018a). The ASX Corporate Governance Council, in the Fourth Edition of its Corporate Governance Principles & Recommendations (2019), indicated its support for IR, and implicitly IR assurance, by introducing a new recommendation (4.3) and including a reference suggesting that companies should consider adopting the <IR> Framework principles when preparing their annual reports, and disclose how their key corporate reports have been verified.

Although the IAASB claimed that the revised ISA 720 will not impose incremental costs on auditors, because auditors are only required to consider the other information based on the work undertaken in the course of the audit, various stakeholders expressed reservations about such assertions (e.g., ICAEW, 2013; KPMG, 2013). Further, under the ISA 720 approach it is not clear how the expanded reporting contained in the Strategic Report and the OFR, which incorporates content elements of IR, has an impact on financial statement auditors' existing responsibilities, and what other credibility-enhancing mechanisms are currently in use in these reports. This is one of the areas in which academic research can potentially add value.

Evolving innovative credibility enhancing and assurance approaches

The integrated nature of the reporting processes and the many broad types of reported information call for innovative forms of credibility enhancement that can accommodate the connectivity between the different components of integrated reports (Ridehalgh, 2010). Outside the current IAASB approaches, we can identify or envisage two additional credibility-enhancing and assurance approaches. The first is commonly referred to as the combined assurance approach, although it does not have the characteristics of an assurance engagement. It is effectively a formal statement from the governing body or audit committee, explaining why the committee or board believe they are in a position to accept responsibility for the information contained in the integrated report. The second approach, which we are calling the integrated report assurance approach, effectively explores whether assurance can be provided to attest to the integrated report appropriately representing the discussions and actions of those charged with governance.

The combined assurance approach

Combined assurance aims to optimize the assurance coverage obtained from management, internal assurance providers, and external assurance providers, in the process ensuring that significant risks facing the company are adequately addressed (Zhou et al., 2019). Under this approach, the audit committee (or governing body) form and communicate their conclusion on the reliability of reported information, outlining their reliance on external and internal assurance, and the effectiveness of risk management and internal controls and processes. A formal statement of this type from the governing body or audit committee, explaining why the committee or board believe they are in a position to accept responsibility for the information contained in the report, may be beneficial in improving the relevance and reliability of reported information, as well as being a potentially more cost-effective credibility-enhancing (but possibly less trusted) mechanism than independent assurance (Simnett et al., 2016).

From its definition, combined assurance can be seen as mainly an internal governance and risk management practice, with assurance implications. There are two ways in which combined assurance enhances the credibility and usefulness of integrated reports: (i) by enhancing risk management and the overall governance of the firm, thus leading to higher reporting quality; and (ii) by enhancing the coordination of assurance providers' activities, thus leading to higher assurance quality. Current academic research supports the view that combined assurance is a credibility enhancing technique that adds value to market participants (Zhou et al., 2019).

In addition to JSE listed companies where the approach of combined assurance is encouraged, this approach is effectively applied to companies listed on the London Stock Exchange (LSE) in the UK via the requirement to disclose the audit committee report. The Financial Reporting Council (FRC) modified the UK Corporate Governance Code and its Guidance for Audit Committees in 2013 to require audit committees to discuss significant issues considered by the committee and how they addressed these issues, including (and focusing on) the issues communicated to the committee by the auditor (FRC, 2013b). Additionally, the auditor is required to include information in the audit report if they are not satisfied with the audit committee's disclosure of the issues communicated by the auditor to the audit committee (FRC, 2013a).

These additional disclosures from auditors and audit committees potentially add credibility and trust to the reported information in the Strategic Report. The existing academic studies have produced mixed results on the effect of the new reporting regime. Reid et al. (2019) find that the new reporting regime is associated with an improvement in audit quality and causes an incremental market reaction, but Gutierrez et al. (2019) find no significant benefit from the new regime.

In Australia, it is advocated that as companies progressively enhance their suite of corporate reporting and share insight into their business model and strategy, which is not subject to assurance by the company's external auditor, the entity should have formal and rigorous processes that safeguard the integrity of its corporate reporting and provide the market with appropriate information to make informed investment decisions. These processes should be disclosed to help the market in assessing the quality of the information included in these corporate reports (ASX, 2019; KPMG, 2018b). The recent update of the ASX Corporate Governance Council's Corporate Governance Principles & Recommendations (in the February 2019 4th Edition) has required the disclosure of the process underpinning the integrity of any periodic corporate report, including integrated reports and sustainability reports, as investors are relying on a broader range of periodic corporate reports than audited or reviewed financial statements to inform their investment decisions (ASX, 2019). This approach shares similar characteristics with the combined assurance approach currently in practice in South Africa.

The integrated report assurance approach

To keep an integrated report concise, the information disclosed should be more strategic in nature, which requires a different application of materiality to that used in financial and sustainability reporting. With the underlying concept to this approach being that the integrated report represents a faithful representation of the matters discussed at the board level, integrated report assurance can become an independent assurance technique to establish that the integrated report is a faithful representation of the business as it really is – its strategy, risks and opportunities, resources and relationships, business model, governance, performance and prospects. This could be characterized as an "integrated report assurance engagement".

It will be important to distinguish between two types of integrated report assurance engagements. The first would be a limited assurance engagement where the assurance procedures are limited to observation and enquiry that the integrated report presents the business as it really is. The second, more challenging but probably more valuable to investors and all other stakeholders, would be a reasonable assurance engagement where the assurance practitioner gathers substantive audit evidence to be able to conclude that the integrated report communicates the business and its operation in practice as it really is.

A reasonable assurance integrated report assurance engagement will involve gathering evidence in order to present conclusions on whether the integrated report reflects the business as designed and in operation. Evidence-gathering approaches may include reading the strategic/business planning documentation and other documentation relating to the business model and governance, risk management, resources and relationships, and board and management reporting; and attending board and management meetings to observe and evaluate whether and how these matters are documented and designed, and whether the documentation reflects their operation in practice.

The advantage of the integrated report assurance approach is that it aligns well with the principles of IR, which are strategic in nature. It would be useful to report users to gain assurance on whether the integrated report produced by the company reflects what is considered most important to the business and the board. Further, other assurance engagements on EER including IR demand a high level of subject matter expertise from practitioners, which can be one of the practical challenges that prevent the widespread adoption of the assurance practice on EER. The integrated report assurance approach, however, could circumvent the restriction as it only requires practitioners to be able to conclude that the items reported were included in Board papers and are faithfully represented in the integrated report.

Future directions and research opportunities

The IAASB is currently focused on developing guidance for EER assurance undertaken in accordance with ISAE 3000. It has been a while since research has been undertaken on the application of ISAE 3000, and how assurance is being provided in practice (Hasan et al., 2005). Therefore, empirical evidence on the usage of ISAE 3000 in practice, and on what subject matter it is currently applied to, can provide useful insights. In addition, ISAE 3000 was developed for separate assurance engagement on non-financial reports, so whether it is fit for purpose for IR, which emphasizes the business and "connectivity" among financial and non-financial information, is an empirical question. Finally, given that assurance engagements on EER reports are commonly performed by practitioners from outside the profession, whether and how ISAE 3000 is used by other practitioners outside the accounting profession is another interesting area to explore. While an increase in the use of ISAE 3000 by other practitioners outside the accounting profession has been identified, these other practitioners do not appear to be following the requirements of ISAE 3000, in that they often fail to disclose the ethics code and quality control framework of the practitioners in their assurance reports (Ge et al., 2019).

In considering the ISA 720 pathway, while EER information contained in mainstream corporate filings is covered under ISA 720, it only requires auditors to identify material inconsistencies during the course of the audit and does not constitute a separate assurance on the EER information. Hence, the level of assurance is far from sufficient to meet user demand and can cause an expectation gap regarding auditors' responsibilities relating to EER information under ISA 720. With the increasing amount of EER information being incorporated into mainstream corporate filings, the impact of EER information on auditors' responsibilities, the audit cost and audit quality of assurance and other credibility-enhancing mechanisms warrant investigation. Further, the impact on user perceptions on auditors' responsibilities and audit quality when EER information is integrated into the annual report represents a fruitful area for research.

Section 4 outlines four different types of assurance approaches that can be used to assure an integrated report. The first three assurance approaches are common in practice, so research can compare and examine user preference and perception of these different approaches. In regard to the visionary integrated report assurance approach, there are questions as to whether and how it can be done, and how strong user demand will be for this approach.

Academic research can contribute to knowledge of appropriate credibility-enhancing techniques by using in-depth field studies, experimental research, and, as the observations become available, archival research (Cohen and Simnett, 2015; Simnett, 2014; Simnett and

Huggins, 2015). At the individual or group decision-making level, there are numerous experimental research opportunities relating to how the credibility-enhancing technique is undertaken, as well as how intended users react to the technique and the way that it is reported. At the organizational level, research opportunities exist around examining how organizations make the decision to produce and assure their IR information, and other organizational characteristics that contribute to these decisions. It may be that different types of experts are involved in an EER assurance engagement, and research could examine factors and techniques, such as familiarization and brainstorming techniques, that may aid engagement team performance. At the market level, using archival research methods as the observations become available, research can examine whether organizations benefit from the different credibility enhancing techniques (Zhou et al., 2019). For example, what will be the effect of assurance on changes in share price, types of investors on share registers, or impact on accuracy (dispersion) of analysts' forecasts? For all research methods, there are great opportunities to contribute to knowledge.

Conclusion

The global movement towards IR brings opportunities as well as challenges to the assurance profession. In particular, as there are different IR journeys, the assurance approach needs to be tailored for different pathways. In this chapter, we have laid out the challenges and issues discussed by practitioners and standard setters, followed by the projects currently undertaken by standard setters in developing non-authoritative guidance on EER assurance, including IR using ISAE 3000.

Depending on the stage of the IR journey that a company is at, different assurance approaches may apply. We discussed four assurance approaches. The ISAE 3000 approach is most suitable for an integrated report. The ISA 720 approach is appropriate when the IR journey starts by augmenting an existing legislated document. The combined assurance approach is flexible, to cater for different IR pathways and is potentially more cost-effective. Finally, there is the visionary integrated report assurance approach, designed for IR, which is strategic in nature, and aims to provide assurance on whether the integrated report reflects the underlying business strategy and operations.

In the meantime, innovative assurance practices continue to emerge in response to the rising demand for EER and EER assurance. Research questions that arise in regard to these assurance approaches include differences in the level of assurance delivered, the cost of the assurance, the user demand and perception of these assurance services, the reasons for choosing different credibility enhancing techniques, and, as we observe these techniques in practice, the impact or market benefits of the various techniques. More research into these innovative assurance approaches to reveal the costs and benefits and the implications of these services will be extremely informative to practitioners and standard setters in moving forward with addressing the challenges associated with the assurance of EER.

Note

1 Extended External Reporting encapsulates many different forms of reporting, including, but not limited to, integrated reporting, sustainability reporting and non-financial reporting about environmental, social and governance matters. Such reports may be prepared under legislative or regulatory requirements and established frameworks, standards and guidance issued by international or national standard setters (IAASB, 2016).

References

ASIC. (2013). *Effective Disclosure in an Operating and Financial Review. Regulatory Guide 247*. Available at: https://asic.gov.au/media/1247147/rg247.pdf (Accessed: 1 August 2019).

ASIC. (2017). *ASIC Calls on Preparers to Focus on Financial Report Quality and New Requirements* [Media release]. Available at: https://asic.gov.au/about-asic/news-centre/find-a-media-release/2017-releases/17-423mr-asic-calls-on-preparers-to-focus-on-financial-report-quality-and-new-require ments/ (Accessed: 1 August 2019).

ASX Corporate Governance Council. (2019). *Corporate Governance Principles and Recommendations 4th Edition*. Available at: www.asx.com.au/documents/asx-compliance/cgc-principles-and-recommenda tions-fourth-edn.pdf (Accessed: 1 August 2019).

Cohen, J., and Simnett, R. (2015). CSR and Assurance Services: A Research Agenda. *Auditing: A Journal of Practice and Theory, 34*(1), 59–74.

Deakin University. (2019). *Submission to the IAASB Extended External Reporting Assurance Consultation Paper*. Available at: www.ifac.org/publications-resources/consultation-paper-extended-external-reporting-assurance (Accessed: 1 August 2019).

Edelman. (2018). *Edelman Trust Barometer 2018 Executive Summary*. Available at: www.edelman.com/research/2018-edelman-trust-barometer (Accessed: 1 August 2019).

FRC. (2013a). *International Standard on Auditing (UK and Ireland) 700: The Independent Auditor's Report on Financial Statements, revised June*. London: FRC.

FRC. (2013b). *Improving the Auditor's Report: Note of a Public Meeting*. Available at: www.frc.org.uk/Our-Work/Publications/Audit-and-Assurance-Team/Consultation-Paper-Revision-to-ISA-%28UK-and-Ireland/Improving-the-auditor-s-report-record-of-public-me.aspx (Accessed: 1 August 2019).

FRC. (2014). *Guidance on the Strategic Report*. Available at: www.frc.org.uk/getattachment/697745ed-d991-4360-a32c-857dc28fb949/Guidance-on-the-strategic-report-2014.pdf (Accessed: 1 August 2019).

FRC. (2018). *Guidance on the Strategic Report*. Available at: www.frc.org.uk/getattachment/fb05dd7b-c76c-424e-9daf-4293c9fa2d6a/Guidance-on-the-Strategic-Report-31-7-18.pdf (Accessed: 1 August 2019).

Ge, Q. L., Simnett, R., and Zhou, S. (2019). The Use of International Standards on Assurance Engagements (ISAEs) by Practitioners from outside the Accounting Profession: Public Interest or Risk to Legitimacy? *Working paper, UNSW Sydney and University of Sydney*.

Gutierrez, E., Minutti-Meza, M., Tatum, K., and Vulcheva, M. (2019). Consequences of Adopting an Expanded Auditor's Report in the United Kingdom. *Review of Accounting Studies*, forthcoming.

Hasan, M., Maijoor, S., Mock, T. J., Roebuck, P., Simnett, R., and Vanstraelen, A. (2005). The Different Types of Assurance Services and Levels of Assurance Provided. *International Journal of Auditing, 9*(July), 91–102.

Hoang, H., and Simnett, R. (2013). *Analysis of Framework – Specific Comments on Question 19 and 20 – Credibility*. Available at: www.theiirc.org/resources2/framework-development/technical-agenda-papers/ (Accessed: 1 August 2019).

IAASB. (2015a). *Exploring Assurance on Integrated Reporting and Other Emerging Developments in External Reporting*. Available at: www.ifac.org/publications-resources/exploring-assurance-integrated-report ing-and-other-emerging-developments (Accessed: 1 August 2019).

IAASB. (2015b). *ISA 720. The Auditor's Responsibilities Relating to Other Information and Related Conforming Amendments*. Available at: www.ifac.org/publications-resources/international-standard-auditing-isa-720-revised-auditor-s-responsibilities–0 (Accessed: 1 August 2019).

IAASB. (2016). *Supporting Credibility and Trust in Emerging Forms of External Reporting: Ten Key Challenges for Assurance Engagements. Discussion Paper*. Available at: www.ifac.org/publications-resources/discus sion-paper-supporting-credibility-and-trust-emerging-forms-external (Accessed: 1 August 2019).

IAASB. (2017a). *IRWG Discussion Paper – Discussion of Responses – Approval of Project Proposal – Agreement to Issue Feedback Statement*. Available at: www.iaasb.org/system/files/meetings/files/20171024-IAAS B_Agenda_Item_4-A-EER_Issues-Paper_Final.pdf (Accessed: 1 August 2019).

IAASB. (2017b). *Emerging Forms of External Reporting. IAASB CAG Meeting, Agenda Item L*. Available at: www.ifac.org/system/files/meetings/files/20170911-IAASB_CAG_Agenda_Item_L-EER-DP-ini tial-analysis-of-responses-Presentation.Marek_.pdf (Accessed: 1 August 2019).

IAASB. (2018a). *IAASB Project Proposal – Guidance on Key Challenges in Assurance Engagements Over Emerging Forms of External Reporting ("EER")*. Available at: www.ifac.org/publications-resources/iaasb-project-proposal-emerging-forms-external-reporting (Accessed: 1 August 2019).

IAASB. (2018b). *Supporting Credibility and Trust in Emerging Forms of External Reporting: Ten Key Challenges for Assurance Engagements*. Available at: www.ifac.org/publications-resources/supporting-credibility-and-trust-emerging-forms-external-reporting-ten-key (Accessed: 1 August 2019).

IAASB. (2019a). *Extended External Reporting (EER) Assurance. IAASB Consultation Paper*. Available at: www.ifac.org/system/files/publications/files/EER-Consultation-Paper.pdf (Accessed: 1 August 2019).

IAASB. (2019b). *IAASB March 2019 Board Meeting Feedback from EER Breakout Sessions. IAASB Main Agenda (June 2019), Agenda Item 8-A*. Available at: www.iaasb.org/system/files/meetings/files/20190617-IAASB-Agenda_Item_8-A-Supplementary-Paper-EER-Assurance-Breakout-Session.pdf (Accessed: 1 August 2019).

IAASB. (n.d.). *International Auditing and Assurance Standards Board*. Available at: www.iaasb.org/ (Accessed: 1 August 2019).

IAASB Integrated Reporting Working Group (IRWG). (2014). *Market Developments in Integrated Reporting and Emerging Assurance Issues Relevant to IAASB*. Available at: www.ifac.org/system/files/meetings/files/20141201-IAASB-Agenda_Item_10-B-IRWG_Briefing_Paper_Market_Developments_Integrated_Reporting_and_Assurance.pdf (Accessed: 1 August 2019).

ICAEW. (2013). *International Standard on Auditing (ISA) 720 (Revised) The Auditor's Responsibilities Relating to Other Information in Documents Containing or Accompanying Audited Financial Statements and the Auditor's Report Thereon*. Available at: www.ifac.org/publications-resources/international-standard-auditing-isa-720-revised-auditor-s-responsibilities-re (Accessed: 1 August 2019).

IIRC. (2013a). *Consultation Draft of the International <IR> Framework*. Available at: http://integratedreporting.org/resource/consultationdraft2013/ (Accessed: 1 August 2019).

IIRC. (2013b). *The International <IR> Framework*. Available at: www.theiirc.org/wp-content/uploads/2013/12/13-12-08-THE-INTERNATIONAL-IR-FRAMEWORK-2-1.pdf (Accessed: 1 August 2019).

IIRC. (2014a). *Assurance on <IR>: An Introduction to the Discussion*. Available at: www.theiirc.org/resources-2/assurance (Accessed: 1 August 2019).

IIRC. (2014b). *Assurance on <IR>: An Exploration of Issues*. Available at: www.theiirc.org/resources-2/assurance (Accessed: 1 August 2019).

IIRC. (2015). *Assurance on <IR>: Overview of Feedback and Call to Action*. Available at: http://integratedreporting.org/wp-content/uploads/2015/07/IIRC-Assurance-Overview-July-2015.pdf (Accessed: 1 August 2019).

Kay, J. (2012). *The Kay Review of UK Equity Markets and Long-Term Decision Making, Final Report*. Available at: www.ecgi.org/conferences/eu_actionplan2013/documents/kay_review_final_report.pdf (Accessed: 1 August 2019).

KPMG. (2013). *The Auditor' Responsibilities Relating to Other Information in Documents Containing or Accompanying Audited Financial Statements and the Auditor's Report Thereon*. Available at: www.ifac.org/publications-resources/international-standard-auditing-isa-720-revised-auditor-s-responsibilities-re (Accessed: 1 August 2019).

KPMG. (2018a). *Corporate Reporting: Rebuilding Trust through Improved Transparency and Insight*. Available at: https://home.kpmg/au/en/home/insights/2018/11/asx-200-corporate-reporting-trends-2018.html (Accessed: 1 August 2019).

KPMG. (2018b). *Credibility and Trust, Delivering Robust Assurance*. Available at: https://home.kpmg/au/en/home/insights/2018/02/credibility-trust-delivering-robust-assurance.html (Accessed: 1 August 2019).

Reid, L., Carcello, J., Li, C., and Neal, T. (2019). Impact of Auditor Report Changes on Audit Quality and Costs: Evidence from the United Kingdom. *Contemporary Accounting Research*, Forthcoming.

Ridehalgh, N. (2010). One Audit—Moving towards 21st Century Integrated Assurance. In: R. G. Eccles, B. Cheng, and D. Saltzman (Eds.), *The Landscape of Integrated Reporting* (p. 144). Boston: Harvard Business School.

Simnett, R. (2014). Assurance of Environmental, Social and Sustainability Information. In: D. Hay, W. R. Knechel, and M. Willekens (Eds.), *Routledge Companion to Auditing* (pp. 325–337). London: Routledge.

Simnett, R., and Huggins, A. (2015). Integrated Reporting and Assurance: Where Can Research Add Value? *Sustainability Accounting, Management and Policy Journal*, 6(1), 29–53.

Simnett, R., Zhou, S., and Hoang, H. (2016). Assurance and Other Credibility Enhancing Mechanisms for Integrated Reporting. In: C. Mio (Ed.), *Integrated Reporting: A New Accounting Disclosure* (pp. 269–314). London: Palgrave.

Wang, R., Zhou, S., and Wang, T. (2019). Corporate Governance, Integrated Reporting and the Use of Credibility-enhancing Mechanisms on Integrated Reports. *European Accounting Review*, 10.1080/ 09638180.2019.1668281.

World Business Council for Sustainable Development (WBCSD). (2016). Assurance: Generating Value from External Assurance of Sustainability Reporting. Available at: www.wbcsd.org/Programs/ Redefining-Value/External-Disclosure/Assurance-Internal-Controls/Resources/Generating-Value-from-External-Assurance-of-Sustainability-Reporting (Accessed: 1 August 2019).

Zhou, S., Simnett, R., and Green, W. (2017). Does Integrated Reporting Matter to the Capital Market? *Abacus*, *53*(1), 94–132.

Zhou, S., Simnett, R., and Hoang, H. (2019). Evaluating Combined Assurance as a New Credibility Enhancement Technique. *Auditing: A Journal of Practice & Theory*, *38*(2), 235–259.

25

INTEGRATED REPORTING AND EARNINGS CALLS

Virtuous circle or benchmarking effect? Preliminary insights

Marco Fasan

Ca' Foscari University

Chiara Mio

Ca' Foscari University

Eduardo Flores

University of Sao Paulo

Abstract

Previous literature on the capital market effects of integrated reporting (IR) suggests that IR helps analysts improve their earnings forecast accuracy. This chapter contributes to this line of research by investigating the extent to which IR and non-IR companies mention IR-related information during earnings conference calls. One could expect that analysts who follow IR companies are interested in having more detailed and updated IR information (virtuous circle view). However, analysts following non-IR companies may also require IR information during conference calls, given its value relevance (benchmarking effect view). Our empirical results support the first view and corroborate the idea that IR provides value-relevant information to investors.

Introduction

According to the International Integrated Reporting Framework (IIRC Framework), one of the main aims of integrated reporting (IR) is to offer value-relevant information to providers of financial capital about the short-, medium- and long-term performance of a company (IIRC, 2013). Previous literature investigating the capital markets effects of IR has focused on the relevance of IR to investors and their advisors; financial analysts. Several studies (Bernardi and Stark, 2018; Flores et al., 2019; Zhou et al., 2017) have found that IR improves disclosure quality, allowing analysts to make more accurate earnings forecasts. These empirical results confirm the predictions of voluntary disclosure (Beyer et al., 2010) and information processing theory (Dhaliwal et al., 2012). Voluntary disclosure theory links earnings forecast accuracy to the quantity of information disclosed, while information processing theory focuses on the quality of such information.

The present chapter contributes to the growing IR literature by adopting a dynamic approach to examining the behaviour of financial analysts after IR information has been disclosed. Specifically, we assess whether financial analysts transform from being passive users of IR information to proactive information seekers, thus triggering a virtuous circle that benefits both investors and companies.

Some of the most relevant IR content elements and guiding principles are the business model and the forward-looking approach, allowing better firm strategy to create value in a long-term view. Both these IR features are grounded in the integrated thinking approach introduced by the IIRC Framework and, consistent with the voluntary disclosure and information processing theories, are relevant to stakeholders in terms of evaluating the ability of the company to create value in the long term. Because previous research has found that IR increases analysts' ability to make predictions, one could expect them to be interested in having more detailed and updated information on topics covered by the IR, such as a long-term view and sustainability strategy. For instance, analysts may learn from IR about some risks connected to the macro economic environment. Given possible external shocks that may have occurred since the publication of the integrated report, analysts may be interested in knowing how the company evaluates such risks in this new economic context, therefore mentioning the issue during earnings conference calls.

We focus on conference calls, which are flexible and informal communication tools (see Huang et al., 2014; Matsumoto et al., 2011). We expect that analysts willing to explore IR-related themes further or simply wishing to be updated about them will employ such a channel in addition to other forms of communication. Our underlying argument is that IR creates a virtuous circle between managers and analysts, where interest in IR themes is growing due to higher information supply (i.e. companies publishing integrated reports) and demand (i.e. analysts requiring IR information during conference calls). On the one hand, analysts ask questions about financial issues during conference calls in order to better forecast performance. On the other hand, IR seeks to offer information to providers of financial capital on the short-, medium- and long-term performance of corporations. Our expectation is that, for companies that publish an integrated report, analysts require information not only about financial issues, but also about IR-related themes. The main idea here is that IR provides new perspectives on companies' issues, allowing analysts to expand their set of questions in the conference calls.

We test our hypothesis by analysing a hand-collected database that includes IR companies that voluntarily issued an integrated report in 2013 or 2014 (IR companies), matched with companies that did not issue an integrated report (non-IR companies). We analyze the conference call transcripts using a content analysis methodology. Our empirical results suggest that IR companies disclose more information about IR themes compared to non-IR companies. This evidence is consistent with the virtuous circle effect and not with the benchmarking effect; the latter predicts that analysts following non-IR companies may have incentives to request information during conference calls because of the value relevance of IR.

Our study contributes to the literature on the capital markets effects of IR (among others, Bernardi and Stark, 2018; Serafeim, 2015; Zhou et al., 2017), focusing in particular on financial analysts and their behavior and incentives after IRs have been published. Our results are of interest to policymakers, as they support the idea that IR positively contributes to the functioning of capital markets. From this perspective, we expect that the decision of the European legislator to issue Directive 2014/95/EU on non-financial disclosure will have a positive impact on both companies and investors.

Background

According to the IIRC Framework, one of the primary aims of IR is to offer information to providers of financial capital about the short-, medium- and long-term performance of a company. One of the main advisors of investors is the financial analyst, who provides information and advice on the future performance of a corporation. According to Ramnath et al. (2008), financial analysts play a central role in capital market functioning and are an important external corporate governance mechanism. According to Kelly and Ljungqvist (2012), financial analysts facilitate the pricing of stocks and serve as information intermediaries between firms and outsiders. One of the most relevant impacts of analyst activity is the reduction of agency problems between managers and shareholders, and of information asymmetry for investors (Boubakri and Bouslimi, 2016; Bowen et al., 2008; Lang et al., 2004).

Analysts use information in order to perform the following activities: conceptual description of the firm's prospects; earnings forecasts over various horizons; price forecasts; and buy-sell-hold recommendations. In their activity, analysts rely on several different sources of information, identified in previous literature as earnings, other information from SEC filings, industry information, macroeconomic information, management communication and other information (for a review, see Ramnath et al., 2008). Our analysis focuses on the input of analyst activity rather than on the outputs. From this perspective, IR can be considered a source of information that analysts use to make decisions. Following the model by Ramnath et al. (2008), integrated reports would be included in the 'management communication and other information' category.

A key variable influencing analysts' forecast accuracy is disclosure quality. Several authors (Hope, 2003; Plumlee, 2003) find that better disclosure quality improves forecast accuracy because it enhances analysts' understanding of companies' performance and outlook. Better disclosure also helps to lower the cost of processing and interpreting information, again leading to improved earnings forecasts (Lehavy et al., 2011). Previous studies find that voluntary disclosure enhances analysts' understanding of companies' prospects (see Beyer et al., 2010). According to Dhaliwal et al. (2012) and Nichols and Wieland (2009), analysts use non-financial information to reduce acquisition and processing costs and therefore reduce forecast errors. The IIRC Framework requires companies to broaden the scope of reporting, including information on companies' capital, governance, business model and strategy. It is therefore likely that analysts will find value-relevant information in IRs. For instance, broader disclosure of the business model or the corporate governance system is fundamental for analysts to understand the value creation process.

We provide some background on the stream of research focusing on the capital market (external) effects of IR, as our paper contributes mainly to this field of study. One of the main results in the literature on the capital market effects of IR is that it increases firm value (Barth et al., 2017; Lee and Yeo, 2016). Both studies motivate their findings with IR, leading to a better information environment. To the best of our knowledge, three IR studies focus on financial analysts, representing one of the most important mechanisms connecting IR to a better information environment (Healy et al., 1999) and therefore to a lower cost of capital. These studies are particularly relevant to the present study and therefore merit discussion.

Zhou et al. (2017) study the South African context and provide evidence that analysts' forecast errors and dispersion decrease as a company's level of alignment with the IIRC Framework increases; in this way, better IR disclosure potentially reduces the impact of information asymmetry in the reduction of forecast errors. The authors also show that this phenomenon leads to a lower cost of capital. Bernardi and Stark (2018) also focus on South Africa, studying the impact of reporting regime changes on analyst forecast accuracy from 2008 to 2012 as a way to evaluate users' perceptions of the usefulness of IR. The authors find that implementing IR changes the relationship between the extent of ESG disclosure and analyst forecast accuracy, and that this association is greater for companies producing an integrated report. The evidence from both of these studies is in line with the idea that IR provides information that improves the information environment, reduces information risk, and enables more accurate and consistent forecasting by analysts.

The study by Abhayawansa et al. (2019) focuses on the relevance of IR to analysts' practices and the reasons for the (ir)relevance; its results conflict with those of Bernardi and Stark (2018) and Zhou et al. (2017). The authors conducted 23 semi-structured interviews with financial analysts covering companies implementing an integrated report. They find that IR is not connected with analysts' practice of firm assessment because the reports do not provide the information required by analysts in sufficient detail or in the preferred format. Flores et al. (2019) test the relationship between IR and analysts' forecast accuracy in an international context; they find that analysts following companies publishing an integrated report are better able to predict future earnings. Furthermore, the authors find that the impact is greater in the US than in the European context, and they interpret this result as an indication that IR can be considered an investor-oriented rather than a stakeholder-oriented tool.

In this context, research has shown that conference calls (Bushee et al., 2004; Frankel et al., 1999), particularly the question and answer portion of the call (Matsumoto et al., 2011; Mayew and Venkatachalam, 2012), provide useful information to capital market participants. Conference calls are periodic (often quarterly) company events spread throughout the year, during which the top management, usually the CFO and CEO, present projections and forward-looking information to investors. The conference call event is usually organized in two phases: the managerial discussion or presentation part, and the question and answer (Q&A) session. Conference calls, together with press releases, websites and other business reports, are the most common form of voluntary disclosure used by listed companies.

Previous literature has documented that institutional investors and analysts are keen to participate in conference calls to get access to specific segments of information and details not disclosed in other releases. Companies prefer conference calls to other disclosure tools because they are more flexible and less formal. In particular, the Q&A session allows analysts to gather all the information they consider necessary to predict earnings. The quantity and quality of information released during earnings conference calls has been widely investigated: prior research (Huang et al., 2014; Matsumoto et al., 2011) has mainly analyzed the content of conference calls in terms of their length, tone or signals launched to the financial markets. Despite the recognition that sustainability information is value relevant, few researchers have considered the sustainability issues included in conference calls (see Cavezzali et al., 2016).

Hypothesis development

Building on previous studies on the capital markets effects of IR, on the relevance of IR to analysts, and on earnings conference calls, we aim at answering the following research question: which companies (IR or non-IR) mention IR-related themes during conference calls to a greater extent? The main idea is to test the reaction of analysts and investors to IR and possible changes in the themes covered during conference calls. As suggested by previous studies, conference calls are flexible disclosure tools, as they allow analysts to pose questions and companies to provide an answer. While most previous studies on IR and capital markets focus on reports and other forms of formal corporate communication, we choose to focus on this less formal and more flexible tool.

Previous literature offers arguments predicting that IR companies will disclose both more and less IR information during conference calls compared to non-IR companies. According to a first view, which we define as the benchmarking view, companies that publish an integrated report set a benchmark that leads financial analysts and investors to expect to receive similar information from every other company. Integrated Reporting enlarges the scope of disclosure to non-financial topics such as strategy, business model or outlook. The IIRC Framework is based on the following content elements: organizational overview and external environment; governance; business model; risks and opportunities; strategy and resource allocation; performance; outlook; basis of preparation; and presentation. Moreover, IR changes the way in which information is provided, making it easier for analysts to take decisions. For instance, the materiality principle requires companies only to disclose information on issues that will impact the ability of the company to create value in the long term, and this is of great help in limiting the risk of information overload. The IIRC Framework is based on the following guiding principles: strategic focus and future orientation; connectivity of information; stakeholder relationships; materiality; conciseness; reliability and completeness; consistency; and comparability.

Building on voluntary information (which leverages on the IIRC Framework content elements) and on information processing theories (which leverage on the IIRC Framework guiding principles), several studies (Bernardi and Stark, 2018; Flores et al., 2019; Zhou et al., 2017) find that analysts are able to make better predictions if they can rely on an integrated report. Because IR increases analysts' ability to make predictions, we would expect IR-related themes to be discussed to a greater extent by non-IR companies. Analysts would have incentives for requiring IR-related disclosure, because it would make their decision-making process easier and their forecasts more accurate.

According to the second view, which we define as the virtuous circle view, one would expect that IR companies disclose more IR-related information during conference calls. Like most corporate reports, an integrated report is published once a year, and analysts may be interested in having more detailed or updated information about the topics covered by IR. For instance, analysts may have learned from an integrated report about a new strategic approach by the company: given possible external shocks that may have occurred since the publication of the integrated report, analysts may be interested to know whether or not the intended strategy is confirmed. The underlying idea is that IR creates a virtuous circle between managers and analysts.

First, according to the virtuous circle view, managers disclose information through integrated reports. This empowers analysts, as it allows them to access information about issues that are not covered by annual or sustainability reports. This is consistent with previous studies that found a positive association between IR and analysts' forecast accuracy. It may be that the triggering element is not the amount of information provided but rather the way in which such information is disclosed, consistent with information processing theory (see Dhaliwal et al., 2012). In this case, information was already disclosed in sustainability or other non-financial reports, but this was not really employed by analysts because of information overload or other constraints in information processing.

The second step of the virtuous circle relies on analysts' activity. By building on the information they have gathered through IR and on other external events that may change the environment in which the company is operating, they may want to discuss some IR-related aspects further. This second step would not be possible without the first.

Relying on the virtuous circle view, which seems to have more support in the literature, we hypothesize that IR companies disclose more information about IR-related themes than non-IR companies.

Methodology

In order to test our hypothesis, we built a hand-collected database including firms that voluntarily issued an integrated report that applies the IIRC Framework in 2013 or 2014. These companies were defined as IR companies, and they represented the treatment sample. They have demonstrated a higher degree of attention towards IR, voluntarily embracing the IR philosophy when it was still at an early stage of development. To identify these companies, we used the information provided by the official IIRC website, which lists companies issuing an integrated report that is compliant with the IIRC Framework. We matched treated to untreated firms using a propensity score matching (PSM) technique based on industry (two-digit SIC code), size (logarithm of total assets), and year of the first IR issuance per company (2013 or 2014) with a caliper of 0.001 for the neighbour approach. We matched every treated firm to one or more non-treated firms, following Almeida et al. (2011), Fleischer et al. (2017), Franzen and Weißenberger (2018), and Hong et al. (2018). We defined these matched companies as non-IR companies: they are companies that did not join the IIRC Framework in 2013 or 2014 that are similar in terms of industry and size to the IR companies. Our data sample can be defined as an unbalanced panel; it included 162 IR companies and 452 non-IR companies.

After we defined our sample, for each company we downloaded from Bloomberg the earnings conference call transcripts from 2014 to 2018. We collected a total number of 1,377 transcripts, 432 for non-IR companies and 945 for IR companies. Conference call transcripts were not available for all the companies in our original sample; therefore our final sample included a total of 89 companies, 56 IR and 33 non-IR.

In order to analyze our data and to determine the topics covered during the conference calls, we relied on content analysis methodology. According to Beattie and Thomson (2007), the importance attached to different categories of information by a reporting entity is assumed to be reflected in the extent of the information disclosed. We applied this logic to conference calls and therefore attributed more importance to topics that were mentioned more often during the call. The higher the number of references to a certain topic, the greater its importance.

In implementing our content analysis, we used NVivo software, which helps in organizing, querying, visualizing, and reporting the analyzed data. NVivo has an autocoded theme function that allows large sets of data to be worked through to produce results rapidly. More specifically, the software identifies common themes in the documents and identifies the specific sentence or paragraph covering the topic. Technically, NVivo groups themes by comparing words with the same stem—for example, house, houses and housing. It then filters the themes and excludes those groups that represent a much smaller proportion of the content. For each group, NVivo uses the most frequently shared phrase or word as the name of the theme. For each of the identified themes, NVivo indicates the number of references, which is the number of times the theme is mentioned during the conference call.

Our main variable of interest was the number of references each theme received, scaled by the total number of words in the call. We wanted to make sure that the number of conference calls or the length of such calls did not bias our results. We called our main dependent variable 'references', and we defined it as the number of times a certain topic was mentioned every 1,000 conference call words. For example, the following conference call sentence was classified by NVivo as belonging to the theme of value: 'so I think it's a better broadened way of ensuring that we can deliver long-term sustainable value to our shareholders, and I'll pass it on Kathy if she wants to add anything'. The following sentence belongs to the theme 'human capital': 'we will show you how we will further enhance our operating model and cost control and strengthen our human capital'. This sentence: 'The third piece, which is the most difficult piece, is client-facing technology where we are, as you know, staying very close to the startup community analysing business models' is classified under the 'business' theme.

We also coded the IIRC Framework (IIRC, 2013), in order to arrive at the most cited themes. These themes, which we defined as 'IR themes', are the topics that are more relevant in the IIRC Framework and therefore the topics that we believe are the closest to the IR philosophy. By using these IR themes, we empirically tested whether there was any significant difference between IR and non-IR companies in terms of number of references devoted to each theme. If IR companies mentioned IR themes more often in their conference calls, we would interpret this as confirmation of our hypothesis.

We performed a parametric test (t-test) and a non-parametric test (Wilcoxon rank sum test) to determine whether the average number of references to IR themes in IR companies was significantly different from non-IR companies. We dropped those IR themes that were never cited by either IR or non-IR companies. We were left with the following ten IR themes: business, capital, effect, value, human capital, key performance indicators, key risks, process, value, and value chain.

We also performed a multivariate analysis, where the dependent variable was the number of mentions of IR themes per 1,000 words for each theme (reference). We used the following regression equation for each of the ten IR themes identified:

$$Reference_{i,t} = \beta_0 + \beta_1 IRcompany_{i,t} + \beta_2 OperatingRev_{i,t} + \beta_3 TotalAsset_{i,t} +$$
$$\beta_4 Employees_{i,t} + \beta_5 ROA_{i,t} + \sum\nolimits^{I} ndustryIndicator + \sum\nolimits^{C} ountryIndicator + \varepsilon_{i,t}$$

where Reference is the number of times the IR topic is mentioned every 1,000 conference call words over the period 2014–2018; IRcompany is an indicator variable which is equal to 1 if the company is an IR company and 0 otherwise; OperatingRev is the average operating revenue of the company in the period 2014–2018; TotalAsset is the average total assets of the company in the period 2014–2018; Employees is the average number of employees of the company in the period 2014–2018; ROA is the average return on assets of the company in the period 2014–2018; and Industry and Country indicators are indicator variables controlling industry and country respectively.

Results and discussion

Our empirical analysis was performed on a sample of 89 firms: 56 IR companies and 33 non-IR companies. Table 25.1 provides some descriptive statistics in terms of the country of origin of our sample companies.

Table 25.2 displays the descriptive statistics on conference calls. On average, IR companies made more conference calls. The mean (median) number of conference calls was 16.87 (18) for IR companies and 13.1 (16) for non-IR companies; this is significantly different at the 1 percent level according to both the t-test and the Wilcoxon rank sum test. Not only did IR companies engage more often than non-IR companies in conference calls, but these calls also lasted longer. The mean (median) number of words per conference call was 9,682 (9,873) for IR companies and 7,868 (7,884) for non-IR companies, which was also significantly different at the 1 percent level according to both the t-test and the Wilcoxon rank sum test. The fact that conference calls had different characteristics for our treated (IR) and control (non-IR) samples may have biased our results. Therefore, we calculated our main variable of interest as the number of references to a certain topic scaled by the total number of words in the conference call.

Table 25.1 The number of firms belonging to both groups (IR and non-IR) for each country

IR companies			Non-IR companies		
Country	*N*	*%*	*Country*	*N*	*%*
Brazil	8	14%	Brazil	12	36%
United States	6	11%	Italy	4	12%
United Kingdom	6	11%	Australia	4	12%
Spain	6	11%	Germany	3	9%
Italy	5	9%	United Kingdom	2	6%
Germany	5	9%	Spain	2	6%
South Africa	3	5%	Netherlands	1	3%
Netherlands	3	5%	Turkey	1	3%
Australia	3	5%	Russian Federation	1	3%
Turkey	1	2%	Denmark	1	3%
Sweden	1	2%	United States	1	3%
South Korea	1	2%	South Africa	1	3%
Russian Federation	1	2%			
Japan	1	2%	**TOTAL**	**33**	**100%**
India	1	2%			
France	1	2%			
Denmark	1	2%			
Chile	1	2%			
Canada	1	2%			
Belgium	1	2%			
TOTAL	**56**	**100%**			

Table 25.2 Some descriptive statistics for IR and non-IR companies conference calls

Variable	Mean (median)		Difference (A)—(B)	T (Wilcoxon test)	
	IR (A)	Non-IR (B)			
Words per conference call	9,682	7,868	1,814	-3.57	***
	(9,873)	(7,884)	1,989	-3.81	***
Number of conference calls	16.87	13.1	3.77	-3.12	***
	(18)	(16)	2	-2.41	***

*, **, and *** represent significance levels of 15 percent, 10 percent, and 5 percent, respectively.

Table 25.3 displays our preliminary evidence based on a univariate analysis. The first column indicates the IR themes autocoded by NVivo from the IIRC Framework. The second and third columns display the mean and median number of references (per 1,000 words) for IR and non-IR companies respectively. Looking at the IR theme 'business', on average the theme was mentioned 0.315 times every 1,000 words by IR companies. Non-IR companies mentioned the topic less often (0.193 times every 1,000

Table 25.3 The mean (median) number of references per 1,000 words for each IR theme in IR and non-IR companies

IR Theme	Mean (median)		Difference (A)—(B)	T (Wilcoxon test)	
	IR (A)	Non-IR (B)			
Business	0.315	0.193	0.122	2.32	***
	(0.267)	(0.118)	0.149	(2.17)	***
Capital	0.141	0.102	0.039	1.08	
	(0)	(0.121)	-0.121	(1.06)	
Effect	0.085	0.042	0.043	1.56	*
	(0)	(0)	0	(1.059)	
Value	0.053	0	0.053	3.61	***
	(0)	(0)	0	(3.71)	***
Human Capital	0.001	0.001	0	-0.26	
	(0)	(0)	0	(0.109)	
Key performance indicators	0	0.001	-0.001	-1.3	
	(0)	(0)	0	(-1.03)	
Key risks	0.001	0	0.001	0.76	
	(0)	(0)	0	(0.76)	
Process	0	0.019	-0.019	-2.15	***
	(0)	(0)	0	(-2.28)	***
Value chain	0.002	0	0.002	1.94	**
	(0)	(0)	0	(2.44)	***

*, **, and *** represent significance levels of 15 percent, 10 percent, and 5 percent, respectively. The table shows the result of the parametric (T-test) and non-parametric tests (Wilcoxon test) on the difference between the mean value of references.

words). The fourth column indicates the differences between the means and medians of IR and non-IR companies. Finally, the last column displays the results of the parametric (t-test) and non-parametric (Wilcoxon rank sum) tests.

Of the ten IR themes under analysis, four (capital, human capital, key performance indicators, key risks) showed no significant difference in terms of references. In other words, IR and non-IR companies mentioned these topics a similar number of times. Another five IR topics (business, effect, value, process, value chain) were mentioned more often by IR companies. Only the IR theme 'process' was mentioned more often by non-IR companies. The results are corroborated by both the t-test and the Wilcoxon rank sum test, which indicate that the difference between the mean number of references for each topic is significantly different for IR and non-IR firms. Therefore, our univariate analysis provides some preliminary evidence supporting our hypothesis.

The multivariate analysis further corroborates our results and suggests the existence of a virtuous circle between IR companies and analysts. Table 25.4 displays the results of our regression equations (one for each IR theme). Consistent with Table 25.3, the number of references for the following IR themes was not significantly influenced by the fact that companies adopt IR: capital (model 2), effect (model 3), human capital (model 5), key

Table 25.4 Regression results

	Dependent variable: number of references to IR themes								
	Business	Capital	Effect	Value	Human Cap.	KPI	Key risks	Process	Value chain
	(1)	(2)	(3)	(4)	(5)	(6)	(7)	(8)	(9)
IR Company	0.136 **	0.013	0.038	0.049 ***	0.001	-0.001	0.001	-0.007 **	0.001 ***
	(0.071)	(0.054)	(0.039)	(0.022)	(0.001)	(0.001)	(0.001)	(0.002)	(0.001)
Operating Revenues	0.001	0.001	0.001 **	0.001 **	0.001	-0.001	-0.001	-0.001	0.001 **
	(0.001)	(0.001)	(0.001)	(0.001)	(0.001)	(0.001)	(0.001)	(0.001)	(0.001)
Total Assets	0.001 ***	0.001 ***	0.001	0.001	0.001	0.001	-0.001	-0.001	-0.001 **
	(0.001)	(0.001)	(0.001)	(0.001)	(0.001)	(0.001)	(0.001)	(0.001)	(0.001)
Employees	0.001 *	0.001	0.001 *	0.001	0.001	0.001	-0.001	-0.001	0.001
	(0.001)	(0.001)	(0.001)	(0.001)	(0.001)	(0.001)	(0.001)	(0.001)	(0.001)
ROA	0.095 **	-0.028	0.005	-0.025 *	-0.001	0.001	-0.001	0.001 *	0.004
	(0.055)	(0.042)	(0.030)	(0.058)	(0.001)	(0.001)	(0.001)	(0.001)	(0.036)
Industry control	Yes	Yes	Yes	Yes	Yes	Yes	Yes	Yes	Yes
Country control	Yes	Yes	Yes	Yes	Yes	Yes	Yes	Yes	Yes
N	89	89	89	89	89	89	89	89	89
R2	0.21	0.27	0.20	0.25	0.04	0.06	0.05	0.10	0.12

*, **, and *** represent significance levels of 15 percent, 10 percent, and 5 percent, respectively. The results of regressing the references of the 9 IR themes on the following variables: IR company (indicator variable with value 1 if the company is IR and 0 otherwise); average 2014–2018 operating revenues; average 2014–2018 total assets; average 2014–2018 employees; and average 2014–2018 return on assets (ROA). All the models include industry and country controls.

performance indicators (model 6) and key risks (model 7). In these models, the coefficient of our main independent variable (IR company) was statistically insignificant. Instead, the coefficients of IR companies were positive and significant (at the 5 percent or 10 percent level) for the following IR themes: business (model 1), value (model 4) and value chain (model 9). This means that whether a company was IR or non-IR did influence the extent to which companies mentioned the three IR themes (business, value and value chain). This effect goes above and beyond that of the other control variables (operating revenues, total assets, employees, ROA, industry and country). The topic 'process' was mentioned to a greater extent by non-IR companies.

The IR topics identified mirror the main concepts of the IIRC Framework. The first is business, which in the IIRC Framework is often mentioned with regard to the business model, defined as 'the chosen system of inputs, business activities, outputs and outcomes that aims to create value over the short, medium and long term' (IIRC, 2013, p. 14). Most of the references in the conference calls, including the example mentioned in the previous paragraph, referred to the concept of the business model. The fact that such a topic was mentioned more often by IR companies is in line with the virtuous circle view, and thus with the idea that analysts require companies that apply IR principles and disclosure to provide more information on the theme.

Similarly, the theme 'effect' is mentioned in the whole IIRC Framework when it discusses the effects of different actions on the different capitals. The idea of measuring all the effects of corporations' activities in an integrated and holistic way is probably one of the most important in the framework. The theme 'capital' is also related to this idea, but results show that there was no significant difference between IR and non-IR companies. This is probably due to the fact that the term 'capital' has a financial meaning, therefore making our results noisier. Also the theme 'value' recalls the idea of a multi-dimensional value creation process that not only refers to shareholders but extends to other categories of stakeholder. References to this topic were significantly more numerous for IR companies. For example, the following is a reference to the theme: 'so I think it's a better broadened way of ensuring that we can deliver long-term sustainable value to our shareholders, and I'll pass it on Kathy if she wants to add anything'. Finally, the theme 'value chain' refers to the IR idea of enlarging the boundaries of the report in order to include suppliers, clients and other stakeholders that influence the ability of the company to create value. In this case, too, IR companies mentioned this topic more than non-IR companies.

Conclusion

This chapter looked at the behaviour of financial analysts after IR information has been disclosed. We were interested in investigating the extent to which IR and non-IR companies mention IR-related information during earnings conference calls. On the one hand, one could expect analysts following IR companies to be interested in having more detailed and up-to-date IR information (virtuous circle view); on the other hand, it may be that analysts following non-IR companies require IR information during conference calls, given its value relevance (benchmarking effect view).

Our results support the virtuous circle view and suggest that IR companies cover IR themes more extensively than non-IR companies. This evidence is in line with the idea that IR helps financial analysts in the decision-making process. Were this not the case and IR was irrelevant to analysts, then we would not have found any significant difference in the references to IR themes between the two samples. Future research may further examine the research issue, adopting different methodologies such as case studies or interviews, which allow an in-depth understanding of the mechanisms underlying the relationship between IR and analysts. One of the limitations of the present study is the variable measuring the link to the IIRC Framework.

References

Abhayawansa, S., Elijido-Ten, E., and Dumay, J. (2019). A practice theoretical analysis of the irrelevance of integrated reporting to mainstream sell-side analysts. *Accounting & Finance, 59*(3), 1615–1647.

Almeida, H., Campello, M., Laranjeira, B., and Weisbenner, S. (2011). Corporate debt maturity and the real effects of the 2007 credit crisis. *Critical Financial Review, 1,* 3–58.

Barth, M. E., Cahan, S. F., Chen, L., and Venter, E. R. (2017). The economic consequences associated with integrated report quality: Capital market and real effects. *Accounting, Organizations and Society, 62,* 43–64.

Beattie, V., and Thomson, S. J. (2007). Lifting the lid on the use of content analysis to investigate intellectual capital disclosures. *Accounting Forum, 31*(2), 129–163.

Bernardi, C., and Stark, A. W. (2018). Environmental, social and governance disclosure, integrated reporting, and the accuracy of analyst forecasts. *The British Accounting Review, 50*(1), 16–31.

Beyer, A., Cohen, D. A., Lys, T. Z., and Walther, B. R. (2010). The financial reporting environment: Review of the recent literature. *Journal of Accounting and Economics, 50*(2-3), 296–343.

Boubakri, N., and Bouslimi, L. (2016). Directors' and officers' liability insurance and analyst forecast properties. *Finance Research Letters, 19,* 22–32.

Bowen, R. M., Chen, X., and Cheng, Q. (2008). Analyst coverage and the cost of raising equity capital: Evidence from underpricing of seasoned equity offerings. *Contemporary Accounting Research, 25*(3), 657–700.

Bushee, B. J., Matsumoto, D. A., and Miller, G. S. (2004). Managerial and investor responses to disclosure regulation: The case of Reg FD and conference calls. *The Accounting Review, 79*(3), 617–643.

Cavezzali, E., Hussain, N., and Rigoni, U. (2016). The integrated reporting and the conference calls content. In: C. Mio (Ed.), *Integrated reporting: A new accounting disclosure* (pp. 231–252). London: Palgrave Macmillan.

Dhaliwal, D. S., Radhakrishnan, S., Tsang, A., and Yang, Y. G. (2012). Nonfinancial disclosure and analyst forecast accuracy: International evidence on corporate social responsibility disclosure. *The Accounting Review, 87*(3), 723–759.

Fleischer, R., Goettsche, M., and Schauer, M. (2017). The Big 4 premium: Does it survive an auditor change? Evidence from Europe. *Journal of International Accounting, Auditing and Taxation, 29,* 103–117.

Flores, E., Fasan, M., Mendes-da-Silva, W., and Sampaio, J. O. (2019). Integrated reporting and capital markets in an international setting: The role of financial analysts. *Business Strategy and the Environment, 28*(7), 1465–1480.

Frankel, R., Johnson, M., and Skinner, D. J. (1999). An empirical examination of conference calls as a voluntary disclosure medium. *Journal of Accounting Research, 37*(1), 133–150.

Franzen, N., and Weißenberger, B. E. (2018). Capital market effects of mandatory IFRS 8 adoption: An empirical analysis of German firms. *Journal of International Accounting, Auditing and Taxation, 31,* 1–19.

Healy, P. M., Hutton, A. P., and Palepu, K. G. (1999). Stock performance and intermediation changes surrounding sustained increases in disclosure. *Contemporary Accounting Research, 16*(3), 485–520.

Hong, P. K., Paik, D. G., and Smith, J. V. D. L. (2018). A study of long-lived asset impairment under U.S. GAAP and IFRS within the U.S. institutional environment. *Journal of International Accounting, Auditing and Taxation, 31,* 74–89.

Hope, O. K. (2003). Disclosure practices, enforcement of accounting standards, and analysts' forecast accuracy: An international study. *Journal of Accounting Research, 41*(2), 235–272.

Huang, X., Teoh, S. H., and Zhang, Y. (2014). Tone management. *The Accounting Review, 89*(3), 1083–1113.

IIRC. (2013). *The International <IR> Framework.* London, UK: IIRC.

Kelly, B., and Ljungqvist, A. (2012). Testing asymmetric-information asset pricing models. *The Review of Financial Studies, 25*(5), 1366–1413.

Lang, M. H., Lins, K. V., and Miller, D. P. (2004). Concentrated control, analyst following, and valuation: Do analysts matter most when investors are protected least? *Journal of Accounting Research*, *42*(3), 589–623.

Lee, K. W., and Yeo, G.-H.-H. (2016). The association between integrated reporting and firm valuation. *Review of Quantitative Finance and Accounting*, *47*(4), 1221–1250.

Lehavy, R., Li, F., and Merkley, K. (2011). The effect of annual report readability on analyst following and the properties of their earnings forecasts. *The Accounting Review*, *86*(3), 1087–1115.

Matsumoto, D., Pronk, M., and Roelofsen, E. (2011). What makes conference calls useful? The information content of managers' presentations and analysts discussion sessions. *The Accounting Review*, *86*(4), 1383–1414.

Mayew, W. J., and Venkatachalam, M. (2012). The power of voice: Managerial affective states and future firm performance. *The Journal of Finance*, *67*(1), 1–43.

Nichols, D. C., and Wieland, M. M. (2009). *Do firms' nonfinancial disclosures enhance the value of analyst services?* Available at: https://ssrn.com/abstract=1463005 (Accessed: 8 August 2019).

Plumlee, M. A. (2003). The effect of information complexity on analysts' use of that information. *The Accounting Review*, *78*(1), 275–296.

Ramnath, S., Rock, S., and Shane, P. (2008). The financial analyst forecasting literature: A taxonomy with suggestions for further research. *International Journal of Forecasting*, *24*(1), 34–75.

Serafeim, G. (2015). Integrated reporting and investor clientele. *Journal of Applied Corporate Finance*, *27*(2), 34–51.

Zhou, S., Simnett, R., and Green, W. (2017). Does integrated reporting matter to the capital market? *Abacus*, *53*(1), 94–132.

26

THE POSSIBILITY OF ACHIEVING SUSTAINABILITY AND FINANCIAL STABILITY THROUGH THE INFLUENCE OF INTEGRATED REPORTING ON INVESTMENT DECISIONS

René de Klerk

Faculty of Economic and Management Sciences, Akademia

Neil Eccles

Institute for Corporate Citizenship, University of South Africa

Derick de Jongh

Albert Luthuli Centre of Responsible Leadership, Department of Business Management, University of Pretoria

Abstract

The International Integrated Reporting Council (IIRC) claims that integrated reporting (IR) will be a force for financial stability and sustainability. It is also clear that improved allocation of capital through IR is central to the IIRC's claim. The purpose of the research was to explore the possibility of achieving financial stability and sustainability through the influence of IR on the providers of financial capital and their investment decisions. The research comprises a qualitative survey. Its results illustrate that there was no indication that providers of financial capital understood that it is their responsibility to achieve financial stability and sustainability through investment decision-making.

Introduction

In 2017, Humphrey et al. (2017, p. 56) made the following statement:

> At present, it is an unproven claim that integrated reporting will serve to direct financial capital to long term, sustainable businesses. It remains largely a belief statement, a testable proposition not a proven fact despite the proliferation of positive views from early integrated reporting adopters.

The International Integrated Reporting Council (IIRC) states that integrated reporting (IR) "will act as a force for financial stability and sustainability" (IIRC, 2013b, p. 2). However, scholars have questioned the potential of IR to lead to sustainability, although some have argued that the IIRC Framework aims to promote sustainability. One of the major concerns in the literature on IR is the fact that the IIRC, the self-proclaimed governing body of IR, has stated that the purpose of an integrated report is to explain to providers of financial capital how an organisation creates value over time (International Integrated Reporting Council, 2013b, p. 4).

Although IR can be viewed as having evolved from broader social and environmental accounting movements, the IIRC Framework specifically names the providers of financial capital as the target audience of integrated reports (Thomson, 2015). The IIRC explains that this decision was based on its understanding that IR would help guide more effective capital allocation decisions and better long-term investment returns (IIRC, 2015). The IIRC further argues that the creation of a sustainable planet depends greatly on the allocation of financial capital. They contend that IR will assist in directing financial capital to sustainable businesses and that this will lead to a stable economy and a sustainable planet (IIRC, 2013a). Providers of financial capital are therefore given the enormous responsibility of achieving financial stability and sustainability through their investment decisions. For this reason, it is essential to understand whether or not providers of financial capital are aware of this responsibility and whether IR is guiding them in making their investment decisions.

A number of emerging studies have investigated the perceptions that providers of financial capital have about IR (Atkins and Maroun, 2015; Stubbs et al., 2014). Stubbs et al.'s (2014) findings indicated that IR was still lacking in terms of supplying the information that providers of financial capital wanted. They noted that the six capitals model, which is key to understanding IR, was not well understood and was not perceived as particularly useful to investment decision making. Like Stubbs et al. (2014), the Association of Chartered Certified Accountants' report noted that there was general misunderstanding regarding IR's six capitals model and its usefulness and possible integration into investment decisions (Slack and Campbell, 2016). The report also found that short-termism is still prevalent in the investment industry (Slack and Campbell, 2016). In contrast, Serafeim (2015) demonstrated that long-term providers of financial capital are more likely than short-term providers of financial capital to invest in companies that integrate Environmental, Social and Governance (ESG) information into their strategy and business model reporting. Serafeim (2015) illustrated that in a sample of 1,114 unique US-listed companies, IR was associated with a longer-term provider of financial capital base. In contrast, research by Stubbs and Higgins (2018), in a follow-up study to Stubbs et al.

(2014), revealed strong overall support for voluntary IR, with many participants indicating that it was too soon to legislate mandatory IR. But, unlike other users of integrated reports, 50 per cent of the providers of financial capital supported the idea of mandatory IR. This demonstrates that providers of financial capital – more so than other participants – supported mandatory reporting. The participants also believed that IR would become the corporate reporting norm if things were left to market forces. This might be a result of the fact that shareholders are prioritised through IR, so it would not be surprising if markets responded positively to that. Stubbs and Higgins (2018) also confirmed that IR privileges financial information over environmental, social and governance (ESG) information and therefore tends to remain stuck in a weak sustainability paradigm (the status quo view of sustainability). This implies that the prioritisation of providers of financial capital and the privileging of financial information over ESG information may well help IR to become the reporting norm, but also that it will not necessarily assist in contributing to broader sustainability.

A recent study by Loprevite et al. (2018) contributed to the discussion concerning the relevance of IR for providers of financial capital in the European context. Their results indicated that companies that produce integrated reports displayed a significant improvement in earnings quality, and that this in turn increased the probability that providers of financial capital would interpret them.

At the heart of the debate in the IR literature lies the issue of whether providers of financial capital will indeed be influenced by IR to such an extent that it changes the way in which they allocate financial capital by making financial stability and sustainability a priority. This idea is well articulated by Humphrey et al. (2017, p. 32, emphasis added):

> the prospects of success for the IIRC's reconfiguration of the corporate reporting field have come to depend centrally on the IIRC being able to instigate institutional change in the rather more distantly related field of mainstream investment. In essence, the IIRC has sought to promote a greater focus on long term, sustainable investment not only by constructing a new form of (integrated) corporate reporting but also by *seeking to reconstruct the identity and interests of the mainstream provider of financial capital* (with the success of the former depending centrally on delivering the latter).

For this reason, it was a worthwhile research endeavour to explore the influence of IR on investment decision making and whether it will specifically lead providers of financial capital to achieve sustainability and financial stability.

The rest of this chapter is structured as follows: First, the methodology that was used to address the research question is described. Second, the findings based on 30 in-depth interviews with providers of financial capital are provided, and, finally, the chapter is concluded with some thoughts about the possibility of achieving sustainability and financial stability through the influence of IR on investment decision making.[1]

Methodology

The research took the form of a qualitative survey (Jansen, 2010) conducted on a sample of providers of financial capital. It is evident from the IIRC's definition that providers of financial capital represent a number of different categories of role players that include the entire investment chain:

[e]quity and debt holders and others who provide financial capital, both existing and potential, including lenders and other creditors. This includes the ultimate beneficiaries of investments, collective asset owners, and asset or fund managers.

(IIRC, 2013b, p. 33)

The sample was drawn from the South African investment community. In terms of IR, South Africa is widely recognised as a global leader (Adams, 2015; Atkins and Maroun, 2015; Brown and Dillard, 2014; Humphrey et al., 2017; Perego et al., 2016; Serafeim, 2015; Tweedie and Martinov-Bennie, 2015). In fact, anecdotally speaking, it seems like the exception to find a paper on IR that does not mention the IR "experiment" in South Africa. The sample was drawn in an explicitly stratified manner with a view to hearing the voices of as many different categories of providers of financial capital as possible. The final sample comprised: seven portfolio managers working for asset management firms (Interviewee codes: P2, P4, P5, P6, P7, P8, P9); six investment analysts, of whom the majority also worked for asset management firms (Interviewee codes: P26, P27, P28, P29, P30); two asset consultants intimately involved in providing advisory services to pension funds (Interviewee codes: P24, P25); six pension fund trustees (Interviewee codes: P13, P14, P15, P16, P17, P18); four pension fund members (Interviewee codes: P19, P20, P21, P22) and three "other" participants (Interviewee codes: P31, P32, P33). All the potential participants were informed of the confidentiality arrangements prior to participation, and all signed informed consent forms.

The interview questions were not provided to participants prior to the interviews. Beyond these preconceived questions, interviews were unstructured and probing questions were asked as the need arose.[2] It is possible that these preconceived questions might seem unnecessarily abstruse. However, opting for these abstruse questions at the beginning of the interview schedule and not providing participants with the questions before the interview was an intentional strategy aimed at mitigating the risk of creating an "artificial awareness" (Öberseder et al., 2011, p. 449) amongst the interviewees, with regard to IR. During the interviews, it became obvious that a number of participants did not even know that IR existed. Integrated reporting was explained to these participants before other questions about IR were asked.

The description of the findings presented in the following section was based on an inductive analysis. Three major themes emerged from the research: the process of investment decision making; perceptions about IR; and perceptions about financial stability and sustainability. Here these themes, together with sub-themes, are discussed.

Findings

The process of investment decision making

The first sub-theme of the process of investment decision making to emerge from the findings was that of sources of information. The findings illustrated that providers of financial capital make use of personal, internal and external sources of information to inform their investment decisions. Interestingly, very few participants referred to integrated reports spontaneously. Although a number of participants referred to company reports and annual reports, only a very small minority referred to IR. Company reports and third-party research reports were mentioned frequently. P8 emphasised the importance of company reports and described such reports as a very *"pure"* form of information. However, P8 did not specifically talk about integrated annual reports: "So there's a whole, there's an array of different sources of information we use. But principally, on a company work, given that we're all experienced, we use company reports because ultimately it's the purest form of information" (P8:4, Asset manager).[3] In contrast to P8's perception that company reports are the *"purest"* form of information, several participants mentioned reservations with regard to company reports. These participants described a sense of distrust towards company reports, describing them as marketing tools. Both P30 and P2 mentioned third-party research, which is done by companies that specialise in investment research. Investors then buy their research reports from these companies. These research companies base their reports on several sources, including news, macro-economic factors and in-depth analysis of companies:

> Okay, so we, from a company's perspective, obviously our main source of information is the annual report and obviously presentations that they do, the company does, so you'll have annual presentations, semi-annual, you'll have reporting. So those kind of things we do and then also conferences they do presentations, so it's all linked to companies, right, but then we also look a lot at the sell-side brokerage, so "Y" banking, all these kind of companies, their analysts look at the companies as well, so we look at their reports on the companies.
>
> *(P30:19, Analyst)*

The findings in this study seem to align with that of Rensburg and Botha (2014), which found that very few stakeholders use integrated reports as their main source of financial and investment information. Stakeholders typically only drew on integrated reports to get extra information about a company (Rensburg and Botha, 2014). It was evident from the study at hand that, if and when integrated reports are used by investment analysts and portfolio managers, it is almost done as a last resort. It was clear that the portfolio managers do not specifically use integrated reports to make investment decisions. Even if they do refer to integrated reports, they seem to only use integrated reports for the purposes of analysing the financials or numbers.

The second sub-theme that arose from the interviews was the theme of *engagement*, which takes place internally, within organisations. Internal engagements typically occur within asset management firms where analysts and portfolio managers work together in teams to make decisions. It was also apparent that the providers of financial capital engage outside of their own organisations, and that these engagements are perceived as part of the investment decision-making process. A topic mentioned a number of times regarding external engagements was proxy voting. It was evident that several participants perceived proxy voting as an important part of their responsibilities. Some participants explained that proxy voting is used as a method to engage companies on ESG issues. It was evident that ESG issues would not determine whether the providers bought a share, but proxy voting was described as the tool used to influence issues relating to ESG in the companies:

> The reason why I have this background in both analysis and portfolio managing, because I'm an old guy, I've been around, I've got the experience, because a lot of these votes [proxy votes], there's not always a clear-cut answer to resolutions at annual general meetings. Like most issues in investments there are lots of grey areas and I have the background, I've made decisions to buy and sell shares and all those kind of things, so.
>
> *(P28:3, Analyst)*

The third and final sub-theme to emerge was the theme of *abdication of investment decision making*. Portfolio managers within asset management firms were described as the ultimate decision makers, but they are governed by investment mandates and investment policies. In the majority of cases examined by this study, the investment mandates and investment policies were compiled by pension fund trustees in consultation with asset consultants. In terms of how the portfolio managers then go about making investment decisions, it was clear that they depend on the models and frameworks used within the organisations they work for. Some participants referred to top-down models, where macro-economic issues are considered first, and others used bottom-up models, where issues in the company are considered first. Nonetheless, the majority of portfolio managers expressed that an important consideration before investing in a company is its management. Investment decision making was also described as an art. The ultimate asset owners, represented in this study by pension fund members, described full abdication of their decision making to their fiduciaries. Interestingly, the pension fund members were the only category of provider of financial capital that described a sense of guilt because of this abdication of responsibility. Not a single participant ever mentioned the consideration of integrated reports or the information in integrated reports specifically in their descriptions of the investment decision-making process. If IR was something that influenced their investment decision making significantly, then surely it would have emerged from these descriptions.

Perceptions of providers of financial capital about IR

From the questions that explored the perceptions of providers of financial capital about IR, four sub-themes arose. The first sub-theme was the extent to which participants were aware of IR. It was obvious that a number of participants did not even know about IR. For example, one participant responded: "Reporting is always very important, and I'm not sure what you mean by integrated reporting. Please explain to me what you mean by integrated reporting" (P7:8, Portfolio manager).

Other participants clearly did not make any distinction between an integrated report and an annual report or company report as they call them. One participant, for example, asked, "Okay, what's the difference between the integrated report and the annual financial statements?" (P7:9, Portfolio manager). It was obvious that for many providers of financial capital the integrated report is still simply a report in which you can find the financial statements of a company.

The second sub-theme was the extent to which integrated reports were used. It was essential to understand whether the providers of financial capital make use of integrated reports, because it is obvious that, if they do not use integrated reports, then they are not influenced by such reports in their investment decision making. The providers' responses to the question of whether they make use of integrated reports could be categorised into three groups: Those who do not use integrated reports at all; those who make use of them sometimes; and those that make use of integrated reports regularly. In response to the question of whether he/she used integrated reports to inform investment decisions, P11, an investment banker, answered: "No ... Because I'm actually too short-term. Like I'm literally thinking one year, two years out" (P11:16, Investment banker). When asked whether they make use of integrated reports, P28 responded "I know the basics of King I, II, III, IV. I sometimes read the integrated report" (P28:21). P4 similarly responded that he/she "sometimes" referred to such reports (P4:10, Portfolio manager).

Participant responses raised questions regarding the idea that IR would encourage providers of financial capital to take a more long-term view (Adams, 2015). A small minority of participants, however, indicated that they absolutely make use of integrated reports. P1, for example, said:

> Yes, absolutely, absolutely. We seldom rely on third party research. Most other asset managers that I find rely only on third party research. The really successful, and I think South Africa to a large extent is an anomaly, but oosh, your US based asset management companies use primarily third party or broker research actually, not independent third party but broker based research and there's a lot of broker based research
>
> *(P1:35, Portfolio manager)*

P1's response was, however, an exception to the rule. P2 indicated that they do make use of integrated reports, but made it clear that such reports are only used for the purposes of analysing the financials:

> so from our point of view, really, if we look at integrated reporting we actually only look at the financial capital part of integrated reporting, so we would look at the assets, the income sheet, the balance sheet, even the cash flow that the client would be able to bring in, that is what we look at. We add, to certain clients, the human capital part, as they are, let's say, directors or employees of companies that provide them with deferred bonus plans and so on. So the human capital part does come into our integrated reporting but not much else comes into it as we only focus on the financial part, really
>
> *(P2:28, Portfolio manager)*

The third sub-theme that arose from the interviews was the extent to which participants were knowledgeable about the goals and purpose of IR. Here, it was especially important to establish whether the providers knew that the declared goals of IR are financial stability and sustainability. Clearly, if providers of financial capital are not even aware of what the goals are, they would not be able to contribute to the achievement of the goals through their actions. Not one of the participants was able to name the goals of IR:

> *Interviewer:* "Okay, and now, do you know what the specific goals or, sort of vision, of integrated reporting is? P2: No. To be very honest, no"
>
> *(P2:31, Portfolio manager)*.

Even though the terms financial stability and sustainability were not explicitly used, one of the portfolio managers (P8) described the goals of IR accurately. He/she stated that:

> I'm just trying to think of these … these whole … addressing some of the requirements that are growing from an ESG point of view, I've spoken of social responsibility investment, but this is the whole ESG. This is the impact on the environment, the social dynamic, governance, you know those are all very important, as, be it your carbon footprint, be it your … just the social side of … the social impact that business is having on society. The impact that business is having on society. So that's kind of what my understanding of the catalyst for a separate

report was, is this growing global requirement of providers of financial capital to ensure institutions invest with social conscience and corporates are run with social conscience and it's not social conscience necessarily from a charitable point of view, just from an impact on society generally. So my understanding of an integrated report is that it addresses those issues. It addresses the more detailed issues like remuneration and board representation, and board governance and empowerment dynamics. So it's just a very broad snapshot of a company, far more than just the numbers

(P8:10, Portfolio manager)

P12, an investment banker, also did not know what the goals of IR are, but described what he/she thought it should be. Nonetheless, P12 touched on an important code that emerged in the sub-themes – the notion of distrust. It is the idea that providers of financial capital do not trust company reports, because they believe companies are not willing to be completely transparent and that companies only produce integrated reports for compliance purposes:

So what it's supposed to do is piggyback on the global trend of giving it 360^0 view of a company, which I think is essential and brilliant if achieved. Are we there yet? We're far from there yet. I think most companies don't do it. Most companies do it as a PR and window dressing exercise

(P12:9, Investment banker)

Because not one of the participants specifically mentioned financial stability and sustainability, it was stated to some of the participants that the IIRC specifically declared that the vision of IR is to achieve financial stability and sustainability. They were then asked whether they would agree that IR is going to achieve these goals. In response to this, participants indicated that IR might be a contributing factor, but that it would require other interventions as well. One portfolio manager opined:

I think it [IR] would assist; I don't think it would be primarily through that, no, it would definitely assist, but you can still hide a lot of things, even in an integrated report, and that is the problem.

(P2:32, Portfolio manager)

The fourth and final sub-theme to emerge was the degree to which IR was perceived as a leadership phenomenon. Here, questions were asked of participants regarding the level of influence that IR has on their decision making, given the common definition of leadership: "a social influence process that motivates and enables a group of individuals to achieve a collective goal or shared purpose" (DeRue, 2011, p. 141). The question of whether they consider IR to be a leadership phenomenon was put to them plainly. Here, very few providers of financial capital indicated that IR really has an influence on their investment decision-making, but many of them agreed that IR is a leadership phenomenon. This might mean that they think it is a leading phenomenon in the corporate reporting space, but it is not leading their decision making, per se. This is an important finding: providers of financial capital, who have been named the primary audience of integrated reports, are not specifically influenced by IR. One asset manager responded:

I think if it, I think the practical implication, you know, of what integrated reporting would like to achieve, if you look at that then I'd say, yes I do think it will have that effect but I don't think it's a leader as such, I think it's more of a, of an extra, or a backup.

(P6:14, Asset manager)

P33 did not really answer the question outright and did not complete his/her entire thought process on the issue, but it was evident that P33 was of the view that IR would only lead providers of financial capital to make different investment decisions if the providers of financial capital took a long-term view:

> I think that providers of financial capital need to attach value to that reporting [IR] before they decide how they ... how important it is for the company to rely on... or how they think around integrated reporting will inform how the company behaves and how it invests in the long-term. If providers of financial capital are taking a long-term view, that's a key point.
>
> *(P33:11, Other)*

This was an important finding in the light of the literature on IR and the dichotomy (Adams, 2015; Flower, 2015) that exists in terms of whether IR is a failure or a success. The authors who argue that IR can still be a success specifically emphasise the idea that IR can shift the providers of financial capital to taking a more long-term view (Adams, 2015). However, this study's findings suggest, firstly, that IR is unlikely to achieve such a shift, since providers of financial capital will only pay attention to IR at all if they already take a long-term view. Secondly, it suggests that, rather than asking whether IR is a general success or failure, it might be more useful to ask to what degree IR has assisted those providers of financial capital who do take a long-term view.

In the Australian study of providers of financial capital, Stubbs et al. (2014) presented a similar finding. Their finding was actually more explicit, in the sense that a fund manager specifically said that IR will be more useful to long-term providers of financial capital and it was made clear that not all providers of financial capital are long-term. Caveats aside, when providers of financial capital were asked whether they considered IR to be a leadership phenomenon, the answer was in no way close to a resounding yes.

Perceptions about financial stability and sustainability

The theme of *perceptions about financial stability and sustainability* emerged automatically because the participants were asked specifically to provide their own definitions and interpretations of these concepts. This was done in order to understand whether they believe these goals can be achieved through investment and whether they consider the achievement of these goals to be one of their responsibilities. It was clear that providers of financial capital mostly held a very constricted view of what financial stability entailed, as financial stability was interpreted to mean the potential future profits of a single company. It was also evident that there is a wide range of perceptions regarding what sustainability means. Only two of the participants had a clear understanding of sustainability that aligned very well with the Brundtland definition of sustainability.[4] Others did not connect sustainability to the future of our species or planet at all, and perceived sustainability through a purely financial lens. On the question of the possible influence of IR on the attainment of financial stability and sustainability through better investment decision making, interviewees were generally of the opinion that it is possible, but that IR will only be one of many factors to have an influence.

Financial stability was described in very myopic terms and none of the participants defined financial stability in a broad macro-economic sense. It was, for example, very obvious from P8 that they perceived financial stability only in the narrow sense of the sustained cash flow and earnings of a single company: "Financial stability I guess is, would be the ability of the company to either sustain its current earnings profile or manageable levels of debt" (P8:11, Portfolio Manager). None of the participants defined financial stability as non-volatility of the entire financial system. P15, a pension fund trustee, also described financial stability along the same narrow lines, but went further in tying it to the past financial performance of a company: "Financial stability. I think financial stability is, in the case of equity, it's more a historic thing. It's based on history, how the company performed over the past" (P15:14, Pension Fund Trustee).

P6, an asset manager, also described financial stability in a narrow way, simply viewing it in terms of his/her job responsibility to grow the portfolio of the client. Not surprisingly, they added a component of managing risk to his/her definition. Risk and return was consistently described as an important code in the findings:

> Well, when it comes to wealth management, financial stability would mean, you know, to see a positive growth every year or not to make, you know, not to expose your clients to severe market volatility, to mitigate, you know, volatility as a risk in the short term.
>
> *(P6:12, Wealth manager)*

P6 in no uncertain terms described financial stability as the management of risk and return with the prerequisite of achieving positive growth. P6's statement also illustrated a short-termist perspective.

Closely linked to the idea of managing risk, one interviewee, an investment expert who specialises in ESG, described financial stability in a slightly different way by referring to the management of externalities. ESG issues are often referred to as externalities and seen as an investment risk, and therefore ESG issues should be considered – to mitigate risk. P33 "would say financial stability is really the management of externalities" (P33:9, Other investment expert).

In describing financial stability, the interviewees typically also did not talk about regulation or how regulation could assist in achieving more stability. This is surprising, seeing that compliance and regulation was a very prominent part of their responses to other questions. This might be an indication that they feel there is enough regulation in this area already. The providers of financial capital also did not mention how they think providers of financial capital could or should play a role in achieving financial stability.

The idea that sustainability simply referred to the sustainability of a business in terms of the continuation of making profits was expressed by a majority of the participants. P8 first indicated that they did not know what was meant by the term, but then continued to describe sustainability as the ability of a business to continue to exist in the future.

Interviewer: Sustainable development.
P8: Ja, I don't know what you mean by that.
Interviewer: Perhaps just sustainability?
P8: Ja, so… Actually I don't know – it's all quite – it feels quite soft, quite a theory. I don't… the ability of business to be around in the next decade.

(P8:12, Portfolio Manager)

P12, an investment banker, also described sustainability in very narrow terms in only focusing on the ability of business to continue to grow in the future: "For me sustainability in a business is ability to continue providing and growing and being around the block for a couple of years to come" (P12:10, Investment banker). P15, a pension fund trustee, provided a description of sustainability that is future-orientated as well, but expressed the idea that one should look at historic performance to estimate future performance. This idea was expressed in the descriptions of financial stability as well. P15, however, included the idea of trust in management as a component to guarantee the sustainability of business. The importance of the management of companies or governance was a code that repeated regularly throughout the interviews: "Sustainability is about looking into the future, getting to be, can this position be sustained? And the, once again, I think the history is an indication of sustainability into the future and so the trust you have in the management" (P15:15, Pension Fund Trustee).

With the exception of two of the participants, the vast majority perceived sustainability as the continuation of profits. The two exceptions described sustainability along the lines of the Brundtland Commission (1987) definition. For example, P9 stated that: "Sustainability to me is to make sure, and these are just my own words, that whatever it is, is handled in a healthy fashion that doesn't detract from the future" (P9:10, Portfolio Manager).

The Brundtland definition (Brundtland Commission, 1987) specifically refers to providing future generations with the ability to have no less than what we have. P33 described sustainability specifically as the impact of business on society. Although this description is not very close to the Brundtland definition, it does present the ideas of responsible citizenship that are aligned to the idea of building a future through responsible behaviour, and these often include the consideration of ESG issues:

> sustainable development is recognizing your role, or the company's role as a responsible corporate citizen and how many touch-points they have in society in relation to the business that they practise. Or the effect on society.
>
> *(P33:10, Other investment expert)*

The description of sustainability provided by P6 can be viewed in some ways as an outlier, but worth mentioning, because P6 specifically excluded the idea that investment can have something to do with sustainability. P6 however emphasised that sustainable development is context specific, but then continued to describe what seems like good governance:

> It's different in every country, but sustainable development in South Africa, that would not have to do with investing specifically, it will have to do with the company investing in itself and the area around it like if you look at the King code.
>
> *(P6:13, Wealth Manager)*

In terms of the question of whether IR could lead to financial stability and sustainability, the overall responses were surprisingly optimistic. This was surprising, because up to the point of actually asking the participants whether they thought IR was a leadership phenomenon, some of them did not even know what IR was. This might just point to the fact that participants perceived it as socially desirable to describe IR as a leadership phenomenon.

The participants' responses were optimistic in the sense that many participants described IR as something that could potentially influence investment decision making to consider more and other information. However, almost none of the participants described IR as something that greatly influences their decision making at the present moment. P8, a portfolio manager, could be described as the most optimistic of all the participants about IR in terms of its influence on investment decision making. They stated:

> But I think the more information that's available, the more information ... integrated reporting has been a big driver of this increase in information. There's no doubt it could lead providers of financial capital to make more informed decisions.
>
> *(P8:13, Portfolio Manager)*

P2 expressed the idea that IR might have an influence, but also stated that it will be one of a number of things – it will not bring about change alone: "I think it would assist. I don't think it would be primarily through that, no, it would definitely assist, but you can still hide a lot of things, even in an integrated report, and that is the problem" (P2:32, Portfolio Manager). Again, as observed throughout the interviews, participants expressed a sense of distrust towards company reports, and then, more specifically, integrated reports. For example, P1 unequivocally stated that integrated reports are "window dressing":

> a lot of those integrated reports is nothing other than window dressing, especially the corporate governance part. It's window dressing and you've got companies with beautiful mission and vision statements but it's only out there in an integrated report, it's not part of the culture really of the company
>
> *(P1:43, Portfolio Manager)*

It might well then be concluded that IR might have the potential to still influence providers of financial capital in the future to make investment decisions in other ways, but that IR has a fairly small influence on the decision-making processes of providers of financial capital at this point.

Conclusion

It was stated in the introduction to this chapter that the primacy of providers of financial capital in relation to IR is unquestionable. It was also emphasised that the IIRC has placed the responsibility of achieving the goals of financial stability and sustainability on the shoulders of providers of financial capital. It is therefore a worthy research endeavour to explore whether providers of financial capital are aware of this responsibility and if they are indeed being influenced by IR to such an extent that it changes the way they allocate financial capital with the view of achieving financial stability and sustainability. Thus, this chapter reported on a study (de Klerk, 2019) that explored the influence of IR on the providers of financial capital, specifically investigating whether investment decision-making is aimed at achieving financial stability and sustainability. The study concluded that many providers of financial capital are not even aware of IR and its goals. It also found that very few providers of financial capital are actually using IR as a source of information to integrate into their investment decision making. A certain level of distrust towards corporate reporting and IR was also reported and IR was even described as "window-dressing". In terms of the question of whether IR will achieve financial stability and sustainability by informing investment decision making, there was almost no indication that providers of financial capital are connecting the dots between IR, their investment decisions, and the achievement of financial stability and sustainability. There was also no suggestion that providers of financial capital understood that it is their responsibility to achieve financial stability and sustainability through investment decision making. Simply put, providers of financial capital still view their role and responsibility in a myopic manner, thinking that it simply means maximising returns and minimising risk.

Notes

1 This chapter reported on findings that emerged from a PhD study (de Klerk, 2019) that focused on IR as a leadership phenomenon for investment decision making and more specifically, providers of financial capital (providers of financial capital) as the proclaimed followers of IR.
2 In terms of the interview schedule, the findings reported in this chapter emerged from answers to the following preconceived questions:

1. Do you see yourself as a provider of financial capital?
2. Could you describe the role you play in investment decision making?
3. Do you take responsibility for any specific steps in the investment decision-making process?
4. Could you describe your fiduciary responsibility and how it informs your decision making?
5. How would you typically make investment decisions?
6. Could you describe what specific investment decisions you make?
7. What sources of information do you use to inform your investment decision making?
8. Do you have any knowledge of integrated reporting?
9. Do you know what the goals of integrated reporting are?
10. Do you make use of integrated reports?
11. Would you say integrated reporting influences your decision making in any way? If so, how?
12. Do you think that integrated reporting might influence your decision making in the future? If so, how?
13. Would you describe integrated reporting as a leadership phenomenon?
14. Do you think integrated reporting can "better" your investment decision making? If so, how?
15. How would you define "better" investment decision making?
16. How would you define financial stability?
17. How would you define sustainable development?
18. Do you think integrated reporting could lead to financial stability and sustainability? If so, how?

3 All reference codes are formatted as follows: participant number: code number in transcript, category of provider of financial capital. The participants are not classified as male or female, to increase their anonymity.
4 The Brundtland definition of sustainable development requires that we "meet the needs of the present without compromising the ability of future generations to meet their own needs" (Brundtland Commission, 1987).

References

Adams, C. A. (2015). The International Integrated Reporting Council: A call to action. *Critical Perspectives on Accounting, 27*, 23–28.

Atkins, J., and Maroun, W. (2015). Integrated reporting in South Africa in 2012: Perspectives from South African institutional investors. *Meditari Accountancy Research, 23*(2), 197–221.

Brown, J., and Dillard, J. (2014). Integrated reporting: On the need for broadening out and opening up. *Accounting, Auditing & Accountability Journal, 27*(7), 1120–1156.

Brundtland Commission. (1987). *Our common future.* Available at: www.un-documents.net/our-common-future.pdf (Accessed: 28 February 2019).

de Klerk, R. L. (2019). The social construction of leadership: A follower centric investigation into integrated reporting. PhD thesis, University of Pretoria.

DeRue, D. S. (2011). Adaptive leadership theory: Leading and following as a complex adaptive process. *Research in Organizational Behavior, 31*, 125–150.

Flower, J. (2015). The International Integrated Reporting Council: A story of failure. *Critical Perspectives on Accounting, 27*, 18–22.

Humphrey, C., O'Dwyer, B., and Unerman, J. (2017). Re-theorizing the configuration of organizational fields: The IIRC and the pursuit of "enlightened" corporate reporting. *Accounting and Business Research, 47*(1), 30–63.

IIRC. (2013a). *Basis for conclusions.* London, UK: IIRC.

IIRC. (2013b). *The International Integrated Reporting Framework.* London, UK: IIRC.

IIRC. (2015). *Creating value: Value to providers of financial capital.* London, UK: IIRC.

Jansen, H. (2010). The logic of qualitative survey research and its position in the field of social research methods. *Forum: Qualitative Social Research, 11*(2), 1–21.

Loprevite, S., Rupo, D., and Ricca, B. (2018). Integrated reporting practices in Europe and value relevance of accounting information under the Framework of IIRC. *International Journal of Business and Management, 13*(5), 1–12.

Öberseder, M., Schlegelmilch, B. B., and Gruber, V. (2011). "Why don't consumers care about CSR?": A qualitative study exploring the role of CSR in consumption decisions. *Journal of Business Ethics, 104*, 449–460.

Perego, P., Kennedy, S., and Whiteman, G. (2016). A lot of icing but little cake? Taking integrated reporting forward. *Journal of Cleaner Production, 136*, 53–64.

Rensburg, R., and Botha, E. (2014). Is integrated reporting the silver bullet of financial communication? A stakeholder perspective from South Africa. *Public Relations Review, 40*(2), 144–152.

Serafeim, G. (2015). Integrated reporting and provider of financial capital clientele. *Journal of Applied Corporate Finance, 27*(2), 34–51.

Slack, R., and Campbell, D. (2016). *Meeting users' information needs: The use and usefulness of integrated reporting.* London, UK: Association of Chartered Certified Accountants.

Stubbs, W., and Higgins, C. (2018). stakeholders' perspectives on the role of regulatory reform in integrated reporting. *Journal of Business Ethics, 147*(3), 489–508.

Stubbs, W., Higgins, C., Milne, M., and Hems, L. (2014). *Financial Capital Providers' Perceptions of Integrated Reporting.* Available at: https://ssrn.com/abstract=2473426 (Accessed: 28 February 2019).

Thomson, I. (2015). "But does sustainability need capitalism or an integrated report": A commentary on "The International Integrated Reporting Council: A story of failure" by Flower, J. *Critical Perspectives on Accounting, 27*, 18–22.

Tweedie, D., and Martinov-Bennie, N. (2015). Entitlements and time: Integrated reporting's double-edged agenda. *Social and Environmental Accountability Journal, 35*(1), 49–61.

PART VII

Sustainable development and integrated reporting

27

MAKING SUSTAINABLE DEVELOPMENT GOALS HAPPEN THROUGH INTEGRATED THINKING AND REPORTING

Cristiano Busco

LUISS Guido Carli, and Roehampton University of London

Fabrizio Granà

ESCP Business School

Maria Federica Izzo

LUISS Guido Carli

Abstract

This chapter analyses the role that organizations can play in the achievement of the UN Sustainable Development Goals (SDGs). Drawing on the experience of three corporate leaders in different industries, we analyse the potential advantages they can obtain by leveraging the interconnections between SDGs, integrated thinking and integrated reporting. In particular, we find that both integrated thinking and SDGs can support organizations in defining risks, prioritizing activities, and developing clear and successful strategies for better and more holistic approaches to sustainable development and value creation.

Introduction

The world is facing massive global economic, social and environmental challenges. From poverty to climate change and clean water access, these issues are affecting our daily activities more than was imagined likely in the past, and require unprecedented and cohesive actions from citizens, governments and organizations. In particular, organizations need to shift from a business-centred approach, focused almost exclusively on financial returns, towards a more sustainable value creation approach. In doing so, organizations are expected to integrate sustainability dimensions (Economic, Social and Environmental dimension), initiatives and targets into their strategic plans, business models and performance measurement systems by radically changing their behaviours and operations.

In parallel, public, private and non-governmental organizations have been directly involved in attempts to ensure more coordinated efforts with regard to the 'sustainability agenda' (see, for example, the UN General Assembly resolution of 2010).

This process was consolidated in 2015, when the General Assembly of the United Nations promoted the 2030 Agenda for Sustainable Development, accompanied by a list of Sustainable Development Goals (SDGs). The goals are universally applicable in developing and developed countries alike, and require governments to translate them into national action plans, policies and initiatives, reflecting the different realities and capacities their countries possess. However, attempting to achieve the SDGs is not just a governmental and societal task – it also requires the involvement of proactive and sustainable organizations. Making SDGs an integral part of organizations' strategies and business models can help to generate new source of revenues, increase supply chain resilience, recruit and retain talent, spawn investors interest and ensure ongoing license to operate.

However, the path towards the integration of Sustainable Development Goals (SDGs) into strategies and business models is not straightforward and requires organizations to directly engage and dialogue with stakeholders and experts on social and environmental issues. As organizations become familiar with the SDGs, the development of innovative management and reporting systems that enable the identification and measurement of key sustainability targets seems necessary and unavoidable.

By drawing on the experience of three corporate leaders in different industries, this chapter aims to analyse the role organizations can play in promoting and realizing SDGs and the potential advantages they can obtain by leveraging the interconnections between SDGs, and integrated thinking and integrated reporting. In particular, we show that integrated thinking and reporting, and SDGs, can support organizations in defining risks, prioritizing activities and developing clear and successful strategies for better and more holistic approaches to sustainable development and value creation.

The chapter is structured as follows. The next section reviews the literature on sustainable development and SDGs, focusing on organizations' role towards the achievement of the Agenda 2030. This is followed by an exploration of the role of integrated thinking and reporting in making SDGs visible and manageable within organizations. The penultimate section illustrates some of the best practices adopted by three organizations that are leaders in different industries (PepsiCo, City Developments Limited and Itaú Unibanco Holdings SA). The final section presents conclusions.

Towards a more sustainable approach to value creation: integrating SDGs in companies' business models

For the past 30 years or so, world leaders and national governments, as well as businesses and civil society as a whole, have embraced sustainability as the cornerstone of long-term development and growth. As widely acknowledged by the literature, the concept of sustainability was defined in 1987 by the World Commission on Environment and Development (WCED) as 'development that meets the needs of the present, without compromising the ability of future generations to meet their own needs' (WCED, 1987).

Since the publication of this first definition of sustainable development, an increasing number of institutions and international bodies have attempted to address issues broadly related to the domain of sustainability (such as extreme poverty, water emergencies, health, climate change, pollution, social inequalities, access to energy and hunger). Since the early 1990s, several major events and initiatives have taken place globally. Among others, the Rio Summit in 1992 laid the foundations for the global institutionalization of the concept of sustainable development by proposing Agenda 21, which set out actions in regard to sustainable development, conservation and management of natural resources.

The 'Earth Summit' in Rio in 1992, organized by the UN Conference on Environment and Development (UNCED), hosted more than 114 heads of state, including over 10,000 representatives from 178 countries and 1,400 non-governmental organizations. Aside from the numbers, the UNCED Conference was a historical moment in which international governments and institutions gathered around a table to further debate issues concerning the economic, social and environmental dimensions of sustainable development as priorities in international politics (Spangenberg et al., 2002). The content of Agenda 21 was revolutionary for that time and laid out a set of principles to be implemented to achieve sustainable development in the long term.

The scope of the 'Earth Summit' and its final product, Agenda 21, had a great impact on successive conferences and definitions of sustainable development. The publication of the United Nations Millennium Declaration in September 2000 committed governments and public institutions to a new global partnership to reduce extreme poverty and set out a series of time-bound targets (eight in total), known as the Millennium Development Goals (MDGs). According to McArthur (2013, p. 20), MDGs were 'the world's first explicit development partnership framework between developed and developing countries'. The aim was to achieve the MDGs by 2015. They included the following eight objectives: (1) Halving extreme poverty; (2) Halting the spread of HIV/AIDS; (3) Providing universal primary education; (4) Eliminating gender disparity in education; (5) Reducing the under-five mortality rate; (6) Reducing the maternal mortality rate and achieving universal access to reproductive health; (7) Developing a global partnership (to address the needs of the poorest countries, to further an open non-discriminatory trade system and to deal with developing country debt); and (8) Ensuring environmental sustainability (by integrating sustainable development into countries' policies and programs, reducing biodiversity loss, improving access to safe drinking water and sanitation, and improving the lives of slum dwellers) (UN, 2010).

In parallel, public, private and non-governmental organizations have been directly involved in attempts to coordinate efforts regarding the sustainability agenda. This process was further consolidated in 2015 when the UN General Assembly adopted the 2030 Agenda for Sustainable Development: a plan of action presenting a list of SDGs (17 objectives and 169 targets) that all countries of the world are encouraged to achieve by 2030[1] (Figure 27.1).

The SDGs build on the results achieved by the MDGs and involve both developed and developing countries. Participating countries are required to embrace a wide range of topics that interconnect across the economic, social and environmental dimensions of sustainable development, which affect all sectors of society in all parts of the world. Although the 17 SDGs are not considered legally binding, governments are expected to take ownership and stimulate actions in areas of critical importance for humanity and the planet, recognizing that a change in the approach is required. To achieve these goals, governments and organizations are asked to combine their efforts to reduce inequalities and poverty worldwide and tackle climate change.

Figure 27.1 The Sustainable Development Goals

In order to implement a successful sustainable development agenda, public and private organizations are encouraged to create inclusive partnerships with governments and place civil society and the planet at the centre of their long-term value creation processes and business models.[2] As suggested by the Oxford Committee for Famine Relief (OXFAM), organizations should embrace three pathways to better integrate SDGs within their strategies and business models (OXFAM, 2017). First, organizations should *prioritize an understanding of sustainable impact*, reviewing their initiatives and strategic objectives to determine the impacts (positive and negative) they have on multiple stakeholders. Second, organizations should *align their core business strategies with the SDGs*. If organizations aim at pursuing the SDGs, they have to broaden and deepen their partnerships, aligning their core business practices and strategies with the principles of sustainable development. Third, organizations should *work together with regulators, governments, investors and citizens* by setting rules (regulators), incentives (governments) and rewards for meaningful SDG engagement (investors) that may improve social responsibilities and ambitions towards a new concept of what meaningful engagement with the SDGs should look like (OXFAM, 2017, p. 3).

The ambition of the SDGs is not only to challenge organizations on the achievement of broader social, environmental, economic and governance issues, but to develop a global movement that reframes the existence and sustainability of entire industries (BSDC, 2017).

Specifically, SDGs suggest managing performance with regard to the three pillars of sustainable development (economic, social and environmental) in a balanced and integrated manner, leading governments' and organizations' actions towards a more inclusive approach to sustainable development. For instance, as shown in a report of the Business Sustainable Development Commission:

> major investments in infrastructure and innovation will be needed to meet the environmental goals set in the SDGs. Links between the social and environmental clusters are also critically important: sustainable management of land and water eco-systems will help improve agricultural productivity and eliminate hunger and malnutrition, while climate action, better housing and less polluted cities will have widespread benefits on health and well-being.
>
> *(BSDC, 2017, p. 23)*

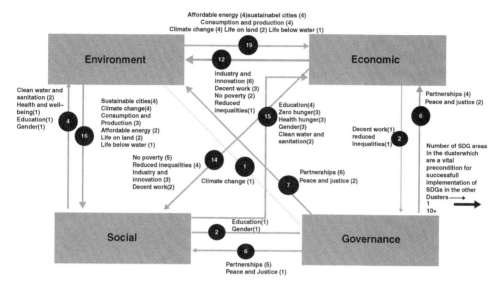

Figure 27.2 Connecting SDGS and their social, environmental and economic effects
Source: Adapted from BSDC (2017, p. 23)

Further, 'effective action on climate change will be essential to achieving the objectives of strong economic growth and ending poverty, while access to affordable energy will help reduce inequality and support sustainable industrialization in the developing world' (BSDC, 2017, p. 23) (see Figure 27.2).

At the same time, the alignment between SDGs and organizations' strategies may help in generating new revenues, increasing supply chain resilience, recruiting and retaining talent, stimulating investor interest, and assuring organizations with licenses to operate.

Achieving the SDGs through integrated thinking and reporting

The integration of SDGs within companies' strategies and business models calls for a more transparent and complete disclosure of information in relation to sustainable development, both in the private and the public sector. With the aim of offering an account of their ongoing attempts made to integrate competitive strategies and sustainable development goals, organizations are expected to provide insightful information beyond their annual key financial data. Since 2015, the number of organizations that have been reporting their contribution to the SDGs has increased significantly. According to the UN Global Compact (2017)[3]: 75 percent of organizations have actions in place to address the SDGs; 55 percent of organizations align their core business strategy with one or more relevant UN goals/ issues; 70 percent of organizations are reporting publicly about their progress with sustainable development; and 55 percent of organizations note that reporting helps them in embedding sustainability into the business.

However, organizations tend to 'cherry pick' the SDGs they address and ignore those that do not fit with their specific corporate priorities or comfort zones. According to a survey published by PwC in 2015, only 1 percent of the organizations surveyed measured and reported their impacts on all 17 SDGs, and 34 percent assessed SDGs in accordance with their relevance to the business (PwC, 2015). For these reasons, organizations' approaches to and reporting on SDGs still do not provide a comprehensive overview of the actions they take with regard to sustainable development, and this is often due to organizations' industry characteristics, competitor policies and expectations of heterogeneous stakeholders that are difficult to satisfy (PwC, 2015) (see Figure 27.3).

Considered as one of the most recent accounting and reporting innovations worldwide, integrated thinking and reporting have been used within organizations to aid understanding of the cause and effect relationships between business models, strategy execution and sustainable value creation. Developed and promoted by the International Integrated Reporting Council (IIRC), integrated reporting refers to organizations' processes of decision making, management and reporting, and is based on the connectivity and interdependencies between a range of capitals (financial, manufacturing, human, intellectual, social and relationship, and natural) that affect an organization's ability to create value and be sustainable.

According to the IIRC (2013), integrated reporting leads to integrated thinking and results from a process of connectivity between a range of factors, including:

- the capitals that the organization uses or affects and their critical interdependencies, including trade-offs between them;
- the capacity of the organization to respond to key stakeholders' needs and interests;
- how the organization tailors its business model and strategy to respond to its external environment and the risks and opportunities it faces;
- the organization's activities, performance (financial and other) and outcomes in terms of capitals – in the past, present and future.

The combination of all these factors makes integrated thinking and reporting a powerful tool for embedding the SDGs within organizations' measurement and disclosure processes, enabling managers to focus on sustainable development (Adams, 2017). Further, integrated thinking and reporting enable managers to better understand how multiple capitals are involved and transformed throughout an organization's value creation process, determining its influence on a multitude of stakeholders and more generally on the external environment, and conversely measuring its impacts on SDGs.

As mentioned by Adams (2017), there are two main advantages in merging integrated thinking and reporting with SDGs. First, aligning business approaches to the SDGs with integrated reporting can redirect investment flows to maximize value creation and enhance knowledge of the impact of business activities on sustainable development. Second, integrating SDGs within performance measurement and reporting systems can help organizations in reducing risk, identifying opportunities, and delivering long-term, innovative solutions and technologies for addressing sustainable development.

To help organizations manage SDGs as strategic objectives to be achieved, Adams (2017) defined a series of steps that need to be applied in a continuous and iterative cycle (See Figure 27.4). In particular, organizations would be required to:

1. *Enlarge their approach to the external environment, explicitly considering risks and opportunities associated with sustainable development.* In this way, organizations are invited to identify the external factors that can both influence and be influenced by organizations' activities.
2. *Define and prioritize sustainable development issues, considering their specific characteristics.* This will lead organizations to identify their material risks, and opportunities to create sustainable value in the long term. In this phase, stakeholder engagement can play a strategic role in defining these material issues, since they are fundamental in the value creation process.

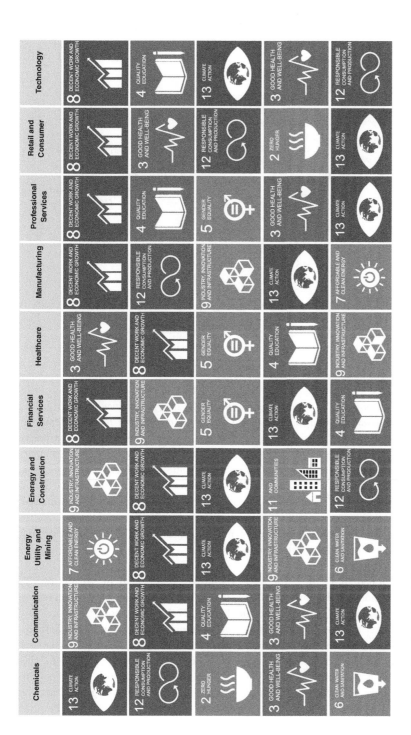

Figure 27.3 Top business impacts by industry

Source: Adapted from PwC (2015, p. 11)

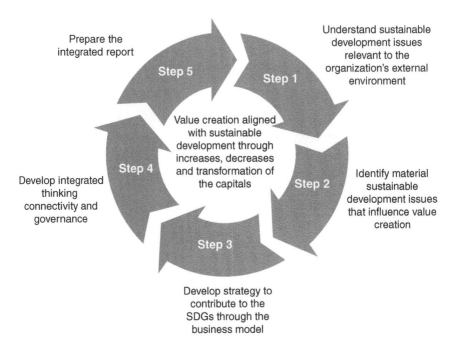

Figure 27.4 SDGs and the value creation process
Source: Adapted from Adams (2017, p. 22)

3. *Incorporate the material issues identified at step two within the strategy definition process.*
4. *Embed all the considerations mentioned above into the process of integrated thinking, facing the trade-offs that exist among different SDGs and different capitals.* Thanks to this approach, organizations will properly consider the connectivity and interdependencies in a range of factors that affect an organization's ability to create value over time.
5. *Inform organization members and stakeholders in a clear way about their contribution to SDGs through the integrated report.* These results should be presented alongside the information about capitals. By adopting integrated thinking and reporting, organizations are able to depict the links and the relationships between the capitals (used and/or affected) and the SDGs, through their value creation process.

The five steps mentioned in Figure 27.4 were graphically represented by Adams (2017) using the value creation model promoted by the International Integrated Reporting Framework (IIRC Framework). As shown in Figure 27.4, organizations' inputs and outcomes are strictly related and represent both the beginning and the end of a business model, which is based on the six capitals promoted by the IIRC. By exploiting a variety of capitals, organizations generate outcomes that may have positive or negative impacts on the organization's external environment, affecting its value creation process over time. For this reason, in order to limit the effects of negative impacts on the society, organizations are required to implement ad hoc strategies that capture social, environmental and economic dimensions as well as the intertwining relationships among them.

As maintained by Adams (2017), integrated reporting and the SDGs potentially follow the same pattern, as both aim at embracing the economic, social and environmental aspects

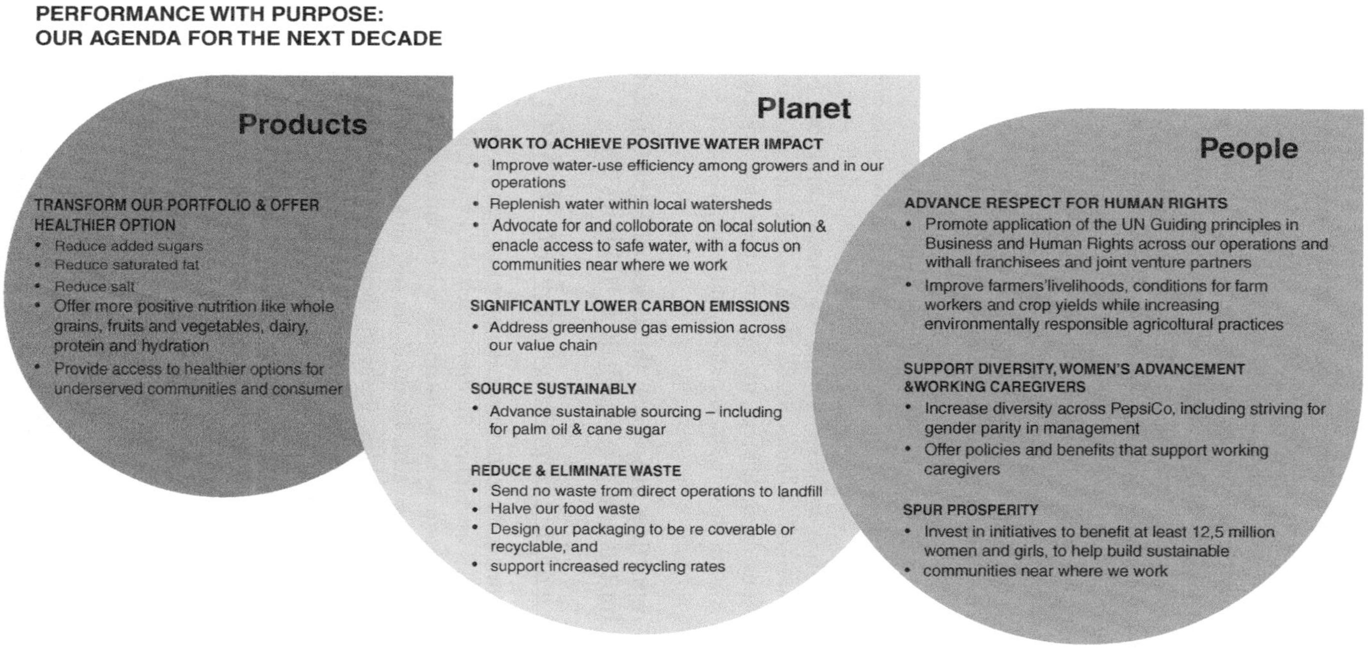

PERFORMANCE WITH PURPOSE:
OUR AGENDA FOR THE NEXT DECADE

Products

TRANSFORM OUR PORTFOLIO & OFFER HEALTHIER OPTION

- Reduce added sugars
- Reduce saturated fat
- Reduce salt
- Offer more positive nutrition like whole grains, fruits and vegetables, dairy, protein and hydration
- Provide access to healthier options for underserved communities and consumer

Planet

WORK TO ACHIEVE POSITIVE WATER IMPACT

- Improve water-use efficiency among growers and in our operations
- Replenish water within local watersheds
- Advocate for and colllaborate on local solution & enacble access to safe water, with a focus on communities near where we work

SIGNIFICANTLY LOWER CARBON EMISSIONS

- Address greenhouse gas emission across our value chain

SOURCE SUSTAINABLY

- Advance sustainable sourcing – including for palm oil & cane sugar

REDUCE & ELIMINATE WASTE

- Send no waste from direct operations to landfill
- Halve our food waste
- Design our packaging to be re coverable or recyclable, and
- support increased recycling rates

People

ADVANCE RESPECT FOR HUMAN RIGHTS

- Promote application of the UN Guiding principles in Business and Human Rights across our operations and withall franchisees and joint venture partners
- Improve farmers'livelihoods, conditions for farm workers and crop yields while increasing environmentally responsible agricoltural practices

SUPPORT DIVERSITY, WOMEN'S ADVANCEMENT &WORKING CAREGIVERS

- Increase diversity across PepsiCo, including striving for gender parity in management
- Offer policies and benefits that support working caregivers

SPUR PROSPERITY

- Invest in initiatives to benefit at least 12.5 million women and girls, to help build sustainable communities near where we work

Figure 27.5 Performance with Purpose at PepsiCo
Source: Adapted from PepsiCo (2015, p. 5)

of sustainable development. The former aims to improve organizations' disclosure and reporting systems, and the latter aims to broaden the spectrum of sustainable development towards better actions and outcomes.

The integration of SDGs within organizations' business models may represent both a substantial opportunity and an important challenge for the whole economic system. It serves as an opportunity since it brings in the benefits of additional investments, skills and innovation from the business sector. However, a challenge may arise as it gives unprecedented power and expectations to organizations as fundamental actors in sustainable development. In this context, organizations are required to meet the SDGs by conducting robust impact assessment analysis and improving their non-financial reporting processes.

The world cannot afford public and private organizations to ignore meeting the 17 SDGs, as major undesirable consequences may occur. The costs of managing global burdens (such as violence and armed conflict, obesity, congestion and climate change) may increase, generating unstable and unequitable societies, and irreversibly damaging the environment. Further, the mismanagement of global burdens may have a cumulative economic impact equal to one-third of global gross domestic product, stimulating governments to produce strong regulations and sanctions that may limit organizations' access to new forms of financing (BSDC, 2017).

The following sections describe how an increasing number of organizations are attempting to align their corporate purpose with the execution of sustainable strategies to comply with the SDGs. In particular, we draw on the experiences of PepsiCo, City Developments Limited and Itaú Unibanco Holdings SA to illustrate how integrated thinking and reporting can help organizations from different sectors (i.e., food and beverage, real estate and banking) embed SDGs within their business models and strategic plans.

Integrating SDGs into reporting processes: the cases of PepsiCo, City Developments Limited and Itaú Unibanco Holdings SA

The case of PepsiCo: mapping corporate strategy with the SDGs

PepsiCo is an American leader in the food and beverage industry that sells products in more than 200 countries. The company was established in 1965 when the Pepsi-Cola Company merged with Frito-Lay, Inc. PepsiCo's attention to sustainable development started in 2006 when the company launched its 'Performance with Purpose' strategy, aimed at expanding the organization's portfolio of more nutritious products, shrinking their environmental footprint, acting as a good global citizen and working to improve employees' and their families' working and living conditions.[4] As illustrated in its 2015 report, PepsiCo has based its 'Performance with Purpose' strategy on three key strategic goals: Products (human sustainability), Planet (environmental sustainability) and People (talent sustainability) – see Figure 27.5.

By focusing on creating and sustaining jobs, stimulating economic growth, transforming the product portfolio, protecting the planet and enhancing the lives of people around the world, PepsiCo believes that impactful contributions to sustainable development will be made through its own business and its value creation process.

More recently, the company decided to align its 'Performance with Purpose' strategy with the most relevant SDGs impacted by the company's traditional activities. In particular, PepsiCo's Sustainability Report 2017 identifies, for each of the three key strategic goals mentioned above, the SDGs impacted and provides examples of the actions implemented in the company's daily activities. Additionally, by aligning the 'Performance with Purpose' strategy and the SDGs, the report aims at explaining the opportunities the company may

SDG	EXAMPLES OF ACTION
Zero Hunger	• Since 2016, we have provided access to 475 million servings of affordable nutritious food and beverages to undeserved to consumers and communities, through products like Quaker *3 Minutos* in Latin America. • Sustainable agricultural practices will be important to meeting the increasing demand for food as the global population grows. As of the end of 2017, 24 percent of our direct crops were sustainably sourced.
Good Health and Well-Being	• The rate of sale growth Everyday Nutrition products outpaced the rate of sales growth in the balance of our product portfolio in 2017. • 43 percent of our beverage portfolio volume in our Top 10 Beverage markets contains 100 Calories of fewer from added sugars per 12-ounce serving.
Gender Equality	• As of the end of 2017, women and men were paid within one percent each other in the 21 countries we have analyzed, based on base compensation and after controlling for legitimate drivers of pay. • In 2016 and 2017, PepsiCo Foundation and invested $ 14,3 millions to support initiatives that benefit women and girls in communities near where we work.
Clean Water and Sanitation	• 95 percent of wastewater from our operations met PepsiCo's highs standard for protection of the environment in 2017. • With the PepsiCo Foundation and its partners, we have provided access to safe water to nearly 16 million people since 2006 in the world's most at-water-risk areas.
Decent Work and Economi Growth	• Through our Sustainable Farming Program (SFP), wee work with partecipating growers to promote the well-being og agricultural workers and surrounding communities, with 79 percent of our directly sourced crops grown by farmes engaged through SFP. • In 2016 and 2017, we enable 6,4 million women and girls to progress through school and be successful in the workforce.
Responsible Consumption and Production	• An estimated 85 percent of our packaging worldwide was recyclable, compostable or biodegradable in 2017. • 95 percent of waste was diverted away from landfill through reuse, recycling or waste-to-energy in 2017.
Climate Action	• In 2017, we reduced Scope 3 GHG emissions by approximately 2,1 million metric tonnes versus our 2015 baseline. This represents approximately seven percent of our 2030 target reduction amount. • Our goal to reduce absolute GHG emissions across our value chain by least 20 percent by 2030 has been validated by the Science Based Target Initiative.

Figure 27.6 Aligning Performance with Purpose to the SDGs

Source: Adapted from PepsiCo (2017, p. 9)

have for improving health, environmental conservation, and education in under-served regions through sustainable development partnerships and programs.

PepsiCo identifies seven SDGs that the company directly affects, which are classified below according to the company's three key strategic areas:

• Products: SDG 2 – Zero hunger – and SDG 3 – Good health and well-being;
• Planet: SDG 6 – Clear water and sanitation – ; SDG 12 – Responsible consumption and production – and SDG 13 – Climate Action;
• People: SDG 5 – Gender equality – and SDG 8 – Decent work and economic growth.

For each SDG impacted by the organization, the report provides detailed accounts of the actions taken and the performance achieved between 2016 and 2017 (see Figure 27.6).

The case of city developments limited: determining the connectivity between capitals and SDGs

City Developments Limited (CDL) is a multinational real estate company listed on the Singapore Stock Exchange. It operates in more than 100 locations and 28 countries around the world. Its investment portfolio comprises residences, offices, hotels, serviced apartments and shopping malls, totalling over 18 million square feet of floor area globally.

Sustainability has historically been a top priority of the company and, from 1990, it has been integrated into CDL's corporate vision and mission to create enhanced value for stakeholders and the business. The company has always recognized environmental, social and governance (ESG) dimensions as central to its value creation process, actively engaging with existing shareholders and potential investors to communicate its business case for ESG integration. As suggested by the Executive Chairman (CDL, 2017 p. 4):

> There has been progressively more evidence that investors are placing greater importance on such [ESG] data, believing in a causal link between good ESG practices and the long-term success and economic value of a company, beyond just pursuing financial returns. Furthermore, research has now shown that investors are actively incorporating such data into investment decisions, reinforcing the business case for sustainability. Businesses must adapt to the increasing importance of sustainability, capitalize on such opportunities and unlock the potential of integrating sustainability into their operations.

More recently, CDL launched a series of projects that have supported a massive move towards integration and strategic alignment with ESG dimensions. In 2015, the company was one of the first developers in Singapore to adopt the integrated reporting approach in its sustainability reporting process. In 2016, the company developed a materiality assessment process that aligned ESG issues with the key SDGs achieved, and finally, in 2017, the company launched a sustainability blueprint guide labelled 'CDL Future Value 2030'.

The 'CDL Future Value 2030' blueprint is an integral part of CDL's integrated sustainability strategy and reporting process. It is based on the six capitals promoted by the IIRC Framework and is also aligned with 13 SDGs (see Figure 27.7). In particular, it illustrates how the organization aims to address the fast-changing environmental and business landscape by making ESG performance financially evaluated (CDL, 2019).

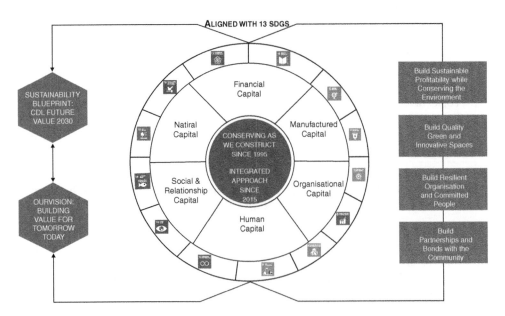

Figure 27.7 CDL value-creation business model
Source: CDL (2019, p. 17)

FUTURE VALUE 2030 GOALS	2030 TARGETS (EFFECTIVE FROM 2018)	INTERIM ANNUAL TARGETS FOR 2018	FY2018 PERFORMANCE
GOAL 1:Building Sustainable Cities and Communication	Archieve Green Marks certification for 80% of CDL owned and/or management building	≥ 75%	75% archieved
	Maintain 100% tenant participation in	Achieve 100%	100% maintained
	Double our commitment to adopt innovations and technology green building	Average of two innovations or new technology adoptions per year	1.Adoption of solution by two sustainability-linked local start-ups, Gush! And UglyGood
			2.Implementation of a food waste treatment system at le Grove Serviced Residences
	Double resources devoted to advocacy of sustainability practices, stakeholder engagement and capacity building	≥ 100 training programmes and events held in the SSA per year	146 comprising 60 trainings and 86 events

Figure 27.8 CDL 2030 strategic goal, targets and performance for 2018

Source: Adapted from CDL (2019, p. 18)

The CDL Future Value 2030 blueprint sets out long-term ESG goals and targets for 2030 and aims at:

- reinforcing CDL's long-established sustainability strategy and best practices in creating value for business, investors, stakeholders, community and the planet;
- setting out clear directions and ESG goals material to CDL's business and stakeholders;
- maintaining CDL's position as a sustainable leader in the real estate management and development sector.

Delivering on three strategic goals, the blueprint provides a set of targets to address ESG issues, while contributing to the UN SDGs. As shown in the 2019 CDL integrated report, the organization's strategic plan is based on three key strategic goals: Building sustainable cities; Reducing environmental impact; and Ensuring Fair, Safe and Inclusive Workplaces. The three goals are monitored annually according to the actual performance achieved and their variation from the future targets (see Figure 27.8). Figure 27.8 also shows the SDGs impacted by each goal and target.

Further, the report introduces a new step of disclosure by integrating capitals, past performances, specific targets and sustainable development goals in the same table. Interestingly, the table, as shown in Figure 27.9, illustrates how the key capitals exploited throughout the organization's value creation process (manufactured; social and relationship; natural; organizational and human) affect the most material SDGs. It also highlights the activities and initiatives performed, the output achieved, and the value created for the business and its stakeholders.

The case of Itaú Unibanco Holdings SA (IUH): integrating the SDGS within the company's business model

Itaú Unibanco Holdings SA (IUH) is a publicly listed company operating in the banking industry. The company provides a range of financial products and services to individual and corporate clients in Brazil and abroad. It is interesting to note how IUH explicitly represents itself in its annual integrated report as a 'bank with a purpose', which has a key role in leading a real change in business towards sustainable development (IUH, 2017, p. 4).

Manufactured Capital	Activities	Innovation and Tecnology	Customer Service	Contributing to SDGs
		Universal Design	Safety Design and Management	
		Cross –sectoral Partnerships	Stakeholder Engagement	
		Quality Management		
Financial Capital	Outputs	Green Buildings	Green Leases	
		CDL Green Lease Partnership Programme	Products Safety and Customer Well-being	
		Green Mark for Healthier Workplaces Scheme	Singapore Sustainability Academy	
Social and Relationship Capital	Value Created	Energy Efficiency		
		Cost Saving		
		Costumer Satisfation		
		Social Impact		

Figure 27.9 CDL capitals, initiatives, outputs, value created and SDGs
Source: Adapted from CDL (2019, p. 34)

Aiming to 'present the progress of business towards the vision of being the leading bank in sustainable performance and customer satisfaction' (IUH, 2017, p. 4), the Itaù Unibanco 2017 Integrated Report illustrates the different capitals that affect the bank's value creation process by: (a) identifying the key material themes and, (b) identifying their impacts on SDGs. Three different categories of impact have been defined according to their relevance to the business: 'impacts of operations' ('direct' social and economic impacts of the jobs created and maintained or income generated); 'catalyzing impacts' (impacts of the operations relating to the top ten products offered), and 'other impacts' (direct, indirect and induced).

Figure 27.10 illustrates the bank business model, showing the cause-effect relationships between capitals, material issues, strategic objectives and SDGs. All these aspects have been represented as parts of a circle known as the 'Sustainable Performance Spiral'. Using this

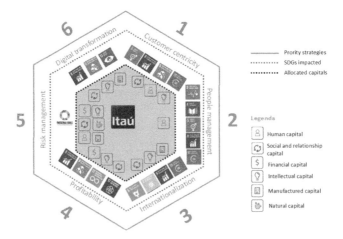

Figure 27.10 Priority strategies, material themes and SDGs
Source: Adapted from IUH (2017, p. 13)

model, the report aims to explain how IUH plays an active role in addressing the SDGs by balancing financial goals and sustainable performance at a global level, finding concrete solutions and providing excellent service to its clients.

The 'Sustainable Performance Spiral', illustrated in Figure 27.10, identifies the six key strategic priorities promoted by the bank (Customer centricity, People management, Internationalization, Profitability, Risk management and Digital transformation), which are determined in accordance with the most material issues for the organization and its stakeholders. Figure 27.10 also points out the SDGs that are most exposed to the company's strategic drivers and material issues. Finally, the base of the whole model illustrates the capitals used by the company to achieve its six strategic objectives.

Conclusion

By drawing on recent studies about the SDGs and their relationships to integrated thinking (Adams, 2017; Busco et al., 2018), this chapter has showed how integrated thinking endeavours to connect financial and nonfinancial performance in the achievement of the SDGs. In particular, we have analysed the cases of PepsiCo, CDL and Itau Unibanco to explain how organizations integrate their strategies and business models with SDGs using different performance measurement and reporting approaches.

All three case studies analysed show that, in order to make SDGs happen, organizations need to change their operational model, looking for systemic change and constant innovation in their performance measurement and reporting practices. In this regard, integrated thinking and reporting can provide guidelines and tools that may allow organizations to improve their management and reporting approaches (Busco et al., 2018) by:

• embedding the SDGs within strategies, risk management and business models, and enabling organizations to focus on sustainable development;
• demonstrating the impact of an organization's value creation process on sustainable development. In other words, integrated reporting may lead toward greater transparency and completeness of disclosure, emphasizing the outcomes that organizations generate with regard to sustainable development.

Organizations still face difficulties in developing standardized performance measurement and reporting methodologies to meet the SDGs and embrace all the different stakeholders' requests. However, their attempts are not necessarily counterproductive. As every business model exploits a different number of capitals, integrated reporting invites organizations to reflect deeply on their own contributions to the SDGs and sustainable development. Each of the companies analysed in this chapter adopted a tailored approach to meet the SDGs by readapting their strategic goals and actions (see PepsiCo), business models and resource allocations with a view to the creation of sustainable value (see respectively Itau Unibanco and CDL).

A cultural shift is required to support such a process and must be rooted in the reorganization of systems, processes and practices, while seeking to meet the SDGs. In this regard, management accounting and reporting tools, such as IR, represent a powerful instrument enabling organizations to move toward novel sustainable growth models that aim to reduce exposure to risks, produce benefits for both organizations and the economic system, and open new opportunities in terms of innovation, reputation and efficiency gains. This is in line with the OXFAM (2017) call for companies to change the way they define the overall purpose of business and their actions. Business structures must play a critical role in determining the trade-off between a focus on profit maximization and sustainable development objectives. They may empower stakeholders' requests relating to key decisions, and resolve trade-offs between multiple stakeholder interests.

Notes

1 www.un.org/sustainabledevelopment.
2 UN 17th Sustainable Development Goal www.un.org/sustainabledevelopment/globalpartnerships/
3 The survey was submitted to all 9,400 organizations participating to the UN Global Compact with a response rate of 22 percent (1,945 respondents in total).
4 www.pepsico.com/sustainability/performance-with-purpose.

References

Adams, C. (2017). *The Sustainable Development Goals, integrated thinking and the integrated report.* Available at: http://integratedreporting.org/resource/sdgs-integrated-thinking-and-the-integrated-report/ (Accessed: 20 August 2019).

BSDC. (2017). *Valuing the SDG prize. Unlocking business opportunities to accelerate sustainable and Inclusive growth.* Available at: http://s3.amazonaws.com/aws-bsdc/Valuing-the-SDG-Prize.pdf (Accessed: 20 August 2019).

Busco, C., Granà, F., and Izzo, M. F. (2018). *Sustainable Development Goals and Integrated Thinking.* London: Routledge-Giappichelli.

CDL. (2017). *Integrated Sustainability Report 2017.* Available at: https://www.cdlsustainability.com/sustainability-reports/ (Accessed: 17 March 2020).

CDL. (2019). *Integrated Sustainability Report 2019.* Available at: https://ir.cdl.com.sg/news-releases/news-release-details/cdl-integrated-sustainability-report-2019-accelerating-action (Accessed: 20 August 2019).

IIRC. (2013). *International <IR> Framework.* Available at: http://integrate-dreporting.org/Resources/ (Accessed: 20 August 2019).

IUH. (2017). *Integrated Report 2017.* Available at: www.itau.com.br/annual-report/integrated-reporting/ (Accessed: 20 August 2019).

McArthur. (2013). Own the Goals: What the Millennium Development Goals Have Accomplished. *Foreign Affairs, 92*(2), 152–162.

OXFAM. (2017). *Raising the BAR. Rethinking the role of business in the Sustainable Development Goals.* Available at: www-cdn.oxfam.org/s3fs-public/dp-raising-the-bar-business-sdgs-130217en_0.pdf (Accessed: 20 August 2019).

PepsiCo. (2015). *GRI 2015 Report.* Available at: www.pepsico.com/docs/album/sustainability-report/2015-csr/pep_gri15_v10.pdf?sfvrsn=297300_4 (Accessed: 20 August 2019).

PepsiCo. (2017). *Sustainability Report 2017.* Available at: www.pepsico.com/docs/album/sustainability-report/2017-csr/pepsico_2017_csr.pdf (Accessed: 20 August 2019).

PwC. (2015). *Make it your business: Engaging with the Sustainable Development Goals.* Available at: www.pwc.com/gx/en/sustainability/SDG/SDG%20Research_FINAL.pdf (Accessed: 20 August 2019).

Spangenberg, J. H., Pfahl, S., and Deller, K. (2002). Towards indicators for institutional sustainability: Lessons from an analysis of Agenda 21. *Ecological Indicators, 2*(1-2), 61–77.

UN Global Compact. (2017). *United Nations Global Compact Progress Report. Business solutions to sustainable development.* Available at: www.unglobalcompact.org/library/5431 (Accessed: 20 August 2019).

United Nation (UN). (2010). *United Nations Millennium Declaration: General Assembly Resolution A/RES/55/2.* Available at: www.un.org/en/development/desa/population/migration/generalassembly/docs/globalcompact/A_RES_55_2.pdf (Accessed: 20 August 2019).

WCED. (1987). *Our Common Future.* Available at: www.un-documents.net/our-common-future.pdf (Accessed: 17 March 2020).

28

INTEGRATED REPORTING AND SUSTAINABLE DEVELOPMENT GOALS IN UNIVERSITIES

James Guthrie

Macquarie University

Ana Rita Domingues

University of Bologna

Francesca Manes-Rossi

University of Naples Federico II

Rebecca L. Orelli

University of Bologna

Abstract

The United Nations (UN) is challenging organizations to integrate the 2030 Sustainable Development Goals (SDGs) into their strategies and operations. The International Integrated Reporting Framework (IIRC Framework) also supports these goals, enabling organizations to incorporate financial and non-financial disclosures in one report. We present a longitudinal analysis of an Italian university's adoption of both the UN SDGs and the IIRC Framework. The analysis allows us to understand the "why" and "how" of one organization's journey in constructing strategies, plans, and operations. Our findings are valuable for both academics and practitioners seeking insights into ways to conform with the SDGs and adopt the IIRC Framework.

Introduction

Integrated reporting (IR) aims to "improve the understanding of the relationship between financial and non-financial factors that determine an organization's performance and of how an organization creates sustainable value in the longer term, disclosing material information about an organization's strategy, governance and performance" (International Integrated Reporting Council (IIRC, 2013)). The International Integrated Reporting Framework (IIRC Framework) is used by a range of organizations to assess and communicate their performance on sustainability-related aspects of their operations. In doing so, it aligns with the United Nations (UN) Sustainable Development Goals (SDGs) by communicating sustainability information within an integrated report. The UN SDGs are a global plan for achieving a sustainable future, addressing global challenges including poverty, inequality, climate change, environmental degradation, prosperity, and peace and justice. The majority of countries worldwide have committed to achieving the 17 SDGs by 2030 (UN, 2016). Both private and public sector organizations have an essential role in achieving these goals. These organizations are required to prepare a report that outlines the process by which the organization has included the SDGs when developing strategies.

Public sector organizations have a responsibility to pursue the SDGs, because of their role in global economic activities, promoting welfare and equity, and because of their regulatory power (Farneti and Guthrie, 2009; Dumay et al., 2010; Bebbington and Unerman, 2018; Farneti et al., 2019). Furthermore, while private sector organizations may be accused of adopting sustainability reporting for the purposes of "greenwashing", for economic reasons, or for legitimizing their behaviour (Gray, 2010), public sector organizations work in the public interest for social good, and sustainability strategy should inform their everyday activities, affecting their performance and relationships with their stakeholders (Dumay et al., 2010).

In turn the IIRC Framework has a role in supporting the communication and operationalization of these goals. Organizations should be able to use the IIRC Framework to demonstrate a connection between selected SDGs and the capitals (i.e., financial, manufactured, intellectual, human, social and relationship, natural capital) that an organization manages in the pursuit of value creation (Adams, 2017a).

This research examines the adoption of the UN SDGs and the IIRC Framework by an Italian university. Universities, like other public sector organizations, work in the public interest to achieve societal good. In Italy, the social report has been used by different public sector organizations (Farneti et al., 2019), including universities. This non-financial report was introduced to conform with national guidelines issued in 2006 by the Prime Minister's Office of Public Affairs, which specifically aimed to develop social reporting in public sector organizations.

In this research, a case approach was used to analyse the adoption of sustainable strategies by an Italian state university, which led it to embrace the UN SDGs and report on them. The university completed the integration of the UN SDGs into its strategy from 2016 and has published UN SDGs annual reports since then. The university faced challenges in reporting the UN SDGs because it had to integrate various SDGs into its organizational strategy, producing a link between strategy and results (reports). This chapter highlights why SDGs have been included in the university's strategy and operational documents and how the process was commenced.

Sustainable development and IR

In recent decades, there has been increasing attention to social and environmental sustainability (Bebbington, 2001). One such initiative is the announcement of the 2030 Agenda for Sustainable Development and its 17 SDGs. Public sector entities are expected to participate in meeting the sustainable development challenges, and incorporating the goals in their strategies and plans (UN, 2016).

Several accounting scholars have investigated managerial and disclosure practices in social and environmental goals (e.g., Mathews, 1984; Gray et al., 1988; Guthrie and Parker, 1990; Gray, 1992). Gray (2010, p. 48) asked "what is this sustainability that we wish to account for and why would we wish to undertake such an accounting?" The question still requires academic consideration, perhaps even more so with the introduction of the UN SDGs.

Of particular interest to researchers are the limitations that stem from the separation of social, environmental and financial disclosure, as well as those resulting from a narrow approach to sustainability (Giovannoni and Fabietti, 2013). Sustainability reporting has gained momentum and reports have been published by both private and public sector entities (according to the GRI database, by May 2019, 54,080 reports had been produced worldwide, involving 13,781 organizations) in recent decades. For instance, Galpin et al. (2015) argue that sustainability is a journey throughout which different transformative stages in the organization might be identified, allowing a progressive alignment of attitudes and behaviours of people involved in the organization towards principles of sustainable development. Through this journey, a sustainability culture should be embedded in the organization's mission, values, goals, and strategies.

Busco (2018) considers the IIRC Framework an opportunity for any organization to extend this journey to develop strategies that align the SDGs with transformation of the capitals that will create value. According to the IIRC (2013, p. 6), IR is an accounting device to communicate "how an organization's strategy, governance, performance and prospects, in the context of its external environment, lead to the creation of value in the short, medium and long term". This aspect of IR has been examined by scholars (e.g., Adams, 2015; Flower, 2015; De Villiers and Sharma, 2018; Rinaldi et al., 2018), global accounting bodies (e.g., ACCA and Eurosif, 2013), and accounting partnerships (PwC, 2015; KPMG, 2017). Several scholars consider the IIRC Framework "an evolution of the provision of social, environmental and financial information in a format where the different kind of disclosure are interconnected' (De Villiers et al., 2017, p. 450). Adams (2017a) proposed a five-step model following a top-down approach to aligning the SDG to the IR value creation process. According to her model, organizations should identify sustainable issues relevant to their context, verify whether these issues affect their value creation process, then develop a strategy to introduce the SDGs, developing integrated thinking, connectivity, and governance.

However, research on the adoption of IR in the public sector context is still scarce (Dumay et al., 2016). In particular, research has not investigated the potential of the IIRC Framework in the context of universities (Adams, 2018; Brusca et al., 2018). The next section provides an overview of previous studies discussing sustainability reporting and IR in universities, which helps to frame our analysis.

Sustainability and IR in universities

Several universities have been involved in sustainable development initiatives (Adams et al., 2018; Ramos et al., 2015). Prior research on universities' sustainability strategies highlights a more formal than substantial alignment of vision and mission to sustainability issues (Lozano, 2011; Lee et al., 2013). However, recent studies (Alonso-Almeida et al., 2015; Brusca et al., 2018) and initiatives (UniversitiesUK, 2011; GUNI, 2018), highlight efforts to define vision, mission, and future strategies and plans linked to sustainability.

Despite these efforts, the total number of universities producing sustainability reporting is still low (Ceulemans et al., 2015); universities preparing a specific report to address sustainability issues are considered early adopters and prior research has discussed the need for guidelines for universities. The main barriers to the adoption of sustainability reporting are universities' governance structures and bureaucracy (Lozano, 2011; Alonso-Almeida et al., 2015). To overcome these barriers a different approach is needed, in which mission, strategies, and plans are linked with governance. Governance is a crucial aspect as it can hinder or facilitate the reporting process (Adams, 2017a).

The British Universities Finance Directors Group (BUFDG) project encourages universities to adopt integrated thinking and reporting (BUFDG, 2016). In 2017 it published a joint report examining annual reports by four universities to identify their stages of integrated thinking (BUFDG and IIRC, 2017). Brusca et al. (2018) found that universities were reluctant to change the name of their annual report to "Integrated Report". It seems that even those universities that have adopted integrated thinking continue to publish their reports as annual reports, as required by law, or under the label "sustainability report". These results echo criticisms of the IIRC, which has been considered guilty of promoting integration of information rather than environmental, sustainability and governance disclosures (Dumay et al., 2017; La Torre et al., 2019).

Public universities – like other public organizations (Guthrie et al., 2017) – may make incremental changes to process and structure, rather than a radical change. A gap between strategies, operation, and what is in the report may result in a "cosmetic change", with no discernible impact on society (Manes-Rossi, 2019).

Economic, social, and environmental sustainability and related forms of disclosure and report are recent phenomena (Alrazi et al., 2016). The number of different frameworks available for reporting non-financial information make it difficult to decide which is the most relevant to use (De Villiers, 1999), and there is a need for examples of good, bad or even ugly practice (Baard and Dumay, 2018).

Research method and case study organization

Making use of Adams' model (2017a), this chapter explores the path followed by the University of Bologna (UniBo) to incorporate various SDGs in its reporting, connecting strategies, actions, and goals. It investigates the "why" and "how" behind the strategy on adopting SDGs in a public sector university.

The research questions are:

RQ1. Why did UniBo incorporate the UN SDGs in its processes?
RQ2. How did a state university go about preparing a UN SDGs report?

To understand "why" a university decides to integrate the UN SDGs in its strategy, plans, and reports and "how" it accounts for these, the chapter uses a case study approach. This longitudinal analysis focuses on the dynamics in a management situation (Eisenhardt and Graebner, 2007), and allows researchers to investigate the phenomenon in a real-life context when the boundaries between events are not evident and in which multiple sources of evidence are used (Yin, 2014). The aim of a longitudinal case study is to provide an understanding of how dynamic contexts affect subject matter over time (De Villiers et al., 2019).

Our case focuses on UniBo, the first and only Italian public sector university to publish a UN SDG report (in 2016). UniBo is the oldest university in Europe (founded in 1088), as well as one of the leading academic institutions in Italy and globally (2019 QS World University Rankings; 2019 THE World University Rankings). UniBo has 85,509 students and 5,715 EFT staff across 33 departments.

UniBo's reporting measures the contribution generated by the different institutional activities carried out to reach the SDGs set by the UN. The report presents the direct and indirect impact of UniBo's activities and how they contribute to the achievement of the SDGs. UniBo's UN SDGs report is the final step in a complex dynamic of change involving strategic plans prepared since 2007, and social reports developed since 2013.

To develop insights, we triangulated sources of data available (Yin, 2014), including strategic plans, social reports, SDGs reports, and documents published on UniBo websites. The types and names of the documents analysed are illustrated in Table 28.1.

To answer the "why" and the "how" questions about the incorporation of UN SDGs in UniBo's strategy and reports we used Adams' five steps model (Figure 28.1). The first step will be used to shed light on both questions, while the other steps will be mainly used to understand the "how" question.

Adams' five steps model (2017a) is used as a framing device to understand UniBo's case. The first step, *Understand sustainable development issues relevant to the organization's external environment*, is about how "The sustainable development issues that the SDGs address impact on the organization's ability to create value for itself and its stakeholders" (Adams, 2017b, p. 23). There are many factors that can increase or decrease value created, one of which is the

Table 28.1 List of documents analysed

Type of document	Name of the document	Language	Date of publication
Strategic Plan	Piano strategico 2007–2009	IT	2007
	Piano strategico 2010–2014	IT	2011
	Strategic Plan 2013–2015	EN	2013
	Piano Strategico 2013–2015	IT	2013
	Strategic Plan 2016–2018	EN	2016
	Piano Strategico 2016–2018	IT	2016
	Piano Strategico 2019–2021	IT	2019
Social Report	Bilancio Sociale 2012 – Le persone al centro della conoscenza	IT	2013
	Bilancio Sociale 2013 – Un bilancio di persone, progetti e risultati	IT	2014
	Bilancio Sociale 2014 – Una eredità dal passato, molti progetti per il futuro	IT	2015
	Bilancio Sociale 2015 – Un impegno verso il futuro	IT	2016
	Bilancio Sociale 2016 – Un percorso verso la sostenibilità	IT	2017
	Bilancio Sociale 2017 – Valore d'uso della conoscenza per la comunità e il territorio	IT	2018
UN SDGs Report	Report on United Nations Sustainable Development Goals 2016	EN	2017
	Report on United Nations Sustainable Development Goals 2017	EN	2018
	Report on United Nations Sustainable Development Goals 2017	EN	2019

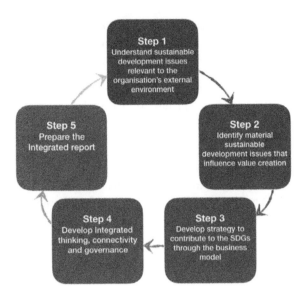

Figure 28.1 Adams' model to align the SDGs to the value creation process
Source: Elaboration on Adams (2017a, p. 22)

quality of relationships with stakeholders. Therefore, consideration of the SDGs, and the sustainable development issues that they address, should be incorporated into the wider consideration of the external environment relevant to the organization's ability to create value. The step requires a clear identification by management of environmental factors affecting the organization's ability to create value, through opportunities and threats. The step presents a link with the IIRC Framework because the identification of a strategy and resource allocation plans are influenced by the external environment and the identified risks and opportunities. They are also influenced by availability of capitals, which are in turn influenced by SDGs.

The second step, *Identify material sustainable development issues that influence value creation*, requires organizations to adjust their mission and strategies following those sustainable development issues that might allow the maximizing of outcomes for the different capitals involved in the value creation process, thus contributing to the achievement of SDGs. In this step, it is essential to identify which of the 17 SDGs are material for the organization, as few organizations are able to contribute to all 17 SDGs (Adams, 2017b, p. 26). Sound governance is critical throughout this step, and senior executives and board members can be engaged to evaluate and prioritize sustainable development or other issues that present risks and opportunities for value creation. The materiality determination implies economic, social and environmental issues are important for stakeholders and can affect the ability of an organization to create value (Adams, 2017b, p. 26).

The third step, *Develop a strategy to contribute to the SDGs through the business model*, involves management defining strategies attuned to support material SDGs through the organization's business model. This step implies the definition of activities, goals, and targets to be achieved in the short, medium, and long term. Having clarified the sustainable development issues relevant for the external environment (first step) and the material sustainable development issues that impact on value creation (second step), an organization can develop a strategy to address them via its business model. To ensure the achievement of strategic objectives, including the outcomes of SDGs, a resource allocation plan has to be prepared (Adams, 2017b, p. 28).

The fourth step, *Develop integrated thinking, connectivity and governance*, is a challenging phase that may require a long period of managerial changes inside the organization and changes in relationships with stakeholders. The IIRC Framework requires linking organizations' strategies to changes in the external environment, including evolving societal expectations and natural resources limitation. It also requires responding to stakeholders' expectations as value is created through relationships with others. Adams (2017b, p. 29) lists the main elements to be considered in the fourth step by those charged with an organization's governance. Those involved must identify material sustainable development issues and ensure that:

- these are incorporated into strategy;
- appropriate goals and targets have been developed;
- the organization develops and nurtures relationships with and between stakeholders in order to enhance collective well-being;
- the organization's business model considers all material sustainable development issues impacting on inputs and outcomes in terms of the six capitals;
- the organization's strategy and business model evolve to reflect past performance with respect to the SDGs.

The fifth and last step consists of the *preparation of the integrated report*, clearly connecting each capital to the SDGs. Organizations are not expected to report on all six capitals; rather on all capitals that are material for them (Adams, 2017b, p. 32).

Results and discussion

"Why" of UN SDGs strategy and reports at UniBo

Before the first UN SDG Report in 2016, UniBo mainly issued Strategic Plans and Social Reports. To understand "why" UniBo incorporated the UN SDGs in its strategy and reports, we need to go back to the beginning of its pathway to integration between financial and non-financial information. Figure 28.2 presents this timeline.

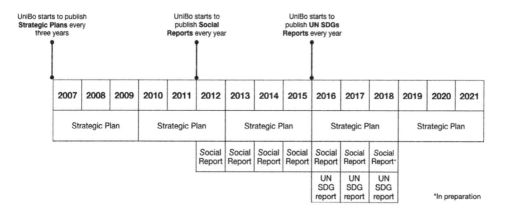

Figure 28.2 Timeline of the development of UniBo reporting tools

Following Adams' (2017a) first step, *Understand sustainable development issues relevant to the organization's external environment*, at UniBo, the quality of relationships with stakeholders is a crucial factor in understanding the reasons behind the incorporation of SDGs in strategy and reports. The path started in 2007 when UniBo prepared and published a three-year voluntary Strategic Plan, allowing UniBo to rethink its mission and fundamental values. The first Strategic Plan was focused on internal stakeholders, defining strategies for students and academics, with no sustainability elements.

> We had to re-think our mission and values, and we defined some main paths, which represent UniBo's way to produce research, teaching, services to students and internationalisation … We performed a strength and weakness analysis under both the Italian and European perspective
>
> *(University of Bologna, 2007, p. 6)*

In 2009 the new Rector developed a new Strategic Plan (2010–2013), embedding considerations of a wider external environment extended to external stakeholders (students and society). Within this Strategic Plan, UniBo highlighted the influence of the external environment on the organization, and its impact on relationships with stakeholders (Adams, 2017b). "Our institution is … an institution that is open to dialogue with people inside and outside its boundaries and that follows its aim with attention to the values of autonomy, respect of diversity and social responsibility" (University of Bologna, 2011, p. 8). During the preparation of the second Strategic Plan it emerged that UniBo's information systems were not able to collect, analyze, and represent the link between the university's actions and sustainability (University of Bologna, 2011, p. 14). For that reason, the Strategic Plan has strategic objectives for the creation of a system of communication with external stakeholders and a set of indicators to measure the results achieved (University of Bologna, 2011, p. 4). The strategic objectives were achieved within a year and a half, and the Rector presented the first UniBo Social Report in 2012 as a mid-term product of his six-year mandate, to legitimize his past and future actions for sustainability and stakeholders. The Rector identified the main aim of the Social Report as: "To add a wider representation of the effects of activities in terms of economic, social and environmental sustainability to traditional forms of disclosure. The Social Report allows UniBo to demonstrate its responsibilities" (University of Bologna, 2013, p. 3). Since 2012, UniBo has prepared an annual Social Report. The six Social Reports published so far use the GRI Guidelines. In 2013, the third UniBo Strategic Plan was prepared for the years 2013–2015.

A new Rector was elected in 2016, at the time of the fourth Strategic Report (2016–2018), and the fifth Social Report for 2016. The Rector decided to align the Strategic Plan 2016–2018 with the UN SDGs and to prepare a UN SDGs Report, as outlined below:

> In order to implement a planning process for tackling the challenges posed by contemporary reality, particularly in relation to sustainable development, the University has decided to integrate the present Strategic Plan with a re-reading of the 17 basic sustainable development goals and their relative 169 targets, as proposed by the 2030 Agenda adopted on 25 September 2015 by the UN General Assembly.
>
> *(University of Bologna, 2016, p. 11)*

> Consistent with the perspective adopted in the Strategic Plan 2016–2018, the University of Bologna proposes an innovative way to report on the contributions generated by its institutional activities, including training, research and social and public engagement, aimed at the achievement of the 17 Sustainable Development Goals (SDGs) of the U.N. 2030 Agenda ... [It] is fully aware that its activities can produce a significant impact, both direct and indirect, on the community and the region.
>
> *(United Nations, 2016, p. 5)*

The commitment of UniBo's Rector to the integration of SDGs into the university's activities was a key driver in the implementation of UN SDGs. This is consistent with the idea that leaders are responsible for driving the effort of internalizing sustainable development considerations (Adams, 2015).

The "how" of UN SDGs strategy and reports at UniBo

The Strategic Plan 2016–2018 gathered information around three main areas of activities: teaching; research; and third mission (to engage with societal needs and market demands by linking the university's activity with its own socio-economic context). The last dimension is a new area that UniBo decided to add after reflecting on those of its activities that have a direct effect on society (Ramos et al., 2015; Adams et al., 2018).

To understand the sustainable development issues relevant to the external environment as required in the first step of Adams' model, *Understand sustainable development issues relevant to the organization's external environment*, UniBo considered the theme of quality of education, as well as other external environmental aspects that affected its operations:

> The University of Bologna is committed to the values of sustainability, such as enhancing and safeguarding the territory, improving community wellbeing, promoting a knowledge-based development economy, social equity, and the ability of those involved to work effectively together for the common good ... not only the connection between the university and the theme of the quality of education but also the possible interconnections with the goals of the UN 2030 Agenda.
>
> *(United Nations, 2016, p. 5)*

The Strategic Plan included UniBo's mission and vision, a positioning analysis, and a SWOT analysis to understand the sustainable development issues relevant to the organization's external environment and identify risks and opportunities (Adams, 2017a).

> The analysis of our positioning represents the first step in the entire strategic planning process. It facilitates a fuller understanding of the reality within which an organisation operates, and the resources it can count upon to optimise its results. It is also fundamental for understanding the nature of the organisation's external commitments and internal limits, and for ensuring that its planning is concrete and feasible.
>
> *(University of Bologna, 2016, p. 17)*

In relation to the second step, *Identify material sustainable development issued that influence value creation*, in 2016 it was possible to identify the material SDGs for UniBo to include in the Strategic Plan. Seven SDGs were included: *SDG 3 Health and Well-being*, to ensure healthy lives and promote well-being for all, at all ages; *SDG 4 Quality Education*, to provide inclusive and equitable quality education and promote lifelong learning opportunities for all; *SDG 5 Gender Equality*, to achieve gender equality and empower all women and girls; *SDG 8 Decent Work and Economic Growth*, to promote sustained, inclusive and sustainable economic growth, full and productive employment and decent work for all; *SDG 9 Industry, Innovation and Infrastructure*, to build resilient infrastructure, promote inclusive and sustainable industrialization and foster innovation; *SDG 10 Reduced Inequalities*, to reduce inequality within and among countries; *SDG 11 Sustainable Cities and Communities*, to make cities and human settlements inclusive, safe, resilient, and sustainable; and *SDG 17 Partnerships for the Goals*, to strengthen the means of implementation and revitalize the Global Partnership for Sustainable Development.

The SDGs were reconsidered for the preparation of the second Strategic Plan 2019–2021 and *SDG 10 Peace, Justice and Strong Institutions*, to promote peaceful and inclusive societies for sustainable development, provide access to justice for all and build effective, accountable and inclusive institutions at all levels, was added.

A vulnerability in the UniBo pathway towards the SDGs is that it is not possible to connect the material SDGs with the IIRC Framework's six capitals. To understand that link, consider UniBo's Social Reports, prepared to show how public resources (beyond financial) are used to achieve specific results to internal and external stakeholders. The Social Reports have been prepared following the guidelines from the Italian Prime Minister's Office of Public Affairs, which refers to social reporting for public administration and the GRI guidelines on sustainability reporting, as well as the research report on social reporting in universities, issued by the Italian Study Group on Social Reports (GBS, 2008). The data disclosed in the Social Reports (e.g. gender equality, work environment, environmental policies related to energy and consumption of resources) link to intellectual capital, and to human, relational and structural capitals, but not to the other IIRC Framework capitals. "The Social Report also represents the intellectual capital of the university, which is human capital, structural capital and relational capital, and the three elements are distributed in the

Figure 28.3 UN SDGs included in the UniBo Strategic Plan 2016–2018

Source: University of Bologna (2016, p. 11)

Table 28.2 The relationship between strategic goals, specific goals, performance indicators, and UN SDGs

Strategic goal	Specific goal	Performance Indicators	UN SDGs
Strategic area: Research			
1. To support basic and applied research, in order to confront major challenges in an international context.	1.1 To qualify and highlight PhD degree programmes in an international perspective	I.1 PhD students with degrees from other Italian or foreign universities I.2 Overall investment in PhD degree programmes	INDUSTRY, INNOVATION AND INFRASTRUCTURE (9)
	1.2 To reinforce the priority of merit in recruitment and career advancement	I.3 Number of new recruits in charge of competitive projects compared to the total number of new recruits I.4 Percentage of new recruits with a VRA (University Research Evaluation) score higher than the median	DECENT WORK AND ECONOMIC GROWTH (8)
	1.3 To improve research quality and productivity	I.5 Comparison of the distribution of UNIBO publications per Single Index compared with total products for VQR Groups 2011/14 (Bibliometric areas) I.6 a) Percentage of Group A publications according to VRA criteria; b) Percentage of publications presented for VRA in proportion to the maximum number of publications allowed per VRA scientific area (NON-bibliometric areas)	INDUSTRY, INNOVATION AND INFRASTRUCTURE (9)
	1.4 Reinforce the infrastructures needed for research purposes	I.7 Investment in research infrastructure and equipment	INDUSTRY, INNOVATION AND INFRASTRUCTURE (9)
2. To invest in distinctive and multidisciplinary fields for our university, on national and international levels	2.1 To enhance the ability to collaborate and to attract research funding from national and international sources	I.8 Per capita funding for Italian and international projects	INDUSTRY, INNOVATION AND INFRASTRUCTURE (9)

(Continued)

Table 28.2 (Cont.)

Strategic goal	Specific goal	Performance Indicators	UN SDGs
	2.2 To develop new projects that will attract international competences, thereby enhancing the university's multidisciplinary heritage	I.9 Degree of implementation of programmed initiatives	DECENT WORK AND ECONOMIC GROWTH (8)
Strategic area: Teaching			
3. To promote the quality of the programme catalogue and invest in distinctive and multidisciplinary fields related to people's needs and society's needs	3.1 To improve the competences acquired during degree courses in order to help graduates enter the world of work, and remain there	I.10 The number of students using Career Guidance Services I.11 Employment/ unemployment after 1/3/5 years	QUALITY EDUCATION (4) DECENT WORK AND ECONOMIC GROWTH (8)
	3.2 To consolidate the regularity of studies while respecting strict evaluation procedures	I.12 Graduates in stable regular employment (number of years) I.13 Continuations with >39 ECTS achieved in the 1st year	QUALITY EDUCATION (4)
	3.3 To improve teaching quality by adopting innovative methods and by training teachers	I.14 Number of hours of training initiatives for teachers per number of teachers I.15 Attending students' satisfaction with teaching methods – Opinion Poll of students	QUALITY EDUCATION (4)
	3.4 To encourage synergies between studies and research in distinctive fields, and in tune with society's needs	I.16 Reports on results of new initiatives programmed in *distinctive* fields (Advanced manufacturing; Health and wellbeing, Agriculture and food, Sustainability and circular economy, Arts and Humanities in the digital era, Cultural interaction, inclusion and social security, Big data & industry 4.0, Creativity)	QUALITY EDUCATION (4)

(Continued)

Table 28.2 (Cont.)

Strategic goal	Specific goal	Performance Indicators	UN SDGs
4. To improve the attractiveness and the international dimension of our teaching offer	4.1 To attract talented students, thanks also to specific career orientation activities	I.17 MA students with 1st level degrees from other universities I.18 Extra-regional mobility I.19 Value of resources committed to rewarding merit	4 QUALITY EDUCATION
	4.2 To increase the number of talented international students and further diversify their geographical provenance	I.20 Incoming exchange students I.21 Students with previous degrees obtained outside Italy	4 QUALITY EDUCATION · 17 PARTNERSHIP FOR THE GOALS
	4.3 To increase the number of graduates who have received an educational experience outside Italy	I.22 Graduates with at least 12 ECTS credits obtained outside Italy I.23 Outgoing Students	4 QUALITY EDUCATION · 17 PARTNERSHIP FOR THE GOALS
	4.4 To strengthen the international dimension of teaching situations and also by developing students' linguistic skills	I.24 Number of months (per person) spent in the university by teachers and researchers from foreign research institutes	4 QUALITY EDUCATION · 17 PARTNERSHIP FOR THE GOALS
5. To enhance the services available to students and actively support policies on the right to higher education	5.1 To reinforce the services intended to ensure improved study and living conditions for students, partly through partnerships with public and private actors	I.25 Qualitative indicators on initiatives in favour of students I.26 Percentage of students satisfied with university infrastructures	3 GOOD HEALTH AND WELL-BEING · 4 QUALITY EDUCATION · 11 AND COMMUNITIES

(*Continued*)

Table 28.2 (Cont.)

Strategic goal	Specific goal	Performance Indicators	UN SDGs
	5.2 To promote study opportunities for disadvantaged students, consolidating coordinated action with local institutions and communities on "right to higher education" issues	I.27 Per capita cost of resources used to facilitate students on the basis of their economic condition and their talent	
	5.3 To improve activities relating to career orientation, for incoming, resident and outgoing students, on the basis of their specific needs	I.28 Number of companies involved in Job placement initiatives I.29 Percentage of graduates with curricular internships I.30 Studies abandoned before the end of the second year	
Strategic area: Third Mission 6. To promote cultural development, plus economic and social innovation	6.1 To qualify and enhance professionalizing and permanent study processes and courses	I.31 Number of students involved in professionalizing and lifelong learning programmes	
	6.2 To improve the impact of research and upgrade technological transfer at regional, national and international levels, partly through entrepreneurial projects	I.32 Number of patents obtained by the entire permanent teaching body I.33 Number of spin-offs and start-ups accredited/active	
	6.3 To promote processes that enhance the environmental and social sustainability of the university's buildings,	I.34 Qualitative indicator on initiatives carried out on "social" and "green" issues	

(*Continued*)

Table 28.2 (Cont.)

Strategic goal	Specific goal	Performance Indicators	UN SDGs
	facilities and community, while also revitalizing the area in synergy with all local institutions		
	6.4 To promote activities offering scientific and cultural popularization	I.35 Qualitative indicator: obtain tools for measuring the impact and send back to be included in the Social Report	11 AND COMMUNITIES
7. To improve relationships with our numerous stakeholders at national and international levels	7.1 To develop and highlight the heritage of knowledge and skill of our graduates and personnel, in order to develop connections and synergies between the university and society	I.36 Qualitative report on activities carried out	17 PARTNERSHIP FOR THE GOALS
	7.2 To strengthen support structures and interfaces between the world of production and the academic community	I.37 Turnover from commissioned scientific activities involving permanent teaching personnel I.38 Qualitative indicator: actions taken to strengthen support and interface structures	8 DECENT WORK AND ECONOMIC GROWTH 9 INDUSTRY, INNOVATION AND INFRASTRUCTURE 17 PARTNERSHIP FOR THE GOALS
	7.3 To create a system for evolving development cooperation activities	I.39 Degree of implementation of planned initiatives, and the need to use instruments for measuring the impact achievement	17 PARTNERSHIP FOR THE GOALS

Source: University of Bologna (2016)

different sections of the report" (University of Bologna, 2018, p. 179). The choice to prepare two separate documents per year; a Social Report and a UN SDGs Report, fragmented the disclosure and the understanding of UniBo's activities. This lack of integrated thinking undermines the organization's strategy and value creation potential.

Table 28.3 The measurement of UniBo's SDGs achievement over time

Strategic area: Teaching	Specific goal/target	UN SDG
Strategic goal/target		
4. To improve the attractiveness and the international dimension of our teaching offer	4.1 To attract talented students, thanks also to specific career orientation activities	4 QUALITY EDUCATION

Performance indicator	2015	2018	2019
I.19 Value of resources committed to rewarding merit	10.8 Mln €	12.2 Mln €	> 12.2 Mln €

Source: University of Bologna (2019b, p. 33)

UniBo developed a strategy to contribute to the UN SDGs based on the three dimensions (i.e. teaching, research, third mission), consistent with Step 3 of Adams' model, *Develop strategy to contribute to the SDGs through the business model*. After defining its mission and vision, and performing a positioning analysis, UniBo selected goals, indicators, and targets to support its action (Figure 28.3).

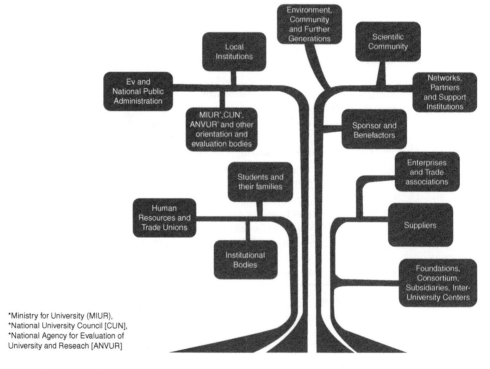

*Ministry for University (MIUR),
*National University Council [CUN],
*National Agency for Evaluation of University and Reseach [ANVUR]

Figure 28.4 Stakeholder groups related to the University of Bologna in the Social Report 2017
Source: University of Bologna (2018, p. 16)

UniBo presents a definition of strategic goals/targets, specific goals/targets and performance indicators to contribute to the SDGs considering the dimensions of teaching, research, and third mission, consistent with Step 3 in Adams' model (Table 28.2).

UNIVERSITY QUALITY ASSURANCE

The University of Bologna has an **Internal Quality Assurance System** involving a self-assessment that allow the University to improve the quality of its study programmes. This process provides an adequate response to the expectations of all actors who have an interest in the offered training service: students, families, companies, institutions, etc.

The system envisages the periodic analysis of significant data (such as the number of graduates in the course, the opinions of the students and the employment status of the graduates) collected both by the University and by the **National Agency for the Evaluation of the University and Research System (ANVUR)**.

TEACHING

375 COURSE UNITS	**29** COLLABORATIONS, TEACHING, MOBILITY	**29,474** ALL STUDENTS	**1,174** ALL COURSE UNITS RELATED TO SDGs

PARAMETERS FOR QUALITY EDUCATION

STUDENT ATTRACTIVENESS	
Students enrolled in Second cycle degree programmes (from other universities)	47.4%
Incoming exchange students	3,100
International students (UE and Extra-UE)	7.2%
SOCIAL INCLUSION	
Value of scholarships (merit and status based) Per Capita	510 €
Students followed by the Service for disabled	654
Enrolled University students by gender (first, second and single cycle degrees)	36,726 M 46,273 F
PROGRAMMES OFFERED AND MAIN RESULTS	
Degree programmes	219
Degree programmes taught in English	52
Masters' programmes and post-graduate/lifelong learning programmes	109
Courses with at least three quarters of students satisfied with the course	76.7 %
Graduates	18,380
Graduates within regular enrollment	67%

Figure 28.5 UN SDGs Report at UniBo (section)
Source: University of Bologna (2019a, p. 19)

In the Strategic Plan 2019–2021, all the targets and indicators identified in the previous Strategic Plan 2016–2018 are measured and new targets for 2019–2021 are set (Table 28.3). For each performance indicator the 2015 and 2018 achievements and the 2019 targets are presented.

To *Develop Integrated Thinking, Connectivity and Governance*, as in Adams' Step 4, requires change inside the organization. Inside UniBo, a change took place with the Social Report preparation as, for the first time, it disclosed the impact of UniBo's activities on the external environment. UniBo's Strategic Plan 2016–2018 was created with the engagement of the academic community and the administration of the university to show how the activities developed in teaching, research, and third mission contributed towards the achievement of the selected SDGs. Mainly internal stakeholders (e.g. researchers, professors, vice-rectors and rector, and administrative staff) were involved in the planning, assessing, and reporting stages of this process. These groups are key stakeholders for the university (Mitchell et al., 1997).

Other stakeholder groups were not directly engaged in the development of the report, but they are considered relevant to the development of the university's Strategic Plans and SDGs Reports. UniBo's governance recently fostered a new approach to stakeholders. The 2017 Social Report (see Figure 28.4) engaged new categories of stakeholders, mainly external to UniBo. This approach can be extended to UniBo's start-up and owned or participated organizations (libraries and museums) at the regional level, beyond their organizational border of a single organization (Dumay et al., 2010). These incremental changes to process and structure were among the drivers of the adoption of integrating thinking at UniBo, instead of a radical change. Similar findings have been reported for other public entities in Italy (Guthrie et al., 2017).

Three reports on UN SDGs for the years 2016, 2017, and 2018 have been published so far, following the same structure (Step 5 *Prepare the integrated report*). They include the university's context and critical features on teaching, research, and third mission and the main outputs of the related-activities for each SDG using indicators (Figure 28.5).

In summary, the UniBo UN SDG Report identifies the different resources used and the impact of its activities, particularly for stakeholders (Busco, 2018), and therefore has significant potential to support organizational learning and change in universities (Ceulemans et al., 2015). As outlined above, incremental changes to process and structure were among the drivers of incorporation of SDGs in Strategy Plans and Social Reports at UniBo and offered the chance to commit to sustainable development through changes to organizational strategy and operational activities. The value created by universities like UniBo is related to their context, and it is vital to understand it to achieve a transition to sustainable development (Godemann et al., 2014). Despite some limitations due to the indirect link between the capitals and the UN SDGs, the UniBo approach offers stakeholders a view of the impact of the university's activities (teaching, research and third mission) in relation to each UN SDG. Both the Strategic Plans and UN SDGs Reports show the adoption of integrated thinking as encouraged by BUFDG (2016).

Conclusions

Organizations are challenged to integrate sustainable development considerations into their organization and reporting (Adams, 2015). The IIRC Framework may provide appropriate guidance for introducing integrated thinking, embedding SDGs in organization strategies and, in turn, fostering SDG achievements.

This chapter sheds light on the journey of UniBo, an Italian public university, which has been a pioneer in the integration and reporting of SDGs. The longitudinal case study of UniBo illustrates integrated thinking in action – its journey enabled it to connect the resources used and outcomes achieved concerning sustainable development and to develop plans and reports according to both SDGs and IR capitals. In the UniBo experience, the antecedents of the reporting of the SDGs were its social reports and the driver was the strong commitment of UniBo's governance to sustainable development. UniBo implemented the UN SDGs by focusing on integrating the SDGs into the strategy of the organization, producing a link between strategy and results (reports).

Using Adams' (2017a) model, this case study sheds light on the path that might be followed to align sustainable development through increases, decreases, and transformations of capital. The introduction of SDGs at UniBo required a change in thinking and a revision of strategy, which then allowed it to develop both a three-year strategic plan and a year-end report based on the SDGs.

The UniBo experience highlights the challenges and issues arising from a sustainable development approach using the SDGs and, to a lesser extent, transformations of the organization's capitals. UniBo's journey has lessons for other public sector organizations embarking on this journey, as well as for academics and practitioners who would like a better understanding of the path of transition from more traditional forms of reporting to the SDGs and its impact on the value creation process and capitals.

References

ACCA and Eurosif. (2013). *What do Investors Expect from Non-financial Reporting?* Available at: www.acca global.com/content/dam/acca/global/PDF-technical/sustainability-reporting/tech-tp-wdir.pdf (Accessed: 4 December 2019).

Adams, C. A. (2015). The International Integrated Reporting Council: A Call to Action. *Critical Perspectives on Accounting*, 27, 23–28.

Adams, C. A. (2017a). *The Sustainable Development Goals, Integrated Thinking and Integrated Report.* Available at: http://integratedreporting.org/resource/sdgs-integrated-thinking-and-the-integrated-report/ (Accessed: 30 October 2019).

Adams, C. A. (2017b). Conceptualising the Contemporary Corporate Value Creation Process. *Accounting, Auditing & Accountability Journal*, 3(4), 906–931.

Adams, C. A. (2018). Debate: Integrated Reporting and Accounting for Sustainable Development Across Generations by Universities. *Public Money & Management*, 38(5), 332–334.

Adams, R., Martin, S., and Boom, K. (2018). University Culture and Sustainability: Designing and Implementing an Enabling Framework. *Journal of Cleaner Production*, 171, 434–445.

Alonso-Almeida, M. D. M., Marimo, F., Casani, F., and Rodriguez-Pomeda, J. (2015). Diffusion of Sustainability Reporting in Universities: Current Situation and Future Perspectives. *Journal of Cleaner Production*, 106, 144–154.

Alrazi, B., De Villiers, C., and van Staden, C. J. (2016). The Environmental Disclosures of the Electricity Generation Industry: A Global Perspective. *Accounting and Business Research*, 46, 665–701.

Baard, V. C., and Dumay, J. (2018). Interventionist Research in Accounting: Reflections on the Good, the Bad and the Ugly. *Accounting and Finance*, Available online: 10.1111/acfi.12409.

Bebbington, J. (2001). Sustainable Development: A Review of the International Development, Business and Accounting Literature. *Accounting Forum*, 25(2), 128–157.

Bebbington, J., and Unerman, J. (2018). Achieving the United Nations Sustainable Development Goals: An Enabling Role for Accounting Research. *Accounting, Auditing and Accountability Journal*, 31(1), 2–24.

Brusca, I., Labrador, M., and Larran, M. (2018). The Challenge of Sustainability and Integrated Reporting at Universities: A Case Study. *Journal of Cleaner Production*, 188, 347–354.

BUFDG. (2016). *Integrated Reporting in Higher Education*. Available at: www.bufdg.ac.uk/ir/ (Accessed: 30 October 2019).

BUFDG and IIRC. (2017). *Integrated Reporting in Four British Universities*. Available at: www.bufdg.ac.uk/ir/ (Accessed: 30 October 2019).

Busco, C. (2018). Make Sustainable Development Goals happen through Integrated Thinking: An Introduction. In: C. Busco, F. Granà, and M. F. Izzo (Eds.), *Sustainable Development Goals and Integrated Reporting* (pp. 1–20). London: Routledge.

Ceulemans, K., Molderez, I., and van Liedekerke, L. (2015). Sustainability Reporting in Higher Education: A Comprehensive Review of the Recent Literature and Paths for Further Research. *Journal of Cleaner Production*, *106*, 127–143.

De Villiers, C. (1999). The Decision by Management to Disclose Environmental Information: A Research Note based on Interviews. *Meditari Accountancy Research*, 7, 33–48.

De Villiers, C., Dumay, J., and Maroun, W. (2019). Qualitative Accounting Research: Dispelling Myths and Developing a New Research Agenda. *Accounting and Finance*, Available online: 10.1111/acfi.12487.

De Villiers, C., Hsiao, P.-C. K., and Maroun, W. (2017). Developing a Conceptual Model of Influences around Integrated Reporting, New Insights and Directions for Future Research. *Meditari Accountancy Research*, *25*(4), 450–460.

De Villiers, C., and Sharma, U. (2018). A Critical Reflection on the Future of Financial, Intellectual Capital, Sustainability and Integrated Reporting. *Critical Perspectives on Accounting*, Available online: 10.1016/j.cpa.2017.05.003.

Dumay, J., Bernardi, C., Guthrie, J., and Demartini, P. (2016). Integrated Reporting: A Structured Literature Review. *Accounting Forum*, *40*(3), 166–185.

Dumay, J., Bernardi, C., Guthrie, J., and La Torre, M. (2017). Barriers to Implementing Integrated Reporting: A Contemporary Academic Perspective. *Meditari Accountancy Research*, *25*(4), 461–480.

Dumay, J., Farneti, F., and Guthrie, J. (2010). GRI Sustainability Reporting Guidelines for Public and Third Sector Organizations: A Critical Review. *Public Management Review*, *12*(4), 531–548.

Eisenhardt, K. M., and Graebner, M. E. (2007). Theory Building from Cases: Opportunities and Challenges. *The Academy of Management Journal*, *50*(1), 25–32.

Farneti, F., and Guthrie, J. (2009). Sustainability Reporting by Australian Public Sector Organisations: Why They Report. *Accounting Forum*, *33*(2), 89–98.

Farneti, F., Guthrie, J., and Canetto, M. (2019). Social Reports of an Italian Local Government: A Longitudinal Analysis. *Meditari Accountancy Research*, 27(4), 580–612.

Flower, J. (2015). The International Integrated Reporting Council: A Story of Failure. *Critical Perspectives on Accounting*, *27*, 1–17.

Galpin, T., Whitttington, J. L., and Bell, G. (2015). Is Your Sustainability Strategy Sustainable? Creating a Culture of Sustainability. *Corporate Governance*, *15*(1), 1–17.

GBS. (2008). *Il bilancio sociale standard La rendicontazione sociale nel settore pubblico, Giuffrè*. Available at: www.gruppobilanciosociale.org/pubblicazioni/la-rendicontazione-sociale-nel-settore-pubblico (Accessed: 20 September 2019).

Giovannoni, E., and Fabietti, G. (2013). What is Sustainability? A Review of the Concept and its Applications. In: C. Busco, M. L. Frigo, A. Riccaboni, and P. Quattrone (Eds.), *Integrated Reporting* (pp. 21–40). Cham: Springer.

Godemann, J., Bebbington, J., Herzig, C., and Moon, J. (2014). Higher Education and Sustainable Development: Exploring Possibilities for Organisational Change. *Accounting, Auditing & Accountability Journal*, *27*(2), 218–233.

Gray, R. (2010). Is Accounting for Sustainability Actually Accounting for Sustainability … And How Would We Know? An Exploration of Narratives of Organisations and the Planet. *Accounting, Organizations and Society*, *35*(1), 47–62.

Gray, R. H. (1992). Accounting and Environmentalism: An Exploration of the Challenge of Gently Accounting for Accountability, Transparency and Sustainability. *Accounting Organizations and Society*, *17*(5), 399–426.

Gray, R. H., Owen, D. L., and Maunders, K. T. (1988). Corporate Social Reporting: Emerging Trends in Accountability and the Social Contract. *Accounting, Auditing & Accountability Journal*, *1*(1), 6–20.

GUNI. (2018). *Sustainable Development Goals: Actors and Implementation A Report from the International Conference*. Available at: www.guninetwork.org/files/guni_sdgs_report_0.pdf (Accessed: 30 October 2019).

Guthrie, J., Manes-Rossi, F., and Orelli, R. L. (2017). Integrated Reporting and Integrated Thinking in Italian Public Sector Organisations. *Meditari Accountancy Research*, *25*(4), 553–573.

Guthrie, J. E., and Parker, L. D. (1990). Corporate Social Disclosure Practice: A Comparative International Analysis. *Advances in Public Interest Accounting, 3,* 159–176.

IIRC. (2013). *The International <IR> Framework.* London: IIRC.

KPMG. (2017). *The KPMG Survey of Corporate Responsibility Reporting 2017.* Available at: http://integrate dreporting.org/wp-content/uploads/2017/10/kpmg-survey-of-corporate-responsibility-reporting-2017.pdf (Accessed: 30 October 2019).

La Torre, M., Dumay, J., Rea, M. A., and Abhayawansa, S. (2019). A Journey Towards a Safe Harbour: The Rhetorical Process of the International Integrated Reporting Council. *The British Accounting Review,* Available online: 10.1016/j.bar.2019.100836.

Lee, K.-H., Barker, M., and Mouasher, A. (2013). Is it Even Espoused? An Exploratory Study of Commitment to Sustainability as Evidenced in Vision, Mission, and Graduate Attribute Statements in Australian Universities. *Journal of Cleaner Production, 48,* 20–28.

Lozano, R. (2011). The State of Sustainability Reporting in Universities. *International Journal of Sustainability in Higher Education, 12*(1), 67–78.

Manes-Rossi, F. (2019). New Development: Alternative Reporting Formats: A Panacea for Accountability Dilemmas? *Public Money & Management, 39*(7), 1–4.

Mathews, M. R. (1984). A Suggested Classification for Social Accounting Research. *Journal of Accounting and Public Policy, 3,* 199–221.

Mitchell, R. K., Agle, B. R., and Wood, D. J. (1997). Toward a Theory of Stakeholder Identification and Salience: Defining the Principle of Who and What Really Counts. *Academy of Management Review, 22*(4), 853–886.

PwC. (2015). *Implementing Integrated Reporting.* Available at: www.pwc.com/gx/en/audit-services/publica tions/assets/pwc-ir-practical-guide.pdf (Accessed: 20 October 2019).

Ramos, T. B., Caeiro, S., Van Hoof, B., Lozano, R., Huisingh, D., and Ceulemans, K. (2015). Experiences from the Implementation of Sustainable Development in Higher Education Institutions: Environmental Management for Sustainable Universities. *Journal of Cleaner Production, 106,* 3–10.

Rinaldi, L., Unerman, J., and De Villiers, C. (2018). Evaluating the Integrated Reporting Journey: Insights, Gaps and Agendas for Future Research. *Accounting, Auditing & Accountability Journal, 31*(5), 1294–1318.

UniversitiesUK. (2011). *Degrees of Value: How Universities Benefit Society.* Available at: www.universitie suk.ac.uk/policy-and-analysis/reports/Pages/degrees-of-value.aspx (Accessed: 30 October 2019).

University of Bologna. (2007). *Piano strategico 2007–2009* (Strategic Plan 2007–2009). Available at: www.unibo.it/en/university/who-we-are/strategic-plan (Accessed: 30 October 2019).

University of Bologna. (2011). *Piano strategico 2010–2014* (Strategic Plan 2010–2014). Available at: www.unibo.it/en/university/who-we-are/strategic-plan (Accessed: 30 October 2019).

University of Bologna. (2013). *Bilancio Sociale 2012* (Social Report 2012). Accessed at: www.unibo.it/en/university/who-we-are/Social-Responsibility-Report (Accessed: 30 October 2019).

University of Bologna. (2016). *Strategic Plan 2016–2018.* Available at: www.unibo.it/en/university/who-we-are/strategic-plan (Accessed: 30 October 2019).

University of Bologna. (2018). *Bilancio Sociale 2017* (Social Report 2017). Available at: www.unibo.it/en/university/who-we-are/Social-Responsibility-Report (Accessed: 30 October 2019).

University of Bologna. (2019a). *AlmaGoals: The University of Bologna for the UN SDGs.* Available at: https://site.unibo.it/almagoals/en (Accessed: 30 October 2019).

University of Bologna. (2019b). *Piano Strategico.* Available at: www.unibo.it/en/university/who-we-are/strategic-plan (Accessed: 30 October 2019).

United Nations (2016). *Compendium of Innovative Practices in Public Governance and Administration for Sustainable Development.* Available at: https://publicadministration.un.org/publications/content/PDFs/Compendium%20Public%20Governance%20and%20Administration%20for%20Sustainable%20Development.pdf (Accessed: 5 May 2019).

Yin, R. K. (2014). *Case Study Research: Design and Methods.* London: Sage Publications.

29

REPORTING ON MORE THAN JUST NATURAL CAPITAL

Michael Büchling

University of the Witwatersrand

Jill Atkins

University of Sheffield

Abstract

This chapter provides an overview of the different biodiversity-related reporting standards that can be used by preparers of integrated reports when disclosing information on an organization's natural capital. Using prior literature, an extinction accounting framework is presented that can be used by organizations in reporting on biodiversity and extinction risk, at a species level. The reporting framework demonstrates how the different capitals are affected by the natural capital of an organization and how biodiversity-related risks (in particular, extinction risk), affect the ability of an organization to continue operating. The use of the framework will enhance accountability and ensure better management of an organization's natural capital.

Introduction

Technological progress over the last 100 years has come at considerable cost to the planet. According to the International Union for Conservation of Nature (IUCN), 872 known species are known to have gone extinct (IUCN, 2019). The vertebrate animal population has decreased by 60 per cent since 1970 (WWF, 2018) and one million species have been identified as being at risk of extinction by the Intergovernmental Science-Policy Platform on Biodiversity and Ecosystem Services (IPBES, 2019b). Threats posed to natural capital include a change in the over-use of land and sea; overexploitation by humans; climate change; pollution; and invasive alien species (see, for example, IPBES (2019a); IPBES (2019c, 2019d); WWF (2018)).

The IPBES (2019d, pp. 3–4) found that the destruction of the natural world may be attributed to "societal values and behaviours that include production and consumption patterns, human population dynamics and trends, trade [and] technological innovations".

Although warnings have been issued by the scientific community (see, for example, Ripple et al., 2017), non-governmental organizations (see, for example, WWF, 2018) and international agencies (see, for example, IPBES, 2019a, 2019b, 2019c, 2019d), business has mainly continued as usual. This is because the capitalist system places profits before the environment (see, for example, Apostolopoulou and Adams, 2015; Büscher et al., 2012). In particular, capitalism makes a case for conservation only when there is a clear business case for protecting the environment and, as part of this, a price can be assigned to ecological goods or services (see, for example, Apostolopoulou and Adams, 2015; Brockington and Duffy, 2010; Büscher et al., 2012).

While capitalism has been accused of exploiting conservation for its own goals, a growing body of work suggests that the traditional focus on financial capital does not have to come at the expense of social and environmental imperatives. Atkins and Maroun (2018) argue that profit-orientated business can drive conservation using a variety of accounting and accountability mechanisms. These include not only sustainability and integrated reporting (IR), but emerging forms of accounting such as biodiversity reporting and emancipatory accounting (see, for example, Atkins and Atkins, 2016; Atkins and Maroun, 2018; Atkins et al., 2018; Büchling and Maroun, 2019; Gray and Milne, 2019; Maroun and Atkins, 2014, 2018).

Despite earlier research in the accounting field proposing radical alternatives involving a complete overhaul of the capitalist system, we consider that reorganizing the economy along Marxist lines is not required; instead, technologies of accounting and accountability are mobilized to draw attention to the state of the natural world and to make the interconnection between financial and so-called non-financial capitals more explicit (Atkins and Maroun, 2018). This involves balancing an anthropocentric perspective with a deep ecological view to frame an organization as part of the broader ecosystem rather than something that only seeks to maximize financial returns. This chapter explores some of the emerging forms of accounting that seek to achieve this objective.

By using an extinction accounting framework, an organization can address some of the criticisms of sustainability and IR (see Atkins and Maroun, 2018). These types of reports do not provide sufficient detail on the importance of biodiversity to the organization and society as a whole (see also Atkins et al., 2015; Dillard and Reynolds, 2008). They include some information on social and environmental issues but stop short of dealing explicitly with material issues such as habitat destruction, climate-change effects and over-population (Atkins and Maroun, 2018; Atkins et al., 2018; Jones and Solomon, 2013; Zhao and Atkins, 2019).

Biodiversity, deep ecology and anthropocentrism

There are different definitions of biodiversity. Most commonly used is the one provided by the GRI (2007, p. 7):

> Biodiversity is the variability among living organisms from all sources and the ecological complexes of which they are part, ranging from birds in the air, fish in the sea, and microorganisms in the soil to genetic variety within agricultural crops and diversity of ecosystems. This variability is essential for ecosystems to function efficiently. Ecosystems provide 'ecosystem services' to organizations and society as a whole, including food, fresh water, wood and fibre, medicines, soil fertility, climate regulation, building materials, inspiration for scientific and technical development, genetic resources, flood regulation, and recreation facilities.

There is no organization that does not make use of one or more of these eco-system services, either directly through their activities or indirectly through supply chain partners.

The GRI definition frames biodiversity as part of a system that provides goods and services to organizations and society as a whole (anthropocentricism). For example, insects, such as bees, provide essential pollination services in agricultural areas (see, for example, Atkins and Atkins, 2016), which are needed to ensure good harvests. Without pollination services, agricultural organizations (or organizations dependent on the agriculture sector), may face declining profits or face threats to their sustainability (see, for example, IPBES, 2019d). Pollination is an essential ecosystem service that is crucial to the survival of the human species. Similarly, fish are a primary source of nutrition for many people, and with fishing stocks depleting at a faster rate than in the past (IPBES, 2019d), industries (and many people) will be impacted (see, for example, Maroun et al., 2018).

With ecosystem services and goods playing such a crucial role in society, attempts have been made to value these goods and services. The valuations can be used to make a case for protecting biodiversity by emphasizing the replacement costs or losses to be incurred if biodiversity collapses (see, for example, Turpie et al., 2017). The natural world should not, however, only be seen as providing monetary value to organizations and society. So-called "natural capital" has an intrinsic value which is independent of the benefits it provides to humanity (see, for example, Chrisitan, 2019; Devall, 1980; Drengson, 1995; Khisty, 2006; Naess, 1973).

Many animal and plant species play an essential role in the healthy functioning of ecosystems and provide services to other flora and fauna, forming part of the ecosystem (see, for example, WWF, 2019). Other animals have cultural significance. For example, giant pandas have become synonymous not only with Chinese culture but also with various agencies aimed at protecting animals species (see, for example, Zhao and Atkins, 2019). The giant panda has also become an indicator species[1] used by scientists to investigate the impact of external factors on ecosystems. In South Africa, the rhinoceros is regarded as both ecologically and culturally significant. As a result, organizations and members of society have taken actions to curb the steep decline in rhinoceros populations caused by poaching even when there is no direct business case for doing so (see, for example, Atkins et al., 2018). This is in keeping with a deep ecological view on biodiversity.

From an ecological perspective, the rhinoceros is a keystone species, according to scientists, which means that the animal plays an essential part in the functioning and health of its ecological environment, being an important herbivore that interacts with the natural vegetation and ecosystem around it. There are, however, identifiable economic incentives for prioritizing rhinoceros conservation given the significance and materiality of eco-tourism to the South African economy, for example. From a more anthropocentric perspective, the mighty rhinoceros defines African heritage and culture. The demise of various rhinoceros species in South Africa and across the continent is eliciting a powerful emotional response from South Africans and people around the world.

According to deep ecologists, organisations cannot continue to operate as if they are independent of nature (Gray and Milne, 2018, 2019). They should actively consider how their business impacts the environment and appreciate that, without nature, commercial activity is impossible. A deep ecological view does not, how-ever, mean that economic dimensions need to be ignored: it may be possible to use the features of existing accounting infrastructure to contribute to improved transparency and accountability and operationalise sustainable development. This can take into consideration the intrinsic value of the natural world (as espoused by deep ecologists) while simultaneously recognising the anthropocentric case for pre-serving so-called 'natural capital'

(Maroun and Atkins, 2018, p. 5)

At a minimum, this requires companies to incorporate biodiversity management into their strategy, operations and reporting (Atkins et al., 2014; Gallhofer and Haslam, 2017), promoting accountability to stakeholders. It also encourages positive change by making companies, and members of society, more aware of the impact of their operations on biodiversity (Gallhofer and Haslam, 2011, 2017; Gallhofer et al., 2013).

Different reporting models have been developed to give effect to the above objectives. The next section discusses some of the emerging forms of accounting and reporting which, in the authors' opinion, could be useful for companies wanting to provide a more detailed analysis of natural capital (flora and fauna) in their integrated reports.

Emerging reporting frameworks

In this section, we consider the frameworks that have emerged from practice as well as from the academic literature.

Biodiversity reporting

The most commonly used framework to account for biodiversity is the Global Reporting Initiative (GRI, 2016). Recommended disclosures are summarized in Table 29.1.

The GRI disclosures have been criticized for not providing sufficient context on the risks associated with biodiversity loss and how these are managed. Grabsch et al. (2012) and van Liempd and Busch (2013) offer a way forward. They suggest that organizations should disclose how their vision and mission to address biodiversity-related risks. A biodiversity risk register should be maintained, which outlines material issues by operational area and the steps taken to manage them. Key performance indicators should be developed, which include biodiversity-related measures. This can include the costs incurred to meet the biodiversity targets, action plans and an analysis of results (Grabsch et al., 2012; van Liempd and Busch, 2013). Clearly, GRI304-4 provides an opportunity and an incentive to account for ways in which species extinctions are being prevented.

In the authors' opinion, biodiversity disclosures should be included in the integrated report rather than only in supporting documents or on webpages. This will ensure that biodiversity-related concerns are understood as a core part of an organization's business model, risk management and stakeholder engagement process (see, for example, Atkins and Maroun, 2018; Atkins et al., 2018; Jones, 1996, 2003). Disclosures should be informed by detailed consultations with the relevant stakeholders, environmental specialists and non-governmental organizations (Grabsch et al., 2012; IIRC, 2013; van Liempd and Busch, 2013).

Table 29.2 summarizes the codes/themes of an expanded biodiversity reporting schematic for inclusion in an organization's integrated report.

Table 29.3 provides a summary of research conducted on biodiversity disclosures. The results are presented by country to demonstrate that the disclosures are not limited to

Table 29.1 Biodiversity disclosure requirements

Indicator	Explanation	Examples
GRI-103	This requires organizations to report on their bio-diversity management policies, providing details that include the impact of their operations on bio-diversity. This can include the inclusion of bio-diversity management strategies into organizations' entire strategies.	• Disclosing the strategic biodiversity targets of an organization and • Including essential biodiversity in key performance indicators.
GRI304-1	Provides the required disclosure regarding the "operational sites owned, leased, managed in, or adjacent to, protected areas and areas of high bio-diversity value outside protected areas".	• Operational areas in sensitive or at-risk ecosystems or biomes; • Protected status per operational area and • The nature of the operations (extractive, harvesting, commercial) per protected area or biome.
GRI304-2	Description of significant impacts of activities, products and services on biodiversity in protected areas and areas of high biodiversity value outside pro-tected areas.	• Rehabilitation of areas damaged by operations; • Removal of invasive alien species and • Reintroduction of flora or fauna to areas.
GRI304-3	Habitats protected or restored.	• Size (or volume) of the area restored and the process used for restoration; • Total number of species, based upon risk, affected by the rehabilitation and • Methods used to determine the extent and success of the rehabilitation.
GRI304-4	IUCN Red List species and national conservation list species with habitats in areas affected by operations.	• Inventory of at-risk species, based on IUCN Red List species categories, per operational site; • IUCN species affected by the operational sites and • Changes in the population size of at-risk species.

Table 29.2 Disclosure matrix

Codes/Themes	Examples
Scene-setting	A description of the organization's definition of biodiversity. This can include disclosure on the status of biodiversity within the operational area of the organization and how biodiversity is included in the vision and mission of the entity.
Species-related	An inventory of the species at risk, based on the IUCN categories per operational site. This can include population numbers and biodiversity mass.
Social and stakeholder engagements	Disclosure on the processes followed to engage with stakeholders. This can also include disclosure on engagements with communities to promote awareness around biodiversity issues.
Performance evaluations – biodiversity specifics	Disclosure on the actions taken to reverse biodiversity loss. This includes the planned and actual results with an analysis of the variance.
Internal management	Information relating to a plan or officer to address biodiversity concerns that stakeholders might have. This can include internal reporting systems or changes made to the control environment to address biodiversity risks.
Risk	This can include disclosure of a risk register, detailing material biodiversity risk and how the disclosed risks impact stakeholders and the organisation. This can include reports on the actual events that have occurred, such as fires or drought.
External reporting	Reference to a biodiversity disclosure framework, such as the GRI or integrated reporting frameworks
Assurance	This includes reporting on assurance services (and assurance providers) used to assure the biodiversity-related information.

specific jurisdictions; existing disclosure frameworks have been adopted by the international community.

As companies become more aware of their social, economic and environmental responsibilities, they should increase their investment in management and accounting systems to provide information to manage and report on environmental responsibilities (see, for example, Alrazi et al., 2015; De Villiers et al., 2017). At the same time, they should engage more actively with stakeholders to ensure that legitimate concerns and information needs are being addressed. This points to the emergence of an emancipatory form of accounting which can promote positive changes in how companies manage biodiversity and reduce the impact of their operations on sensitive areas (Gallhofer and Haslam, 2017; Russell et al., 2017). Extinction accounting is an excellent example.

Extinction accounting

Seen as a logical development from biodiversity reporting (Atkins et al., 2018), extinction accounting is an emerging form of accounting, which requires organizations to report on the extinction of species. The accounting addresses concerns raised by the academic community that organizations only report on species that are of use to humans (Rimmel and Jonäll, 2013; Samkin et al., 2014). Also, biodiversity disclosure requirements seldom

Table 29.3 Summary of biodiversity reporting trends

Country	Findings
Denmark	van Liempd and Busch (2013) find that Danish companies view biodiversity as a moral and ethical issue, even when biodiversity has no immediately apparent intrinsic value. However, analysis of biodiversity reporting shows that Danish companies fail to report adequately on both qualitative and quantitative aspects of biodiversity. The study suggests that regulators and accounting standard-setters should work together to develop a comprehensive reporting framework to increase the quality of biodiversity-related reporting.
Sweden	In Sweden, Rimmel and Jonäll (2013) find that biodiversity disclosures are usually included in annual reports but are limited to a discussion on the biodiversity risks in geographical areas. Few companies disclose the risks and actions plans taken to address biodiversity concerns. The total number of companies that reported on biodiversity increased over the period under review, but this was limited to organizations in low-risk industries. Under-developed internal management and accounting systems impede detailed biodiversity reporting. Most companies rely on external reporting guidelines, such as those issued by the GRI, with only limited engagement with stakeholders
United Kingdom	Atkins, Barone, Maroun, and Atkins (2018) explored disclosures on bees by a sample of prominent companies listed on the LSE. Companies in the food, cosmetics and agrochemical chemical industries provided the most disclosures, usually on their webpages. There is relatively little biodiversity-related information in annual or sustainability reports. While there is room for improvement, disclosures are intended to be informative and raise awareness about the risks posed by the loss of bees.
South Africa	Maroun (2016) finds that corporate South Africa has not considered the importance of pollination services in South Africa. The integrated reports of the 19 largest farming, food and retail companies did not include information on pollination services. Low levels of disclosure are attributed to a lack of reporting guidelines and time required by organizations to move from a shareholder-centric approach in reporting to a stakeholder-centric approach. The findings raise the concern that the investor community may be unaware of the risks posed by a decline in pollinator species.
	The findings are corroborated by Mansoor and Maroun (2016) who find little evidence of biodiversity reporting in the integrated and sustainability reports of mining entities, food producers and retailers listed on the local stock exchange. This is concerning given the fact that South Africa has championed the use of integrated reporting and has a long history of including non-financial information in corporate reports. The research questions the sincerity of the disclosures made by organizations in specific industries. It calls for existing frameworks to include a clear definition of biodiversity and provide guidance on what organizations should include in a biodiversity account. Findings from South African reports are not, however, entirely negative. Usher and Maroun (2018) show that hat there has been an increase in biodiversity-related disclosures, suggesting that organizations realise the importance of disclosing non-financial information and have started appreciating the importance of preserving biodiversity to ensure long-term sustainability. There is room for improvement when it comes to the quality of biodiversity reporting, but there is evidence of companies beginning to internalise the relevance of biodiversity for their business models and the need for effective reporting to stakeholders (see also Maroun et al., 2018).
Various	Boiral and Heras-Saizarbitoria (2017) explore the drivers of biodiversity conservation in mining and forestry organisation by performing a content analysis on a sample of sustainability reports in different jurisdictions. The research finds that organizations are motivated to report on biodiversity to gain legitimacy. Organizations achieve this by addressing ethical concerns in their disclosures, applying good corporate governance practises and improving relationships with stakeholders

deal with internal processes adopted to include biodiversity in a company's strategy, risk management and monitoring processes (see, for example, Mansoor and Maroun, 2016; Samkin et al., 2014; Tregidga, 2013; van Liempd and Busch, 2013). Biodiversity is also dealt with in anthropocentric terms; sincere attempts to protect biodiversity on deep ecological grounds are not a primary consideration (see, for example, Atkins et al., 2014; Atkins and Maroun, 2018; Atkins et al., 2018).

To address the concerns raised above, extinction accounting requires organizations to collect and analyse information on the impacts their business activities have on biodiversity and the risk of species loss. The aim is to place the focus on the importance of the environment for long-term business sustainability *and* continuity of all forms of life (see, for example, Brown et al., 2015; Gallhofer and Haslam, 2011, 2017; Maroun and Atkins, 2018; Tinker, 1984). This does not require a complete rejection of capitalism. As explained by Gallhofer and Haslam (2017, p. 6), dealing with emancipatory forms of accounting,

> there is a move away ... from the position that emancipatory accounting – if still, a radically progressive notion – necessarily reduces to an accounting that is an instrument of revolutionary or grand radical transformation consistent with the position suggested in the Marx-inspired line of thought pursued by [critical theorists].

Instead, the emancipatory project aims to provide a complete account of the relationship between organizations and the undeniable dependence of contemporary business on the environment.

Importantly, extinction accounting is grounded in pragmatism and attempts to take a middle road, or middle-range thinking through praxis (Laughlin, 1995). It attempts to balance deep ecological and anthropocentric views. Although a subset of biodiversity reporting, it provides additional information on biodiversity that can be used to prevent extinction (Atkins and Maroun, 2018). This builds on suggestions for accounting researchers to adopt middle-range thinking specifically about Laughlin's (1995) recommendations regarding change and critique in accounting research and implications for policy and practice arising from such research:

> the medium position on change keeps open the possibility that in certain circumstances critique and ultimate change are important but not in other situations. This more conditional approach to critique and change is clearly more complex than either the deliberate exclusion as with the Comteans or the ontological necessity for exclusion as with the Fichteans. It requires a deliberate and deliberated evaluatory policy to decide when critique and change are appropriate
>
> *(Laughlin, 1995, p. 82)*

We feel that in developing a more open-ended approach to accounting for biodiversity and to the development of extinction accounting frameworks, it is essential that there is no attempt to straight-jacket such frameworks into either a positivist frame considering only "natural capital" and its economic implications (which adopts a no change/status quo approach to the current capitalist system), or a more extreme deep ecology view, which might prefer to do away with our capitalist, finance and accounting systems altogether (a position of extreme change/critique). Our approach is aligned with the concept and ethos of middle-range thinking. This approach, we feel, is consistent with Laughlin's view that:

the argument for the "medium" position is because of its greater balance in its attitude to the status quo. The argument for "high" levels of change assumes that everything is basically in need of change. Nothing is satisfactory or acceptable or worthy of preservation. At the "low" end of the change continuum, everything is satisfactory and in need of preservation. There is nothing wrong with anything. Both positions are arguably untenable and very extreme. Again the "medium" position holds open the possibility that the status quo should continue while also keeping open that change is required. This more balanced perspective, which neither argues that everything is right nor that it is wrong, calls for a rather more sophisticated model of change to make this judgement. It is this change model which is central to this "medium" position on the change dimension

(Laughlin, 1995, p. 84)

Thus, extinction accounting seeks to build on existing frameworks, to work within the established systems and mechanisms of capitalism, but to bring about a change in focus and a more critical perspective by incorporating a deep ecology mindset and a more intrinsic value appreciation of the value of flora and fauna into the accounting system. We would like to think that our extinction accounting represents, in Laughlin's words, a "rather more sophisticated model of change" than others "in the market" at present.

Consequently, extinction accounting builds on the GRI (2016) and the International Integrated Reporting Council's (IIRC) Integrated Reporting Framework. The academic research draws on the social constructivist traditions, developing a framework that shows the interconnection between extinction risk (at a species level), the action plans to address the risk and the analysis of outcomes (Atkins et al., 2018; Büchling and Maroun, 2019; Mansoor and Maroun, 2016; Maroun and Atkins, 2018).

The disclosure of financial capital does not dominate the extinction accounting framework; it places natural capital at the centre of the reporting model to show the interconnection between economic, environmental and social factors. Extinction accounting is grounded in an iterative process which involves reporting on steps taken to prevent extinction, reflecting on successes and failures and using these to inform the refinement of operational and management changes. This should not lead to the monetization of extinction but to tangible changes in the business model and interactions with other organizations and stakeholders (Atkins et al., 2018; Maroun and Atkins, 2018).

While not widespread, there is evidence of extinction accounting taking shape, especially where IR is more mature. Atkins et al. (2018), for example, examine reporting on the extinction of the rhinoceros by South African listed companies. The integrated reports of organizations provided disclosure explaining the risks faced by the species, steps taken to lower the extinction risk and an assessment of the action plans. The research finds that the disclosure demonstrates a sincere concern for the rhino and that the disclosure is not only motivated by impression management. Key elements of the extinction accounts include

- Educational-focused initiatives;
- Direct wildlife protection initiatives;
- Partnership and collaborative corporate initiatives;
- Customer-focused initiatives for rhinoceros conservation and preservation;
- Stakeholder-focused initiatives and
- Genuine concern for native wildlife and cultural heritage (Atkins et al., 2018):

Table 29.4 Elements in an extinction accounting framework

Element	Purpose
Element 1: Extinction accounting context	This element requires the organization to provide disclosure on risks of extinction at a species level. The disclosure should be done per geographical or operational area to demonstrate how the entity's operations affect biodiversity in different biomes. The vision and mission of the organization need to demonstrate how the organization seeks to manage biodiversity.
Element 2: Action-focused reporting	This element requires disclosure on how the extinction risks are to be managed and what plans have been implemented. This process will need to incorporate disclosure on a species and habitat level (depending on the nature of the organisation's operations).
Element 3: Partnership reporting	Organizations do not function in a vacuum and should include disclosure on how local communities, stakeholders, NGOs and other parties were consulted or incorporated into the extinction management plan of the entity.
Element 4: Analysis and reflection	The disclosure should include the assessment performed over planned actions and should include discussion on favourable and unfavourable outcomes. The outcomes should be measured, and proposed adjustments should be disclosed.
Element 5: Assessment	An independent assessment should be performed over the information disclosed to assure that the information is accurate. This can include annual biodiversity assessments.
Element 6: Reporting	Provide an account of the progress made to date on preventing or mitigating extinction, planned future actions and risk exposure. This should include disclosure on how extinction accounting has been integrated into the organization's strategy.

Maroun and Atkins (2018) refine the above elements using the guidance provided by the GRI and IIRC. Table 29.4 provides an outline of the extinction accounting schematic.

Maroun and Atkins (2018), drawing on the existing principles of the GRI, IIRC and extinction accounting framework, demonstrate how extinction accounting can be operationalized as part of a broader IR and thinking philosophy. See Figure 29.1.

Figure 29.1 provides a framework for organizations to account for the extinction of species as part of their reporting on natural capital. The model is informed by the GRI (2016) and Cuckston (2017, 2018), who recommend that organizations disclose biodiversity (species and ecosystems) per area of operation (B). The location (A) should describe the natural capital of an organization and provide information on the risks faced by biodiversity (C1), drawing on the extinction risk category as per the IUCN (C2). The information provided by C1 and C2 can then be used to create a risk accounting, which demonstrates how business operations affect biodiversity (C3). Where there have been failures in conserving biodiversity, resulting in fines, penalties or possible contingent liabilities, disclosure needs to be provided. This is to enhance accountability and provide a sense of the costs of non-compliance (C4).

Maroun and Atkins (2018) and Büchling and Maroun (2019) find that the disclosure should not be limited to natural capital or financial capital but should deal with the

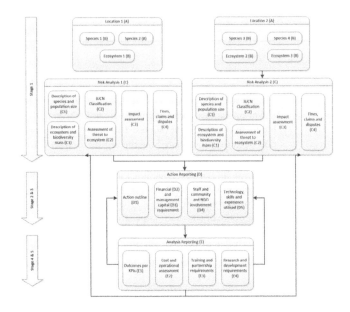

Figure 29.1 A natural capital reporting framework

Reproduced from: Maroun and Atkins (2018, p. 13)

organization's capitals as a whole. For example, employees may require training (human capital) or new information systems or machinery (manufacturing capital) to report on or conserve biodiversity. In some cases, research on how best to address extinction risks may need to be undertaken (intellectual capital) and supported by detailed engagement with environmental specialists and non-governmental organizations (relationship capital).

Drawing on the logic followed by the IIRC (2013), reporting on the different capitals affected by and required in order to address the loss of species provides both managers and stakeholders with a better sense of the interconnection among the different capitals. The process of demonstrating how the different capitals affect the natural capital can be used to demonstrate how a multi-capital approach to managing biodiversity has been incorporated into the action plans (D1). Providing an account on how the different capitals are used to address biodiversity can inform the organization of resource requirements and changes required to information systems (D2 and D3). Where a shortage of capital exists, the account can guide management processes and help to identify where partnerships may be required to assist in the biodiversity management action plan (D4). The action plans may also require more intellectual capital (in the form of research and development) to address the weaknesses identified in the biodiversity management action plan (D5).

As the different capitals of organizations become more involved in managing biodiversity risk, those charged with corporate governance should monitor and assess the performance of the capitals used (IOD, 2016). This will require key performance indicators (E1) to be developed by the governance body to monitor the costs and operational structure of action plans (E2). This will include an evaluation of partnerships (social and human capital) and research and development functions (intellectual capital), addressing the requirements of E3 and E4. Where performance has not been satisfactory and has not addressed the risks, the action plans, and the risks, have to be reassessed accordingly (see, for example, Büchling and

Maroun, 2019). The model, therefore, requires the process to be iterative, with the organization engaging with stakeholders.

Büchling and Maroun (2019) analysed annual reports of South African National Parks (SANParks) to determine whether the disclosures can be used to build an extinction account of an organization that is required to conserve biodiversity. The analysis suggests that SANParks actively monitors the biodiversity in its operational areas and acts to address risks of extinction. Disclosures demonstrate that a detailed analysis is performed by SANParks to assess action plans and that variances, favourable and unfavourable, are explained. The disclosures in SANParks' annual reports can be used to construct an account of how the organization manages not only its biodiversity but also extinction risks.

Extinction accounting is not without limitations. For example, in the UK public sector, different accounting practices are used to analyse and report on species loss and the success of recovery actions. Nevertheless, an economic logic impinges on ecological decision-making, undermining the emancipatory potential of extinction accounts (Weir, 2018). In the private sector, Adler et al. (2018) show that many of the world's most prominent organizations are hesitant to provide detailed reports on biodiversity and steps being taken to mitigate the risk of extinction. Zhao and Atkins (2019) deal with a more context-specific scenario. They explore the extent of biodiversity disclosures in Chinese companies and whether or not they are accounting for the extinction of the giant panda. The researchers find that Chinese companies are reporting little information on biodiversity initiatives. This is attributed to a lack of public awareness and under-developed reporting frameworks.

Even when guidelines are more detailed, there is usually room for interpretation. This makes it possible for organizations to address environmental issues symbolically (see, for example, Milne et al., 2009; Tregidga et al., 2014). For example, research on how oil companies report on the impact of their operations on polar bears indicated an increase in the amount of biodiversity disclosure but, in the absence of a well-functioning extinction accounting model, accountability is not enhanced. Instead, organizations use existing disclosure frameworks to paint a positive picture in order to bolster legitimacy (Jonäll and Sabelfeld, 2019). In this way, the accounting fails to internalize the impact of extinction and create a potential for changes in the way in which business is conducted (Gray and Milne, 2018).

Concluding remarks

Biodiversity reporting and extinction accounting are emerging forms of accounting, aimed at enhancing organizations' accountability to stakeholders. These types of accounting are part of a broader emancipatory movement aimed at strengthening stakeholder engagement processes on sustainability and environmental matters to promote change (Laine and Vinnari, 2017). The emancipatory project borrows from existing reporting frameworks, such as IR, to develop frameworks that can bring about change in organizations (Atkins and Atkins, 2019; Atkins et al., 2018). To be effective, extinction accounting requires natural capital to be placed at the centre of the business model. The organization should demonstrate how the other capitals are affected by a change in natural capital. Importantly, extinction accounting does not have to be limited to only the integrated report; it can include information contained on social media platforms and organizations' websites to produce a type of consolidated account.

Maroun and Atkins (2018) suggest borrowing from sustainability and IR frameworks to guide the development and application of extinction accounting. Jonäll and Sabelfeld (2019) and Zhao and Atkins (2019) recommend that national-level regulation is required to ensure that organizations comply with biodiversity standards.

As concerns about biodiversity loss mount, an international response is also required. There have already been some achievements. The Aichi Conference (CBD, 2011), hosted by the Convention on Biological Diversity (CBD), has proposed 20 targets aimed at protecting biodiversity. This includes a biodiversity reporting framework, which should be developed by the national governments and applied by the private and public sectors to drive responsible environmental practices (CBD, 2011). This provides environmental accounting academics with an excellent opportunity to inform practice.

As discussed above, the approach adopted by extinction accounting arises from attempts to embed middle-range thinking within accounting academia, especially concerning change/ critique. Our approach to developing extinction accounting falls between maintaining the status quo of accounting and the capitalist system we find ourselves in, and developing a new system to replace the status quo. Extinction accounting seeks to alter the current system by integrating deep ecology and intrinsic value while maintaining the structures and mechanisms already in place.

The following are possible areas for future research:

- Providing empirical evidence of entities in the private and public sector attempting to apply extinction accounting and analysing the challenges encountered;
- Exploring the role of regulation in promoting an awareness of and more detailed reporting on the loss of biodiversity;
- Obtaining an understanding of stakeholders' information needs and developing a more refined view on what companies and the public sector should be included in their extinction accounts;
- Examining in more detail how natural capital affects organizations' business models and how best to manage the consequences of a loss of species.

Note

1 Indicator species are species that function as proxies for ecological processes (for example habitat loss) or biological species that assists in determining the impact of external biological factors on the broader ecosystem (Lindenmayer et al., 2000).

References

Adler, R., Mansi, M., and Pandey, R. (2018). Biodiversity and threatened species reporting by the top Fortune Global companies. *Accounting, Auditing & Accountability Journal, 31*(3), 787–825.

Alrazi, B., de Villiers, C., and van Staden, C. J. (2015). A comprehensive literature review on, and the construction of a framework for, environmental legitimacy, accountability and proactivity. *Journal of Cleaner Production, 102*, 44–57.

Apostolopoulou, E., and Adams, W. M. (2015). Neoliberal capitalism and conservation in the post-crisis era: The dialectics of "green" and "un-green" grabbing in Greece and the UK. *Antipode, 47*(1), 15–35.

Atkins, J., and Atkins, B. (2019). What is mass extinction and can we stop it? In: J. Atkins, and B. Atkins (Eds.), *Around the World in 80 Species: Exploring the Business of Extinction.* London: Routledge.

Atkins, J., and Atkins, B. C. (2016). *The Business of Bees: An Integrated Approach to Bee Decline and Corporate Responsibility.* Sheffield: Greenleaf Publishing.

Atkins, J., Atkins, B. C., Thomson, I., and Maroun, W. (2015). "Good" news from nowhere: Imagining utopian sustainable accounting. *Accounting, Auditing & Accountability Journal, 28*(5), 651–670.

Atkins, J., Gräbsch, C., and Jones, M. (2014). Corporate biodiversity reporting: Exploring its anthropocentric nature. In: M. Jones (Ed.), *Accounting for Biodiversity* (pp. 215–244). London: Routledge.

Atkins, J., and Maroun, W. (2018). Integrated extinction accounting and accountability: Building an ark. *Accounting, Auditing & Accountability Journal, 31*(3), 750–786.

Atkins, J., Maroun, W., Atkins, B. C., and Barone, E. (2018). From the Big Five to the Big Four? Exploring extinction accounting for the rhinoceros. *Accounting, Auditing & Accountability Journal, 31*(2), 674–702.

Boiral, O., and Heras-Saizarbitoria, I. (2017). Corporate commitment to biodiversity in mining and forestry: identifying drivers from GRI reports. *Journal of Cleaner Production, 162,* 153–161.

Brockington, D., and Duffy, R. (2010). Capitalism and conservation: The production and reproduction of biodiversity conservation. *Antipode, 42*(3), 469–484.

Brown, J., Dillard, J., Hopper, T., Gallhofer, S., Haslam, J., and Yonekura, A. (2015). Accounting as differentiated universal for emancipatory praxis. *Accounting, Auditing & Accountability Journal, 28*(5), 846–874.

Büchling, M. C., and Maroun, W. (2019). Extinction accounting by the public sector: South African National Parks (SANParks). In: J. Atkins, and B. Atkins (Eds.), *Around the World in 80 Species: Exploring the Business of Extinction* (pp. 201–218). Oxford: Routledge.

Büscher, B., Sullivan, S., Neves, K., Igoe, J., and Brockington, D. (2012). Towards a synthesized critique of neoliberal biodiversity conservation. *Capitalism Nature Socialism, 23*(2), 4–30.

CBD. (2011). *Strategic Plan for Biodiversity 2011–2020 and the Aichi Targets.* Available at: www.cbd.int/doc/strategic-plan/2011-2020/Aichi-Targets-EN.pdf (Accessed: 28 October 2019).

Chrisitan, J. (2019). A deep ecology perspective on extinction. In: J. Atkins, and B. Atkins (Eds.), *Around the World in 80 Species: Exploring the Business of Extinction* (pp. 91–118). London: Routledge.

Cuckston, T. (2017). Ecology-centred accounting for biodiversity in the production of a blanket bog. *Accounting, Auditing & Accountability Journal, 30*(7), 1537–1567.

Cuckston, T. (2018). Making extinction calculable. *Accounting, Auditing & Accountability Journal, 31*(3), 849–874.

De Villiers, C., Hsiao, P.-C. K., and Maroun, W. (2017). Developing a conceptual model of influences around integrated reporting, new insights and directions for future research. *Meditari Accountancy Research, 25*(4), 450–460.

Devall, B. (1980). The deep ecology movement. *Natural Resources Journal, 20*(2), 299–322.

Dillard, J., and Reynolds, M. (2008). Green owl and the corn maiden. *Accounting, Auditing & Accountability Journal, 21*(4), 556–579.

Drengson, A. (1995). The deep ecology movement. *Trumpeter, 12*(3), 2–7.

Gallhofer, S., and Haslam, J. (2011). Emancipation, the spiritual and accounting. *Critical Perspectives on Accounting, 22*(5), 500–509.

Gallhofer, S., and Haslam, J. (2017). Some reflections on the construct of emancipatory accounting: Shifting meaning and the possibilities of a new pragmatism. *Critical Perspectives on Accounting, 63,* 1–18.

Gallhofer, S., Haslam, J., and Yonekura, A. (2013). Further critical reflections on a contribution to the methodological issues debate in accounting. *Critical Perspectives on Accounting, 24*(3), 191–206.

Grabsch, C., Jones, M. J., and Solomon, J. F. (2012). *Accounting for Biodiversity in Crisis: A European Perspective.* Working Paper, Kings College London.

Gray, R., and Milne, M. J. (2018). Perhaps the dodo should have accounted for human beings? Accounts of humanity and (its) extinction. *Accounting, Auditing & Accountability Journal, 31*(3), 826–848.

Gray, R., and Milne, M. J. (2019). Species extinction and closing the loop of argument: Imagining accounting and finance as the potential cause of human extinction. In: J. Atkins, and B. Atkins (Eds.), *Around the World in 80 Species: Exploring the Business of Extinction* (pp. 119–132). Oxford: Routledge.

GRI. (2007). B*iodiversity: A GRI reportingresource.* Available at: http://www.globalreporting.org/resourcelibrary/Biodiversity-A-GRI-Resource-Document.pdf (Accessed: 28 October 2019).

GRI. (2016). *Consolidated Set of GRI Sustainability Reporting Standards (2016).* Available at: www.globalreporting.org/standards/gri-standards-download-center/?g=ae2e23b8-4958-455c-a9df-ac372d6ed9a8 (Accessed: 28 October 2019).

IIRC. (2013). *The International Integrated Reporting Framework.* London: IIRC.

IOD. (2016). *King IV Report on Governance for South Africa.* Johannesburg, SA: Lexis Nexus.

IPBES. (2019a). *The Assessment Report on Pollinators, Pollination and Food Production*. Available at: https://ipbes.net/assessment-reports/pollinators (Accessed: 9 May 2019).

IPBES. (2019b). *Nature's Dangerous Decline 'Unprecedented'; Species Extinction Rates Accelerating* [Press release]. Available at: www.ipbes.net/news/Media-Release-Global-Assessment (Accessed: 28 October 2019).

IPBES. (2019c). *The Regional Assessment Report on Biodiversity and Ecosystem Services for Africa*. Available at: www.ipbes.net/system/tdf/spm_africa_2018_digital.pdf?file=1&type=node&id=28397 (Accessed: 28 October 2019).

IPBES. (2019d). *Summary for Policymakers of the Global Assessment Report on Biodiversity and Ecosystem Services of the Intergovernmental Science-Policy Platform on Biodiversity and Ecosystem Services*. Available at: www.ipbes.net/sites/default/files/downloads/spm_unedited_advance_for_posting_htn.pdf (Accessed: 28 October 2019).

IUCN. (2019). *IUCN Red List*. Available at: www.iucnredlist.org/search/stats?redListCategory=ew (Accessed: 28 October 2019).

Jonäll, K., and Sabelfeld, S. (2019). Accounting for survival of polar bears. In: J. Atkins, and B. Atkins (Eds.), *Around the World in 80 Species: Exploring the Business of Extinction* (pp. 337–358). London: Routledge.

Jones, M. J. (1996). Accounting for biodiversity: A pilot study. *The British Accounting Review*, *28*(4), 281–303.

Jones, M. J. (2003). Accounting for biodiversity: Operationalising environmental accounting. *Accounting, Auditing & Accountability Journal*, *16*(5), 762–789.

Jones, M. J., and Solomon, J. F. (2013). Problematising accounting for biodiversity. *Accounting, Auditing & Accountability Journal*, *26*(5), 668–687.

Khisty, C. J. (2006). Meditations on systems thinking, spiritual systems, and deep ecology. *Systemic Practice and Action Research*, *19*(4), 295–307.

Laine, M., and Vinnari, E. (2017). The transformative potential of counter accounts: A case study of animal rights activism. *Accounting, Auditing & Accountability Journal*, *30*(7), 1481–1510.

Laughlin, R. (1995). Empirical research in accounting: Alternative approaches and a case for "middle-range" thinking. *Accounting, Auditing & Accountability Journal*, *8*(1), 63–87.

Lindenmayer, D. B., Margules, C. R., and Botkin, D. B. (2000). Indicators of biodiversity for ecologically sustainable forest management. *Conservation Biology*, *14*(4), 941–950.

Mansoor, H., and Maroun, W. (2016). An initial review of biodiversity reporting by South African corporates: The case of the food and mining sectors. *South African Journal of Economic and Management Sciences*, *19*(4), 592–614.

Maroun, W. (2016). No bees in their bonnet: On the absence of bee-reporting by South African listed companies. The business of bees: An integrated approach to bee decline and corporate responsibility. J. Atkins and B. Atkins. Aizlewood's Mill, Greenleaf, 317–325.

Maroun, W., and Atkins, J. (2014). Section 45 of the Auditing Profession Act: Blowing the whistle for audit quality? *The British Accounting Review*, *46*(3), 248–263.

Maroun, W., and Atkins, J. (2018). The emancipatory potential of extinction accounting: Exploring current practice in integrated reports. *Accounting Forum*, *42*(1), 102–118.

Maroun, W., Usher, K., and Mansoor, H. (2018). Biodiversity reporting and organised hypocrisy: The case of the South African food and retail industry. *Qualitative Research in Accounting & Management*, *15*(4), 437–464.

Milne, M., Tregidga, H., and Walton, S. (2009). Words not actions! The ideological role of sustainable development reporting. *Accounting, Auditing and Accountability Journal*, *22*(8), 1211–1257.

Naess, A. (1973). The shallow and the deep, long-range ecology movement: A summary. *Inquiry*, *16*(1–4), 95–100.

Rimmel, G., and Jonäll, K. (2013). Biodiversity reporting in Sweden: Corporate disclosure and preparers' views. *Accounting, Auditing & Accountability Journal*, *26*(5), 746–778.

Ripple, W. J., Wolf, C., Newsome, T. M., Galetti, M., Alamgir, M., Crist, E., Mahmoud, M. I., and Laurance, W. F. (2017). World scientists' warning to humanity: A second notice. *BioScience*, *67*(12), 1026–1028.

Russell, S., Milne, M. J., and Dey, C. (2017). Accounts of nature and the nature of accounts: Critical reflections on environmental accounting and propositions for ecologically informed accounting. *Accounting, Auditing & Accountability Journal*, *30*(7), 1426–1458.

Samkin, G., Schneider, A., and Tappin, D. (2014). Developing a reporting and evaluation framework for biodiversity. *Accounting, Auditing & Accountability Journal, 27*(3), 527–562.

Tinker, T. (1984). *Social Accounting for Corporations: Private Enterprise versus the Public Interest*. Manchester: Manchester University Press.

Tregidga, H. (2013). Biodiversity offsetting: Problematisation of an emerging governance regime. *Accounting, Auditing & Accountability Journal, 26*(5), 806–832.

Tregidga, H., Milne, M., and Kearins, K. (2014). (Re)presenting 'sustainable organizations'. *Accounting, Organizations and Society, 39*(6), 477–494.

Turpie, J. K., Forsythe, K. J., Knowles, A., Blignaut, J., and Letley, G. (2017). Mapping and valuation of South Africa's ecosystem services: A local perspective. *Ecosystem Services, 27*, 179–192.

Usher, K., and Maroun, W. (2018). A review of biodiversity reporting by the South African Sea Food Industry. *South African Journal of Economic and Management Sciences, 21*(1), 1–12.

van Liempd, D., and Busch, J. (2013). Biodiversity reporting in Denmark. *Accounting, Auditing & Accountability Journal, 26*(5), 833–872.

Weir, K. (2018). The purposes, promises and compromises of extinction accounting in the UK public sector. *Accounting, Auditing & Accountability Journal, 31*(3), 875–899.

WWF. (2018). *Living Planet Report 2018*. Available at: https://wwf.panda.org/knowledge_hub/all_publi cations/living_planet_report_2018/ (Accessed: 28 October 2019).

WWF. (2019). *Black Rhino*. Available at: www.worldwildlife.org/species/black-rhino (Assessed: 28 October 2019).

Zhao, L., and Atkins, J. (2019). Panda accounting and accountability. In: J. Atkins, and B. Atkins (Eds.), *Around the World in 80 Species: Exploring the Business of Extinction* (pp. 359–388). Oxford: Routledge.

30

INTEGRATED REPORTING AND THE NEED FOR SPECIFICITY

Lessons from city-based greenhouse gas measurement and reporting

Parvez Mia, James Hazelton and James Guthrie

Macquarie University

Abstract

The International Integrated Reporting Council (IIRC) aims to provide a global measuring and reporting framework for environmental, social and governance performance. However, the absence of reliable and relevant metrics and key performance indicators for social, environmental and governance issues remain a big challenge for Integrated Reporting (IR). There is an urgent call from stakeholders for standard setters to solve inconsistency and build better alignment in metrics, especially concerning climate change reporting. Hence, this chapter focuses on an especially important metric – greenhouse gas emissions. We argue that a revised greenhouse gas management protocol would provide a useful focal point for standardizing accounting and reporting frameworks for cities' greenhouse gas emissions.

Introduction

The primary purpose of reporting under the International Integrated Reporting Council (IIRC) Framework is to encourage organizations to take an integrated approach to thinking, planning and reporting on how they create value (IIRC, 2016, p. 6). In order to disseminate these benefits as widely as possible, the IIRC has been advocating for Integrated Reporting (IR) to be the global norm for organizational reporting (Bernardi and Stark, 2018). Integrated Reporting is promoted as a solution to the shortcomings of the traditional financial reporting model, because it combines environmental, social and governance performance along with financial information (Dumay et al., 2016; Eccles and Kiron, 2012).

Although initially developed for the corporate sector, the IIRC also suggest that IR should be adopted by the public sector, as the emphasis of IR on value beyond profit has many benefits for public sector organizations (IIRC, 2016). Public sector organizations are critical players both in terms of their long-term social and environmental impacts as well as their sheer size: the public sector encompasses some of the largest reporting entities in the world (IIRC, 2016, p. 5). Growing demand for more non-financial performance, along with financial information to support better decision-making, means that public sector organizations need to rethink the way that they present their accounts (CIMA, 2015). They are under constant pressure to develop better reporting (KPMG, 2013). Hence, adopting IR, which incorporates non-financial information, key performance indicators (KPIs) and financial data, can help public sector organizations address these challenges and advance greater understanding of the way in which they create value. For these reasons, the IIRC (2016, p. 5) claims that public sector adoption of IR can deliver substantial benefits and that:

> Public sector leaders are looking for tools and frameworks to help them demonstrate effective resource allocation, and accountability – communicating not just for the sake of "being transparent" – but to ensure all stakeholders understand how their organisation is creating value in the short, medium and long term.

Some of the IIRC's claimed benefits from public sector adoption of IR include increased understanding of performance and value creation, improved decision making, and better internal organizational connections. Similarly, the Chartered Institute of Management Accountants (2015, p. 6) suggests that the "more flexible" approach of IR enables public sector organizations "to focus clearly on how they and their stakeholders define value in the short, medium and long term."

Integrated Reporting research, however, does not entirely validate the IIRC's enthusiasm regarding the application of IR to the public sector. While there has been limited academic research to date on the public sector and IR, the early indications are that while there are benefits, substantial operational challenges remain. For example, Caruana and Grech (2019, p. 8) report that integrated thinking may have significant benefits for the provision of public services, but the lack of guidelines for report preparers is a noteworthy limitation. Cohen and Karatzimas (2015) suggest that the "transplant" of IR from the private to the public sector must be via a process of adaptation, with their preferred hybrid approach termed "Integrated Popular Reporting." Manes-Rossi (2018, p. 186) argues that IR "does not provide sufficient support for public sector entities for it to be considered the primary reference for accountability purposes. Thus, further effort should be made to interpret the peculiarity of public sector organisations."

A particular weakness of IR has been the absence of reliable and relevant metrics and KPIs for social, environmental and governance issues (Adams and Simnett, 2011). The IIRC's 2017 consultation process – which received more than 400 submissions from 19 countries – identified IIRC collaboration with others to develop suitable metrics and measurement approaches as a possible way forward (IIRC, 2017). Corporate Reporting Dialogue[1] consultation findings reaffirmed an urgent call from stakeholders for standard setters to solve inconsistency and build better alignment in metrics, especially in relation to climate change reporting (IIRC, 2019). This warning resonates with other authors who bemoan the lack of measurement and specific metrics to support IR (Burke and Clark, 2016; Dumay et al., 2017).

In this chapter, we explore the debate regarding IR metrics in the context of greenhouse gas (GHG) reporting by large cities. Scientific evidence suggests that GHG emissions accelerate global climate change, causing significant risk to the planet (IPCC, 2015; Rosenzweig et al., 2010; Shao et al., 2016). Activities taking place within cities account for more than 70 per cent of GHG emissions (Dahal and Niemelä, 2017; World Bank, 2010). Greenhouse gas emissions must be cut to net zero levels by 2050 to avoid catastrophic climate change impacts (IPCC, 2018; Stern, 2018; Watts, 2018). City governments play a crucial role in producing, as well as reducing, GHG emissions by cities. Moreover, as centres of economic activity, population migration and energy consumption, cities should play a significant role in tackling global climate change (Meng et al., 2014). Accounting and reporting of cities' GHG emissions is an essential basis for management and action on climate change (Ibrahim et al., 2012; Kennedy et al., 2012; Rauland and Newman, 2015) and city governments (e.g., City of Johannesburg, City of Melbourne) are beginning to use IR as a contemporary communication tool (Manes-Rossi, 2018). Planning for mitigation actions at the city scale starts with the compilation of a GHG inventory that is also the first step toward developing a comprehensive emissions reduction strategy (Sanna et al., 2014).

The outcome of our review is to suggest that if city-based IR reporting is to be useful, the method for reporting the GHG element needs to be specified in order that reports have both internal and external validity, which adds further credence to prior calls for greater specificity in the IIRC Framework (Adams and Simnett, 2011; Burke and Clark, 2016; Dumay et al., 2017). To achieve this, we suggest that the IIRC needs to closely collaborate with GHG reporting standard-setters - such as CDP, the Climate Disclosure Standards Board, the GRI and the Sustainability Accounting Standards Board – to provide consistent guidance for GHG reporting.

To develop this argument, we explore two aspects of city-based GHG reporting. The next section reviews the two major GHG accounting approaches discussed in the academic literature: the production-based (PB) and consumption-based (CB) approaches (Andrade et al., 2018; Chen et al., 2019; Ibrahim et al., 2012). The third section reviews a selection of other aspects of reporting that can result in material differences in reporting practices; namely reporting boundaries, data availability, GHG selection completeness and verification. The final section provides our conclusions and highlights avenues for further research.

GHG accounting: production- vs consumption-based approaches

In order to understand its impact on climate change, an organization – or city – depends on its ability to account for its GHG emissions and to report reliable data (Talbot and Boiral, 2018). Accounting and reporting of GHG emissions are crucial for organizations, policymakers and others concerned about the issue of climate change to develop strategies and to act to reduce GHG emissions. Monitoring, tracking and managing GHG emissions is essential (Mia et al., 2018) to identify opportunities to reduce emissions, save energy and increase awareness about potential and future climate change-related risks.

Maintaining a GHG inventory can help policymakers track emission trends, develop mitigation strategies and policies and assess progress. A GHG inventory can help city governments identify their current levels of emissions, as well as the sources and activities within their physical boundaries that are responsible for those emissions. Further, a GHG inventory can help in setting goals and targets for future reductions and engage residents and businesses in initiatives to reduce GHG emissions. It can also serve as the basis for developing an action plan or to quantify the benefits and track the progress of activities that reduce emissions (EPA, 2018). Identifying principal emissions sources, implementing reliable emissions accounting systems and developing emissions inventories all serve to establish robust climate strategies and actions for cities (Dahal and Niemelä, 2017).

Prior studies show that organizations generally include scope 1 and 2 emissions in their inventories (Andrew and Cortese, 2011; Matisoff et al., 2013; Mia et al., 2019). The GPC and PAS 2070 both provide limited guidelines in measuring scope 3 emissions (Wiedmann et al., 2016). Excluding any scope from an emissions inventory can lead to significant carbon under-reporting from cities (Andrew and Cortese, 2011). Therefore, a standardized guideline for scope 3 emissions from various sources can help cities to estimate their emissions inventories more accurately.

Moreover, a comparable and accurate accounting of GHG emissions, similar to financial reporting rules and standards, is required for emissions disclosure, so that stakeholders receive an accurate and fair representation of an organization's carbon footprint and its efforts in emissions reduction strategies and actions (Gibassier and Schaltegger, 2015). Hence, it is necessary to have global city-scale GHG accounting guidelines and standards to facilitate consistency and comparability between city inventories.

The range of available guidelines means that different cities can choose the way they calculate GHG emissions. While measurement of GHG emissions is a positive step, inconsistency of measurement has several disadvantages. Prior studies suggest that the use of different guidelines can change the amount of disclosed total emissions significantly (Andrew and Cortese, 2011; Kolk et al., 2008; Mia et al., 2019). Moreover, variations in guidelines do not allow comparability of an entity's emissions. Such variations can also prevent policy coordination between cities. Dhakal and Shrestha (2010) notes that having standard guidance for GHG accounting could improve the reliability of emissions comparisons and may generate a more accurate understanding of cities' contributions to global emissions. It is also difficult to identify best practices and policies if there is no comparative analysis between cities (Sovacool and Brown, 2010). The abundance of initiatives and significant overlap between GHG guidelines has led different organizations to come together to develop a standard GHG accounting guideline for communities and cities called the Global Protocol for Community-Scale GHG Emissions (GPC).

Production-based (PB) and consumption-based (CB) are the two primary accounting approaches to estimate cities' GHG inventory (Chen et al., 2019; C40, 2018; Dhakal and Shrestha, 2010; Wang et al., 2018). The PB approach allocates GHG emissions to the producer, whereas the CB approach allocates emissions to the final consumer (Wang et al., 2018). The following example from Wiebe and Yamano (2016, p. 6) illustrates the difference between the PB and CB accounting approaches.

> A wooden table is bought by a final consumer in France. It was transported by a German logistics company from Poland, where it was assembled from screws (produced in China) and wooden planks (produced in Lithuania). China provides the tools to cut the timber from Finland into wooden planks. The tools were manufactured from metal, which was produced in the UK using iron ore from Australia and machinery from Germany.

Production-based accounting here registers the emissions from the screws in China, the machinery in Germany and so on; whereas CB accounting allocates the emissions entirely to France (Duus-Otterström and Hjorthen, 2019).

A PB GHG inventory calculates the GHG emissions based on production, regardless of where the product is used or consumed (Athanassiadis et al., 2018). The production principle is extensively used in global climate change agreements. The United Nations

Framework Convention on Climate Change (UNFCCC), for example, requires countries to measure their GHG inventory using the PB accounting approach (Afionis et al., 2017; Lombardi et al., 2017). Cities also use the PB accounting approach in measuring their GHG inventory (Chen et al., 2019; Dahal and Niemelä, 2017). However, it is argued that a national PB accounting approach has little relevance in measuring city-scale GHG inventory (Chen et al., 2019; Ibrahim et al., 2012). Cities serve 50 per cent of the world's population with only approximately 3 per cent of land mass, which means they have to outsource a large number of emissions from outside the city boundary (Grimm et al., 2008). Traditional PB methodology, which was initially developed for national reporting, fails to account for GHG emissions occurring outside the study boundary but as a result of the activity of the territory.

This is a significant limitation of PB accounting. It fails to recognize and address emissions generated from production of commodities in one geographical area (often smaller industrial towns), generally created primarily to satisfy the demand for those commodities in other areas (typically larger cities) (Afionis et al., 2017; Rauland and Newman, 2015). A significant amount of emissions embodied in international trade are ignored (Franzen and Mader, 2018; Shao et al., 2016). This has led to increased calls for a switch to, or an amalgamation with, CB accounting (Afionis et al., 2017).

Consumption-based accounting offers an alternative to PB accounting. Consumption-based emissions comprise:

> emissions arising within a city's boundaries, minus those emissions associated with the production of goods and services exported to meet demand outside the city, plus emissions arising in supply chains for goods and services produced outside the city but imported for consumption by its residents.
>
> *(C40, 2018, p. 4)*

Prior studies argue that CB accounting offers broader emissions coverage and provides a more accurate representation of a city's emissions profile (Afionis et al., 2017; Shao et al., 2016).

The choice between the two accounting approaches has significant implications for GHG emissions inventory and climate change mitigation strategy. C40 cities has calculated the CB GHG emissions of its 79 partner cities and found a substantial difference between PB and CB emissions as a result of international trade (C40, 2018). Shao et al. (2016) also found a similar result when calculating and comparing CB and PB emissions for Beijing. The substantial difference between CB and PB emissions may be the result of low emissions cities transferring their emissions, via the production of goods, to high emissions cities (Franzen and Mader, 2018).

Although the CB approach provides a more accurate representation of a city's emissions profile, it nonetheless has significant methodological, political and other uncertainties (Afionis et al., 2017). Cities may not have much direct control over the emissions intensity of energy used in the manufacturing process or transport methods of an imported product (C40, 2018); nor are they able to influence consumer behaviour in relation to the end-product. Access to reliable data from international trade is another challenge. Hence, CB emissions accounting is unlikely to replace its established PB counterpart, at least in the foreseeable future (Afionis et al., 2017).

To counter one of the major criticisms of the PB accounting approach – that it does not recognize cities' transboundary (indirect) emissions or emissions related to supply chains – in 2014, the WRI, ICLEI and C40 launched the GPC to address cities' transboundary emissions. The GPC standard outlines three scopes for emissions calculation. Scope 1 extends to territory-based emissions and covers emissions from sources located within the city boundaries, while scope 2 includes grid-supplied energy, which may or may not cross city boundaries (Fong et al., 2015). Scope 3 includes all indirect CB emissions excluding those in scopes 1 and 2, but includes all indirect emissions that occur outside the city boundary as a result of activities within the city boundary (Wiedmann et al., 2016). The total sum of emissions falling within scopes 1, 2 and 3 is referred to as the carbon footprint or CB emissions of a city (Dahal and Niemelä, 2017; Yetano et al., 2014).

The GPC requires cities first to define an emissions inventory boundary that includes physical or geographic area, period, gases and emission sources (Fong et al., 2015). The physical boundary can be the administrative boundary of a local government, a ward or borough within a city, a combination of administrative divisions, a metropolitan area, or another geographically identifiable entity (Fong et al., 2015; Sovacool and Brown, 2010). Regarding period, the GPC is designed to account for GHG emissions in a single reporting year. The inventory must cover a continuous period of 12 months, ideally aligning to either a calendar year or a financial year, consistent with the periods most commonly used by the city. With regard to GHGs, cities are required to include emissions of the seven gases covered by the Kyoto Protocol: carbon dioxide (CO_2), methane (CH_4), nitrous oxide (N_2O), hydrofluorocarbons (HFCs), perfluorocarbons (PFCs), sulphur hexafluoride (SF_6) and nitrogen trifluoride (NF_3). Cities also need to include emissions from six main sectors, including stationary energy, transportation, waste, industrial processes and product use (IPPU), agriculture, forestry and other land use (AFOLU) and any other emissions occurring outside the geographic boundary as a result of the city's activities (collectively referred to as other scope 3).

The GPC only provides guidance for a limited number of scope 3 emission sources, including transmission and distribution losses associated with grid-supplied energy, waste disposal and treatment outside the city boundary, and transboundary transportation. The GPC allows cities the inclusion of "other scope 3"; however, the guidelines for measuring these scope 3 emissions in a robust and consistent manner are yet to be written (Fong et al., 2015; Wiedmann et al., 2016). Such guidelines would encourage more holistic GHG emissions assessments, enable decision makers to consider a wider range of opportunities to reduce global GHG emissions and provide an additional perspective from which to engage other stakeholders in climate action (C40, 2018; Dahal and Niemelä, 2017).

Prior research shows that cities generally include scope 1 and 2 emissions in their GHG inventory (Dahal and Niemelä, 2017; Mia et al., 2019). These studies indicate that significant emissions are embedded in the supply chain; therefore, ignoring scope 3 emissions will result in a significant under-reporting of GHG inventory (Hertwich and Wood, 2018; Yetano et al., 2014). Inclusion of scope 3 with scopes 1 and 2 would capture PB GHG emissions and those associated with the largest supply chains serving cities. Including this requirement with the IIRC Framework – or at the very least providing strong encouragement in those publications aimed to promote public sector IR reporting – would significantly enhance the quality of public sector GHG emissions reporting.

Challenges for measurement and recognition of emissions

In addition to the challenge of accounting for GHG using a PB or CB approach, a number of other factors influence the quality of public sector GHG reporting and are therefore worthy of specific consideration by the IIRC Framework. These issues are reporting boundaries, data availability, GHG selection completeness and verification, and are considered in turn below.

Cities need to establish physical or geographic boundaries that identify the spatial dimension or physical perimeter of the inventories' boundaries (Fong et al., 2015). City boundaries may comprise different aspects, such as territorial boundaries (e.g., boundaries of the settlement) or administrative boundaries. However, there is no uniform or global definition of what constitutes an urban or city boundary (Meng et al., 2014). The United Nations (UN) allows countries to establish their definitions for urban or city areas according to their own needs (Meng et al., 2014; Parshall et al., 2010). The GPC also allows cities to establish their boundaries depending on the purpose of the inventory. Most cities estimate GHG emissions based on their administrative boundaries (CDP, 2018).

The government often defines an urban district based on the administrative boundary for a political purpose - this may not properly represent the urban area (Zhang and Seto, 2011). Also, defining an urban area as a discrete entity with a fixed administrative boundary fails to capture the dynamic process of urban development (Meng et al., 2014). Therefore, more rigorous boundary mapping is required. Several studies suggest that night-time light imagery is appropriate both in defining the urban boundary and estimating GHG emissions at an urban scale (Meng et al., 2014; Parshall et al., 2010). Wiedmann et al. (2016) proposed a "city carbon map" concept to identify the emissions boundary and estimate a city's GHG inventory.

Data availability is closely linked with the boundary issue. While establishing boundaries for emissions, cities also need to consider whether data is available for that boundary. There is a continuous tension between data acquisition and data quality when compiling a GHG inventory (Lombardi et al., 2017; Yetano et al., 2014). Moreover, it is expensive and time consuming to build, maintain, validate and evaluate local level data (Ahlers and Driscoll, 2016). Quality data is vital for an accurate and reliable emissions inventory. The public sector, in particular, suffers from a lack of adequate information technology and management systems suitable for the collection of accurate data on how entire operations are managed (Manes-Rossi, 2018). Data on a range of activities, such as the fuel consumption of a power plant, local cement production or electricity consumption are commonly not available at the regional or local level (Kennedy et al., 2009; Meng et al., 2014).

Data collection can be done in two ways: a bottom-up or a top-down approach. The bottom-up approach collects data at a local level, guaranteeing a relatively accurate inventory. However, this process is costly and time-consuming. Several relevant activities may also take place outside the territory (e.g., waste disposal), so data may not be available (Bader and Bleischwitz, 2009). The top-down approach can be used to estimate GHG emissions, especially where there is a lack of available data (Meng et al., 2014). This approach scales from national statistics but is disadvantaged in reflecting the national average for a certain emission source while not being necessarily compatible with the reporting requirements of a city-level emissions inventory (Ahlers and Driscoll, 2016). Cities, therefore, face a trade-off between compiling an inventory as accurately as possible on the one hand and limiting the time needed for the undertaking on the other hand. A mixed approach – that is, a combination of the top-down and bottom-up approach – may help to determine GHG emissions tied to activity and consumption within a city (Sanna et al., 2014). City authorities may be able to improve their data collection and management systems over time to adopt a mixed approach and more accurately record GHG emissions.

A third critical issue in relation to GHG reporting quality is the inclusion (or lack thereof) of all relevant greenhouse gasses. Cities that plan to create an inventory of GHG emissions must decide whether to include all seven greenhouse gases as well as direct and indirect emissions in the GHG inventory. The UNFCCC urges cities to account for emissions of seven gases: CO_2, CH_4, N_2O, HFCs, PFCs, SF_6 and NF_3 (CDP, 2018). However, a recent study of cities' GHG emissions inventory suggests that many cities do not include all seven gases in their GHG inventory (Mia et al., 2019). The more types of gases and emission sources included, the more accurately the inventory reflects overall GHG emissions. Sometimes even small quantities of a powerful gas such as N_2O can have a significant impact on the climate footprint of cities, as N_2O is 310 times more potent than CO_2 (Bader and Bleischwitz, 2009). Gases are normally converted to CO_2 equivalents for the purposes of an emissions inventory, based on the global warming potential of gases identified by the IPCC. However, use of the IPCC default global warming potential may not provide an accurate value for cities (Ahlers and Driscoll, 2016).

A final core issue in relation to the quality of GHG reporting is verification. As with the corporate sector, most cities do not verify their GHG inventory (Mia et al., 2019). The CDP, the GPC and the C40 do not require cities to verify their emissions but recommend that cities should choose the level and type of verification that meets their needs and capacity. Verification involves a third-party assessment of the completeness and accuracy of reported data and compliance with the relevant guidelines (Bellassen and Cochran, 2015). Verification of cities' GHG inventory demonstrates that their calculations meet the requirements of the GPC or other standards and provide confidence to users that the disclosed GHG emissions are a fair reflection of a city's activities. This can be used to increase the credibility of publicly reported emissions information with external audiences and increase confidence in the data used to develop climate action plans, set GHG targets and track progress. However, the GPC does not provide any guidelines to verify emissions inventory.

To address the challenges outlined above, as with the PB- and CB-approaches discussed in the section on production- vs consumption-based approaches, providing guidance on each of these four matters in the IIRC Framework as to expected reporting practices would significantly enhance the quality of public sector GHG emissions reporting. Of course, cities are developing their own reporting guidelines in collaboration with governmental agencies, other cities, universities and research institutions. However, we believe a common approach is necessary to avoid variations in the calculation methods, and to encourage the IIRC to build upon frameworks such as the GPC to improve IR practice.

Conclusion

The IIRC Framework offers an opportunity for public sector organizations to provide information related to financial, environmental and social performance, as well as governance issues, in a clear, concise, consistent and comparable format in one document (Manes-Rossi, 2018). However, prior studies have pointed to the lack of reliable and relevant metrics for a series of social, environmental and governance issues (Adams and Simnett, 2011; Burke and Clark, 2016; Dumay et al., 2017).

We have explored the debate regarding IR metrics in the context of GHG reporting by large cities. We suggest that effective reporting under the IIRC Framework will only occur with greater specificity in relation to a number of reporting elements: consumption- versus production-based reporting; reporting boundaries; data availability; GHG selection completeness; and verification. Extending the analysis from cities, we suggest that the basis of GHG reporting be standardized via further congruence of the reporting requirements of the main sustainability standard-setters, including the IIRC together with bodies such as the CDP, the Climate Disclosure Standards Board, the GRI, GPC and the Sustainability Accounting Standards Board. In order to optimize the utility of GHG disclosures, these requirements should include both PB and CB reporting and explicitly require both public and private sector entities to give equivalent attention to PB (scopes 1 and 2) and CB (scope 3) reporting.

Future research could usefully focus on the appropriate specification of GHG reporting under the IIRC framework and the usefulness of this reporting to both external and internal stakeholders. In particular, further research is acutely needed on how IR might both enhance and be enhanced by integrated thinking, the facilitation of which is the core objective of the IR project (IIRC, 2016, p. 6).

Note

1 The Corporate Reporting Dialogue is an initiative, convened in June 2014 by the IIRC, designed to respond to market calls for greater coherence, consistency and comparability between corporate reporting frameworks, standards and related requirements.

References

Adams, S., and Simnett, R. (2011). Integrated Reporting: An Opportunity for Australia's Not-for-Profit Sector. *Australian Accounting Review, 21*(3), 292–301.

Afionis, S., Sakai, M., Scott, K., Barrett, J., and Gouldson, A. (2017). Consumption-based Carbon Accounting: Does It Have a Future? *WIREs Climate Change, 8*(1), 1–19.

Ahlers, D., and Driscoll, P. (2016). Understanding Challenges in Municipal Greenhouse Gas Emission Inventories. *ICE/IEEE International Technology Management Conference 2016.*

Andrade, J. C. S., Dameno, A., Pérez, J., de Andrés, J. M., and Lumbreras, J. (2018). Implementing City-level Carbon Accounting: A Comparison between Madrid and London. *Journal of Cleaner Production, 172,* 795–804.

Andrew, J., and Cortese, C. (2011). Carbon Disclosures: Comparability, the Carbon Disclosure Project and the Greenhouse Gas Protocol. *Australasian Accounting, Business and Finance Journal, 5*(4), 5–18.

Athanassiadis, A., Christis, M., Bouillard, P., Vercalsteren, A., Crawford, R. H., and Khan, A. Z. (2018). Comparing a Territorial-based and a Consumption-based Approach to Assess the Local and Global Environmental Performance of Cities. *Journal of Cleaner Production, 173,* 112–123.

Bader, N., and Bleischwitz, R. (2009). Measuring Urban Greenhouse Gas Emissions: The Challenge of Comparability. *Survey and Perspectives Integrating Environment and Society, 2*(3), 7–21.

Bellassen, V., and Cochran, I. (2015). Introduction: Key Notions and Trade-Offs Involved in MRVing Emissions. In: V. Bellassen, and N. Stephan (Eds.), *Accounting for Carbon Monitoring, Reporting and Verifying Emissions in the Climate Economy* (pp. 1–18). Cambridge, UK: Cambridge University Press.

Bernardi, C., and Stark, A. W. (2018). Environmental, Social and Governance Disclosure, Integrated Reporting, and the Accuracy of Analyst Forecasts. *The British Accounting Review, 50*(1), 16–31.

Burke, J. J., and Clark, C. E. (2016). The Business Case for Integrated Reporting: Insights from Leading Practitioners, Regulators, and Academics. *Business Horizons, 59*(3), 273–283.

C40. (2018). *Consumption Based GHG Emissions of C40 Cities* [Press release]. Available at: www.c40.org/researches/consumption-based-emissions (Accessed: 12 November 2018).

Caruana, J., and Grech, I. (2019). Tweaking Public Sector Reporting with Integrated Reporting (IR) concepts. *Public Money & Management, 39*(6), 409–417.

CDP. (2018). *CDP Disclosure Insight Action.* Available at: www.cdp.net/en (Accessed: 25 April 2018).

Chartered Institute of Management Accountants (CIMA). (2015). *Integrated Reporting in the Public Sector.* Available at: https://integratedreporting.org/resource/cima-integrated-reporting-in-the-public-sector/ (Accessed: 6 August 2019).

Chen, G., Shan, Y., Hu, Y., Tong, K., Wiedmann, T., Ramaswami, A., Guan, D., Shi, L., and Wang, Y. (2019). Review on City-level Carbon Accounting. *Environmental Science & Technology*, *53*(10), 5545–5558.

Cohen, S. and Karatzimas, S. (2015). Tracing the Future of Reporting in the Public Sector: Introducing Integrated Popular Reporting. *International Journal of Public Sector Management*, *28*(6), 449–460.

Dahal, K., and Niemelä, J. (2017). Cities' Greenhouse Gas Accounting Methods: A Study of Helsinki, Stockholm, and Copenhagen. *Climate*, *5*(2), 1–14.

Dhakal, S., and Shrestha, R. M. (2010). Bridging the Research Gaps for Carbon Emissions and their Management in Cities. *Energy Policy*, *38*(9), 4753–4755.

Dumay, J., Bernardi, C., Guthrie, J., and Demartini, P. (2016). Integrated Reporting: A Structured Literature Review. *Accounting Forum*, *40*(3), 166–185.

Dumay, J., Bernardi, C., Guthrie, J., and Torre, M. (2017). Barriers to Implementing Integrated Reporting: An Contemporary Academic Perspective. *Meditari Accountancy Research*, *25*(4), 461–480.

Duus-Otterström, G., and Hjorthen, F. D. (2019). Consumption-based Emissions Accounting: The Normative Debate. *Environmental Politics*, *28*(5), 866–885.

Eccles, R., and Kiron, D. (2012). Get Ready: Mandated Integrated Reporting is the Future of Corporate Reporting. *MIT Sloan Management Review*, *53*(3), 1–5.

EPA. (2018). *U.S. Environmental Protection Agency.* Available at: www.epa.gov/ (Accessed: 27 April 2018).

Fong, W. K., Sotos, M., Michael, D. M., Schultz, S., Marques, A., and Deng-Beck, C. (2015). *Global Protocol for Community-scale Greenhouse Gas Emission Inventories.* New York, USA: World Resources Institute.

Franzen, A., and Mader, S. (2018). Consumption-based Versus Production-Based Accounting of CO2 Emissions: Is there Evidence for Carbon Leakage? *Environmental Science & Policy*, *84*, 34–40.

Gibassier, D., and Schaltegger, S. (2015). Carbon Management Accounting and Reporting in Practice: A Case Study on Converging Emergent Approaches. *Sustainability Accounting, Management and Policy Journal*, *6*(3), 340–365.

Grimm, N. B., Faeth, S. H., Golubiewski, N. E., Redman, C. L., Wu, J., Bai, X., and Briggs, J. M. (2008). Global Change and the Ecology of Cities. *Science*, *319*(5864), 756–760.

Hertwich, E. G., and Wood, R. (2018). The Growing Importance of Scope 3 Greenhouse Gas Emissions from Industry. *Environmental Research Letters*, *13*(10), 1–11.

Ibrahim, N., Sugar, L., Hoornweg, D., and Kennedy, C. (2012). Greenhouse Gas Emissions from Cities: Comparison of International Inventory Frameworks. *Local Environment*, *17*(2), 223–241.

IIRC. (2016). *Focusing on Value Creation in the Public Sector.* Available at: http://integratedreporting.org/wp-content/uploads/2016/09/Focusing-on-value-creation-in-the-public-sector-_vFINAL.pdf (Accessed: 5 August 2019).

IIRC. (2017). *Framework Implementation Feedback: Integrated Reporting.* Available at: https://integratedreporting.org/wp-content/uploads/2017/10/Framework_feedback_Sum2017.pdf (Accessed: 30 June 2019).

IIRC. (2019). *Corporate Reporting Dialogue Consultation Reveals Urgent Market Call for Indicator Alignment on Climate.* Available at: https://integratedreporting.org/news/corporate-reporting-dialogue-consultation-reveals-urgent-market-call-for-indicator-alignment-on-climate/ (Accessed: 30 June 2019).

Intergovernmental Panel on Climate Change (IPCC). (2015). *Climate Change 2014: Mitigation of Climate Change.* Cambridge, UK: Cambridge University Press.

Intergovernmental Panel on Climate Change (IPCC). (2018). *IPCC Special Report on Global Warming of 1.5°C.* France: Office for Climate Education.

Kennedy, C., Demoullin, S., and Mohareb, E. (2012). Cities Reducing their Greenhouse Gas Emissions. *Energy Policy*, *49*, 774–777.

Kennedy, C., Steinberger, J., Gasson, B., Hansen, Y., Hillman, T., Havranek, M., and Mendez, G. V. (2009). Greenhouse Gas Emissions from Global Cities. *Environmental Science & Technology*, *43*(19), 7297–7302.

Kolk, A., Levy, D., and Pinkse, J. (2008). Corporate Responses in an Emerging Climate Regime: The Institutionalization and Commensuration of Carbon Disclosure. *European Accounting Review*, *17*(4), 719–745.

KPMG. (2013). *Applying Integrated Reporting Principles in the Public Sector.* UK: KPMG International.

Lombardi, M., Laiola, E., Tricase, C., and Rana, R. (2017). Assessing the Urban Carbon Footprint: An Overview. *Environmental Impact Assessment Review*, *66*, 43–52.

Manes-Rossi, F. (2018). Is Integrated Reporting a New Challenge for Public Sector Entities? *African Journal of Business Management*, *12*(7), 172–187.

Matisoff, D. C., Noonan, D. S., and O'Brien, J. J. (2013). Convergence in Environmental Reporting: Assessing the Carbon Disclosure Project. *Business Strategy and the Environment*, *22*(5), 285–305.

Meng, L., Graus, W., Worrell, E., and Huang, B. (2014). Estimating CO2 (Carbon Dioxide) Emissions at Urban scales by DMSP/OLS (Defense Meteorological Satellite Program's Operational Linescan System) Nighttime Light Imagery: Methodological Challenges and a Case Study for China. *Energy*, *71*, 468–478.

Mia, P., Hazelton, J., and Guthrie, J. (2018). Measuring the Climate Actions: A Disclosure Study of World Ten Megacities. *Meditari Accountancy Research*, *26*(4), 550–575.

Mia, P., Hazelton, J., and Guthrie, J. (2019). Greenhouse Gas Emissions Disclosure by Cities: The Expectation Gap. *Sustainability Accounting, Management and Policy Journal*, *10*(4), 685–709.

Parshall, L., Gurney, K., Hammer, S. A., Mendoza, D., Zhou, Y., and Geethakumar, S. (2010). Modeling Energy Consumption and CO2 Emissions at the Urban Scale: Methodological Challenges and Insights from the United States. *Energy Policy*, *38*(9), 4765–4782.

Rauland, V., and Newman, P. (2015). Counting Carbon in Cities. In: V. Raul, and P. Newman (Eds.), *Decarbonising Cities* (pp. 117–130). Basel, Switzerland: Springer International.

Rosenzweig, C., Solecki, W., Hammer, S. A., and Mehrotra, S. (2010). Cities Lead the Way in Climate-change Action. *Nature*, *467*(7318), 909–911.

Sanna, L., Ferrara, R., Zara, P., and Duce, P. (2014). GHG Emissions Inventory at Urban Scale: The Sassari Case Study. *Energy Procedia*, *59*, 344–350.

Shao, L., Chen, B., and Gan, L. (2016). Production-based and Consumption-based Carbon Emissions of Beijing: Trend and Features. *Energy Procedia*, *104*, 171–176.

Sovacool, B. K., and Brown, M. A. (2010). Twelve Metropolitan Carbon Footprints: A Preliminary Comparative Global Assessment. *Energy Policy*, *38*(9), 4856–4869.

Stern, N. (2018). *We must Reduce Greenhouse Gas Emissions to Net Zero or Face More Floods*. Available at: www.theguardian.com/environment/2018/oct/08/we-must-reduce-greenhouse-gas-emissions-to-net-zero-or-face-more-floods (Accessed: 20 November 2018).

Talbot, D., and Boiral, O. (2018). GHG Reporting and Impression Management: An Assessment of Sustainability Reports from the Energy Sector. *Journal of Business Ethics*, *147*(2), 367–383.

Wang, Z., Li, Y., Cai, H., and Wang, B. (2018). Comparative Analysis of Regional Carbon Emissions Accounting Methods in China: Production-based Versus Consumption-based Principles. *Journal of Cleaner Production*, *194*, 12–22.

Watts, J. (2018). *We have 12 Years to Limit Climate Change Catastrophe, Warns UN*. Available at: www.theguardian.com/environment/2018/oct/08/global-warming-must-not-exceed-15c-warns-land mark-un-report (Accessed: 15 November 2018).

Wiebe, K. S., and Yamano, N. (2016), Estimating CO_2 Emissions Embodied in Final Demand and Trade Using the OECD ICIO 2015: Methodologyand Results. *OECD Science, Technology and Industry Working Papers*, pp. 1–39. doi:10.1787/5jlrcm216xkl-en

Wiedmann, T. O., Chen, G., and Barrett, J. (2016). The Concept of City Carbon Maps: A Case Study of Melbourne, Australia. *Journal of Industrial Ecology*, *20*(4), 676–691.

World Bank. (2010). *Cities and Climate Change: An Urgent Agenda*. Available at: https://openknowledge.worldbank.org/handle/10986/17381 (Accessed: 4 December 2019).

Yetano, R. M., Lechtenböhmer, S., Fischedick, M., Gröne, M. C., Xia, C., and Dienst, C. (2014). Concepts and Methodologies for Measuring the Sustainability of Cities. *Annual Review of Environment and Resources*, *39*, 519–547.

Zhang, Q., and Seto, K. C. (2011). Mapping Urbanization Dynamics at Regional and Global Scales using Multi-temporal DMSP/OLS Nighttime Light Data. *Remote Sensing of Environment*, *115*(9), 2320–2329.

For Product Safety Concerns and Information please contact our EU
representative GPSR@taylorandfrancis.com Taylor & Francis Verlag GmbH,
Kaufingerstraße 24, 80331 München, Germany

Printed and bound by CPI Group (UK) Ltd, Croydon, CR0 4YY
08/05/2025
01864358-0012